TEACHER PREP

MERRILL
PRENTICE HALL

Teacher Preparation Classroom

See a demo at
www.prenhall.com/teacherprep/demo

Your Class. Their Careers. Our Future. Will your students be prepared?

We invite you to explore our new, innovative and engaging website and all that it has to offer you, your course, and tomorrow's educators! Preview this site today at www.prenhall.com/teacherprep/demo. Just click on "go" on the login page to begin your exploration.

Organized around the major courses pre-service teachers take, the Teacher Preparation site provides media, student/teacher artifacts, strategies, research articles, and other resources to equip your students with the quality tools needed to excel in their courses and prepare them for their first classroom.

This ultimate on-line education resource will provide you and your students access to:

Online Video Library. More than 250 video clips—each tied to a course topic and framed by learning goals and Praxis-type questions—capture real teachers and students working in real classrooms.

Student and Teacher Artifacts. More than 200 student and teacher classroom artifacts—each tied to a course topic and framed by learning goals and application questions—provide a wealth of materials and experiences to help make your students observe children's developmental learning.

Lesson Plan Builder. Offers step-by-step guidelines and lesson plan examples to support students as they learn to build high quality lesson plans.

Articles and Readings. Over 500 articles from ASCD's renowned journal *Educational Leadership* are available. The site also includes Research Navigator, a searchable database of additional educational journals.

Strategies and Lessons. Over 500 research-supported instructional strategies appropriate for a wide range of grade levels and content areas.

Licensure and Career Tools. Resources devoted to helping your students pass their licensure exam; learn standards, law, and public policies; plan a teaching portfolio; and survive their first year of teaching.

How to ORDER *Teacher Prep* for you and your students:

For students to receive a *Teacher Prep* Access Code with this text, instructors **must** provide a special value pack ISBN number on their textbook order form. To receive this special ISBN, please email **Merrill.marketing@pearsoned.com** and provide the following information:

- Name and Affiliation
- Author/Title/Edition of Merrill text

Upon ordering *Teacher Prep* for their students, instructors will be given a lifetime *Teacher Prep* Access Code.

TEACHING YOUNG ADOLESCENTS

Methods and Resources for Middle Grades Teaching

Fifth Edition

Richard D. Kellough
Noreen G. Kellough
California State University at Sacramento

PEARSON

Merrill
Prentice Hall

Upper Saddle River, New Jersey
Columbus, Ohio

Library of Congress Cataloging-in-Publication Data
Kellough, Richard D. (Richard Dean)
  Teaching young adolescents : methods and resources for middle grades teaching/Richard D. Kellough, Noreen G. Kellough. —5th ed.
    p. cm.
  Includes bibliographical references and index.
  ISBN 0-13-199617-7 (alk. paper)
  1. Middle school teaching—United States. 2. Middle schools—United States. I. Kellough, Noreen G. II. Title
  LB1737.5.U6K45 2008
  373.1102—dc22   2006024665

Vice President and Executive Publisher: Jeffery W. Johnston
Executive Editor: Debra A. Stollenwerk
Development Editor: Christina Robb
Production Editor: Alexandrina Benedicto Wolf
Production Coordination: Carlisle Publishing Services
Photo Coordinator: Monica Merkel
Design Coordinator: Diane C. Lorenzo
Cover Designer: Janna Thompson-Chordas
Cover art: Corbis
Production Manager: Susan W. Hannahs
Director of Marketing: David Gesell
Senior Marketing Manager: Darcy Betts Prybella
Marketing Coordinator: Brian Mounts

This book was set in New Baskerville by Carlisle Publishing Services, Ltd. It was printed and bound by Banta Book Group. The cover was printed by Phoenix Color Corp.

Pearson Education Ltd.   Pearson Education Australia Pty. Limited
Pearson Education Singapore Pte. Ltd.   Pearson Education North Asia Ltd.
Pearson Education Canada, Ltd.   Pearson Educación de Mexico, S.A. de C.V.
Pearson Education—Japan   Pearson Education Malaysia, Pte. Ltd.

10 9 8 7 6 5 4
ISBN: 0-13-199617-7

Preface

Welcome to the fifth edition of *Teaching Young Adolescents: Methods and Resources for Middle Grades Teaching*. The purpose of this book is to provide a practical and concise guide for college and university students who are preparing to become competent middle grades teachers. Others who may find it useful are experienced teachers who want to continue developing their teaching skills, as well as curriculum specialists and school administrators who want a current, practical, and concise text of methods, guidelines, and resources for teaching young adolescents (children ages 9–14, typically in grades 5–8).

NEW TO THIS EDITION

- The inside front cover presents **Strategies and Materials You Can Use in Classroom Teaching**.
- INTASC principles on the inside back cover correlate text material with the text.
- Exercises that we believe would be useful additions to your professional portfolio are marked with a **(PP)**

Increased or Added Emphasis. Focal points of the text include

- Reflective teaching
- Personalized and integrated learning
- Working with young adolescents regardless of how or where they are housed

Reorganization of Content to Increase Flexibility of Usage. While providing comprehensive coverage of methods of instruction enhanced with exercises for active learning, both continuing hallmarks of this resource guide, this edition has been reorganized to increase flexibility of usage.

- The text has been condensed from 12 to 9 chapters.
- Part openers have been deleted.
- The chapter on assessment now follows the instructional planning chapter.

- Topics on the basic skills of thinking and questioning are combined in Chapter 3.
- Strategies are now found in Chapters 8 and 9.
- Information on media and technology is integrated throughout the text and is emphasized in Chapter 2.
- References are listed at the end of the book.
- More interactive scenarios, "Teaching in Practice," vignettes, tables, figures, and quotations of significance are found throughout the text.
- Relevant Internet resources are listed at the end of each chapter.

OUR BELIEFS: HOW AND WHERE THEY ARE REFLECTED IN THIS BOOK

In preparing this book, we saw our task as providing relevant guidelines and current resources to improve your teaching effectiveness. You may choose from these resources and build upon what works best for you. Nobody can assuredly tell you what will work with your students; you will know them best. We do share what we believe to be the best of practice, the most useful of recent research findings, and the richest of experiences. Preparing this new edition presented us with an opportunity to reexamine and share our own beliefs about middle level teaching. The boldface statements that follow present those beliefs and describe briefly how they are embraced in this book.

The best learning occurs when the learner actively participates in the process, which includes having ownership in both the process and the product of the learning. Consequently, this book continues to be designed to engage you in hands-on and minds-on learning about effective teaching of young adolescents in the classroom. For example, rather than simply reading a chapter devoted to the important topic of cooperative learning, in each chapter you will become involved in cooperative and collaborative learning. In essence, via the exercises found in every chapter, you will practice cooperative learning, talk about it, practice it some more, and finally, through the process of doing it, learn a great deal about it. This book involves you in it. To maintain these exercises as an integral part of the book, we have resisted moving them to the Internet as is becoming an increasingly common practice in publishing.

The best strategies for learning about teaching young adolescents are those that model those very strategies. It is our belief that integrated learning is the cornerstone of effective teaching of young adolescents, and that is a premise upon which this resource guide is designed.

To be most effective today, a teacher must use an eclectic style in teaching. Rather than focusing your attention on particular models of teaching, we emphasize the importance of an eclectic model—that is, one in which you select and integrate the best from various instructional approaches. For example, sometimes you will want to use a direct, expository approach, perhaps through a mini-lecture; more often you will want to use an indirect, social-interactive, or student-centered approach, perhaps through project-based learning. This book provides guidelines to help you not only decide which approach to use at a particular time but also to develop your skill in using specific approaches. You will learn the importance of being able to combine both direct and indirect approaches, using what we refer to as *multilevel instruction.*

Learning should be active, pleasant, fun, meaningful, and productive. Our desire is to present this resource in an enthusiastic, positive, and cognitive-humanistic way, in part by providing rich experiences in social-interactive learning. How this is done is perhaps best exemplified by the active learning exercises embedded in relevant locations throughout the book. Exercises were developed to ensure that you become an active participant in learning the methods and procedures that are most appropriate in facilitating the learning of active, responsive young adolescents.

Teaching skills can be learned. In medicine, certain knowledge and skills must be learned and developed before the student physician is licensed to practice with patients. In law, certain knowledge and skills must be learned and developed before the law student is licensed to practice with clients. So it is in teacher preparation. It is our continuing belief that knowledge and skills must be learned and developed before the teacher candidate is licensed to practice the art and science of teaching young people. We would never allow just any person to treat our child's illness or to defend us in a legal case; the professional education of teachers is no less important! Receiving a professional education on how to teach young people is absolutely necessary, and certain aspects of that education must precede any interaction with students if teachers are to become truly competent professionals.

ORGANIZATION OF THIS BOOK: AN OVERVIEW

Competent teaching of young adolescents in the classroom is a kaleidoscopic, multifaceted, eclectic process. When preparing and writing a book for use in teacher preparation, by necessity one must separate that kaleidoscopic process into separate parts, which is not always possible to do in a way that makes the most sense to everyone using the book. For that reason it is *not* necessary for users to follow our chapter-by-chapter organization, and that is a major reason we have made every effort to increase the flexibility of usage. Although we organized the book in a way that makes sense to us, we readily agree that there are other ways that are no less sensible. Here is a chapter-by-chapter synopsis of how we have organized the content.

Chapter 1, with two exercises, presents an **overview** of the reality and challenge of middle level teaching today, including a review of the developmental characteristics of young adolescents.

Chapter 2, focusing on the **teacher as a reflective decision maker**, presents the **expectations, responsibilities, and behaviors of competent middle level teachers**, and includes brief attention to certain legal guidelines and use of basic resources and media for instruction. It contains five exercises.

Chapter 3 focuses attention on **questioning and thinking**, two significantly important skills for intelligent behavior and necessary for meaningful learning. It contains seven exercises, including the first of two micro peer teaching exercises in the book.

Chapter 4, with six exercises, focuses on **classroom management**.

Chapter 5, with 12 exercises, focuses on **curriculum**: the rationale for planning and selecting the content of the curriculum; information about the national, state, and local documents that provide benchmarks for learning and that guide content selection; and describes preparing goals and learning targets and using them in planning for and assessment of learning.

Chapter 6, with four exercises, is devoted to **unit and lesson planning**.

Chapter 7 focuses attention on the **assessment** of what students know or they think they know prior to, during, and following the instructional experience. To complete your instructional planning (begun in Chapter 6) you will necessarily be referring to the content of not only Chapter 7 but Chapters 8 and 9 as well. It contains one exercise.

Chapter 8, with three exercises, presents guidelines for **grouping students, using project-centered teaching,**

assignments and homework, ensuring classroom equity, and writing across the curriculum. Chapter 8 ends with a section you may find useful for years to come—a popular and updated annotated listing of more than 125 motivational strategies and ideas for lessons, interdisciplinary teaching, transcultural studies, and student projects, followed by an extended list of Internet sites containing teaching ideas for your subject field.

Chapter 9 presents guidelines for using **teacher talk, demonstrations, discovery and inquiry, and educational games**. It contains two exercises.

CONTINUING SPECIAL FEATURES OF THIS RESOURCE GUIDE

It is our belief that for you to achieve professional competency, you need guided learning, guided practice, productive feedback, encouragement, opportunity for reflection, and positive reinforcement. To provide you with resources and encouragement to make you an effective and confident teacher, this book is organized with the following features:

- **A strong, current, and broad research base.** This is evidenced by the references throughout the text.
- **Advance organizers.** The objectives found in the introduction of each chapter serve as advance organizers; that is, they establish a mind-set for that which is to come in the chapter.
- **Exercises for active learning.** Found throughout are exercises we consider to be fundamental to your learning. We continue in our belief that for this book exercises are best placed within the content of the chapter rather than at the chapter end or even worse, on a remote website. Each exercise requires that you deal in some descriptive, analytical, or self-reflective manner with text concepts and actual practice. Each is designed to encourage continual assessment of and reflection on your progress in building your teaching competencies and skill development and involve you in collaborative and cooperative learning. It is unlikely that all exercises in this book could be (or should be) completed in a one-semester course. Since some exercises necessitate a school visit, review the exercises early so you can plan your visits and work schedule. In fact, because certain exercises build upon previous ones or suggest that help be obtained from teachers in the field, we advise that all exercises be reviewed at the outset of your course so you and your course instructor can decide which are most appropriate for your situation and training.
- **Perforated pages.** Pages of the book are perforated for easy removal of the exercises. Exercises and some forms that are likely to be removed begin on separate pages so that they can be removed without disturbing text.

- **Performance assessment.** Assessment of your developing competencies is encouraged by two micro peer teaching (MPT) exercises found in Chapters 3 (Exercise 3.7) and 9 (Exercise 9.2).
- **Situational case studies, teaching vignettes, interactive teaching scenarios, and questions for class discussion.** For extended class discussions, situational case studies are presented in Chapter 4. Relevant scenarios for reflection and teaching vignettes are distributed throughout. Questions for Class Discussion appear at the end of each chapter.
- **Outstanding practices and exemplary programs.** To let you gain further insight or to visit exemplary programs, middle level schools recognized as having exemplary programs are identified throughout the text.
- **Internet resources.** At the end of each chapter you will find a current list of Internet sites and references that we can recommend. Each site was visited and checked by us in 2005 but because the Internet is anything but static, Web addresses may change. To determine if the information is still available for any outdated address, type the title of the Web page into a search engine and check the results.
- **For further reading.** At the conclusion of each chapter are additional sources, both current and classic, to deepen and broaden your understanding of particular topics.
- **Glossary and Index.** The text concludes with a glossary of terms, list of references, and an index.

Additionally, an **Instructor's Manual** is available online and addresses each chapter in three ways: a detailed outline of the chapter, chapter notes containing additional information or suggestions about particular content, and examination questions and answers. Additionally, it contains a more complex summative MPT that may be preferred by some users of the book. These materials are available at www.prenhall.com on the book's description page under Instructor Resources.

ACKNOWLEDGMENTS

We would never have been able to complete this fifth edition had it not been for the valued help of many individuals, including former students in our classes, teachers who have shared their experiences with us, administrators and colleagues who have talked and debated with us, and authors and publishers who have graciously granted permission to reprint materials and who are acknowledged in the book. To each we offer our warmest thanks.

Although we take full responsibility for any errors or omissions in this book, we are deeply grateful to others for their cogent comments and important contributions that led to the development of this book. We thank the following reviewers: Madge Holden Kibler, Piedmont College; Ron Towery, Arkansas State University;

J. L. High, Lipscomb University; and Eva Weisz, DePaul University.

We express our deepest admiration for and appreciation to the highly competent professionals at Merrill/Prentice Hall with whom we have had a long and rewarding relationship.

We are indeed indebted and grateful to all the people in our lives, now and in the past, who have interacted with us and reinforced what we have known since the days we began our careers as teachers: Teaching is the most rewarding profession of all.

Richard D. Kellough
Noreen G. Kellough

Brief Contents

Contents

Note: Every effort has been made to provide accurate Internet information in this book. However, the Internet and information posted on it are constantly changing, so it is inevitable that some of the Internet addresses listed in this textbook will change.

CHAPTER 1

Teaching Young Adolescents
Recognizing and Understanding the Challenge

Anna Vega/Merrill

Welcome to the exciting and ever-changing world of teaching young adolescents. Whether you are in your early twenties and starting your first career or older and beginning a new career, this book is for you—that is, for any person interested in becoming a classroom teacher of young adolescents, that is of children who are experiencing the developmental stage of early adolescence, generally who are in the age range of 9 to 14, of children who are in their middle level years of K–12 education.

The bell rings, and the students enter your classroom, a kaleidoscope of personalities, all peerless and idiosyncratic, each a bundle of energy, with different focuses, experiences, dispositions, learning styles, and learning capacities, differing proficiencies in use of the English language—different challenges. What a formidable task it is to understand and teach 25 or so unique individuals, all at once, and do it for six hours a day, five days a week, 180 days a year! What a challenge it is today, to be a middle level teacher. To prepare yourself for this challenge, consider the information provided in this chapter about schools and about the diverse characteristics and needs of young adolescents, for it is well known that their academic achievement is greatly dependent upon how well their other developmental needs are understood and satisfied. We have to begin this journey somewhere, so let's do it with the following clarification of terms and purpose. We hope you enjoy and benefit from your quest.

CLARIFICATION OF TERMS AND PURPOSE

Young adolescents typically are found in schools in what traditionally have been referred to as grades 5 to 8. Those grades today in the United States may be housed in a number of ways. The **elementary school**, for example, sometimes includes students from kindergarten through grade 8, although some stop with grades 5 or 6. An **intermediate school** commonly houses children of grades 4–6. **Middle schools** most often house children of grades 6 through 8. There are, as you will learn in this chapter, other arrangements.

Regardless of where or how young adolescents are housed or of the cognomen of the school in which they are housed, this resource guide is about preparing you to teach those children in the classroom. Most often, when referring to grades and schools that house young adolescents, we use the term *middle level*. This is not in any way to be construed that we, the authors of this resource guide, are not supporters of the middle school concept because WE ARE! However, the purpose of this resource guide is to help you in your pursuit of excellence as a teacher of young adolescents, not to explain everything you might want or need to know about the middle school. There are, as indicated in the suggested readings at the end of each chapter, other good sources for that.

If you are now in a program of teacher preparation, then perhaps near the completion of the program you likely will be offered your first teaching contract. We use the optimistic "likely" because there is in the profession a general agreement and concern that for the next several years in the United States there will be an acute shortage of teachers (Heller, 2004). You will be excited and eager to sign the contract and begin your new career. Yet after the initial excitement, you will have time to reflect. Many questions will then begin forming in your mind. If in a multiple-school district, to which school will I be assigned? Will it be a traditional school or will it be a *magnet* or *theme school*, that is, a school that specializes in a particular area of the curriculum, such as the visual and performing arts, or science, mathematics, and technology, or international studies? Or a school might be a *charter school*, that is, a public school that is freed from many of the usual rules while still accountable for results (Weertz, 2002). Or a *full-service school*, a school that serves as a hub for quality education and comprehensive social services all beneath one roof (e.g., Black, 2004; Dryfoos, 2002). Or an *International Baccalaureate Middle School*, that is, one with a curriculum approved by the International Baccalaureate Organization (IBO), a worldwide nonprofit educational foundation that is based in Switzerland. Or perhaps it might be another type or combination of these, for example, a charter-magnet school. Although in different ways and with varying terminology, the historical practice of providing different routes for students with different needs and different vocational and academic aspirations continues.

Will it be a school that has its start in the fall, as is traditional, or will it be an extended-year (one that extends longer than the usual 180 days) or a year-round school? Which subjects will I be assigned to teach? What specific grade levels will I have or what will be the age range of my students? How many different preparations will I have? Will I be a member of a teaching team? Will I have core curriculum teaching responsibilities? What advisory and supervision responsibilities might I have? What will the students be like? What will their parents or guardians will be like? How will I get along with the rest of the faculty? What textbooks and curricular materials will I use, and when can I expect to see them? How should I prepare? How can I prepare when there are so many unanswered questions? What school district policies do I need to learn about now? What support services can I expect? How extensive are the school's rules and regulations? Will there be an orientation and an induction program for new and beginning teachers? How can I prepare for students I know little to nothing about?

Those questions, and many others, are often the concerns of beginning teachers. To guide you through this initial experience and help answer some of your questions, this chapter offers a first glimpse into today's world of middle level teaching. This chapter provides an orientation and basis for your planning and selecting learning activities presented in subsequent chapters. Enjoy your quest toward becoming the best teacher you can be.

OBJECTIVES

Upon completion of this first chapter you should be able to:

1. Define middle school.
2. Describe key characteristics that identify a school as being exemplary for the learning of young adolescent students.
3. Describe the middle school concept, how it came to be, its contributions to public K–12 education, and its status today.
4. Describe similarities and differences between the exemplary middle school and the traditional junior high school.
5. Describe the purposes and characteristics of the small learning community concept.

6. Demonstrate understanding of the term *developmentally appropriate*, particularly as related to young adolescents.
7. Recall key developmental characteristics of youth within the age range of 9–14 years.
8. Describe the meaning of the phrase "quality education for each student."
9. Describe the meaning of "teacher as a reflective decision maker."
10. Describe current trends, problems, and issues in public education, particularly as related to middle level education.
11. Describe key principles of the *No Child Left Behind Act* and how that act is likely to affect your work as a middle level classroom teacher.
12. Describe efforts made by today's middle level schools and their teachers to involve parents, guardians, and the community in the children's education.

THE CLASSROOM IN A NATION OF DIVERSITY AND SHIFTING DEMOGRAPHICS: UNDERSTANDING YOUR CHALLENGE

Engaging a New Generation of Citizens

Immigrant students might find the U.S. concept of democracy difficult to grasp. How can a school make students with different languages, ethnicities, races, and complex personal histories understand the importance of the democratic tradition even as they pursue individual dreams of achievement?

The answer: Make learning student-centered and activity- and project-based. Allow immigrant students to communicate in both English and native languages and work in small groups to create a play, collaborate on a work of art, or hash out a mathematical concept.

Rick Allen (2003, p. 8)

Central to your challenge as a classroom teacher is the concept of *multicultural education*, the recognition and acceptance of students from a variety of backgrounds. As stated by Banks (1999, pp. 8–10) an important goal of this concept

is to educate citizens who can participate successfully in the workforce and take action in the civic community to help the nation actualize its democratic ideals . . . Schools should be model communities that mirror the kind of democratic society we envision [where] the curriculum reflects the cultures of the diverse groups within society, the languages and dialects that students speak are respected and valued, cooperation rather than competition is fostered among students and students from diverse racial, ethnic and social-class groups are given equal status.

The variety of individual differences among students requires classroom teachers to use teaching strategies and tactics that accommodate those differences. To most effectively teach students who are different from you, you need skills in:

- establishing a classroom climate in which all students feel welcome and they can learn and are supported in doing so (Chapter 4)
- techniques that emphasize cooperative and social-interactive learning and de-emphasize competitive learning (Chapter 8)
- building upon students' learning styles, capacities, and modalities (Chapter 6)
- strategies and techniques that have proven successful for students of specific characteristics and differences (Chapters 1 and 8).

As indicated, this resource guide has been planned to help you understand and begin developing skills in those four areas as well as with young adolescents in general.

To help you meet the challenge, a wealth of information is available. As a licensed and highly qualified teacher you are expected to know it all, or at least know where you can find all necessary information—and review it when needed. Certain information you have stored in memory will surface and become useful at the most unexpected times. While concerned about all students' safety and physical well-being, you will want to remain sensitive to each student's attitudes, values, social adjustment, emotional well-being, and cognitive development. You must be prepared not only to teach one or more subjects but also do it effectively with students of different cultural backgrounds, diverse linguistic abilities, and varying learning styles, as well as with young adolescents who have been identified as having exceptionalities or special needs. It is, indeed, a challenge!

The United States truly is a multilingual, multiethnic, and multicultural nation. Of children in young adolescent years, approximately one out of every six speaks a language other than English at home. Many of those children have only limited proficiency in the English language (i.e., conversational speaking ability only). The term *English Language Learner (ELL)* is used to refer to students who are non- or limited-English proficient (also known as NEP and LEP). Although 80 percent of ELLs speak Spanish as their first language, there are 5.5 million ELLs in the U.S. public schools who altogether speak more than 400 different languages. In most large school districts, more than 100 languages are represented, with as many as 20 or more different primary languages found in some classrooms. An increasing ethnic, cultural, and linguistic diversity is quickly and strongly affecting schools all across the country, not only the large urban areas but also traditionally homogeneous suburbs and small rural communities.

The overall picture that emerges is a diverse student population that challenges teaching skills. Teachers who traditionally have used direct instruction (such as by lecturing and whole-class discussions) as the dominant mode of instruction have done so with the assumption their students were relatively homogeneous in terms of experience, background, knowledge, motivation, and facility with the English language. However, no such assumption can be made today in classrooms of such cultural, ethnic, and linguistic diversity. As a classroom teacher today, you must be knowledgeable and skilled in using teaching strategies that recognize, celebrate, and build upon that diversity. In a nutshell, that is your challenge.

There may be another recent occurring dimension to this challenge. As we prepare this fifth edition of the book we read and hear of teachers being expected, even instructed, by their supervisors to do more rather than less direct instruction in order to help students score well on the state's standardized achievement tests. Although increasing the amount of direct instruction may or may not help learners score well on tests, it is, as you will learn as you work your way through this resource guide, inconsistent with what is known about instilling meaningful, long-lasting learning, and most especially when working with young adolescents. Please read on!

ORIENTATION: NO SINGLE SHOE FITS ALL

The rapid and dramatic changes occurring throughout modern society, as well as what has been learned in recent years about intelligence and learning, are reflected in the equally rapid and dramatic changes occurring in today's schools. The school in which you are or soon will be teaching may bear little resemblance to the school with the same or similar grade levels that you attended—in its curriculum, its student body, its methods of instruction, its size, or its physical appearance. Two things seem clear: Regardless of organizational patterns, to become and to remain an exemplary school, the school must be in a continual mode of inquiry, reflection, and change; the advantage of utilizing a combination of practices concurrently is usually greater in helping all students succeed in school than is the gain from using any singular practice by itself. The bottom line? Schools and the teachers must constantly change; there is no single shoe that best fits all children in all neighborhoods. America is too large and too diverse for that to ever be possible.

So, what does this mean for you as a teacher of young adolescents? It means that from the moment you set foot onto a school campus, you will want to keep your sensory input channels broadly open, learning as much as you can about the school, its organization, its students and their parents/guardians, the administration, and its support staff. Although it is perhaps only the beginning to your learning about teaching, this resource guide does offer information and resources that you will want to refer to time and again, perhaps long after the initial course for which it is used is over.

Start of the School Year Orientation

As a beginning teacher, you will likely be expected to participate in orientation meetings. When not in meetings, you will have time to prepare your assigned classroom(s) for instruction.

Some school districts start the school year with a district-wide orientation, whereas others schedule on-site orientations at each school. Many school districts do both, with perhaps a district-wide morning meeting followed by school on-site meetings in the afternoon. Such meetings provide you with the opportunity to meet other teachers and establish new collegial friendships and professional relationships, some which may last forever. Many school districts sponsor beginning teacher induction programs that provide special assistance to new teachers. Of course, the scheduling and planning of orientation meetings will vary by district and by school. The objectives for all orientation meetings, however, should be similar to those as discussed in the following paragraphs.

You should become familiar with the district's (or school's) written statement of its unique beliefs and goals—its statement of mission (or philosophy)—and what that statement means to people affiliated with the district or school. [*Note:* Although the terms *mission statement, philosophy statement,* and *vision statement* are often used interchangeably, and while in our opinion the first two are synonymous, the vision statement is or should be a statement of intention that extends beyond the immediate mission of the school and gives future direction to the school's stated mission.] Sample mission statements are shown in Figure 1.1.

You will be encouraged to become knowledgeable about policies of the school and its district. Numerous policies usually cover a wide range. There are policies for procedures relating to students who are injured at school; for what to do during disasters whether natural, such as earthquakes, flooding, and severe storms, or those caused by humans, such as terrorist attacks; regarding students who need to take prescribed medications; for finding illegal drugs and weapons; for campus intruders; for parking on campus; for leaving campus during the school day; for classroom conduct; for school programs, field trips, and parties in the classroom; for mandatory testing and grading practices; for completing absentee and tardy forms; for sending students to the office; and for chaperoning and sponsoring student activities. And these examples are just the beginning.

You will learn about the myriad forms that teachers must fill out. There are forms for injuries that occur while at school, for textbook loans, equipment loans, key loans, attendance, student academic deficiencies and achievements, working with students with special needs, sponsoring student activities, field trips, and referrals of students for inappropriate behavior, to name just a few.

You will learn about the approved curriculum that defines what teachers are mandated to teach and what students are expected to learn. This means that you must familiarize yourself with the curriculum frameworks and learning benchmarks, courses of study, curriculum guides, resource units, teacher's manuals, student textbooks, media programs, testing schedules, and supplementary materials—all of which should reflect the school's mission statement, approved curriculum, and advisory program. You will learn about the school or district plan for monitoring, assessing, and supervising implementation of the curriculum, and about available resource materials and equipment.

You will learn about the school library/media resource center, its personnel, and its procedures, and you will meet district and school personnel and become familiar with the many services that support you in the classroom. You will meet campus security personnel, resource officers, and other ancillary personnel and learn about their functions and locations.

Figure 1.1 Sample middle school mission statements. *(By permission)*

- The mission of **Brandon Middle School** (Virginia Beach, VA) is to provide a challenging, supportive, caring, and safe environment that promotes academic and physical excellence for lifelong learning.
- **Timothy Edwards Middle School** (South Windsor, CT) is a place where children are inspired to grow and learn in an atmosphere of respect, love, and caring. We believe that our charge as educators is (a) to offer intellectual challenge in order to promote academic development, (b) to address the needs of each student as an individual, (c) to foster in each child a sense of belonging and appreciation for self and others, and (d) to help students to become contributing citizens of the world. We . . . are committed to these goals—the keys to a healthy, interesting, and prosperous environment where a child's positive self-concept is cultivated through academic, physical, and social/emotional growth.
- The mission of **Toby Johnson Middle School** (Elk Grove, CA) is to challenge students to maximize their potential as learners, achievers, and productive world citizens. To that end, we will provide for all students:
  - rigorous standards-based curricula in preparation for advanced educational opportunities
  - career paths to provide a "school to career" link with employment and higher education
  - the knowledge and skill necessary to attain optimal health and physical fitness and to maintain both throughout their lives
  - opportunity for personal development through cultural, athletic, and extra-curricular activities
  - an atmosphere that fosters mutual respect, acceptance of diversity, and cooperative, collegial behavior
  - opportunity to contribute positively to their society and community
  - curriculum that incorporates the use of technological skills necessary for academic and career success.

As a student in a program for teacher preparation, you may be expected to participate in an orientation meeting at your college or university. The meeting may be held at the beginning of the program, just before the beginning of your field experiences, or both times. Perhaps this meeting will be a function of one of your college or university courses. You will receive your school assignment, the name of the school and the school district, the school's location, the date when you should report to that assignment, the name of your cooperating teacher(s), the grade level(s), the subject(s), and perhaps the name of your college or university supervisor. You will probably be encouraged to follow many of the objectives just discussed as well as to meet other teacher candidates.

When you arrive at your assigned school and after introductions have been made, you should familiarize yourself with the school campus and the way the school is organized. Walk around the campus, perhaps with a copy of the school map, and learn the location of your classroom(s). Also locate the nearest restrooms for girls, for boys, and for adult men and women. You may be loaned one or several keys—one for the classroom, one for a restroom, and perhaps one for a faculty workroom. Become familiar with such areas as the teachers' workroom, the faculty room, and the faculty lunchroom (which may or may not be a single area—a large school may have several faculty rooms scattered about the campus).

Thoroughly investigate this campus environment. Where do students eat their lunches? Is there a multipurpose room—a room used for lunch as well as for educational purposes? Is there a school nurse? Where is the nurse's station? When is the nurse available? Where is the nearest first aid and emergency equipment? How do you notify maintenance and security personnel quickly and efficiently? Where are the written procedures for fire drills and other emergencies? Where is information about the school's emergency warning system? Is there a plan posted in a conspicuous place for all to see? Where are the various administrative offices? Where are the counseling and guidance offices? Is there an office of student activities? Where are the library, the media center, the resources room, gymnasium(s), and the auditorium? Where are textbooks stored, and how are students expected to use them? Are the textbooks to be checked out and distributed? If so, how? Where is the attendance office? Are there resource specialists, and if there are, what are their functions and where are their offices located?

At an orientation session, you may meet the grade level or department chairperson or the team leader and members of that team. How can you discover where those persons are to be found at various times during the school day? Where are teaching materials and laboratory supplies kept, and how do you obtain them? Have you located your faculty mailbox and the place to check in or out when you arrive at school or leave at the end of the day? What procedures do you follow if you are absent because of illness or if you know you are going to arrive late? Do you have the necessary phone numbers? Is there a school website? If there is, how extensive and current is it? Not of least importance, if you drive a vehicle to school, where do you park? Otherwise, what is the best local transportation available for getting to and from school each day?

The School Calendar Year

School years vary from state to state, district to district, and school to school. Most school years begin in August and continue through late May or mid-June. However, to accommodate more students without a significant increase in capital costs and to better sustain student learning, some schools have eliminated the traditional long summer break by switching to year-round education (YRE). Some schools that are called year-round simply start a week or two earlier than is traditional and end a week or two later and still have a summer break of two or more months. Although year-round schooling is increasing in popularity (George, 2005), for most teachers and students in the United States the school year is still approximately 180 days.

In a school with year-round operation, a teacher might teach for three-quarters of the year and be off for one-quarter or teach in a 45/15 program which means nine weeks of school (45 days) "on track" followed by three weeks of school (15 days) "off track" throughout the year. In a 45/15 arrangement, teachers and students are on tracks, referred to as an A Track, a B Track, and so on, with starting and ending times that vary depending on the track and time of year. At any one time there is usually at least one track that is on vacation. Intersession programs may be held during off-track times, at which time students might participate in classes designed for remediation, exploration, or enrichment.

Beginning about 8:00 A.M. the school day lasts until about 3:00 P.M. During hot summer months, some schools begin earlier, say at 7:15, and end around 2:00. District and state laws vary, but generally teachers are expected to be in the classroom no less than 15 minutes prior to the start of school and to remain in their classrooms no less than 15 minutes after final dismissal of students. Many schools use what is commonly called a *freeze time*, a scheduled time each week, such as 2:30–3:30 P.M. every Monday, when all teachers are in their classrooms to help students and meet with parents. Typically no other activities, such as athletic practices or club meetings, are supposed to be scheduled during freeze time.

Drawing upon studies of adolescent sleep patterns as well as the need to find ways to deal with crowded schools or to cut transportation costs by reducing the number of busses and drivers needed, some schools are experimenting with later than usual starting times, or because no single schedule can accommodate the desires and needs of everyone, with multiple starting times.

Laura Bolesta/Merrill

Teaching Teams

Traditionally, elementary school teachers taught their groups of children in their self-contained classrooms for most of the school day and junior high and senior high school teachers taught their subject disciplines as often as seven or eight times each day to as many groups of students. At all levels, teachers taught in their assigned classrooms while fairly isolated from other teachers and school activities—not unlike the parallel play of preschool children, that is, playing side-by-side but not really together. In some schools, that is still the case. Increasingly, however, middle level teachers especially are finding themselves members of a **collaborative teaching team** in which several teachers work together to reflect, plan, and implement a curriculum for a common cohort of students. [*Note:* A distinction must be made between *teaching teams* and *team teaching:* team teaching refers to two or more teachers simultaneously providing instruction to students in the same classroom. Members of a teaching team may participate in team teaching.]

The teaching team may comprise of only a few teachers, for example, all seventh-grade teachers or all the teachers who teach the same cohort of sixth-grade students. They may meet regularly to plan curriculum for the particular cohort of students, or they may meet periodically to plan a curriculum and learning activities around a common theme. For example, the grade-level teaching teams at Eual J. Landry Middle School (Hahnville, LA) meet daily for 45 minutes, at which time they plan their monthly project-based interdisciplinary units. Sometimes teaching teams are comprised of one teacher each from the curriculum areas of English/reading/language arts (known also as literacy), history/social studies/geography, mathematics, and science. In addition, other teachers may be part of the team, including teachers of physical education, the visual and performing arts, and even special education teachers and at-risk specialty personnel or school counselors. As a visiting or continuing member of this *interdisciplinary team organization* (ITO), a team may invite a community-resource person.

These teams are commonly called *inter-disciplinary teaching teams* or simply *interdisciplinary teams.*

The Community of Learners Concept

An interdisciplinary teaching team and its common cohort of students is sometimes referred to as the community of learners, or *learning community* (also called *school-within-a-school, village, pod, academy, family, neighborhood, house,* or just plain *team*) concept, where each team of teachers is assigned each day to the same cohort of students for a common block of time. Within this block of time, teachers on the team are responsible for the many professional decisions necessary, such as how school can be made developmentally responsive (i.e., most meaningful) to students' lives, what specific responsibilities each teacher has each day, which students need special attention, and how students will be grouped for instruction. Members of such a team become "students of their students" and thereby build the curriculum and instruction around their students' interests, perspectives, and perceptions. The team and their students truly become a community of learners.

The community of learners concept helps students make important and meaningful connections among disciplines. It also provides them with both peer and adult group identification, which provides an important sense of identity and belonging. In some schools, using an arrangement called **looping** (also referred to variously as *banding, family-style grouping, multiyear grouping, multiyear instruction, multiyear placement, persisting groups,* and *teacher-student progression*), the cohort of students and teachers remain together as a group for several or all of the years a student is at that school. Spending more than the usual one school year with a group of students allows their teacher or the teaching team to acquire greater knowledge of the students' personalities, learning styles and capacities, and their needs.

The advantages to being a member of a teaching team in a learning community environment are numerous. For example, the combined thinking of several teachers creates an expanded pool of ideas, enhances individual capacities for handling complex problems, and provides intellectual stimulation and emotional support. The combination of talents produces an energy that has a positive impact on the instructional program. A beginning teacher who joins a team has the benefit of support from more experienced teammates. When a team member is absent, other members of the team work closely with the substitute, resulting in less loss of instructional time for students. More and better planning for students occurs as teachers discuss, argue, and reach agreement on behavioral expectations, curriculum emphasis, instructional approaches, and materials.

For a teaching team to plan effectively and efficiently, members must meet together frequently. This is best accomplished when they share a *common planning time*. This means in addition to each member's daily planning time, members of a team share a common time to plan curriculum and discuss the progress and needs of individual students within the cohort.

Each team assigns a member to be a team facilitator, or a *lead teacher*. The lead teacher organizes the meetings and facilitates discussions during the common planning time. Usually, this teacher also acts as a liaison with the administration to assure the team has the necessary resources to put its plans into action. A team's lead teacher (or another member designated by the team) may also serve on the school leadership team, a group of teachers and administrators, and sometimes students (Fiscus, 2005), designated by the principal or elected by the faculty (and student body) to assist in the leadership of the school.

Nontraditional Scheduling

To maximize the learning time, to allow for more instructional flexibility, and to accommodate common planning time for teachers, an increasing number of middle level schools use some form of *block scheduling*. Block scheduling means, for at least a portion of the school day, or of the week, blocks of time ranging from 70 to 140 or more minutes replace the traditional structure of 50-minute-long instructional periods. The possible variations are nearly limitless.

For example, for some schools, the school year consists of three 12-week-long trimesters, and each school day is divided into five 70-minute-long class periods. Such a schedule is referred to as a 5×3×7 block plan. Some schools use a 4×3×4 block plan, whereby students take four 85–90-minute-long *macroperiods* (or macroclasses) each day, each semester. Other schools use an alternating-day block plan, sometimes called the *A-B plan*, where classes meet every other day for the entire school year for 90-minute blocks.

Using extended periods, or macroperiods, allows the teacher to supervise and assist students with assignments and project work as well as with their reading, writing, thinking, and study skills. Macroperiods provide more time for student inquiry, project work, and for interactive and interdisciplinary thematic instruction that might otherwise be difficult or impossible to accomplish in shorter instructional periods.

Block Scheduling: Advantages and Disadvantages

Consistently reported in the research of schools using block scheduling—where students and teachers work together in longer but fewer classes at a time—are: greater satisfaction among teachers and administrators

and improvement in both the behavior and the learning of all students (Black, 1998). In block schedule students do more writing, pursue issues in greater depth, enjoy classes more, feel more challenged, and gain deeper understandings. There is more time for learning via projects, for review, to effectively differentiate the instruction, and for the teacher to get to know the students better and to respond to a student's needs with greater care (Kalina, 2004). In studies of schools using block scheduling as opposed to traditional scheduling, researchers report equal or better mastery and retention of material, and a significant reduction in suspension and dropout rates (Shortt & Thayer, 1998).

Other benefits of the block plans over a traditional seven- or eight-period daily schedule include: in one school year the total hours of instruction is significantly greater; each teacher teaches fewer courses during a semester and is responsible for fewer students. Therefore, student-teacher interaction is more productive and the school climate is positive with fewer discipline problems and fewer dropouts; and, because planning periods are longer, there is more time for teachers to plan and interact with parents and guardians.

Block scheduling arrangements often produce serendipitous benefits. For example, students may not have to carry as many books and may go to their lockers fewer times a day to exchange textbooks and materials between blocks. In some schools, except perhaps for physical education and shop classes, student lockers are not used at all. On the other hand, prompted by the number of heavily loaded book bags lying in the aisles of classrooms—making the aisles difficult to traverse and causing safety concerns during emergencies—some schools request that students leave book bags in their lockers during the school day rather than carry them around from classroom to classroom.

Also, the reduction of bells ringing from as many as eight times a day to perhaps only two or three times a day, or not at all, creates less disturbance. Some middle level schools use no passing bells or signals at all.

Because students are not roaming halls for three to five minutes five or six times a day, teachers can more easily supervise unstructured time and thereby have improved control over portions of the subtle but powerful message systems within schools referred to as the **hidden** (or *covert, informal*) **curriculum**. The messages of the hidden curriculum are the school climate, the feelings projected from the teacher and other adults to students and from the students to one another, not only in classrooms but before and after school, at social events, school programs, club meetings, and in the halls, restrooms, lunch areas, and other places on the school campus not monitored as closely as the classrooms. Now do Exercise 1.1.

EXERCISE 1.1: WHAT MESSAGE IS BEING CONVEYED?

INSTRUCTIONS: Although it is seldom planned and almost never assessed, students do learn through the hidden or covert curriculum. For this exercise, your task is two-fold. First, identify what you believe to be the hidden message, if any, that is conveyed to the students by behaviors of each of the following teachers. Then, share and discuss your responses with your classmates. Later in the course, you might like to revisit this exercise and think about what, if anything, in each instance would have been a more appropriate teacher behavior.

1. Ms. Tai is a middle school teacher of mathematics. After visiting her classroom, the principal suggested that she brighten the classroom and decorate its walls with a display of student work. When the principal returned to the classroom two weeks later, Ms. Tai had put up a display that consisted solely of a chart of the homework and test records of students.

   Hidden message sent by Ms. Tai: _____

   _____

2. Mr. Lever has decorated one wall of his classroom with pictures and stories of famous scientists, all of whom are men.

   Hidden message sent by Mr. Lever: _____

   _____

3. While Ms. Gushé is talking to her classroom of students, the school principal walks into the room. Ms. Gushé stops her talk and walks over to greet the principal and find out what the principal wants.

   Hidden message sent by Ms. Gushé: _____

   _____

4. Mr. Latte is nearly always late in arriving to his class that meets the period after lunch, seldom beginning class until at least five minutes past the scheduled start time.

   Hidden message sent by Mr. Latte: _____

   _____

5. Three minutes into the planned ten minutes of silent reading, Ms. Silencia asks for everyone's attention, verbally reprimands two students for fooling around, and then writes out a referral for each of the two students.

   Hidden message being sent by Mrs. Silencia: _____

   _____

6. Can you recall an example to present to your classmates for a discussion?

   _____

   _____

FOR YOUR NOTES

Nontraditional school schedules are not without their problems. Problems that sometimes arise from block scheduling are: there may be a mismatch between content actually covered and what is expected by state-mandated tests and the dates those tests are given to students; content coverage in a course may be less than what was traditionally covered (certainly neither of these first two is an unimportant issue in this day of high-stakes, exterior-developed academic achievement testing); some teachers may be unhappy if classes meet less frequently than in the traditional once-a-day, five-days-a-week schedule; and when the instructional strategy is developmentally inappropriate (such as if the teacher uses formal teacher talk for the entire length of a macroperiod) students are likely to become bored, restless, frequently late to class or absent, and mischievous, that is, the students become turned-off to learning.

Using a *modified block schedule*, some schools have successfully combined schedules, thus satisfying teachers who prefer block scheduling and those who prefer the traditional schedule. A modified block schedule can provide both traditional 40-minute periods (sometimes called *split-block periods*) that meet daily and have longer blocks. A modified block schedule centers on a day consisting of seven or eight 45- or 40-minute periods along with alternate longer blocks. In a modified block schedule, all students might start the day with a 30- or 40-minute-long first period that serves as an advisory time (known also as *homeroom, homebase,* or *advisor-advisee*). From there, some students continue the morning attending traditional-length periods while others move into a morning block class. Throughout the day, teachers and students may pass from block classes to those of traditional length or vice versa.

Some schools use a *flexible block schedule*. The daily schedule is a seven-period day with all seven classes meeting on Monday. Periods one through four meet for 75 minutes, while periods five through seven meet for 30 minutes. Periods one through four meet for 105 minutes each on Tuesdays and Thursdays, and periods five through seven meet for 120 minutes each on Wednesdays and Fridays. A 30-minute advisory period is held at the same time each day, perhaps first thing in the morning or immediately after lunch.

In short, there is little doubt that longer blocks of instructional time can be a positive factor contributing to students' meaningful learning, especially when combined with year-round education, curriculum integration, interdisciplinary thematic instruction, and project-based learning.

Quality Education for Every Student

Smaller learning communities and nontraditional scheduling are efforts to organize schools in ways that will deliver quality education for every student. The curriculum of a quality education school is one seen by students as having meaning and usefulness in their lives and is delivered via activity-oriented instruction. Rather than dictating procedures, ordering students to work, and berating them when they do not, in a quality school the teachers provide a stimulating learning environment and are seen by the students as being positive, encouraging, respectful, and supportive.

Today's movement to transform all schools into caring and responsive learning communities has, as its sole purpose, helping each and every child to make the transitions necessary to succeed in school and in life.

Responsive Practices for Helping Each Child Succeed

Because of the enormous diversity of students, the advantage from utilizing a combination of practices concurrently is usually greater in helping all children succeed in school than is the gain from using any singular practice by itself. School reorganization and the restructuring of schedules, then, represent two of the transformation efforts to help all students make successful transitions.

Other important responsive practices, most of which are discussed in various ways throughout this resource guide, are:

- a perception, shared by all teachers and staff, that every child can learn when given adequate support, although not all students need the same amount of time to learn the same thing
- attention to the emotional development and the coping skills of each child
- engagement of parents and guardians as partners in their child's education
- high, although not necessarily identical, expectations for all students
- highly qualified teachers, specialist teachers, and smaller schools with smaller classes
- peer tutoring and cross-age coaching
- personal attention, adult advocacy, and scheduling and learning plans to help students learn in a manner by which they best learn
- time and guided attention to basic skills—especially those of literacy, thinking, and social—rather than solely on rote memory.

MIDDLE LEVEL SCHOOLS

When you receive your teaching credential, you may or may not be certified to teach at the middle school level. In some states, an elementary school credential certifies a person to teach in any grade, kindergarten through grade eight. In some states, a secondary school credential certifies a person to teach a particular subject at any grade level, kindergarten through grade 12. In other states, such a credential qualifies a person to teach only grades 7 through 12. However, at least 33 states provide a middle school teaching credential to candidates who have successfully completed a program specifically designed to prepare teachers for that level.

At this point, you should note there are two sometimes quite different types of schools, both of which may be called middle schools. One is the traditional junior high school with perhaps a few minor changes, such as changing its name to "middle school." The second is the exemplary middle school, which is, as shown in Table 1.1, quite different from the traditional junior high school.

Used historically from about 1880, the term *junior high school* most commonly refers to schools having grades seven and eight or grades seven, eight, and nine, in which a program is designed to approximate the type of education commonly found in traditional high schools. Thus, a junior high school might be considered a "not-quite-yet-but-trying-to-be" high school. Students graduating from a junior high school would often then move on to a senior high school.

Beginning in the 1960s, the term *middle school* gained favor as a result of the movement away from the concept of "junior" high school. Reasons for the reorganization away from the concept of junior high school and the adoption of a middle school education include: (a) providing a program specifically designed for young adolescents, (b) setting up a more effective transition between the elementary school and the high school, and (c) moving ninth graders to the high school or, as has happened in some school districts in recent years, to a location designed solely for ninth graders, such as the Minne Howard School for ninth graders (Alexandria, VA) or the Ninth Grade Success Academies (Philadelphia, PA). Proponents of the separate facility for ninth graders argue that having a separate school improves their academic and social transition to high school (Reents, 2002).

Although any combination of grades four through nine may be included in a middle school, the most common configuration is grades six through eight. Including sixth graders and excluding ninth graders is a reflection of the recommendation of the National Middle School Association in its official position paper, *This We Believe* (NMSA, 1982, rev. 1995).

The term *middle level education* identifies school organizations based on a philosophy that incorporates curricula and instructional practices specifically designed to meet the developmental needs of young adolescent students, that is, of students "between the ages of 10 and 15." This philosophy is referred to as the *middle school concept* (NMSA, 1995).

The middle school movement began to grow in the 1960s, especially with the publication of W. M. Alexander's, "The Junior High: A Changing View," in *Readings in Curriculum*, edited by G. Hass and K. Wiles (Boston: Allyn & Bacon, 1965), D. H. Eichhorn's *The Middle School* (New York: The Center for Applied Research in Education, 1966), and W. M. Alexander's, ed., *The Emergent Middle School* (New York: Holt, Rinehart & Winston, 1969).

Since the emergence of the middle school concept in the 1960s, the needs of young adolescents have been studied, researched, and analyzed in greater detail and sophistication than ever before. Over the years, youngsters of middle school age have been designated by various nomenclatures, including *transescent, preadolescent, preteen, prepubescent, in-betweenager,* and *tweenager,* defined as the stage of development that begins before

Table 1.1 Summary of Differences between Middle Schools and Traditional Junior High Schools	Characteristic	Junior High School	Middle School
	Most common grade-span organization	7–8 or 7–9	6–8
	Scheduling	Traditional 50-minute periods, six-period day	Flexible, usually block
	Subject organization	Departmentalized	Intergrated and thematic; interdisciplinary, usually language arts, math, science, and social studies
	Guidance/counseling	Separate sessions with counselor on individual or "as-needed" basis; full-time counselors	Advisor-advisee relationship between teacher and student in homeroom or home base
	Exploratory curriculum	Electives by individual choice	Common "wheel" of experiences for all students
	Teachers	Subject-centered; grades 7–12 certification	Interdisciplinary teams; student-centered; grades K–8 or 6–8 certification
	Instruction	Traditional; lecture, skills, and repetition	Thematic units; discovery techniques; study skills
	Athletics	Interscholastic sports emphasizing competition	Intramural programs emphasizing participation

the onset of puberty and extends through the early stages of adolescence. Although the term used is perhaps inconsequential, some understanding of the various developmental stages associated with this group of youngsters is essential if an educational program and its instruction are to be appropriately tailored to address their needs. That understanding is reviewed in the final section of this chapter.

In recent years, some school districts, especially large, urban school districts, perhaps from equating low achievement test scores with the middle school concept have searched for ways to more effectively improve the academic achievement of its young adolescent students, such as closing middle schools and returning to the neighborhood K–8 elementary school concept. Their reasoning includes: (a) their belief that teachers get to know children better and can more effectively share important information about the children and about the curriculum when children are at the same school for eight or nine years rather than just three or four years, (b) children in a K–8 school can be continuously assessed and will therefore progress more smoothly and successfully through the curriculum than when there is a break due to changing schools, (c) more effective modeling behaviors occur as the young adolescents realize their responsibility resulting from the younger children adulating them, and (d) the stress of early adolescence is less magnified than when only young adolescents are together in a school (Arth, 2004; Herman, 2004).

MIDDLE SCHOOL WITHIN A K–8 SCHOOL

The idea that middle school has to be either a place of academic rigor or of nurturing is a false dichotomy. It must be both.
Linda Perlstein (2004, p. 60)

Still another emerging arrangement is the middle school within a K–8 school, such as Cordova Middle School (Phoenix, AZ), where Cordova Primary and Middle Schools are separate units within a K–8 school, each with its own principal. While enabling a middle school program to develop (for example, with its characteristic common planning time, block scheduling, elective enrichment programs, and instruction appropriate for young adolescents), the separate schools share the same campus as well as music, art, and physical education teachers.

THE FUNDAMENTAL CHARACTERISTIC OF QUALITY MIDDLE LEVEL EDUCATION

Wherever and however the young adolescent students are housed, and regardless of other responsive practices, in the end it is the dedication, commitment, and nature of the understanding of the involved adults—the teachers, administrators, bus drivers, cooks, grounds crew,

security staff, custodial staff, and support personnel—that remains the incisive element. That, in our opinion, is the fundamental characteristic of quality public education—that is, to celebrate and build upon the diverse characteristics and needs of students. This resource guide continues in its commitment to that premise.

Committed Teachers

Middle level teachers represent myriad individual personalities—perhaps impossible to capture in generalizations. Let us imagine a teaching colleague mentions that Pat Gomez, in Room 17, is a "fantastic teacher," "one of the best teachers in the district," "super," and "magnificent." What might be some of the characteristics you would expect to see in Pat's teaching behaviors? (A detailed presentation of teacher responsibilities and behaviors is the topic of the chapter that follows.)

Perhaps foremost is that Pat constructs positive, accepting, respectful, and trusting relationships with students and their families. Additionally, we can expect Pat to:

- be knowledgeable about the developmental characteristics of the young adolescent students under Pat's supervision
- be understanding of, and committed to, the school's statement of philosophy or mission
- know the curriculum and how best to teach it
- be enthusiastic, motivated, and well organized
- demonstrate effective communication and interpersonal skills
- be willing to listen to the students and to risk trying their ideas
- acknowledge students' strengths, not their limitations
- be a reflective and responsible decision maker.

Students need teachers who are well organized and who know how to establish and manage an active and supportive learning environment, even with its multiple instructional demands. Young adolescents respond best to teachers who provide leadership and who enjoy their function as role models, advisors, mentors, and reflective decision makers.

Reflective Decision Making

During any school day you will make hundreds of nontrivial decisions, many of them instantaneously. In addition, you will have already made many decisions in preparation for the teaching day. During one school year a teacher makes literally thousands of decisions, many of which can and will affect the lives of her or his students for years to come. As in the nearly poetic words of Brown and Mofett (1999, p. 24), "We [teachers] influence students in myriad, unperceived ways that affect them and the lives of people with whom they interact like the widening circles extending from a stone tossed into a tranquil pond." This may seem to you to be an awesome responsibility; indeed it is!

Initially, of course, you will make errors in judgment, but you will also learn that your students are resilient and there are experts available who can guide you to help ensure the students are not harmed severely by your mistakes. You can and should learn from your errors. Keep in mind the sheer number of decisions you make each day will mean not all will be the best decisions you could have made if you had more time and better resources for planning.

While pedagogy is based on scientific principles, good classroom teaching is as much an art as it is a science. Few rules apply to every teaching situation. The writers of published curriculum programs wrote for students of a particular age in general; they did *not* know your students specifically. In fact, real decisions about the selection of content, instructional objectives and materials, teaching strategies, a teacher's response to student misbehavior, and the selection of techniques for assessment of the learning experiences are all the result of subjective judgments.

Although many decisions are made at a somewhat unhurried pace when you are planning for your instruction, many others will be made intuitively and *tout de suite*. Once the school day has begun, there is rarely time for making carefully thought-out judgments. At your best, you base your decisions on your teaching style, which, in turn, is based on your knowledge of school policies, pedagogical research, the curriculum, and the unique characteristics of the young adolescents in your classroom. You will also base your decisions on instinct, common sense, and reflective judgment. The better your understanding and experience with schools, the curriculum, and the students, and the more time you give for thoughtful reflection, the more likely it will be your decisions will result in the children meeting the educational goals. You will reflect upon, conceptualize, and apply understandings from one teaching experience to the next. As your understanding about your classroom experiences accumulates, your teaching will become more routinized, predictable, refined, and steadily effective. This discussion of reflective decision making, a basic concept about which this book is designed, is continued at the beginning of the chapter that follows; to learn more about the reality of teaching, now do Exercise 1.2, Conversation with a Classroom Teacher.

EXERCISE 1.2: CONVERSATION WITH A CLASSROOM TEACHER

INSTRUCTIONS: The purpose of this exercise is to interview one or more middle level teachers, perhaps one who is relatively new to the classroom and one who has been teaching for 10 or more years. Use the following questions. You may make duplicate blank copies of this form. Share the results with others in your class.

1. Name and location of school _____

_____

_____

2. Total enrollment _____

_____

_____

3. Grade span of school _____

_____

_____

4. Date of interview _____

_____

_____

5. Name of interviewee _____

_____

_____

6. In which area(s) of the school's curriculum do you work? _____

_____

_____

7. Tell me one or two factors in your life or in your education that led you to choose teaching as a career.

_____

_____

8. What were the circumstances that led you to teach at this level? _____

_____

_____

9. Please describe the preparation or training that you had for this teaching. _____

_____

_____

10. What do you like the most about your work? _____

_____

_____

EXERCISE 1.2   *(continued)*

11. What do you like the least about your work? _____

_____

_____

12. What would you say is the most important thing for me to know in order to be an effective teacher of young adolescents? _____

_____

_____

13. What advice about preparation can you offer me? _____

_____

_____

14. Is there any other advice you have for those who are entering the teaching profession?

_____

_____

School Leadership

As a new or visiting member of the faculty, one of your tasks is to become familiar with the administrative organization of your school and district. The roles of principals, superintendents, and other educational leaders have changed significantly in recent years, with a much larger focus today on teaching and learning, professional development, achievement testing, and accountability. Now, because only since mid-2003 all 50 states, plus the District of Columbia and Puerto Rico, had approved accountability plans in place for the *No Child Left Behind (NCLB) Act* (Signed into law by President Bush in January 2002, NCLB is discussed in the next section), those plans will most assuredly be areas of major focus for years to come.

One person significantly responsible for the success of any school is its principal (or in the case of a teacher-led school, the teacher leader). What are the characteristics of an effective school principal or teacher leader? Perhaps foremost is that the person has a vision of what a quality school is and strives to bring that vision to life. Improvement of student learning is the effective school leader's constant theme. Because exemplary educators today believe in the innate potential of every child, rather than of dumbing down standards and expectations, they modify the key variables of time, grouping, and instructional strategies to help individual children achieve quality learning, nearly impossible to do without a supportive, forward, and positive-thinking school principal or leader.

In addition to the school principal there may be vice, assistant, or grade level principals, persons with specific responsibilities and oversight functions, such as student activities, school discipline and security, transition programs, and curriculum and instruction. A school might also employ a school manager, a person who assumes a variety of administrative tasks so as to free the principal or teacher leader to focus on education. Blurring the traditional lines that separated administrators and teachers, for the purposes of improving instruction and ultimately the scores of students on high-stakes assessments, more and more school districts are giving select teachers leadership roles beyond their own classrooms.

THE COMMUNITY SERVED BY THE SCHOOL

Today's exemplary educators are making major efforts to enhance the connections among the home, school, local, and global communities to promote the success of every child.

The No Child Left Behind Act

Indeed, enhanced connections between home and school is a key provision of the *No Child Left Behind Act of 2001*, a massive federal education policy initiative (a revised version of the *Elementary and Secondary Education Act*, the central federal law in precollegiate education

first enacted in 1965) that impacts nearly all aspects of public education. It has been called the most significant and controversial change in federal education policy since the federal government assumed a major role in American education nearly half a century ago (Sunderman & Kim, 2004). Signed into law by President Bush in January 2002, aspects of the law include:

- an annual report of school-by-school data that show a range of information
- annual testing that must demonstrate all groups of disadvantaged children making substantial progress every year in every school, thus narrowing the gap between advantaged and disadvantaged students and among all subgroups of students
- annual testing of children in reading and mathematics in grades 3 through 8 with tests that are aligned with state academic standards
- dialogue between schools and families, especially in low-income communities, and for states, districts, and schools to notify parents/guardians about their children's progress and about their options for transferring out of low-performing schools. [*Note:* The number of parents opting to transfer their children to better schools has been quite low, for example, just 215 out of 204,000 eligible in Los Angeles; 1,097 out of 279,000 in Chicago; 6,828 out of 230,000 in New York City (Helfand & Rubin, 2004).]
- federal school funding changes
- paraprofessionals hired with Title I funds who must have completed at least two years of college, obtained an associate's degree or higher, or passed an evaluation to demonstrate knowledge and teaching ability
- scientific, research-based reading programs for children in grades K–3
- states must bring all students up to the "proficient" level on state tests by the year 2013–14
- teachers in core content areas must be highly qualified. [*Note:* As defined by NCLB, core content areas are English, reading or language arts, mathematics, science, foreign languages, civics and government, economics, art, history, and geography. Although each state can determine its own definition of "the arts," it most likely will include music, visual arts, and dance.] As defined by NCLB, "highly qualified" means the teacher has (1) full state certification, which can be "alternative certification," as defined by a state, (2) at least a bachelor's degree, and (3) demonstrated subject matter competence in the core academic subjects taught.]
- and, along with the requirement to have content standards in science in place by the 2005–06 school year, beginning in the 2007–08 school year, states must test students in science once in each of three grade spans: 3–5, 6–9, and 10–12. The NCLB Act however does not specify that states must include science-test results in measuring adequate yearly progress.

A rebellion has been stirring in relation to certain aspects of NCLB and/or to its cost, with some school districts refusing federal funding rather than complying with NCLB mandates (Frahm, 2004; Paulson, 2004). Several states have requested federal waivers on certain requirements. Although the legislation is up for reauthorization in 2007, it is probably reasonable to expect modifications to the NCLB Act of 2001 to occur not only then but also for years to come.

Home and School Connections

It is well known that parental and family involvement in a child's education can have a positive impact on the student's achievement at school. When parents or guardians of children who are not doing well in school get involved, the student benefits with more consistent attendance at school, more positive attitudes and actions, better grades, increased motivation, and higher test scores. Recognizing the positive effect parent and family involvement has on student achievement and success, the National PTA published National Standards for Parent/Family Involvement Programs (Sullivan, 1998).

Although not all schools have a parent/guardian organization, many schools have adopted formal policies about home and community connections. These policies usually emphasize that parents/guardians should be included as partners in the educational program, that teachers and administrators will inform parents/guardians about their child's progress, about the school's family involvement policy, and about any programs in which family members can participate. Schools' efforts to foster parent/guardian and community involvement are as varied as the people who participate, and include:

- enrollment of not only students but of entire families as members of a learning team
- home visitation programs
- homework hotlines
- involvement of community leaders in the classroom as mentors, aides, and role models
- involvement of students in community service learning
- newsletters, workshops, and electronic hardware and software for parents/guardians to help facilitate their children's learning
- parent/guardian volunteers as "co-teachers" in the classroom
- regular phone calls and personal notes home about a student's progress
- student-teacher-parent contracts and assignment calendars, sometimes available via the school's webpage
- use of adult coordinators to serve as liaisons between home and school.

Community Service Learning

Through community service learning students learn and develop during active participation in thoughtfully organized and curriculum-connected experiences that meet community needs. Community members, geographic features, buildings, monuments, historic sites, and other places in a school's geographic area constitute one of the richest instructional laboratories that can be imagined. To take advantage of this accumulated wealth of resources, as well as to build school-community partnerships, once hired by a school district you should start a file of community resources as related to subject areas in which you work. For instance, you might include files about the skills of the students' parents and other family members, noting those that could be resources for the study occurring in your classroom. You might also include files on various resource people who could speak or present to the class, on free and inexpensive materials, on sites for field trips, and on what other communities of teachers, students, and adult helpers have done.

It is a useful idea to start your professional resources file now, and to maintain it throughout your professional career; for that, see Figure 1.2. Many

Figure 1.2 Beginning my professional resources file.

A professional resources file is a project you could begin now and continue throughout your professional career. Begin your resources file either on a computer database program or on color-coded file cards listing: (1) the name of the resource, (2) how and where to obtain the resource, (3) description of how to use the resource, and (4) evaluative comments about the resource.

Organize the file in a way that makes sense to you. Cross-reference or color-code your system to accommodate the following categories of resources.

- CD/DVD titles
- Community resources
- Free/inexpensive materials
- Games
- Guest speakers/presenters
- Internet resources
- Media sources
- Motivational ideas
- Print resources
- Printed visuals
- Resources to order
- Software titles
- Student worksheets
- Test items
- Thematic units/ideas
- Unit/lesson plans/ideas
- Video titles
- Miscellaneous/other

resource ideas and sources are mentioned and listed throughout this resource guide.

THE EMERGENT OVERALL PICTURE: CURRENT ACTIONS, TRENDS, PROBLEMS, AND ISSUES AFFECTING MIDDLE LEVEL EDUCATION

Certainly, no facet of education receives more attention from the media, causes more concern among parents and teachers, or receives larger headlines than that of a decline (factual or fanciful) in students' achievement in the public schools. Reports are issued, polls are taken, debates are organized, blue ribbon commissions are formed, and legislation is enacted. Community members write letters to local editors about it, news editors devote editorial space to it, television anchors comment about it, and documentaries and specials focus on it in full color. We read, "Schools put in program for failing academic standards," "30,000 facing summer school: Student failures push city to revert to K–8 school organization," and so on. What initiated this attention that began at least three decades ago and continues today (Bracey, 2003)? We are not sure, but it has never been matched in its political interest and participation, and it has affected and continues to affect both the public schools and programs in higher education that are directly or indirectly related to teacher preparation and certification.

In response to the reports, educators, corporations and local businesspersons, and politicians acted and continue acting. Around the nation, their actions have resulted in:

- changes in standards for teacher certification
- an emphasis on education for cultural diversity and ways of teaching and working with English-language learners
- an emphasis on helping students make connections between what is being learned and real life, as well as connections between subjects in the curriculum and between academics and vocations
- an emphasis on helping students make effective transitions from home to school, from one level of schooling to the next, and from school to life
- an emphasis on raising test scores, increasing quality instructional time, and changing curricula
- an emphasis on standards-based education
- an improvement of school-home-community connections
- school district reorganization.

Key Trends and Practices

Listed here are key trends and practices in education today, all of which either directly or indirectly affect middle level education, some of which are discussed in subsequent chapters (see index for topic locations).

Perhaps you and members of your class can identify other key trends and practices.

- A continuing influx of immigrant and language-minority students throughout the United States; in rural, suburban, and urban areas.
- Dividing the student body and faculty into smaller cohorts.
- Encouraging the practices of reflective thinking and self-discipline.
- Facilitating the students' social skills as they interact, relate to one another, identify and solve meaningful problems, develop skills in conflict resolution, and foster peaceful relationships and friendships.
- Finding ways to reduce the so-called summer regression, which is the loss of students' skills and content knowledge due to the traditional summer layoff. One such move is away from the traditional "agrarian school calendar" to a 45/15 year-round or modified year-round calendar, while another is through the use of looping and assigning summer homework.
- Holding high expectations, although not necessarily identical expectations, for all students by establishing benchmark academic standards, teaching toward those standards, and assessing student achievement against those standards.
- Increased movement to grades K–8 and 9–12 school organization, that is, to a two-school (elementary and high school) rather than a three-school organization (elementary, middle, and high school).
- Increased requirements for high school graduation. For example, an increasing number of states (at least 21) require students to pass algebra to graduate, and an increasing number are requiring exit examinations (20 in 2004 with 5 more expected by 2009), that is, tests that students must pass to graduate. It is expected that by 2009, exit exams will affect about 70% of all public school students and 80% of all minority students (Center for Education Policy, 2004).
- Individualizing (personalizing) the instruction.
- Integrating the subjects of the curriculum.
- Involving parents/guardians and communities in the education of the children.
- Involving students in the self-assessment of their learning.
- Providing students with the time and the opportunity to think and be creative, rather than simply memorizing and repeating information.
- Provision of meaningful curriculum options with multiple pathways for academic success.
- Redefining giftedness to include nonacademic as well as traditional academic abilities.
- School-based community learning centers that also provide social services.
- Statewide accountability systems for all students.

- Teaching and assessing for higher-order thinking skills.
- Transformation of large schools into smaller learning communities.
- Use of nontraditional scheduling.
- Using heterogeneous small-group learning, peer coaching, and cross-age tutoring as instructional strategies.
- Using the Internet as a communication tool and learning resource.

Major Problems and Issues

Major problems and issues plague our nation's schools. Some of the most pressing are:

- alternatives to grade retention and social promotion
- outdated buildings in need of retrofitting
- concern about the anxiety shown in youth, with the concomitant knowledge that anxiety is counterproductive to positive academic performance
- concern that while schools are spending more time on reading and mathematics, implementation of NCLB legislation is causing less time being spent on students' learning of other subjects in the curriculum
- concern that with the increased emphasis in mathematics on critical and conceptual thinking and practical problem solving, there has been a corresponding de-emphasis on skills of arithmetic and calculation; a trend that weakens math performance in general and makes math less useful for students who go on to college
- controversy over the value and effects of the NCLB Act and the concomitant high-stakes standardized testing
- controversy over what is the actual percentage of students who complete high school and the concomitant concern that the percentage is decreasing and that a child's potential for incompletion of school is recognizable as early as the sixth grade
- controversy over whether charter schools are doing as well at educating young people as had been hoped, or even as well as noncharter public schools
- controversy regarding the value of the child-centered middle school concept
- debate regarding the extent to which a school should impose dress code standards on its students
- the funding gap in many states, with a nationwide per-student expenditure disparity between high-poverty and low-poverty school districts
- impedance of immigrant parental/guardian involvement in school activities due to the school's difficulty in bridging cultural and communication barriers
- the potential misdiagnosis of children as intellectually or behaviorally challenged.

- recruiting and retaining the best teachers and school administrators
- resegregation that is occurring in schools
- a rush to mainstream children identified as limited English proficient
- scarcity of male teachers—the lowest percentage in four decades
- security and the related problems of bias, bullying, crime, drugs, harassment, prejudice, violence, and weapons on school campuses and in school neighborhoods
- the scarcity of minority teachers to serve as role models for youth
- the education of teachers to work effectively with young people, who may be too overwhelmed by personal problems to focus on learning and to succeed in school
- the use of standardized test scores and statistics to judge and reward the performance of schools and teachers, thereby creating a disincentive for teachers and administrators to work with particular groups of youth.

Perhaps you and your classmates can identify and describe other issues and problems faced by our nation's schools, particularly those in your immediate geographic area.

MEETING THE CHALLENGE: RECOGNIZING AND PROVIDING FOR STUDENT DIFFERENCES

To provide learning experiences that are consistent with what is known about young adolescents (see Figure 1.3) and their ways of learning and knowing, consider the following general guidelines. These guidelines are the main focus of subsequent content in this resource guide. Begin now by making notes to yourself as you read on.

- As frequently as is appropriate, and especially for skills development, plan the learning activities so they follow a step-by-step sequence from concrete to abstract.
- Communicate with students in a clear, direct, respectful, and consistent manner.
- Even when teaching a mandated curriculum, concentrate on using student-centered instruction, by using project-centered learning, discovery and inquiry strategies, and include simulations and role-play.
- Establish multiple learning centers within the classroom.
- Maintain high expectations, although not necessarily identical, for every student; establish high standards and teach toward them without wavering.
- Plan interesting activities to bridge learning, activities that help students connect what is being learned with their real world.

- Provide a structured learning environment with well-understood and frequently rehearsed procedures.
- Provide ongoing and frequent monitoring of individual student learning.
- Provide tiered assignments, with optional due dates, that are based on individual student abilities and interests.
- Use direct instruction to teach to the development of observation, generalization, and other thinking and learning skills.
- Use interactive computer programs and multimedia.
- Use interdisciplinary thematic instruction.
- Use multilevel instruction.
- Use reciprocal peer coaching and cross-age tutoring.
- Use small-group and cooperative learning strategies.
- With students, collaboratively plan challenging and engaging classroom learning activities and assignments.

YOUNG ADOLESCENT YEARS: TIME OF RAPID CHANGE AND GREAT VARIABILITY

Their honesty, their belief that they are invincible, and their desire to make a difference in the world are all characteristics that separate middle school adolescents from other age groups.

Erika Daniels (2005, p. 53)

Although generalizations are risky, from many years of experience and research, experts have come to accept certain precepts about young adolescents. These are developmental characteristics of young adolescents regardless of their individual genetic or cultural differences. Adapted from *Caught in the Middle: Educational Reform for Young Adolescents in California Public Schools* (California Middle Grades Task Force, 1987, pp. 144–148), they are presented in Figure 1.3 in five categories: intellectual, physical, emotional/psychological, social, and moral/ethical [see also "Characteristics of Young Adolescents," *This We Believe: Developmentally Responsive Middle Level Schools* (NMSA, 1995, pp. 35–40)]. Each category is accompanied by practices that are developmentally appropriate for middle level curriculum and instruction, adapted by permission from *The New American Middle School* (Wiles & Bondi, 2001, pp. 33–36).

It is important to emphasize that early adolescence is a period of tremendous variability among individuals of the same gender and chronological age, and that dissimilar rates of growth are common in all areas of development. It would be erroneous, for example, to draw a conclusion that states "All seventh graders are. . . ." In addition, the five areas of development are "inexorably entwined" (NMSA, 1995, p. 6).

Figure 1.3 Characteristics of young adolescents and their implications for developmentally appropriate practice.

Intellectual Development. Young adolescents tend to

1. Be egocentric; argue to convince others; exhibit independent, critical thought.
2. Be intellectually at risk; that is, they face decisions that have the potential to affect major academic values with lifelong consequences.
3. Be intensely curious.
4. Consider academic goals as a secondary level of priority, whereas personal-social concerns dominate thoughts and activities.
5. Display a wide range of individual intellectual development as their minds experience change from the concrete-manipulatory stage to the capacity for abstract thought. This change makes possible
   a. Ability to project thought into the future, to expect, and to formulate goals.
   b. Analysis of the power of a political ideology.
   c. Appreciation for the elegance of mathematical logic expressed in symbols.
   d. Consideration of ideas contrary to fact.
   e. Insight into the nuances of poetic metaphor and musical notation.
   f. Insight into the sources of previously unquestioned attitudes, behaviors, and values.
   g. Interpretation of larger concepts and generalizations of traditional wisdom expressed through sayings, axioms, and aphorisms.
   h. Propositional thought.
   i. Reasoning with hypotheses involving two or more variables.
6. Experience the phenomenon of metacognition—that is, the ability to think about one's thinking, and to know what one knows and does not know.
7. Exhibit strong willingness to learn what they consider to be useful, and enjoy using skills to solve real-life problems.
8. Prefer active to passive learning experiences; favor interaction with peers during learning activities.

(continued)

Figure 1.3   (*continued*)

Implications for Developmentally Appropriate Practice (DAP). Regarding the intellectual development of young adolescents, developmentally appropriate actions include

- The use of a wide variety of approaches and materials for instruction, that is, an eclectic approach (a theme found throughout this resource guide), including physical movement with small-group discussions and learning centers.
- Curricula organized around real-life concepts (e.g., conflict, competition, peer-group influence). Activities in formal and informal situations that are designed to improve reasoning powers. Studies of the community and environment are particularly relevant for young adolescents.
- Organized discussions of ideas and feelings in peer groups to facilitate self-understanding. Provision of experiences for individuals to express themselves by writing and participating in creative dramatics.
- Opportunities for enjoyable studies in the arts. Encouragement of self-expression in all subjects.

Physical Development.   Young adolescents tend to

1. Be concerned about their physical appearance.
2. Be physically at risk; major causes of death are homicide, suicide, accident, and leukemia.
3. Experience accelerated physical development marked by increases in weight, height, heart size, lung capacity, and muscular strength.
4. Experience bone growth faster than muscle development; uneven muscle/bone development results in lack of coordination and awkwardness; bones may lack protection of covering muscles and supporting tendons.
5. Experience fluctuations in basal metabolism, which at times can cause either extreme restlessness or listlessness.
6. Face responsibility for sexual behavior before full emotional and social maturity has occurred.
7. Have ravenous appetites and peculiar tastes; may overtax digestive system with large quantities of improper foods.
8. Lack physical health; have poor levels of endurance, strength, and flexibility; as a group are more overweight and less healthy.
9. Mature at varying rates of speed. Girls are often taller than boys for the first two years of early adolescence and are ordinarily more physically developed than boys are.
10. Reflect a wide range of individual differences that begin to appear in prepubertal and pubertal stages of development. Boys tend to lag behind girls at this stage, and there are marked individual differences in physical development for both boys and girls. The greatest variation in physiological development and size occurs at about age 13.
11. Show changes in body contour, including temporarily large noses, protruding ears, and long arms; have posture problems.

Implications for Developmentally Appropriate Practice. Regarding the physical development of young adolescents, developmentally appropriate actions include

- A health and science curriculum that emphasizes self-understanding about body changes. Guidance counseling and community resource persons to help students understand what is happening to their bodies.
- Advising parents to insist that students get proper rest; overexertion should be discouraged.
- Providing an opportunity for daily exercise and a place where students can be children by playing and being noisy for short periods.
- Encouraging activities such as special-interest classes and hands-on learning. Students should be allowed to move about physically in classes and avoid long periods of passive work.
- Providing snacks to satisfy between-meal hunger as well as nutritional guidance specific to the needs of young adolescents.

Emotional/Psychological Development.   Young adolescents tend to

1. Be easily offended and are sensitive to criticism of personal shortcomings.
2. Be erratic and inconsistent in their behavior; anxiety and fear are contrasted with periods of bravado; feelings shift between superiority and inferiority.
3. Be moody, restless; often feel self-conscious and alienated; lack self-esteem; be introspective.
4. Be optimistic, hopeful.
5. Be psychologically at risk; at no other point in human development is an individual likely to meet so much diversity in relation to self and others.
6. Be searching for adult identity and acceptance even in the midst of intense peer-group relationships.
7. Be searching to form a conscious sense of individual uniqueness—"Who am I?"
8. Be vulnerable to naive opinions, one-sided arguments.

Figure 1.3 *(continued)*

9. Exaggerate simple occurrences and believe that personal problems, experiences; and feelings are unique to themselves.
10. Have an emerging sense of humor based on increased intellectual ability to see abstract relationships; appreciate the *double entendre*.
11. Have chemical and hormonal imbalances, which often trigger emotions that are frightening and poorly understood; may regress to more childish behavior patterns at this point.

Implications for Developmentally Appropriate Practice. Regarding the psychological development of young adolescents, developmentally appropriate actions include

- Encouragement of self-assessment.
- Activities designed to allow students to play out their emotions.
- Helping students to understand their feelings of superiority and inferiority.
- Avoiding the pressuring of students by adults in the school to explain their emotions. Occasional childlike behavior is not ridiculed. Sarcasm by adults is avoided.
- Encouragement of students to assume leadership in group discussions and to experience frequent success and recognition for personal efforts and achievement.
- A general atmosphere of friendliness, relaxation, concern, and group cohesiveness.
- Numerous opportunities to release emotional stress.
- Use of sociodrama to enable students to see themselves as others see them.
- Readings that deal with problems similar to their own to help them see that many of their problems are not unique.

Social Development.   Young adolescents tend to

1. Act out unusual or drastic behavior at times; may be aggressive, daring, boisterous, and argumentative.
2. Be confused and frightened by new school settings that are large and impersonal.
3. Be fiercely loyal to peer-group values; sometimes cruel or insensitive to those outside the peer group.
4. Be impacted by the high level of mobility in society; may become anxious and disoriented when peer-group ties are broken because of family relocation.
5. Be rebellious toward parents but still strongly dependent on parental values; want to make their own choices, but the authority of the family is a critical factor in final decisions.
6. Be socially at risk. Adult values are largely shaped conceptually during adolescence; negative interactions with peers, parents, and teachers may compromise ideals and commitments.
7. Challenge authority figures; test limits of acceptable behavior.
8. Experience low-risk trust relationships with adults who show lack of sensitivity to adolescent characteristics and needs.
9. Experience often traumatic conflicts because of conflicting loyalties to peer group and family.
10. Refer to peers as sources for standards and models of behavior. Media heroes and heroines are also singularly important in shaping both behavior and fashion.
11. Sense the negative impact of adolescent behaviors on parents and teachers; realize the thin edge between tolerance and rejection. Feelings of adult rejection can drive the adolescent into the relatively secure social environment of the peer group.
12. Strive to define sex role characteristics; search to set up positive social relationships with members of the same and opposite sex.
13. Want to know and feel that significant adults, including parents and teachers, love and accept them; need frequent affirmation.

Implications for Developmentally Appropriate Practice. Regarding the social development of young adolescents, developmentally appropriate actions include

- Scheduling debates, plays, play days, and other activities to allow students to show off in a productive way.
- Role-playing and guidance exercises that provide the opportunity to act out feelings. Providing opportunities for social interaction between the sexes—parties and games, but not dances in the early grades of middle school.
- Establishing a student government so students can develop their own guidelines for dress and behavior. Adults should be encouraged not to react with outrage when students display extreme dress or mannerisms.
- Fostering peer teaching and community service projects.
- Planning large group activities rather than boy-girl events. Intramurals can be scheduled so students can interact with friends of the same or opposite sex.

(continued)

Figure 1.3 *(continued)*

Moral and Ethical Development. Young adolescents tend to

1. Ask broad, unanswerable questions about the meaning of life; not expecting absolute answers but being turned off by trivial adult responses.
2. Be at risk in the development of moral and ethical choices and behaviors; depend on the influences of home and church for moral and ethical development; explore the moral and ethical issues that are met in the curriculum, in the media, and in daily interactions with their families and peer groups.
3. Be idealistic; have a strong sense of fairness in human relationships.
4. Be reflective, introspective, and analytical about their thoughts and feelings.
5. Experience thoughts and feelings of awe and wonder related to their expanding intellectual and emotional awareness.
6. Face hard moral and ethical questions for which they are unprepared to cope.

Implications for Developmentally Appropriate Practice. Regarding the moral and ethical development of young adolescents, developmentally appropriate actions include

- Encouraging mature value systems by providing opportunities for students to examine options of behavior and to study consequences of various actions.
- Providing opportunities to students to accept responsibility in setting standards for behavior.
- Helping students to develop values when solving their problems.

SUMMARY

Despite the many commissions, writers, and politicians that have and continue to vilify the failures of public education, thousands of committed teachers, administrators, parents and guardians, and members of the community struggle daily, year after year, to provide our youth with a quality education. Regardless of all the legislation and other responsive school practices, in the end it is the dedication, commitment, and nature of the understanding of the involved adults—the teachers, administrators, bus drivers, cooks, grounds crew, security staff, custodial staff, and support personnel—that remains the incisive element in children's learning. And, from the work of many researchers, it has been made clear that teachers' actions in their classrooms can have a much far greater impact on student achievement than do school matters of curriculum, assessment, staff collegiality, and community involvement (Marzano & Marzano, 2003). This resource guide is designed to help you with your understandings and to develop your teaching competencies.

In beginning to plan for developing your teaching competencies, you have read an overview of today's schools, characteristics of young adolescents, and of the characteristics of some of the adults who work in the schools, of trends and practices, and of problems, issues, and challenges that continue to plague our nation's schools. That background knowledge will be useful in your assimilation of the content explored in the chapters that follow, beginning in the next chapter with descriptions of teacher behaviors and the responsibilities necessary for meeting the challenges.

QUESTIONS FOR CLASS DISCUSSION

1. Describe how you would know if you were at an exemplary middle level school.
2. Some educators advocate the use of high-stakes standardized assessments of students' knowledge in the arts, such as painting and music. Explain why you would or would not support such an assessment.
3. Describe the major ethnic, racial, and/or cultural groups that live in the geographic area in which you plan to teach. Have the percentages of the represented groups changed in the past 15 years? What implications are there in these social realities for your work as a public school teacher?
4. Have you personally experienced organized course learning on the Internet, or e-learning as it is sometimes called? Some believe that within only a few years as much as 50 percent of public school learning will happen online. What do you see in the near future for distance online learning? Do you see yourself as a participant, either as a teacher or a student, or both? Discuss this with your classmates, especially the pluses and minuses of learning online by youth.
5. Some experts fear that using test scores as the sole indicator of students' and teachers' knowledge and skills is harming students and causing students to drop out of school and driving the best teachers from the profession. What is your opinion on this issue? Find support for your opinion and share your findings with your classmates.
6. It has been predicted (see page 67 of the February 7, 2000, issue of *Business Week* magazine) that by the year 2020, for-profit corporations will run approximately one-fourth of the U.S. public schools. Are, in fact, for-profit public schools increasing in number from the approximately 200 such schools in the year 2000? Why or why not,

do you suppose, is the for-profit public school alternative growing in popularity? Does the issue have any special significance for you and your career? Discuss these questions and your thoughts with your classmates.

7. Assume that you are a middle school teacher and that your teaching schedule includes three sections of world history. Furthermore, assume that students at your school are tracked and that one of your classes is a so-called college prep class with 27 students; another is a regular education class with 32 students, 3 of whom have special needs because of disabilities; and the third is a sheltered English class with 13 students, 7 of whom are Hispanics with limited proficiency in English, 3 from Russia with very limited proficiency in English, and 4 of whom are Southeast Asians, 2 with no ability to use English. Will one lesson plan using direct instruction (such as by lecture, discussion, and worksheets) as the primary instructional strategy work for all three sections? If so, explain how. If not, explain what you will need to do and why. [*Note:* Save your response to this question, as you will be returning to it later.]

8. As is being discovered by those involved, dividing a large school into smaller learning communities of, say, no more than 400 students each, is far from being an uncomplicated task that automatically solves the problems experienced when and because the school was larger. For example, when implementing the learning community, urban areas often have difficulty finding suitable locations for the new smaller schools and finding teachers with the wanted qualifications. Also, smaller schools may have a more limited range of course offerings. Discover if there are middle level schools in your area that are making the transition from large to smaller learning communities and inquire about problems they have encountered and steps they have taken to revolve those problems. Share your findings with your classmates.

9. With each member of your class responsible for researching one of the websites given below, share findings with the whole class. Arrange to continue doing this for each chapter of this resource guide.

10. More than 40 years ago sociologist Edgar Friedenberg (1963) wrote: "School ought to be a place where you can not only learn to be a scholar, a fighter, a lover, a repairman, a writer, or a scientist, but learn that you are good at it, and in which your awareness and pride in being good at it become a part of your sense of being you." What to you is the significance of Friedenberg's statement? Is his point any less or any more true today?

INTERNET RESOURCES

Consortium for School Networking **http://cosn.org**

First Amendment Schools
   http://www.firstamendmentschools.org

International Baccalaureate Organization **http://www.ibo.org**

KIPP (Knowledge is Power Program) schools **http://www.kipp.org**

Knowledge Loom **http://www.knowledgeloom.org**

Making Schools Work **http://www.sreb.org**

Middle Web **http://www.middleweb.com**

National Association for Single Sex Public Education
   http://www.singlesexschools.org

National Association for Year-Round Education
   http://www.nayre.org

Renaissance 2010 **http://www.cps.k12.il.us/**

Teacher Talk
   http://education.indiana.edu/cas/tt/tthmpg.html

Teachers Helping Teachers **http://www.pacificnet.net/~mandel**

United States Charter Schools **http://www.uscharterschools.org**

United States Department of Education
   http://www.ed.gov/index.jhtml?src=a

Yahoo! Education Directory **http://www.yahoo.com/Education**

To learn more about teaching young adolescents please go to the Teacher Prep website at **www.prenhall.com/teacherprep.**

FOR FURTHER READING

Abrams, J., & Ferguson, J. (2005). Teaching students from many nations. *Educational Leadership, 62*(4), 64–67.

Anfara, Jr., V. A., & Buehler, A. (2005). Grade configurations and the education of young adolescents. *Middle School Journal, 37*(1), 53–59.

Beane, J., & Lipka, R. (2006). Guess again: Will changing the grades save middle-level education? *Educational Leadership, 63*(7), 26–30.

Boice, M., & Rypka, S. (2005). Scheduling with a purpose: Professional learning communities. *Middle Ground, 8*(4), 14–16.

Cushman, K. (2006). Help us make the 9th grade transition. *Educational Leadership, 63*(7), 47–52.

Daniels, E. (2005). On the minds of middle schoolers. *Educational Leadership, 62*(7), 52–54.

Essex, N. L. (2004). Zero tolerance and student dress codes. *Principal, 84*(1), 54–57.

Green, D.G. (2006). Welcome to the house system. *Educational Leadership, 63*(7), 64–67.

Hackmann, D. G. (2004). Constructivism and block scheduling: Making the connection. *Phi Delta Kappan, 85,* 697–702.

Hadi-Tabassum, S. (2005). The balancing act of bilingual immersion. *Educational Leadership, 62*(4), 50–54.

Herman, B. E. (2004). *The revival of K–8 schools.* Fastback 519. Bloomington, IN: Phi Delta Kappa Educational Foundation.

Howe, F., & Simmons, B. J. (2005). *Nurturing the parent-teacher alliance.* Bloomington, IN: Phi Delta Kappa Educational Foundation.

Jackson, A. W., & Davis, G. A. (2000). *Turning points 2000: Educating adolescents in the 21st century.* New York: Teachers College Press.

Kugler, E. G., & Albright, E. M. (2005). Increasing diversity in challenging classes. *Educational Leadership, 62*(5), 42–45.

McEwin, C. K., Dickinson, T. S., & Jacobson, M. G. (2004). *Programs and practices in K–8 schools: Do they meet the educational needs of young adolescents?* Westerville, OH: National Middle School Association.

McLeod, J. (2005). Kick-off, half-time, and over-time. *Middle Ground, 8*(4), 12–13.

Mizelle, N. B. (2005). Moving out of middle school. *Educational Leadership, 62*(7), 56–60.

Perlstein, L. (2003). *Not much, just chillin': The hidden lives of middle schoolers.* New York: Farrar, Straus, & Giroux.

Rettig, M. D. (2004). Four-block scheduling: Meeting middle-level needs. *Middle Matters, 12*(2), 1–3.

San Antonio, D. (2004). *Adolescent lives in transition: How social class influences the adjustment to middle school.* Albany, NY: SUNY Press.

San Antonio, D. (2006). Broadening the world of early adolescents. *Educational Leadership, 63*(7), 8–13.

Spielhagen, F. R. (2006). How tweens view single-sex classes. *Educational Leadership, 63,* 68–72.

Williams-Boyd, P. (2005). Middle schools that make a difference. *Childhood Education, 82,* 278.

Yecke, C. P. (2006). Mayhem in the middle: Why we should shift to K–8. *Educational Leadership, 63*(7), 20–25.

CHAPTER 2

Professional Responsibilities of Teachers of Young Adolescents

Anthony Magnacca/Merrill

The primary expectation of any teacher is to facilitate student learning. As an effective classroom teacher of young adolescents your professional responsibilities will extend well beyond the ability to work effectively in a classroom from approximately 8:00 A.M. until mid- to late afternoon. In this chapter, you will learn about the many responsibilities you will assume and the competencies and behaviors necessary for fulfilling them. Four categories of responsibilities and 22 competencies are identified. [*Note:* You may want to compare the four categories and 22 competencies that are identified here with other lists such as the four domains (organizing content knowledge for student learning, creating an environment for student learning, teaching for student learning, and teacher professionalism) and 19 criteria of Educational Testing Service's Praxis Series. See relevant websites at end of this chapter.]

The four categories are: (1) responsibility as a reflective decision maker, (2) commitment to young adolescent children and to the profession, (3) noninstructional responsibilities, and (4) instructional responsibilities and fundamental teaching behaviors. As these four categories and the 22 competencies are presented, you are guided through the reality of these expectations as they exist for today's middle level classroom teacher.

OBJECTIVES

Specifically, upon completion of this chapter you should be able to:

1. Describe the four decision-making and thought-processing phases of instruction and the types of decisions you must make during each.

2. Demonstrate an operational awareness of the variety of materials and resources for use in your teaching.

3. Demonstrate knowledge of copyright laws for using printed and media materials for teaching.

4. Demonstrate an understanding about using community resources, speakers, and field trips.

5. Demonstrate competency in using standard classroom tools for teaching.

6. Describe the importance of the concept of *locus of control* and its relationship to your professional responsibilities.

7. Demonstrate your understanding of the depth and breadth of the *instructional* and the *noninstructional responsibilities* of being a classroom teacher.

8. Demonstrate knowledge of certain basic safety and legal guidelines for the classroom teacher.

9. Contrast teacher use of *praise* and of *encouragement* and describe situations in which each is more appropriate.

10. Compare and contrast teacher *facilitating behaviors* with *instructional strategies*.

11. Demonstrate your growing understanding of the concept of *teaching style* and its relevance to the classroom instruction of young adolescent learners.

12. Demonstrate your understanding of the importance of *reflection* to the process of constructing skills and understandings.

13. Demonstrate your growing understanding of the concept of *multilevel instruction* and describe how you would use multilevel instruction in your work with young adolescents.

THE TEACHER AS A REFLECTIVE DECISION MAKER

During any single school day, you will make hundreds of decisions. Some decisions will have been made prior to

> It is this decision-making obligation and privilege that defines the teacher as an artist and classroom teaching as a profession.

meeting your students for instruction, others will be made during the instructional activities, and yet others are made later as you reflect on the instruction for that day.

Let's consider further these decision-making and thought-processing phases of instruction, the basis for the organization of this resource guide.

Decision-Making Phases of Instruction

Instruction can be divided into four decision-making and thought-processing phases: (1) the planning or preactive phase, (2) the teaching or interactive phase, (3) the analyzing and evaluating or reflective phase, and (4) the application or projective phase (Costa, 1991).

The planning or preactive phase consists of all those intellectual functions and decisions you will make prior to actual instruction. This includes decisions

Scott Cunningham/Merrill

about content selection, the goals and objectives, homework assignments, what students already know and can do, appropriate learning activities, questions to be asked (and possible answers), and the selection and preparation of instructional materials.

The teaching or interactive phase includes all the decisions made during the immediacy and spontaneity of the teaching act. This includes maintaining student focus, questions to be asked by the teacher, types of feedback given to the students, and ongoing adjustments to the lesson plan. As said before, decisions made during this phase are likely to be more instinctive and routine than those made during the planning phase.

The analyzing and evaluating or reflective phase is the time you will take to reflect on, analyze, and judge the decisions and behaviors that occurred during the interactive phase. (See questions for self-reflection in Figure 2.1.) It is during reflection that you make decisions about student learning, student marks and grades, feedback given to parents and guardians, and adjustments on what and how next to teach.

As emphasized by Schon (1983) more than two decades ago, it is not that we learn so much from our experience, but from our reflection on our experience. As a result of this teacher self-reflection, decisions are made to use what was learned in subsequent teaching actions. At this point, you are in the application or projective phase, abstracting from your reflection and projecting your analysis into subsequent teaching behaviors. It is suggested that one reason some teachers are not as effective as they might be is because of their lack of attention to any sustained self-reflection (Danielson & McGreal, 2000). What is the characteristic of a "sustained self-reflection"? It is when a teacher asks her or his self questions like those of Figure 2.1, thoughtfully answers the questions, and then acts accordingly.

Reflection, Locus of Control, Sense of Self-Efficacy, and Teacher Responsibility

During the reflective phase, teachers have a choice of whether to assume full responsibility for the instructional

Figure 2.1 Questions for self-reflection.

- What is my overall opinion about today's lesson—good, fair, or bad? What specifically made me feel this way?
- Were I a student in my class today, would I look forward to tomorrow's class? Why or why not?
- Did students seem to enjoy the lesson? What specifically makes me think so?
- Did the objectives seem to be met? What evidence is there?
- What aspects of the lesson went well? What makes me believe so?
- Were I to repeat the lesson, what changes might I make?
- Which students seemed to do well? Which ones didn't? What should I do about that?
- To what extent was this lesson personalized for the students? Could I do more in this regard? If so, what? If not, then why not?
- To what extent did this lesson engage various learning modalities? Should more have been done in this area? Why or why not?
- Did the students seem to have sufficient time to think and apply? Why or why not?
- Would I have wanted my own child present as a student in this class? Why or why not?
- Would I have been proud had the school district superintendent been present to observe this lesson? Why or why not?

outcomes or to assume responsibility for only the positive outcomes of the planned instruction while placing the blame for the negative outcomes on outside forces (e.g., district, state or federal requirements, parents and guardians or society in general, colleagues, administrators, textbooks or lack thereof). Where the responsibility for outcomes is placed is referred to as *locus of control.* A person with an internal locus of control typically is more likely to persist against formidable odds (see "intelligent behaviors" in Chapter 3). Furthermore, a teacher who believes he or she can, generally will, a characteristic called *efficacy.* Teachers who have a strong sense of self-efficacy (feeling of "I can") are more likely to instill in their students the same sense of empowerment (Ashton & Webb, 1986).

However, just because a teacher thinks he or she "can" teach doesn't mean he or she "will." If many of the teacher's students are not learning, then that teacher is not competent. In the words of the late Madeline Hunter, "To say that I am an effective teacher, and acknowledge that my students may not be learning is the same as saying I am a great surgeon, but most of my patients die" (Villa & Thousands, 1995). Teachers who are intrinsically motivated and competent tend to assume full responsibility for instructional outcomes, regardless of whether or not the outcomes are as intended from the planning phase.

Of course, every teacher realizes there are factors which the teacher cannot control, such as the negative effects on children from poverty, bullying, gangs, alcohol, and drug abuse, so they must do what they can within the confines of the classroom and resources of the school and district. History brims with examples of how a relatively few, but positive, moments with a truly caring and knowledgeable adult can drastically change for the better the life of a young person, whom until then had a history of mostly negative experiences.

Now, further your understanding of the responsibilities of a classroom teacher by completing Exercises 2.1 and 2.2.

TEACHING IN PRACTICE

Once upon a time there was a life science student teacher that, to teaching colleagues and the university supervisor, seemed to always be complaining. "Too many students in the class." "Not enough microscopes." "Textbooks are outdated." "Half the students in this class shouldn't be in here." "Many of them can't or don't read the textbook." "Their parents don't care; the kids don't care!" "Supply budget is inadequate." "I can't get any help from my cooperating teacher; I never even see him." Finally, one day, out of frustration, the student teacher's university supervisor said, "For crying out loud, stop complaining. You now have the one thing you have been working for—a class of life science students. If you are a teacher, then teach them!"

Questions for Reflection and Discussion

1. What thoughts, if any, came to you immediately after reading this brief scenario?

2. From what little you know, do you think the supervisor was out of line or right on?

3. Have you ever heard stories of teachers who had their students make their own textbooks? Make their own microscopes with bamboo rods and a drop of water in each end? Or litmus indicators made from flower petals?

4. Do you have any additional thoughts about the essence of this scenario?

FOR YOUR NOTES

EXERCISE 2.1: THE TEACHER AS REFLECTIVE DECISION MAKER

INSTRUCTIONS: The purpose of this exercise is to learn more about the nature of the decisions and the decision-making process used by teachers. To accomplish this, you are to observe one middle level teacher for one hour while that teacher is teaching. Tabulate as accurately as possible the number of decisions the teacher makes during that time period, then share the results with your classmates. Obtain permission from a cooperating teacher by explaining the purpose of your observations. You will need to have a follow-up discussion with the cooperating teacher regarding your tabulations. A follow-up thank-you letter is appropriate.

School, teacher, and class observed: _____

_____

_____

_____

_____

1. Use the following format for your tabulations. You may first want to make your tabulations on a separate blank sheet of paper and then organize and transfer those tabulations to this page. Tabulate and identify each decision. To tabulate the decisions made before and after instruction, confer with the teacher after class.

DECISION MADE BEFORE INSTRUCTION

Examples

- Objectives of lesson
- Amount of time to be devoted to particular activities
- Classroom management procedures

_____

_____

_____

_____

_____

_____

DECISIONS MADE DURING INSTRUCTION

Examples

- Called on Roberta to answer a question
- Teacher remained silent until students in back corner got quiet
- Talked with tardy student

_____

_____

_____

_____

_____

_____

EXERCISE 2.1 *(continued)*

DECISIONS MADE AFTER INSTRUCTION

Examples

- To review a particular concept tomorrow
- To arrange a conference with Sean to talk with him about his hostility in class
- To make a revision in Friday's homework assignment

_____

_____

_____

_____

_____

2. What was the total number of decisions made by this teacher before instruction? _____ during instruction? _____ after instruction? _____
Compare your results with those of others in your class.

3. Did you observe any evidence that this teacher assumed full responsibility for the learning outcomes of this class session? Describe the evidence. _____

_____

_____

_____

_____

_____

4. What percentage of all decisions by this teacher were planned? _____ were spontaneous? _____

5. Did you share your results of this exercise with the cooperating teacher? His or her reaction? _____

_____

_____

_____

_____

_____

6. Your conclusions from this exercise: _____

_____

_____

_____

_____

EXERCISE 2.2: REFLECTIVE DECISION MAKING: THE PREACTIVE PHASE OF INSTRUCTION

INSTRUCTIONS: Mentally rehearsing your actions before meeting the students is absolutely essential for effective teaching and learning. The purpose of this exercise is to stress the importance of clearly and fully thinking about what you will do and say in the classroom and to demonstrate how mental rehearsal of a lesson can identify possible problems. Follow these steps:

1. Select a grade level (5–8) you are currently teaching or that you would like to teach. _____

   _____

2. Objective of lesson: Students will design name tags for their desks during a 20-minute time frame.

3. *Without looking ahead at step 4,* on separate paper write a lesson plan for this activity. (Although you have not yet learned the details of lesson planning, outline the steps you would follow and things you would say to your students in order to accomplish the objective of step 2.)

4. To analyze the thoroughness of your preactive thinking, respond to the following questions.

   a. Are materials listed in your plan? _____

   b. Are those materials readily available in your classroom? _____

   c. Will paper or tagboard need to be precut? _____

   d. How large can the name tags be? _____

   e. How and where will they be attached to each desk? _____

      _____

   f. Should they be flat or three-dimensional? _____

   g. Will you supply markers or crayons, or are the students expected to have them? _____

   h. Will students need scissors?_____

   i. Will you have left-handed scissors available if needed? _____

   j. Should name tags have first name, last name, last initial? _____

      _____

   k. Can other words or designs be added? _____

   l. When and how will materials be distributed? Collected? _____

      _____

   m. What plan do you have for absent or tardy students? _____

      _____

5. Share the results of your steps 1–4 with others in your class. Did members of your class come up with other questions relevant and necessary to the preplanning for this instructional period? If so, share them with the rest of the class. _____

   _____

Conclusion: A teacher who practices thorough preactive planning should have planned answers for each of these questions.

FOR YOUR NOTES

SELECTED LEGAL GUIDELINES

Among teachers and teacher candidates, the topic of teacher and student rights generates discussions and concerns. You are, or will be, interested in teacher tenure laws, retirement laws, professional organizations, collective bargaining, legal requirements with respect to student discipline, teacher liability and insurance, and teacher negligence—topics this resource guide cannot pursue or discuss in depth.

Nevertheless, you must be knowledgeable about legal matters regarding teaching and supervising minors, as well as about copyright laws. Such knowledge can minimize the possibility of making errors that abuse the rights of children, that cause emotional or physical trauma to a student, and that could result in litigation and an abrupt and unpleasant break or end to your teaching career. The content in this chapter gives only some very basic information.

Student Rights

Students should be informed of their rights by their schools, and they should be encouraged to report any suspected violations of their rights to the school principal or other designated person. Many schools provide students with a printed document of their rights.

Right Against Discrimination

Federal law Title VI of the Civil Rights Act of 1964 prohibits any discrimination that is based on race, color, national origin, or gender. The Americans With Disabilities Act of 1990 prohibits discrimination against individuals with disabilities. Federal law Title IX of the Education Act Amendments of 1972 prohibits discrimination among students on the basis of their gender. In all aspects of school, students must be treated the same. This means, for example, that a teacher must not pit males against females in a subject content quiz game—or for any other activity or reason. Further, no teacher, student, administrator, or other school employee should make sexual advances toward or sexually harass a student (i.e., speaking or touching in a sexual manner). The school atmosphere must be one of trust, dignity, and respect among students and the adult staff.

Cellular Phones and Other Handheld Electronic Devices in the Classroom

The right for students to possess and to use cellular phones, pagers, and other mobile devices while at school varies from state to state, from district to district, and from school to school. You will need to clearly understand and adhere to whatever policy is in force at the school where you teach.

While in the recent past students were prohibited from possessing these devices on school property, for a variety of reasons, not the least of which have included shootings on school campuses and the terrorist attack in September, 2001, on New York City, Pennsylvania, and Washington, DC, there is pressure from many parents and guardians for children to have access to cell phones while at school. More and more school districts are relaxing restrictions but generally insisting that cell phones are off while students are in classes (Danforth, 2003).

A problem some classroom teachers have experienced, besides the obvious distraction made when a phone rings, is that of student inattentiveness to the lesson because the student was reading text messages, viewing photos, or playing games on the cell phone rather than attending to the instruction. It seems to us that whatever the school and district policy, as a classroom teacher you should have the policy common in theaters and concerts, and that is students are expected, upon entering your classroom, to turn their electronic devices completely off and keep them off until they are dismissed from your classroom.

Teacher Liability and Insurance

Credentialed teachers and student teachers in public schools are usually protected by their school districts against personal injury litigation (i.e., a negligence suit filed as the result of a student being injured at school or at a school-sponsored activity). Although not all schools receive federal funding, Title II of the *Elementary and Secondary Education Act of 1965* (ESEA), as reauthorized by the *No Child Left Behind Act of 2001*, ensures that teachers can undertake reasonable actions to maintain order and discipline in the classroom without the fear of litigation. Student teachers and credentialed teachers should investigate carefully the extent of their tort (i.e., any private or civil wrong for which a civil suit can be brought) liability coverage in districts where they work. If it is decided that the coverage provided is insufficient, a teacher may obtain additional liability coverage through private insurance agents and through affiliation with national teacher's organizations.

Teachers sometimes find themselves in situations where they are tempted to transport students in their own private automobiles, such as for field trips and other off-campus activities. Before ever transporting students in your automobile—or in private automobiles driven by others—you and other drivers should inquire from your insurance agents whether you have adequate automobile insurance liability coverage to do so and if any written permissions or release from liability is needed. Our advice to you is to *not* use your private vehicle for transporting students for school events; after all, if it is an important educational activity, then in our opinion the school district should provide the necessary transportation support.

Inevitably, teachers take personal items to school, such as purses, cameras, cell phones, and various other electronic devices. It is unlikely that the school's insurance policy covers your personal items if stolen or damaged. A homeowner's or apartment renter's policy might. Our advice: To the extent possible, avoid taking valuable personal items to school. Otherwise, keep the items in a secure location and out of sight so as to not tempt thievery.

TEACHING STYLE

Teaching style is the way teachers teach, which includes their distinctive mannerisms complemented by their choices of teaching behaviors and strategies. A teacher's style affects the way that teacher presents information and interacts with the students. The manner and pattern of those interactions with students clearly determines a teacher's effectiveness—or lack thereof—in promoting student learning, positive attitudes about learning, and students' self-esteem.

A middle level teacher's style is determined by the teacher's personal characteristics (especially the teacher's own preferred learning style), experiences, and knowledge of research findings about how young adolescents learn. Teaching style can be altered, intentionally or unintentionally, as a result of changes in any of these three areas.

While there are other ways to label and to describe teaching styles, let's consider two contrasting styles—the *traditional* and the *facilitating style* (see Table 2.1) to emphasize that although today's teacher of young adolescents must use aspects from each (i.e., be eclectic in style choice), there must be a very strong inclination toward the facilitating style. What we refer to as "traditional" and "facilitating" styles of teaching are often referred to in the literature as "didactic" and "constructivist" teaching, although constructivism (or "constructionism" as it is sometimes referred) is a theory of learning rather than a precise method of teaching (Smerdon, Burkam, & Lee, 1999).

Multilevel Instruction: Individualizing the Instruction

Students in your classroom have their own independent ways of knowing and learning. It is important to try to attend to how each student best learns and to where each student is developmentally—in other words, to *individualize both the content and the methods of learning*. In essence, although perhaps not as detailed as those prepared for special education students, at various times during the school year you will be developing personalized educational plans for each student. These may be

Table 2.1 A Contrast of Two Teaching Styles

		Traditional Style	*Facilitating Style*
Teacher		Autocratic	Democratic
		Curriculum-centered	Student-centered
		Direct	Indirect
		Dominative	Interactive
		Formal	Informal
		Informative	Inquiring
		Prescriptive	Reflective
Classroom		Teacher-centered	Student-centered
		Linear (seats facing front)	Grouped or circular
Instructional modes		Abstract learning	Concrete learning
		Teacher-centered discussion	Discussions
		Lectures	Peer and cross-age coaching
		Competitive learning	Cooperative learning
		Some problem solving	Problem solving
		Demonstrations by teacher	Student inquiries
		From simple to complex	Start with complex tasks and use instructional scaffolding and dialogue
		Transmission of information from teacher to students	Reciprocal teaching (using dialogue) between teacher and a small group of students, then among students

prepared in collaboration with members of your teaching team. To accomplish this personalized instruction, you can use *multilevel instruction,* that is, where individual students and groups of students are working at different tasks to accomplish the same objective or at different tasks to accomplish different objectives. For example, while some students may be working independently of the teacher—that is, within the facilitating mode—others may be receiving direct instruction—that is, more within the traditional mode.

When personalizing and integrating student learning, multilevel instruction is an important and useful, perhaps even necessary, strategy. Project-centered teaching is an instructional method that easily allows for the provision of multilevel instruction.

The Theoretical Origins of Teaching Styles and Their Relation to Constructivism

Constructivism and the integration of curriculum are certainly not new concepts. The importance of constructivism and of curriculum integration approaches are found, for example, in the writings of Arthur W. Combs (1962) and Jean Piaget (1970), and a century ago in the writings of John Dewey (1902, 1910).

Instructional styles are deeply rooted in certain theoretical assumptions about learners and their development, and although it is beyond the scope of our intent for this resource guide to explore deeply those assumptions, three major theoretical positions with research findings, each of which is based on certain philosophical and psychological assumptions, suggest

different ways of working with children. The theoretical positions are described in the next three paragraphs. (See Table 2.2.)

Tied to the theoretical positions of *romanticism-maturationism* is the assumption that the learner's mind is neutral-passive to good-active, and the main focus in teaching should be the addition of new ideas to a subconscious store of old ones. Key persons include Jean J. Rousseau and Sigmund Freud; key instructional strategies include classic lecturing with rote memorization.

Tied to the theoretical position of *behaviorism* is the assumption that the learner's mind is neutral-passive with innate reflexes and needs, and the main focus in teaching should be on the successive, systematic changes in the learner's environment to increase the possibilities of desired behavior responses. Key persons include John Locke, B. F. Skinner, A. H. Thorndike, Robert Gagné, and John Watson; key instructional strategies include practice and reinforcement as in workbook drill activities and programmed instruction.

Tied to the theoretical position of *cognitive-experimentalism* (including constructivism) is the assumption that the learner is a neutral-interactive, purposeful individual in simultaneous interaction with physical and biological environments. The main focus in teaching should be on facilitating the learner's gain and construction of new perceptions that lead to desired behavioral changes and ultimately to a more fully functioning individual. [*Note:* A person with a "fully functioning self" can be described only in terms of ideal behavior. As explained by Earl C. Kelley, those characteristics

Theoretical Position	Philosophical Assumption about Learner's Mind	Main Focus in Teaching	Key Persons	Key Instructional Strategies
Romanticism-maturationism	neutral-passive to good-active	Addition of new ideas to subconscious store of old ones	J. J. Rousseau S. Freud	Classic lecturing with rote memorization
Behaviorism	neutral-passive	Systematic changes to learner's environment to increase desired behaviors	J. Locke B. F. Skinner A. H. Thorndike R. Gagné J. Waston	Practice and reinforcement, workbook and drill exercises, programmed instruction
Cognitive-experimentalism, including constructivism	neutral-interactive	Facilitating learner's change in perceptions to become a more fully functioning self	J. Dewey L. Vygotsky J. Bruner J. Piaget A. W. Combs	Discovery, inquiry, project, cooperative learning, integrated curriculum

Table 2.2 Comparison of Three Theoretical Origins of Teaching Styles

include: thinks well of himself and of others; sees his stake in others; sees himself as a part of a world in movement—in process of becoming; sees the value of mistakes; develops and holds human values and knows of no other way to live except in keeping with his values; and sees himself as cast in a creative role (Combs, 1962, pp. 17–20).] Key persons include John Dewey, Lev Vygotsky, Jerome Bruner, Jean Piaget, and Arthur W. Combs; key instructional strategies include discovery, inquiry, project-centered teaching, cooperative and social-interactive learning, and integrated curriculum.

It is our opinion that with a diverse group of students, to be most effective, a teacher of young adolescents must be eclectic—but with a strong emphasis toward cognitive-experimentalism-constructivism because of its divergence in learning and the importance given to learning as a change in perceptions—utilizing at appropriate times the best of strategies and knowledgeable instructor behaviors, regardless of whether individually they can be classified within any style dichotomy, such as "direct vs. indirect," "formal vs. informal," "traditional vs. progressive," or "didactic vs. facilitative."

Now, to further your understanding of teaching styles, complete Exercises 2.3 and 2.4. After you finish those exercises, we will review the category of commitment and professionalism.

EXERCISE 2.3: USING OBSERVATION OF CLASSROOM INTERACTION TO ANALYZE ONE MIDDLE GRADE TEACHER'S STYLE*

INSTRUCTIONS: The purpose of this exercise is to visit a classroom to observe and identify the instructional style for that particular day. Be certain first to obtain permission and then to explain to the teacher that you are observing, not evaluating, for teaching style. The host teacher may be interested in discussing with you the results of your observation. A follow-up thank-you letter is appropriate.

1. Class, grade level, and school visited: _____

2. Date of visit: _____

3. From the start of your classroom observation, observe at 1-minute intervals for a period of 10 minutes what the teacher is doing at that very moment, marking the appropriate traditional or facilitating teacher behavior on the chart below. Continue for the entire class meeting for as many 10 1-minute intervals as you can.

					Minutes						
Traditional teacher behaviors	1	2	3	4	5	6	7	8	9	10	*Totals*
Prescribing (giving advice or directions; being critical, evaluative; offering judgments)											
Informing (giving information; lecturing; interpreting)											
Confronting (directly challenging students)											

Traditional Behaviors Total _____

Facilitating teacher behaviors	1	2	3	4	5	6	7	8	9	10	*Totals*
Relaxing (releasing tension; using humor)											
Mediating (asking for information; being reflective; encouraging self-directed problem solving)											
Supporting (approving; confirming; validating; listening)											

Facilitating Behaviors Total _____

4. Total traditional (T) behaviors divided by total facilitating (F) behaviors = T/F ratio. T/F ratio for this observation = _____

5. Conclusions about the host teacher's style on this day: _____

_____

_____

_____

_____

_____

6. Did you discuss your observations with the host teacher? _____

_____

* Adapted from J. Heron, *Six Category Intervention Analysis* (Guildford, England: Centre of Adult Education, University of Surrey, 1975).

FOR YOUR NOTES

PP **EXERCISE 2.4: USING A QUESTIONNAIRE TO DEVELOP A PROFILE AND A STATEMENT ABOUT MY OWN EMERGING TEACHING STYLE**

INSTRUCTIONS: The purpose of this exercise is to help you clarify and articulate your own assumptions about teaching and learning. You will develop a profile of your emerging teaching style, and from that a statement representative of your current thinking about teaching and learning especially about teaching young adolescents. Proceed with the following five steps.*

Step 1. Read each of the 50 statements and rate your feelings about each, giving a *1* if you strongly agree, a *2* if you are neutral, and a *3* if you strongly disagree.

Remember: *1* = strongly agree; *2* = neutral; *3* = strongly disagree

_____ 1. Most of what students learn, they learn on their own.

_____ 2. Students should be concerned about other students' reactions to their work in the classroom.

_____ 3. An important part of schooling is learning to work with others.

_____ 4. Students learn more by working on their own than by working with others.

_____ 5. Students should be given opportunities to participate actively in class planning and implementation of lessons.

_____ 6. In an effective learning environment, grades are inappropriate.

_____ 7. Students enjoy working in a classroom that has clearly defined learning objectives and assessment criteria.

_____ 8. I favor teaching methods and classroom procedures that maximize students' independence to learn from their own experiences.

_____ 9. Most of what students learn is learned from other students.

_____ 10. Students should be concerned with getting good grades.

_____ 11. An important part of teaching and learning is learning how to work independently.

_____ 12. A teacher should not be contradicted or challenged by a student.

_____ 13. Interchanges between students and a teacher can provide ideas about content better than those found in a textbook.

_____ 14. For students to get the most out of a class, they must be aware of the primary concerns and biases of the teacher.

_____ 15. Students should not be given high grades unless they are clearly earned.

_____ 16. Learning should help the student to become an independent thinker.

_____ 17. Most of what students learn is learned from their teachers.

_____ 18. A teacher who makes students do things they don't want to do is an ineffective teacher.

_____ 19. Learning takes place most effectively under conditions in which students are in competition with one another.

_____ 20. A teacher should try to persuade students that particular ideas are valid and exciting.

_____ 21. To do well in school, students must be assertive.

*Adapted from William H. Berquist and Steve R. Phillips, *A Handbook for Faculty Development* (Washington, DC: The Council for Independent Colleges, June 1975), 25–27.

☞

EXERCISE 2.4 *(continued)*

_____ 22. Facts in textbooks are usually accurate.

_____ 23. I favor the use of teaching methods and classroom procedures that maximize students and teacher interaction.

_____ 24. Most of what students learn is learned from books.

_____ 25. A teacher who lets students do whatever they want is incompetent.

_____ 26. Students can learn more by working with an enthusiastic teacher than by working alone.

_____ 27. I favor the use of teaching methods and classroom procedures that maximize students' learning of basic subject matter content.

_____ 28. Ideas of other students are useful for helping a student understand the content of lessons.

_____ 29. A student should study what the teacher says is important and not necessarily what is important to that student.

_____ 30. A teacher who does not motivate students' interest in subject content is incompetent.

_____ 31. An important part of education is learning how to perform under testing and evaluation conditions.

_____ 32. Students can learn more by sharing their ideas than by keeping their ideas to themselves.

_____ 33. Teachers tend to give students too many assignments that are trivial.

_____ 34. Ideas contained in the textbook should be the primary source of the content taught.

_____ 35. Students should be given high grades as a means of motivating them and increasing their self-esteem.

_____ 36. The ideas a student brings into a class are useful for helping him or her to understand subject content.

_____ 37. Students should study what is important to them and not necessarily what the teacher claims is important.

_____ 38. Learning takes place most effectively under conditions in which students are working independently of one another.

_____ 39. Teachers often give students too much freedom of choice in content, methods, and procedures.

_____ 40. Teachers should clearly explain what it is they expect from students.

_____ 41. Students' ideas about content are often better than those ideas found in textbooks.

_____ 42. Classroom discussions are beneficial learning experiences.

_____ 43. A student's education should help the student to become a successful and contributing member of society.

_____ 44. Learning takes place most effectively under conditions in which students are working cooperatively with one another.

_____ 45. Teachers often are too personal with their students.

_____ 46. A teacher should encourage students to disagree with or challenge that teacher in the classroom.

_____ 47. Students have to be able to work effectively with other people to do well in school.

_____ 48. For students to get the most out of school, they must assume at least part of the responsibility for their learning.

_____ 49. Students seem to enjoy discussing their ideas about learning with the teacher and other students.

_____ 50. A student's education should help him or her to become a sensitive human being.

EXERCISE 2.4 *(continued)*

Step 2. From the list of 50 items, write the items (by their number) in two columns, those with which you held strong agreement, and those with which you strongly disagreed, ignoring those items you gave a *2* (were neutral).

Strongly agreed   *Strongly disagreed*

Step 3. In groups of three or four, discuss your lists (in step 2) with your classmates. From the discussion, you may rerank any items you wish.

Step 4. You now have a finalized list of those items with which you were in agreement, and those with which you disagreed. On the basis of those two lists, write a paragraph that summarizes your philosophy about teaching and learning. It should be no longer than one-half page in length. That statement is a theoretical representation of your present philosophy about teaching, especially about teaching young adolescents.

_____

_____

_____

_____

_____

_____

_____

EXERCISE 2.4   *(continued)*

_____

_____

_____

_____

_____

_____

_____

Step 5. Compare your philosophical statement with the three theoretical positions as discussed prior to this exercise. Can you clearly identify your position? Name it: _____

_____

_____

Explain your rationale: _____

_____

_____

_____

_____

_____

_____

_____

_____

_____

_____

_____

_____

_____

_____

_____

At the completion of this course, you may wish to revisit your philosophical statement, perhaps even to make revisions to it. It will be useful to have your educational philosophy firmly implanted in your memory for teaching job interviews at a later date.

COMMITMENT AND PROFESSIONALISM

The middle level classroom teacher is expected to demonstrate commitment to both the school's stated mission and to the emotional, physical, social, and intellectual development of the students. Not only do competent middle level teachers expect and receive positive results in learning from their students while in the classroom, they are also interested and involved in the activities of the students outside the classroom, willing to sacrifice personal time to give them attention and guidance.

Noninstructional Responsibilities

There seems to be no end to the duties required of teachers. Is this the career that a 22-year-old English major envisions when he or she contemplates the joys of sharing his or her passion with new students?

D. A. Heller (2004, p. 4)

The aspects of the teacher as a decision maker with professional commitments take on a very real dimension when you consider specific noninstruction-related and instruction-related responsibilities of the classroom teacher. Shown in Figure 2.2 are 13 categories of items that should alert you to the many noninstructional matters with which you should become familiar, especially during your first year of teaching. Their importance and the amount of time they require are often underestimated by beginning teachers.

STUDENT PHYSICAL SAFETY: RULES AND GUIDELINES

One item (item number nine) on the list in Figure 2.2 includes the responsibility of providing an environment that is safe for the children, both psychological and physical. While the psychological aspect is discussed later in this chapter and continues in Chapter 4, the physical safety aspect is discussed here.

Teachers are responsible for preventing accidents and ensuring that the learning environment is as safe as possible. Nevertheless, accidents and resulting injuries do occur to children at school. For example, during a language arts lesson, a student is injured by glass from a falling windowpane when the teacher forces the opening of a jammed window. A student in life science is helicoptered to the hospital after, on a dare, he devoured a preserved frog. A student falls on the playground and has an eye injury due to a sprinkler head that remained upright even though the sprinkler system was off. Students on the playing field were injured by a falling goal post that had been damaged below the ground level by termites.

So, you need to understand what you can do as a teacher to prevent accidents from happening. Also, you need to know what you should and should not do when an accident does happen. See the classroom safety rules and guidelines in Figure 2.3, and use the items as a basis for discussion with your classmates. The school in which you teach will, of course, have its own written rules and guidelines that may be more or

Figure 2.2 Noninstructional responsibilities of the classroom teacher.

1. Knowledgeable about activities of interest to the students.
2. Familiarity with the school campus and community.
3. Acquainted with members of the faculty and the support staff.
4. Knowledgeable about school and district policies.
5. Familiar with the backgrounds of the students.
6. Knowledgeable about procedures for such routine matters as planning and scheduling of before- and after-school activities; restroom regulations; distribution and collection of textbooks and other school materials; class dismissal; ordering of supplies; fire drills and severe weather; daily attendance records; school assemblies; sharing of instructional space with other teachers; arranging for and preparing displays for common areas of the school.
7. Expected role in teaching common elements of the curriculum, such as reading, writing, thinking, social skills, and study skills.
8. Expected role in the advisory program.
9. Classroom duties such as maintaining a cheerful, pleasant, and safe environment; obtaining materials needed for each lesson; keeping supplies orderly; supervising students who are helpers.
10. Expected role in the parent-teacher organization and other community participation activities.
11. The many conferences that will be needed, such as those between teacher and teacher; teacher and student; teacher and parent or guardian; teacher, student, and parent/guardian; teacher and administrator; and teacher and community representative.
12. Professional meetings, such as those of the interdisciplinary teaching team; other school and district committees; parent-teacher and community groups; and local, regional, state, and national professional organizations.
13. Time to relax and enjoy family, friends, and hobbies.

Figure 2.3   Safety procedures and guidelines for the classroom.

1. If an accident occurs, notify the school office immediately by contacting the office.
2. Give first aid *only* when it is necessary to save a minor's life or limb. When life or limb is not at risk, then follow school policy by referring the minor immediately to professional care. When immediate professional care is unavailable and you believe that immediate first aid is necessary, you can take prudent action, as if you were that child's parent or legal guardian. However, you must be cautious and knowledgeable about what you are doing, so as to not cause further injury to the child.
3. Unless you are a licensed medical professional, you should *never* give medication to a minor, whether prescription or over the counter (OTC). Refer to your school's policy on this. Be alert for students who have allergies or other medical problems, and be aware of what you can and must do if a particular student is having a medical problem while under your supervision.
4. For special situations, such as in classrooms for teaching laboratory science and physical education, rules and procedures should be taught to the students, posted in a conspicuous place, and reviewed and rehearsed often.
5. When escorting students on a field trip, solicit adult volunteer help, even if the destination is only a short distance from the school. Unless otherwise specified in your school policies, a recommended guideline is one or more responsible adults for every 10 students.
6. Maintain a neatly organized classroom working environment, with aisles kept clear and books, coats, and backpacks in designated storage areas. In classrooms used for laboratory science and shop instruction, in particular, students should not wear coats or any loose-fitting clothing that can easily knock over or become entangled in equipment.
7. Be aware of, model, and enforce eye safety precautions and regulations regarding eye protection.
8. Avoid using flammable materials and alcohol burners. Use lighted candles and hot plates only with extreme care.
9. Maintain a well-supplied first aid kit in the classroom, even if you must supply it with your own funds.
10. With emergency procedures posted conspicuously in the classroom, be sure you know exactly what to do in emergency situations.
11. Every classroom should have an adequately charged ABC-type fire extinguisher readily available.
12. Use proper waste disposal procedures. Learn school district policies regarding disposal of various waste materials relevant to your classroom activities.
13. Maintain accurate labels on all drawers, cupboards, closets, and containers.
14. Students should never be encouraged and allowed to taste unknown substances.
15. Avoid having dangerous plants, animals, chemicals, and apparatus in the classroom.
16. Instruct students to *never* handle or bring dead animals into the classroom.
17. Handle pets with care and caution. For example, birds can carry psittacosis and salmonella bacteria. Everyone should wash their hands thoroughly after handling bird feeders. Turtles and other animals also can carry salmonella bacteria. Dogs, rabbits, and other animals may harbor parasites. Some children are allergic to animal dander.
18. Do not store heavy items on shelves above the heads of students.
19. Do not allow students to climb or allow them to be in positions where they may fall.
20. Do not leave dangerously sharp objects, or those that may shatter, where students can obtain them without approval and supervision.
21. Avoid allowing students to overheat or to overexert themselves.
22. Never leave students unattended, for any reason, in the classroom, on the school campus, or during a field trip.
23. Inspect electrical equipment for frayed cords and, if frayed, do not use until repaired.
24. Avoid overloading an electrical circuit. When in doubt, don't use it until it is checked and approved by maintenance.
25. Disconnect electrical appliances, especially heating appliances, when they are not being used. Make sure the appliance is in the off position before disconnecting or connecting any electrical appliance.
26. Avoid poking around the back of a computer, television monitor, projector equipment, or any electrical appliance when the appliance is plugged into an outlet.
27. Never touch an electrical cord with wet hands or when standing or leaning in water.
28. Keep magnets away from computers and other electronic devices.
29. Use extra caution when you or your students are using any mechanical equipment with moving parts.
30. Under no circumstances should human body fluids be used for science investigation or for any other reason.

less extensive than those presented here. Safety guidelines for a shop class or a gymnasium, for example, will be more extensive.

Instructional Responsibilities

The items illustrated in Figure 2.4 categorize the instructional responsibilities you will have as a classroom teacher. The 16 categories of instructional responsibilities are the primary focus of study of the remainder of this resource guide. After you have reviewed both the lists of instructional and noninstructional responsibilities of the classroom teacher, complete Exercise 2.4, which is a model of cooperative learning.

Figure 2.4   Instructional responsibilities of the middle level classroom teacher.

1. Becoming knowledgeable about the expected target learning outcomes.
2. Planning units and lessons.
3. Learning the needs and interests of the students so lessons will reflect those needs and interests.
4. Incorporating relevant learning styles and learning modalities into the lessons.
5. Reading student papers.
6. Assessing and recording student progress.
7. Preparing the classroom.
8. Providing classroom instruction.
9. Thinking about professional growth and development, which may include attending university courses, attending workshops and other presentations offered by the school district or professional organizations, and reading professional literature.
10. Developing an effective classroom management system.
11. Becoming reacquainted with the developmental characteristics of young adolescents.
12. Learning the backgrounds of students with special problems who might cause concerns in the learning environment.
13. Developing strategies and plans for cross-age tutoring, peer coaching, cooperative learning, project-based learning, and other developmentally appropriate learning strategies.
14. Identifying resources and sources.
15. Devoting time to team planning.
16. Holding conferences with individual students, parents, and guardians.

FOR YOUR NOTES

EXERCISE 2.5 REVIEWING THE PROFESSIONAL RESPONSIBILITIES OF A FIRST-YEAR MIDDLE LEVEL TEACHER

INSTRUCTIONS: The purpose of this exercise is to review the responsibilities of a first-year teacher. Have the class of teacher candidates divide into groups of four. Within each group, one member should play each of the following roles: (1) group facilitator, (2) recorder, (3) materials manager, and (4) reporter. Each group is to choose one of these six categories of responsibilities:

1. Audiovisual/media
2. Classroom environment
3. Clerical
4. Instructional
5. Professional activities
6. Advisory/supervision

Each group then will read the responsibilities for their selected category listed on the following cards and arrange them in prioritized order, beginning with the most important. The group facilitator will lead this discussion. Under the guidance of the materials manager, the group may cut the cards apart so they can be physically manipulated as priorities are discussed. The recorder should take notes of the groups's work, which can then be discussed in order to develop the report that will be made to the class.

After a prearranged discussion time, recall the entire class and ask each reporter to share the group's (1) prioritized order of responsibilities and (2) estimate of the amount of time that a beginning teacher might devote to these responsibilities each week.

As each group reports, all members of the class should enter its list of priorities and time estimates on the Recap Sheet.

After completion of this exercise, the class may wish to discuss the group dynamics of this model of cooperative learning (see Chapter 8). For discussion in either large or small groups, key questions might be

1. Would you use this form of discussion in your own teaching?
2. How would you divide a class into groups of four?

Other questions may be generated by the group work.

FOR YOUR NOTES

CARD FOR EXERCISE 2.5
Audiovisual/Media Responsibilities

Selecting, ordering, and returning cassettes, films, videodiscs, and other materials

Preparing and operating equipment	Reviewing selected materials
Planning class introduction to the audiovisual materials	Other audiovisual responsibilities as determined

Estimated hours a beginning teacher will devote to audiovisual/media responsibilities each week = _____

CARD FOR EXERCISE 2.5
Classroom Environment Responsibilities

Planning and constructing displays	Preparing bulletin boards
Reading, announcing, and posting class notices	Managing a classroom library
Opening and closing windows, arranging furniture, cleaning the writing board	Other classroom environment responsibilities as determined

Estimated hours a beginning teacher will devote to classroom environment responsibilities each week = _____

CARD FOR EXERCISE 2.5
Clerical Responsibilities

Maintaining attendance and tardy records	Entering grades, scores, or marks into a record book or onto the computer
Preparing progress and grade reports	Typing, drawing, and duplicating instructional materials
Locating resource ideas and materials to support lessons	Other clerical responsibilities as determined

Estimated hours a beginning teacher will devote to clerical responsibilities each week = _____

FOR YOUR NOTES

CARD FOR EXERCISE 2.5
Instructional Responsibilities

Giving additional instruction (e.g., to students who need one-to-one attention, those who have been absent, or small review groups)	Correcting student work
Preparing special learning materials	Preparing, reading, and scoring tests; helping students self-evaluate
Writing information on the board	Preparing long-range and daily lesson plans
Grouping for instruction	Other instructional responsibilities as determined

Estimated hours a beginning teacher will devote to instructional responsibilities each week = _____

CARD FOR EXERCISE 2.5
Professional Activities Responsibilities

Researching and writing teacher reports	Attending teachers' and school district meetings
Planning and attending parent-teacher meetings	Attending local teachers' organization meetings
Attending state, regional, and national professional organizations; taking university classes	Other professional activities responsibilities as determined

Estimated hours a beginning teacher will devote to professional activities each week = _____

CARD FOR EXERCISE 2.5
Advisory/Supervision Responsibilities

Supervising before- or after-school activities	Supervising hallways, lunchrooms, and bathrooms
Supervising student assemblies	Advisory meetings
Supervising laboratory activities	Settling students' disputes

Other supervision responsibilities as determined

Estimated hours a beginning teacher will devote to supervision responsibilities each week = _____

FOR YOUR NOTES

EXERCISE 2.5: RECAP SHEET

AUDIOVISUAL/MEDIA RESPONSIBILITIES

1. _____
2. _____
3. _____
4. _____
5. _____

Estimated hours = _____

CLASSROOM ENVIRONMENT RESPONSIBILITIES

1. _____
2. _____
3. _____
4. _____
5. _____
6. _____

Estimated hours = _____

CLERICAL RESPONSIBILITIES

1. _____
2. _____
3. _____
4. _____
5. _____
6. _____

Estimated hours = _____

INSTRUCTIONAL RESPONSIBILITIES

1. _____
2. _____
3. _____
4. _____
5. _____
6. _____
7. _____
8. _____

Estimated hours = _____

☞

PROFESSIONAL ACTIVITIES RESPONSIBILITIES

1. _____
2. _____
3. _____
4. _____
5. _____
6. _____

　Estimated hours = _____

ADVISORY/SUPERVISION RESPONSIBILITIES

1. _____
2. _____
3. _____
4. _____
5. _____
6. _____
7. _____

　Estimated hours = _____

IDENTIFYING AND BUILDING YOUR INSTRUCTIONAL COMPETENCIES

The overall purpose of this resource guide is to assist you in building your instructional competencies so you can be a most effective professional. In order to do that, we need a starting place and this is it: the identification and presentation of 22 specific competencies. [*Note:* The following list of 22 competencies has evolved from its earliest inception as a simple (not annotated) listing of 20 "Characteristics of the Competent Teacher" (Kim & Kellough, 1983) to the current annotated list of 22 characteristics of the competent teacher (Kim & Kellough, 1991; Kellough & Roberts, 1994; Kellough, 1994; Kellough & Kellough, 1999).]

Characteristics of the Competent Classroom Teacher: An Annotated List

Students learn a lot from the company they keep—including the intellectual habits of their teachers.

Deborah Meier (2005, p. 7)

Please do not feel overwhelmed by the list; it may well be that no teacher expertly models all the characteristics that follow. The characteristics do, however, represent an ideal to strive for. You will continue to reflect on and build upon these competencies throughout your study of the remaining chapters of this book and, indeed, throughout your professional career.

1. *The teacher is knowledgeable about the subject matter.* You should have both historical understanding and current knowledge of the structure of the subject content you are expected to teach, and of the facts, principles, concepts, and skills needed for that subject matter.

2. *The teacher is an "educational broker."* You will learn where and how to discover information about content you are expected to teach. You cannot know everything there is to know about each subject or topic—indeed, you will not always be able to predict all that is learned—but you should become knowledgeable about where and how to best research it and how to assist your students in developing those same skills.

3. *The teacher is an active member of professional organizations, reads professional journals, dialogues with colleagues, and maintains currency in methodology and about the students and the subject content the teacher is expected to teach.* While this resource guide offers valuable information about teaching and learning, it is much closer to the start of your professional career than it is to the end. As a teacher, you are a learner among learners. Plan to spend your career in a perpetual mode of reflection and learning through workshops, advanced course work, coaching and training, reading and study, and collaboration with and role modeling of significant and more experienced colleagues.

4. *The teacher understands the processes of learning.* You will ensure that students understand classroom procedures, your expectations, and the lesson's target objectives. Students must feel welcome in your classroom and involved in learning activities, and they should have some control over the pacing of their own learning. Furthermore, when preparing your lessons, you will: (a) consider the unique learning characteristics of each student; (b) see that content is presented in reasonably small doses—and in a logical and coherent sequence—while using visual, verbal, tactile, and kinesthetic learning activities with opportunities for coached practice and reinforcement; and (c) scaffold the learning (providing temporary support) by frequently checking for student comprehension to assure each student is getting it.

5. *The teacher uses effective modeling behaviors.* Your own behaviors *must* be consistent with those expected of your students. If, for example, you want your students to demonstrate regular and punctual attendance, to have their work done on time, to have their materials each day for learning, to demonstrate cooperative behavior and respect for others, to maintain an open and inquisitive mind and attitude, to demonstrate critical thinking, and to use proper communication skills, then you will do likewise, modeling those same behaviors and attitudes for the students. As a classroom teacher, you serve as a very important role model for your students. Whether you realize it or not, your behavior sends important messages to students that complement curriculum content. You serve your students well when you model inclusive and collaborative approaches to learning. The importance of effective modeling is one of several recurring themes in this resource guide.

6. *The teacher is open to change, willing to take risks, and to be held accountable.* If there were no difference between what is and what can be, then formal schooling would be of little value. A competent teacher knows not only of historical and traditional values and knowledge, but also of the value of change. The teacher thus is willing to carefully plan and experiment, to move between that which is known and that which is not. Realizing that little of value is ever achieved without a certain amount of risk and employment of personal strength of convictions, the competent teacher stands ready to be held accountable, as the teacher undoubtedly will be, for assuming such risks. As stated so clearly elsewhere, "no coward ever got the Great Teacher Award" (Wassermann, 1999).

7. *The teacher is nondiscriminatory toward gender, sexual preference, ethnicity, skin color, religion, physical disabilities, socioeconomic status, learning disabilities, national origin, or any other personal characteristic.* Among other things, this means no sexual innuendoes, religious or ethnic jokes, or racial slurs. It means being cognizant of how teachers, male and female, black or white, heterosexual or homosexual, U.S. born or not, Christian or

other, knowingly or unknowingly, historically have mistreated certain students, and of how to avoid those same errors in your own teaching. It means learning about and attending to the needs of individual students in your classroom. It means maintaining high, although not necessarily identical, expectations for all students.

8. *The teacher organizes the classroom and plans lessons carefully.* Long-range plans, no matter whether they include interdisciplinary thematic units or standard units, and daily lessons, no matter whether student-centered or teacher-centered, are prepared thoughtfully, reflected on, revised, and competently implemented with creative, motivating, and effective strategies and skills. Much of this resource guide is devoted specifically to assisting in your development of this competency.

9. *The teacher is a capable communicator.* The competent teacher uses thoughtfully selected words, carefully planned questions, expressive voice inflections, useful pauses, meaningful gestures, and productive and nonconfusing body language. Some of these expressions are carefully and thoughtfully planned during the preactive phase of instruction and others, through practice and reflection, become second-nature skills. Throughout this resource guide, you will find useful suggestions for your development of this competency.

10. *The teacher functions effectively as a decision maker.* The exemplary middle level classroom is a complex place, busy with fast-paced activities. In a single day you may engage in a thousand or more interpersonal exchanges with students, to say nothing about the numerous exchanges possible with the many adults with whom you will be in contact. The competent teacher is in control of classroom events rather than controlled *by* them. The teacher initiates, rather than merely reacts, is proactive and in control of her or his interactions, having learned how to manage time to analyze and develop effective interpersonal behaviors.

11. *The teacher is in a perpetual learning mode, striving to further develop a repertoire of teaching strategies.* Competent teachers are good students, continuing their own learning by reflecting on and assessing their work, attending workshops, studying the work of others, and communicating with students, parents and guardians, and colleagues.

12. *The teacher demonstrates concern for the safety and health of the students.* The competent teacher consistently models safety procedures, ensuring precautions necessary to protect the health and emotional and physical safety of the students. The teacher strives to maintain a comfortable room temperature with adequate ventilation and to prevent safety hazards in the classroom. Students who are ill are encouraged to stay home and to get well. If a teacher suspects a student may be ill or may be suffering from neglect or abuse at home, the teacher appropriately and promptly acts upon that suspicion by referring it to the appropriate school official.

13. *The teacher demonstrates optimism for the learning of every student, while providing a constructive and positive environment for learning.* Both common sense and research tell us clearly that young adolescents enjoy and learn better from a teacher who is positive and optimistic, encouraging, nurturing, and happy, rather than from a teacher who is negative and pessimistic, discouraging, uninterested, and grumpy.

14. *The teacher demonstrates confidence in each student's ability to learn.* For a young adolescent, nothing at school is more satisfying than having a teacher who demonstrates confidence in that student's abilities. Unfortunately, for some children, a teacher's show of confidence may be the only positive indicator that child ever receives. Each of us can recall with admiration a teacher (or other significant person) who demonstrated confidence in our ability to accomplish seemingly formidable tasks. A competent teacher demonstrates this confidence with each and every student, and tries to do so every school day. This doesn't mean you must personally like every student with whom you will ever come into contact; it does mean that you accept each one as a person of dignity and who is worthy of receiving your respect as a young adolescent in process of development and the benefits of your professional training and experiences.

15. *The teacher is skillful and fair in the employment of strategies for the assessment of student learning.* The competent teacher is knowledgeable about the importance of providing immediate, intensive intervention when learning problems become apparent, implementing appropriate learning assessment tools while avoiding the abuse of power afforded by the assessment process.

16. *The teacher is skillful in working with parents and guardians, colleagues, administrators, and the support staff, and maintains and nurtures friendly and ethical professional relationships.* Teachers, parents and guardians, administrators, cooks, custodians, secretaries, school bus drivers, security personnel, and other adults of the school community all share a common purpose, and that is to serve the education of the students. It is done best when they do it knowledgeably, pensively, and cooperatively.

17. *The teacher demonstrates continuing interest in professional responsibilities, challenges, and opportunities.* Knowing that ultimately each and every school activity has an effect upon the classroom, the competent teacher assumes an active interest in the school community. The purpose of the school is to serve the education of the students, and the classroom is the primary, but most certainly not only, place where this occurs. Every committee meeting, school event, advisory meeting, faculty meeting, school board meeting, office, program, and any other planned function related to school life shares in the ultimate purpose of better serving the education of the children who attend that school.

18. *The teacher exhibits a wide range of interests.* This includes interest in the activities of the children and the many aspects of the school and its surrounding community. The competent teacher is interesting because of his or her interests; a teacher with varied interests more often motivates and captures the attention of more students. A teacher with no interests outside his or her subject area and the classroom is likely, for young adolescent students, to be an exceedingly dull person.

19. *The teacher shares a healthy sense of humor.* The positive effects of appropriate humor (i.e., humor that is not self-deprecating or disrespectful of others) on learning are well established: increases immune system activity and decreases stress-producing hormones; pulse rate drops; reduces feelings of anxiety, tension, and stress; activates T cells for the immune system, antibodies that fight against harmful microorganisms, and gamma interferon—a hormone that fights viruses and regulates cell growth; and increases blood oxygen. Because of these effects, humor is a stimulant to not only healthy living, but to creativity and higher-level thinking. As they should, young adolescents appreciate and learn more from a teacher who shares a sense of humor and laughs with them. Additionally, and certainly not unimportantly, considerable evidence exists to show the importance of a healthy sense of humor to the development of a teacher's resilience and career longevity (Bobek, 2002).

20. *The teacher is quick to recognize a child who may be in need of special attention.* A competent teacher is alert to recognize any child who demonstrates behaviors indicating a need for special attention, guidance, or counseling. The teacher knows how and where to refer the student, doing so with minimal class disruption and without embarrassment to the child. For example, a pattern of increasingly poor attendance or of steady negative-attention seeking behaviors are two of the more obvious early signals of the student who is potentially at risk of dropping out of school.

21. *The teacher makes specific and frequent efforts to demonstrate how the subject content may be related to the students' lives.* A potentially dry and dull topic is made significant and alive when taught by a competent teacher. Regardless of topic, somewhere competent teachers are teaching that topic, and one of the significant characteristics of their effectiveness is they make the topic alive and relevant to themselves and to their students. Time and again studies point out what should be obvious: Young adolescent students don't learn much from dull, meaningless "drill and kill" exercises and assignments. Such uninspired teaching may be at the root of the reason why some children lose interest in formal schooling. Obtaining ideas from professional journals, attending workshops and conferences, such as those sponsored by the National Middle School Association, communicating with colleagues either personally or via e-bulletin boards and websites, and using project-based and interdisciplinary thematic instruction are ways of discovering how to make a potentially dry and boring topic interesting and alive for students (and for the teacher).

22. *The teacher is reliable.* The competent teacher can be relied on to fulfill professional responsibilities, promises, and commitments. A teacher who cannot be relied on is quick to lose credibility with children and with colleagues and administrators. Regardless of a teacher's credential qualifications and potential for effectiveness, an unreliable teacher is an incompetent teacher and should be released from duties unless he or she improves in reliability.

Specific teacher behaviors are discussed in the following section; guidelines and resources to assist you in your development of these competencies permeate this resource guide.

TEACHER BEHAVIORS NECESSARY TO FACILITATE STUDENT LEARNING

Your ability to perform your instructional responsibilities effectively is directly dependent upon your knowledge of young adolescents and how they best learn and your knowledge of, and the quality of, your teaching skills. Directly related to teacher competencies discussed in the preceding section are specific teacher behaviors that are necessary to facilitate student learning. As was said at the beginning of this chapter, development of your strategy repertoire along with your skills in using specific strategies should be ongoing throughout your teaching career. To be most effective, you need a large repertoire from which to select a specific strategy for a particular goal with a distinctive group of students. In addition, you need skill in using that strategy. This section of the chapter is designed to help you begin building your strategies repertoire and to develop your skills in using these strategies. Like intelligences, teaching style is neither absolutely inherited nor fixed, but continues to develop and emerge throughout one's professional career.

Three Basic Rules for Becoming a Competent Teacher of Young Adolescents

First, you must know why you have selected a particular strategy. An unknowing teacher is likely to use the teaching strategy most common in college classes—the lecture. However, as many beginning teachers have discovered the hard way, the traditional lecture is seldom, if ever, an effective or appropriate way to instruct young adolescents. As a rule, unlike many college and university students, not many young adolescents are strong auditory learners by preference and by adeptness. For most of them, learning by sitting and listening is difficult. Instead, young adolescents learn best when physically (hands-on) and intellectually (minds-on) active—that is, when using tactile and kinesthetic experiences, touching objects, feeling shapes and textures, moving objects, and when together they are able to talk about and share what they are learning, that is by learning *collaboratively*.

Second, basic teacher behaviors create the conditions needed to enable students to think and to learn, whether the learning is a further understanding of concepts, the internalization of attitudes and values, the development of cognitive processes, or the actuating of the most complex behaviors. The basic teacher behaviors are those that produce the following results: (a) students who are physically and mentally engaged in the learning activities, (b) instructional time that is efficiently used, and (c) minimal classroom distractions and interruptions.

Third, the effectiveness with which a teacher carries out the basic behaviors can be measured by how well the students learn.

The basic teacher behaviors that facilitate student learning, discussed in detail next, are: structuring the learning environment, accepting and sharing instructional accountability, demonstrating withitness and overlapping, providing a variety of motivating and challenging lessons, modeling appropriate behaviors, facilitating student acquisition of data, creating a psychologically safe environment, clarifying whenever necessary, using periods of silence, and questioning thoughtfully.

Facilitating Behaviors and Instructional Strategies: A Clarification

Clearly, at least some of the 10 basic behaviors are also instructional strategies. Questioning is one example. The difference is while the behaviors must be in place for the most effective teaching to occur, strategies are more or less discretionary; that is, they are pedagogical techniques from which you may select but may not be obligated to use. For example, questioning and the use of silence are fundamental teaching behaviors, whereas lecturing and showing videos are not. Thus, your task is two-fold: (1) develop your awareness of and skills in using the fundamental teaching behaviors, and (2) develop your repertoire and skills in selecting and using appropriate instructional strategies.

Starting now and continuing throughout your teaching career, you will want to evaluate your developing competency for each of the 10 fundamental facilitating behaviors and improve in areas where you need help. Consider the following descriptions and examples, and discuss them with your classmates. [*Note:* The meaning of key terms may be found in the glossary of this resource guide; additional discussion of key strategies may be found via the index.]

Structuring the Learning Environment

Structuring the learning environment means establishing an intellectual, psychological, and physical environment that enables all students to act and react productively. Specifically, you:

- Attend to the organization of the classroom as a learning laboratory to establish a positive (inviting), safe, and efficient environment for student learning.
- Establish and maintain clearly understood classroom procedures, definitions, instructions, and expectations.
- Help students to clarify the learning expectations and to establish clearly understood learning objectives.
- Help students assume tasks and responsibilities, thereby empowering them in their learning.
- Organize the students, helping them to organize their learning. Help students in their identifying and understanding of time and resource constraints.

Provide instructional scaffolds, such as building bridges to student learning by helping students connect what is being learned with what the students already know or think they know and have experienced.

- Plan and implement techniques for schema building, such as providing content and process outlines, visual diagrams, and opportunities for thinking process mapping.
- Use techniques for students' metacognitive development, such as: *think-pair-share*, in which students are asked to think about an idea, share thoughts about it with a partner, and then share the pair's thoughts with the entire class; *think-write-pair-share*, in which each student writes his or her ideas about the new word and then shares in pairs before sharing with the entire class; and *jigsaw*, in which individuals or small groups of students are given responsibilities for separate tasks which lead to a bigger task or understanding, thereby putting together parts to make a whole (as done in this chapter with Exercise 2.5).
- Plan units and lessons that have clear and concise beginnings and endings with at least some of the planning done collaboratively with the students.
- Provide frequent summary reviews, often by using student self-assessment of what is being learned. Structure and facilitate ongoing formal and informal discussion based on a shared understanding of the rules of discourse.

Accepting and Sharing Instructional Accountability

While holding students accountable for their learning, the teacher is willing to be held accountable for the effectiveness of the learning process and outcomes (the "locus of control" as discussed at the start of this chapter). Specifically, you:

- Assume a responsibility for professional decision making and the risks associated with that responsibility. Share some responsibility for decision making and risk taking with the students. A primary goal in the students' education must be to see that students become accountable for themselves as learners and as citizens. Teachers are advised to work with their students as partners in their learning and development. One dimension of the partnership is shared accountability. One way of doing that is by using student portfolios.
- Communicate clearly to parents/guardians, administrators, and colleagues.
- Communicate to students that the accomplishment of learning goals and objectives is a responsibility they share with you.
- Plan exploratory activities that engage students in the learning.

- Provide continuous cues for desired learning behaviors and incentives contingent upon desired performance, such as grades, points, rewards, and privileges. Establish a clearly understood and continuous program of assessment that includes reflection and self-assessment.
- Provide opportunities for the students to demonstrate their learning, to refine and explore their questions, to inquire, and to share their thinking and results.

Demonstrating Withitness and Overlapping

First described by Jacob Kounin (1970), withitness and overlapping are separate but closely related behaviors. Withitness is the teacher's awareness of the whole group (i.e., the ability to remain alert in the classroom, to spot quickly and redirect potential student misbehavior, which is analogous to having "eyes in the back of your head"). Overlapping is the ability to attend to several matters simultaneously.

Specifically, you:

- Attend to the entire class while working with one student or with a small group of students, communicating this awareness with eye contact, hand gestures, body position and language, and clear but private verbal cues.
- Continually and simultaneously monitoring all classroom activities to keep students at their tasks and to provide students with assistance and resources.
- Continue monitoring the class during any distraction, such as when a visitor enters the classroom or while the students are on a field trip.
- Demonstrate an understanding of when comprehension checks and instructional transitions are appropriate or needed.
- Dwell on one topic only as long as necessary for the students' understanding.
- Quickly intervene and redirect potential undesirable student behavior.
- Refocus or shift activities for a student when that student's attention begins to fade.

GUIDELINES FOR DEVELOPING WITHITNESS

Consider the follow guidelines for developing classroom withitness.

- Avoid spending too much time with any one student or group; in classes of 20 or more students, longer than 30 seconds may be approaching "too much time."
- Avoid turning your back to all or a portion of the students, such as when writing on the writing board.
- If two or more errant behaviors are occurring simultaneously in different locations, attend to the

most serious first, while giving the other(s) a non-verbal gesture showing your awareness (e.g., by eye contact) and displeasure (e.g., with a frown).

- Involve all students in the act, not just one student or small group. Avoid concentrating on only those who appear most interested or responsive, sometimes referred to as the "chosen few."
- Keep students alert by calling on them randomly, asking questions and calling on an answerer, circulating from group to group during team learning activities, and frequently checking on the progress of individual students.
- Maintain constant visual surveillance of the entire class, even when talking to or working with an individual or small group of students and when meeting a classroom visitor at the door.
- Move around the room. Be on top of potential misbehavior and quietly redirect student attention before the misbehavior occurs or escalates.
- Try, during whole-class direct instruction, to establish eye contact with each student about once every minute. Although that may sound impossible to do, it is not; it is a skill that can be developed with practice.

A prerequisite to being withit is the skill to attend to more than one matter at a time. This is referred to as overlapping ability, which today is called *multitasking*. The teacher with overlapping skill uses body language, body position, and hand signals to communicate with students. Consider the following examples.

- Rather than bringing their papers and problems to her desk, the teacher expects students to remain seated and to raise their hands as the teacher circulates in the room monitoring and attending to individual students.
- The teacher takes care of attendance while visually and/or verbally monitoring the students during their warm-up activity.
- While attending to a messenger who has entered the room, the teacher demonstrates verbally or by gestures that the teacher expects the students to continue their work.
- While working in a small group, a student raises a hand to obtain the teacher's attention. The teacher, while continuing to work with another group of students, with a hand signals to the student that the teacher is aware that the student wants his or her attention and will get to the student soon, which the teacher does.
- Without missing a beat in her or his talk, the teacher aborts a potentially disruptive behavior of a student by gesturing, making eye contact, or moving closer to the student (using what is referred to as *proximity control*).

Providing a Variety of Motivating and Challenging Activities

The effective teacher uses a variety of activities that motivate and challenge all students to work to the utmost of their abilities, and that engage and challenge the preferred learning styles and learning capacities of more of the students more of the time. Specifically, you:

- Demonstrate optimism toward each student's ability.
- Demonstrate an unwavering expectation that each student will work to the best of her or his ability.
- Show pride, optimism, and enthusiasm in learning, thinking, and teaching.
- View teaching and learning as an organic and reciprocal process that extends well beyond that which can be referred to as the traditional 2 by 4 by 6 curriculum—that is, a curriculum that is bound by the two covers of the textbook, the four walls of the classroom, and the six hours of the school day.
- Collaborate with the students to plan exciting and interesting learning activities, including those that engage the young adolescents' natural interest in the mysterious and the novel.

Modeling Appropriate Behaviors

Effective teachers model the very behaviors expected of their students. Specifically, you:

- Are prompt in returning students' papers and offer comments that provide instructive and encouraging feedback.
- Arrive promptly in the classroom and demonstrate on-task behaviors for the entire class meeting.
- Demonstrate respect for all students. For example, you do not interrupt when a student is showing rational thinking, even though you may disagree with or frown upon the words used or the direction of the student's thinking.
- Demonstrate that making "errors" is a natural event while learning and during problem solving, and readily admit and correct mistakes you have made.
- Model and emphasize the skills, attitudes, and values of higher-order intellectual processes. Demonstrate rational problem-solving skills and explain to the students the processes being engaged while problem solving.
- Model professionalism by spelling correctly, using proper grammar, and writing clearly and legibly.
- Practice communication that is clear, precise, and to the point. For example, use "I" when referring to yourself, "we" when "we" is meant. And, as another example, rather than responding to student contributions with simply "good" or "okay," tell specifically what about the response was good, or what made it okay.

- Practice moments of silence (see the section "Using Periods of Silence" that follows), thus modeling thoughtfulness, reflectiveness, and restraint of impulsiveness.
- Realize that students are also models for other students, reinforce appropriate student behaviors, and intervene when behaviors are inappropriate.

Facilitating Student Acquisition of Data

The teacher makes sure that data are accessible to students as input they can process. Specifically, you:

- Create a responsive classroom environment with direct learning experiences.
- Ensure that major ideas receive proper attention and emphasis.
- Ensure that sources of information are readily available to students for their use.
- Select books, media, and other resource materials that facilitate student learning.
- Assure to the extent you can that equipment and materials are readily available for students to use.
- Identify and use resources beyond the walls of the classroom and the boundaries of the school campus.
- Provide clear and specific instructions.
- Provide feedback and feedback mechanisms about each student's performance and progress.
- Encourage students to organize and maintain devices to self-monitor their progress in learning and thinking.
- Select anchoring (also called model or benchmark) examples of student work that help students bridge what is being learned with what they already know and have experienced.
- Serve as a resource person and use collaborative and cooperative learning, thus regarding students as resources too.

Creating a Psychologically Safe Environment

To encourage the positive development of student self-esteem, to provide a psychologically safe learning environment, and to encourage the most creative thought and behavior, the teacher provides a positive, attractive, and stimulating classroom environment and appropriate nonjudgmental responses. (Chapter 4 is devoted to this theme.) Specifically, you:

- Avoid negative criticism. Criticism is often a negative value judgment, and "when a teacher responds to a student's ideas or actions with such negative words as 'poor,' 'incorrect,' or 'wrong,' the response tends to signal inadequacy or disapproval and ends the student's thinking about the task" (Costa, 1991, p. 54).
- Frequently use minimal reinforcement (i.e., nonjudgmental acceptance behaviors, such as nodding head, writing a student's response on the board, or saying "I understand"). Whereas elaborate or strong praise is generally unrelated to student achievement, minimal reinforcement, using words like "right," "okay," "uh-huh," and "thank you," does correlate with achievement.

However, as implied in the previous discussion about "modeling," be careful with a too frequent and thereby ineffective and even damaging use of the single word "good" following student contributions during a class discussion. Use the word only when the contribution was truly that—good—and better yet, say not only "good" but tell what specifically was good about the student's contribution. That provides a more powerful reinforcement by demonstrating that you truly heard the student's contribution and, thus, indeed thought it was good.

- Infrequently use elaborate or strong praise. By the time students are beyond primary grades, teacher praise, a positive value judgment, has little or no value as a form of positive reinforcement. When praise is used for young adolescents it should be mild, private, and for student accomplishment, rather than for effort; for each child, the frequency in using praise should be gradually reduced. When praise is reduced, a more diffused sociometric pattern develops; that is, more of the children become directly and productively involved in the learning. Praise should be simple and direct, delivered in a natural voice without dramatizing (Good & Brophy, 2003).

Let's take pause to consider this point. Probably no statement in this resource guide raises more eyebrows than the statement that praise for most children beyond primary years has little or no value as a form of positive reinforcement. After all, praise may well motivate some people. However, at what cost? Praise and encouragement are often confused and considered to be the same (see Figure 2.5), but they are not, and they do not have the same long-term results. [*Note:* Some researchers distinguish between praise that is "ineffective" and praise that is "effective," with the latter considered synonymous with the term *encouragement.* For clarity, we prefer to use simply the terms *praise* (which is generally ineffective) versus *encouragement* (which *is* effective).] This is explained as follows:

> For many years there has been a great campaign for the virtues of praise in helping children gain a positive self-concept and improve their behavior. This is another time when we must "beware of what works." Praise may inspire some children to improve their behavior. The problem is that they become pleasers and approval "junkies." These children (and later these adults) develop self-concepts that are totally dependent on the opinions of others. Other children resent and rebel against praise, either because

Figure 2.5 Statements of praise versus encouragement.

Statement of Praise	Statement of Encouragement
1. Your painting is excellent.	1. It is obvious that you enjoy painting.
2. I am delighted that you behaved so well on our class field trip.	2. I am so delighted that we all enjoyed the class field trip.
3. You did a good job on those word problems.	3. I can tell that you have been working and are enjoying it more.
4. Your oral report on your project was well done.	4. I can tell that you got really interested in your topic for the oral report on your project.
5. Great answer, Louis!	5. Louis, your answer shows that you gave a lot of thought to the question.

they don't want to live up to the expectations of others or because they fear they can't compete with those who seem to get praise so easily. The alternative that considers long-range effects is encouragement. The long-range effect of encouragement is self-confidence. The long-range effect of praise is dependence on others. (Nelsen, 1987, p. 103)

In summary, then, while being cautious with the use of praise, do reinforce student efforts by recognizing specific personal accomplishments (Marzano, Pickering, & Pollock, 2001).

- Perceive your classroom as the place where you work and where students learn, and make that place of work, and the tools available, a place of pride—as positive, stimulating, and practical as possible.
- Plan within the lessons behaviors that show respect for the cultures, experiences, and ideas of individual students.
- Provide positive individual student attention as often as possible. Write sincere, reinforcing, personalized comments on student papers.
- Use nonverbal cues to show awareness, empathy, and acceptance of individual students. Use paraphrasing and reflective listening. Use empathic acceptance of a student's expression of feelings; demonstrate by words and gestures that you understand the student's position, and that you truly care about how the student is doing. Perceiving the teacher as a truly caring adult can go a long way in supplying a student with motivation to learn (Littky, 2004, Murdock & Miller, 2003).

Clarifying Whenever Necessary

Your responding behavior seeks further elaboration from a student about that student's idea or comprehension. Specifically, you:

- Help students to connect new content to what was previously learned. Help students relate content of a lesson to students' other school and nonschool

experiences. Help students make learning connections between disciplines.
- Politely invite a student to be more specific, to elaborate on or rephrase an idea, or to provide a concrete illustration of an idea.
- Provide frequent opportunities for summary reviews.
- Repeat or paraphrase a student's response, allowing the student to correct any other person's misinterpretation of what the student said or implied.
- Select instructional strategies that help students recognize and correct, or improve upon, their prior notions about a topic.

Using Periods of Silence

Competent teachers use periods of silence in the classroom. Specifically, you:

- Actively listen when a student is talking.
- Allow sufficient think time, sometimes as long as seven seconds (Rowe, 1974; Tobin, 1984), after asking a question or posing a problem.
- Keep silent when students are working quietly or attending to a visual display, and maintain classroom control with use of nonverbal signals and indirect intervention strategies.
- Pause while talking to allow for thinking and reflection.
- Use teacher silence, supported by body language and nonverbal gesturing (i.e., a nod of the head, a thumbs up), to stimulate group discussion.

Questioning Thoughtfully

Thoughtfully worded questions induce learning and stimulate thinking and the development of students' thinking skills. Specifically, you:

- Encourage student questioning without judging the quality or relevancy of a student's question. Attend to student questions, and respond and encourage other students to respond, often by building upon the content of a student's questions and student responses.

- Help students develop their own questioning skills and provide opportunities for students to explore their own ideas, obtain data, and find answers to their own questions and solutions to their problems.
- Plan questioning sequences that elicit a variety of thinking skills and that maneuver students to higher levels of thinking and doing.
- Use a variety of types of questions.
- Use questions to help students explore their knowledge, develop new understandings, and discover ways of applying their new understandings.

Questioning, an important instructional strategy as well as a basic facilitating behavior, is discussed in great detail in the chapter that follows. But before we leave this chapter about teacher professionalism, let's consider one final topic and that is the teacher's responsibilities as related to tools for instruction.

TOOLS FOR INSTRUCTION

This final section of this chapter focuses your attention on the important responsibility you have for using the cognitive tools available for helping students construct their understandings. You will be pleased to know that there is a large variety of useful and effective educational media, aids, and resources—electronic, print, and objects—from which to draw on as you plan your instructional experiences. On the other hand, you could also become overwhelmed by the variety and sheer quantity of materials available for classroom use. You could spend a lot of time reviewing, sorting, selecting, and practicing with these materials and tools. Although nobody can make the job easier for you, information in this final section of this chapter may expedite the process.

Long ago, when humankind was young and writing had not yet been invented, men and women taught their children by means of very simple tools. Telling children what they should know was an important teaching technique, but there were other teaching and learning methods, too. Children learned to hunt by practicing with spears, by throwing sticks, and by simulating hunts of simulated animals. Parents taught geography by maps drawn in the sand and religion by pictures drawn on the walls of caves. Dance and drama portrayed the history, customs, and lore of a group. From the very earliest times, teachers have depended on diverse teaching tools to make their teaching interesting and effective. Today, teachers still depend on a variety of teaching tools. In some respects, modern teaching tools are much more sophisticated than those of older times. Yet we use our new tools for the same purposes and in much the same ways that our ancestors used theirs: to make things clear, to make instruction real, to spice up the learning process, and to make it possible for students to teach themselves. Teaching would be impossible without some instructional aids.

TECHNOLOGY IN THE CLASSROOM
Past, Present, and Future

In 1922, Thomas Edison predicted that "the motion picture is destined to revolutionize our educational system and . . . in a few years it will supplant largely, if not entirely, the use of textbooks." In 1945, William Levenson of the Cleveland public schools' radio station claimed that "the time may come when a portable radio receiver will be as common in the classroom as is the blackboard." In the early 1960s, B. F. Skinner believed that with the help of the new teaching machines and programmed instruction, students could learn twice as much in the same time as with the same effort in a standard classroom.

Questions for Class Discussion

1. Did motion pictures, radio, programmed instruction, and television revolutionize education?

2. Will computers and the accompanying electronic technology become as much a part of the classroom as writing boards?

3. What do you predict the public school classroom of the year 2040 will be like, that is, at the time when you will be well into your career and likely thinking about retirement? Will the role of a teacher be different in any way than it is today? Will electronic distance education via the Internet replace face-to-face instruction?

As you peruse this final topic in this chapter we remind you again, as we did in Chapter 1 (Figure 1.2), about starting your professional resources file.

The Internet

The Internet Originated from a Department of Defense project (called ARPAnet, named after the federal government's Advanced Research Projects Agency) at the University of California, Los Angeles, computer science department in 1969, to establish a computer network of military researchers. The federally funded Internet (also known as the "information superhighway" and "cyberspace" or just simply the "net") has as you undoubtedly know, become an enormous, steadily expanding, worldwide system of connected computer networks. The Internet provides literally millions of resources to explore, with thousands more added nearly every day. Today you can surf the Internet and find many sources about how to use it, and you can walk into almost any bookstore and find hundreds of recent titles, most of which give their authors' favorite websites. However, new technologies are steadily emerging and the Internet changes every day, with some sites and resources disappearing or not kept current, others having changed

TEACHING VIGNETTE
Natural Disasters

Let us suppose that the students from your "house" have been working nearly all year on an interdisciplinary thematic unit titled "surviving natural disasters" (returning to the discussion in Chapter 5 regarding ITU themes). As a culmination to their study, they "published" a document titled *Natural Disaster Preparation and Survival Guide for (name of their community)* and proudly distributed the guide to their parents and members of the community.

Long before preparing the guide, however, the students had to do research about the history of various kinds of natural disasters that had occurred or might occur locally and about the preparations a community should take for each kind of disaster. Students searched sources on the Internet, such as federal documents, scientific articles, and articles from newspapers around the world where natural disasters had occurred. They also searched in the local library and the local newspaper's archives to learn about floods, tornadoes, and fires that had occurred during the past 200 years. Much to their surprise, they also learned that their community is located very near the New Madrid Fault and did, in fact, experience a serious earthquake in 1811, although they have had none since. As a result of that earthquake, two nearby towns completely disappeared; the Mississippi River flowed in reverse; and the river's course changed and caused the formation of a new lake.

From published and copyrighted sources, including websites, the students found many useful photographs, graphics, and articles that they included in whole or in part in their *Natural Disaster Preparation and Survival Guide*. They did so without obtaining permission from the original copyright holders or even citing those sources.

You and the other members of your teaching team and other people in the community were so impressed with the student's work that the students were encouraged to publish the document on the school's website. In addition, the students decided to place it for sale in local retail outlets. This would help defray the original cost of duplication and enable them to continue to supply the guides.

---

their location and undergone reconstruction, and other new ones appearing. Therefore, it would be superfluous for us in this book, which will be around for several years, to get too enthused about sites that we personally have viewed and can recommend as teacher resources. Nevertheless, recommended sites are listed at the end of each chapter.

CAUTIONS AND GUIDELINES FOR USING THE INTERNET

If you have yet to learn to use the Internet, we shall leave the mechanics of that to the many resources available to you, including the experts that can be found among your peers, on your college or university staff, and among members of any public school faculty. The remaining pages of this section address the "how" of using the Internet from an academic perspective. Let's begin with the fictitious, although feasible, Teaching Vignette: Natural Disasters, illustrated in the accompanying box.

In the above scenario, there are both a desirable aspect and a not-so-desirable aspect. It was good that the students used a worthy technological tool (the Internet) to research a variety of sources, including many primary ones. But when they published their document on the Internet and when they made copies of their guide to be sold, they did so without permission from original copyright holders, and were thus infringing copyright law. Although it would take an attorney to say for sure, with this scenario it is probable that the students, teacher, school, and the school district would be liable. As is true for other documents (such as published photos, graphics, and text), unless there is an explicit statement that materials taken from the Internet are public domain, it is best to assume that they are copyrighted and should not be republished without permission from the original source.

There is such a proliferation of information today, from both printed materials and from information on the Internet, how can a person determine the validity and currency of a particular piece of information? When searching for useful and reliable information on a particular topic, how can one be protected from wasting valuable time sifting through all the information? Students need to know that just because information is found on a printed page or is published on the Internet doesn't necessarily mean that the information is accurate or current.

Teaching all students how to access and assess websites adds to their repertoire of skills for lifelong learning. Consider allowing each student or teams of students to become experts on specific sites during particular units of study. It might be useful to start a chronicle of student-recorded log entries about particular websites to provide comprehensive long-term data about those sites.

When students use information from the Internet, require that they print copies of sources of citations and materials so you can check for accuracy. These copies may be maintained in their portfolios.

Student work published on the Internet should be considered intellectual material and protected from plagiarism by others. Most school districts post a copyright notice on their home page. Someone at the school usually is assigned to supervise the school website to see that district and school policy and legal requirements are observed.

Professional Journals and Periodicals

Figure 2.6 lists examples of the many professional periodicals and journals that can provide useful teaching ideas and website information and that carry information about instructional materials and how to get them. Some of these may be in your university or college library and accessible through Internet sources. Check there for these and other titles of interest to you.

The ERIC Information Network

The Educational Resources Information Center (ERIC) system, established by the United States Office of Education, is a widely used network providing access to information and research in education. The site underwent renovation in 2004.

Copying Printed Materials

Remember that although on many webpages there is no notice, the material is still copyrighted. Copyright law protects original material; that is just as true for the intellectual property created by a minor as it is for that of an adult.

Although space here prohibits full inclusion of United States legal guidelines, your local school district should be able to provide a copy of current district policies for compliance with copyright laws. District policies should include guidelines for teachers and students in publishing materials on the Internet. If no district guidelines are available, adhere to the guidelines shown in Figure 2.7 when using printed materials.

When preparing to make a copy you must find out whether the law under the category of "permitted use" permits the copying. If not allowed under "permitted use," then you must get written permission to reproduce the material from the holder of the copyright. If

Figure 2.6 Selected professional journals and periodicals for teachers.

American Biology Teacher	The Middle School Journal
American Music Teacher	Modern Language Journal
Childhood Education	Negro Educational Review
Computing Teacher, The	OAH Magazine of History
Educational Horizons	Phi Delta Kappan
Educational Leadership	Physical Education
Edutopia	Reading Teacher
English Journal	Reading Today
English Language Teaching Journal	School Arts
Hispania	School Library Journal
History Teacher	School Science and Mathematics
Horn Book	Science
Instructor	Science Activities
Journal of Adolescent and Adult Literacy	Science and Children
Journal of Geography	Science Scope
Journal of Learning Disabilities	Social Education
Journal of Physical Education and Recreation	Social Studies
Journal of Teaching in Physical Education	Teacher Magazine
Language Arts	Teaching Pre K–8
Language Learning	TESOL Quarterly
Learning and Instruction	Voices from the Middle
Mathematics Teacher	

Figure 2.7   Guidelines for copying printed materials that are copyrighted.

Permitted Uses—You May Make
1. Single copies of
   - A chapter of a book.
   - An article from a periodical, magazine, or newspaper.
   - A short story, short essay, or short poem whether or not from a collected work.
   - A chart, graph, diagram, drawing, or cartoon.
   - An illustration from a book, magazine, or newspaper.
2. Multiple copies for classroom use (not to exceed one copy per student in a course) of
   - A complete poem if less than 250 words.
   - An excerpt from a longer poem, but not to exceed 250 words.
   - A complete article, story, or essay of less than 2,500 words.
   - An excerpt from a larger printed work not to exceed 10 percent of the whole or 1,000 words.
   - One chart, graph, diagram, cartoon, or picture per book or magazine issue.

Prohibited Uses—You May Not
1. Copy more than one work or two excerpts from a single author during one class term (semester or year).
2. Copy more than three works from a collective work or periodical volume during one class term.
3. Reproduce more than nine sets of multiple copies for distribution to students in one class term.
4. Copy to create, replace, or substitute for anthologies or collective works.
5. Copy "consumable" works (e.g., workbooks, standardized tests, or answer sheets).
6. Copy the same work year after year.

Source: Section 107 of the 1976 Federal Omnibus Copyright Revision Act.

the address of the source is not given on the material, addresses may be obtained from various references, such as *Literary Market Place, Audio Visual Market Place,* and *Ulrich's International Periodical's Directory.*

The Classroom Writing Board

As is true for an auto mechanic or a brain surgeon or any other professional, as a teacher a professional responsibility is to know when and how to use the tools of the trade. One of the tools available to almost every classroom teacher is the writing board. Can you imagine a classroom without a writing board? In this section you will find guidelines for using this important tool.

They used to be, and in some schools still are, slate blackboards (slate is a type of metamorphic rock). In today's classroom, however, the writing board is more likely to be either a board that is painted plywood (chalkboard), which, like the blackboard, is also becoming obsolete, to some extent because of the need to be concerned about the dust created from using chalk; or a white or colored (light green and light blue are common) *multipurpose dry-erase board* on which you write with special marking pens and erase with any soft cloth. In addition to providing a surface upon which you can write and draw, the multipurpose board can be used as a projection screen and as a surface to which figures cut from colored transparency film will stick. It may also have a magnetic backing.

Extending the purposes of the multipurpose board and correlated with modern technology is an *electronic whiteboard* that can transfer information that is written on it to a connected computer and monitor, which in turn can save the material as a computer file. The electronic whiteboard uses dry-erase markers and special erasers that have optically encoded sleeves that enable the device to track their position on the board. The data are then converted into a display for the computer monitor, which may then be printed, cut and pasted into other applications, sent as an e-mail or fax message, or networked to other sites.

Each day, each class, and even each new idea should begin with a clean board, except for announcements that have been placed there by you or another teacher. At the end of each class, clean the board, especially if another teacher follows you in using that room (professional courtesy).

Use colored chalk or marking pens to highlight your board talk. This is especially helpful for students with learning difficulties. Beginning at the top left of the board, print or write neatly and clearly, with the writing intentionally positioned to indicate content relationships (e.g., causal, oppositional, numerical, comparative, categorical, and so on). Use the writing board to acknowledge acceptance and to record student contributions. Print instructions for an activity on the board, in addition to giving them orally. At the top of the board frame, you might find clips for hanging posters, maps, and charts.

Learn to use the board without having to turn your back entirely on students and without blocking their view of the board. When you have a lot of material to put on the board, do it before class and then cover it, or better yet, put the material on transparencies and use the overhead projector or use a PowerPoint™ presentation rather than the board, or use both. Be careful not to write too much information.

The Classroom Bulletin Board

Bulletin boards also are found in nearly every classroom, and, although sometimes poorly used or not used at all, they can be relatively inexpensively transformed into attractive and valuable instructional tools. Among other uses, the bulletin board is a convenient location to post reminders, assignments and schedules, and commercially produced materials, and to celebrate and display model student work and anchor papers. To plan, design, and prepare bulletin board displays, some teachers use student assistants or committees, giving those students guidance and responsibility for planning, preparing, and maintaining bulletin board displays.

When preparing a bulletin board display, keep these guidelines in mind: The display should be simple, emphasizing one main idea, concept, topic, or theme, and captions should be short and concise; illustrations can accent learning topics; verbs can vitalize the captions; phrases can punctuate a student's thoughts; and alliteration can announce anything you wish on the board. Finally, as in all other aspects of the classroom learning environment, remember to ensure that the board display reflects gender and ethnic equity.

The Community as a Resource

One of the richest resources for learning is the local community and the people and places in it. You will want to build your own file of community resources—speakers, sources for free materials, and field trip locations. Your school may already have a community resource file available for your use. However, it may need updating. A community resource file should contain information about (a) possible field trip locations; (b) community resource people who could serve as guest speakers, presenters, or mentors; and (c) local agencies that can provide information and instructional materials. (See Figure 2.8).

There are many ways of using community resources, and a variety is demonstrated by the schools specifically mentioned throughout this book (see Schools in the index). Here the discussion is limited to two often used, although sometimes abused, instruc-

tional tools: (a) guest speakers or presenters and (b) out-of-classroom and off-campus excursions, commonly called field trips.

GUEST SPEAKER OR PRESENTER

Bringing outside speakers or presenters into your classroom can be a valuable educational experience for students, but not automatically so. In essence, guest speakers can be classified within a spectrum of four types, two of which should not be considered: (a) Ideally, a speaker is both informative and inspiring; (b) a speaker may be inspiring but with nothing substantive to offer, except for the possible diversion it might offer from the usual rigors of classroom work; (c) the speaker might be informative, but boring to students; (d) at the worst end of this spectrum is the guest speaker who is both boring and uninformative. So, just like any other instructional experience, to make a guest speaking experience most effective takes your careful planning. To make sure that the experience is beneficial to student learning, consider the following guidelines.

- If at all possible, meet and talk with the guest speaker in advance to inform him or her about your students and your expectations for the presentation and to gauge how motivational and informative he or she might be. If you believe the speaker might be informative but boring, then perhaps you can help structure the presentation in some way to make the presentation a bit more inspiring. For example, stop the speaker every few minutes and involve the students in questions and discussions of points made.
- Prepare students in advance with key points of information that you expect them to obtain.
- Prepare students with questions to ask the speaker, things the students want to find out, and information you want them to inquire about.
- Follow up the presentation with a thank-you letter to the guest speaker and perhaps further questions that developed during class discussions subsequent to the speaker's presentation.
- Be sure you have a backup lesson plan in the eventuality the guest is late or fails to show.
- Consider briefing the guest ahead of time about any dos and don'ts and any particular sensitivities among your students.

FIELD TRIPS

What is the most memorable field trip that you were ever on as a student? Do you recall what made it memorable? You may want to discuss these questions and others like them and their responses with your classmates or members of your teaching team.

Figure 2.8 Community resources for speakers, materials, and field trips.

Airport	Highway patrol station
Apiary	Historical sites and monuments
Aquarium	Industrial plant
Archeological site	Legislature session
Art gallery	Levee and water reservoir
Assembly plant	Library and archive
Bakery	Mass transit authority
Bird and wildlife sanctuary	Military installation
Book publisher	Mine
Bookstore	Museum
Broadcasting and TV station	Native American reservation
Building being razed	Newspaper plant
Building under construction	Observatory
Canal lock	Oil refinery
Cemetery	Park
Chemical plant	Poetry reading
City or county planning commission	Police station
Courthouse	Post office and package delivery company
Dairy	Recycling center
Dam and floodplain	Retail store
Dock and harbor	Sanitation department
Factory	Sawmill or lumber company
Farm	Shopping mall
Fire department	Shoreline (stream, lake, wetland, ocean)
Fish hatchery	Telecommunications center
Flea market	Town meeting
Foreign embassy	Universities and colleges
Forest and forest preserve	Utility company
Freeway under construction	Warehouse
Gas company	Water reservoir and treatment plant
Geological site	Weather bureau and storm center
Health department and hospital	Wildlife park and preserve
Highway construction site	Zoo

Today's schools often have very limited funds for the transportation and liability costs for field trips. In some cases, there are no funds at all, in which case student field trips are electronic, or online only. At times, parent-teacher groups and business, and civic organizations help by providing financial resources so that children get valuable first-hand experiences that field trips so often afford.

To prepare for and implement a successful field trip, there are three important stages of planning—before, during, and after—and critical decisions to be made at each stage. Consider the following guidelines.

Before the Field Trip.   When the field trip is your idea (and not the students), discuss the idea with your teaching team, principal, or department chair (especially when transportation will be needed) *before* mentioning the idea to your students. Also, you may discover that the place you had in mind is in fact an overused sight for field trips and many or most of your students have already been there. Also, carefully consider the worth of

the proposed field trip; don't use valuable resources for field trips for trivial learnings. The bottom line is that there is no cause served by getting students excited about a trip before you know if it is feasible.

Once you have obtained the necessary, but tentative, approval from school officials, take the trip yourself (or with team members), if possible. A previsit allows you to determine how to make the field trip most productive and what arrangements will be necessary. For this previsit you might consider taking a couple of your students along for their ideas and help. If a previsit is not possible, you still will need to arrange for travel directions, arrival and departure times, parking, briefing by the host (if there is one), storage of students' personal items, such as coats and lunches, provisions for eating and rest rooms, and fees, if any.

If there are fees, you need to talk with your administration about who will pay the fees. If the trip is worth taking, the school should cover the costs. If that is not possible, perhaps students can plan a fund-raising activity or financial assistance can be obtained from some other source. If this does not work, you might consider an alternative that does not involve financial costs.

Arrange for official permission from the school administration. This usually requires a form for requesting, planning, and reporting field trips. After permission has been obtained, you can discuss the field trip with your students and arrange for permissions from their parents or guardians. You need to realize that although parents or guardians sign official permission forms allowing their children to participate in the trip, these only show that the parents or guardians are aware of what will take place and give their permission for their child to participate. Although the permission form should include a statement that the parent or guardian absolves the teacher and the school from liability should an accident occur, it does not lessen the teacher's and the school's responsibilities should there be negligence by a teacher, driver, or chaperone.

Arrange for students to be excused from their other classes while on the field trip. Using an information form prepared and signed by you and perhaps by the principal, the students should then assume responsibility for notifying their other teachers of the planned absence from classes and for assuring them that whatever work is missed will be made up. In addition, you will need to make arrangements for your own teaching duties to be covered. In some schools, teachers cooperate by filling in for those who will be gone. In other schools, substitute teachers are hired. Unfortunately, in some cases, sometimes teachers must hire their own substitute.

Arrange to have a cell phone available for your use during the trip. Some schools have a cell phone available for just that purpose. If not, and you don't have your own, perhaps one of the drivers or other adult chaperones has one. Check this out prior to the field trip.

Arrange for whatever transportation is needed. Your principal, or the principal's designee, will help you with the details. In many schools, someone else is responsible for arranging transportation. In any case, the use of private automobiles is ill advised, because you and the school could be liable for the acts of the drivers.

Arrange for the collection of money that is needed for fees. If there are out-of-pocket costs to be paid by students, this information needs to be included on the permission form. No students should ever be excluded from the field trip because of a lack of money. This can be a tricky issue, because there may be some students who would rather steal the money for a field trip than admit they don't have it. Try to anticipate problems;

hopefully the school or some organization can pay for the trip so that fees need not be collected from students and therefore potential problems of this sort are avoided.

Plan details for student safety and the monitoring of their safety from departure to return. Included should be a first-aid kit and a system of student control, such as a buddy system whereby students must remain paired throughout the trip. The pairs sometimes are given numbers that are recorded and kept by the teacher and the chaperones, and then checked at departure time, periodically during the trip, at the time of return, and again upon return. Only adult chaperones should accompany students. As a general rule, there should be one adult chaperone for every 10 students. Some districts have a policy regarding this. While on a field trip, at all times all students should be under the direct supervision of a dependable adult.

Plan the complete route and schedule, including any stops along the way. If transportation is being provided, you will need to discuss the plans with the provider.

Establish and discuss, to the extent you believe necessary, the rules of behavior your students should follow. Included in this might be details of the trip, its purpose, directions, what they should wear and bring, academic expectations of them (for example, consider giving each student a study guide), and follow-up activities. Also included should be information about what to do if anything should go awry, for example, if a student is late for the departure or return, loses a personal possession along the way, gets lost, is injured, becomes sick, or misbehaves. For the latter, never send a misbehaving student back to school alone. Involve the adult chaperones in the previsit discussion. All of this information should also be included on the parental permission form.

If a field trip is supposed to promote some kind of learning, as undoubtedly will be the case unless the sole purpose is something like an end-of-the-term or end-of-unit celebration, then to avoid leaving it to chance, the learning expectations need to be clearly defined and the students given an explanation of how and where they may encounter the learning experience. Before the field trip, students should be asked questions such as, "What do we already know about _____?" "What do we want to find out about _____?" "How can we find out?" and then, with their assistance, an appropriate guide can be prepared for the students to use during the field trip.

To further ensure learning and individual student responsibility for that learning, you may want to assign different roles and responsibilities to students, just as would be done in cooperative learning, ensuring that each student has a role with responsibility.

You may want to take recording equipment so the field trip experience can be relived and shared in class upon return. If so, roles and responsibilities for the equipment and its care and use can be assigned to students as well.

During the Field Trip.   If your field trip has been carefully planned according to the preceding guidelines, it should be a valuable and safe experience for all. Enroute, while at the trip location, and on the return to school, you and the adult chaperones should monitor student behavior and learning just as you do in the classroom.

After the Field Trip.   Plan the follow-up activities. As with any other lesson plan, the field trip lesson is complete only when there is both a proper introduction and a well-planned and executed closure. All sorts of follow-up activities can be planned as an educational wrap-up to this educational experience. For example, a bulletin board committee can plan and prepare an attractive display summarizing the trip. Students can write about their experiences in their journals or as papers. Small groups can give oral reports to the class about what they did and learned. Their reports can then serve as springboards for further class discussion, and perhaps further investigations. Finally, for future planning, all who were involved should contribute to an assessment of the experience.

Media Tools

Media tools are instructional devices that depend upon electricity to project light and sound and to focus images on screens. Included are projectors of various sorts, computers, CD-ROMs, DVDs, sound recorders, and video recorders. The aim here is not to provide instruction on how to operate equipment but to help you develop a philosophy for using it and to provide strategies for using media tools in your teaching. Consequently, to conserve space in this book, except for the overhead projector, which in some respects is more practical than the writing board, we devote no attention to traditional/audiovisual (AV) equipment, such as film projectors, VCRs, and opaque projectors. There are staff members on any school faculty who gladly will assist you in locating and using those tools if you so desire or need.

It is important to remember that the role of media tools is to aid student learning, not to teach for you. You must still select the objectives, orchestrate the instructional plan, assess the results, and follow up the lessons, just as you learn to do with various other instructional strategies. If you use media tools prudently, your teaching and students' learning will benefit. Like a competent brain surgeon or a competent auto mechanic, a competent teacher knows when and how to select and use the right tools at the right time. Would you want to be operated on by a surgeon who was unfamiliar with the tools used in surgery? The education of youth should be no less important.

TEACHING IN PRACTICE

What Is Mr. Klutz's Problem and How Can It Be Resolved?

Although Mr. Klutz is considered to be a good beginning teacher, things rarely work well for him when he uses materials and media. Right in the middle of a lesson, he often discovers that he is missing an important piece of equipment or material he needs to complete the lesson, or a machine breaks down. Once, he was going to demonstrate how a candle extinguishes when covered with a glass jar. He had the candles and the jar all right, but he forgot to bring matches. Another time, he planned to use an overhead projector, only to find at the last minute that the electrical cord was not long enough to reach the wall outlet, and he did not have an extension cord. Yesterday, while he was demonstrating on the overhead screen with a computer, the computer froze. Such situations always seemed to happen at the most unexpected time to surprise Mr. Klutz and spoil his plans and lesson presentations.

Questions for Class Discussion

1. Does Mr. Klutz remind you of any teacher you have known?

2. Is it possible for Mr. Klutz' carelessness to result in other, more serious, problems?

3. What action would you take to avoid such unexpected and unwanted outcomes?

4. Is it possible for a teacher who is classed as "highly qualified" to also be grossly incompetent?

WHEN EQUIPMENT MALFUNCTIONS

When using media equipment, it is nearly always best to set up the equipment and have it ready to go before students arrive. This helps avoid problems in classroom management that can occur when there is a delay because the equipment is not ready. After all, if you were a surgeon ready to begin an operation and your tools and equipment weren't ready, your patient's life would likely be placed in extra danger. Like any other competent professional, a competent teacher is ready when the work is to begin.

Of course, delays may be unavoidable when equipment breaks down or if a videotape breaks. Remember Murphy's Law, which states if anything can go wrong, it will. It is particularly relevant when using audiovisual equipment. You want to be prepared for such emergencies. Effectively planning for and responding to this eventuality is an important element of your system of movement management and takes place during the planning phase of instruction. That preparation includes consideration of a number of factors.

When equipment malfunctions, three principles should be in mind: (a) avoid dead time in the instruction; (b) avoid causing permanent damage to equipment; and (c) avoid losing content continuity of a lesson. So, what do you do when equipment breaks down? Again, the answer is: Be prepared for the eventuality.

If a projector bulb expires, quickly insert another. That means you should have an extra bulb on hand. If the computer screen freezes during direct, whole-class instruction, you should probably quickly move to an alternate activity. If it is during multilevel instruction, while maintaining your classroom withitness, you can probably take the time to treat this as a teachable moment and show the student who is working on the computer what to do, which probably would be simply how to restart the computer. If it occurs during a PowerPoint™ presentation, then you might be able to continue simply by moving to an available overhead projector or to the writing board.

If, during surgery, a patient's cerebral artery suddenly and unexpectedly ruptures, the surgeon and the surgical team are ready and make the necessary repair. If, while working on an automobile a part breaks, the mechanic obtains a replacement part. If, while teaching, a computer program freezes or aborts on the screen, or if a fuse blows or for some other reason you lose power and you feel that there is going to be too much dead time before the equipment is working again, that is the time to go to an alternate lesson plan. You have probably heard the expression "go to Plan B." It is a useful phrase; what it means is that without missing a beat in the lesson, to accomplish the same instructional objective or another objective, you immediately and smoothly switch to an alternate learning activity. For you, the beginning teacher, it does not mean that you must plan two lessons for every one, but that when planning a lesson that uses media equipment, you should plan in your lesson an alternative activity, just in case. Then, you move your students into the planned alternative activity quickly and smoothly. Your state of preparedness and smoothness in your action will impress your students, with them seeing you as a competent and well-prepared teacher.

THE OVERHEAD PROJECTOR

In addition to a writing board and a bulletin board, nearly every classroom is equipped with an overhead projector. The overhead projector is a versatile, effective, and reliable teaching tool. Except for the bulb burning out, not much else can go wrong with an overhead projector. There is no film to break or program to crash.

The overhead projector projects light through objects that are transparent. A properly functioning overhead projector usually works quite well in a fully lit room. Truly portable overhead projectors are available that can be carried easily from place to place in their compact cases.

Other types of modern-day overhead projectors include rear-projection systems that allow the teacher to stand off to the side rather than between students and the screen and overhead video projectors that use video cameras to send images that are projected by television monitors. Some schools use overhead video camera technology that focuses on an object, pages of a book, or a demonstration, while sending a clear image to a video monitor with a screen large enough for an entire class to clearly see.

In some respects, the overhead projector is more practical than the writing board, particularly for a teacher who is nervous. Using the overhead projector rather than the writing board can help avoid tension by decreasing the need to pace back and forth to the board. By using an overhead projector rather than a writing board, a teacher can maintain both eye contact and physical proximity with students, both of which are important for maintaining classroom control.

GUIDELINES FOR USING THE OVERHEAD PROJECTOR

As with any projector, find the best place in your classroom to position it. If there is no classroom projection screen, you can hang white paper or a sheet, use a white multipurpose board, or use a white or near-white wall.

Have you ever attended a presentation by someone who was not using an overhead projector properly? It can be frustrating to members of an audience when the image is too small, out of focus, partially off the screen, or partially blocked from view by the presenter. To use this teaching tool in a professional manner:

- Place the projector so the projected white light covers the entire screen and hits the screen at a 90-degree angle, and then focus the image to be projected.
- Face the students while using the projector. The fact that you do not lose eye contact with your students is a major advantage of using the overhead projector rather than a writing board. (A PowerPoint™ presentation provides the same advantage.) What you write as you face your students will show up perfectly (unless out of focus or off the screen).
- Lay the pencil directly on the transparency with the tip of the pencil pointing to the detail being emphasized rather than using your finger to point to the detail or pointing to the screen (thereby turning away from your students).
- Lessen distractions by turning the projector off when you want student attention shifted back to you.

For writing on overhead projector transparencies, ordinary felt-tip pens are not satisfactory. Select a transparency-marking pen available at an office supply store. The ink of these pens is water-soluble, so keep the palm of your hand from resting on the transparency or you will have ink smudges on your transparency and on your hand. Non-water-soluble pens—permanent markers—can be used, but the transparency must be cleaned with an alcohol solvent or a plastic eraser. When using a cleaning solvent, you can clean and dry the transparency with paper toweling or a soft rag. To highlight the writing on a transparency and to organize student learning, use pens in a variety of colors. Transparency pens tend to dry out quickly, and they are relatively expensive, so the caps must be taken on and off frequently, which is something of a nuisance when working with several colors. Practice writing on a transparency, and also practice making overlays. You can use an acetate transparency roll or single sheets of flat transparencies. Flat sheets of transparency come in different colors—clear, red, blue, yellow, and green—which can be useful in making overlays.

Some teachers prepare lesson outlines in advance on transparencies, which allows more careful preparation of the transparencies and means that they are then ready for reuse at another time. Some teachers use an opaque material, such as a 3×5 note card, to block out prewritten material and then uncover it at the moment it is being discussed. For preparation of permanent transparencies, you will probably want to use permanent marker pens, rather than those that are water-soluble and easily smudged. Heavy paper frames are available for permanent transparencies; marginal notes can be written on the frames. Personal computers with laser printers and thermal processing (copy) machines, probably located in the teachers' workroom or in the school's main office, can be used to make permanent transparencies.

Another function of the overhead projector is made possible by the fact that transparent objects can be placed on the platform and displayed on the screen, objects such as transparent rulers, protractors, and Petri dishes for science activities; even opaque objects can be used if you want to simply show silhouette, as you might in math and art activities.

The overhead projector can also be used for tracing transparent charts or drawings into larger drawings on paper or on the writing board. The image projected onto the screen can be made smaller or larger by moving the projector closer or farther away, respectively, and then traced when you have the size you want. An overhead projector can be used also as a light source (spotlight) to highlight demonstrations.

THE DOCUMENT CAMERA

Although more expensive than overhead projectors, document cameras are increasing in popularity in classrooms across the country. When connected to a computer and projector, the document camera becomes a very versatile presentation tool. In addition to displaying text you can project 3-D objects, slides, and other microscopic objects, and you can zoom in on objects.

MULTIMEDIA PROGRAM

A multimedia program is a collection of teaching and learning materials involving more than one type of medium and organized around a single theme or topic. The types of media involved vary from rather simple kits—perhaps including CDs, games, activity cards, student worksheets, and manuals of instructions for the teacher—to sophisticated packages involving building-level site-licensed computer software, student handbooks, reproducible activity worksheets, classroom wall hangings, and online subscriptions to telecommunication networks. Some kits are designed for teacher use, others by individual or small groups of students; yet many more are designed for the collaborative use of students and teachers. Teachers sometimes incorporate multimedia programs with learning activity centers.

TELEVISION, VIDEOS, AND DVDs

Everyone knows that television, videos, and DVDs represent a powerful medium. What follows are some general guidelines for their use.

Review Material Before Using.   It's important that you remember *always* to review the material before using it with your students. Any teacher who has been in the profession for long can share horror stories of the lazy and incompetent teacher who used a medium with students without first previewing it. For example, there was the tenured middle school teacher who showed movies literally every day, any that had arrived at school regardless of what they were about or who ordered it.

TELEVISION PROGRAMMING

For purposes of professional discussion, television programming can be divided into three categories: instructional television, educational television, and general commercial television. Instructional television refers to programs specifically designed as classroom instruction. Educational television refers to programs of cable television and of public broadcasting designed to educate in general, but not aimed at classroom instruction. Commercial television programs include the entertainment and public service programs of the television networks and local stations.

Watch for announcements for educational programs in professional journals. And, of course, television program listings can be obtained from your local commercial, educational, or cable companies or by writing directly to network stations. Some networks sponsor Internet websites.

Combined with a television monitor, the DVD player is one of the most popular and frequently used tools in today's classroom. DVD programs can do nearly everything that the former 16-mm films could do.

A TV camera and recorder makes it possible to record students during activities, practice, projects, and demonstrations as well as yourself when teaching. It gives students a marvelous opportunity to self-assess as they see and hear themselves in action.

Entire course packages, as well as supplements, are available on DVDs. The schools where you student teach and where you eventually are employed may have a collection of such programs. Some teachers make their own.

Carefully selected programs enhance student learning. For example, DVDs and CD-ROMs offer quick and efficient accessibility of thousands of visuals, thus providing an appreciated boost to teachers of students with limited language proficiency. With the use of frame control, students can observe phenomena, in detail, that previous students only read about.

Computers and Computer-Based Instructional Tools

As a teacher, the computer can be valuable to you in several ways. For example, the computer can help you manage the instruction by obtaining information, storing and preparing test materials, maintaining attendance and grade records, and preparing programs to aid in the academic development of individual students. This category of uses of the computer is referred to as *computer-managed instruction* (CMI).

The computer can also be used for instruction by employing various instructional software programs, and it can be used to teach about computers and to help students develop their metacognitive skills as well as their skills in computer use. When the computer is used to assist students in their learning, it is called *computer-assisted instruction* (CAI) or *computer-assisted learning* (CAL).

THE PLACEMENT AND USE OF COMPUTERS: THE ONLINE CLASSROOM

Teachers looking to make their classrooms more student-centered, collaborative, and interactive, continue to increasingly turn to telecommunications networks. Webs of connected computers allow teachers and students from around the world to reach each other directly and gain access to quantities of information previously unimaginable. Students using networks learn new inquiry and analytical skills in a stimulating environment, and they can also gain an increased awareness of their role as world citizens. Just imagine, for example,

students in a classroom in Kansas in direct online communication with scientists working at the North Pole or at the bottom of the Pacific Ocean; possibilities only dreamed of just a generation ago.

How you use the computer for instruction and learning is determined by several factors, including your knowledge of and skills in its use, the number of computers that you have available for instructional use, where computers are placed in the school, the software that is available, printer availability, and the telecommunications capabilities (that is, wiring and phone lines, modems, and servers).

Schools continue to purchase or to lease computers and to upgrade their telecommunications capabilities. Regarding computer placement and equipment and technological support available, here are some possible scenarios and how classroom teachers work within each.

Scenario 1. With the assistance of a computer lab and the lab technician, computers are integrated into the whole curriculum. In collaboration with members of interdisciplinary teaching teams, in a computer lab students use computers, software, and sources on the Internet as tools to build their knowledge, to write stories with word processors, to illustrate diagrams with paint utilities, to create interactive reports with hypermedia, and to graph data they have gathered using spreadsheets.

Scenario 2. In some middle schools, students take a computer class as an elective or exploratory course. Students in your classes who are simultaneously enrolled in such a course may be given special computer assignments by you that they can then share with the rest of the class.

Scenario 3. Some classrooms have a computer connected to a large-screen video monitor. The teacher or a student works the computer, and the entire class can see the monitor screen. As they view the screen, students can verbally respond to and interact with what is happening on the computer.

Presentation software, such as Microsoft's PowerPoint™, can help teachers and students create powerful on-screen presentations. First developed for use in the world of business for reports at sales meetings and with clients, educators quickly became aware of the power provided by presentation software to display, illustrate, and elucidate information. From the world of business, presentation software made its way into university classrooms and then into K–12 classrooms to where today it is not uncommon for it to be used even by kindergarten children in their own presentations. Whenever students are using modern presentation software, it is the teacher's responsibility to ensure that students don't become so fixated on fonts and formats and other aspects of the technology that insufficient thinking is given to the content of their presentation. Of course, that is not more a concern for electronic presentations than when students are using any other format to display their work, such as an interactive, student-created bulletin board.

Scenario 4. You may be fortunate to have one or more computers in your classroom for all or a portion of the school year, computers with Internet connections and CD-ROM playing capabilities, an overhead projector, and a liquid crystal display (LCD) projection system. Coupled with the overhead projector, the LCD projection system allows you to project onto your large wall screen (and TV monitor at the same time) any image from computer software or a videodisc. With this system, all students can see and verbally interact with the multimedia instruction.

Scenario 5. Many classrooms have at least one computer with telecommunications capability, and some have many. When this is the case in your classroom, then you most likely will have one or two students working at the computer sta-

tion while others are doing other learning activities (multi-level teaching). Computers can be an integral part of a learning center and an important aid in your overall effort to personalize the instruction within your classroom.

Using Copyrighted Video, Computer, and Multimedia Programs

You have a responsibility to be knowledgeable about the laws on the use of copyrighted videos and computer software materials. Although space here prohibits full inclusion of U.S. legal guidelines, your local school district undoubtedly can provide you with a copy of current district policies to ensure your compliance with all copyright laws. As was discussed earlier in the discussion about the use of printed materials that are copyrighted, when preparing to make any copy you must find out whether the law under the category of "permitted use" permits the copying. If not allowed under "permitted use," then you must get written permission to reproduce the material from the holder of the copyright. Figures 2.9 and 2.10 present guidelines for the copying of videos and of computer software.

Usually, when purchasing CD-ROMs, DVDs, and other multimedia software packages intended for the school's use, you are also paying for a license to modify and use its contents for instructional purposes. However, not all CD-ROMs and DVDs include copyright permission, so always check the copyright notice on any package you purchase and use. Whenever in doubt, don't use it until you have asked your district media specialists about copyrights or have obtained necessary permissions from the original source.

Anthony Magnacca/Merrill

Figure 2.9 Fair-use guidelines for off-air videotaping.

Permitted Uses—You May
1. Request your media center or audiovisual coordinator to record a program for you if you cannot or if you lack the equipment.
2. Keep a videotaped copy of a broadcast (including cable transmission) for 45 calendar days, after which the program must be erased.
3. Use the program in class once during the first 10 school days of the 45 calendar days, and a second time if instruction needs to be reinforced.
4. Have professional staff view the program several times for evaluation purposes during the full 45-day period.
5. Make a few copies to meet legitimate needs, but these copies must be erased when the original videotape is erased.
6. Use only a part of the program if instructional needs warrant.
7. Enter into a licensing agreement with the copyright holder to continue use of the program.

Prohibited Uses—You May *Not*
1. Videotape premium cable services such as HBO without express permission.
2. Alter the original content of the program.
3. Exclude the copyright notice on the program.
4. Videorecord before a request for use is granted—the request to record must come from an instructor.
5. Keep the program, and any copies, after 45 days.

Figure 2.10   Copyright law for use of computer software.

Permitted Uses—You May
1. Make a single back-up or archival copy of the computer program.
2. Adapt the computer program to another language if the program is unavailable in the target language.
3. Add features to make better use of the computer program.

Prohibited Uses—You May *Not*
1. Make multiple copies.
2. Make replacement copies from an archival or back-up copy.
3. Make copies of copyrighted programs to be sold, leased, loaned, transmitted, or given away.

Source: December, 1980, Congressional amendment to the 1976 Copyright Act.

Figure 2.11   Fair-use guidelines for using multimedia programs.

1. For portions of copyrighted works used in your own multimedia production for use in teaching, follow normal copyright guidelines (e.g., the limitations on the amount of material used, whether it be motion media, text, music, illustrations, photographs, or computer software).
2. You may display your own multimedia work using copyrighted works to other teachers, such as in workshops. However, you may *not* make and distribute copies to colleagues without obtaining permission from copyright holders.
3. You may use your own multimedia production for instruction over an electronic network (e.g., distance learning) provided there are limits to access and to the number of students enrolled. You may *not* distribute such work over any electronic network (local area or wide area) without expressed permission from copyright holders.
4. You must obtain permissions from copyright holders before using any copyrighted materials in educational multimedia productions for commercial reproduction and distribution or before replicating more than one copy, distributing copies to others, or for use beyond your own classroom.

A general rule of thumb for use of any copyrighted material is to treat the work of others as you would want your own material treated were it protected by a copyright (see Figure 2.11).

Distance Learning

Distance learning (or *distance education*) is the term used when referring to any instructional situation in which the learner is separated in time or space from the point of instruction. Although telecommunications technologies have provided courses (e.g., by mail correspondence) and workshops (e.g., by video) for industry training, medical organizations, and higher education for many years, recent developments have created a renewed interest in distance education. In fact, some predict that learning and instruction over the Internet will be the driving force for educational changes in the 21st century, with an accompanying change in the role of the classroom teacher from less of a deliverer of instruction to more of a facilitator of learning both by providing individual tutoring and by helping students work together in groups (Schank, 2000).

With the technology of distance education, students in small rural schools can receive instruction in courses that, because of limited local resources, might otherwise have been unavailable to them; via the Internet all students can interact in real time with people from around the world.

SUMMARY

You have reviewed the realities of the responsibilities of today's classroom teacher. Being a good teacher of young adolescents takes time, commitment, concentrated effort, and just plain hard work. Nobody truly knowledgeable about it ever said that good teaching was easy.

You have learned that your professional responsibilities as a classroom teacher will extend well beyond the four walls of the classroom, the six hours of the school day, the five days of the school week, and the 180 or so days of the school year. You learned of the many expectations. As you have read and discussed these responsibilities, you should have begun to fully comprehend the challenge and reality of being a competent classroom teacher of young adolescents.

Teaching style is the way teachers teach, their distinctive mannerisms complemented by their choices of teaching behaviors and strategies. Style develops from tradition, from one's beliefs and experiences, and from one's knowledge of research findings. You analyzed your own beliefs, observed one teacher and that teacher's style for that lesson, and began the development of your philosophy about teaching and learning—a philosophical statement that should be useful to you during later job interviews.

Exciting research findings continue to emerge from several, and related, areas—about learning, conceptual development, and thinking styles—and from neurophysiology. The findings continue to support the hypothesis that a middle level teacher's best teaching style choice is eclectic with a strong bent toward facilitating collaborative learning, at least until the day arrives when students of certain thinking styles can be practically matched to teachers with particular teaching styles. Future research will undoubtedly shed additional light on the relationships among pedagogy, pedagogical styles, and student thinking and learning.

Today, there seems to be much agreement that the essence of the learning process is a combined self-awareness, self-monitoring, and active reflection. Young adolescents learn these skills best when exposed to teachers who effectively model those same behaviors. The most effective teaching and learning is an interactive process, which involves not only learning, but also thinking about the process of learning.

You have learned of the variety of tools available to supplement your instruction and enhance student learning. When used wisely, these tools will help you reach more of your students more of the time. As you know, teachers must meet the needs of a diversity of students, many who are linguistically and culturally different. The material selected and presented in this and subsequent chapters should be of help to your doing that. The future will undoubtedly continue bringing technological innovations that will be even more helpful.

You should remain alert to developing technologies for your teaching. New instructional technologies are advancing at an increasingly rapid rate. You and your colleagues must maintain vigilance over new developments, constantly looking for those that will not only help make student learning meaningful and interesting, and your teaching effective, but that are cost effective as well.

The next chapter focuses your attention on the development and use of two critically important skills for teaching and learning—thinking and questioning.

QUESTIONS FOR CLASS DISCUSSION

1. More than four decades ago, a publication entitled *Six Areas of Teacher Competencies* (Burlingame, CA: California Teachers Association, 1964) identified six roles of the classroom teacher: director of learning, counselor and guidance worker, mediator of the culture, link with the community, member of the school staff, and member of the profession. When compared with that, have the roles changed for today's classroom teacher? If so, how?

2. Recall a teacher whom you admired when you were a middle school student. What characteristics did this teacher possess? Do you see or would you like to see any of those same qualities in yourself? Explain.

3. Return to your response to question number 7 at the end of Chapter 1. Modify it, if necessary, and keep it for review later in this course. Share your modifications with those of your classmates.

4. Before studying this chapter were you fully aware of the extent of a classroom teacher's professional responsibilities? Explain what, if anything, new you learned and your feelings and concerns about it.

5. Explain the difference between the teacher's use of praise and the use of reinforcement. Explain how you feel about that difference. Is it, in your mind, a significant difference? Explain why it is or is not.

6. Explain how your effective use of the writing board and of the bulletin board can help students to understand relationships among verbal concepts or information.

7. Has the purchase of new textbooks and library books become stagnated as schools use their available funds for technology? Have music and art programs suffered as a result of expenditures on technology (as well as the focus on standardized testing)? How are school districts finding funds necessary for the cost of technology, such as for the cost of wiring classrooms for networking and for updating computers, for the planning, installation, and maintenance of complex computer networks? Or are districts finding the necessary funds? In this respect, is the "playing field" even or are some districts worse off or better off than others? Is this an issue? In order to learn some answers, do some inquiring in the local schools where your are likely to do your student teaching and/or become employed.

8. The local school board is concerned about copyright law and how it relates to instruction. You have been asked to make a presentation on the topic to the board. Prepare that presentation and present it to your classmates as if they were school board members.

9. Young adolescents today have grown up having become accustomed to modern technology. Some teachers have discovered that they can temporarily "wow" their students and teach them by using old media tools. For example, one teacher set up a filmstrip projector and showed a filmstrip from the 1950s. While advancing the frames slowly, projecting the images onto a whiteboard, the teacher emphasized points with dry-erase markers. Can you think of old media equipment and how you might be able to use it as a motivating instructional tool? Or would you even be interested in doing it? Share your thoughts with your classmates, perhaps even finding old equipment and preparing and presenting lessons using that equipment.

10. Peer bullying and harassment are, and perhaps always have been, a problem in many schools and communities. However, using the Internet as a medium in which to bully or harass is a new phenomenon. The Internet has become a relatively unsupervised place where bullies can belittle, torment, and frighten others. What, if anything, should the classroom teacher know and be prepared to do about this problem?

INTERNET RESOURCES

- *Answers.com* **http://www.answers.com**
- *California Instructional Technology Clearinghouse* **http://clrn.org/home**

- *Center for Children and Technology*
  http://www2.edc.org/CCT/index.asp
- *Children's Partnership*
  http://www.childrenspartnership.org
- *ClassNotesOnline* **http://www.ClassNotesOnline.com**
- *Consortium for School Networking* **http://www.cosn.org**
- *Copyright guidelines and information*
  **http://www.lib.washington.edu/help/guides/
  copyright.html**
- *Database tutorial* **http://www.quasar.ualberta.ca/edit202/
  tutorial/database/database.htm**
- *Deep Web information source* **http://www.deepweb.com**
- *Document camera* **http://www.elmousa.com**
- *Electronic boards: Cognitive Systems Technologies*
  http://www.cogsystech.com; *GTCO CalComp*
  http://www.gtcocalcomp.com; *Interactive Products
  Division of Numonics* **http://www.interactivewhiteboards.
  com;** *Smart Technologies* **http://www.smarttech.com**
- *Electronic Reference Formats Recommended by the American
  Psychological Association* **http://www.apa.org**
- *Finding information on the Internet*
  **http://www.lib.berkeley.edu/TeachingLib/Guides/
  Internet/FindInfo.html**
- *Free government materials* **http://www.ed.gov/free**
- *Gateway to Educational Materials (GEM)*
  http://www.thegateway.org
- *Interactive Frog Dissection*
  http://teach.virginia.edu/go/frog
- *International Telementor Program*
  http://www.telementor.org
- *Learn the Net* **http://www.learnthenet.com**
- *Mathematics Archives* **http://archives.math.utk.edu**
- *National Archives and Records Administration*
  http://www.Archives.gov
- *National Geographic Map Machine*
  http://www.nationalgeographic.com
- *National Middle School Association (NMSA)*
  http://www.nmsa.org
- *NBPTS standards* **http://www.nbpts.org**
- *NetDay* **http://www.netday.org**
- *No Child Left Behind Act*
  http://www.ed.gov/legislation/esea02
- *Online field trips* **http://www.thinkport.org**
- *PDA use* **http://scilib.ucsd.edu/bml/pda/intro.htm**
- *PowerPoint™ use*
  http://www.electricteacher.com/tutorial3.htm *and*
  http://staff.philau.edu/bells/ppt.html *and*
  http://www.bitbetter.com/powertips.htm
- *Professional development online*
  http://www.apexlearning.com
- *Search engines for children*
  **http://www.bhsu.edu/education/edfaculty/lturner/
  Search%20Engines.htm**
- *Software Information & Industry Association*
  http://www.siia.net
- *Spreadsheet tutorials* **http://teachers.teach-nology.com/
  themes/comp/spreadsheets**
- *State education resource organizations directory*
  http://www.ed.gov/Programs/bastmp/SEA.htm

- *Teacher's Network* **http://www.teachnet.org**
- *Tech Corps* **http://techcorps.org**
- *U.S. Department of Education, Office of Technology*
  http://www.ed.gov/Technology/index.html
- *Word Processing Tutorials*
  **http://www.tutorialfind.com/tutorials/computerbasics/
  wordprocessing**

To learn more about the professional responsibilities of teaching young adolescents, please go to the teacher preference website at **www.prenhall.com/teacherpref**

FOR FURTHER READING

Beane, J., & Lipka, R. (2006). Guess again: Will changing the grades save middle-level education? *Educational Leadership, 63*(7), 26–30.

Bomar, L. (2006). iPods as reading tools. *Principal, 85*(5), 52–53.

Buck, F. (2005). The basics of blogging. *Principal, 85*(2), 54–55.

Caine, R. N., Caine, G., McClintic, C., & Klimek, K. (2005). *12 brain/mind learning principles in action.* Thousand Oaks, CA: Corwin Press.

Clement, M. C. (2004). Hiring the best middle school teachers with behavior-based interviewing. *Middle School Journal, 35*(4), 25–32.

Csikszentmihalyi, M. (1990). *Flow: The psychology of optimal experience.* New York: Harper and Row.

Fay, K., & Whaley, S. (2005). The gift of attention. *Educational Leadership, 62*(4), 76–79.

Freiberg, H. J. (Ed.). (1999). *Perceiving, behaving, becoming: Lessons learned.* Alexandria, VA: Association for Supervision and Curriculum Development.

Howe, F., & Simmons, B. J. (2005). *Nurturing the parent-teacher alliance.* Bloomington, IN: Phi Delta Kappa Educational Foundation.

Kellough, R. D. (2005). *Your first year of teaching: Guidelines for success.* 3d ed. New Jersey: Merrill Prentice Hall.

Maxwell, J. C. (2001). *The 17 essential qualities of a team player: Becoming the kind of person every team wants.* Nashville, TN: Thomas Nelson.

Morgan, B., & Odom, D. (2006). Stories from tween classrooms. *Educational Leadership, 63,* 38–41.

Sheehy, M. (2003). Illuminating constructivism: Structure, discourse, and subjectivity in a middle school classroom. *Reading Research Quarterly, 37,* 278–305.

Tomlinson, C. A., & Doubet, K. (2005). Reach them to teach them. *Educational Leadership, 62*(7), 8–15.

Turner, J., & Foshay, J. (2005). *Student television is authentic context.* Fastback 531. Bloomington, IN: Phi Delta Kappa Educational Foundation.

Vega, E. S., & Schnackenberg, H. L. (2006). Integrating technology, art, and writing to create comic books. *Middle School Journal, 37*(4), 30–36.

Weinthal, E. (2005). Using photographs as teaching tools. *Principal, 85*(1), 60–61.

Wormelik, R. (2006). Differentiating for tweens. *Educational Leadership, 63,* 14–19.

CHAPTER 3

Thinking and Questioning
Skills for Meaningful Learning

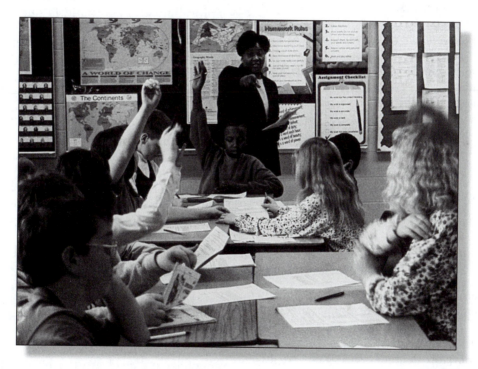

Anne Vega/Merrill

The key to meaningful learning is thinking. Skills of thinking can be taught and learned. Those same skills can and should be modeled by the teacher for the students. The key to thinking effectively is, as introduced in Chapter 2, the strategy of questioning. In this chapter we focus your attention on skills for teaching thinking and for using questioning, skills that we believe should be a primary focus when teaching young adolescents.

In this chapter you will also be introduced to the first of two micro peer teaching exercises that are in this resource guide. Micro peer teaching (MPT) is a skill-development strategy used for professional development

by both preservice (prior to credentialing) and also for inservice (credentialed and employed) teachers. It is a scaled-down teaching experience involving a (a) limited objective, (b) brief interval for teaching the lesson, (c) lesson taught to a few (usually 8 to 10) peers (as the students), and (d) lesson that focuses on the use of one to several instructional strategies. Often a predictor of later teaching effectiveness in a regular classroom, more importantly the MPT can provide an opportunity to develop and improve specific teaching behaviors. A videotaped MPT allows you to see yourself in action for self-evaluation and diagnosis. The final exercise of this resource guide is one that puts what you have learned together in what can be thought of as a final performance assessment for what you have learned.

In many ways this chapter and the final chapter of this book are complementary. Having the first and the final micro peer teaching exercises is only one way. Their combined focus on thinking, intelligent behavior, and integrated learning is another.

OBJECTIVES

Specifically, upon completion of this chapter you should be able to:

1. Demonstrate how you will help young adolescents learn to think and behave intelligently.
2. Demonstrate your developing understanding of the relationship between thinking, questioning, and learning.
3. Compare and contrast ways of thinking with levels of questioning.
4. Demonstrate knowledge and developing skill in the use of questioning.
5. Demonstrate an understanding of the types of cognitive questions.
6. Describe ways of helping students to develop their metacognitive skills.
7. Explain the educational value of using students' questions.
8. Identify categories of purposes for which questioning can be used as an instructional strategy.
9. Describe and demonstrate at least 10 characteristics of intelligent behavior.

TEACHING THINKING FOR INTELLIGENT BEHAVIOR

Pulling together what has been learned about learning and brain functioning, teachers of young adolescents are encouraged to integrate explicit thinking instruction into daily lessons. In other words, teachers should help students develop their thinking skills. As their thinking skills develop students develop a sense of "I can," with an accompanying feeling of "I enjoy." Art Costa (1991, p. 19) expresses it this way:

> In teaching for thinking, we are interested not only in what students know but also in how students behave when they don't know. . . . Gathering evidence of the performance and growth of intelligent behavior . . . requires "kid-watching": observing students as they try to solve the day-to-day academic and real-life problems they encounter. . . . By collecting anecdotes and examples of written, oral, and visual expressions, we can see students' increasingly voluntary and spontaneous performance of these intelligent behaviors.

Characteristics of Intelligent Behavior

Characteristics of intelligent behavior that you should model, teach for, and observe developing in your students, as identified by Costa and Kallick (2000), are described in the following paragraphs. [*Note:* See also Armstrong's (1998) 12 qualities of genius—curiosity, playfulness, imagination, creativity, wonderment, wisdom, inventiveness, vitality, sensitivity, flexibility, humor, and joy.]

Drawing on knowledge and applying it to new situations. A major goal of formal education is for students to apply school-learned knowledge to real-life situations. To develop skills in drawing on past knowledge and applying that knowledge to new situations, students must be given opportunities to practice doing that very thing. Problem recognition, problem solving, and project-based learning are significantly important ways of providing that opportunity to students.

Finding humor. The positive effects of humor on the body's physiological functions are well established (see Chapter 2). Humor liberates creativity and provides high-level thinking skills, such as anticipation, finding novel relationships, and visual imagery. The acquisition of a sense of humor follows a developmental sequence similar to that described by Piaget (1972) and Kohlberg (1981). Initially, young children and immature adolescents (and some immature adults) may find humor in all the wrong things—human frailty, ethnic humor, sacrilegious riddles, and ribald profanities. Later, creative young adolescents thrive on finding incongruity and will demonstrate a whimsical frame of mind during problem solving.

Creating, imagining, innovating. All students must be encouraged to do and discouraged from saying "I can't." Students must be taught in such a way as to encourage intrinsic motivation rather than reliance on extrinsic sources. Teachers must be able to offer criticism in a way that the student understands that the criticism is not a criticism of self. In exemplary educational programs, students learn the value of feedback. They learn the value of their own intuition, of guessing—they learn "I can."

Listening with understanding and empathy. Some psychologists believe that the ability to listen to others, to empathize with and to understand their point of view, is one of the highest forms of intelligent behavior. Empathic behavior, nearly the exact opposite of egoism, is an important skill for conflict resolution. In class and advisory meetings, brainstorming sessions, think tanks, town meetings, advisory councils, board meetings, and in legislative bodies, people from various walks of life convene to share their thinking, to explore their ideas, and to broaden their perspectives by listening to the ideas and reactions of others.

Managing impulsivity. When young adolescents develop impulse control, they think before acting. Impulsive behavior can worsen conflict and inhibit effective problem solving (Goos & Galbraith, 1996). Students can be taught to think before shouting out an answer, to wait their turn, to raise their hand to be called on before answering, to think before beginning a project or task, and before arriving at conclusions with insufficient data. One of several reasons that teachers should routinely expect a show of student hands before selecting a student to respond or question is to help students develop control over the impulsive behavior of shouting out in class (Brandt, 2000; Harrington-Lueker, 1997). Indeed, research clearly indicates that the quality of one's emotional intelligence—that is, to exercise self-control, to empathize with others, to work collaboratively and cooperatively—is a much more significant predictor of success in the workplace than is any analytical measure of intelligence (Goleman, Boyataiz, & McKee, 2002).

Persisting. Persistence is staying with a task until it is completed. People with an internal locus of control (discussed in Chapter 2) tend to show more persistence. Consider the examples shown in Figure 3.1.

Remaining open to continuous learning. Intelligent people are in a continuous learning mode, always eager to learn and find new ways.

Responding with wonderment and awe. Young children express wonderment, an expression that should never be stifled. Your students can be helped to recapture that sense of wonderment as you guide them into a sense of "I can," and an expression of the feeling of "I enjoy."

Striving for accuracy. Growth in this behavior is demonstrated when students take time to check their work, review the procedures, and hesitate to draw conclusions when they possess only limited data.

Taking responsible risks: Venture forth and explore ideas beyond the usual zone of comfort. Such exploration, of course, must be done with thoughtfulness; it must not be done in ways that could put the student at risk psychologically or physically. Using the analogy of a turtle going nowhere until it sticks its neck out, teachers of young adolescents should model this behavior and provide opportunities for students to develop this intelligent behavior by using techniques such as brainstorming strategies, divergent-thinking questioning, think-pair-share, cooperative learning, inquiry, and project-based learning.

Thinking and communicating with clarity and precision. Strive for clarity and accurate communication in both written and oral form. Shown in Figure 3.2 are humorous sample sentences (taken from newspapers) that lack clarity and precision in written expression. A useful academic exercise is to have students, perhaps in dyads, read and then rewrite sentences such as these, and then share and compare their rewrites.

Thinking about thinking (metacognition). Learning to plan, monitor, assess, and reflect on one's own thinking is another characteristic of intelligent behavior. Small group learning, journals, student-led portfolio conferences, self-assessment, and thinking aloud in dyads, are strategies that can be used to help students develop this intelligent behavior (Stright & Supplee, 2002). Your own thinking aloud is good modeling for your students, helping them to develop their cognitive skills of thinking, learning, and reasoning (Astington, 1998).

Thinking flexibly. Sometimes referred to as *lateral thinking* (De Bono, 1970), flexibility in thinking is the ability to approach a problem from "the side," or from a new angle, using a novel approach. With modeling by the teacher, students can develop this behavior as they learn to consider alternative points of view and to deal with several sources of information simultaneously.

Figure 3.1   Examples of persistence.

- *Rachel Carson.* Refusing to be intimidated by powerful external forces, Carson was persistent in her pursuit to educate society about the ill effects of pesticides. Her book, *Silent Spring,* published in 1963, was the seed for the beginning of the development of a more responsible ecological attitude.
- *Amelia Earhart.* Born in 1898, Earhart demonstrated from the time she was a young girl that she was creative, curious, and persistent. Learning to fly in 1920, in just eight more years she became the first woman to fly the Atlantic Ocean, thereby paving the way for other women to become active in aviation.
- *Lewis H. Latimer.* Born in 1848 the son of slaves, Latimer served in the U.S. Navy during the Civil War. After the war he studied drafting, eventually becoming chief draftsman for both General Electric and Westinghouse. Among his career achievements were his patent drawings for Alexander Graham Bell's first telephone; his invention of a method to make a carbon filament for a light bulb that was made by one of Thomas Edison's competitors; and supervision of the installation of the first electric lights in New York City, Philadelphia, Montreal, and London. Later, in 1884, he went to work for Edison.
- *Wilma Rudolf.* As the result of childhood diseases, Rudolf, at the age of 10 could not walk without the aid of leg braces. Just 10 years later, at the age of 20, she was declared to be the fastest running woman in the world, having won three gold medals in the 1960 World Olympics.

Figure 3.2   Sample sentences that lack clarity and precision.

1. The burglar was about 30 years old, white, 5' 10", with wavy hair weighing about 150 pounds.
2. The family lawyer will read the will tomorrow at the residence of Mr. Carlson, who died June 19 to accommodate his relatives.
3. Mrs. Maureen Doolittle, who went deer hunting with her husband, is very proud that she was able to shoot a fine buck as well as her husband.
4. Organ donations from the living reached a record high last year, outnumbering donors who are dead for the first time.
5. The dog was hungry and made the mistake of nipping a 2-year-old that was trying to force feed it in his ear.
6. We spent most of our time sitting on the back porch watching the cows playing Scrabble and reading.
7. Hunting can also be dangerous, as in the case of pygmies hunting elephants armed only with spears.

Tom Watson/Merrill

Thinking interdependently. Real-world problem solving has become so complex that seldom can any person go it alone. As stated by Elias (2001, p. 2), "We live in an interdependent world; there is no such thing, in any practical sense, as independence and autonomy. We live lives of synergy and linkage." Not all young adolescents come to school knowing how to work effectively in groups. They may exhibit competitiveness, narrow-mindedness, egocentrism, ethnocentrism, or criticism of others' values, emotions, and beliefs. Listening, consensus seeking, giving up an idea to work on someone else's, empathy, compassion, group leadership, cooperative learning, knowing how to support group efforts, and altruism—those are behaviors indicative of intelligent human beings, and they can be learned by children at school and in the classroom.

Using all the senses. As emphasized throughout this resource guide—as often as is appropriate and feasible—to best learn, children should be encouraged to use and develop all of their sensory input channels (i.e., verbal, visual, tactile, and kinesthetic).

Questioning and posing problems. Young adolescents are usually full of questions, and, unless discouraged, they do ask them. As educators, we want students to be alert to, and recognize, discrepancies and phenomena in their environment and to freely inquire about their causes. In exemplary middle level programs, students are encouraged to ask questions and then from those questions to develop a problem-solving strategy to investigate their questions.

We should strive to help our own students develop these characteristics of intelligent behavior. In Chapter 2 you learned of specific teacher behaviors that facilitate this development. Now, let's review additional research findings that offer important considerations in the facilitation of student learning and intelligent behaving.

Direct Teaching for Thinking and Intelligent Behavior

The curriculum of any school includes the development of skills that are used in thinking, skills such as *questioning, classifying, comparing* and *contrasting, concluding, generalizing,* and *inferring.* Because the academic achievement of students increases when they are taught thinking skills directly, many researchers and educators concur that direct instruction should be given to all students on how to think and behave intelligently.

Several research perspectives have influenced today's interest in the direct teaching of thinking. The *cognitive view of intelligence* asserts that intellectual ability is not fixed but can be developed. The *constructivist approach to learning* maintains that learners actively and independently construct knowledge by creating and coordinating relationships in their mental repertoire. The *social psychology view of classroom experience* focuses on the learner as an individual who is a member of various peer groups and a society. The *perspective of information processing* deals with the acquisition, elaboration, and management of information.

Rather than assuming young adolescents have developed thinking skills, middle level teachers of all disciplines should devote classroom time to teaching them directly. When teaching a thinking skill directly, the subject content becomes the vehicle for thinking. For example, a social studies lesson can teach students how to distinguish fact and opinion; a language arts lesson instructs students how to compare and analyze; and a science lesson can teach students how to set up a problem for their inquiry.

Because it is so important, and because it is so frequently used and abused, the remainder of this chapter is devoted to assisting you in the development of your skills in using questioning as a tool for thinking, teaching, and learning.

PURPOSES FOR USING QUESTIONING

You will adapt the type and form of each question to the purpose for which it is asked. The purposes that questions serve can be separated into five categories, as follows:

1. *To politely give instructions.* An example is, "Mariya, would you please turn out the lights so we can better view what's on the screen?" Although they probably should avoid doing so, teachers sometimes also use rhetorical questions for the purpose of regaining student attention and maintaining classroom control. For example, "Mario, would you please attend to your work?" Rhetorical questions can sometimes backfire on the teacher. In this case, for example, Mario might say "No"; then the teacher would have a problem that could have been avoided had the teacher been more direct and simply told Mario to attend to his work, rather than asking if he would.

2. *To review and remind students of classroom procedures.* For example, if students continue to talk when they shouldn't, you can stop the lesson and ask, "Class, I think we need to review the procedure we agreed on for when someone is talking. Who can tell me what is the procedure that we agreed upon?"

3. *To gather information.* Examples are: "How many of you have finished the assignment?" or, to find out whether a student knows something, "Kaiya, can you please explain for us the difference between a synonym and an antonym?"

4. *To discover student knowledge, interests, or experiences.* An example might be, "How many of you think you know the process by which water in our city is made drinkable?"

5. *To guide student thinking and learning.* It is this category of questioning that is the focus for your learning in this chapter. In teaching, questions in this category are used to:

- *Build the curriculum.* It is the students' questions that provide the basis for the learning that occurs in an effective program that is inquiry-based and project-centered. More on this subject follows later in "Questions from Students: The Question-Driven Curriculum."

- *Develop appreciation.* For example, "Do you now understand the ecological relationship between that particular root fungus, voles, and the survival of the large conifers of the forests of the Pacific Northwest?"

- *Develop student thinking.* For example, "What do you suppose the effects to the ecology are when standing water is sprayed with an insecticide that is designed to kill all mosquito larvae?"

- *Diagnose learning difficulty.* For example, "What part of the writer's argument don't you understand, Sarah?"

- *Emphasize major points.* For example, "If no one has ever been to the sun, how can we be confident that we know of what the sun is made?"

- *Encourage students.* For example, "OK, so you didn't remember the formula for glucose. What really impressed me in your essay is what you did understand about photosynthesis. Do you know specifically what part that was?"

- *Establish rapport.* For example, "We have a problem here, but I think we can solve it if we work together. What do you think ought to be our first step?"

- *Evaluate learning.* For example, "Siobhan, what is the effect when two rough surfaces are rubbed together?"

- *Give practice in expression.* For example, "Yvonne, would you please share with us the examples of shadowing that you found?"

- *Help students in their metacognition.* For example, "Yes, something did go wrong. Do you still think your original hypothesis is correct? If not, then where was the error in your thinking? Or if you still think your hypothesis is correct, then where might the error have been? How might we verify?"

- *Help students interpret materials.* For example, "Something seems to be wrong with this compass. How do you suppose we can find out what it might be? For example, if the needle is marked N and S in reverse, how can we find out if that is the problem?"

- *Help students organize materials.* For example, "If you really want to test your idea, then we are going to need certain materials. We are going to have to deal with some strategic questions here, such as, what do you think we will need, where can we find those things, who will be responsible for getting them, and how will we store and arrange them once we are ready to start the investigation?"

- *Provide drill and practice.* For example, "Team A has prepared some questions that they would like to use as practice questions for our upcoming unit exam, and they are suggesting that we use them to play the game of *Jeopardy* on Friday. Is everyone in agreement with their idea?"

- *Provide review.* For example, "Today, in your groups, you are going to study the unit review questions. After each group has studied and prepared its answers to these written questions, your group will pick another group and ask them your set of review questions. Each group has a different set of questions. Members of Team Alpha are going to keep score, and the group that has the highest score from this review session will receive free tickets to Friday night's game. Ready?"

- *Show agreement or disagreement.* For example, "Some of you believe that the United States should not have invaded Iraq. Explain why you agree or disagree with that conclusion."
- *Show relationships,* such as cause and effect. For example, "What do you suppose would be the global effect, if any, if just one inch of the total Antarctic ice shelf were to melt rather suddenly?"
- *Build the curriculum.* It is the students' questions that provide the basis for the learning that occurs in an effective program that is inquiry-based and project-centered. More on this subject follows later in the section of this chapter titled "Questions from Students: The Question-Driven Curriculum."

Questions to Avoid Asking

Before going further, while it is important to avoid asking rhetorical questions, questions for which you do not want a response, you should also avoid asking questions that call for little or no student thinking, such as those that can be answered with a simple yes or no or some other sort of alternative answer response. Unless followed up with questions calling for clarification, questions that call for simple responses have little or no learning and diagnostic value; they encourage guessing and inappropriate student responses that can cause classroom control problems for the teacher.

> Never deliberately ask questions for the purpose of embarrassing or punishing a student, that in any way deny the student's dignity.

Questions that embarrass or punish tend to damage the student's developing self-esteem and serve no meaningful academic or instructional purpose. Questioning is an important instructional tool that should be used by the teacher only for academic reasons. Although it is not always possible to predict when a student might be embarrassed by a question, a teacher should never deliberately ask questions for the purpose of embarrassment or punishment. For example, avoid asking a student a content question when you sense the student was not paying attention and/or does not know the answer. When done deliberately to punish or embarrass, that teacher's action borders on abuse!

TYPES OF COGNITIVE QUESTIONS: A GLOSSARY

Let's now define, describe, and provide examples for each of the types of cognitive (or mental) questions that you will use in teaching. Please note that although we refer to these in the traditional fashion as cognitive questions, any question type could relate to any of the three domains of learning (cognitive, affective, or psychomotor). In the section that follows, your attention is focused on the levels of cognitive questions.

Analytic Question

The analytic question is used to encourage students to analyze and even critique information before them. For example, "In what way was the news headline misleading?" and "How could we improve the initial sentence?"

Clarifying Question

The clarifying question is used to gain more information from a student to help the teacher better understand a student's ideas, feelings, and thought processes. Often, asking a student to elaborate on an initial response will lead the student to think more deeply, restructure his or her thinking, and while doing so, discover a fallacy in the original response. Examples of clarifying questions are "What I hear you saying is that you would rather work alone than in your group. Is that correct?" "So, Denise, you think the poem is a sad one, is that right?" There is a strong positive correlation between student learning, the development of metacognitive skills (i.e., their thinking about thinking), and the teacher's use of questions that ask for clarification (Costa, 1991). In addition, by seeking clarification, you are likely to be demonstrating an interest in the student and in the student's thinking, and that is good.

Convergent-Thinking Question

Convergent-thinking questions, also called *narrow questions* are low-order thinking questions that have a single correct answer (such as recall questions, discussed further in the next section). Examples of convergent-thinking questions are "If the circumference of a circle is 31 meters, what is its radius?" "What engineering feat allowed Xerxes to invade Greece in 481 B.C.E.?" When using questions of this type, try to come back with follow-up questions so the student answering can demonstrate thinking beyond rote memory.

Cueing Question

If you ask a question to which, after sufficient *wait time*, that is longer than two seconds and as long as seven (Rowe, 1974; Tobin, 1984), no students respond or to which their responses indicate they need more information, then you can ask a question that cues the answer or response you are seeking. In essence, you are going backward in your questioning sequence, in order to cue the students. For example, as an introduction to a lesson on the study of prefixes, a teacher asks students, "How many legs each do crayfish, lobsters, and shrimp have?" and there is no accurate response. The teacher might then cue the answer with the following information and question, "Those animals belong to the class Decapoda. Does that give you a clue about the number of legs they have?" If that clue is not enough, and after allowing sufficient time for students to think (two to seven seconds), then the teacher might ask, "What is a decathlon?" or "What is the decimal system?" or "What is a decimeter?" or "What is a decibel?" or "What is a decade?" or "What is the Decalogue?" and so on.

When questioning students over reading material, you can use the *question answer relationship* (QAR) strategy (McIntosh & Draper, 1996). QAR involves asking a question and, if a student is unable to respond, providing one of three types of cues. "Right there" is used for questions for which the answer can be found explicitly stated in the sentence or paragraph. "Search and think" means the answer is not directly stated and therefore must be inferred. "On your own" is used for critical thinking questions for which the answers are neither explicit nor inferred in the text (Choate & Rakes, 1998).

Divergent-Thinking Question

Divergent-thinking questions (also known as *broad, reflective,* or *thought questions*) are open-ended (i.e., usually having no singularly correct answer), high-order thinking questions (requiring analysis, synthesis, or evaluation), which require students to think creatively and to leave the comfortable confines of the known and reach out into the unknown. Examples of questions that require divergent thinking are "Do you believe our school should have a dress code?" or "What measures could be taken to reduce crime in our neighborhood?"

Evaluative Question

Whether convergent or divergent, some questions require students to place a value on something or to take a stance on some issue; these are referred to as *evaluative questions*. If the teacher and the students agree on certain premises, then the evaluative question would also be a convergent question. If original assumptions differ, then the response to the evaluative question would be more subjective, and therefore divergent. Examples of evaluative questions are "Is it right for 18-year-olds to serve in the military but still be unable to buy a beer?" or "Is the legal age for obtaining a driver's license too low?" and "Should the Electoral College be abolished?"

Focus Question

A focus question is any question that focuses student thinking. For example, the last question of the preceding paragraph can be a focus question when the teacher asking it is attempting to focus student attention on the concept of a democracy.

Probing Question

Similar to a clarifying question, the probing question requires student thinking to go beyond superficial first-answer or single-word responses. An example of a probing question is "Why, Eloy, do you think it is the case that every citizen has the right to have a gun?"

Probing questions are effective for encouraging and engaging student thinking *before* a particular learning experience, that is, for establishing a mindset. For example, "How many consecutive drops of water do you predict we could place on this coin before any water would run off the edge?"

SOCRATIC QUESTIONING

In the fifth century B.C.E., Socrates, the famous Athenian teacher, used the art of questioning so successfully that to this day we still hear of the Socratic method (Elder & Paul, 1998; Phillips, 2000; Schneider, 2000). What, exactly, is the Socratic method? Socrates' strategy was to ask his students a series of leading questions that gradually snarled them up to the point where they had to look carefully at their own ideas and think rigorously for themselves. Today, that strategy is referred to as the Socratic approach or method.

Socratic discussions were informal dialogues taking place in a natural, pleasant environment. Although Socrates sometimes had to go to considerable lengths to ignite his students' intrinsic interest, their response was natural and spontaneous. In his dialogues, Socrates tried to aid students in developing ideas. He did not impose his own notions on the students. Rather, he encouraged them to develop their own conclusions and draw their own inferences. Of course, Socrates may have had preconceived notions about what the final learning should be and carefully aimed his questions so that the students would arrive at the desired conclusions. Still, his questions were open-ended, causing divergent rather than convergent thinking. The students were free to go mentally wherever the facts and their thinking led them.

Throughout history, teachers have tried to adapt that which they believe to be the methods of Socrates to the classroom. In some situations, they have been quite successful and are a major mode of instruction. However, it's important to understand that Socrates used this method in the context of a one-to-one relationship between the student and himself. Some teachers have adapted it for whole-class, direct instruction by asking questions first of one student and then of another, moving slowly about the class. This technique may work, but it is difficult because the essence of the Socratic technique is to build question on question in a logical fashion so that each question leads the student a step further toward the understanding sought. When you distribute the questions around the classroom, you may find it difficult to build up the desired sequence and to keep all the students involved in the discussion. Sometimes you may be able to use the Socratic method by directing all the questions at one student—at least for several minutes—while the other students look on and listen in. That is how Socrates did it. When the topic is interesting enough, this technique can be quite successful and even exciting, but in the long run, the Socratic method works best when the teacher is working in one-on-one coaching situations or with small groups of students, rather than in whole-class, direct instruction.

In using Socratic questioning the focus is on the questions, not the answers, and thinking is valued as the quintessential activity (Brogan & Brogan, 1995). In essence, to conduct Socratic questioning, with the student or class, identify a problem (either student- or teacher-posed) and then ask the students a series of probing questions designed to cause them to examine critically the problem and potential solutions to it. The main thrust of the questioning and the key questions must be planned in advance so that the questioning will proceed logically. To think of quality probing questions on the spur of the moment is too difficult. It is the Socratic method that you will be using in a micro peer teaching exercise later in this chapter (Exercise 3.7).

LEVELS OF COGNITIVE QUESTIONS AND STUDENT THINKING

Questions posed by you are cues to your students to the level of thinking expected of them, ranging from the lowest level of mental operation, requiring simple recall of knowledge (convergent thinking), to the highest, requiring divergent thought and application of that thought. It is important that you are aware of the levels of thinking, that you understand the importance of attending to student thinking from low to higher levels of operation, and that you understand that what for one student may be a matter of simple recall of information, may for another require a higher-order mental activity, such as figuring something out by deduction.

You should structure and sequence your questions (and assist students in developing their own skill in structuring and sequencing their questions) in a way that is designed to guide students to higher levels of thinking. For example, when students respond to questions in complete sentences that provide supportive evidence for their ideas, it is fairly safe to assume that their thinking is at a higher level than were the response an imprecise and nondescriptive single-word answer.

To help your understanding, three levels of questioning and thinking are described as follows. [*Note:* Others have described this three-tiered model of thinking variously. For example, in Eisner's *The Educational*

Imagination (Macmillan, 1979), the levels are "descriptive," "interpretive," and "evaluative."] You should recognize the similarity between these three levels of questions and the six levels of thinking and doing from Bloom's taxonomy of cognitive objectives (Chapter 5). For your daily use of questioning it is just as useful but more practical to think and behave in terms of these three levels, rather than six.

1. *Lowest level: Gathering and recalling information.* At this level, questions are designed to solicit from students concepts, information, feelings, or experiences that were gained in the past and stored in memory. Sample key words and desired behaviors are:

> *complete, count, define, describe, identify, list, match, name, observe, recall, recite, select*

Thinking involves receiving data through the senses, followed by the processing of those data. Inputting without processing is brain-dysfunctional. Information that has not been processed is stored only in short-term memory.

2. *Intermediate level: Processing information.* At this level, questions are designed to draw relationships of cause and effect, to synthesize, analyze, summarize, compare, contrast, or classify data. Sample key words and desired behaviors are:

> *analyze, classify, compare, contrast, distinguish, explain, group, infer, make an analogy, organize, plan, synthesize*

Thinking and questioning that involve processing of information can be conscious or unconscious. When students observe the teacher thinking aloud, and when they are urged to think aloud, to think about their thinking, and to analyze it as it occurs, they are in the process of developing their intellectual skills.

At the processing level, this internal analysis of new data may challenge a learner's preconceptions (and misconceptions or what are sometimes referred to as *naïve theories*) about a phenomenon. The learner's brain will naturally resist this challenge to existing beliefs. The greater the mental challenge, the greater will be the brain's effort to draw upon data already in storage. With increasing data, the mind will gradually examine existing concepts and ultimately, as necessary, develop new mental concepts.

If there is a match between new input and existing mental concepts, no problem exists. Piaget called this process *assimilation* (Piaget, 1977). If, however, in processing new data there is no match with existing mental concepts, then the situation has created what Piaget called *cognitive disequilibrium*. The brain does not "like" this disequilibrium and will drive the learner to search for an explanation for the discrepancy. Piaget called this process *accommodation*. However, although learning is enhanced by challenge, in situations that are threatening the brain is less flexible in accommodating new ideas.

As we discuss in Chapter 4, that is why each student must feel welcomed in the classroom and learners must perceive the classroom environment as challenging but nonthreatening, what is referred to as an environment of *relaxed alertness* (Caine, 2000).

Questions and experiences must be designed to elicit more than merely recall memory responses (assimilation). Many middle level teachers find it useful to use discrepant events to introduce concepts. **Discrepant events** are phenomena that cause cognitive disequilibrium, thus stimulating higher-level mental functioning. However, merely exposing students to a discrepant event will not in itself cause students to develop new conceptual understandings. It simply stirs the mind into processing, without which mental development does not occur (See Figure 3.3).

3. *Highest level: Applying and evaluating in new situations.* Questions at the highest level encourage learners to think intuitively, creatively, and hypothetically, to use their imagination, to expose a value system, or to make a judgment. Sample key words and desired behaviors are:

> *apply, build, evaluate, extrapolate, forecast, generalize, hypothesize, imagine, judge, predict, speculate*

You must use questions at the level best suited for the purpose, use questions of a variety of different levels, and structure questions in a way intended to move student thinking to higher levels.

With the use of questions as a strategy to move student thinking to higher levels, the teacher is facilitating the students' intellectual development. Developing your skill in using questioning requires attention to detail and practice. The following guidelines will provide that detail and some practice, but first, do Exercise 3.1 to check your understanding of the levels of questions.

Figure 3.3   Example of a discrepant event demonstration.

Balloon Will Not Pop

Practice this first. Partially blow up a balloon, and tie it off. Take a large but sharp sewing needle and slowly push it into the balloon. Because the needle immediately plugs the hole, the balloon remains filled. Sure, you say, students have seen this done by magicians or birthday party clowns. But wait. Now for the real discrepant event: slowly remove the needle, and voila! The balloon does not collapse. The balloon material expands to plug the hole. Make several holes. Take a long needle (as used in doll making) and push it through the balloon and out through the other side, keeping the needle in both holes. The balloon stays filled. (Hint: Push the needle into the thickest portion of the balloon, opposite the opening.) If students believe you are using a fake balloon, take the same needle and quickly puncture the balloon, popping it.

When teachers use higher-level questions, their students tend to score higher on tests of critical thinking and on standardized tests of achievement (Newton, 1978; Redfield & Rousseau, 1981).

EXERCISE 3.1: IDENTIFYING THE COGNITIVE LEVELS OF QUESTIONS—
A SELF-CHECK EXERCISE

INSTRUCTIONS: The purpose of this exercise is to test your understanding and recognition of the levels of questions. Mark each of the following questions with a

1, if it is at the lowest level of mental operation, gathering and recalling data.
2, if it is at a middle level, processing data.
3, if it is at the highest level, applying or evaluating data in a new situation.

Check your answers against the key that follows. Resolve problems by discussing them with your classmates and instructor.

_____ 1. Do you recall the differences between an Asian elephant and an African elephant?

_____ 2. How are the natural habitats of the Asian and African elephants similar? How are they different?

_____ 3. Which of the elephants do you think is more interesting?

_____ 4. For what do you think the elephant uses its tusks?

_____ 5. Do all elephants have tusks?

_____ 6. Did the trick ending make the story more interesting for you?

_____ 7. How might these evergreen needles be grouped?

_____ 8. How do these two types of pine needles differ?

_____ 9. For how many years was the Soviet Union a communist-dominated nation?

_____ 10. How many republics do you believe will be in the new Commonwealth of Independent States (the former Soviet Union) by the year 2020?

_____ 11. Why do you think the city decided to move the zoo?

_____ 12. How would the park be different today had the zoo been left there?

_____ 13. How do zoos today differ from those of the mid-nineteenth century?

_____ 14. Should a teacher be entitled to unemployment benefits during the summer or when school is not in session?

_____ 15. If $4X + 40 = 44$, what is X?

_____ 16. What happens when I spin this egg?

_____ 17. How does this poem make you feel?

_____ 18. What will happen when we mix equal amounts of the red and yellow solutions?

_____ 19. What is the capital of West Virginia?

_____ 20. What will be the long-term global effects if the rain forests continue to be removed at the present rate?

Answer Key: 1 = 1 (recall); 2 = 2 (compare); 3 = 3 (judge); 4 = 3 (imagine); 5 = 3 (extrapolate); 6 = 3 (evaluate); 7 = 2 (classify); 8 = 2 (contrast); 9 = 1 (recall); 10 = 3 (predict); 11 = 2 (explain cause and effect); 12 = 3 (speculate); 13 = 2 (contrast); 14 = 3 (judge); 15 = 1 (recall of how to work the problem); 16 = 1 (observe); 17 = 1 (describe); 18 = 3 (hypothesize); 19 = 1 (recall); 20 = 3 (speculate or generalize).

GUIDELINES FOR USING QUESTIONING

As emphasized many times in several ways throughout this resource guide, as a teacher of young adolescents your goals are to help your students learn how to solve problems; make decisions and value judgments; think creatively and critically; and feel positive about themselves, their schools, and their learning—rather than simply to fill their minds with bits and pieces of information that will likely last only a brief time in the students' short-term memory. Important to the realization of these goals are how you construct your questions and how you implement your questioning strategy.

Constructing Questions

When constructing questions, consider the guidelines presented in the following paragraphs.

Key cognitive questions should be planned, thoughtfully worded, and written into your lesson plan. Thoughtful construction of questions helps to assure that they are clear and specific, not ambiguous, that the vocabulary is appropriate, and that each question matches its purpose. Incorporate questions into your lessons as instructional devices, welcomed pauses, attention grabbers, and as checks for student comprehension. Thoughtful teachers even plan questions that they intend to ask specific students, targeting questions to the readiness level, interest, or learning profile of a student.

Match questions with their target purposes. Carefully prepared questions allow them to be sequenced and worded to match the levels of cognitive thinking expected of students. To help students in developing their thinking skills, you need to demonstrate how to do this. To demonstrate, you must use terminology that is specific and that provides students with examples of experiences consonant with the meanings of the cognitive words. You should demonstrate this every day so students learn the cognitive terminology. As stated by Brooks and Brooks, "framing tasks around cognitive activities such as analysis, interpretation, and prediction—and explicitly using those terms with students—fosters the construction of new understandings" (Brooks & Brooks, 1993, p. 105). See the three examples in Figure 3.4.

Implementing Questioning

Careful preparation of questions is half the skill in questioning. Implementation is the other half. Here are guidelines for effective implementation.

Ask your well-worded question before calling on a student for a response. A common error made is when the teacher first calls on a student and then asks the question, such as "Sean, would you please tell us what you believe the author meant by the title 'We are One'?" Although probably not intended by the teacher, as soon

Figure 3.4 Questions that use appropriate cognitive terminology.

Instead of	Say
"How else might it be done?"	"How could you apply . . .?"
"Are you going to get quiet?"	"If we are going to hear what Joan has to say, what do you need to do?"
"How do you know that is so?"	"What evidence do you have?"

as the teacher called on Sean, that signaled to the rest of the students in the classroom that they were released from having to pay further attention and from having to think about the question. The preferred strategy is to phrase the question, allow time for all students to think, and then call on Sean and other students for their interpretations of the author's meaning of the title.

Avoid bombarding students with too much teacher talk. Sometimes teachers talk too much. This could be especially true for teachers who are nervous, as might be the case for many during the initial weeks of their student teaching. Knowing the guidelines presented here will help you avoid that syndrome. Remind yourself to be quiet after you ask a question that you have carefully formulated. Some teachers even put a reminder per se in their lesson plans. Sometimes, due to lack of confidence, and especially when a question hasn't been carefully planned, the teacher asks the question and then, with a slight change in wording, asks it again, or asks several questions, one after another. That is too much verbiage. It's called "machine gun questioning" and only confuses students, allowing too little time for them to think.

After asking a question, provide students with adequate time to think. The pause after asking a question is called wait time (or **think time**). Knowing the subject better than the students know it and having given prior thought to the subject, too many teachers fail to allow students sufficient time to think after asking a question. In addition, by the time they have reached the middle grades, students have learned pretty well how to play the "game"—that is, they know that if they remain silent long enough the teacher will probably answer his or her own question. After asking a well-worded question you should remain silent for a while, allowing students time to think and to respond. If you wait long enough, they usually will. You may need to rehearse your students on this procedure.

After asking a question, how long should you wait before you do something? You should wait at least two seconds, and perhaps as long as seven or sometimes even longer (when it appears that students are still thinking). Stop reading now and look at a timepiece to get a feeling for how long two seconds is. Then, observe how long seven seconds is. Did seven seconds seem like a long time? Because most of us are not used to silence in the classroom, two seconds of silence can seem quite long, while seven seconds may seem eternal. If, for some reason, students have not responded after a period of two to seven seconds of wait time, then you can ask the question again (but don't reword an already carefully worded question or else students are likely to be confused, thinking perhaps it is a new question). Pause for several seconds; then if you still haven't received a response you can call on a student, then another, if necessary, after sufficient wait time. Soon you will get a response that can be built upon. Avoid answering your own question!

Now, to better understand the art of questioning, the importance of well-worded questions and well-prepared and clear instructions, and of allowing students time to think, do Exercise 3.2.

EXERCISE 3.2: THINK TIME AND THE ART OF QUESTIONING: AN IN-CLASS EXERCISE

INSTRUCTIONS: The purpose of this exercise is to further your understanding of the art and power of questioning, the importance of well-worded questions with well-prepared and clear instructions, and the need to give students time to think. A secondary purpose is to experience and discuss the use of role-play simulations in learning.

1. Role-play simulation: From your class ask for three volunteers. One volunteer will read the lines of the teacher, Angel, a second will read the one line of the student, while the third volunteer uses a stop watch to direct Angel and the student to speak their lines at the designated times. The rest of your class can pretend to be students in Angel's English class.

1:00	*Angel:* "Think of a man whom you admire, perhaps a father figure, and write a three-sentence paragraph describing that person." Students begin their writing.
1:00:05	*Angel:* "Only three sentences about someone you admire. It might be your father, uncle, anyone."
1:00:07	*Student:* "Does it have to be about a man?"
	Angel: "No, it can be a man or a woman, but someone you truly look up to."
1:01	Angel works the rows, seeing that students are on task.
1:01:10	*Angel:* "Three sentences are all you need to write."
1:01:15	*Angel:* "Think of someone you really admire, and write three sentences in a paragraph that describes that person."
1:01:30	*Angel:* "Someone you would like to be like."
1:02	Angel continues walking around helping students who are having difficulty. All students are on task.
1:04	*Angel:* "Now I want you to exchange papers with the person behind or beside you, read that person's description of the person they admire, and describe a setting that you see their person in. Write a paragraph that describes that setting."
1:04–1:05	Students exchange papers; teacher walks around seeing that everyone has received another student's paper.
1:05	*Angel:* "Where do you see that person being? Below the paragraph I want you to write a new paragraph describing where you see this person, perhaps in an easy chair watching a ball game, on a porch, in a car, or in the kitchen cooking."
1:05:10	*Angel:* "Describe a scene you see this person in."
1:05:15	*Angel:* "After you read the description, I want you to create a setting for the person described."
1:05:18	Students seem confused either about what they are reading (e.g., asking the writer what a word is or means) or what they are supposed to do.
1:05:19	*Angel:* "Anything is fine. Use your imagination to describe the setting."
1:05:22	*Angel:* "Describe a setting for this person."
1:09	*Angel:* "Now I want you to exchange papers with yet another person and after reading the previous two paragraphs written by two other students, write a third paragraph describing a problem you think this admired person has."

2. After the role-play simulation, hold a whole-class discussion or small-group discussions and use the following as a springboard for your discussion: Describe what you believe are the good points and weak points of this portion of Angel's lesson and her implementation of it.

3. Lastly, hold a discussion sharing opinions and experiences about role-play simulations as a strategy for teaching/learning.

Practice gender equity. To practice gender equity, here are four rules to follow when using questioning: (a) Avoid going to a boy to bail out a girl who fails to answer a question, (b) avoid going to a boy to improve upon a girl's answer (For the first, without seeming to badger, try to give the student clues until she can answer with success. For the second, hold and demonstrate high expectations for all students.), (c) allow equal wait time regardless of student gender, and (d) call on boys and girls equally.

Practice calling on all students. Related to the last rule of the preceding paragraph, you must call on not just the quick or the slow, not just the boys or the girls, not only those in the front or middle of the classroom, but all of them. To do these things is important and may take your concentrated effort. To ensure that students are called on equally, some teachers have in hand laminated copies of their seating charts, perhaps on bright, neon-colored clipboards (giving students a visual focus), and, with an erasable marker, make a mark next to the name of the student each time that student is called on. With the seating chart laminated, and using erasable markers, the marks can be erased at the end of the day and the seating chart used over and over.

Give the same minimum amount of wait time (think time) to all students. This, too, will require concentrated effort on your part, but is important to do. A teacher who waits for less time when calling on a slow student or students of one gender, is showing a prejudice or a lack of confidence in certain students, both of which are detrimental when a teacher is striving to establish for all students a positive, equal, and safe environment for classroom learning. Show confidence in all students, and never discriminate by expecting less or more from some students than from others. Although some students may take longer to respond, it is not necessarily because they are not thinking or they have less ability. There may be cultural differences to think about, in that some cultures simply allow more wait time than others do. There may also be learning disabilities to consider. But the important point here is to *individualize* to allow students who need more time to have it. Variation in wait time allowed should not be used to single out some students and to lead to lower expectations but rather to allow for higher expectations.

Require students to raise their hands and be called on. Of course there are always possible and reasonable exceptions to most any rule, including this one, but as a general and important procedure for when you ask questions, instead of allowing students to randomly shout out their answers, expect them to raise their hands and to be called on before they respond. Establish that procedure and stick with it. If/when you do relax the rule (such as you might in small group instruction) let the students know. Using the rule, however, helps to assure both that you call on all students equally, fairly

distributing your interactions with the students, and that girls are not interacted with less because boys tend to be more obstreperous. Even in same-gender classrooms, some students tend to be more vocal while others are less so and, when allowed by the instructor, tend to monopolize and control the flow of the verbal interactions. Every teacher has the responsibility to guarantee a nonbiased classroom and an equal distribution of interaction time in the classroom. That is impossible to do when students are allowed to speak at will.

Another important reason for this advice is to aid students in learning to control their impulsivity. Controlling one's impulsivity is a characteristic of intelligent behavior discussed earlier in this chapter. One of your many instructional responsibilities is to help students develop this intelligent behavior.

Actively involve as many students as possible in the questioning-answering discussion session. The traditional method of the teacher asking a question and then calling on a student to respond is essentially a one-on-one interaction. Many students, those not called on, are likely to view that as their opportunity to disengage in the lesson at hand. Even though you call on one student, you want the other students to not mentally disengage. There are many effective ways to keep all engaged. Consider the following.

To keep all students mentally engaged, you will want to call on students who are sitting quietly and have not raised their hands as well as those who have, but avoid badgering or humiliating an unwilling participant. When a student has no response, you might suggest he or she think about it and even write down his or her thoughts, and you will come back to the student to assure he or she is mentally engaged, and eventually understands or has an answer to the original question.

By dividing a single question into several parts, the number of students involved can be increased. For example, "What are the causes of the Civil War? Who can give one?" followed then by "Who can give another?" Or, you can involve several students in answering a single question. For example, ask one student for an answer, such as to the question "What was the first battle of the Civil War?" and ask a second student to read the text aloud to verify the student's answer, and then ask a third student to explore the reason or thinking that makes it the accepted answer.

Carefully gauge your responses to students' responses to your questions. The way you respond to students' answers influences students' subsequent participation. Responses by the teacher that encourage student participation include probing for elaboration, discussing student answers, requesting justification, asking how answers were arrived at, and providing positive reinforcement.

In gauging your responses to students' responses to your questions you must be cognizant of cultural characteristics and differences of your students. How students respond to questioning is in part culturally dependent and understanding these differences can be very helpful toward your effectiveness in using questioning. For example, among many Native American groups, once one student gives an incorrect answer, no student following that student will give the correct answer; not because they do not know it, but because it would be culturally inappropriate to "upstage" the shamed student. Also, for many minority cultures, giving a "guess" answer when one is not one hundred percent sure is disrespectful. This can have an impact on how a student responds in class. Having relevant knowledge about the cultural heritage of children in your particular classroom will help you become more reflective and responsive in using questioning.

Use strong praise sparingly. Although a teacher's use of strong praise is sometimes okay, when you want students to think divergently and creatively, you should be stingy with the use of strong praise to student responses. Strong praise from a teacher tends to terminate divergent and creative thinking. Strong praise can also cause children to become dependent on external sources of praise—to become "praise junkies." (As discussed in Chapter 2 about "praise versus encouragement.")

One of your goals is to help students realize **intrinsic** sources for **motivation**, that is, an inner drive of intent or desire that causes them to want to learn. Use of strong praise tends to build conformity, causing students to depend on outside forces—that is, the giver of praise—for their worth rather than upon themselves. An example of a strong praise response is "That's right! Very good." On the other hand, passive acceptance responses, such as, "Okay, that seems to be one possibility," keep the door open for further thinking, particularly for higher-level, divergent thinking.

Another example of a passive acceptance response is one used in brainstorming sessions, when the teacher says, "After asking the question and giving you time to think about it, I will hear your ideas and record them on the board." Only after all student responses have been heard and recorded does the class begin its consideration of each. That kind of nonjudgmental acceptance of all ideas in the classroom will generate from the students a great deal of expression of high-level thought.

QUESTIONS FROM STUDENTS: THE QUESTION-DRIVEN CURRICULUM

Student questions can and should be used as springboards for further questioning, discussions, and investigations. Students should be encouraged to ask questions that challenge the textbook, the process, or other persons' statements, and they should be encouraged to seek the supporting evidence behind a statement.

> *The most intellectually demanding tasks lie not so much in solving problems as in posing questions. The kind of schools we need would be staffed by teachers who are as interested in questions students ask after a unit of study as they are in the answers students give.*
>
> Elliot W. Eisner (2002, p. 579)

Being able to ask questions may be more important than having right answers. Knowledge is derived from asking questions. Being able to recognize problems and to formulate questions is a skill and the key to problem solving and critical thinking skill development (Ciardiello, 2000). You have a responsibility to encourage students to formulate questions and to help them word their questions in such a way that tentative answers can be sought. That is the process necessary to build a base of knowledge that can be drawn upon whenever necessary to link, interpret, and explain new information in new situations.

Questioning: The Cornerstone of Critical Thinking, Real-World Problem Solving, and Meaningful Learning

With real-world problem solving, there are usually no absolute right answers. Rather than "correct" answers, some are simply better than others. The student with a problem needs to learn how to:

1. recognize the problem
2. formulate a question about that problem
3. collect data
4. arrive at a temporarily acceptable answer to the problem, while realizing that at some later time new data may dictate a review of the former conclusion.

For example, if a biochemist believes she has discovered a new enzyme, there is no textbook or teacher or any other outside authoritative source to which she may refer to inquire if she is correct. Rather, on the basis of her self-confidence in problem identification, asking questions, collecting data, and arriving at a tentative conclusion based on those data, she assumes that, for now, her conclusion is safe.

Help students learn the difference between asking questions that are descriptive and those that are comparative. An example descriptive question is "How many people live in lower altitude deserts of the world?" Changing that to a comparative question we could have "Are low desert populations of people fewer in number than populations living in high deserts?" From the first question the asker would likely get a simple number whereas changing the question to a comparative one opens new avenues for further learning. A simple comparative question might lead to a unit of study lasting weeks and that overlaps many disciplines.

Encourage students to ask questions about content and process. As emphasized in *Tried and True* (United States Department of Education, 1997), question asking often indicates that the inquirer is curious, puzzled, and uncertain; it is a sign of being engaged in thinking. And, yet, in too many classrooms too few students ask questions. Students should be encouraged to ask questions. From young adolescent students, there is no such thing as a "dumb" question. Sometimes students, like everyone else, ask questions that could just as easily have been looked up, are truly irrelevant, or show lack of thought or sensitivity. Those questions can consume precious class time. For a teacher, they can be frustrating. A teacher's initial reaction may be to quickly and mistakenly brush off that type of question with sarcasm, while assuming that the student is too lazy to look up an answer. In such instances, you are advised to think before responding and to respond kindly and professionally, although in the busy life of a classroom teacher, that may not always be so easy to remember to do. However, be assured, there is a reason for a student's question. Perhaps the student is signaling a need for recognition or simply demanding attention.

In large schools, it is sometimes easy for a student to feel alone and insignificant (although this seems less the case with schools that use a school-within-a-school plan and where teachers and students work together in interdisciplinary teams, or, as in looping, where one cadre of teachers remains with the same cohort of students for two or more years). When a student makes an effort to interact with you, that can be a positive sign, so gauge carefully your responses to those efforts. If a student's question is really off track, off the wall, out of order, and out of context with the content of the lesson, consider this as a possible response: "That is an interesting question (or comment) and I would very much like to talk with you more about it. Could we meet at freeze time, or at some other time that is mutually convenient?"

Avoid bluffing an answer to a question for which you do not have an answer. Nothing will cause you to lose credibility with young adolescent students any faster than faking an answer. There is nothing wrong with admitting that you do not know. It helps students realize that you are human. It helps them maintain an adequate self-esteem, realizing that they are okay. What is important is that you know where and how to find possible or tentative answers and that you help students develop that same knowledge and those same process skills.

Now, to reinforce your understanding, do Exercises 3.3 through 3.7.

EXERCISE 3.3: EXAMINING COURSE MATERIALS FOR LEVEL OF QUESTIONING AND EXPECTED THINKING

INSTRUCTIONS: It is often reported that a very high percentage of the questions found in textbooks, teacher guides, student workbooks, electronic materials, and tests are low level; that is they are devoted to factual recall. The purpose of this exercise is for you to examine course materials for the levels of questions presented to students and to learn what you can do to raise the level of expected student thinking. For a subject and grade level you intend to teach, examine materials mentioned for the questions posed to the students. Complete the exercise that follows; then share your findings with your classmates. Use additional paper if necessary.

1. Materials examined (include date of publication and grade level of target students): _____

   _____

   _____

2. Questions at the recall (lowest) level: _____

   _____

   _____

   _____

   _____

3. Questions at the processing (intermediate) level: _____

   _____

   _____

   _____

   _____

4. Questions at the application (highest) level: _____

   _____

   _____

   _____

   _____

5. Approximate percentage of questions at each level: _____
   a. Recall = _____%
   b. Processing = _____%
   c. Application = _____%

6. Did you find evidence of question-level sequencing? If so, describe it. _____

   _____

   _____

   _____

   _____

EXERCISE 3.3   *(continued)*

7. After sharing and discussing your results with your classmates, what do you conclude from this exercise?

_____

_____

_____

_____

8. When using instructional materials that you believe have a disproportionately high percentage of questions at the input (or recall) level, in addition to the two examples provided, what should or could you do?

Example 1: Have students scan chapter subheadings and develop higher-level cognitive questions based on the subheadings, which they would then answer through their reading.

Example 2: Require students to defend their answers to low-level cognitive chapter review and end-of-chapter questions with textual information and experience.

_____

_____

_____

_____

EXERCISE 3.4: OBSERVING THE COGNITIVE LEVELS OF CLASSROOM VERBAL INTERACTION

INSTRUCTIONS: The purpose of this exercise is to develop your skill in recognizing the levels of classroom questions. Arrange to visit a middle level classroom. In the spaces provided here, tally each time you hear a question (or statement) from the teacher that causes students to gather or recall information, to process information, or to apply or evaluate data. In the left-hand column you may want to write additional key words to assist your memory. After your observation, compare and discuss the results of this exercise with your colleagues.

School and class visited: _____

Date of observation: _____

Level	*Tallies of Level of Question or Statement*
Recall level (key words: *complete, count, define, describe,* and so on)	
Processing level (key words: *analyze, classify, compare,* and so on)	
Application level (key words: *apply, build, evaluate,* and so on)	

FOR YOUR NOTES

EXERCISE 3.5: PRACTICE IN RAISING QUESTIONS TO HIGHER LEVELS

INSTRUCTIONS: The purpose of this exercise is to further develop your skill in raising questions from one level to the next higher level. Complete the blank spaces with questions at the appropriate levels (for the last series, create your own recall question and then vary it for the higher levels). Share and discuss your responses with your classmates.

Recall Level	*Processing Level*	*Application Level*
1. How many of you read a newspaper today?	1. Why did you read a newspaper today?	1. Do you think the time will come when nobody reads a newspaper?
2. What was today's newspaper headline?	2. Why was that so important as to be a headline?	2. Do you think that news item will be in tomorrow's paper?
3. Who is the vice president of the United States today?	3. How does the work this vice president has done compare with that done by the previous vice president?	3. _____ _____ _____ _____ _____
4. How many presidents has the United States had?	4. _____ _____ _____ _____	4. _____ _____ _____ _____
5. _____ _____ _____ _____	5. _____ _____ _____ _____	5. _____ _____ _____ _____

FOR YOUR NOTES

EXERCISE 3.6: PRACTICE IN CREATING COGNITIVE QUESTIONS

INSTRUCTIONS: The purpose of this exercise is to provide practice in writing cognitive questions. Read the following passage. Then compose three questions about it that cause students to identify, list, and recall; three that cause students to analyze, compare, and explain; and three that cause students to predict, apply, and hypothesize. Share and check your questions with your peers.

We Are One

Truth, love, peace, and beauty,
We have sought apart
    but will find within, as our
Moods—explored, shared,
    questioned, and accepted—
Together become one and all.

Through life my friends
We can travel together,
for we now know
each could go it alone.

To assimilate our efforts into one,
While growing in accepting,
and trusting, and sharing the
    individuality of the other,
Is truly to enjoy our greatest gift—
Feeling—knowing love and compassion.

Through life my friends
We are together,
for we must know
we are one.

—R. D. Kellough

RECALL QUESTIONS

1. To identify _____

_____

_____

_____

2. To list _____

_____

_____

_____

3. To recall _____

_____

_____

_____

EXERCISE 3.6   *(continued)*

PROCESSING QUESTIONS

1. To analyze _____

   _____

   _____

   _____

   _____

2. To compare _____

   _____

   _____

   _____

   _____

3. To explain _____

   _____

   _____

   _____

   _____

   _____

APPLICATION QUESTIONS

1. To predict _____

   _____

   _____

   _____

   _____

2. To apply _____

   _____

   _____

   _____

   _____

3. To hypothesize _____

   _____

   _____

   _____

   _____

EXERCISE 3.7: A COOPERATIVE LEARNING AND MICRO PEER TEACHING EXERCISE IN THE USE OF QUESTIONING—MICRO PEER TEACHING I

INSTRUCTIONS: The purpose of this exercise is to practice preparing and asking questions that are designed to lead student thinking from the lowest level to the highest. Before class, prepare a five-minute lesson for posing questions that will guide the learner from lowest to highest levels of thinking. Teaching will be one-on-one, in groups of four, with each member of the group assuming a particular role—teacher, student, judge, or recorder. Each of the four members of your group will assume each of those roles once for five minutes. (If there are only three members in a group, the roles of judge and recorder can be combined during each five-minute lesson; or, if there are five members in the group, one member can sit out each round, or two can work together as a judge.) Each member of the group should have his or her own tally sheet.

Suggested Lesson Topics

- Teaching styles

- Characteristics of young adolescents

- Learning styles of students

- Evaluation of learning achievement

- A skill or hobby

- Teaching competencies

- A particular teaching strategy

- Student teaching and what it will really be like

Each of your group members should keep the following role descriptions in mind:

- *Teacher (sender).*   Pose recall (input), processing, and application (output) questions related to one of the topics above or to any topic you choose.

- *Student (receiver).*   Respond to the questions of the teacher.

- *Judge.*   Identify the level of each question or statement used by the teacher *and* the level of the student's response.

- *Recorder.*   Tally the number of each level of question or statement used by the teacher (S = sender) as indicated by the judge; also tally the level of student responses (R = receiver). Record any problems encountered by your group.

EXERCISE 3.7   *(continued)*

		TALLY SHEET			
		Minute	**Input**	**Processing**	**Output**
Sender _____ (Teacher)		1 S			
Receiver _____ (Student)		R			
		2 S			
		R			
		3 S			
		R			
		4 S			
		R			
		5 S			
		R			

		TALLY SHEET			
		Minute	**Input**	**Processing**	**Output**
Sender _____ (Teacher)		1 S			
Receiver _____ (Student)		R			
		2 S			
		R			
		3 S			
		R			
		4 S			
		R			
		5 S			
		R			

SUMMARY

Central to helping young adolescents in their learning and in their learning to learn is helping them to understand and develop their intelligent behaviors. This chapter presented a great deal of information about one teaching strategy in particular, which will be perhaps the most important one in your instructional repertoire. Questioning is the cornerstone to meaningful thinking, communication, learning, and real-world problem solving. The art of its use in instruction is something you will continue to develop throughout your teaching career.

This completes our look at the preactive phase of teaching and learning today. You are now ready to begin the planning phase. For that, the next chapter focuses attention on ways of planning and establishing an effective classroom environment within which to carry out your professional responsibilities.

QUESTIONS FOR CLASS DISCUSSION

1. Explain some specific ways you can help students develop their skills in thinking and learning. Explain how you will determine that students have raised their skill level in thinking and learning.
2. Have you ever noticed that some teachers seem to anticipate a lower-level response to their questions from particular students? Discuss your answer and the reasons for such teacher behavior with your classmates.
3. Do you believe a teacher should verbally respond to every student's comment or question? Explain why or why not. If not, on what basis does the teacher decide when and how to respond?
4. Explain the meaning of this statement: Rather than looking for what students can reiterate, we should look for what they can demonstrate and produce. Explain why you agree or disagree with the concept.
5. To what extent should (or can) a middle level classroom teacher allow student questions to determine content studied? To what extent should students' initial interest, or lack of interest, in a topic determine whether the topic gets taught?
6. It is claimed that questions stimulate certain kinds of thought responses. What mental operations must students engage in to answer this question: What is the most important reason that sea level deserts have a relatively small population of humans? (That is, what would the student need to know and in what sequence would they have to process information in order to answer the question?)
7. Explain why you believe it is or is not a good idea to assign reflective questions (i.e., open-ended, "thought" questions) for homework. What research evidence can you find to support or refute your opinion?
8. Is there ever a time when it is okay for a teacher to bluff an answer to a student's question? Explain and discuss your response with your classmates.
9. In groups of four, discuss with your classmates the extent to which, during your education, you personally have experienced exposure to high-level questioning. Discuss to what extent that experience will or will not strengthen your own ability to use questioning as an instructional tool. Discuss whether or not you feel that ability was strengthened further by the work you did for this chapter.
10. Have you ever witnessed a teacher using rapid-fire questioning, so rapid coming were the questioning and responses that there seemed little time for many students to think or to register any learning? Discuss the pros and cons of such classroom interaction.

INTERNET RESOURCES

Creative Teaching Associates **http://www.mastercta.com/**

Critical thinking about what is found on the Web
    http://www.ithaca.edu/library/training/think.html

Teacher Created Materials
    http://myconsumerguide.com/teacher_created_materials.htm

The Critical Thinking Co. **http://www.criticalthinking.com**

FOR FURTHER READING

Armone, M. P. (2003). *Using instructional design strategies to foster curiosity.* ED479842. Syracuse, NY: ERIC Clearinghouse on Information & Technology.

Becker, R. R. (2000). The critical role of students' questions in literacy development. *Educational Forum, 64*(3), 261–271.

Bintz, W. P., & Williams, L. (2005). Questioning techniques of fifth and sixth grade reading teachers. *Middle School Journal, 37*(1), 45–52.

Black, S. (2001). Ask me a question: How teachers use inquiry in a classroom. *American School Board Journal, 188*(5), 43–45.

Caine, G., McClintic, C., & Klimek, K. (2005). *12 brain/mind learning principles in action.* Thousand Oaks, CA: Corwin Press.

Chin, C., Brown, D. E., & Bruce, B. C. (2002). Student-generated questions: A meaningful aspect of learning in science. *International Journal of Science Education, 24,* 521–549.

Copeland, M. (2005). *Socratic circles.* Portland, ME: Stenhouse.

Costa, A. L. (Ed.). (2001). *Developing minds: A resource book for teaching thinking.* 3d ed. Alexandria, VA: Association for Supervision and Curriculum Development.

Cuccio-Schirripa, S., & Steiner, H. E. (2000). Enhancement and analysis of science question level for middle school students. *Journal of Research in Science Teaching, 37,* 210–224.

Gauthier, L. R. (2000). The role of questioning: Beyond comprehension's front door. *Reading Horizons, 40,* 239–252.

Harris, R. L. (2000). Batting 1,000: Questioning techniques in student-centered classrooms. *Clearing House, 74*(1), 25–26.

Kohn, A. (2004). Challenging students—and how to have more of them. *Phi Delta Kappan, 86,* 184–194.

Koufetta-Menicou, C., & Scaife, J. (2000). Teachers' questions—types and significance in science education. *School Science Review, 81*(296), 79–84.

Martinez, M. E. (2006). What is metacognition? *Phi Delta Kappan, 87,* 696–699.

Morocco, C. C., Walker, A., & Lewis, L. R. (2003). Access to a schoolwide thinking curriculum: Leadership challenges and solutions. *Journal of Special Education Leadership, 16*(1), 5–14.

Reeves, C. A., & Reeves, R. (2003). Encouraging students to think about how they think! *Mathematics Teaching in the Middle School, 8,* 374–378.

Vavilis, B., & Vavilis, S. L. (2004). Why are we learning this? What is this stuff good for, anyway? *Phi Delta Kappan, 86,* 282–287.

Walsh, J. A., & Sattes, B. D. (2005). *Quality questioning.* Thousand Oaks, CA: Corwin Press.

4

The Learning Environment
Planning and Managing the Classroom

Scott Cunningham/Merrill

> After considering what experienced others have to say, the final decision is one of many that you as teacher must make and will be influenced by your own thinking and unique situation. That fact is what makes a teacher a professional.

To become and to remain an effective teacher with a minimum of distractions in the classroom, you must: (a) apply your knowledge of the characteristics and needs of young adolescents (knowledge gained from your prior coursework and reviewed in Chapter 1); (b) initiate, practice, develop, and model the behaviors that facilitate their learning (Chapters 2 and 3); and (c) do so in a conducive

learning environment. The latter is the principal focus of this chapter.

A successful school is an inviting, supportive, and safe place, a joyful community that promotes in-depth learning and enhances students' physical and emotional well-being.
National Middle School Association (2003, p. 12)

As you are probably becoming quite aware that although competent teaching may be as much an intuitive art as it is a science, still it does not just happen. It begins with (a) the deliberative planning and arranging of

109

the learning environment and continues with (b) selection of the curriculum and (c) the thoughtful planning of each phase of the learning process. This chapter deals with the first of these, with the planning, establishing, and managing of a classroom environment most conducive to young adolescent student learning. Selection of the curriculum and planning each phase of the learning process follows beginning with Chapter 5.

To say that a learning environment is "conducive" means it is one that is caring and responsive, that has as its sole purpose that of aiding each learner in making the transitions necessary to succeed in school and in life. The planning, establishment, and managing of a conducive classroom learning environment derives from one's knowledge about young adolescents and how they learn, and from careful thought and planning, and should never be left for the beginning teacher to learn on the job in a sink-or-swim situation.

A *conducive classroom learning environment* is one that is emotionally safe, that helps students to perceive the importance of what is being taught, that helps them realize they can achieve, and is instructive and supportive in the procedures for doing it. While important that they develop emotionally, that they learn impulse control and to delay their need for gratification young adolescents are more willing to spend time on a learning task when they perceive value or reward in doing so, when they possess some ownership in planning and carrying out the task, and when they feel they can, in fact, accomplish the task.

The teacher who goes the extra mile to earn a child's trust, who offers a nuanced response to each learner and each classroom, may account for far more variation in children's performance than the exact method of instruction used.

Deborah Meier (2005, p. 8)

Thoughtful and thorough planning of your procedures for classroom management is as important an element of your preactive phase of instruction as is the planning of the curriculum with its units and lessons. Indeed, from an analysis of half a century of research studies it is concluded that establishment and management of the classroom learning environment is the single most important factor influencing student learning (Want, Haertel, & Walberg, 1993).

This chapter presents guidelines and resources to help you establish and manage a classroom environment that is emotionally safe and conducive to the learning of each and every student.

OBJECTIVES

Specifically, upon completion of this chapter you should be able to:

1. Distinguish between the concepts of consequences and punishment as related to classroom management.

2. Describe a teacher's reasonable first reaction to various student behaviors, such as one who is aggressively violent, one who is bullying another student, one who habitually lies, one who is defiant, one who tosses paper from across the room towards the wastebasket, one who knowingly steals, and one who is just sitting and staring out the window.

3. Use examples to describe how each of the following contributes to effective classroom control: a positive approach, well-planned lessons, a productive start of the school term, classroom procedures and rules, consistency but with professional judgment in enforcing procedures and rules, correction of student misbehavior, and classroom management.

4. Describe ways you can help students establish and maintain self-control.

5. Describe important perceptions that must be in place.

6. Describe planning you would do for the first week of school.

7. Describe the importance of transitions and the characteristics of an effective instructional transition.

8. Describe the meaning and give an example of *sequenced consequences* as used in response to inappropriate student behavior.

9. Differentiate between direct and indirect intervention to refocus a student and describe situations where you would be most likely to use each.

10. Prepare an initial draft of your proposed classroom management system.

THE IMPORTANCE OF PERCEPTIONS

We all know of, or have heard of, teachers who obtain the very best from their students, even from those students many teachers find most challenging to teach. Regardless of individual circumstances, those teachers

- know, when given adequate support, all children can learn
- expect the best from each student
- establish a classroom environment that motivates students to do their best
- manage their classrooms so class time is efficiently used, that is, with the least amount of distraction to the learning process.

> Unless you believe your students can learn, they will not. Unless you believe you can teach them, you will not. Unless your students believe they can learn and until they want to learn, they will not.

Regardless of how well planned you are for the instruction, certain perceptions by students must be in place to support the successful implementation of those plans. It is the teacher's duty to help children develop and sustain these perceptions; it is the task of this chapter to illustrate how best to perform that duty. Students must perceive

- the classroom environment as being supportive of their efforts
- that you care about their learning
- that you respect them as human beings
- that they are welcome in your classroom
- the expected learning as being challenging, but not impossible
- the target learning outcomes as being worthy of their time and effort to try and achieve.

CLASSROOM CONTROL—ITS MEANING— PAST AND PRESENT

Classroom control frequently is of the greatest concern to beginning teachers—and they have cause to be concerned. Even experienced teachers sometimes find control difficult, particularly in schools where so many students come to school with so much psychological baggage and have already become alienated as a result of negative experiences in their lives.

In one respect, being a classroom teacher is analogous to being a truck driver who must remain alert while going down a steep and winding grade; otherwise, the truck will most assuredly get out of control, veer off the highway, and crash. This chapter has been thoughtfully designed to help you with your concerns about control—and to help you avoid a crash.

Historical Meaning of Classroom Control

To set the stage for your comprehension, consider what the term *classroom control* has meant historically and what it means today. In the 1800s, instead of classroom control, educators spoke of classroom discipline, and that meant punishment. Such an interpretation was consistent with the then-popular learning theory that assumed children were innately bad and that inappropriate behavior could be prevented by strictness, or treated with punishment. Schools of the mid-1800s have been described as being "wild and unruly places," and "full of idleness and disorder" (Hyman & D'Allessandro, 1984, p. 24).

By the early 1900s, educators were asking, "Why are the children still misbehaving?" The accepted answer was that they were misbehaving because of the rigid punitive system. On this point, the era of progressive education began, providing students more freedom to decide what they would learn. The teacher's job, then, became one of providing a rich classroom of resources and materials to stimulate the student's natural curiosity. And since the system no longer would be causing misbehavior, punishment would no longer be necessary. Classes of the 1930s that were highly permissive, however, turned out to cause more anxiety than the restrictive classes of the 1800s.

Today's Meaning of Classroom Control and the Concept of Classroom Management

Today, rather than classroom "discipline," educators speak of classroom control, the process of controlling student behavior in the classroom. The most effective teacher is one who is in control of classroom events rather than controlled by them. Classroom control is an important aspect of the broader concept of classroom management. Classroom control is a component of a management plan designed to:

- prevent inappropriate student behavior
- help children develop self-control
- suggest procedures for dealing with inappropriate student behavior.

Effective teaching requires a well-organized, businesslike classroom in which motivated students work diligently at their learning tasks, free from distractions and interruptions. Providing such a setting for learning requires careful thought and preparation, and is called *effective classroom management*. Effective classroom management is the process of organizing and conducting a classroom so that it maximizes student learning. As a new teacher, it is important you not underestimate how difficult this process can be. Please read on with interest and attention.

A teacher's procedures for classroom control reflect that teacher's philosophy about how young adolescents learn and the teacher's interpretation and commitment to the school's stated mission. In sum, those procedures represent the teacher's concept of classroom management. Although often eclectic in their approaches, today's teachers of young adolescents share a concern for selecting management techniques that enhance student self-esteem and that help students learn how to assume control of their behavior and ownership of their learning.

Although some middle level schools subscribe heavily to one approach or another, many others are more eclectic, having evolved from the historical works of several leading authorities. Let's consider what some authorities have said. To assist your understanding, refer to Table 4.1, which illustrates the main ideas of each authority and provides a comparison of their recommended approaches. As was said in the preceding paragraph, the guidelines and suggestions that are presented throughout this chapter represent an eclectic approach, borrowing from many of these authorities.

Classroom Management: Contributions of Some Leading Authorities

You are probably familiar with the term *behavior modification*, which describes several high-control techniques for changing behavior in an observable and predictable way; with **B. F. Skinner's** (Skinner, 1968, 1971) ideas about how students learn and how behavior can be modified by

Table 4.1   Comparing Approaches to Classroom Management

Authority	To Know What Is Going On	To Provide Smooth Transitions
Canter/Jones	Realize that the student has the right to choose how to behave in your class with understanding of the consequences that will follow his or her choice.	Insist on decent, responsible behavior.
Dreikurs/Nelsen/Albert	Realize that the student wants status, recognition, and a feeling of belonging. Misbehavior is associated with mistaken goals of getting attention, seeking power, getting revenge, and wanting to be left alone.	Identify a mistaken student goal; act in ways that do not reinforce these goals.
Ginott	Communicate with the student to find out his/her feelings about a situation and about him/herself.	Invite student cooperation.
Glasser/Gordon/Sprich/Marshall	Realize that the student is a rational being; he/she can control his/her own behavior.	Help the student make good choices; good choices produce good behavior, and bad choices produce bad behavior.
Kounin	Develop *withitness,* a skill enabling you to see what is happening in all parts of the classroom at all times.	Avoid jerkiness, which consists of thrusts (giving directions before your group is ready), dangles (leaving one activity dangling in the verbal air, starting another one, and then returning to the first activity), flip-flops (terminating one activity, beginning another one, and then returning to the first activity you terminated).
Skinner	Realize value of nonverbal interaction (i.e., smiles, pats, and handshakes) to communicate to students that you know what is going on.	Realize that smooth transitions may be part of your procedures for awarding reinforcers (i.e., points and tokens) to reward appropriate behavior.

using reinforcers (rewards); and with how his principles of behavior shaping have been extended by others.

Behavior modification begins with four steps: (a) identify the behavior to be modified; (b) record how often and under what conditions that behavior occurs; (c) cause a change by reinforcing a desired behavior with a positive reinforcer; and (d) choose the type of positive reinforcers to award—*activity* or *privilege reinforcers*—such as choice of playing a game, decorating the classroom, choice at a classroom learning center, freed without penalty from doing an assignment or test, running an errand for the teacher; *social reinforcers,* such as verbal attention or private praise, and nonverbal such as proximity of teacher to student, and facial expression of approval, such as a wink or smile, or bodily expression of approval, such as a thumbs up or high five; *graphic*

reinforcers, such as numerals and symbols; *tangible reinforcers,* such as edibles, badges, certificates, stickers, or books; and *token reinforcers,* such as points, stars, or script that can be accumulated and cashed in later for a tangible reinforcer, or tickets that can be used for something like a school athletic or musical event.

Using an approach that emphasizes both reinforcement for appropriate behaviors and punishment or consequences for inappropriate behaviors, **Lee Canter** and **Marlene Canter** developed their *assertive discipline* model that emphasizes four major points (Canter & Canter, 1992). First, as a teacher, you have professional rights in your classroom and should expect appropriate student behavior. Second, your students have rights to choose how to behave in your classroom, and you should plan limits for inappropriate behavior. Third, an

To Maintain Group Alertness	To Involve Students	To Attend to Misbehavior
Set clear limits and consequences; follow through consistently; state what you expect; state the consequences, and why the limits are needed.	Use firm tone of voice; keep eye contact; use nonverbal gestures as well as verbal statements; use hints, questions, and direct messages in requesting student behavior; give and receive compliments.	Follow through with your promises and the reasonable, previously stated consequences that have been established in your class.
Provide firm guidance and leadership.	Allow students to have a say in establishing rules and consequences in your class.	Make it clear that unpleasant consequences will follow inappropriate behavior.
Model the behavior you expect to see in your students.	Build student's self-esteem.	Give a message that addresses the situation and does not attack the student's character.
Understand that class rules are essential.	Realize that classroom meetings are effective means for attending to rules, behavior, and discipline.	Accept no excuses for inappropriate behavior; see that reasonable consequences always follow.
Avoid slowdowns (delays and time wasting) that can be caused by overdwelling (too much time spent on explanations) and by fragmentation (breaking down an activity into several unnecessary steps). Develop a group focus (active participation by all students in the group) through accountability (holding all students accountable for the concept of the lesson) and by attention (seeing all the students and using unison responses as well as individual responses).	Avoid boredom by providing a feeling of progress for the students, by offering challenges, by varying class activities, by changing the level of intellectual challenge, by varying lesson presentations, and by using many different learning materials and aids.	Understand that teacher correction influences behavior of other nearby students (the ripple effect).
Set rules, rewards, and consequences; emphasize that responsibility for good behavior rests with each student.	Involve students in "token economies," in contracts, and in charting own behavior performance.	Provide tangibles to students who follow the class rules; represent tangibles as "points" for the whole class to use to "purchase" a special activity.

assertive discipline approach means you clearly state your expectations in a firm voice and explain the boundaries for behavior. And fourth, you should plan a system of positive consequences (e.g., positive messages home, awards and rewards, special privileges) for appropriate behavior, and establish consequences (e.g., time-out, withdrawal of privileges, parent/guardian conference) for inappropriate student misbehavior, and you follow through in a consistent way.

In his *logical consequences* approach, **Rudolf Dreikurs** emphasized six points (Dreikurs & Cassel, 1972; Dreikurs, Grunwald, & Pepper, 1982). First, be fair, firm, and friendly, and involve students in developing and implementing class rules. Second, students need to clearly understand the rules and the logical consequences for misbehavior. For example, a logical conse-

quence for a student who has written graffiti on a school wall would be to either clean the wall or pay for a school custodian to do it. Third, allow the students to be responsible not only for their own actions but also for influencing others to maintain appropriate behavior in your classroom. Fourth, encourage students to show respect for themselves and for others, and provide each student with a sense of belonging to the classroom. Fifth, recognize and encourage student goals of belonging, gaining status, and gaining recognition. And sixth, recognize but do not reinforce correlated student goals of getting attention, seeking power, and taking revenge.

Continuing the work of Dreikurs, **Linda Albert** (1989, rev. 1996) developed a *cooperative discipline* model. The cooperative discipline model makes use of Dreikurs' fundamental concepts, with emphasis added on the "three C's": capable, connect, and contribute. Also building upon the work of Dreikurs, **Jane Nelsen** (Nelsen, 1987; Nelsen, Lott, & Glenn, 1993) provides guidelines for helping children develop positive feelings of self. Key points made by Nelsen and that are reflected throughout this resource guide, include: (a) use natural and logical consequences as a means to inspire a positive classroom atmosphere, (b) understand that children have goals that drive them toward misbehavior (attention, power, revenge, and assumed adequacy), (c) use kindness (student retains dignity) and firmness when administering consequences for a student's misbehavior, (d) establish a climate of mutual respect, (e) use class meetings to give students ownership in problem solving, and (f) offer encouragement as a means of inspiring self-evaluation and focusing on the student's behaviors.

William Glasser (1965, 1969, 1986, 1990, 1993) developed his concept of *reality therapy* (i.e., the condition of the present, rather than of the past, contributes to inappropriate behavior) for the classroom. Glasser emphasizes that students have a responsibility to learn at school and to maintain appropriate behavior while there. He emphasizes that with the teacher's help, students can make appropriate choices about their behavior in school—can, in fact, learn self-control. Finally, he suggests holding classroom meetings that are devoted to establishing rules and identifying standards for student behavior, matters of misbehavior, and the consequences of misbehavior. Since the publication of his first book in 1965, Glasser has expanded his message to include the student needs of belonging and love, control, freedom, and fun, asserting that if these needs are ignored and unattended at school, students are bound to fail (Glasser, 1997).

Today's commitment to *quality education* is largely derived from the recent work of Glasser and the corresponding concept of the *personal-centered classrooms* as advanced by **Carl Rogers** and **H. Jerome Freiberg** in their 1994 book *Freedom to Learn* (Columbus, OH: Merrill). In schools committed to quality education and the person-centered classroom, students feel a sense of belonging, enjoy some degree of power of self-discipline, have fun learning, and experience a sense of freedom in the process (Freiberg, 1997, 1999; Jackson & Davis, 2000).

Paul Gathercoal built his *judicious discipline* model on a synthesis of professional ethics, good quality educational practice, and democratic principles and students' constitutional rights as outlined especially in the 1st, 4th, and 14th Amendments to the U.S. Constitution (Gathercoal, 1997). By allowing students the opportunity to experience individual freedoms and encouraging them to learn and practice the responsibilities emanating from their individual rights, students learn how to govern themselves. A number of schools report success in reducing student hostile behaviors by using a combination of judicious discipline and class meetings (Freiberg, 1999; McEwan & Gathercoal, 2000).

Haim G. Ginott emphasized ways for teacher and student to communicate in his communication model. He advised a teacher's sending a clear message (or messages) about situations rather than about the child. Ginott also emphasized that teachers must model the behavior they expect from their students. Ginott's suggested messages are those that express feelings appropriately, acknowledge students' feelings, give appropriate direction, and invite cooperation (Ginott, 1971; Manning & Bucher, 2001).

Thomas Gordon (1989) emphasizes influence over control, and decries use of reinforcement (i.e., rewards and punishment) as an ineffective tool for achieving a positive influence over a child's behavior. Rather than using reinforcements for appropriate behavior and punishment for inappropriate behaviors, Gordon advocates encouragement and development of student self-control and self-regulated behavior. To have a positive influence and to encourage self-control, the teacher (and school) should provide a rich and positive learning environment with rich and stimulating learning activities. Specific teacher behaviors include active listening (exemplified, for example, by maintaining eye contact, rephrasing what the student has said, and asking relevant questions), sending I-messages (rather than you-messages), shifting from I-messages to listening when there is student resistance to an I-message, clearly identifying ownership of problems to the student when such is the case (i.e., not assuming ownership if it is a student's problem), and encouraging collaborative problem solving.

Fredric Jones (1987) also promotes the idea of helping students support their own self-control, essentially, however, by way of a negative reinforcement method—rewards follow wanted behavior. Preferred activity time (PAT), for example, is an invention derived from the Jones model. The Jones model makes four recommendations. First, you should properly structure your classroom so students understand the rules (the expectation standards for classroom behavior) and procedures (the means for accomplishing routine tasks). Second, you maintain control by selecting appropriate instructional strategies. Third, you build patterns of cooperative work. Finally, you develop appropriate backup methods for dealing with inappropriate student behavior.

Jacob Kounin (1970) is well known for his identification of the *ripple effect* (i.e., the effect of a teacher's response to one student's misbehavior on students whose behavior was appropriate) and of *withitness* and *overlapping ability* (both of which are discussed in Chapter 2).

Figure 4.1   Developing the personal classroom management system.

MY EMERGING PLAN FOR CLASSROOM MANAGEMENT

Grade level (or range) _____   My name _____

Plans Before the First Day

1. Describe your classroom with respect to the physical room arrangement and organization and the positive and caring classroom community that you aim to create.
2. Describe communication you will initiate with your students and their families prior to the first day of school.
3. Describe characteristics of your classroom that will signal to the students that it is a friendly and safe place to be.
4. Describe how you will get to know the students and what you will do to help the students get to know you and each other.

The First Day

5. Describe how you will greet the students when they arrive for the first day.
6. Describe the rules or procedural expectations that you will have already in place and how they will be presented to the students.
7. Describe how you will have students contribute to these rules and expectations.
8. Describe your classroom procedures for
   - absences; making up missed work and instruction
   - assigning helpers for classroom jobs such as taking care of pets, plants, the calendar, bathroom monitor, and so forth
   - being in the classroom before and after school, and at recess and lunch time
   - bringing plants and pets into the classroom
   - collecting notes, money, and forms
   - distributing and collecting papers and materials
   - eating and drinking in the classroom
   - going to the bathroom
   - late arrival and early dismissal
   - movement in the halls
   - storing personal belongings
   - taking attendance
   - using the classroom sink (if there is one)
   - using the pencil sharpener
   - using the teacher's desk
   - using the water fountain
   - using other materials and equipment
   - wearing hats and other articles of clothing in the classroom
   - what to do in an emergency situation
   - when a visitor comes into the classroom
9. Describe the class or morning opening; the class or day's closure.

Managing the Curriculum

10. Describe how you will help the students with their organization and assignments.
11. Describe your homework expectations. Will there be homework? How much and how often? Will parents and guardians be informed? If so, how? What is their involvement to be? Is there a school homework hotline?
12. Describe your procedure for incomplete, unacceptable, or incorrect student work? Is there a recovery option?
13. Do you plan to provide comments feedback, or corrections on student work?
14. Will you use marks of some sort—grades, value words, figures, and so forth?
15. Will students be rewarded for their group work? How will you assess group learning? How will you assess individual learning from group work?
16. Describe the student portfolio expectation. Where will the portfolios be stored? When will students work on their portfolios?
17. Describe your plan for communication with parents/guardians.

(continued)

Figure 4.1 (*continued*)

Maintaining Classroom Relations and Personal Behavior

18. Describe how you will bring an off-task student back on task.
19. Describe how students will know what is and what is not an appropriate level of classroom noise.
20. Describe how you will signal a need for hands and when, if ever, it is okay to call out without using hands.
21. Describe how you will indicate your support for appropriate student behavior.
22. Describe how you will discourage inappropriate student behavior.
23. Describe your order of indirect and direct behavior intervention strategies.
24. Describe how you will signal your need for attention from the class from a distracted student.
25. Describe how you will respond when two errant behaviors are happening simultaneously but at opposing locations in the classroom.

When the Going Gets Tough

26. Describe your pattern of escalating consequences.
27. Describe how you will deal with disrespectful, inappropriate comments from students.
28. Describe how you will respond to remarks that are sexist or racist or that stereotype people in inappropriate and cruel ways.
29. Describe how you will respond to serious and dangerous student behaviors.
30. Identify one adult you can go to for support.

DEVELOPING YOUR OWN EFFECTIVE APPROACH TO CLASSROOM MANAGEMENT

As you review these contributions to today's approaches to effective classroom management, the expert opinions as well as the research evidence will remind you of the importance of doing the following:

1. concentrating your attention on desirable student behaviors
2. quickly and appropriately attending to inappropriate behavior, especially that which is lingering or likely to become disruptive
3. maintaining alertness to all that is happening in your classroom
4. providing smooth transitions, keeping the entire class on task, and preventing dead time (i.e., time when students have nothing to do)
5. involving students by providing challenges, class meetings, ways of establishing rules and consequences, opportunities to receive and return compliments, and chances to build self-control and self-esteem.

Using the criteria of your own perceptions, philosophy, feelings, values, knowledge, and perceptions, you are encouraged to construct a classroom environment and management system that is positive and effective for you and your students, and then to consistently apply it while still being willing to modify it as time and circumstances dictate. Use the guidelines shown in Figure 4.1 to begin the thinking process for developing your personal plan for classroom management—the process that begins now and continues in Exercise 4.3 and throughout your professional career.

PROVIDING A SUPPORTIVE LEARNING ENVIRONMENT

It is probably no surprise to you to hear that teachers whose classrooms are pleasant, positive, and challenging but supportive places to be, find that their students learn and behave better than do the students of teachers whose classroom atmospheres are harsh, negative, repressive, and unchallenging. What follows now are specific suggestions for making your classroom a pleasant, positive, and challenging place, that is, an environment that encourages and supports student learning.

Consider the Physical Layout

There is much in the arrangement of the classroom that can either contribute to or help prevent classroom management problems. Certainly, there is no one best way to arrange a classroom. To the extent allowed by the room, the arrangement should be kept flexible so students may be deployed in the ways most suitable for accomplishing specific tasks. The primary guideline, however, is simple. Just as is true with adults, when young adolescents are seated side by side or facing one another, it is perfectly natural for them to talk to each other. Therefore, if your desire is to encourage social interaction, as when using small-group learning, seat students of groups close together; if you would rather they work interdependently, such as when taking independent achievement tests, separate them to the extent possible.

Some teachers have students at the start of the school year design personal space dividers to provide privacy during testing and other independent activities. Attaching three approximately 8 × 10-inch rectangular sections of cardboard can make space dividers. The divider is placed standing in front of the student making it impossible for neighboring students to see over or around. Dividers can be made from cardboard boxes or heavy folders of various sorts. Students enjoy being allowed to personalize their dividers.

It is unreasonable to place students in situations that encourage maximum interaction and then admonish or berate them for interacting, for whispering and talking. Sometimes, so as not to disturb the learning going on in neighboring classrooms, you may need to remind the students to keep their voices down. Some teachers even have a sign hung in the classroom where all can see that clearly designates the expected noise level on a given day or for a particular activity, such as *0* for *complete silence* (no talking), *1* for *whispering*, and a *2* for *talking aloud in a normal voice* (but within reason).

Create a Positive Ambiance

All students should feel welcome in your classroom and accepted by you as individuals of worth and dignity. Although these feelings and behaviors should be reciprocal, that is, expected of the children as well, they may have to begin with your frequent modeling of the behaviors expected of the students. You must help children know that any denial by you of a child's specific behavior is not a denial of that individual as a worthwhile person who is still welcomed into your classroom to learn as long as the child agrees to follow expected procedures.

Specific things you can do to create a positive classroom ambiance, some of which are repeated from preceding chapters and others that are addressed in later chapters, include:

- Admonish behavior, not persons.
- Assure that no discrimination is ever displayed against any individual student.

- Assure that every student in the classroom can see and hear all that he or she should be seeing or hearing. For example, students who have to strain to hear a teacher or other presenter may simply tune out and become increasingly inattentive and perhaps mischievous.
- Attend to the classroom's physical appearance and comfort—it is your place of work, show pride in that fact. Consider this: a study with eighth-grade students suggests that in a classroom atmosphere enhanced with a pleasant scented fragrance students require fewer redirections of their behavior from the teacher (Gabriel, 1999).

Questions for Self-Reflection for Establishing a Conducive Learning Environment

Does Your Classroom Attractively Display . . .

- Agreed-upon classroom rules and procedures, a few major ones?
- Benchmark curriculum standards, perhaps the most important ones, with scoring rubrics?
- Helpful information about the expected mechanics for writing?
  - Photographs of happy and proud students—current and past—in action?
  - Reminders about procedures and deadlines for homework?
  - Samples of exemplary student work, including writing and long-term projects (with or without student names, depending on school policy)?
- Student-created murals and collages that include all students, helping each feel that he or she belongs?

- In encouraging desirable student behavior, phrase directions in positive rather than negative language, using "dos" rather than "do nots."
- Be an interesting person and an optimistic and enthusiastic teacher.
- Encourage students to set high yet realistic goals for themselves, and then show them how to work in increments toward meeting their goal—letting each know that you are confident in the child's ability to achieve.
- Help students develop the skills necessary for collaborative and cooperative learning.
- Involve students in every aspect of their learning, including the planning of learning activities, thereby giving them partial ownership and responsibility in their learning.
- Make the learning enjoyable and even fun, at least to the extent possible and reasonable.
- Recognize and reward truly positive behaviors and individual successes, no matter how meager they might seem to be.

- Send positive and easily understood messages home to parents or guardians, even if you have to get help to write the message in the language of the student's home.
- Use varied, interesting, developmentally appropriate, and motivating learning activities.

Behaviors to Avoid when Using Encouragement to Motivate Children.   Two items in the preceding list are statements about giving encouragement. When using encouragement to motivate student learning, there are a few important behaviors that you should *avoid* because they inhibit learning.

- Avoid comparing one child with another, or one class of students with another.
- Avoid encouraging competition among students except when all students have equal opportunity to win, when winning is determined primarily by degree of effort (and perhaps a degree of luck) rather than by ability level, and when reactions to the outcome emphasize the positive (i.e., winners are congratulated but losers are not criticized or ridiculed; the accomplishments of the class as a whole, not just of the winners, are acknowledged) (Good & Brophy, 2003).
- Avoid ever giving up or appearing to give up on any child.
- Avoid telling a student how much better he or she could be.
- Avoid using qualifying statements, such as "I like what you did, but . . ." or "It's about time."

Get to Know Your Students as People

For classes to move forward smoothly and efficiently, they should fit the learners' learning styles, learning capacities, developmental needs, and interests. To make the learning meaningful and longest lasting, build curriculum around student interests, capacities, perceptions, and perspectives. Therefore, you need to know your students well enough to be able to provide learning experiences that they will find interesting, valuable, intrinsically motivating, challenging, and rewarding. Knowing your students is at least as important as knowing subject-matter content (Hoffman & Levak, 2003). Of course, looping and small learning communities help teachers to get to know their students as people. Whether or not those opportunities immediately avail themselves, the following paragraphs describe a number of things you can do to get to know your students as people.

Quickly Learn and Use Student Names.   Like everyone else, young adolescents appreciate being recognized and addressed by name. Quickly learning and using their names is an important motivating strategy.

Be certain you use the name the student wishes to be called by; young adolescents in particular seem to be prone to frequent changing of their given names and will act insulted when called by something other than what they prefer. Some teachers avoid the problem by using only surnames. One technique for learning names quickly is to take snapshot photographs of each student on the first day. Later, students could use the photographs as a portion of the covers of their learning portfolios or desktop space dividers. Another technique for learning names quickly is to use a seating chart. Laminate the seating chart onto an attractive, neon-colored (gives students a visual focus) clipboard that you can carry in class. Many teachers prefer to assign permanent seats and then make seating charts from which they can unobtrusively check the roll while students are doing seatwork. It is usually best to get your students into the lesson before taking roll and before doing other housekeeping chores. Ways of assigning student seating are discussed later in this chapter (see "The First Day").

Addressing students by name every time you speak to them helps you to learn and remember their names. Be sure to quickly learn to pronounce their names correctly; that helps in making a positive impression. Another helpful way to learn student names is to return papers yourself by calling student names and then handing the papers to them, paying careful attention to look at each student and make mental notes that may help you associate names with faces.

Classroom Sharing During the First Week of School. During the first week of school many teachers take time each day to have students present information about themselves and/or about the day's assignment. For instance, perhaps five or six students are selected each day to answer questions such as "What name would you like to be called by?" "Where did you attend school last year?" "Tell us about your hobbies and other interests, or about your summer." "What interested you about last night's reading, or yesterday's lesson?"

How the student answers such questions or participates in such activities can be as revealing as is the information (or the lack thereof) that the student does share. From the sharing, you sometimes get clues about additional information you would like about the student.

Observe Students in the Classroom—Develop and Practice Your Withitness.   During learning activities the wise teacher is constantly moving around the classroom and is alert to the individual behavior (nonverbal and verbal) of each child in the class, whether the student is on task or gazing off and perhaps thinking about other things. Be cautious, however; just because a student is gazing out the window does not automatically mean the student is not thinking about the learning task. During group work is a particularly good time to observe students and get to know more about each one's skills and interests.

Observations of and Conversations with Students Outside the Classroom.

Another way to learn more about students is from observing them outside class, for example at athletic events, performing arts presentations, lunch time (teachers find this is an excellent time to get to know their students as well as to provide informal guidance/counseling by opening their classrooms at noon for a brown-bag lunch with any students who wish to come), intramural activities, during advisory or homeroom or freeze time, in the hallways, from home visits, and at club meetings. Observations made from outside the classroom can give information about student personalities, friendships, interests, and potentialities. For instance, you may find that a student who seems phlegmatic, lackadaisical, or uninterested in the learning activities in your classroom is a real fireball on the playing field, or a major mover and shaker on the school's student council, or at some other student gathering.

Conferences and Interviews with Students.

Conferences with students, and sometimes with family members as well, afford yet another opportunity to show that you are genuinely interested in each student as a person as well as a student. Some teachers and teaching teams plan and conduct a series of conferences, even home visits, during the first few weeks in which, individually or in small groups of three or four, students are interviewed by the teacher or by members of the teaching team. Block scheduling is especially conducive to teacher-parent/guardian-student conferences. Such conferences and interviews are managed by using open-ended questions. The teacher indicates by the questions, by listening and by nonjudgmental and empathic responses (i.e., being able to "step into the shoes" of the student, thereby understanding from where the student is coming), a genuine interest in the students. Keep in mind, however, that students who feel they have been betrayed by prior adult associations may at first be distrustful of your sincerity. In such instances, don't force it. Be patient, but do not hesitate to take advantage of the opportunity afforded by talking with individual students outside of class time. Investing a few minutes of time in a positive conversation with a student, during which you indicate a genuine interest in that student, can pay real dividends (although it may not always be immediately obvious) when it comes to that student's interest and learning in your classroom.

When using interviews with students, consider having the students individually write one or two questions that they would like you to answer in the interview. This ensures that the student is an active participant in the interview.

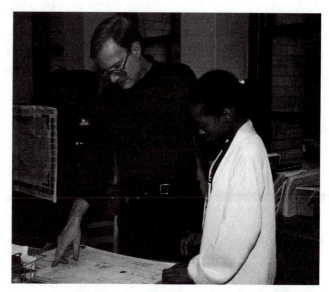

Laima Druskis/PH College

Student Writing and Questionnaires.

Much can be learned about students by what they write. It is important to encourage writing in your classroom, and (with varying degrees of intensity) to read everything that students write and submit to you, and to ask for clarification when needed. Useful for this are portfolios and journals (see index for locations).

Some teachers use open-ended, interest-discovering questionnaires. Student responses to questionnaires can provide ideas about how to tailor assignments for individual students. However, you must assure students that their answers are optional and that you are not invading their privacy.

In an interest-discovering questionnaire, students are asked to answer questions such as "When you read for fun or pleasure, what do you usually read?" "What are your favorite movies or TV shows?" "Who are your favorite performers?" "Athletes?" "Describe your favorite hobby or other nonschool-related activity."

Cumulative Record, Discussions with Colleagues, Experiential Backgrounds, Community and Home Visits.

The cumulative record for each child is maintained in the school office, and it contains information recorded from year to year by teachers and other school professionals. The information covers the student's academic background, standardized test scores, and extracurricular activities. However, the Family Educational Rights and Privacy Act (FERPA) of 1974, and its subsequent amendments and local policies, may forbid your viewing the record, except perhaps in collaboration with an administrator or counselor when you have a legitimate educational purpose for doing so. Although you must use discretion before arriving at any conclusion about information contained in the cumulative record, the record may afford information for getting to know a particular child better. Remember, though, a child's past is history and should not be held against that student, but used as a means for improved understanding of a student's experiences and current perceptions.

To better understand a student it is sometimes helpful to talk with other school personnel to learn of their perceptions and experiences with the student. Yet another way of getting to know students is to spend time in the neighborhoods in which they live, while, of course, always keeping your personal safety utmost in mind. Observe and listen, finding and noting things that you can use as examples, connections, or as learning activities.

Visiting the student's home is yet another strategy that can enable the teacher to better know a student. When doing a home visit it is a good idea to always be accompanied by another adult, perhaps another member of your teaching team.

PREPARATION PROVIDES CONFIDENCE AND SUCCESS

For successful classroom management, beginning the school term well may make all the difference in the world. Remember that you have only one opportunity to make a first and lasting impression. Therefore, you should appear at the first session as well prepared and as confident as possible.

Perhaps in the beginning you will feel nervous and apprehensive, but being ready and well prepared will help you at least to appear confident. It is probable that every beginning teacher is nervous and apprehensive to some degree; the secret is to not appear nervous. Being well prepared goes a long way in providing the confidence necessary to cloud feelings of nervousness. A slow, under-the-breadth counting to 10 at the start can be helpful, too. Then, if you proceed in a businesslike, matter-of-fact way, the impetus of your well-prepared beginning will, most likely, cause the day, week, and year to proceed pretty much as desired.

Effective Organization and Administration of Activities and Materials

In a well-managed classroom student movement about the classroom is routinized, controlled, and purposeful to the learning activities; students know what to do, have the materials needed to do it well, and remain on task while doing it. The classroom atmosphere is supportive; the assignments and procedures for doing them are clear; and the materials of instruction current, interesting, and readily available. At all times, the teacher is in control of events, rather than controlled by them, ensuring that students are spending their time on appropriate tasks. For your work—your teaching—to be most effective you must be skilled in managing that which occurs in your workplace—your classroom.

Natural Interruptions and Disruptions to Routine

As you devise and prepare to implement your management system (which will, by the way, be ever-evolving), you must also be aware of your own moods and high-stress days, and knowing that your own tolerance levels may vary some. Your students, too, are susceptible to personal problems and events that can be the sources of high stress. As you come to know your students well, you will be able to ascertain when certain children are under an inordinate amount of stress and anxiety, come to school sleepy or hungry, or are emotionally distraught from unfortunate happenings at home or elsewhere.

You must understand that classroom routines may be interrupted occasionally, especially on certain days and at certain times during the school year. Students will not have the same motivation and energy level on each and every day. Energy level also varies throughout the school day. Your anticipation of—and thoughtful and carefully planning during the preactive phase of instruction—periods of high- or low-energy levels will help protect your own mental health. Depending on a number of factors, periods of high-energy level might be:

- at the beginning of each school day
- before a field trip, a holiday, or a school event—such as a social event, picture day, athletic event, or a school assembly
- returning to school from a field trip
- a holiday, such as Valentine's Day or Halloween
- a day following a holiday
- a day a substitute teacher is present
- grade report day
- immediately before and/or after lunch
- on a minimum day
- toward the end of each school day, toward the end of school each Friday afternoon, and toward the end of the school term or year.

Although there may be no hard evidence, many experienced teachers will tell you that particularly troublesome days for classroom control are those days when there is a strong north wind or a full moon. One teacher jokingly (we suspect) said that on days when there is both a strong north wind and a full moon, she calls in sick.

How should you prepare for these so-called high-energy days? There are probably no specific guidelines that will work for all teachers in all situations in each instance from the list. However, these are days to which you need to pay extra attention during your planning, days that students could possibly be restless and more difficult to manage, days when you might need to be especially forceful and consistent in your enforcement of procedures, or even compassionate and more tolerant than usual. Plan instructional activities that might be more readily accepted by the students. In no instance is it our intent to imply that learning ceases and playtime takes over. What little instructional time is available to a teacher during a school year is too precious for that ever to happen.

CLASSROOM PROCEDURES AND GUIDELINES FOR ACCEPTABLE BEHAVIOR

It is impossible to overemphasize the importance of getting the school term off to a positive and productive beginning, so this section begins with a presentation of how that is done.

Starting off the School Term Well

There are but a few important key reminders to getting the school term off to an excellent beginning. Perhaps most important are for you to be *prepared* and to be *fair*. Preparation for the first day of school should include the determination of your classroom procedures and basic expectations for the behavior of the students while they are under your supervision. The procedures and expectations must be consistent with school policy, seem reasonable to your students, and in enforcing them you must be a fair and consistent professional. However, being coldly consistent is not the same as being fair and professional. As a teacher, you are a professional who deals in matters of human relations and who must exercise professional judgment. You are not a robot, nor are any of your students. Human beings differ from one another, and seemingly similar situations can vary substantially because the people involved are different. Consequently, your response, or lack of response, to each of two separate, but quite similar, situations may differ. To be most effective, learning must be enjoyable for students; it cannot be enjoyable when a teacher consistently acts like a marine drill sergeant. If a student infracts upon a rule, rather than assuming why, or seeming to not care why, or to overreact to the infraction, find out why before deciding your response.

In preparing your classroom management system, remember that too many rules and detailed procedures at the beginning can be a source of trouble. To avoid trouble, it is best at first to present only the minimum number of procedural expectations necessary for an orderly start to the school term. By the time students reach middle grades, unless they are recent newcomers to the United States, they likely already know the expected procedures, that is, the general rules of expected behavior, although some of their prior teachers may not always have been consistent or even fair about applying these expectations. And, too, your general rules of expected behavior might just be in conflict with the rules or lack thereof in a student's home life. However, you have to start somewhere, and by establishing and sticking

to a few explained general expectations (see discussion that follows under "The First Day") and to those that may be specific to your grade level or subject area, you can leave yourself some room for judgments and maneuvering.

Finally, consequences for not following established procedures must be reasonable, clearly understood, and fairly applied. The procedures should be quite specific so that students know exactly what is expected and what is not and what the consequences are when procedures are not followed.

Procedures Rather Than Rules; Consequences Rather Than Punishment

To encourage a constructive and supportive classroom environment, we encourage you (and your students) to practice thinking in terms of *procedures* (or *expectations*, or *standards and guidelines*) rather than of "rules," and of *consequences* rather than "punishment." The rationale is this: To many people, the term *rules* has a more negative connotation than does the term *procedures* (Queen, Blackwelder, & Mallen, 1997). When working especially with a cohort of students, some rules are necessary but some people feel that using the term *procedures* has a more positive ring to it. For example, a classroom rule might be that when one person is talking we do not interrupt that person until he or she is finished. When that rule is broken, rather than reminding students of the rule, the emphasis can be changed to a procedure simply by reminding the students and asking, "What is our procedure (or expectation) when someone is talking?"

We agree with those who believe that thinking in terms of and talking about *procedures* and *consequences* are more likely to contribute to a positive classroom ambiance than using the terms *rules* and *punishment*. Of course, some argue that by the time students are in middle school, you might as well tell it like it is. Especially if your group of students is linguistically and culturally mixed, you will need to be as direct and clear as possible to avoid sending confusing or mixed signals. Like always, after considering what experienced others have to say, the final decision is one of many that you must make and will be influenced by your own thinking and situation. It might be a decision made in collaboration with members of your teaching team. It is, however, important that expectations are communicated clearly to the students and followed consistently by you and other members of your teaching team.

Once you have decided on your initial expectations, you are ready to explain them to your students and to begin rehearsing a few of the procedures on the very first day of class. You will want to do this in a positive way. Students work best in a positive atmosphere, when teacher expectations are clear to them, when procedures are stated in positive terms, are clearly understood and agreed upon and have become routine, and when consequences for behaviors that are inappropriate are reasonable, clearly understood, and fairly applied.

The First Day

On the first day you will want to cover certain major points of common interest to you and the students. The following paragraphs offer guidelines and suggestions for meeting your students the first time.

Greeting the Students and First Activity.   While standing at the door welcome your students with a smile as they arrive, and then greet the entire class with a friendly but businesslike demeanor. You should not be frowning or off in a corner of the room doing something else as students arrive. As you greet the students, tell them to take a seat and start on the first activity at their desk.

After your greeting, begin the first meeting immediately with some sort of assignment, perhaps with a written assignment already on each student desk. This assures that students have something to do immediately upon arriving in your classroom. That first assignment might be a questionnaire each student completes. This is a good time to instruct students on the expected standard for heading their papers. After giving instructions on how papers are to be handed in, rehearse the procedure by collecting this first assignment.

Student Seating.   One option for student seating is to have student names on the first assignment paper and placed at student seats when students arrive to their first class session. Or, you may prefer to have a seating chart displayed on the screen. Either way allows you to have a seating chart ready on the first day, from which you can quickly take attendance and begin learning student names. Let them know, too, that from time to time you will redo the seating arrangement (if that is true).

Information About the Class.   After the first activity has been completed, discussed, and collected, explain to students about the class—what they will be learning and how they will learn it (covering work and study habits and your expectations regarding the quantity and quality of their work). This is a time you may choose to obtain student input into the course content (discussed in the next chapter), to give students a sense of empowerment or ownership. We advise you to put this information in a course syllabus, give each student a copy, and review it with them, specifically discussing your expectations about how books will be used; about student notebooks, journals, portfolios, and assignments; about what students need to furnish; and about the location of resources in the classroom and elsewhere.

Classroom Procedures and Endorsed Behavior.   Now discuss in a positive way your expectations regarding classroom behavior, procedures, and routines (discussed next). Young adolescent students work best when teacher expectations are well understood with established routines. In the beginning it is important that there be no more procedures than necessary to get the class moving effectively for daily operation. Five or fewer expectations should be enough, such as those shown in Figure 4.2.

Too many procedural expectations at first can be restricting and even confusing to students. Unless they are recent newcomers, most middle grades students already know these things so you shouldn't have to spend much time on the topic, except for those items specific to your course, such as dress and safety expectations for science, art classes, and physical education. Be patient with yourself on this, for finding and applying the proper level of control for a given group of children is one of the skills that you will develop with experience. And remember this: for even the most competent and experienced teachers, activities in the classroom don't always run smoothly.

Although some middle level schools traditionally have posted in the halls and in the classrooms a list of prohibited behaviors, exemplary schools and teachers tend to focus on the positive, on endorsed attitudes and behaviors. Displaying a list of "do nots" does not encourage a positive school or classroom atmosphere; a list of "dos," such as those in Figure 4.2, does.

First Homework Assignment and Dismissal.   End the first class session with a positive statement about being delighted to be working with them and then give the first homework assignment. The first homework assignment should perhaps be one that will not take too much student time and that each student can achieve maximum credit on with minimal effort. Be sure to allow yourself sufficient time to demonstrate where assignments will regularly be posted, and to make assignment instructions

Figure 4.2   Sample list of expectations for classroom behavior.

Our Classroom List of Dos

- Do arrive promptly and remain on task until excused by (teacher's name)
- Do demonstrate appreciation for the rights and property of others
- Do listen attentively when others have the floor
- Do show mutual respect
- Do use appropriate language

clearly understood by every student, including a reminder of how you expect students to head their papers. This time is also good to explain to your students your expectations regarding help from home, if any, on homework. (An identical explanation should be given to parents/guardians at the first contact with them.)

When you are ready to dismiss students this first day and every day hereafter, our advice is to do so by moving to the classroom exit and then verbally excuse the students and give each a smile as they leave the classroom.

Procedural Matters: More on What Students Need to Understand from Early On

When establishing classroom behavior expectations and procedures, remember this point: The learning time needs to run efficiently (i.e., with no "dead time" when students have nothing to do), smoothly (i.e., routine procedures are established and transitions between activities are smooth), and with minimum distraction. As you prepare the guidelines, standards, and expectations for classroom behavior, you (and, if relevant, your teaching team) should consider some of the specifics about what students need to understand from the beginning. These specific points, then, should be reviewed and rehearsed with the students, sometimes several times, during the first week of school and then followed consistently throughout the school term. Important and specific things that students need to know from the start will vary considerably, depending on your specific situation, but generally each of the following paragraphs describes things that all students need to understand from the beginning of the school term.

Signaling for Your Attention and Help. At least at the start of the school term, most teachers who are effective classroom managers expect students to raise their hands until the teacher acknowledges (usually by a nonverbal gesture, such as eye contact, a nod, or with a raised forefinger) that the student's hand has been seen. With that acknowledgment, the student is expected to lower his or her hand and return to work. Whereas a teacher with less than, say, 15 students may indeed relax this expectation—although in many public schools a class of 15 or fewer students is far from common—the expectation should not be ignored, for two of the three reasons given in the following two paragraphs.

There are a number of important reasons for expecting students to raise their hands to be acknowledged before speaking. Two are that it allows you to (a) control the noise and confusion level and (b) be proactive in deciding who speaks. Even with a small group of children (15 or fewer), the latter is important if you are to be in control of classroom events, rather than controlled by them, and you are to manage a classroom with equality—that is, with equal attention to individuals regardless of their gender, ethnicity, proximity to the teacher, or another personal characteristic. We are *not* talking about students having to raise their hands before talking with their peers during group work. We *are* talking about disallowing students shouting across the room to get your attention and boisterously talking out freely and rudely interrupting others during whole-class discussions and instruction.

Another important reason for expecting students to raise their hands and be recognized before speaking is to discourage impulsive outbursts and to promote their emotional and intellectual maturity. An instructional responsibility shared by all teachers is, as emphasized in the preceding chapter, to help children develop intelligent behaviors. Learning to control one's impulsivity is an intelligent behavior.

> Helping young adolescents learn how to control their impulsivity is a highly important responsibility that, in our opinion, is too often neglected by too many teachers (and too many parents and guardians); the ramifications of which are frightening.

Some teachers employ the *three-before-me* (or similar) procedure to avoid dependence on the teacher and having too many students raising their hands for the teacher's attention and to encourage positive interaction among the students. The procedure is: When a student has a question or needs help, the student must quietly ask up to three peers before seeking help from the teacher. Again, as a beginning teacher, you need to learn about what other teachers do; try ideas to find what works best for you in your unique situation. And, of course, as you will learn with experience, what works best for you with one group of children will not always work best the following year with another group of children.

Entering and Leaving the Classroom. From the time that the class is scheduled to begin, teachers who are effective classroom managers expect students to be in their assigned seats or at their assigned learning stations and to be attentive to the teacher or to the learning activity until excused by the teacher. And remember, teachers, not bells or clocks, excuse students. For example, in our opinion, students should not be allowed to begin meandering toward the classroom exit in anticipation of the passing bell or the designated passing time; otherwise, their meandering toward the door will begin earlier and earlier each day and the teacher will increasingly lose control. Besides, it is a waste of a very valuable and very limited resource—instructional time.

Maintaining, Obtaining, and Using Materials for Learning and Items of Personal Use. Students need to know where, when, and how to store, retrieve, and care for items—such as their outer garments, backpacks, books, pencils, and medicines—how to get papers and materials, and when to use the pencil sharpener and wastebasket and classroom sink when there is one. Classroom control is easiest to maintain when:

- items that students need for class activities and for their personal use are neatly and safely arranged (e.g., backpacks stored under tables or chairs rather than in aisles) and located in places that require minimum foot traffic
- there are established procedures that students clearly expect and understand
- there is the least amount of student off-task time
- students do not have to line up to wait for anything.

Therefore, you will want to plan the room arrangement, equipment and materials storage, preparation of equipment and materials, and transitions between activities, to avoid needless delays, confusion, and safety hazards. Remember this well: For a beginning teacher in particular, problems in classroom control will most certainly occur whenever some or all students have nothing to do, even if only briefly.

Leaving Class for a Personal Matter. Normally, students should be able to take care of the need for a drink of water or to go to the restroom between classes; however sometimes they do not, or for medical reasons or during long block classes cannot. Reinforce the notion that they should do those things before coming into your classroom or during the scheduled times, but be flexible enough for the occasional student who has an immediate need. Whenever permitting a student to leave class for a personal reason, follow established school procedures, which may, for reasons of personal security, mean that students can only leave the room in pairs and with a hall pass, or when accompanied by an adult.

Reacting to a Visitor or an Intercom Announcement. Unfortunately, class interruptions do occur, and in some schools they occur far too often and for reasons that are not as important as interrupting the teaching and learning process would imply. For an important reason, an administrator or some other person from the school's office may interrupt the learning to see the teacher or a student or to make an announcement to the entire class. Students need to understand what behavior is expected of them during those interruptions. When there is a visitor to the classroom, the expected procedure should be for students to continue their learning task unless directed otherwise by you. To learn more about class interruptions, do Exercise 4.1 now.

EXERCISE 4.1: OBSERVING A CLASSROOM FOR FREQUENCY OF EXTERNAL INTERRUPTIONS

INSTRUCTIONS: The purpose of this exercise is for you to observe a classroom for frequency of externally caused interruptions to the learning. A second and perhaps even more important purpose is described at the end of the next paragraph. It is disconcerting to realize how often teachers and, therefore, student learning in the classrooms of some schools are interrupted by an announcement over the intercom, a phone call, or a visitor at the door. After all, no one would even consider interrupting a surgeon during the most climactic moments of an open heart operation, nor a defense attorney at the climax of her or his summation. Far too often, though, teachers are interrupted at a critical point in a lesson just when they have their students in "the palm of their hand." Once lost because of an interruption, student attention and that teachable moment are nearly impossible to recapture.

School administrators and office personnel must sometimes be reminded that the most important thing going on in the school is what teachers have been hired to do—teach—and that the act of teaching must not be frivolously interrupted. Except for absolutely critical reasons, teachers should never be interrupted after the first five minutes of a class period or before the last five minutes. That policy should be established and rigidly adhered to. Otherwise, after many years of being a student, the lesson learned is that the least important thing going on at the school is what is going on in the classroom. No wonder then that it is so difficult for teachers in some schools to gain student attention and respect. That respect must be shown, beginning with the school's central office. The need to turn around and refocus on this is the reason for this exercise.

Arrange to visit a classroom (grade 5–8) and observe for interruptions created from outside the classroom.

1. School and class (including grade level) visited: _____

_____

2. Time (start and end of class period):

3. Interruptions (tally for each interruption):
   a. intercom:
   b. phone:
   c. visitor at door:
   d. emergency drill:
   e. other (specify):

4. Total number of interruptions: _____

5. My conclusion:

6. Share and compare your results with your classmates.

7. Describe any further conclusion (and resolve) that you and your classmates draw as a result of sharing your experiences with this exercise.

FOR YOUR NOTES

Figure 4.3 Sample model of consequences for inappropriate student behavior. [*Note:* Whether offenses subsequent to the first are those that occur on the same day or within a designated period of time, such as one week, is one of the many decisions that must be made by a teacher, by members of a teaching team or department, or by the entire faculty at the school. And, of course, it is quite clear in the policy of most schools and districts that there are some offenses (such as having a weapon on campus) for which there is *zero tolerance*, that is, that will result in direct suspension or expulsion regardless of whether it is a first offense.]

FIRST OFFENSE results in a direct, but unobtrusive (probably nonverbal), reminder to the student.

SECOND OFFENSE results in a private, but direct (verbal) reminder of expected behavior and the consequences of continued inappropriate behavior.

THIRD OFFENSE results in the student being given a time-out in a supervised isolation area followed by a private teacher-student conference and the student's subsequent return to class. Parent/guardian notification may occur.

FOURTH OFFENSE results in a suspension from class until there is a student-parent/guardian-teacher (and perhaps the counselor or a school administrator) conference.

FIFTH OFFENSE results in the student being referred to the appropriate administrator or counselor (depending on the school's policy), sometimes followed by a limited or permanent suspension from that class or move to another school or an expulsion from school.

When Late to Class or Leaving Early. You must abide by school policies on early dismissals and late arrivals. Make your own procedures routine so students clearly understand what they are to do if they must leave your class early (e.g., for a medical appointment) or when they arrive late. Procedures in your classroom, and indeed throughout the school, should be such that late-arriving and early-dismissal students do not disturb you or other teachers or the learning in progress.

When students are allowed to interrupt the learning in progress because the teacher has not established such procedures, and these interruptions happen repeatedly and regularly, then the covert message conveyed, at least in that classroom if not by the hidden curriculum of the entire school, is that on the list of matters of importance academic instruction ranks relatively low.

Consequences for Inappropriate Behavior. Most teachers who are effective classroom managers routinize their procedures for handling inappropriate behavior and assure that the students understand the consequences for inappropriate behavior. The consequences, which work best when consistent throughout the school, are posted in the classroom and may be similar to the five-step model shown in Figure 4.3.

Emergency Situations, Practice and Real. Students need to clearly understand what to do, where to go, and how to behave in emergency conditions, such as those that might occur because of a fire, storm, earthquake, or because of a disruptive campus intruder. Students (and teachers, too) must behave well during practice drills, as well as in real emergencies.

To further your understanding of classroom management, and to begin the development of your own management system, now do Exercises 4.2 and 4.3.

FOR YOUR NOTES

EXERCISE 4.2: TEACHERS' CLASSROOM MANAGEMENT SYSTEMS

INSTRUCTIONS: The purpose of this exercise is to interview two teachers (grades 5–8) to discover how they manage their classrooms. Use the outline format that follows, conduct your interviews, and then share the results with your classmates, perhaps in small groups. You may duplicate blank copies of this form.

1. Teacher interviewed: _____

2. Date: _____   4. School: _____

3. Grade level: _____   5. Subject(s): _____

6. Please describe your classroom management system. Specifically, I would like to know your procedures for the following:

  a. How are students to signal that they want your attention and help? _____

     _____

     _____

  b. How do you call on students during question and discussion sessions? _____

     _____

     _____

  c. How and when are students to enter and exit the classroom? _____

     _____

     _____

  d. How are students to obtain the materials for instruction? _____

     _____

     _____

  e. How are students to store their personal items? _____

     _____

     _____

  f. What are the procedures for students going to the drinking fountain or bathroom? _____

     _____

     _____

  g. What are the procedures during class interruptions? _____

     _____

     _____

  h. What are the procedures for tardies or early dismissal? _____

     _____

     _____

EXERCISE 4.2   *(continued)*

i. What are the procedures for turning in homework? _____
_____
_____

7. Describe your expectations for classroom behavior and the consequences for misbehavior. _____
_____
_____
_____
_____
_____
_____
_____
_____
_____

In a discussion with classmates following the interviews, consider the following:

Many modern teachers advocate the use of a highly structured classroom, and then, as appropriate over time during the school year, they share more of the responsibility with the students. Did you find this to be the case with the majority of teachers interviewed? Was it more or less the case with any particular grade level or subject areas?

PP EXERCISE 4.3: BEGINNING THE DEVELOPMENT OF MY CLASSROOM MANAGEMENT SYSTEM

INSTRUCTIONS: The purpose of this exercise is to begin preparation of the management system that you will explain to your students during the first day or week of school. Answer the questions that follow and share those answers with your peers for their feedback. Then make changes as appropriate. (Upon completion of this chapter, you may want to revisit this exercise to make adjustments to your management plan, as you will from time to time throughout your professional career.)

1. My teaching subject area and anticipated grade level: _____

_____

2. Attention to procedures. Use a statement to explain your procedural expectation for each of the following:

   a. How are students to signal that they want your attention and help? _____

   _____

   _____

   b. How do you call on students during question and discussion sessions? _____

   _____

   _____

   c. How and when are students to enter and exit the classroom? _____

   _____

   _____

   d. How are students to obtain the materials for instruction? _____

   _____

   _____

   e. How are students to store their personal items? _____

   _____

   _____

   f. What are the procedures for students going to the drinking fountain or bathroom? ____

   _____

   _____

   g. What are the procedures during class interruptions? _____

   _____

   _____

   h. What are the procedures for tardies or early dismissal? _____

   _____

   _____

EXERCISE 4.3 *(continued)*

   i. What are the procedures for turning in homework? _____

_____

_____

3. List of student behavior expectations that I will present to my class (no more than five):

   Rule 1: _____

_____

_____

   Rule 2: _____

_____

_____

   Rule 3: _____

_____

   Rule 4: _____

_____

_____

   Rule 5: _____

_____

_____

4. Explanation of consequences for broken rules: _____

_____

_____

_____

_____

5. How procedures, rules, or consequences may vary (if at all) according to the grade level taught or according to

any other criteria, such as in team teaching: _____

_____

_____

_____

_____

_____

USING POSITIVE REWARDS AS MOTIVATORS

Reinforcement theory contends that a person's gratification derived from receiving a reward strengthens the tendency for that person to continue to act in a certain way, while the lack of a reward (or the promise of a reward) weakens the tendency to act that way. For example, according to the theory, if students are promised a reward of "preferred activity time (PAT) on Friday" if they work well all week long, then the students are likely to work toward that reward, thus improving their standards of learning. Some educators argue that: (a) once the extrinsic reinforcement (i.e., the reward from outside the learner) has been removed, the desired behavior tends to diminish; and that (b) rather than extrinsic sources of reinforcement, focus should be on increasing the student's internal sense of accomplishment, an intrinsic reward. Further, rewarding students for complying with expected/standard behavior sends the wrong message. It reinforces the mentality of, "What do I get (for doing what I am supposed to do)?" If common as a school practice, it carries over into home situations and eventually into adulthood. A principal does not reward a teacher for showing up on time, attending a faculty meeting, or having report cards prepared on time. Those are expected standard, professional behaviors. [*Note:* There are, however, persons who favor bestowing financial rewards on schools, administrators, and teachers for successfully doing what they are supposed to do—teach children.] Perhaps, for the daily work of a teacher in a classroom of many diverse youngsters, the practical reality is somewhere between. After all, the reality of classroom teaching is less than ideal, and all activities cannot be intrinsically rewarding. Further, for many young adolescents intrinsic rewards are often seemingly too remote to be effective.

The promise of extrinsic rewards is not always necessary or beneficial. Students generally will work harder to learn something because they want to learn it (i.e., it is intrinsically motivating) than they will merely to earn PAT, points, grades, ice cream, stickers, or some other form of reward (called an extrinsic motivator). In addition, regarding the promise of PAT on Friday, many young adolescents are so preoccupied with "the here and now" that for them the promise on Monday of preferred activity time on Friday probably will have little desired effect on their behavior on Monday. On Monday, Friday seems a long way off.

Activities that are interesting and intrinsically rewarding are not served by the addition of extrinsic rewards. Adding extrinsic incentives to learning activities that are already highly motivating tends to actually reduce student motivation. Generally, for most young adolescent learners, the use of extrinsic motivators should be minimal and is probably most useful in skills learning where there is likely to be a lot of repetition and the potential for boredom. If students are working diligently on a highly motivating student-initiated project of study, extrinsic rewards are not necessary and could even have negative effects (Kohn, 1993).

MANAGING CLASS SESSIONS

The guidelines for the first session with your students hold true for every session thereafter. When it is time for the class period to begin, you should start the learning activities at once. By beginning the class session without delay, you discourage the kind of fooling around and time wasting that might otherwise occur. To minimize problems with classroom control, you must practice this from the very first day of your teaching career. [*Note:* If student teaching is an element of the program you are in, then at the beginning of your student teaching you may need to follow the opening procedures already established by your cooperating teacher. If your cooperating teacher's procedures for classroom management are largely ineffective, or counter to what you believe they should be, then perhaps you should talk with your university supervisor about an alternative placement.]

Once class has begun, the pace of activities should be lively enough to keep students alert and productively busy, without dead time, but not so fast as to discourage or lose some students. The effective teacher manages a classroom where at no time does any student sit or stand around with nothing to do. To maintain a smooth and brisk pace, and to lessen distractions and prevent dead time, consider the guidelines that follow.

Opening Activities

Although there are many schools today that do not use a bell system to denote the beginning and ending of every class period, teachers still sometimes refer to the initial class activity as the *bell activity*. More frequently, perhaps, as well as more correctly, it is referred to as the *warm-up activity* or simply as the *opener*.

At the beginning of each class period, in order to take attendance and to attend to other routine administrative matters, most teachers expect the students to be in their assigned seats. You should greet the students warmly and start their learning quickly. Unless you really want responses, it is perhaps best to avoid greeting the entire classroom of students with a rhetorical question such as "How was your weekend?" If you are teaching in a school where you must monitor attendance at the beginning of each class period and you are not yet comfortable with your ability to multitask, an effective management procedure is to have the overhead projector on when students arrive in class, with the day's agenda and immediate assignment or warm-up activity

TEACHING IN PRACTICE

Beginning the Class Period in Mr. Scott's Class

On the first day of school, two students arrived a half-minute late to Mr. Scott's class. On the second day, three students were a minute late, and Mr. Scott waited to begin class until they were in their seats. On the third day, four students were each from one to three minutes late, and again Mr. Scott waited to begin class. By the end of the first week, Mr. Scott was delaying the start of the class for seven minutes after the bell because students continued to amble in throughout this time period.

Questions for Class Discussion

1. What do you predict will be the situation by the end of the second week? Why?

2. What alternatives are open to Mr. Scott for Monday of the second week?

3. Which of the alternatives are likely to lead to a worse situation? Why?

4. Which of the alternatives promise to lead to improvement? Why?

clearly displayed on the screen, which is then referred to after your greeting. Once administrative tasks are completed (usually in a matter of a minute or two, although we kid not when we say we once knew a middle school teacher—an entirely ineffective one we might add—who spent the entire class period doing attendance while students did a worksheet), the day's lesson should begin, which could mean that students will move to other stations within the classroom.

When there are no announcements or other administrative matters to cover, you should try to begin the day's lesson immediately. Then, within a few minutes after the students have begun their lesson activities, take attendance. Perhaps the best routine, one that requires practice and overlapping skill, is to do both simultaneously—take attendance while starting the day's instructional activities. Whichever the case, once

the class period has begun, routines and lesson activities should move forward briskly and steadily until the official end of the class period, or, in the event of extended class periods or blocks, until a scheduled break.

Warm-up activities include any variety of things, such as a specific topic or question each student responds to by writing in his or her journal or the same topic or question that pairs (dyads) of students discuss and write about in their journals. Other activities include a problem to be solved by each student or student pair, the exchange and discussion of a homework assignment, the completion of the write-up of a laboratory activity, and the writing of individual or student dyad responses to worksheet or textbook questions.

Now do Exercise 4.4 to learn further how experienced teachers open their class sessions.

EXERCISE 4.4: OBSERVATION AND ANALYSIS OF HOW EXPERIENCED TEACHERS OPEN CLASS MEETINGS

INSTRUCTIONS: The purpose of this exercise is to learn how experienced teachers open class meetings and, from that, to begin building your own repertoire of options. Select three experienced teachers, all of the same grade level (grades 5, 6, 7, or 8) and subject, and observe how they begin their class meetings. Observe only the first 10 minutes of each period. After collecting these data, share, compile, and discuss the results as follows:

1. Grade level and subject discipline I observed: _____

2. Normal time duration of class period: (example 9:00–10:50 A.M.) _____

    Time that I observed: (example, 9:00–9:10 A.M.) _____

3. Make a check for each of the following observations that you make. For each teacher indicate by numbering 1, 2, 3, etc., the things that he or she did first, second, third, etc., during the initial 10 minutes from the time students began entering the classroom until after the official clock start of class (i.e., when class is supposed to begin).

	✓	Teacher 1	Teacher 2	Teacher 3
Greeting the students	____	____	____	____
Warm and friendly?	____	____	____	____
Giving an assignment (i.e., a warm-up activity)	____	____	____	____
Taking attendance	____	____	____	____
Talking with another adult	____	____	____	____
Talking with one or a few students	____	____	____	____
Readying materials or equipment	____	____	____	____
Working at desk	____	____	____	____
Handing out student papers or materials	____	____	____	____
Other (specify)	____	____	____	____

4. For these three teachers, was there a common way in which they began class?

5. Compile your results with those of your classmates. Write the results here.

6. Compare the results of observations for all similar subjects/grade level combinations. What are the similarities and differences?

7. As a group can you reach any conclusions about teachers of particular grade levels and subject disciplines, and how they spend the first 10 minutes of the class meeting?

FOR YOUR NOTES

Smooth Implementation of the Lesson

The lesson should move forward briskly and purposefully, with natural transitions from one lesson activity to the next and with each activity starting and ending conclusively, especially when using direct (teacher-centered) instruction. Transitions (discussed in the section that follows), in particular, are a most troublesome time for many novice teachers.

When giving verbal instructions to students, do so quickly and succinctly, without talking too long and giving so much detail that students begin to get restless and bored. Young adolescents soon become bored with long-winded, verbal instructions from a teacher.

> Helping students see and understand connections is a continuing responsibility for every classroom teacher.

Once students are busy at their learning tasks, avoid interrupting them with additional verbal instructions, statements, or announcements that distract and get them off task, and that could as easily be written on the board or overhead transparency; interventions should be communicated to a student privately without disturbing the rest of the class. Most young adolescents are easily distracted; do not be the cause of their distractions.

With whole-class instruction, before starting a new activity, be sure that most students satisfactorily complete the present one. Students who finish early can work on an anchor or transitional activity. End each activity conclusively before beginning a new activity, and with a relevant and carefully prepared transition, bridge the new activity with the previous one, so students understand the connection.

With skill in withitness, you will carefully and continuously monitor all students during the entire class period. If one or two students become restless and inattentive, quietly redirect their attention without distracting and interrupting the learning activities of the other students.

To help in the prevention of dead time and management problems, especially when using multiple learning tasks and indirect (student-centered) instruction, you will want to establish and rehearse the students in the use of anchor or transitional activities, which are discussed next.

Transitions within Lessons

> It is probable that the greatest number of discipline problems occur during times of transitions.

Transitions within lessons are the moments between activities or topics, times of change. It will probably take you a while to sharpen the skill of smooth transitions. Planning and consistency in execution are critical to mastering this important but difficult skill. With careful planning, a dependable schedule, and consistent routines, transitions usually occur efficiently and automatically, without disruption. Still, it is probable that for classroom teachers the greatest number of discipline problems occur during times of transitions, especially when students must wait for the next activity. To avoid problems during transitions, eliminate wait times by thinking and planning ahead. During your preactive phase of instruction, plan your transitions and write them into your lesson plan.

Transitions in lessons are of two types, and at times, both are used. The first is achieved by the teacher's connecting one activity to the next so that students understand the relationship between the two activities. That is a *lesson transition.* The second type of transition occurs when some students have finished a learning activity but must wait for others to catch up before starting the next. This, as mentioned in the preceding section, is an *anchor* or *transitional activity. Anchor* or *transitional activities* are ongoing, relevant tasks that students automatically move to whenever they have completed their individual or small-group learning activities, thus allowing no time where students have nothing to do but wait. A common example is when some students have finished a test while others have not. The wise and effective teacher plans a transitional activity and gives instructions or reminders for that activity or an ongoing activity *before* students begin the test.

During the planning (preactive phase) of instruction you should plan and rehearse nearly every move you and the students will make, thinking ahead to anticipate and avoid problems in classroom control. Transitions are planned and students are prepared for them by clearly established transition routines. While in transition and waiting for the start of the next activity, students engage in these transitional activities. You can plan a variety of transitional activities relevant and appropriate to the topics being studied, although not necessarily related to the next activity of that particular day's lesson. Transitional activities may include any number of meaningful activities, such as journal writing, worksheet activities, lab reports, portfolio work, homework, project work, and even work for another class.

As a beginning teacher, it will take time to develop finesse in your application of these guidelines for effective lesson management; during your student teaching experience, your cooperating teacher and college or university supervisor will understand that it takes time and will help you develop and hone your skills.

INAPPROPRIATE STUDENT BEHAVIOR

Student behavior in the classroom that is inappropriate can range from minor acts to very serious ones. Sometimes student behaviors seen by the teacher as inappropriate are simply the demonstration of behaviors that are learned and even encouraged in the child's home. Sometimes the causes of student misbehavior are the result of problems that originated from outside the classroom and spilled over into it. Others are simply behaviors that result from the fact that whenever a group of young adolescents are together for a period of time, mischief or fooling around will likely occur. Still others are the result of something the teacher did or did not do. Pay attention to the guidelines and hints that follow in the remaining pages of this chapter. Described next, in order of increasing seriousness, are categories of student misbehavior that teachers sometimes experience and must deal with.

Transient Nondisruptive Behaviors

This least-serious category includes these common and usually nondisruptive behaviors: chatting with a neighbor; momentarily being off task; fooling around but not really bothering anyone; emotional outburst because the student is really "into the lesson"; brief whispering during a lesson; short periods of apparent inattentiveness, perhaps accompanied by visual wandering or daydreaming. Fortunately, in most instances, this type of behavior is transient, and sometimes it might even be best if you pretend for a moment or so to be unaware of it.

If the off-task behavior persists, all it may take to get the student back on task is an unobtrusive (private) redirection as means of keeping students focused. Examples of unobtrusive redirection, or what may be referred to as *signal interference*, are eye contact, body language, gradual movement to a position closer in proximity to the student, smile or frown, quick use of the student's name without missing a beat in the lesson, and hand gestures. If this doesn't work, go to the next level of intervention (one that is obtrusive) by calling on the student by name and reminding the student of the correct procedure or of what the student is supposed to be doing.

Avoid asking an off-task student any question, such as a content question (for example, "John, what are the raw materials of photosynthesis?" when you know full well that John is not paying attention), or an inquiry ("John, why are you doing that?" John probably doesn't know why.) Also, avoid making a threat such as "John, if you don't turn around and attend to your work, I will send you to the office."

The bottom line is this: It is important you not make "mountains out of molehills," or you could cause more problems than you would resolve. Make every effort to maintain students' focus on the lesson rather than on the off-task behavior.

Disruptions to Learning

This category includes incessant talking out of turn, walking about the room aimlessly and without permission, clowning, and throwing objects, all of which young adolescents know are behaviors that are unacceptable in the classroom. In responding to such misbehaviors, it is important that you have explained their consequences to students, and then, following your stated procedures, promptly and consistently deal with the violations. Too many teachers tend to ignore these misbehaviors (seemingly in the hope that, if not recognized, they will discontinue). Although it is important that you always think before you react to disruptive behavior, totally not reacting to such misbehavior is, in fact, giving it your approval. You must not ignore infractions of this type, for if you do, they most likely will escalate beyond your worst nightmare. Without displaying any anger (otherwise students are winning the battle for control), simply and quickly enforce understood consequences and maintain focus on the lesson, rather than the inappropriate behavior. In other words, you want to maintain your control of classroom events rather than to become controlled by them.

There is sometimes a tendency, especially when they have a problem with students goofing off and being disruptive, for teachers to assume that the entire classroom of students is being unruly, when, most likely, it is only one, two, or maybe three students. You want to avoid saying to the entire group of students anything that implies you perceive them all as being unruly if, in fact, they are not. Such a false accusation will only serve to alienate the students who are being attentive to the learning task.

Defiance, Cheating, Lying, and Stealing

When a student refuses to do what you say, the student's defiance may be worthy of temporary or permanent removal from the classroom. Depending upon your judgment of the seriousness of the act of defiance, you may simply give the student a time-out or you may suspend the student from class until there has been a conference about the situation, perhaps involving you, members of your teaching team, the student, the student's parent or guardian, and a school official.

Any cheating, lying, and stealing may be an isolated act, and the student may only need a one-on-one talk to find out what precipitated the behavior and what might be done to prevent it from occurring again as well as what the consequences would be if it did occur again. Indeed, whenever observing these behaviors and before responding you must consider the personal characteristics and developmental characteristics or level of the student. So, gauge your responses carefully.

A student who habitually exhibits any of these immoral behaviors may need to be referred to a specialist. Our advice for when you suspect immoral behavior is that you discuss your concern with members of your teaching team and a school official.

Bullying, Fighting, Sexual Misconduct, and Violence

Acts in this category usually extend well beyond the purview and responsibility of one classroom teacher. For example, California state law *mandates* five offenses for which a student must be immediately expelled: possessing a firearm, brandishing a knife, selling a controlled substance, committing sexual assault or battery, and possessing an explosive. Please do not think you must be capable of handling alone every act of student misbehavior, especially those of this category. To seek assistance is a sign of wisdom, not a weakness.

In many ways, teaching is clearly different than it used to be. More and more often teachers are confronted with major problems of inappropriate behavior that have ramifications beyond the classroom or that began elsewhere and spill over into the classroom. If this happens, you may need to ask for help and should not hesitate to do so. Be certain that at your school you know where and how to obtain quick assistance when needed. As a student teacher or a newly employed teacher, one of the first things you will want to do is to find out what you should do in the event of such acting out. As a teacher, you must remain alert.

Today's schools are adopting a variety of types of school-wide and classroom instructional programs designed to reduce or eliminate violent, aggressive student behaviors and to help all children succeed in school and to make the transitions necessary for success into adulthood. Strategies include to teach social competence, to create a positive, calm environment, to establish standards of acceptable behavior, and to establish rules and regulations for responding to violence (Schwartz, 1999).

TEACHER RESPONSE TO STUDENT MISBEHAVIOR

Rather than to punish, the goal in responding to student misbehavior should be to calmly intervene and redirect the student's focus, and as we have said previously to do so successfully with the least amount of classroom disturbance. Typically, teachers respond to student classroom misbehaviors in one of three ways: hostile, assertive, or nonassertive. The teacher's response should be assertive. Hostile and nonassertive responses should be avoided. Unlike a hostile response, an assertive response is not abusive or derogatory to the student. Unlike a nonassertive response, an assertive response is a timely and clear communication to the student of what the teacher expects (Edwards, 1997).

Direct versus Indirect Assertive Intervention Strategies: A Clarification

Appropriate assertive intervention strategies can be separated into two categories:

- *direct,* usually a verbal command from the teacher (in years past the direct intervention might have been more physical)
- *indirect,* such as eye contact, body language and proximity (moving closer to the student), nonverbal

gesturing (teacher's finger to the lips, raised hand, pointing to both eyes to indicate "eyes on me," or pointing to the screen or writing board to direct the student's focus).

Too often, teachers intervene with direct intervention, when indirect intervention strategies are less obtrusive or disruptive and often more effective in redirecting a misbehaving student. Although the offense might be identical, the teacher's intervention for one student might have to be direct, while for another student indirect intervention is enough to put a stop to the student's inappropriate behavior.

Order of Behavior Intervention Strategies

To redirect a student's attention, your usual *first effort* should be indirect intervention. Your *second effort* could be the simplest (i.e., the most private, least obtrusive) direct intervention (e.g., simply saying the student's name in a normal voice, or if you believe necessary, "Nelson, please follow procedures" which is slightly more obtrusive than simply saying "Nelson!"). Your *third effort,* one that, in time interval, closely follows the second (i.e., within the same class period), should follow your procedures as outlined in your management system, which might mean a time-out or detention and a phone call to the student's parent or guardian (in private, of course—see scenario "Phone Call Home"). Normally, such a third effort is not necessary. A *fourth effort,* still rarer, is to suspend the student from class (and/or school) for some period of time until decisions about the future of that student in this school are made by school officials in consultation with the student, the parents or guardians, and other professionals such as the school psychologist.

The use of direct intervention beyond that of mere namedropping ("Nelson!") should be reserved for repetitive and serious misbehavior. When using direct intervention, you should give a direct statement ("Nelson, please follow procedures."), either reminding the student of what he or she is supposed to be doing or telling the student what to do. You should avoid asking rhetorical questions, such as "Nelson, why are you doing that?"

When giving students directions about what they are supposed to be doing, you may be asked by a student, "Why do we have to do this?" To that query, you may give a brief academic answer, but do not become defensive or make threats or be silly. As a matter of fact, because understanding reasons for doing something is so central to positive motivation, it may sometimes be beneficial to stop and truly explore with the students a satisfactory answer to the question (Vavilis & Vavilis, 2004).

One reason that direct intervention should be held in reserve is because by interrupting the lesson to verbally intervene, you are doing exactly what the student who is being reprimanded was doing—interrupting the lesson. Not only is that poor modeling but it can create a host of management problems beyond your wildest

TEACHING IN PRACTICE
Phone Call Home

Margaret was in the fourth week of her student teaching semester, teaching a sixth-grade language arts/social studies block. Margaret's cooperating teacher was recognized as one of Emerson Junior High's finest and most respected teachers. So far, the sixth-grade children have not accepted/respected Margaret as their teacher and have been giving her a difficult time. Today was an especially difficult day and out of frustration during class, in the presence of all the students, using her cell phone Margaret phoned Nelson's parent telling how he was misbehaving in class and asking for the parent's suggestion of what to do.

Questions for Class Discussion

1. Can you identify with Margaret's situation?

2. What do you think about what Margaret did?

3. From what little you can detect from the scenario, was what Margaret did a wise choice? How else might she have handled Nelson?

4. Have you ever observed a similar situation? If so, how was it handled? What were the outcomes?

5. What, if anything, did you learn from the discussion of this scenario that might be useful in your own teaching?

---

nightmares. Another reason for holding direct intervention in reserve is that, when used too frequently, direct intervention loses it effectiveness.

TEACHER-CAUSED STUDENT MISBEHAVIOR

As a classroom teacher, one of your major responsibilities is to model appropriate behavior and not to contribute to or be the cause of problems in the classroom. Some student misbehaviors and problems in classroom control are caused or escalated by the teacher and could have been prevented or easily rectified had the teacher behaved or acted differently. Consider the information that follows, first in scenarios for case study review followed by a presentation of mistakes to avoid.

Scenarios for Case Study Review

In addition to sometimes ignoring certain transient student behaviors, you should also avoid using negative methods of rule enforcement and ineffective forms of punishment, as exemplified in each of the following scenarios. We suggest you and your classmates treat these scenarios as case studies for small groups to consider and then discuss before the whole class. During your discussions, consider for each case (1) to what degree, if any, the teacher's action created a potential legal problem and (2) whether you consider the situation as relevant to the subject and grade level you intend to teach.

- *Capricious.* Because of her arbitrary and inconsistent enforcement of classroom expected procedures, eighth-grade language arts teacher Fran Fickle has lost the respect and trust of her students as well as control of her classes. Her students are constantly testing Fran to see how much they can get away with.

- *Extra Assignments.* When students in Margaret Malopropros's seventh-grade reading class misbehave, she habitually assigns extra reading and written work as punishment, even for the most minor offenses. This behavior has simply reinforced the view of many of her students that school is drudgery, so they no longer look forward to her classes, and behavior problems in her class have steadily increased since the beginning of the school year.

- *Embarrassment.* When eighth-grade social studies teacher Denise Degradini was having difficulty controlling the behavior of one of her students, she got on the classroom phone and called the student's parent while the entire class of 33 students could overhear the conversation. She told the parent about the child's behavior in class and how she was going to have to give the student a referral if the student's behavior did not improve. From that one act, Denise lost all respect of her students. Class academic achievement grades plummeted for the rest of the year.

- *Group Punishment.* Because Fred Flock has not developed his withitness and overlapping skills, he has the unfortunate habit of punishing the entire group for every instance of misbehavior. Yesterday, for example, because some students were noisy during a video presentation, he gave the entire class an unannounced quiz on the content of the film. He has lost the respect of the students, students are hostile toward him, and his problems with classroom control are steadily growing worse.

- *Harsh and Humiliating Punishment.* Vince Van Pelt, a physical education teacher, has lost control of his classes and the respect of his students. His thrashing, whipping, tongue-lashing, and use of humiliation are ineffective and indicative of his loss of control. Parents have complained, and one is suing him. The district has given Mr. Van Pelt official notice of the nonrenewal of his contract.

- *Loud Talk.* The noisiest person in Steve Shrill's class is Mr. Shrill. His constant and mistaken efforts to talk over the students have led to his own yelling and screaming, to complaints from neighboring teachers about the noise in his classes, and to a reprimand from the principal.

- *Lowered Marks.* Eunice Erudite, an eighth-grade language arts/social studies teacher, has a policy of writing a student's name on the board each time the person is reprimanded for misbehavior. Then, when a student has accumulated five marks on the board, she lowers the student's academic grade by one letter. As a result of her not separating their academic and social behaviors, her students are not doing as well as they were at the start of the year. Parents and students have complained about this policy to the administration, arguing that the grades Ms. Erudite is giving do not reflect the students' academic progress or abilities.

- *Nagging.* Social studies teacher Paul Peck's continual and unnecessary scolding and criticizing of students upsets the recipient students and arouses resentment from their peers. His nagging resolves nothing, and, like a snowball building in size as it rolls down the hill, causes Mr. Peck more and more problems in the classroom.

- *Negative Direct Intervention.* In the seventh-grade humanities block class, Joshua swears more and more frequently and with graphic and startling language. Other students are beginning to behave similarly. Rather than giving Joshua alternative ways of expressing his feelings, Polly Premio, one team teacher, verbally reprimands Joshua each time this happens and threatens to notify his parents about it. Ms. Premio doesn't realize that by giving her attention to Joshua's swearing she is rewarding, reinforcing, and causing the increase in Joshua's unacceptable behavior.

- *Negative Touch Control.* When middle school student Ezzard, a bully, pushes and shoves other students out of his way for no apparent reason other than to physically manipulate them, his teacher, Tony Trenchant, grabs Ezzard and yanks him into his seat. What "roughneck" Tony the teacher doesn't realize is that he is using the very behavior (physical force) that he

is trying to stop Ezzard from using. This simply confuses students and teaches them (especially Ezzard) that the use of physical force is okay if you are bigger or older than the recipient of that force. In this situation, unfortunately, hostility begets hostility.

- *Overreact.* Randall was reading a magazine in class when his language arts teacher, Harriet Harshmore, grabbed it from Randall's hands, called it "pornographic," ripped out the offending pages, and tossed them into a waste basket. The magazine was *National Geographic*, and the "pornographic article" was on evolution and included drawings of unclothed humans. Harriet was later reprimanded by the school superintendent who said that, although he supported her right to put a stop to what she considered a class disruption, Ms. Harshmore had crossed the line when she damaged the magazine. The magazine, apparently a rare collector's issue, had been brought from Randall's home at his teacher's encouragement to bring reading material from home.

- *Physical Punishment.* Mr. Fit, a geography teacher, punishes students by sending them outside to run around the school track when they misbehave in his class. Last week, Sebastian, a student whom he told to go out and run four laps for "mouthing off in class," collapsed and died while running. Mr. Fit has been placed on paid leave and is being sued for negligence by Sebastian's parents.

- *Premature Judgments and Actions.* Because of Kathy Kwik's impulsiveness, she does not think clearly before acting, and more than once she has reprimanded the wrong student. Because of her hasty and faulty judgments, students have lost respect for her. For them, her mathematics class has become pure drudgery.

- *Taped Mouths.* Miss Ductless taped the mouths of 20 of her middle school students in order to keep them quiet. Later in the school day several of the students went to the school nurse complaining of allergic reactions caused by the duct tape. Until a full investigation is made, Miss Ductless has been relieved of her teaching duties.

- *Threats and Ultimatums.* Threats and ultimatums from algebra teacher Bonnie Badger are known to be empty; because she does not follow through, her credibility with the students has been lost. Like wildfire, the word has spread around—"We can do whatever we want in old Badger's class."

- *Too Hesitant.* Because Tim Timideo is too hesitant and slow to intervene when students get off task, his classes have increasingly gotten further and further out of his control, and it is still early in the school year. As a result, neighbor teachers are complaining about the noise from his shop class and Tim has been writing more and more referrals.

- *Writing as Punishment.* Because they were "too noisy," science teacher Sam Scribe punished his class of 28 students by requiring each one to hand-copy 10 pages from encyclopedias. When the students submitted the completed assignment, he immediately tore up the pages in front of the students and said, "I hope you have learned your lesson and from now on will be quiet." Upon hearing about this, all six teachers of the school's English department signed and filed a complaint with the principal about Mr. Scribe's use of writing for punishment.

Preventing a Ship from Sinking Is Much Easier Than Is Saving a Sinking One: Mistakes to Avoid

During your beginning years of teaching, no one, including you, should expect you to be perfect. You should, however, be aware of common mistakes teachers make that often are the causes of student inattention and misbehavior. It is our estimation that as much as 95 percent of classroom control problems are teacher-caused or teacher aggravated and are preventable. In this section, you will find descriptions of mistakes commonly made by teachers. To have a most successful beginning to your career, you will want to develop your skills so to avoid these mistakes. To avoid making these mistakes requires both knowledge of the potential errors and a reflection upon one's own behaviors in relation to them.

The items are mostly grade level and subject-matter neutral, although clearly some may be more relevant to you than others, depending on your own particular teaching situation.

1. *Inadequately attending to long-range and daily planning.* A teacher who inadequately plans ahead is heading for trouble. Inadequate long-term and sketchy daily planning is a precursor to ineffective teaching and, eventually, to teaching failure. Students are motivated best by teachers who clearly are working intensely and intelligently for them.

Many beginning teachers plan their lessons carefully at first and their students respond well, and that is good. Then, sometimes after finding a few strategies that seem to work their lesson planning becomes increasingly sketchy. They fall into a rut of doing pretty much the same thing day after day—lecture, discussion, videos, and worksheets seem all too common for these teachers. They fail to consider and plan for individual student differences. By mid-semester they have stopped growing professionally and begin to experience increasing numbers of problems with students.

2. *Emphasizing the negative.* Too many warnings to students for their inappropriate behavior—and too little recognition for their positive behaviors—do not help to establish the positive classroom ambiance needed for the most effective learning to occur. Reminding students of procedures is more positive and will bring you

quicker success than reprimanding students when they do not follow procedures.

Too often, teachers try to control students with negative language, such as "There should be no talking," and "No gum or candy in class or else you will receive detention," and "No getting out of your seats without my permission." Teachers sometimes allow students, too, to use negative and disrespectful language on each other, such as "Shut up!" Such language does not help instill a positive classroom climate. To encourage a positive atmosphere, use concise, positive, language. Tell students precisely what they are supposed to do rather than what they are not supposed to do. Disallow the use of disrespectful and negative language in your classroom.

3. *Not requiring students to raise hands and be acknowledged before responding, especially during large- and whole-group instruction.* While ineffective teachers often are ones who are controlled by class events, competent teachers are in control of class events. You cannot be in control of events and your interactions with students if you allow students to shout out their comments, responses, and questions the moment they feel like it. Successful teachers quickly establish their control of classroom events.

In addition, to reiterate a point made in Chapter 2, indulging their natural impulsivity is not helping students to grow intellectually or emotionally. When students develop the intelligent and mature behavior of impulse control, they think before acting. Students can and should be taught to think before acting or shouting out an answer. One of several reasons that teachers should insist on a show of student hands before a student is acknowledged to respond or question is to discourage students from the impulsive, disruptive, immature, disrespectful, and irritating behavior of shouting out in class.

4. *Allowing students' hands to be raised too long.* When students have their hands raised for long periods before you recognize them and attend to their questions or responses, you are providing them with dead time, which is time to fool around. Although you need not call on every student as soon as they raise a hand, you should acknowledge the student quickly, such as with a nod or a wave of your hand, so the student can lower their hand and return to work. Then you should get to the student as quickly as possible. Procedures for this should be clearly understood by the students and followed by you.

5. *Spending too much with one student or one group and not monitoring the entire group.* Spending too much time with any one student or small group of students is, in effect, ignoring the rest of the students. As a novice teacher you cannot afford to ignore the rest of the class, even for a moment. Wise teachers steadily practice and develop their overlapping skill.

6. *Beginning a new activity before gaining the students' attention.* A teacher who consistently fails to insist that students follow procedures and who does not wait until

all students are in compliance before starting a new activity is destined for major problems in classroom control. You must establish and maintain classroom procedures. Starting an activity before all students are in compliance is, in effect, telling the students that they don't have to follow expected procedures. You cannot afford to tell students one thing and then do another (see number 51).

Our insistence on adhering to established procedures is not to imply that procedures came before human beings; they didn't. Sometimes procedures need to be changed. If that notion becomes apparent, then don't fear talking about it with your students. But once procedures are agreed upon, everyone should comply.

7. *Pacing teacher talk and learning activities too fast (or, in some instances, too slow).* Pacing of the learning activities is one of the more difficult skills for beginning teachers. (It is also a skill that even skilled and experienced teachers sometimes fail to apply.) Young adolescents need time to disengage mentally and physically from one activity before engaging in the next. You must remember that this takes more time for a room of 25 or so students than it does for just one person, you. This is a reason we advise that transitions be planned and written into your lesson plan.

8. *Using a voice level that is always either too loud or too soft.* A teacher's voice that is too loud day after day can become irritating to some students, just as one that cannot be heard or understood can become frustrating. If the latter is the case, then as discussed in number 39, you may want to consider investing in a portable sound amplification system.

9. *Assigning a journal entry without giving the topic prudent thought.* If the question or topic about which students are supposed to write is ambiguous or obviously hurriedly prepared—without your having given consideration to how students will interpret and respond to it—students will judge that the task is busywork (i.e., only something to keep them busy while you take attendance). If they do it at all, it will be with a great deal of commotion and much less enthusiasm than if they were writing on a topic meaningful to them.

10. *Standing too long in one place.* Most of the time in the classroom, you should be gently mobile, and, "working the crowd."

11. *Sitting while teaching.* Unless you are physically unable to stand, or to do so for long periods of time, in most situations there is no time to sit while teaching. Unless sitting on a tall stool on a raised platform in the middle of your classroom, it is difficult to monitor the class while seated. You cannot afford to appear that casual.

12. *Being too serious and no fun.* No doubt, competent teaching is serious business. But young adolescents are motivated by and respond best to adults who obviously enjoy working with them, helping them learn, and who are sentient of their interests and lives.

13. *Falling into a rut by using the same teaching strategy or combination of strategies day after day.* The teacher's classroom will likely become boring. Because of their multitude of differences, young adolescents are motivated by and respond best to a variety of well-planned and meaningful learning activities.

14. *Inadequately using quiet wait time after asking a content question.* When expected to think deeply about a question, students need time to do it. A teacher who consistently gives insufficient time for students to think is teaching only superficially and at the lowest cognitive level and is destined for problems in student motivation and classroom control.

15. *Poorly or inefficiently using instructional tools.* The ineffective use of teaching tools such as books, writing board, and computer says to students that you are not a competent teacher. Would you want an auto mechanic who did not know how to use the tools of that trade when servicing your automobile? Would you want a brain surgeon who did not know how to use the tools of the trade to remove your brain tumor? Working with children in a classroom is no less important. Like a competent automobile mechanic or a competent surgeon, and as we emphasized in Chapter 2, a competent teacher selects and effectively uses the best tools available for the job to be done.

16. *Ineffectively using facial expressions and body language.* As said earlier (see number 6), your gestures and body language communicate more to students than your words do. For example, one teacher didn't understand why his class of seventh graders would not respond to his repeated expression of "I need your attention." In one 15-minute segment, he used that expression eight times. Studying video recording of that class period helped him understand the problem. His dress was very casual, and he stood most of the time with his right hand in his pocket. At 5′ 7″, with a slight build, a rather deadpan facial expression, and a nonexpressive voice, he was not a commanding presence in the classroom. After seeing himself on tape, he returned to the class wearing a tie and began using his hands and face more expressively. Rather than saying "I need your attention," he waited in silence for the students to become attentive. It worked, making him a more effective teacher.

17. *Relying too much on teacher talk.* Some have a tendency to rely too much on teacher talk. Too much teacher talk can be deadly. Unable to discern between the important and the unimportant verbiage, students will quickly tune a teacher out.

Some teachers rely too much on obtrusive verbal intervention and too little on nonverbal intervention techniques. For example, to verbally reprimand a student for the student's interruptions of class activities is to reinforce the very behavior you are trying to stop. In addition, verbally reprimanding a student in front of the student's peers can cause repercussions you don't want. Instead, develop your indirect, silent intervention techniques.

18. *Inefficiently using teacher time.* During the planning phase of instruction, think carefully about what you are going to be doing during every minute of instruction, and then plan for the most efficient and therefore the most productive use of your time in the classroom. Consider the following example. During a language arts brainstorming session a teacher is recording student contributions on a large sheet of butcher paper that has been taped to the wall. The teacher solicits student responses, acknowledges those responses, holds and manipulates the writing pen, walks to the wall, and records responses on the paper. Each of those actions requires decisions and movements that consume precious instructional time and that can distract the teacher from the students. An effective alternative should be to have a reliable student helper do the writing while the teacher handles the solicitation and acknowledgment of student contributions. That way the teacher has fewer decisions and fewer actions to distract, and the teacher does not lose eye contact and proximity with the classroom of students.

19. *Talking to and interacting with only half the class.* While leading a class discussion, there is a tendency among some teachers to favor (by their eye contact and verbal interaction) only 40 to 65 percent of the students, sometimes completely ignoring the others for an entire class period. Knowing (consciously or not) that they are being ignored, those students will, in time, become uninterested, restless, and perhaps unruly. Remember to spread your interactions and eye contact throughout the entire class. If you are teaching in block or hour-long classes, our advice to you is to establish eye contact with each student at least once each hour. And when we say to "establish" eye contact, we mean that the student knows that you are looking at her or him. Of course there are always exceptions to rules, such as, for example, you need to be sensitive to a student from a culture where extended eye contact may be unwanted or less common.

20. *Collecting and returning student papers before assigning students a task.* If, while turning in papers or waiting for their return, students have nothing else to do, they become restless and inattentive. It is best if students have something to do (for example an anchor activity), while papers are being collected or returned.

21. *Interrupting students while they are on task.* It is not easy to get an entire classroom of young adolescent students on task. Once they are on task, you do not want to be a distracter. Try to give all instructions before students begin their work. The detailed instructions should be written in your lesson plan; that way you are less likely to forget anything. Once on task, if there is an important point you wish to make, write it on the board. If you want to return papers while students are working, do so in a way and at a time that is least likely to interrupt students from their learning task.

22. *Using "shhh" to quiet students.* Using "shhh" makes the teacher sounds unprofessional and something like a balloon with a slow leak, adding a distracting noise to the classroom. Do not use "shhh" in the classroom.

23. *Using poor body positioning.* Develop your skill of withitness by positioning your body so you can continue visually monitoring the entire class even while talking to and working with one student or a small group. Avoid turning your back for more than a second to even a portion of the class.

24. *Settling for less when you should be trying for more— not getting the most from student responses.* The most successful schools are those with teachers who expect and get the most from all students. Don't hurry a class discussion; "milk" student responses for all you can, especially when discussing a topic that students are obviously interested in. Ask a student for clarification or reasons for his or her response. Ask for verification of data. Have another student paraphrase what a student said. Seek deeper thought and meaning. Too often, the teacher will ask a question, get an abbreviated—often one word and low cognitive level—response from a student, and then move on to new content. Instead, follow up a student's response to your question with a sequence of questions, prompting and cueing to elevate the student's thinking to higher levels.

25. *Using threats.* Avoid making threats of any kind. One teacher, for example, told the students that if they continued with their inappropriate talking they would lose their break time. The teacher should have had that consequence as an understood procedure and consequence and then taken away the break time for some students if warranted. A reminder of procedures and consequences is different than is the use of a threat. The difference between making a threat and reminding students of procedures and consequences is *not* minor. Read on!

26. *Punishing the entire class for the misbehavior of a few.* Although the rationale behind such action is clear (i.e., to get group pressure working for you), often the result is the opposite. Students who have been behaving well are alienated from the teacher because they feel they have been punished unfairly. Those students expect the teacher to be able to deal with the misbehaving students without punishing those who are not misbehaving, and of course they are right!

27. *Using global praise.* Global praise is nearly useless. An example is: "Class, your rough drafts were really wonderful." This is hollow and says nothing; it is useless verbalism. Instead, be informative by being specific—tell what it was about their drafts that made them so wonderful. As another example, after a student's oral response to the class, rather than simply saying "Very good," tell what about the student's response was so good.

28. *Using color meaninglessly.* The use of color on the writing board, transparencies, or a PowerPoint™ presentation is nice but will shortly lose its effectiveness unless the colors have meaning. If, for example, everything in the classroom is color-coded and students understand the meaning of the code, then use of color can serve a useful organizational function as well as an important mnemonic to student learning.

29. *Verbally reprimanding a student from across the classroom.* Not only is it a needless interruption of all students, by embarrassing the recipient student in presence of the student's peers it is likely to increase the "you versus them" syndrome and that is something you don't want. Reprimand if necessary, but do so quietly and privately.

30. *Interacting with only a "chosen few" students rather than spreading interactions around to all.* As a beginning teacher, especially, it is easy to fall into a habit of interacting with only a few students, especially those who are vocal and who seem to you to have significant contributions. Your job, however, is to teach every student assigned to your classroom. To do that, you must be proactive, not reactive, in your interactions.

31. *Not intervening quickly enough during inappropriate student behavior.* Except for those minor misbehaviors that are momentary and nondisruptive, inappropriate student behavior only gets worse, not better. It's best to nip it in the bud quickly and resolutely. A teacher who ignores inappropriate and disruptive behavior, even briefly, is in effect approving it. In turn, that approval reinforces the continuation and escalation of inappropriate behaviors.

32. *Not learning and using student names.* As someone once said, hearing your own name being used in a positive way is one of the sweetest sounds in the world. A teacher who does not know or use names when addressing students is viewed by the students as impersonal and uncaring.

33. *Reading student papers only for correct (or incorrect) answers and not for process and thinking.* Reading student papers only for correct responses reinforces the false notion that the process of arriving at answers or solutions is unimportant and that alternative solutions or answers are impossible or unimportant. In effect, it negates the importance of the individual and the very nature and purpose of learning.

34. *Not posting time plans.* Yelling out how much time is left for an activity interrupts student thinking; it implies that to you, at least, their thinking is unimportant. Avoid interrupting students once they are on-task. Show respect for their on-task behavior. In this instance, write on the board before the activity begins how much time is allowed and the time it is to end. If during the activity a decision is made to change the end time, then post the new time by writing it on the board.

35. *Asking global questions that nobody likely will answer.* Examples are "Does everyone understand?" and "Are there any questions?" and "How do you all feel about . . . ?" It is a brave young adolescent who, in presence of peers, is willing to admit ignorance. It is a waste of precious instructional time to ask such questions. If you truly want to check for student understanding or opinions, then do a spot check by asking specific questions, allow think time, and then call on students.

36. *Failing to do frequent comprehension checks (every few minutes during most direct instruction situations) to see if students are understanding.* Too often, teachers simply plow through a big chunk of the lesson, or the entire lesson, assuming that students understand. Or, in the worst-case scenario, teachers hurry through a lesson without even seeming to care whether students are getting it. Students are quick to recognize teachers who don't care or who, by their actions, don't appear to care.

37. *Not monitoring for understanding during seatwork.* Frequent comprehension checks should be done, too, when students are doing seatwork. When assigning seatwork, be sure that your instructions include specifics about what is to be learned, how it is to be learned, and how the content is connected to previous material that students learned. Then, during the seatwork, monitor students not only to keep them on task but to check for individual understandings.

38. *Using poorly worded, ambiguous questions.* Key questions you will ask during a lesson should be planned and written into your lesson plan. Refine and make precise the questions by asking them to yourself or a friend, and try to predict how students will respond to a particular question.

39. *Trying to talk over student noise.* This simply tells students that their making noise while you are talking is acceptable behavior. When this happens, everyone, teacher included, usually gets increasingly louder during the class period. About all you will accomplish when trying to talk over a high student noise level is a sore throat by the end of the school day and, over a longer period of time, an increasing potential for nodules on your vocal cords.

Incidentally, because teachers experience voice problems with far greater severity and frequency than do most other workers, many school districts now install either portable (system is worn by the teacher) or infrared wireless voice enhancement systems. Some teachers purchase their own system. Such systems help not only teachers' vocal health but also an increase in student academic achievement (McCarty, Ostrem, & Young, 2004).

40. *Wanting to be liked by students.* Forget about being liked! If you are a teacher, then teach! Respect is earned as a result of your effective teaching. Liking you may come later. You are *not* your students' peer; you *are* their teacher—a professional and a very important adult role model.

41. *Permitting students to be inattentive to an educationally useful media presentation.* This usually happens

because the teacher has failed to give the students a written handout of questions or guidelines for what they should acquire from the program. Sometimes students need an additional focus. Furthermore, a media presentation is usually audio and visual. To reinforce student learning, add the kinesthetic, such as the writing aspect when a handout of questions is supplied.

42. *Starting in stutters.* A *stutter start* is when the teacher begins an activity, is distracted, begins again, is distracted again, tries again to start, and so on. During stutter starts, students become increasingly restless and inattentive, and sometimes even amused by the teacher's futility, making the final start almost impossible for the teacher to achieve. Avoid stutter starts. Begin an activity clearly and decisively. This is most easily accomplished when lesson plans are prepared thoughtfully and in detail. Also important to the prevention of stutter starts is the teacher's overlapping (multitasking) ability. For example, a teacher who accepts the admit slip from an incoming tardy student without missing a beat in giving warm-up instructions or the lecture has developed overlapping skill. As another example, the teacher who can stop the ensuing inappropriate behavior of a student with the use of a nonverbal gesture (e.g., prolonged eye contact, a quick pause in vocal delivery, or a change of proximity such as moving and standing adjacent to the student) without interrupting the content discussion or distracting other students has overlapping skill.

43. *Introducing too many topics simultaneously.* It is important that you not overload young adolescent students' capacity to engage mentally by introducing different topics simultaneously. See, for example, the scenario "Too Many Topics Introduced at Once."

44. *Failing to give students a pleasant greeting on the first day of the school year, or on each Monday, or the day back following a holiday, or to remind them to have a pleasant weekend or holiday.* Students are likely to perceive such a teacher as indifferent or unfriendly.

45. *Sounding egocentric.* Whether you are or are not egocentric, you want to avoid seeming so. Sometimes the distinction is subtle, although apparent, such as when a teacher says, "What I am going to do now is . . ." rather than "What we are going to do now is . . ." If you want to strive for group cohesiveness—a sense of "we-ness"—then teach not as if you are the leader and your students are the followers, but rather in a manner that empowers your students in their learning.

46. *Taking too much time to give verbal instructions for an activity.* Young adolescent students become impatient and restless during long verbal instructions from the teacher. It is better to give brief instructions (a minute or two should do it) and get the students started on the task. For more complicated activities, teach three or four students the instructions and then have those students do mini-workshops with five or six students in each workshop group. This frees you to monitor the progress of each group.

47. *Taking too much time for an activity.* No matter what the activity, during your planning think carefully about how much time students can effectively attend to the activity. A general rule for most classes is that when only one or two learning modalities are involved (e.g., auditory and visual), the activity should not extend

---

TEACHING IN PRACTICE
Too Many Topics Introduced at Once

During the first 10 minutes of class a teacher started by introducing a warm-up activity, which was a journal write with instructions clearly presented on the screen from the overhead projector. The teacher also verbally explained the activity, although the teacher could have simply pointed to the screen, thereby nonverbally instructing students to begin work on the activity (without disturbing the thinking of those who had already begun). One minute later, the teacher was telling students about their quarter grades and how later in the period they would learn more about those grades. Then the teacher returned to the warm-up activity, explaining it a second time (third time if one counts the detailed explanation already on the screen). Next, the teacher reminded students of the school's new tardy rules (thereby introducing a third topic). At this time, however, there was much commotion with most of the students talking about what the teacher had said about quarter grades, a few were working on the warm-up activity, and hardly any were listening to the teacher talking about the new tardy rules.

Questions for Class Discussion

1. What were your initial thoughts after reading this scenario?

2. What do you predict for the rest of the year for this teacher?

3. What specifically, if anything, should the teacher have done differently?

beyond about 15 minutes; when more than two modalities are engaged (e.g., add tactile or kinesthetic), then the activity might extend longer, say for 20 to 30 minutes.

48. *Being uptight and anxious.* Consciously or subconsciously, students are quick to detect a teacher who worries that events will not go well. It's like a contagion; if you are uptight and anxious, your students will likely become the same. To prevent such corruption, at least to the extent it damages your teaching and your students' learning you must prepare lessons carefully, thoughtfully, and thoroughly. Unless there is something personal going on in your life that is causing your anxiety, you are more likely to be in control and confident in the classroom when your lessons are well prepared. How do you know when a lesson is well prepared? You'll know! Usually, it's when you have developed a written lesson plan that you are truly excited about, proud of, and very eager to implement.

If you do have a personal problem in your life that is distracting and causing you anxiety (and occasionally most of us do), you need to concentrate on ensuring that your anger, hostility, fear, or other negative emotions do not adversely affect your teaching and your interactions with students. Regardless of your personal problems, your students will face you each day expecting to be taught whatever it is you are supposed to be helping them learn.

49. *Failing to apply the best of what is known about how young adolescents learn.* Too many middle level teachers unrealistically seem to expect success having all students in the classroom doing the same thing at the same time rather than having several alternative activities simultaneously occurring (called multilevel instruction) in the classroom. For example, a student who is not responding well, who is being inattentive and disruptive, to a class discussion might behave better if given the choice of moving to a quiet learning center to work alone. If, after trying this alternative activity, the student continues to be disruptive, then you may have to try still another alternative activity. You may have to send the student to another supervised location out of the classroom, to a place previously arranged by you, until you have time after class or after school to talk with the student about the problem.

50. *Overusing punishment for classroom misbehavior—jumping to the final step without trying alternatives.* Teachers sometimes mistakenly either ignore inappropriate student behavior (see number 31) or they skip steps for intervention, resorting too quickly to punishment. They immediately send the misbehaving student outside to stand in the hall (not a wise choice if the student is not supervised) or too quickly assign detention (a usually ineffective consequence). Being quick to use punishment is not a lesson we should be teaching our youth. In-between steps to consider include the use of alternative activities in the classroom (as in number 49). It is useful to keep in mind that every young adolescent is a work in progress. When a child errs it is very important that the child has an opportunity to recover and to learn from the error.

51. *Being vague and inconsistent.* Perhaps one of the most frequent causes of problems for beginning teachers derives from when they fail to say what is meant or to mean what they said. A teacher who gives only vague instructions or is inconsistent in his or her behaviors only confuses students (e.g., does not enforce that teacher's own classroom procedural expectations). If a teacher's verbal communication conflicts with his or her nonverbal messages, students can become not only confused but even resentful, and this too can affect their learning. And when there is a discrepancy between what the teacher says and what that teacher does, the teacher's nonverbal signal will win every time. Actions do speak louder than words! A teacher, for example, who emphasizes the importance of students getting their assignments in on time but then takes forever to read, evaluate, and return those same papers to the students is using inappropriate modeling. Or, as another example, a teacher who has just finished a lesson on the conservation of energy and does not turn off the room lights upon leaving the classroom for recess or lunch, has, by his or her inappropriate modeling behavior, created cognitive disequilibrium and sabotaged the real purpose for the lesson. And yet another example, a teacher who asks students not to interrupt others when they are on task but who repeatedly interrupts students when they are on task, is confusing students with that teacher's contradictory words and behavior. To avoid confusing students, think through what it is you really expect from your students and then ensure that your own verbal and nonverbal behaviors are consistent with those expectations.

Now do Exercise 4.5 and then direct your attention to other specific instances of teacher behaviors, some of which reinforce or cause student misbehavior, by completing Exercise 4.6.

FOR YOUR NOTES

EXERCISE 4.5: AVOIDING SENDING OPPOSING MESSAGES

INSTRUCTIONS: In the text preceding this exercise, you read about the importance of a teacher's verbal and nonverbal messages being consistent or confluent, and not confusing the students. Three examples were presented in that discussion. It is the purpose of this exercise to heighten your own awareness about the importance of consistency between what you say and what you do as a teacher to better ensure consistency.

1. Think of a recent real-life example where, in your opinion, a classroom teacher's nonverbal behavior and verbal message were inconsistent. Without being intrusive, describe in detail the situation (including grade level, K–college) and the differing messages you believe that teacher conveyed to the students.

2. Describe the results of the inconsistency. In other words, how you could tell that the students were confused by the mixed signals sent by that teacher.

3. Did the teacher become aware that he or she sent contradictory messages? If so, was the situation clarified, and if so, how? Was the situation improved by the clarification?

4. Share this incident (steps 1–3) with your classmates.

5. Finally, after sharing incidents, describe what precautions you will take as a classroom teacher to avoid sending mixed messages and thus confusing your students.

Example: Instruct my students to inform me whenever they catch me being inconsistent in the messages I convey, and provide some sort of recognition or incentive for their alertness.

FOR YOUR NOTES

EXERCISE 4.6: IDENTIFYING TEACHER BEHAVIORS THAT CAUSE STUDENT MISBEHAVIOR—A SELF-CHECK REVIEW EXERCISE

INSTRUCTIONS: The purpose of this exercise is to practice your awareness of the kinds of teacher behaviors to avoid—namely, those that tend to reinforce or cause student misbehavior. Place a check next to each of the following situations you believe illustrate teacher behaviors that cause or reinforce student misbehavior. Then identify what the teacher should do instead. Share your responses with your classmates. An answer key follows.

_____ 1. Ms. Rodriquez is nearly always late in arriving to her eighth-grade English class that meets immediately after lunch, seldom beginning class until at least five minutes past the time it is supposed to start.

_____

_____

_____

_____

_____

_____

_____

_____ 2. Mr. Beyer ignores brief whispering between two students during a quiet activity in his seventh-grade history class.

_____

_____

_____

_____

_____

_____

_____

_____ 3. While lecturing to her biology class, Ms. Whyte ignores brief talking between two students.

_____

_____

_____

_____

_____

EXERCISE 4.6 *(continued)*

_____ 4. During a class discussion in Mr. Stephen's social studies class, one student appears to be daydreaming and just staring out the window.

_____

_____

_____

_____

_____

_____

_____ 5. During quiet study time in Mr. Orey's seventh-grade reading class, Mr. Orey asks for everyone's attention, verbally reprimands two students for horsing around, and then writes out a referral for each of the two students.

_____

_____

_____

_____

_____

_____

_____

_____ 6. Ms. Fueyo advises her students to pay attention during the viewing of a film or else she will give them a quiz on the film's content.

_____

_____

_____

_____

_____

_____ 7. Ms. Lee tells a student that because of his behavior in class today he must come in after school and be detained with her for 10 minutes, the same amount of time that he disturbed the class.

_____

_____

_____

_____

_____

EXERCISE 4.6   *(continued)*

_____ 8. When Mr. Murai sees a student cheating on a science test, he walks over to the student, picks up the student's test paper, and tears it up in front of the student and the rest of the class.

_____

_____

_____

_____

_____

_____

_____

_____

_____ 9. While Ms. Wong is talking to her eighth-grade language arts class, the school principal walks into the room. Ms. Wong stops her lecture and walks over to greet the principal and find out what the principal wants.

_____

_____

_____

_____

_____

_____

_____

_____

_____ 10. While a student learning team is giving its oral report to the health science class, Mr. Edwards, the teacher, begins a conversation with several students in the back of the room.

_____

_____

_____

_____

_____

_____

_____

_____

EXERCISE 4.6 *(continued)*

Answer Key

You should have checked situations 1, 3, 5, 6, 7, 8, 9, and 10; these are teacher behaviors that reinforce or cause student misbehavior. For some situations, reasonable teachers will disagree. You should talk about these disagreements with your classmates and arrive at common understandings. Here are some thoughts on each of the 10 situations:

1. Ms. Rodriquez's behavior is poor modeling for her students. She must model what she expects—as well as what the school expects—of students. In this instance, she should model arriving and starting on time.
2. Minor infractions, such as this, are often best ignored, as long as the whispering is brief and not disturbing.
3. This should not be ignored. Students are expected to give their attention to the teacher or whoever has the floor at the moment—a show of common courtesy. By not attending to these students (perhaps by eye contact, proximity, name dropping, or some other form of indirect intervention), Ms. Whyte is saying that it is OK for students to be discourteous and to talk during the teacher's lecture. In this instance, Ms. Whyte is not following through with classroom behavioral expectations. Her lack of follow-through will cause further and increasingly disturbing management problems.
4. Minor infractions are sometimes best ignored. Perhaps the student is really thinking about ideas presented in the discussion.
5. By his disruption of the class learning activity, Mr. Orey is reinforcing the very behavior he considers inappropriate from his students. This lack of consistency will cause continued problems in management for Mr. Orey.
6. Threats are unacceptable behaviors, from students or from teachers. And tests should never be administered as punishment. Ms. Fueyo could recommend that students take notes (mental or written) during the film, and that these notes will serve as a focus for discussion after the film's showing. And she could advise them that there will be a follow-up quiz later.
7. By giving the student even more individual attention after school, Ms. Lee is reinforcing and rewarding the student's misbehavior that caused the problem in the first place. Besides, this may not be safe for Ms. Lee to do. Detention, supervised by someone other than this teacher, is a better alternative.
8. Mr. Murai has taken no time to diagnose and to prescribe and thus is reacting too hastily and with hostility. This sort of teacher behavior reinforces the notion that the student is guilty until proven innocent and the notion that process is of greater importance than is the individual student. In addition, Mr. Murai violated this student's right to due process.
9. The error here is that by stopping her lesson, Ms. Wong and the principal are reinforcing the notion that classroom disruptions are acceptable—that the act of teaching is less important than other school business.
10. Mr. Edwards's behavior is both disrespectful and an example of poor modeling. Mr. Edwards and his class should be giving their full attention to the student's report. Mr. Edwards is not modeling the very behavior that he undoubtedly expects from his students when he is leading the class.

SITUATIONAL CASE STUDIES FOR ADDITIONAL REVIEW

To provide further insight into the day-by-day events that occur in teaching, as well as to stimulate your thinking about what you might do in similar situations, the following 10 case studies are presented. Each is a situation that actually occurred. Analyze and discuss these in your class, using the accompanying questions to guide your thinking.

CASE 1

The Boy Who Hangs Around

BACKGROUND

Bill is male, age 13, in life science. He is tall and awkward and has poor skin. His classmates consider him "crazy." He has minor police offenses and is apparently in conflict with his father. He has taken a liking to the life science teacher and spends many extra hours in the classroom. He is energetic and displays an inquisitive nature. He is quick to get interested in projects but almost as quick to lose interest. He likes to run the video projector for the teacher, but he does not like to participate in discussions with the rest of the class. He likes personal chats with the teacher but feels that the other students laugh at him.

THE SITUATION

Bill's IQ is recorded to be 95. The teacher attempted to work with Bill in improving his feelings of inadequacy and had frank talks with him about his gangliness and his acne. What follows is actual material as written by Bill during the first semester of school:

September: "I want to make the best out of the time I am on earth. I want to be somebody, not just exist either. . . . The members of this class influence me and what I think of doing. . . . They also make me feel real low. Their teasing me has changed me. . . . The teacher of my science class has helped me very much. . . . My greatest problem is in holding my head up and fighting for myself. . . ."

October: "I have made a lot of headway in the past weeks. . . . I think I have done a good choice in the subject I am studying. . . . I also thank my teacher's actions toward me, that we may get to be very good friends, and learn a lot to know that teachers are human too, that they also have problems to solve and goals to head for."

November: "I don't have to fear anybody or anything on the idea of getting up and saying what I feel I have accomplished in this class and I have learned to make my own decisions on what I will study or maybe do when I get out of school."

December: "I have learned that I have confidence in others only when I have confidence in myself."

January: "I have my report on the affect of geabriilic acid on plants. . . . I told (the class) about all my failures and they were quite interested. I told them that I had failed four times . . . that my science teacher told me I should not give up at this point and that a seintice [scientist] does not give up. I had no longer stated that fact and they all seemed like they could help in some way. I think the report went over well."

So the student developed courage to stand in front of his peers, holding his head high, and confidently reporting to the class how he kept at his plant experiment, even after four failures. He was proud of what he had learned about the work of the scientist. And he was even more proud that the students no longer teased and laughed at him.

Questions for Class Discussion
1. How did you feel after reading this case?
2. Did Bill learn anything that semester? What?
3. Did he learn science?
4. What did the teacher do to facilitate Bill's learning?
5. What is ahead for Bill in school?

CASE 2

The Bully

BACKGROUND

Tony is considered by his peers to be one of the "tough guys." He is 14 and in the eighth grade at Green Middle School. Tony is prone to bullying, frequently quarreling with his fellow students and teachers, and is considered by his parents to be disobedient. He has a record of minor offenses that range from truancy to destruction of property to drunkenness and offensive behavior. In general, Tony gets satisfaction in ways that are damaging and unfair to others.

It is obvious to school officials that Tony is beyond parental control. Tony's mother has no apparent ability to control Tony's behavior. His father frequently beats him.

Tony is not a member of any school organization, nor does he participate in co-curricular activities. His mid-term progress shows that he is failing in three subjects.

THE SITUATION

One of the subjects Tony is failing is English. Tony is a discipline problem in class, and although it makes the teacher feel guilty, she cannot help but be pleased when Tony is absent from class.

Questions for Class Discussion

1. Where is the problem?
2. Where is Tony heading?
3. What can and should be done, if anything? By whom?
4. What is the role for Tony? His teachers? His peers? The school administration? His parents? Society in general?
5. Is it too late for Tony?

CASE 3

The Problem of Mary

BACKGROUND

Mary has been characterized by her peers and by her teachers as being lonely, indifferent, and generally unhappy. She avoids both students and teachers. She will lie and cheat to avoid attention. Her "close" friends describe her as thoughtless and unkind. She often uses damaging remarks about members of her class, calling them conceited, teacher's pets, and so on. She considers members of her class to be thoughtless, unkind, and uninterested in her.

Mary will do what she has to do to achieve average success in her studies. Her association with adults, her parents, and her teachers would be described as one of "getting along," doing what "I have to do in order not to get too much attention."

THE SITUATION

One of Mary's friends is another 14-year-old girl, Jane. Jane is an above-average student in school, seemingly well adjusted, and interested in people. She has gotten to know Mary because they are neighbors and walk together to school. Because of Jane's interest in other people and her closeness to Mary, she has become interested in "trying to bring Mary out of her shell."

Mary has told Jane that she feels her teachers are unreasonably severe. Mary said, "The teachers are only interested in the popular kids." Jane disagreed. Mary said, "You only disagree because you are pretty and popular." At this point, the conversation was broken by a boy running up and saying, "Hey, Jane, you're late for the council meeting."

Questions for Class Discussion

1. Where is the problem?
2. What if you were Mary's teacher?
3. How did you feel after reading this case?

CASE 4

The Stabbing Victim

Ron King, who claims he was stabbed in the back during a class, wants $100,000 in damages from his school and student Richard Decarlo.

According to the action, filed by King's mother, the incident occurred last February. King says he was stabbed by Decarlo and lost his spleen as a result.

The suit says there was no teacher in the classroom when the stabbing took place and that the school was negligent in not providing supervision.

The action also contends that school officials knew that Decarlo secretly carried deadly weapons with him on the school grounds.

Question for Class Discussion

1. After reading this case, how did you feel and what were you thinking?

CASE 5

From a Deadly Dare

In a life science class the students were just starting a lab involving the dissection of triple latex-injected formaldehyde-preserved bullfrogs. While the teacher was busy talking with a few students off to one side of the room—answering their questions and helping them get started on their work—she heard screaming and a commotion from the far side of the room. She looked up and immediately saw Robert vomiting and convulsing. On a dare from other students, he had eaten one of the preserved bullfrogs, completely devouring it. Immediately the teacher sent a runner to the office (there was no phone in the classroom). Someone dialed 911, and an ambulance and paramedics soon arrived to take Robert to a nearby hospital, where his stomach was pumped and other treatment was administered. For the next 24 hours Robert was listed in serious condition.

Questions for Class Discussion
1. What were your thoughts after reading this case?
2. Could the incident have been prevented?

CASE 6

Student Has a Crush on Teacher

During his first year of teaching it had become obvious that one of Mr. Kline's female seventh-grade students had developed a serious crush on him. One day, after class was over and all other students had left the room, she approached Mr. Kline and politely asked him if he had a photograph of himself that she could have.

Questions for Class Discussion
1. Is this a potentially serious situation?
2. How should Mr. Kline respond to the student's request?

CASE 7

Science Teacher Solicits Students for Marijuana for Experiment

A teacher gave $30 to a student for a quantity of marijuana with the intention of putting the marijuana in a bowl with goldfish so students could study the effects on the fish. Before the experiment ever took place, other students reported the teacher's action to the school principal. The teacher was placed on administrative leave. After pleading guilty to charges of contributing to the delinquency of a minor, the teacher was sentenced to 45 days in jail and two years of probation. Apparently, the experiment was to be a repeat of one done earlier at the school by police officers, but with cutbacks and restraints the teacher decided to use her own money to repeat the experiment.

Questions for Class Discussion
1. After reading this, what were your thoughts?
2. What, if anything, did you learn from this situation that might be helpful to you during your own teaching career?

[*Note:* Perhaps the teacher should have searched for an alternative active. For example, see R. N. Russo & S. Parrish. (January 1990). Toxicology for the middle school. *Journal of Chemical Education, 72*(1), 49–50.]

CASE 8

Student Complains to a Student Teacher about Continued Sexual Harassment by a Peer

During the first week after John began his student teaching in eighth-grade history, one of his female students came to him after class and complained that a boy in the class has continued to sexually harass her even after she had reported it to the school vice principal. She says that the harassment is beyond just verbal abuse and she wants it stopped.

Questions for Class Discussion
1. After reading this case, what were your thoughts?
2. What, if anything, should John do?
3. What, if anything, did you learn from this situation that might be helpful to you during your own teaching career?

CASE 9

Students Use the Internet for Extracurricular Activity

During project work time in a seventh-grade language arts/social studies block, the classroom teacher discovers a group of three students at a computer workstation viewing a graphic sex website.

Questions for Class Discussion
1. After reading this, what were your immediate thoughts?
2. What should the teacher do?
3. How could the problem have been avoided?
4. What, if anything, did you learn from this case that might be helpful to you during your own teaching career?

CASE 10

Used the "N-Word" In Class*

Janine teaches English/language arts at a large inner-city school. It is her first year of teaching and the first day of classes following the summer break. As students are arriving in her classroom she overhears several students using the "n-word" as they call to and greet each other. Janine, a white teacher, does not react.

Questions for Class Discussion
1. After reading this scenario, what were your immediate thoughts?
2. What, if anything, should Janine have done differently? And/or what would you have done differently, were you the teacher?
3. Do you believe there is anything a teacher should or should not do depending on whether the teacher hears the "n-word" used in each of these instances: without malice in the classroom, with malice in the classroom, in the hall, on the school campus?
4. What, if anything, did you learn from this case that might be helpful to you during your own teaching career?
[*The inspiration for this case came from Luttrell & Ward (2004).]

SUMMARY

In this chapter, you learned ways to cope with the daily challenges of classroom teaching and of guidelines for effectively managing young adolescents in the classroom. Within that framework, your attention was then focused on specific approaches and additional guidelines for effective classroom management and control of the learning environment. You were offered advice for setting up and maintaining a classroom environment that is favorable to student learning, and for establishing procedures for efficiently controlling student behavior, helping students establish self-control, and for encouraging their learning. To become an accomplished classroom manager for the learning of young adolescents takes thoughtful and thorough planning, consistent and confident application, and reflective experience. Be patient with yourself as you accumulate the prerequisite knowledge and practice and hone the necessary skills.

From this knowledge about establishing the most effective learning environment, in the next two chapters you will be guided through important considerations for selecting the content and planning units of instruction and lessons.

QUESTIONS FOR CLASS DISCUSSION

1. Explain why you believe it is better to be strict with students at first and then relax once your control has been established, or to be relaxed at first and then tighten the reins later if students misbehave, or why, if the case, you believe it doesn't really matter.
2. Explain what you would do if two errant behaviors occurred simultaneously in different locations in your classroom.
3. Explain what you would do if a student from one of your classes came to you and reported that fellow students were harassing him by throwing objects at him, slapping him, pulling his chair out from under him, and pretending to rape him.
4. Sometimes, teachers encourage disruptive student behavior or even misbehavior by what they do or don't do, or by what they say. Teachers may not even be aware that students find their behavior irritating and that it "gets on their nerves." As you observe teachers (even college teachers will suffice), take notice of any teacher behaviors or idiosyncrasies that seem to encourage student hostility. Share what you discover with your classmates and discuss your findings and how they might relate to your own professional development.
5. You have undoubtedly read and heard much about the importance of modeling consistency when implementing the expected classroom procedures and the consequences for inappropriate behavior. When it comes to procedures and consequences, is there a danger in a teacher being too rigid or inflexible? Explain your answer.
6. It is not uncommon to find that a particular student achieves well and behaves well in one teacher's class but not in another. Discuss with your classmates what explanations there can be for such a difference in a young adolescent student's behavior and achievement.
7. To what extent does the environment of the classroom contribute to student behaviors such as stealing, lying, cheating, belligerence, and lack of consideration for others? Many believe the contribution to be substantial. With each of the following classroom situations, note what you would predict to be the consequences in the classroom. Discuss your notations with your classmates.
   - A teacher leaves money lying around on his desk.
   - A teacher stores her purse on the floor next to her desk.
   - Assignments are unreasonably excessive, with embarrassing consequences for noncompletion.
   - Testing situations are poorly supervised.
   - The classroom ambiance is one of high tension and anxiety; students are constantly edgy and easily irritated.
   - The teacher makes negative or destructively critical comments.
   - There are few opportunities to relax and enjoy social interaction.
   - There are many competitive situations in which students are pitted against each other and enjoy excelling or "beating" their classmates.
8. From your current observations and fieldwork as related to this teacher preparation program, clearly identify one example of educational practice that seems contradictory to exemplary practice or theory as presented in this chapter. Present your explanation for the discrepancy.
9. Knowledge held by other teachers about a student can be valuable for your insight about a particular student you have. But as a new teacher in particular you must use such information judiciously. In small groups, work with your classmates to see if you can come up with a few useful guidelines for distinguishing information from other school personnel that may be helpful from that which is not.
10. What are your thoughts about food and drink in your classroom? Will you or will you not allow it? Consider the following five examples concluding then with which teacher you would most identify:
    - Teacher A maintains the rule that no food or drink is allowed in the classroom.
    - Teacher B has the same rule although Mr. B does bring his own coffee (or other drink—your choice) to class.
    - Teacher C brings her coffee (or other drink—your choice) to class and allows students to bring water bottles with the understanding that water spills are to be quietly and quickly cleaned up by the responsible person.
    - Teacher D allows students to bring snacks and drinks, including sodas, to class.
    - Teacher E does not allow food or drink to be brought to class although Ms. E occasionally reward students with candy.

INTERNET RESOURCES

Bell activity **http://www.dailybite.com**

Bullying **http://www.bullying.org** *and*
http://www.bullyfreeme.com

California Home Visiting Center
   http://www.scusd.edu/cahvcenter

Marshall's raising responsibility at
   http://www.MarvinMarshall.com

Randy Sprick's Safe and Civil Schools
   http://www.safeandcivilschools.com

Sound amplification systems

   Audio Enhancement **http://www.audioenhancement.com**

   Califone International **http://www.califone.com**

   Phonic Ear **http://www.phonicear.com**

   Voice Academy **http://www.voiceacademy.org**

FOR FURTHER READING

Anderman, L. H., Patrick, H., & Ryan, A. M. (2004). Creating adaptive motivational environments in the middle grades. *Middle School Journal, 35*(5), 33–39.

Apter, T. (2006). Resolving the confidence crisis. *Educational Leadership, 63*(7), 42–46.

Crawford, G. B. (2004). *Managing the adolescent classroom.* Thousand Oaks, CA: Corwin Press.

Dougherty, J. W. (2002). *Classroom management and the middle school philosophy.* Fastback 500. Bloomington, IN: Phi Delta Kappa Educational Foundation.

Dougherty, J. W. (2004). *Torts and liability: An educator's short guide.* Fastback 527. Bloomington, IN: Phi Delta Kappa Educational Foundation.

Lindberg, J. A., Kelley, D. E., & Swick, A. M. (2005). *Common-sense classroom management for middle and high school teachers.* Thousand Oaks, CA: Corwin Press.

Littky, D. (2004). *The big picture.* Alexandria, VA: Association for Supervision and Curriculum Development.

Marshall, M., & Weisner, K. (2004). Using a discipline system to promote learning. *Phi Delta Kappan, 85,* 498–507.

Smith, R. (2005). *Conscious classroom management.* Thousand Oaks, CA: Corwin Press.

Stone, R. (2005). *Best classroom management practices for reaching all learners.* Thousand Oaks, CA: Corwin Press.

Sussman, G. L. (2006). The violence you don't see. *Educational Leadership, 63,* 1–7. Helping All Students Succeed, ASCD online journal at www.ascd.org:80/portal/site/ascd.

5

The Curriculum

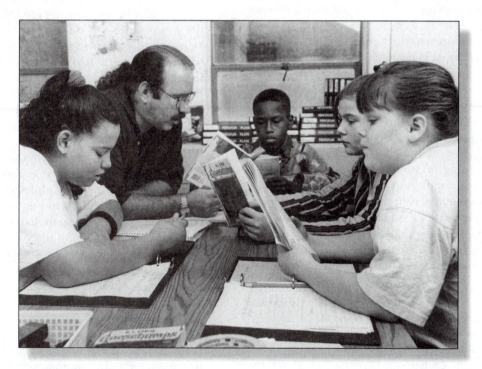

Scott Cunningham/Merrill

An effective curriculum is based on criteria of high quality and includes learning activities that create opportunities for students to "pose and answer questions that are important to them." Such a curriculum provides "direction for what young adolescents should know and be able to do and helps them achieve the attitudes and behaviors needed for a full, productive, and satisfying life."
National Middle School Association (2003, pp. 19 & 24)

Effective teaching of young adolescents does not just happen, it is produced through the thoughtful planning of each phase of the learning process. Most effective teachers begin their planning months before

meeting their students for the first time. Daily lessons form parts of a larger scheme, which is designed to accomplish the teacher's long-range curriculum goals for the semester or year and to mesh with the school's mission and goals standards.

If learning is defined only as the accumulation of bits and pieces of information, then we already know everything about how to teach and how students learn. However, the accumulation of pieces of information is at the lowest end of a spectrum of types of learning. Discoveries are still being made about the processes involved in higher forms of learning—that is, for meaningful understanding and the reflective use of that understanding. The results of recent research support the use of instructional strategies that help students make connections as they learn (Findley, 2002). These strategies include discovery learning, inquiry, collaborative and cooperative learning, interdisciplinary thematic instruction, and project-based learning, with a total curriculum that is integrated and connected to students' life experiences.

As said in Chapter 2, the methodology uses what is referred to as **hands-on** and **minds-on** learning—that is, the learner is learning by doing and is thinking about what she or he is learning and doing. When thoughtfully coupled, these approaches help construct, and often reconstruct, the learner's perceptions. Hands-on learning engages the learner's mind, causing questioning, turning a learner's mind on. Hands-on/minds-on learning encourages students to question and then, with the teacher's guidance, devise ways of investigating satisfactory, although sometimes only tentative, answers to their questions.

As a classroom teacher of young adolescents, your instructional task then is twofold: (1) to plan hands-on experiences, providing the materials and the supportive environment necessary for students' meaningful exploration and discovery and (2) to facilitate the most meaningful and longest-lasting learning possible once the learner's mind has been engaged by the hands-on learning—including, although not necessarily limited to, student learning of any curriculum which may be mandated by your state and local school district. To accomplish this requires your knowledge about curriculum, and competence in the use of varied and developmentally appropriate methods of instruction. To assist you in the acquisition of that knowledge and competence is the primary purpose of this resource guide.

Middle level (teacher) candidates analyze local, state, and national curriculum standards based on their knowledge of content and early adolescent development. They . . . design curriculum and select materials that are integrative, challenging, and grounded in the ideas, interests, and experiences of all.

National Middle School Association (2004)

Competent middle level teaching is a kaleidoscopic, multifaceted, eclectic process. When preparing and writing a book to prepare one to teach, by necessity its authors must separate that kaleidoscopic process into separate topics, which is not always possible to do in a way that makes equal sense to all users of the book. So, here is the plan and our advice for you. This chapter and the next address the instructional planning aspect, first the necessary planning of the curriculum and then, following in Chapter 6 is the detailed instructional planning necessary to bring the planned curriculum to

fruition. As you proceed through these chapters and begin the development of your instructional plans, from time to time you will want to refer to particular topics in Chapters 7 through 9. The rationale for careful planning and the components of that planning are topics pursued now in this chapter.

OBJECTIVES

Specifically, upon completion of this chapter you should be able to:

1. Anticipate controversial topics and issues that may arise while teaching, and what you might do if and when they do arise.
2. Demonstrate ability to select and plan the sequence of content for instruction in a particular subject that is typically taught in a classroom of young adolescents.
3. Demonstrate an understanding of the rationale for planning for instruction, the levels of planning, and the components of a total instructional plan.
4. Demonstrate knowledge of the value of various types of documents that can be resources for middle level curriculum and instructional planning.
5. Demonstrate understanding of how to help students to develop meaningful understandings while still scoring well on standardized achievement tests.
6. Demonstrate understanding of the concept of integrated curriculum, and its relevance to curriculum and instruction for young adolescents.
7. Demonstrate an understanding of the distinction between curriculum content that is *essential* and that which is *supplemental*.
8. Demonstrate an understanding of the value and limitations of a syllabus, textbook, and other print resources for student learning.
9. Describe the relationship of instructional planning to the preactive and reflective thought-processing phases of instruction.
10. Differentiate among diagnostic assessment, formative assessment, and summative assessment and explain the place and use of each in instructional planning.
11. Explain both the value and the limitations afforded by using instructional objectives.
12. Explain the difference and the relationship between hands-on and minds-on learning.
13. Explain the connection among curriculum standards, instructional objectives, and assessment of student learning.
14. Explain the value of students being empowered with some decision making about course planning.
15. Prepare learning objectives for each of the three domains of learning and at various levels within each domain.

PROGRAM ORGANIZATION: PROVIDING SUCCESSFUL TRANSITIONS

Within the framework of middle level school organization lie several components that form a comprehensive, albeit ever-changing, program. Central to the school's purpose and its organizational structure is the concerted effort to see that all students make successful transitions from one level to the next, from one grade to the next, from one school to the next, and ultimately from high school to work and/or postsecondary education. Every aspect of the school program is, in some way, designed to guide students in their making successful transitions. Combining to form the program that students experience are two terms you will frequently encounter, *curriculum* and *instruction*. Let us next clarify those terms as they are used in this resource guide.

CURRICULUM AND INSTRUCTION: CLARIFICATION OF TERMS

Originally derived from a Latin term referring to a racecourse for the Roman chariots, among educators the term *curriculum* still has no singularly accepted definition. Some define it as the planned subject-matter content and skills to be presented to students. Others say that the curriculum is only what students actually learn. Still others hold the broad definition that the curriculum is all experiences students encounter, whether planned or unplanned, learned or unlearned.

Four programs are identified that contribute in different ways to student learning, that do, in fact, comprise the broadest definition of curriculum:

(a) the program of studies (subjects studied; courses offered)
(b) the program of student activities (e.g., sports, clubs, and organizations)
(c) the program of services (e.g., transportation, meals, counseling, nurse station)
(d) the hidden curriculum (i.e., the unplanned and subtle message systems within schools, as discussed in Chapter 1).

This working definition considers curriculum as the *entire school program*. Accepting this broad definition of curriculum, the National Middle School Association describes curriculum of developmentally responsive middle level schools as being all that is intentionally designed to accomplish the school's mission. The curriculum embraces every planned aspect of a school's educational program, including the classes that are designed specifically to advance skills and knowledge and school-wide services such as guidance, clubs and interest groups, visual and performing arts productions, student government, fund-raising events, and athletic programs (National Middle School Association, 2003, p. 19).

Instruction, too, has several definitions, some of which are not clearly distinguishable from curriculum. Whereas curriculum is usually associated with the content of the learning, instruction is associated with *methods* or *strategies*—that is, with ways of presenting content, conveying information, and facilitating student learning. Obviously, curriculum and instruction must be in tandem to affect student learning.

Curriculum Domains and Their Components

Looking at the total school program (the curriculum) and analyzing its various component parts, or domains, you can readily see the importance of studying curriculum and instruction. In one such study, Hough (1989) identified six domains that affect young adolescent student learning experiences (see Figure 5.1).

Although the six domains do not address the hidden (unplanned) curriculum, it is understood that various amounts and degrees of unplanned learning occur within each of the domains. In addition, whereas some schools include certain specialty classes as part of the core curriculum, others do not. In other words, any school's philosophy forms the underpinnings for the development of its curriculum. The middle school philosophy asserts that the needs of young adolescents are different from those of other stages of human development and require a curriculum that attends to these needs. Based on this principle, the various parts of middle school curricula can be grouped into three areas that combine all programs, components, and domains into a comprehensive and challenging middle school educational program. The three areas are the core curriculum, exploratory opportunities, and co-curricular student activities. A brief review of each of these three areas follows.

Core Curriculum

Core subjects of the curriculum as defined by the *No Child Left Behind Act of 2001* are English, reading or language arts, mathematics, science, foreign languages, civics and government, economics, arts, history, and geography. It is within these subjects, individually or in some combination, that *interdisciplinary thematic units* (ITUs) are taught. The purpose of teaching subject matter on a central theme is to avoid a departmentalized mentality that all too often communicates the wrong message to students—that learning is piecemeal and separate from one experience to another. To the contrary, the core curriculum facilitates the integration of subjects of the thematic units taught in tandem by the teaching team.

Figure 5.1 Middle school curriculum domains and their components.

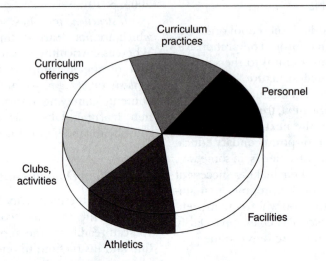

1. Domain of *curriculum offerings* (content)

   - Core subjects—English/language arts/reading (literacy), history/social studies/geography, mathematics, science, arts and foreign languages
   - Specialty classes—advisor-advisee
   - Exploratory opportunities—academic and nonacademic, graded and nongraded classes, sometimes taught for a shorter period of time by teachers, parents, and community members and designed to provide special opportunities for students to discover learning outside the core and the traditional academic format. Exploratories include intramural sports, health, clubs, student government, home economics, technological arts, independent study projects, speech, drama, careers, hunter safety, yearbook and newspaper, consumer education, creative writing, computer, captive breeding, film study, calligraphy, and many more.

2. Domain of *curriculum practices* (instruction)

   - Cooperative learning
   - Electives
   - Individual development
   - Interdisciplinary
   - Learning how to learn
   - Mastery learning
   - Mini-classes and experimental projects
   - Mission statement
   - Parental and community involvement
   - Project-centered
   - Service learning (see Chapter 1)

3. Domain of specialized *personnel* (faculty and staff)

   - Administrators
   - Cafeteria staff
   - Coaches
   - Community volunteers, mentors
   - Counselors
   - Custodial and grounds crew staff
   - Hall monitors and security personnel
   - Librarians
   - Nurse and other health specialists
   - Physical education teachers
   - Visual and performing arts teachers

4. Domain of *clubs and activities*

   - Assemblies
   - Cheerleading
   - Clubs
   - Dances and parties
   - School newspaper and yearbook
   - Student government

5. Domain of *athletics*

   - Interscholastic (competitive between schools)
   - Intramural (noncompetitive and open to all students of the school)

6. Domain of *facilities*

   - Auditorium
   - Athletic field
   - Concession stand
   - Grounds
   - Gymnasium
   - Nature area

Curriculum Content: Essential versus Supplemental

Content that is specified by mandated state curriculum standards is that which is required, that *must* be covered by instruction—it is *essential*. On the other hand, *supplemental content* is *not* mandated by the state standards, but rather is curriculum that is arbitrary and dependent upon the discretion of the teacher or teaching team.

Exploratory Opportunities

Usually, by middle grades, exploratory opportunities have become a substantial part of the school curriculum. The purpose of exploratory opportunities is to provide a variety of experiences to assist students in their discovery of areas of interest for future pursuit that will perhaps develop into a lifelong passion. Allowing students opportunities to discover and explore unusual and novel topics can spawn or rekindle interests in life and school. Exposing them to a range of academic, vocational, and recreational subjects for career options, community service, enrichment, and enjoyment, exploratories build on the inherent curiosity of young adolescents.

Co-Curricular versus Extracurricular

Traditionally, especially in junior high schools and high schools, student activities involving clubs and athletics have been commonly referred to as "extracurricular." That is because they are considered separate from the academic learning of the regular school day. However, in exemplary middle level education many activities are significant components of the total educational program and are "co-curricular," rather than extracurricular. *Co-curricular* means that regardless of whether they occur before, during, or after school, or in some combination, the activities are vital to the total curriculum. They are integral to the total school experience and to the needs of the students, not simply add-ons or extras. Example co-curricular program components are intramurals, study skills, and advisory (discussed next).

The sports program in the exemplary middle level schools in particular emphasizes intramural participation rather than interscholastic competition (Wiles & Bondi, 2001). Some middle level schools try to offer both, but most experts of middle level curricula agree that emphasis on an intramural program is better suited to the needs of all students (McEwin, Jenkins, & Dickinson, 1996). Intramural sports programs are developed to promote participation by all students. The emphasis is on fun, teamwork, socialization, and peer relationships in an unthreatening and relaxed environment. Assessment is based on a student's willingness to cooperate with others and to participate, rather than on the student's skill or performance. Through intramurals, all students can recognize and feel that they are members of a cohesive group, that they are of value as individuals, and that more important than skilled performance is regular, physical exercise.

Advisory Program

The advisory (also called "homebase") program in many middle level schools is usually a separate class, ideally of 8 to 12 students (although, in reality, closer to 15 to 25) that meets daily for no less than 20 minutes, without interruptions, often at the beginning of the school day. The primary purpose of the advisory is to ensure adult advocacy for each student, that each student is known well by at least one adult who can give positive and constructive individual attention to that student. In fact, in some schools the homebase teacher remains with the same students throughout their years at that school.

Regardless of its housing and its label, the advisory program should promote a student's feeling of belonging to a group and is not intended to be used for mechanical tasks (although, in reality, it is sometimes a time for announcements and other maintenance tasks). The program is for purposeful, individual and small-group activities that deal with students' social relationships, transitioning, health education, and emotional/psychological development and well-being. The program should be a vehicle for dealing with students' affective needs and for teaching skills in organization and studying, thinking, problem solving, decision making, violence prevention, and for ensuring meaningful contacts with parents and guardians. In short, for the student, the advisory program, with its planned adult advocacy for each student, can be a very significant aspect of the total school curriculum.

PLANNING FOR INSTRUCTION: THREE LEVELS

As a classroom teacher, planning for instruction is a major professional responsibility. You will be responsible for planning at three levels—the school year, the units, and the lessons—with critical decisions to be made along the way and at each level.

You need not do all your instructional planning from scratch, and you need not do all your planning alone. As a matter of fact, much of the time you *should not* do all your planning alone. In many middle level schools, teams of teachers develop the curricula. Teams of teachers collectively plan special programs for their specific cohorts of students. Team members either plan together or split the responsibilities and then share their individual plans. A final plan is then developed collaboratively.

Some middle level schools subscribe to packaged curriculum programs, especially in reading and mathematics, which are pre-planned and sometimes highly scripted for teacher use. The teacher's manual for the program includes an actual script and specifies the time to spend on a particular activity. The writers of published scripted curriculum programs wrote for students of a

> The most effective education of young adolescents is the result of the combined efforts of competent teachers using the best tools, not the result of tools alone.

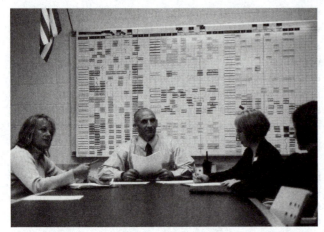

Liz Moore/Merrill

particular developmental level in general; they did not know your students specifically. As a teacher using a scripted program, you still should tweak the program to address the needs of your particular group of students, making decisions about the content, instructional objectives, materials, teaching strategies, your responses to student behaviors, and assessments of the learning experiences. Without making such adjustments for a particular group of students, it would be impossible for any teacher to differentiate the instruction so as to adequately attend to the personal needs and differences of individual students.

In summary, regardless of whether planning is done alone and from scratch, or in collaboration with others, or from a commercially published, scripted program, the heart of productive planning is good decision making. To some degree or another, for every plan and at each of the three levels, you and your team must make decisions about educational standards to be addressed, goals and learning objectives to be set, the subject to be introduced, materials and equipment to be used, methods to be adopted, assessments to be made, and the tools to be used for those assessments. This decision-making process is complicated because so many options are available at each level. Decisions made at all three levels result in a total plan.

> It is, at least in our opinion, this decision-making obligation and privilege that defines the teacher as an artist and classroom teaching as a profession.

Although the planning process continues year after year, the task becomes somewhat easier after the first year as you learn to recycle plans. The process is also made easier via research and communication—by reviewing documents and sharing ideas and plans with other teachers.

Teacher-Student Collaborative Team Planning

Even with the current emphasis on standardized achievement testing, exemplary middle level classrooms tend to be more project-oriented and student- and group-centered than the common teacher- and subject-centered classroom of the past, in which the teacher served as the primary provider of information. Although most assuredly the teacher today is no less a determiner of what is ultimately learned by the students, today's students more actively participate in their learning in collaboration with the teacher or teaching team (Weasmer & Woods, 2000). The teacher and teaching team provide some structure and assistance, but the *collaborative approach* requires that students inquire and interact, generate ideas, seriously listen and talk with one another, and recognize that their thoughts and experiences are valuable and essential to learning that is most meaningful and longest lasting.

Many teachers and teaching teams encourage their students to participate in the planning of some phase of their learning. Such participation tends to give students a proprietary interest in the activities, to satisfy the developmental need to explore knowledge, and a sense of ownership to their learning, thereby increasing their motivation for learning. What students have contributed to the plan often seems more meaningful to them than what others have planned for them. And students like to see their own plans succeed. Thus, teacher-student collaboration in planning is usually a very effective motivational tool.

Reasons for Planning

Planning is done for a number of important reasons, perhaps foremost of which is to ensure curriculum coherence, that is, to ensure that what is supposed to be learned is, in fact, learned. Periodic lesson plans are an integral component of a larger plan, represented by school- and district-wide mission statements and target standards, and by grade level and course goals and objectives. Students' learning experiences are thoughtfully planned in sequence and then orchestrated by teachers who understand the rationale for their respective positions in the curriculum. Such plans do not preclude, of course, an occasional diversion from predetermined activities.

Another reason for planning is to assure that the curriculum is developmentally appropriate for the intended students, that is, to give consideration to students' experiential backgrounds, developmental needs, learning capacities and styles, reading abilities, and exceptionalities. Without careful planning it would be impossible for any teacher to individualize the instruction and adequately attend to students' needs and differences.

Planning is necessary to ensure efficient and effective teaching with a minimum of classroom-control problems. After deciding what to teach, you face the important task of deciding how to teach it. To efficiently use precious instructional time, planning should be accomplished with two goals in mind: to not waste anyone's time during the time allotted for instruction and to select strategies that most effectively promote the anticipated student learning. As emphasized throughout this resource guide, a large portion of the instruction will be via student-centered, indirect instruction, although not exclusive of direct instruction. (See, for example, the discussion "Degrees of Directness" in Chapter 6.)

Planning helps ensure program continuation. The program must continue even if you are absent and a substitute teacher is needed. Planning provides a criterion for reflective practice and self-assessment. After a learning activity and at the end of a school term, you can reflect on and assess what was done and how it affected student learning. Your plans represent a criterion recognized and evaluated by supervisors and administrators.

Not only does good planning provide a boost to your own feelings of confidence and self-assuredness but also from the preceding you realize there are many other reasons a teacher must plan carefully. With those experienced in such matters, it is clear that inadequate planning is usually a precursor to incompetent teaching. Put simply, failing to plan is planning to fail.

Components of an Instructional Plan

A total instructional plan has several major components, described as follows.

Rationale component. This is a statement about why the content of the plan is important and about how students will learn it. The statement should be consistent with the school's mission statement and with the school district's benchmark curriculum standards.

Goals and objectives (standards) component. The goals and objectives represent the learning targets, that is, the specific knowledge, skills, and attitudes to be gained from the study. The plan's learning targets should be consistent with the rationale statement. This topic is discussed in the section that follows, titled "Curriculum Standards."

Articulation component. The articulation component shows the plan's relationship to the learning that preceded and the learning and experiences that will follow. This is referred to as *vertical articulation*. The plan should also indicate its *horizontal articulation*, which is its connectedness with other learning and activities occurring simultaneously across the grade level. Writing and literacy and thinking skills development are examples. Vertical and horizontal articulation representations are usually illustrated in curriculum documents and programs by scope and sequence charting.

Learning activities component. This is the presentation of organized and sequential units and lessons

appropriate for the subject, and for the age and diversity of the learners.

Resources component. This is a listing of resources needed, such as print and electronic resources, artifacts (or realia), and community resource ideas, such as guest speakers or presenters, service learning projects, and field trip locations.

Assessment component. This is the appraisal of student learning and occurs as three parts: (a) before instruction begins, a *preassessment* (or diagnostic assessment) of what students already know or think they know about the topic; (b) during the instruction (*formative assessment*) to uncover whether students are learning that which is intended; and (c) at the end of the instruction (*summative assessment*) to determine the extent the students actually did learn.

Special considerations component. This is a place to make notes to remind yourself to consider special populations of students in your classroom, such as gifted learners, challenged learners (students with exceptionalities), and English language learners.

Curriculum Content Selection: Documents That Provide Guidance

---

A Continuing Dilemma for the Classroom Teacher
Breadth versus Depth of Content Coverage

Many more things are worth teaching than we have time to teach in school, so breadth of topic coverage must be balanced against depth of development of each topic. This is an enduring dilemma that can only be managed in sensible ways, not a problem that can be solved once and for all. School curricula have drifted into addressing far too many topics and including too many trite or pointless details. Analyses in all of the subject areas suggest the need for teacher decision making about how to reduce breadth of coverage, structure the content around powerful ideas, and develop these ideas in depth.

(Good & Brophy, 2003, p. 410)

Whether for a semester, a school year, or some other interval of time, when planning the content of the curriculum you should decide what specifically is to be accomplished in that time interval. To help in setting goals, you will examine school and other resource documents for mandates and guidelines; communicate with colleagues to learn of common expectations; and probe, analyze, and translate your own convictions, knowledge, and skills into behaviors that foster the intellectual and psychological, and in some instances, the physical, development of your students.

With the guidance provided by Exercises 5.1–5.4, you will examine major documents that assist you in selecting the content of your curriculum. These are: national and state curriculum standards, school or district benchmark standards, curriculum frameworks and courses of study, and school-adopted materials. Sources for your examination of these documents include the Internet (see website listings at end of this chapter), your college or university library, and personnel at local schools.

CURRICULUM STANDARDS

What are curriculum standards? **Curriculum standards** are a definition of what students should know (content) and be able to do (process and performance). At the national level, curriculum standards did not exist until those developed and released for mathematics education by the National Council of Teachers of Mathematics in 1989 (revised in 2000). Shortly after the release of the mathematics standards, support for national goals in education was endorsed by the National Governors Association, and the National Council on Education Standards and Testing recommended that in addition to those for mathematics, national standards for subject matter content in K–12 education be developed for the arts, civics/social studies, English/language arts/reading, geography, history, and science. The U.S. Department of Education provided initial funding for the development of national standards. In 1994, the United States Congress passed the *Goals 2000: Educate America Act*, which was, in 1996, amended with an Appropriations Act that encouraged states to set curriculum standards. Long before, however, as was done for mathematics, national organizations devoted to various disciplines were already defining standards.

What are the national standards? The national standards represent the best thinking by expert panels, including teachers from the field, about what are the essential elements of a basic core of subject knowledge that all K–12 students should acquire. They serve not as national mandates but rather as voluntary guidelines to encourage curriculum development to promote higher student achievement.

National Curriculum Standards by Content Area

The following paragraphs describe current national curriculum standards and the related professional organizations for teachers specifically relevant to the middle grades. Relevant websites are listed at the end of this chapter.

Arts (visual and performing). The National Standards for Arts Education were developed jointly by the American Alliance for Health, Physical Education, Recreation, and Dance (AAHPERD), the National Art Education Association (NAEA), the National Dance Association, and the Music Educators National Conference.

English/language arts/reading. Standards for English education were developed jointly by the International Reading Association (IRA), the National Council of Teachers of English (NCTM), and the University of Illinois Center for the Study of Reading.

Foreign languages. Standards for Foreign Language Learning: Preparing for the 21st Century was developed by the American Council on the Teaching of Foreign Languages (ACTFL).

Geography. Standards for geography education were developed jointly by the Association of American Geographers, the National Council for Geographic Education (NCGE), and the National Geographic Society.

Health. National Health Education Standards: Achieving Health Literacy was developed by the Joint Committee for National School Health.

History/civics/social studies. The Center for Civic Education and the National Center for Social Studies developed standards for civics and government, and the National Center for History in the Schools developed the standards for history.

Mathematics. The document *Curriculum and Evaluation Standards for School Mathematics* was developed by the National Council of Teachers of Mathematics (NCTM).

Physical education. The National Association of Sport and Physical Education (NASPE) published *Moving into the Future: National Standards for Physical Education.*

Science. With input from the American Association for the Advancement of Science (AAAS) and the National Science Teachers Association (NSTA), the National Research Council's (NRC) National Committee on Science Education Standards and Assessment published the standards for science education.

Technology. With initial funding from the National Science Foundation (NSF) and the National Aeronautics and Space Administration (NASA), and in collaboration with the International Technology Education Association, National Educational Technology Standards were developed.

Supplements to the national standards are available from the Bureau of Indian Affairs (BIA) for the arts (dance, music, theater, and visual), civics and government, geography, health, language arts, mathematics, science, and social studies. *The American Indian Supplements* may be used by Indian nations as guides in their preparation of tribally specific local standards. They are also useful to school districts serving American Indian children in adapting state standards to be more culturally relevant to their communities.

State Curriculum Standards

Strongly influenced by the national standards, nearly all states have completed or are implementing at least some of their own standards for the various disciplines. For example:

- For the state of Massachusetts, standards are found in eight curriculum frameworks: arts, English language arts, comprehensive health, mathematics, science and technology/engineering, history and social sciences, foreign languages, and English language proficiency.

- For the state of Florida, standards are found in documents in subject areas of the arts (dance, music, theater, and visual), foreign languages, health, language arts, mathematics, physical education, science, and social studies.
- For the state of Idaho, standards are found in documents for health, humanities, language arts/communications, mathematics, science, and social studies.
- The North Carolina Standard Course of Study presents curriculum in arts education, computer/technology skills, English/language arts, English language development, healthful living, information skills, mathematics, science, second-language studies, social studies, and workforce development.
- And, for the state of Texas, the Texas Essential Knowledge and Skills (TEKS) are in the foundation areas of English-language arts and reading, mathematics, science, social studies, Spanish language arts and English as a Second Language, and in the enrichment areas of languages other than English, fine arts, health education, physical education, and technology applications.

Curriculum Standards and High-Stakes Testing

Both national and state standards, accessible on the Internet (see listings at end of this chapter), provide guidance to the developers of the standardized tests that are used in what is referred to today as high-stakes testing, that is, the tests being given to determine student achievement, promotion, rewards to schools and even to individual teachers, and, in about half the 50 states, as a requirement for graduation from high school.

The adoption of tougher learning standards throughout the United States coupled with an emphasis on increased high-stakes testing to assess how schools and teachers are doing with respect to helping their students meet those standards has provoked considerable debate, actions, and reactions among educators, parents, politicians, and from the world of business. Some argue that this renewed emphasis on testing means too much "teaching to the test" at the expense of more meaningful learning, that it ignores the leverage that home, community, and larger societal influences have over the education of children and young people today. In the words of Lauren Sosniak (2001),

> We need to find ways to ask what our communities, corporations, media, and all of our organizations and institutions are doing to promote the development of readers, writers, historians, scientists, artists, musicians, designers and crafts persons. Schools cannot do this

work alone, in the 9% of [a child's K–12 lifetime in school] allotted to them. If this is only 'school work,' it is hard to imagine that our students will see it as a meaningful part of their lives and their futures.... For too long our schools have been held accountable for too much, with too little acknowledgement of the responsibilities of the rest of society.

Nevertheless, responding to the call for increased accountability, especially although not exclusively when state and federal funding may be withheld and/or jobs are on the line for schools, teachers, and administrators where students do not score well, teachers in some schools put aside the regular curriculum for several weeks in advance of the testing date and concentrate on the direct preparation of their students for the test.

Although the interest has been rekindled in recent years, this oft-called "drill and kill" practice is certainly not new. For example, one of the authors can recall as a high school student in Ohio in the early 1950s being given the *Every Pupil Test*, twice a year, one version in December, another version in April. For several weeks before the scheduled test, each teacher would set aside the regular curriculum to prepare the students directly for those tests by distributing and reviewing with them older versions of the tests. Today's interest in annual statewide testing caused us to consider how it compares with past practices.

When comparing standardized testing of today with that of about half a century ago, it is probably safe to conclude: (a) the purpose for statewide standardized testing remains unchanged—it is to determine how well children are learning, at least to the extent determined by the particular test instrument; (b) test design is accomplished today with much greater precision and accuracy; but (c) today's focus on testing is taking precious time away from the most creative aspects of teaching and learning; and (d) the manner in which test results are being used today, and the long-term results of that use, may have ramifications considerably more serious than at any time before.

In schools with the required technology, that subscribe to software programs such as eduTest.com and Homeroom.com, and that have the appropriate number of computers necessary to provide access time to individual students, students can practice and prepare for the state-mandated tests online. Proponents of such online preparation argue that a major advantage is the immediate scoring of practice testing with feedback about each student's areas of weakness, thereby providing the teacher with information necessary for immediate remediation. If the arguments are accurate, then it would seem axiomatic that children of such technology-rich schools would clearly be at an advantage over children in schools where this technology is not available. [*Note:* The disparity between those who have computer access and those who do not is sometimes referred to as *digital inequality* or the *digital divide.*] It would only follow that district and government agencies that mandate the standards and specific assessment practices should provide avenues and tools to assure equity and success for all children toward reaching the expected learning outcomes within the designated learning time. Is in fact this so-called digital divide closing? According to recent studies, "there is no doubt that more American children of all incomes and backgrounds are using computers and the Internet than ever before. But it is also clear that some groups of young people—primarily low income and minority youth—have poorer access to technology than others" (Henry J. Kaiser Family Foundation, 2004, p. 1).

Proceed now to Exercises 5.1, 5.2, 5.3, and 5.4, through which you will explore a variety of types of curriculum documents.

EXERCISE 5.1: EXAMINING NATIONAL CURRICULUM STANDARDS

INSTRUCTIONS: The purpose of this exercise is to become familiar with national curriculum standards for the subject(s) you intend to teach. Using the Internet addresses provided at the end of this chapter, review the standards that interest you. Use the following questions as a guideline for subject-area, small-group discussions. Following the small-group discussion, share the big ideas about the standards and perceptions of your group with the rest of your class.

Subject area (you may duplicate this form for each subject examined):

_____

1. Title of the standards document reviewed, year of publication, and development agency:

2. Major educational goals as specified by the national standards:

3. Are the standards specific as to subject-matter content for each level of schooling, K–12? Explain.

4. Do the standards offer specific strategies for instruction? Describe.

5. Do the standards offer suggestions for teaching students who are culturally different, for students with special needs, for English-language learners, and for students who are intellectually gifted and talented? Describe.

6. Do the standards offer suggestions or guidelines for dealing with controversial issues and topics? Give an example.

7. Do the standards documents or their accompanying materials offer suggestions for specific resources? Describe.

8. Do the standards refer to assessment? Describe.

9. Do the standards promote or discourage inquiry, discovery learning, and/or critical thinking? If so, describe.

10. Is there anything else about the standards you would like to discuss and present?

FOR YOUR NOTES

EXERCISE 5.2: EXAMINING STATE CURRICULUM STANDARDS

INSTRUCTIONS: The purpose of this exercise is to become familiar with your state curriculum standards for the subject(s) you intend to teach. Using the Internet addresses provided at the end of this chapter, review the standards that interest you. Use the following questions as a guideline for subject-area, small-group discussions. Following the small-group discussion, share the big ideas about the standards and perceptions of your group with the rest of your class.

Subject area (you may duplicate this form for each subject examined):

_____

1. Title of the standards document reviewed, year of publication, and development agency:

2. Major educational goals as specified by the national standards:

3. Are the standards specific as to subject-matter content for each level of schooling, K–12? Explain.

4. Do the standards offer specific strategies for instruction? Describe.

5. Do the standards offer suggestions for teaching students who are culturally different, for students with special needs, for English-language learners, and for students who are intellectually gifted and talented? Describe.

6. Do the standards offer suggestions or guidelines for dealing with controversial issues and topics? Give an example.

7. Do the standards documents or their accompanying materials offer suggestions for specific resources? Describe.

8. Do the standards refer to assessment? Describe.

9. Do the standards promote or discourage inquiry, discovery learning, and/or critical thinking? If so, describe.

10. Is there anything else about the standards you would like to discuss and present?

FOR YOUR NOTES

EXERCISE 5.3: EXAMINING STATE CURRICULUM FRAMEWORKS

INSTRUCTIONS: The purpose of this exercise is to become familiar with curriculum documents published by your state department of education. You must determine if that department publishes a curriculum framework for various subjects taught in schools. State frameworks provide valuable information about both content and process, and teachers need to be aware of these documents. You may want to duplicate this form so you can use it to evaluate several documents. After examining documents that interest you, use the following questions as a guideline for small- or large-group class discussions.

1. Are there state curriculum documents available and relevant to middle school teachers for your state? If so, describe them and explain how they can be obtained.

   Title of document:

   Source:

   Most recent year of publication:

   Other pertinent information:

2. Examine how closely the document follows the components presented in this chapter. Are any components omitted? Are there additional components? Specifically, check for these components:

	Yes	No
a. Rationale?	_____	_____
b. Goals and objectives?	_____	_____
c. Schemes for vertical articulation?	_____	_____
d. Schemes for horizontal articulation?	_____	_____
e. Recommended instructional procedures?	_____	_____
f. Recommended resources?	_____	_____
g. Assessment strategies?	_____	_____

   Other:

3. Are the documents specific as to subject-matter content for each grade level? Describe evidence of both vertical and horizontal articulation schemes.

4. Do the documents offer specific strategies for instruction? If yes, describe.

EXERCISE 5.3 *(continued)*

5. Do the documents offer suggestions and resources for working with students who are culturally different, for students with special needs, for English-language learners, and for students who are intellectually gifted and talented? Describe.

6. Do the documents offer suggestions or guidelines for dealing with controversial topics? If so, describe.

7. Do the documents distinguish between what shall be taught (mandated) and what can be taught (permissible)?

8. Do the documents offer suggestions for specific resources?

9. Do the documents refer to assessment strategies? Describe.

10. Is there anything else about the documents you would like to discuss in your group?

EXERCISE 5.4: EXAMINING LOCAL CURRICULUM DOCUMENTS

INSTRUCTIONS: The purpose of this exercise is to become familiar with curriculum documents prepared by local school districts. A primary resource for what to teach is referred to as a *curriculum guide*, or *course of study*, which normally is developed by teachers in a school or district. Samples may be available in your university library or in a local school district resource center. Or perhaps you could borrow them from teachers you visit. Obtain samples from a variety of sources and then examine them using the format of this exercise. (You may duplicate this form for each document examined.) An analysis of several documents will give you a good picture of expectations. If possible, compare documents from several school districts and states.

Title of document: _____

District or school: _____

Date of document: _____

1. Does the document contain the following?

	Yes	*No*
a. Statement of rationale?	_____	_____
b. Goals and objectives?	_____	_____
c. Schemes for vertical articulation?	_____	_____
d. Schemes for horizontal articulation?	_____	_____
e. Recommended instructional procedures?	_____	_____
f. Recommended resources?	_____	_____
g. Assessment strategies?	_____	_____

2. Does the document list expected learning outcomes? If so, describe what they are. _____

_____

_____

_____

3. Does the document contain detailed unit plans? If so, describe them by answering the following questions:

a. Are the units interdisciplinary? _____

b. Do they contain initiating activities (how to begin a unit)? _____

c. Do they contain specific learning activities? _____

d. Do they contain suggested enrichment activities (as for gifted and talented students)? _____

e. Do they contain culminating activities (activities that bring a unit to an end)? _____

f. Do they contain assessment procedures (for determining student achievement)? _____

g. Do they contain activities for learners with special needs? for English-language learners, or for learners who are different in other respects? _____

h. Do they contain activities that address learning styles or learning capacities? _____

EXERCISE 5.4   *(continued)*

4. Does it provide bibliographic entries for

   • The teacher? _____

   _____

   _____

   _____

   • The students? _____

   _____

   _____

   _____

   _____

5. Does it list audiovisual, media, and other materials needed? _____

   _____

   _____

   _____

   _____

   _____

   _____

6. Does the document clearly help you understand what the teacher is expected to teach? _____

   _____

   _____

   _____

   _____

   _____

7. Are there questions not answered by your examination of this document? If so, list them for class discussion.

   _____

   _____

   _____

   _____

   _____

   _____

STUDENT TEXTBOOKS

As schools grow more diverse, so too must our understanding of what it means to be literate.
—Dana G. Thames & Kathleen C. York (2003, p. 609)

For several reasons—recognition of the diversity of learning styles, capacities, and modalities of students; changing concepts about literacy and habits of thought; enhanced graphics capabilities; economic pressures in the publishing industry; and the availability of electronic and other nonprinted materials—textbook appearance, content, and use has changed considerably in recent years and in all likelihood will continue to change.

Within the span of your teaching career, you will likely witness and even be a contributor to a revolution in the continuing redesign of school textbooks. Already some schools allow teachers in certain disciplines the option of choosing between traditional printed textbooks, textbook-loaded laptop computers, and interactive computer programs, or some combination of these (Gordon, 2002).

With the continuing developments in electronics and microcomputer chip technology, textbooks may take on a whole new appearance. With that will come dramatic changes in the importance and use of text as well as new problems for the teacher, some that are predictable, and others we can't even imagine. On the positive side, it is probable that the classroom teacher will have available a variety of "textbooks" to better address the reading levels, interests, abilities, and perhaps even the primary language of individual students. With these changes, the distribution and maintenance of reading materials could create a greater demand on the teacher's time. Regardless, dramatic and exciting events have begun to affect the teaching tool that had not changed much throughout the twentieth century. The textbook of the not-so-distant future may become a handheld, multimedia, interactive, and personal tool that encompasses digitized text, sound, and video and allows for global communications.

Still, today, printed textbooks regulate a large percentage of the learning activity in the middle grades classrooms. School districts periodically adopt new textbooks (usually every five to eight years). If you are a student teacher or a first-year teacher, this will most likely mean that someone will tell you, "Here are the books you will be using."

Benefit of Textbooks to Student Learning

It is unlikely that anyone could rationally argue that textbooks are of no benefit to student learning. Textbooks can provide: (a) an organization of basic or important content for the students that includes and is built around state curriculum standards, (b) a basis for deciding content emphasis, (c) previously tested activities and suggestions for learning, (d) information about other readings and resources to enhance student learning, and (e) a foundation for building higher-order thinking activities (e.g., inquiry discussions and student research) that help develop critical thinking skills. The textbook, however, should not be the "be all and end all" of the instructional experiences.

Problems with Reliance on a Single Textbook

The student textbook is only one of many teaching tools, and not the ultimate word. Of the many ways in which you may use textbooks for student learning, the *least* acceptable is to show a complete dependence on a single book and require students simply to memorize material from it. This is the lowest level of textbook use and learning; furthermore, it implies that you are unaware of other significant resources and have nothing more to contribute to student learning.

Another potential problem brought about by reliance upon a single textbook is that because textbook publishers prepare books for use in a larger market—that is, for national or statewide use—a state- and district-adopted book may not adequately address issues of special interest and importance to the community in which you teach. That is one reason why some teachers and schools provide supplementary printed and electronic resources.

Still another problem brought about by reliance upon a single source is that the adopted textbook may not be at the appropriate reading level for many students. In today's heterogeneous classrooms, the level of student reading can easily vary by as much as two-thirds of the chronological age of the students. This means that if the chronological age is 12 years (typical for seventh graders), then the reading-level range would be eight years—that is, the class may have some students reading at only the preschool level, if at all, while others have college-level reading ability. Think about that for a moment!

Now examine student textbooks and teacher's editions of those books by doing Exercise 5.5.

FOR YOUR NOTES

EXERCISE 5.5: EXAMINING STUDENT TEXTBOOKS AND TEACHERS' EDITIONS

INSTRUCTIONS: The purpose of this exercise is to become familiar with textbooks that you may be using in your teaching. Student textbooks are usually accompanied by a teacher's edition that contains specific objectives, teaching techniques, learning activities, assessment instruments, test items, and suggested resources. Your university library, local schools, and cooperating teachers are sources for locating and borrowing these enhanced textbooks. For your subject field of interest, select a textbook that is accompanied by a teacher's edition and examine the contents of both, using the following format. If there are no standard textbooks available for your teaching field (such as might be the case for art, music, and physical education), then select a field in which there is a possibility you might teach. Beginning teachers are often assigned to teach in more than one field—sometimes, unfortunately, in fields for which they are untrained or have only minimal training. After completion of this exercise, share the book and your analysis of it with your colleagues.

Title of book: _____

Author(s): _____

Publisher: _____

Date of most recent publication: _____

	Yes	*No*
1. Analyze the teacher's edition for the following elements:		
a. Are its goals consistent with the goals of local and state curriculum documents?	_____	_____
b. Are there specific objectives for each lesson?	_____	_____
c. Does the book have scope and sequence charts for teacher reference?	_____	_____
d. Are the units and lessons sequentially developed, with suggested time allotments?	_____	_____
e. Are there any suggested provisions for individual differences?	_____	_____
for reading levels?	_____	_____
for students with special needs?	_____	_____
for students who are gifted and talented?	_____	_____
for students who have limited proficiency in English?	_____	_____
f. Does it recommend specific techniques and strategies?	_____	_____
g. Does it have listings of suggested aids, materials, and resources?	_____	_____
h. Are there suggestions for extension activities (to extend the lessons beyond the usual topic or time)?	_____	_____
i. Does the book have specific guidelines for assessment of student learning?	_____	_____
2. Analyze the student textbook for the following elements:		
a. Does it treat the content with adequate depth?	_____	_____
b. Does it treat ethnic minorities and women fairly?	_____	_____
c. Is the format attractive?	_____	_____
d. Does the book have good-quality binding with suitable type size?	_____	_____
e. Are illustrations and visuals attractive and useful?	_____	_____
f. Is the reading clear and understandable for the students?	_____	_____
g. Is the content current and accurate?	_____	_____

EXERCISE 5.5   *(continued)*

3. Would you like to use this textbook? Give reasons why or why not.

_____

_____

_____

_____

_____

_____

_____

_____

_____

_____

_____

_____

_____

_____

_____

_____

_____

_____

_____

_____

_____

_____

_____

_____

_____

_____

_____

_____

_____

_____

_____

_____

_____

Guidelines for Textbook Use

Generally speaking, students benefit by having their own copies of a textbook in the current edition. However, because of budget constraints, this may not always be possible. The book may be outdated or quantities may be limited. When the latter is the case, students may not be allowed to take the books home or perhaps may only occasionally do so. In some high-poverty area schools, students are not allowed to take textbooks from the classroom. In other classrooms, because of inadequate or misappropriated funding, there may be no textbook at all.

Encourage students to respect books by covering and protecting them and not marking in them. In many schools this is a rule; at the end of the term, students who have damaged or lost their books are charged a fee. As a matter of fact, this is why, as said in the previous paragraph, that in some high-poverty area schools books are not issued at all. If their students lose or damage their books and are charged a fee, the fee goes unpaid because neither the students nor their parents/guardians can afford to pay it.

Yet, in classrooms of some school districts, there are two sets of the textbook, one set that remains for use in the classroom and another set that is assigned to students to use for studying at home. With that arrangement, students don't have to carry around in their backpacks the heavy books used for many subjects taught in today's middle schools. The paragraphs that follow offer general guidelines for using the textbook as a learning tool.

Progressing through a textbook from the front cover to the back in one school term is not necessarily an indicator of good teaching. The textbook is one resource; to enhance their learning, students should be encouraged to use a variety of resources. Encourage students to search additional sources to update the content of the textbook. This is especially important in certain disciplines such as the sciences and social sciences, where the amount of new information is growing rapidly and students may have textbooks that are several years old. The library and sources on the Internet should be researched by students for the latest information on certain subjects, always keeping in mind, however, that just because something is found in print or on the Net doesn't mean that the information is accurate or even true. Maintain supplementary reading materials for student use in the classroom. School and community librarians and resource specialists usually are delighted to cooperate with teachers in the selection and provision of such resources.

Individualize the learning for students of various reading abilities. Consider differentiated reading and workbook assignments in the textbook and several supplementary sources (see "Multitext and Multireadings Approach," a topic that follows). Except to make life simpler for the teacher, there is no advantage in all students working out of the same book and exercises. Some students benefit from the drill, practice, and reinforcement afforded by workbooks or software programs that accompany textbooks, but this is not true for all students, nor do all students benefit from the same activity. In fact, the traditional printed workbook may eventually become extinct, as it is replaced by the modern technology afforded by electronic software. Computers and other interactive media provide students with a psychologically safer learning environment where they have greater control over the pace of the instruction, can repeat instruction if necessary, and can ask for clarification without the fear of having to do so publicly.

Creative teachers continue to invent methods to help students develop their higher-level thinking skills and their comprehension of expository material. Some of these methods are shown in Figure 5.2.

> Just because it is found in print or on the Internet or on broadcast news doesn't mean it's accurate or even true.

Encourage students to be alert for errors in the textbook, both in content and printing—perhaps offering some sort of credit reward when they bring an error to your attention. This can help students develop the skills of critical reading, critical thinking, and healthy skepticism.

Multitext and Multireadings Approach

Rather than a single textbook approach, consider using a strategy that incorporates many readings that vary in difficulty, detail, and vocabulary but have a common focus. Whatever the unit, teachers can include a wide range of materials: informational picture and chapter books; biographies and photographic essays; and Internet, newspaper, and magazine articles. Giving students a choice in what they read, the multiple reading source strategy helps all students become a part of the same community of readers (Robb, 2002). Especially useful for interdisciplinary thematic instruction, the strategy also allows for differences in reading ability and interest level and stimulates a sharing of what is read and being learned. By using a teacher's guide, such as the sample in Figure 5.3, all the students can be directed toward specific information and concepts, but they do not have to all read the same selections.

BEGINNING TO THINK ABOUT THE SEQUENCING OF CONTENT

As you have reviewed the rationale and components of instructional planning, examined curriculum standards, curriculum documents, and student reading

Figure 5.2   Methods for helping students develop their higher-level thinking skills and their comprehension of expository material.

- KQHL: Students ask what they want to know (K) about a topic, ask what questions (Q) do we need/want answered, ask how (H) might we find answers, and then later identify what they have learned (L) (Long, Drake & Halychyn, 2004).
- KWL: Students recall what they already know (K) about a topic, determine what they want to learn (W), and later assess what they have learned (L) (Ogle, 1986).
- KWLQ: Students record what they already know about a topic (K), formulate questions about what they want to learn about the topic (W), search for answers to their questions (L), and ask questions for further study (Q) (source unknown).
- KWHLS: Students identify what they already know about the topic of study (K), what they want to learn (W), how they plan to learn it (H), then what they learned (L), and finally how they will share that new knowledge with others (S) (source unknown).
- POSSE: *Predict* ideas, *organize* ideas, *search* for structure, *summarize* main ideas, and *evaluate* understanding (Englert & Mariage, 1991).
- PQRST: *Preview, question, read, state* the main idea, and *test* yourself by answering the questions you posed earlier (Kelly, 1994).
- QAR: Helping children understand *question* and *answer relationships* (Mesmer & Hutchins, 2002).
- RAP: *Read* paragraphs, *ask* questions about what was read, and *put* in your own words (Schumaker, Denton, & Deshler, 1984).
- Reciprocal teaching: Students are taught and practice the reading skills of summarizing, questioning, clarifying, and predicting (Palincsar & Brown, 1984).
- SQ3R: *Survey* the chapter, ask *questions* about what was read, *read, recite*, and *review* (Robinson, 1961).
- SQ4R: *Survey* the chapter, ask *questions* about what was read, *read* to answer the questions, *recite* the answers, *record* important items from the chapter into their notebooks, then *review* it all (source unknown).
- SRQ2R: *Survey, read, question, recite*, and *review* (Walker, 1995).

materials, you have undoubtedly reflected on your own opinion regarding content that should be included in a subject at a particular grade level. Now it is time to obtain some practical experience in long-range planning.

While some authors believe that after selecting the content the first step in preparing to teach is to prepare the objectives, others believe that a more logical starting point is to prepare a sequential topic outline—the next step in this chapter—from which you can then prepare the major target objectives (benchmark standards). With today's pressure on teachers to work from established and mandated benchmark standards it may well be that many teachers today do, in fact, begin their curriculum development from those objectives.

Regardless of the approach used, the curriculum plan should satisfy three organizational requirements:

1. The plan should be organized around important ideas, concepts, and questions, all of which should correlate with mandated content standards.

2. The plan should reflect the interests and concerns of the recipient students.

3. The plan should be oriented toward the assessments and tasks that will be used for students in demonstrating what they have learned.

The curriculum plans, topic outlines, and instructional objectives may be presented to most beginning teachers with the expectation that they will teach from them. For you this may be the case, but someone had to have written those outlines and objectives and that someone was one or more present or former classroom teachers. As a new teacher, you must know how this is done, for someday it will be your task. To experience preparing a full semester content outline for a subject and grade level that you intend to teach, do Exercise 5.6 now.

Figure 5.3   Sample multiple readings guide and student's book bibliography to assist students in multiple readings about America's Revolutionary times in 1776.

- Purpose: To engage students in multiple readings, critical thinking, and problem solving related to America's Revolutionary times in 1776.
- Activities:

1. By reading and browsing through several books and by carefully observing several illustrations of people in this particular time period and geographic area, the students can engage in critical thinking and problem solving by working in small groups. The bibliography that follows includes books related to America in 1776 that are suitable for a wide range of reading levels. Students can respond to the following focus questions after multitext reading:
   a. What features of the land (features of government, society, etc.) seem to be important to the people in 1776?
   b. What occupations seem to be most important? What inventions (tools, machines) appear to be most useful?
   c. What do the answers to these questions tell us about the way of life of the people who lived in this time period (geographic area)?
2. Back with the whole group, have the students from each group report on the responses to the questions. Engage students in dictating or writing a paragraph summarizing the responses to the questions.
3. Students can meet with response partners to read their individually written paragraphs aloud to one another and provide suggestions to each other for rewriting the paragraphs.

- Bibliography [*Note:* The bibliography shown here is not intended to be inclusive, only to show how a multiple readings guide might appear]:

African American

Davis, B. *Black Heroes of the American Revolution.* (San Diego: Harcourt J, 1976). Nonfictional account depicting contributions of African Americans during the Revolutionary War. Includes drawings, etchings, bibliography, and an index.

Hansen, J. *The Captive.* (New York: Scholastic, 1994). Based on a journal written in the late 1700s, this is about Kofi, the 12-year-old son of an Ashanti chief. Kofi is sold and sent to America after a family slave murders his father. Kofi and others escape from the farmer in Massachusetts and return to Africa. An epilogue relates his good life when he returned to Africa.

Millender, D. H. *Crispus Attucks: Black Leader of Colonial Patriots.* (New York: Macmillan, 1986). Biographical portrayal of the life of a Colonial African American and his contribution to the American Revolution.

European

Wade, M. D. *Benedict Arnold.* (New York: Franklin Watts, 1995). Biographical story of Arnold's life; his heroic deeds, including his leadership at the battle of Saratoga; his later traitorous actions; and his death in London. Includes information about his wife, Peggy Shippen.

Female Image

DePaul, L. G. *Founding Mothers: Women in America in the Revolutionary Era.* (Boston: Houghton Mifflin, 1975). Nonfictional account of the contributions of women during the revolution.

McGovern, A. *Secret Soldier: The Story of Deborah Sampson.* (New York: Scholastic, 1991). Story of a young woman who disguised herself as a boy and joined the army to serve in America's War for Independence.

Latino/Hispanic

Anderson, J. *Spanish Pioneers of the Southwest.* Illustrated by G. Ancona. (New York: Dutton, 1989). Nonfictional account of the lives of the colonists on the east coast contrasted with the lives of the members of a pioneer family in a Spanish community in New Mexico in the 1700s and the family's hard work, harsh living conditions, and traditions.

Native American

Hudson, J. *Dawn Rider.* (New York: Putnam, 1990). Fictional account of 16-year-old Kit Fox, a Blackfoot, forbidden to ride horses. She disobeys and her riding skills help her people when their camp is attacked.

Kinsey-Warock, N. *Wilderness Cat.* Illustrated by Mark Graham. (Minneapolis: Cobblehill, 1992). Lives of colonists are contrasted with the lives of Serena's family members when they moved to Canada in the 1700s. Even though the family trades with the Indians, they do not have enough to eat; Papa and Serena's brother leave to find work. Historical fiction.

Religious Minority

Faber, D. *The Perfect Life: The Shakers in America.* (New York: Farrar, Straus, & Givoux, 1974). Escaping from England, Mother Ann and several followers voyage to America and set up the first settlement in New York in 1776. Nonfictional account detailing the Shaker influence on furniture construction, mechanical inventions, and their religious beliefs.

FOR YOUR NOTES

EXERCISE 5.6: PREPARING A FULL SEMESTER CONTENT OUTLINE

INSTRUCTIONS: The purpose of this exercise is for you to organize your ideas about subject content and the sequencing of content for one semester. Unless instructed otherwise by your instructor, you should select the subject (e.g., algebra, science, English/language arts) and the grade level (5–8).

With *three levels of headings* (see the example that follows), prepare a sequential topic outline (on a separate piece of paper, as space is not provided here) for a subject and grade level you intend to teach. Identify the subject by title, and clearly state the grade level. This is an outline of topic content only and does *not* need to include student activities associated with learning that content (i.e., do not include experiments, assignments, or assessment strategies).

For example, for the study of earth science, three levels of headings might include

I. The earth's surface
   A. Violent changes in earth's surface
      1. Earthquakes
      2. Volcanoes.
   B. Earth's land surface
      1. Rocks
         etc.

If the study of earth science is just one unit for a grade level's study of the broader area of "science," then three levels of headings for that study might include

I. Earth science
   A. The earth's surface
      1. Violent changes in earth's surface
         etc.

Share your completed outline to obtain feedback from your colleagues and university instructor. Because content outlines are never to be "carved in stone," make adjustments to your outline when and as appropriate.

CONTENT OUTLINE ASSESSMENT CHECKLIST

For the development of your own outline and the assessment of outlines by others, following is a content outline assessment checklist:

- Does the outline align with relevant curriculum standards? Yes _____ No _____
  Comment: _____

- Does the outline follow a logical sequence, with each topic logically leading to the next? Yes _____
  No _____ Comment: _____

- Does the content assume prerequisite knowledge or skills that the students are likely to have? Yes _____
  No _____ Comment: _____

- Is the content inclusive, and to an appropriate depth? Yes _____ No _____ Comment: _____

- Does the content consider individual student differences? Yes _____ No _____ Comment: _____

- Does the content allow for interdisciplinary studies? Yes _____ No _____ Comment: _____

EXERCISE 5.6   *(continued)*

- Is the outline complete? Yes _____ No _____ Are there serious content omissions? Yes _____

  No _____ Comment: _____

  _____

- Is there content that is of questionable value for this level of instruction? Yes _____ No _____

  Comment: _____

Save your content outline and this completed exercise for later when you are working on Exercise 5.12 and Exercises 6.3 and 6.4 in Chapter 6.

PREPARING FOR AND DEALING WITH CONTROVERSY

Controversial content and issues abound in teaching, in most disciplines. For example:

- continuing debate over sex education and to what extent, if at all, it should be approached in public schools
- in science, over biological evolution (Joiner, 2003, Terry, 2004).
- in social studies, over moral issues
- in English/reading, over certain books—see Exercise 5.7B— [*Note:* Although efforts to censor books used in schools is nothing new, challenges seem to be escalating (Franklin, 2002)]

As a general rule, if you have concern that a particular topic or activity might create controversy, it probably will. During your teaching career, you undoubtedly will have to make decisions about how you will handle such matters. When selecting content that might be controversial, consider the paragraphs that follow as guidelines.

Maintain a perspective with respect to your own goal, which is at the moment to obtain your teaching credential, and then a teaching job, and then tenure. Student teaching, in particular, is not a good time to become embroiled in controversy. If you communicate closely with your cooperating teacher and your college or university supervisor, you should be able to prevent major problems dealing with controversial issues.

Sometimes, during normal discussion in the classroom, a controversial subject will, however, emerge spontaneously, catching the teacher off guard. If this happens, think before saying anything. You may wish to postpone further discussion until you have a chance to talk over the issue with members of your teaching team or your supervisors. Controversial topics can seem to arise from nowhere for any teacher, and this is perfectly normal. Your young adolescent students are in the process of developing their moral and value systems, and they need and want to know how adults feel about issues that are important to them, particularly those adults they hold in esteem—their teachers. Our youth need to discuss issues that are important to society, and there is absolutely nothing wrong with dealing with those issues as long as certain guidelines are followed.

First, students should learn about all sides of an issue. Controversial issues are open-ended and should be treated as such. They do not have "right" answers or "correct" solutions. If they did, there would be no controversy. [*Note:* As used in this discussion, an "issue" differs from a "problem" in that a problem generally has a solution, whereas an issue has many opinions and several alternative solutions.] Therefore, the focus should be on process as well as on content. A major goal is to show students how to deal with controversy and to mediate wise decisions on the basis of carefully considered information. Another goal is to help students learn how to disagree without being disagreeable—how to resolve conflict. To that end, students need to learn the difference between conflicts that are destructive and those that can be constructive, in other words, to see that conflict (disagreement) can be healthy and that it can have value. A third goal, of course, is to help students learn about the content of an issue so, when necessary, they can make decisions based on knowledge, not on ignorance.

Second, as with all lesson plans, one dealing with a topic that could lead to controversy should be well thought out ahead of time. Potential problem areas and resources must be carefully considered and prepared for in advance. Problems for the teacher are most likely to occur when the plan has not been well conceived.

Third, at some point all persons directly involved in an issue have a right to input: students, parents and guardians, community representatives, and other faculty. This does not mean, for example, that people outside of the school necessarily have the right to censor a teacher's plan, but it does mean that parents or guardians and students should have the right *sans penalty* to not participate and to select an alternate activity. Most school districts have written policies that deal with challenges to instructional materials. As a beginning teacher, you should become aware of policies of your school district. In addition, professional associations such as the NCTE, NCSS, NBTA, and NSTA publish guidelines for dealing with controversial topics, materials, and issues.

Fourth, there is nothing wrong with students knowing a teacher's opinion about an issue as long as it is clear that the students may disagree without reprisal or penalty of any sort. However, it is probably best for a teacher to wait and give her or his opinion only after the students have had full opportunity to study and report on facts and opinions from other sources. Sometimes it is helpful to assist students in separating facts from opinions on a particular issue being studied by setting up on the overhead or writing board a fact-opinion table, with the issue stated at the top and then two parallel columns, one for facts, the other for related opinions, as shown here.

Issue: _____	
FACTS	OPINIONS

A characteristic that makes this nation so great is the freedom for all its citizens to speak out on issues. We agree with others in that this freedom proffered by the First Amendment of the Bill of Rights of the U.S. Constitution should not be excluded from public school classrooms (Haynes, Chaltain, Ferguson, Hudson, & Thomas, 2003). Teachers and students should be encouraged to express their opinions about the great issues of today, to study the issues, to suspend judgment while collecting data, and to form and accept each other's reasoned opinions. We must understand the difference between teaching truth, values, and morals, and teaching about truth, values, and morals.

As a teacher of young adolescents in a public school there are limits to your academic freedom, much greater than are the limits, for example, on a university professor working with college students. You must understand this fact. The primary difference is that the students with whom you will be working are not yet adults; because they are juveniles they must be protected from dogma and allowed the freedom to learn and to develop their values and opinions, free of coercion from those who have power and control over their learning.

Now that we have shared our opinion and suggested guidelines, what do you think about this topic, which should be important to you as a teacher? Use Exercises 5.7A and 5.7B for the development and expression of your opinion.

EXERCISE 5.7A DEALING WITH CONTROVERSIAL CONTENT AND ISSUES

INSTRUCTIONS: The purpose of this exercise is for you to discover controversial content and issues that you may face as a teacher and to consider what you can and will do about them. After completing this exercise, share it with members of your class.

1. After studying current periodicals and talking with colleagues in the school you visit, list two potentially controversial topics that you are likely to encounter as a teacher. (Two examples are given for you.)

Issue	*Source*
Rose Casement, "Breaking the Silence: The Stories of Gay and Lesbian People in Children's Literature"	*New Advocate, 15*(3), 205–213 (Summer 2002)
"Human Cloning"	*New York Times 8/22/01*

2. Take one of these issues, and identify opposing arguments and current resources. _____

_____

_____

_____

_____

_____

3. Identify your own positions on this issue. _____

_____

_____

_____

_____

_____

4. How well can you accept students (and parents or guardians) who assume the opposite position? _____

_____

_____

_____

_____

_____

EXERCISE 5.7A *(continued)*

5. Share the preceding with other teacher candidates. Note comments that you find helpful or enlightening.

_____

_____

_____

_____

_____

EXERCISE 5.7B CENSORSHIP: BOOKS THAT ARE SOMETIMES CHALLENGED

INSTRUCTIONS: Continuing with the topic introduced in Exercise 5.7A, this exercise concentrates on certain books that, although frequently used in public schools, are sometimes challenged by members of some communities. Book censorship becomes a concern when literature is the base for integrated teaching since there may be attempts to censor and ban books and curricular materials in the schools. Books that have been challenged include the following:

A Light in the Attic (Shel Silverstein)
Adventures of Huckleberry Finn, The (Mark Twain)
Annie on My Mind (Nancy Garden)
Are You There, God? It's Me, Margaret (Judy Blume)
Arizona Kid, The (Ron Koertge)
Blubber (Judy Blume)
Bridge to Terabithia (Katherine Paterson)
Catcher in the Rye, The (J. D. Salinger)
Chocolate War, The (Robert Cormier)
Christine (Stephen King)
Color Purple, The (Alice Walker)
Fallen Angels (Walter Dean Myer)
Flowers for Algernon (Daniel Keyes)
Flowers in the Attic (V. C. Andrews)
Forever (Judy Blume)
Giver, The (Lois Lowry)

Go Ask Alice (Anonymous)
Handmaids's Tale, The (Margaret Atwood)
I Know Why the Caged Bird Sings (Maya Angelou)
Kaffir Boy: The True Story of a Black Youth's Coming of Age in Apartheid South Africa (Mark Mathabane)
Lord of the Flies (William Golding)
My Brother Sam Is Dead (James Lincoln Collier and Christopher Collier)
Of Mice and Men (John Steinbeck)
Outsiders, The (S. E. Hinton)
Running Loose (Chris Crutcher)
Scary Stories to Tell in the Dark (Alvin Schwartz)
Slaughterhouse-Five (Kurt Vonnegut)
To Kill a Mockingbird (Harper Lee)
Witches, The (Roald Dahl)

We leave the organization of this exercise for your class to decide; we recommend that you assign small groups to review certain books, then report to the entire class so that all the books on the list are addressed.

AIMS, GOALS, AND OBJECTIVES: THE ANTICIPATED LEARNING OUTCOMES

Now that you have examined content typical of the curriculum, have experienced preparing a tentative content outline for a subject that you intend to teach, and understand some important guidelines for dealing with controversial topics, you are ready to write instructional objectives for that content learning.

Instructional objectives are statements describing what the student will be able to do upon completion of the planned learning experience. Whereas some authors distinguish between *instructional objectives* (hence referring to objectives that are not behavior specific) and *behavioral* or *performance objectives* (objectives that *are* behavior specific), the terms are used here as if they are synonymous to emphasize the importance of writing instructional objectives in terms that are measurable.

As a teacher, you frequently will encounter the compound structure that reads "goals and objectives," as you likely found in the curriculum documents that you reviewed (Exercises 5.1–5.4). A distinction needs to be understood. The easiest way to understand the difference between the two words, *goals* and *objectives*, is to look at your *intent*.

Goals are ideals that you intend to reach, that is, ideals that you would like to have accomplished. Goals may be stated as teacher goals, as student goals, or, collaboratively, as team goals. Ideally, in all three, the goal is the same. If, for example, the goal is to improve students' reading skills, it could be stated as follows:

"To help students develop their reading skills"	*Teacher or course goal*
or	
"To improve my reading skills"	*Student goal*

Educational goals are general statements of intent and are prepared early in course planning. [*Note:* Some writers use the phrase "general goals and objectives," but that is incorrect usage. Goals *are* general; objectives are specific.] Goals are useful when planned cooperatively with students and/or when shared with students as advance mental organizers to establish a mind-set. The students then know what to expect and will begin to prepare mentally to learn it. From the goals, objectives are prepared. Objectives are *not* intentions. They are the actual behaviors that students are expected to display. In short, objectives are what students *do*.

The most general educational objectives are often called *aims*; the objectives of schools, curricula, and courses are called *goals*; the objectives of units and lessons are called *instructional* or *target objectives*. Aims are more general than goals and goals are more general than objectives. Instructional objectives are quite specific. Aims, goals, and objectives represent the targets, from general to specific statements of learning expectations, to which curriculum is designed and instruction is aimed.

Instructional Objectives and Their Relationship to Aligned Curriculum and Authentic Assessment

As implied in the preceding paragraphs, goals guide the instructional methods; objectives drive student performance. Assessment of student achievement in learning should be an assessment of that performance. When the assessment procedure matches the instructional objectives, that is sometimes referred to as assessment that is *aligned* or *authentic*. [*Note:* If the term *authentic assessment* sounds rather silly to you, we concur. After all, if the objectives and assessment don't match, then that particular assessment should be discarded or modified until it does match. In other words, assessment that is not authentic is "poor assessment" and should not be used.] When objectives, instruction, and assessment match the stated goals we have what is referred to as an *aligned curriculum*. (Again, a curriculum that does not align is nonsensical and should be either corrected or discarded. You can even find in some literature the terms *authentic instruction* and *authentic teaching*. The rule still applies, and that is, instruction or teaching that is not authentic . . . Need we say more?)

Goals are general statements, usually not even complete sentences, often beginning with the infinitive "to," which identify what the teacher intends the students to learn. Objectives, stated in performance terms, are specific actions and should be written as complete sentences that include the verb "will" *to indicate what each student is expected to be able to do as a result of the instructional experience*. The last portion of the previous sentence is emphasized because when writing instructional objectives for their unit and lesson plans, one of the most common errors made by teachers is to state what *they*, the teachers, intend to do rather than what the anticipated student performance is. The value of stating learning objectives in terms of student performance is well documented by research (Baker & Martin, 1998; Good & Brophy, 2003).

While instructional goals may not always be quantifiable (i.e., readily measurable), instructional objectives should be measurable. Furthermore, those objectives then become the essence of what is measured for in instruments designed to assess student learning; they are the learning targets. Consider the examples shown in Figure 5.4.

Learning Targets and Goal Indicators

One purpose for writing objectives in performance terms is to be able to assess with precision whether the instruction has resulted in the desired behavior. In

Figure 5.4 Examples of goals and objectives.

Goals

1. To acquire knowledge about the physical geography of North America.
2. To develop an appreciation for music.
3. To develop enjoyment for reading.

Objectives

1. On a map, the student will identify specific mountain ranges of North America.
2. The student will identify 10 different musical instruments by listening to an audio recording of the Boston Pops Symphony Orchestra and identify which instrument is being played at specified times as determined by the teacher.
3. The student will read two books, three short stories, and five newspaper articles at home, within a two-month period. The student will maintain a daily written log of these activities.

many schools the educational goals are established as **learning targets,** competencies that the students are expected to achieve, and that were derived from the district and state curriculum standards. These learning targets are then divided into performance objectives, sometimes referred to as goal indicators. Instruction is designed to teach toward those objectives. When students perform the competencies called for by these objectives, their education is considered successful. This is known variously as *criterion-referenced, competency-based, performance-based, results-driven,* or *outcome-based education.* When the objectives are aligned with specific curriculum standards, as they usually are or should be, then it can also be referred to as **standards-based education.** Expecting students to achieve one set of competencies before moving on to the next set is called **mastery** (or **quality**) **learning.** The success of the student achievement, teacher performance, and the school may each be assessed according to these criteria.

Overt and Covert Performance Outcomes

Assessment is not difficult to accomplish when the desired performance outcome is overt behavior, which can be observed directly. Each of the sample objectives of the preceding section is an example of an overt objective. Assessment is more difficult to accomplish when the desired behavior is covert, that is, when it is not directly observable. Although certainly no less important, behaviors that call for "appreciation," "discovery," or "understanding," for example, are not directly observable because they occur within a person, and so are covert behaviors. Since covert behavior cannot be observed directly, the only way to tell whether the objective has been

achieved is to observe behavior that may be indicative of that achievement. The objective, then, is written in overt language, and evaluators can only assume or trust that the observed behavior is, in fact, reasonably close to being indicative of the expected learning outcome.

Furthermore, when assessing whether an objective has been achieved—that learning has occurred—the assessment device must be consistent with the desired learning outcome. Otherwise, the assessment is not aligned; it is invalid. When the measuring device and the learning objective are compatible, we say that the assessment is authentic. For example, a person's competency to teach specific skills in mathematics to seventh graders is best (i.e., with highest reliability) measured by directly observing that person *doing* that very thing—teaching specific skills in mathematics to seventh graders. Using a standardized paper-and-pencil test of multiple-choice items to determine a person's ability to teach specific math skills to seventh-grade students is not authentic assessment. Although the particular multiple-choice item assessment device might be valid, it is *not* authentic.

Balance of Behaviorism and Constructivism

While behaviorists (behaviorism) assume a definition of learning that deals only with changes in overt behavior, constructivists hold that learning entails the construction or reshaping of mental schemata and that mental processes mediate learning. Thus, people who adhere to constructivism or cognitivism or constructionism are concerned with both overt and covert behaviors (DeLay, 1996; *Educational Leadership,* 1999; Geelan, 1997). Does this mean that you must be one or the other, a behaviorist or a constructivist? Probably not. For now, the point is that when writing instructional objectives, you should write most or all of your basic expectations (minimal competency expectations) in overt terms (the topic of the next section). On the other hand, you cannot be expected to foresee all learning that occurs nor to translate all that is learned into performance terms—most certainly not before it occurs.

Teaching toward Multiple Objectives, Understandings, and Appreciations: The Reality of Classroom Instruction

Any effort to write all learning objectives in performance terms is, in effect, to neglect the individual learner for whom it purports to be concerned; such an approach does not allow for diversity among learners. Learning that is most meaningful to students is not so neatly or easily predicted or isolated. Rather than teaching one objective at a time, much of the time you should direct your teaching toward the simultaneous learning of multiple objectives, understandings, and appreciations. However, when you assess for learning, assessment is cleaner when objectives are assessed one at a time. More on this matter of objectives and their use in teaching and learning follows later in this chapter. Let's now consider how objectives are prepared.

PREPARING INSTRUCTIONAL OBJECTIVES

When preparing instructional objectives, you must ask yourself, "How is the student to demonstrate that the objective has been reached?" The objective must include an action that demonstrates that the objective has been achieved. Inherited from behaviorism, this portion of the objective is sometimes called the *anticipated measurable performance*.

Components of a Complete Objective

When completely written in performance terms, an instructional objective has four components, although in practice you are unlikely to use all four. To aid your understanding and as a mnemonic for remembering, you can refer to these components as the ABCDs of writing objectives.

One component is the *audience*. The *A* of the ABCDs refers to the student for whom the objective is intended. To address this, sometimes teachers begin their objectives with the phrase "The student will be able to . . . ," or, to personalize the objective, "You will be able to . . . ," [*Note:* To conserve space and to eliminate useless language, in examples that follow we delete the "be able to,"

and write simply "The student will . . ." As a matter of fact, we prefer use of "will" over "be able to." For brevity, writers of objectives sometimes use the abbreviation "TSWBAT . . ." for "The student will be able to . . ." or more simply "TSW . . ." for "The student will . . .")

The second component is the expected *behavior*, the *B* of the ABCDs. It is this second component that represents the learning target. The expected behavior (or performance) should be written with verbs that are measurable—that is, with action verbs—so that it is directly observable that the objective, or target, has been reached. As discussed in the preceding section, some verbs are too vague, ambiguous, and not clearly measurable. When writing overt objectives, you should avoid verbs that are not clearly measurable, covert verbs such as "appreciate," "comprehend," and "understand" (see Figure 5.5). For the three examples given earlier, for Objectives 1 and 2 the behaviors (action or overt verbs) are "will *identify*," and, for Objective 3, the behaviors are "will *read* and *maintain*."

Now do Exercise 5.8 to assess and to further your understanding.

Figure 5.5   Verbs to avoid when writing overt objectives.

appreciate	enjoy	indicate	like
believe	familiarize	know	realize
comprehend	grasp	learn	understand

EXERCISE 5.8: RECOGNIZING VERBS THAT ARE ACCEPTABLE FOR OVERT OBJECTIVES— A SELF-CHECK EXERCISE

INSTRUCTIONS: The purpose of this exercise is to check your recognition of verbs that are suitable for use in overt objectives. In the list of verbs below, circle those that *should not* be used in overt objectives—that is, those verbs that describe covert behaviors that are not directly observable and measurable. Check your answers against the answer key that follows. Discuss any problems with the exercise with your classmates and instructor.

1. apply	11. design	21. know
2. appreciate	12. diagram	22. learn
3. believe	13. enjoy	23. name
4. combine	14. explain	24. outline
5. comprehend	15. familiarize	25. predict
6. compute	16. grasp*	26. realize
7. create	17. identify	27. select
8. define	18. illustrate	28. solve
9. demonstrate	19. indicate	29. state
10. describe	20. infer	30. understand

Answer Key for Exercise 5.8:

The following verbs should be circled: 2, 3, 5, 13, 15, 16, 21, 22, 26, 30. If you missed more than a couple, then you need to read the previous sections again and discuss your errors with your classmates and instructor.

*Note: words in English often have more than one meaning. For example, grasp as listed here could mean to take hold, or it could mean to comprehend. For the former it would be an acceptable verb for use in overt objectives; for the latter it would not.

EXERCISE 5.9:   RECOGNIZING THE PARTS OF CRITERION-REFERENCED INSTRUCTIONAL OBJECTIVES—A SELF-CHECK EXERCISE

INSTRUCTIONS: The purpose of this exercise is to practice your skill in recognizing the four components of an instructional objective. In the following two objectives, identify the parts of the objectives by underlining

once the *audience,*

twice the *performance (behavior),*

three times the *conditions,* and

four times the *performance level* (that is, the degree or standard of performance).

Check your answers against the answer key that follows, and discuss any problems with this exercise with your classmates and instructor.

1. Given a metropolitan transit bus schedule, at the end of the lesson the student will be able to read the schedule well enough to determine at what times buses are scheduled to leave randomly selected locations, with at least 90 percent accuracy.
2. Given five rectangular figures, you will correctly compute the area in square centimeters of at least four, by measuring the length and width with a ruler and computing the product using an appropriate calculation method.

	Objective 1	Objective 2
Audience	the student	you
Behavior	will be able to read the schedule	will compute
Conditions	given a metropolitan transit bus schedule	given five rectangular figures
Performance level	well enough to determine (and) with at least 90 percent accuracy	correctly compute the area in square centimeters of at least four (80 percent accuracy)

Answer Key for Exercise 5.9:

EXERCISE 5.10: RECOGNIZING OBJECTIVES THAT ARE MEASURABLE—A SELF-CHECK EXERCISE

INSTRUCTIONS: The purpose of this exercise is to assess your ability to recognize objectives that are measurable. Place an *X* before each of the following that is an overt, student-centered behavioral objective, that is, a learning objective that is clearly measurable. Although "audience," "conditions," or "performance levels" may be absent, ask yourself, "As stated, is this a student-centered and measurable objective?" If it is, place an *X* in the blank. A self-checking answer key follows. After checking your answers, discuss any problems you had with the exercise with your classmates and instructor.

_____ 1. To develop an appreciation for literature.

_____ 2. To identify those celestial bodies that are known as planets.

_____ 3. To provide meaningful experiences for the students.

_____ 4. To recognize antonym pairs.

_____ 5. To convert Celsius temperatures to Fahrenheit.

_____ 6. To analyze and compare patterns of data or specific quartile maps.

_____ 7. To develop skills in inquiry.

_____ 8. To identify which of the four causes is most relevant to the major events leading up to the Civil War.

_____ 9. To use maps and graphs to identify the major areas of world petroleum production and consumption.

_____ 10. To know the causes for the diminishing ozone concentration.

Answer Key for Exercise 5.10:

You should have marked items 2, 4, 5, 6, 8, and 9.

Items 1, 3, 7, and 10 are inadequate because of their ambiguity. Item 3 is not even a student learning objective; it is a teacher goal. "To develop" and "to know" can have too many interpretations.

Although the conditions are not given, items 2, 4, 5, 6, 8, and 9 are clearly measurable. The teacher would have no difficulty recognizing when a learner had reached those objectives. Discuss any problem you had with this exercise with your classmates and instructor.

Most of the time, when writing objectives for your unit and lesson plans, you will not bother yourself with including the next two components. However, as you will learn, they are important considerations for assessment.

The third component is the *conditions,* the *C* of the ABCDs—the setting in which the behavior will be demonstrated by the student and observed by the teacher. Conditions are forever changing; although the learning target should be clearly recognizable long before the actual instruction occurs, the conditions may not. Thus, in curriculum documents in particular, conditions are not often included in the objectives. However, when preparing to assess student learning toward specific objectives, you must consider the conditions within which the performance will be displayed. For the first sample objective, the conditions are: "on a map." For the second sample objective, the conditions are: "by listening to an audio recording of the Boston Pops Symphony Orchestra," and "specified times as determined by the teacher." For the third sample, for "the student will read. . . . ," the conditions are: "at home within a two-month period."

The fourth component, again, that is not always included in objectives found in curriculum documents, is the *degree* (or *level*) *of expected performance*—the *D* of the ABCDs. This is the ingredient that allows for the assessment of student learning. When mastery learning is expected, the level of expected performance is usually omitted (because it is understood). In teaching for mastery learning, the performance-level expectation is 100 percent. In reality, however, the performance level will most likely be 85–95 percent, particularly when working with a group of students, rather than with an individual student. The 5 to 15 percent difference allows for human error, as can occur when using written and oral communication. As with conditions, the level of performance will vary depending on the situation and purpose and thus is not normally included in the unit and lessons that teachers prepare. Now, to check your comprehension, do Exercise 5.9.

Performance level is used to assess student achievement, and sometimes it is used to evaluate the effectiveness of the teaching. Student grades might be based on performance levels; evaluation of teacher effectiveness might be based on the level of student performance. Indeed, with today's use of state-mandated, standardized testing, schools, administrators, and teachers are evaluated on the basis of student performance on those tests.

Now, with Exercise 5.10, try your skill at recognizing student learning objectives that are measurable.

Classifying Instructional Objectives

When planning instructional objectives, it is useful to consider the three domains of learning objectives:

cognitive domain—involves intellectual operations from the lowest level of simple recall of information to complex, high-level thinking processes;

affective domain—involves feelings, emotions, attitudes, and values, and ranges from the lower levels of acquisition to the highest level of internalization and action;

psychomotor domain—ranges from the simple manipulation of materials to the communication of ideas, and finally to the highest level of creative performance.

The Domains of Learning and the Developmental Characteristics of Young Adolescents

Educators attempt to design learning experiences to coincide with the five areas of developmental characteristics and needs of the young adolescent that were discussed in Chapter 1: intellectual, physical, emotional/psychological, social, and moral/ethical. As a teacher, you must include objectives that address learning within each of these categories. While the intellectual needs are primarily within the cognitive domain and the physical are within the psychomotor, the other three categories mostly are within the affective domain.

Too frequently, teachers focus on the cognitive domain while only assuming that the psychomotor and affective will take care of themselves. If the current nationwide focus on standardized achievement testing sustains, this may become even more so. Many experts argue, however, that teachers should do just the opposite; that when the affective is directly attended to, the psychomotor and cognitive naturally develop. They argue that unless the social and emotional needs of students are adequately addressed, little happens cognitively (Hopping, 2000). Whether the domains are attended to separately or simultaneously, you should plan your teaching so your students are guided from the lowest to highest levels of operation within each domain.

The three developmental hierarchies are discussed next to guide your understanding of each of the five areas of needs. Notice the illustrative verbs within each hierarchy. These verbs help you fashion objectives when you are developing unit plans and lesson plans. (To see how goals and objectives are fit into one lesson plan, see Figure 6.10 in Chapter 6, "Multiple-Day, Project-Centered, Interdisciplinary and Transcultural Lesson Using WorldWide Communication via the Internet.") However, caution is urged, for there can be considerable overlap among the levels at which some action verbs may appropriately be used. For example, as shown in Figure 5.6, the verb *identifies* is appropriate in each of the objectives at different levels (identified in parentheses) within the cognitive domain.

Cognitive Domain Hierarchy

In a widely accepted taxonomy of objectives, Bloom and his associates (Bloom, 1984) arranged cognitive objectives into classifications according to the complexity of the skills and abilities they embodied. The result was a

Figure 5.6 Sometimes the same action verb may be used appropriately in objectives at different cognitive levels.

The student will identify the correct definition of the term *osmosis*. (knowledge)

The student will identify examples of the principle of osmosis. (comprehension)

The student will identify the osmotic effect when a cell is immersed into a hypotonic solution. (application)

The student will identify the osmotic effect on turgor pressure when the cell is placed in a hypotonic solution. (analysis)

---

ladder ranging from the simplest to the most complex intellectual processes. Within each domain, prerequisite to a student's ability to function at one particular level of the hierarchy is the ability to function at the preceding level or levels. In other words, when a student is functioning at the third level of the cognitive domain, that student is automatically also functioning at the first and second levels. Rather than an orderly progression from simple to complex mental operations, as illustrated by Bloom's taxonomy, other researchers prefer an organization of cognitive abilities that ranges from simple information storage and retrieval, through a higher level of discrimination and concept attainment, to the highest cognitive ability to recognize and solve problems (Gagné, Briggs, & Wager, 1994).

The six major categories (or levels) in Bloom's taxonomy of cognitive objectives are: (a) knowledge—recognizing and recalling information; (b) comprehension—understanding the meaning of information; (c) application—using information; (d) analysis—dissecting information into its component parts to comprehend their relationships; (e) synthesis—putting components together to generate new ideas; and (f) evaluation—judging the worth of an idea, notion, theory, thesis, proposition, information, or opinion. In this taxonomy, the top four categories or levels—application, analysis, synthesis, and evaluation—represent what are called higher-order cognitive thinking skills. [*Note:* Compare Bloom's higher-order cognitive thinking skills with R. H. Ennis's, "A Taxonomy of Critical Thinking Dispositions and Abilities," and Qellmalz's "Developing Reasoning Skills," both in Barron and Sternberg (1987), and with Marzano's "complex thinking strategies" (Marzano, 1992).]

While space limitation prohibits elaboration here, Bloom's taxonomy includes various subcategories within each of these six major categories. It is probably less important that an objective be absolutely classified than it is to be cognizant of hierarchies of thinking and doing and to understand the importance of attending to student intellectual behavior from lower to higher

levels of operation in all three domains. Discussion of each of Bloom's six categories follows.

Knowledge.   The basic element in Bloom's taxonomy concerns the acquisition of knowledge—that is, the ability to recognize and recall information. (As discussed in Chapter 3, this is similar to the *input level* of thinking and questioning.) Although this is the lowest of the six categories, the information to be learned may not itself be of a low level. In fact, it may be of an extremely high level. Bloom includes here knowledge of principles, generalizations, theories, structures, and methodology, as well as knowledge of facts and ways of dealing with facts.

Action verbs appropriate for this category include: *choose, complete, cite, define, describe, identify, indicate, label, list, locate, match, name, outline, recall, recognize, select,* and *state.*

The following are examples of objectives at the knowledge level. Note especially the verb (in italics) used in each example:

- From memory, the student *will recall* the letters in the English alphabet that are vowels.
- The student *will list* the organelles found in animal cell cytoplasm.

The remaining five categories of Bloom's taxonomy of the cognitive domain deal with the *use* of knowledge. They encompass the educational objectives aimed at developing cognitive skills and abilities, including comprehension, application, analysis, synthesis, and evaluation of knowledge. As said previously, the last four categories—application, analysis, synthesis, and evaluation—are referred to as *higher-order thinking skills*, as are the higher categories of the affective and psychomotor domains.

Comprehension.   Comprehension includes the ability to translate, explain, or interpret knowledge and to extrapolate from it to address new situations. Action verbs appropriate for this category include: *change, classify, convert, defend, describe, discuss, distinguish, estimate, expand, explain, generalize, give example, infer, interpret, paraphrase, predict, recognize, retell, summarize,* and *translate.* Examples of objectives in this category are:

- From a sentence, the student *will recognize* the letters that are vowels in the English alphabet.
- The student *will describe* each of the organelles found in animal cell cytoplasm.

Application.   Once learners understand information, they should be able to apply it. Action verbs in this category of operation include: *apply, calculate, compute, demonstrate, develop, discover, exhibit, manipulate, modify, operate, participate, perform, plan, predict, relate, show,* *simulate, solve,* and *use.* Examples of objectives in this category are:

- The student *will use* in a sentence a word that contains at least two vowels.
- The student *will predict* the organelles found in plant cell cytoplasm.

Analysis.   This category includes objectives that require learners to use the skills of analysis. Action verbs appropriate for this category include: *analyze, arrange, break down, categorize, classify, compare, contrast, debate, deduce, diagram, differentiate, discover, discriminate, group, identify, illustrate, infer, inquire, organize, outline, relate, separate,* and *subdivide.* Examples of objectives in this category are:

- From a list of words, the student *will differentiate* those that contain vowels from those that do not.
- Using the microscope, the student *will identify* the organelles found in animal cell cytoplasm.

Synthesis.   This category includes objectives that involve such skills as designing a plan, proposing a set of operations, and deriving a series of abstract relations. Action verbs appropriate for this category include: *arrange, assemble, categorize, classify, combine, compile, compose, constitute, create, design, develop, devise, document, explain, formulate, generate, hypothesize, imagine, invent, modify, organize, originate, plan, predict, produce, rearrange, reconstruct, revise, rewrite, summarize, synthesize, tell, transmit,* and *write.* Examples of objectives in this category are:

- From a list of words, the student *will rearrange* them into several lists according to the vowels contained in each.
- The student *will devise* a classification scheme of the organelles found in animal cell and plant cell cytoplasm according to their functions.

Evaluation.   This, the highest category of Bloom's cognitive taxonomy, includes offering opinions and making value judgments. Action verbs appropriate for this category include: *appraise, argue, assess, choose, compare, conclude, consider, contrast, criticize, decide, describe, discriminate, estimate, evaluate, explain, interpret, judge, justify, predict, rank, rate, recommend, relate, revise, standardize, summarize, support,* and *validate.* Examples of objectives in this category are:

- The student *will listen to and evaluate* other students' identifications of vowels from sentences written on the board.
- While observing living cytoplasm under the microscope, the student *will justify* his or her interpretation that certain structures are specific organelles of a plant or animal cell.

Affective Domain Hierarchy

Krathwohl, Bloom, and Masia (1964) developed a useful taxonomy of the affective domain. The following are their major levels (or categories), from least internalized to most internalized: (a) *receiving*—being aware of the affective stimulus and beginning to have favorable feelings toward it; (b) *responding*—taking an interest in the stimulus and viewing it favorably; (c) *valuing*—showing a tentative belief in the value of the affective stimulus and becoming committed to it; (d) *organizing*—placing values into a system of dominant and supporting values; and, (e) *internalizing*—demonstrating consistent beliefs and behavior that have become a way of life. Although there is considerable overlap from one category to another within the affective domain, these categories do give a basis by which to judge the quality of objectives and the nature of learning within this area. A discussion of each of the five categories follows.

Receiving.   At this level, which is the least internalized, the learner exhibits willingness to give attention to particular phenomena or stimuli, and the teacher is able to arouse, sustain, and direct that attention. Action verbs appropriate for this category include: *ask, choose, describe, differentiate, distinguish, give, hold, identify, locate, name, point to, recall, recognize, reply, select,* and *use.* Examples of objectives in this category are:

- The student *listens attentively* to the instructions for the project assignment.
- The student *demonstrates sensitivity* to the property, beliefs, and concerns of others.

Responding.   At this level, learners respond to the stimulus they have received. They may do so because of some external pressure, because they find the stimulus interesting, or because responding gives them satisfaction. Action verbs appropriate for this category include: *answer, applaud, approve, assist, command, comply, discuss, greet, help, label, perform, play, practice, present, read, recite, report, select, spend (leisure time in), tell,* and *write.* Examples of objectives at this level are:

- The student *completes* the project assignment.
- The student *cooperates* with others during group learning activities.

Valuing.   Objectives at the valuing level deal with learner's beliefs, attitudes, and appreciations. The simplest objectives concern the acceptance of beliefs and values; the higher ones involve learning to prefer certain values and finally becoming committed to them. Action verbs appropriate for this level include: *argue, assist, complete, describe, differentiate, explain, follow, form, initiate, invite, join, justify, propose, protest, read, report, select, share,* *study, support,* and *work.* Examples of objectives in this category are:

- The student *protests* against reinstitution of the military draft.
- The student *argues* a position against abortion or pro-choice for women.

Organizing. This fourth level in the affective domain concerns the building of a personal value system. Here the learner is conceptualizing and arranging values into a system that recognizes their relative importance. Action verbs appropriate for this level include: *adhere, alter, arrange, balance, combine, compare, defend, define, discuss, explain, form, generalize, identify, integrate, modify, order, organize, prepare, relate,* and *synthesize.* Examples of objectives in this category are:

- The student *recognizes* the value of serendipity when problem solving.
- The student *defends* the values of a particular subculture.

Internalizing. This is the last and highest category within the affective domain, at which the learner's behaviors have become consistent with his or her beliefs. Action verbs appropriate for this level include: *act, complete, discriminate, display, influence, listen, modify, perform, practice, propose, qualify, question, revise, serve, solve,* and *verify.* Examples of objectives in this category are:

- The student's behavior *displays* self-assurance in working alone.
- The student *practices* cooperative behaviors in group activities.

Psychomotor Domain Hierarchy

Whereas identification and classification within the cognitive and affective domains are generally agreed upon, there is less agreement on the classification within the psychomotor domain. Originally, the goal of this domain was simply to develop and categorize proficiency in skills, particularly those dealing with gross and fine muscle control. The classification of the domain presented here follows this lead, but includes at its highest level the most creative and inventive behaviors, thus coordinating skills and knowledge from all three domains. Consequently, the objectives are in a hierarchy ranging from simple gross locomotor control to the most creative and complex, requiring originality

and fine locomotor control—for example, from simply turning on a computer to designing a software program. From Harrow is the following taxonomy of the psychomotor domain: (a) *moving,* (b) *manipulating,* (c) *communicating,* and (d) *creating* (Harrow, 1977). [*Note:* A similar taxonomy is that of Simpson (1972).]

Moving. This level involves gross motor coordination. Action verbs appropriate for this level include: *adjust, carry, clean, grasp, jump, locate, obtain,* and *walk.* Sample objectives for this category are:

- The student *will jump* a rope 10 times without missing.
- The student *will carry* the microscope to the desk correctly.

Manipulating. This level involves fine motor coordination. Action verbs appropriate for this level include: *assemble, build, calibrate, connect, play, thread,* and *turn.* Sample objectives for this category are:

- The student *will assemble* a kite.
- The student *will turn* the fine adjustment until the microscope is in focus.

Communicating. This level involves the communication of ideas and feelings. Action verbs appropriate for this level include: *analyze, ask, describe, draw, explain,* and *write.* Sample objectives for this category are:

- The student *will draw* what he or she observes on a slide through the microscope.
- The student *will describe* his or her feelings about cloning.

Creating. Creating is the highest level of this domain, and of all domains, and represents the student's coordination of thinking, learning, and behaving in all three domains. Action verbs appropriate for this level include: *create, design,* and *invent.* Sample objectives for this category are:

- The student will *create, choreograph,* and *perform* a dance pattern.
- The student *will design* and build a kite pattern.

Now, using Exercise 5.11, assess your recognition of performance objectives according to which domain they belong. Then, with Exercise 5.12, begin writing your own objectives for use in your teaching.

EXERCISE 5.11: ASSESSING RECOGNITION OF OBJECTIVES ACCORDING TO DOMAIN—A SELF-CHECK EXERCISE

INSTRUCTIONS: The purpose of this exercise is to assess your ability to identify objectives correctly according to their domain: For each of the following instructional objectives, identify by the appropriate letter the domain involved: (*C*) cognitive, (*A*) affective, (*P*) psychomotor. Check your answers and discuss the results with your classmates and instructor.

_____   1. The student will shoot free throws until he or she can complete 80 percent of the attempts.

_____   2. The student will identify on a map the mountain ranges of the eastern United States.

_____   3. The student will summarize the historical development of the Democratic party in the United States.

_____   4. The student will demonstrate a continuing desire to learn more about using the classroom computer for word processing by volunteering to work at it during free time.

_____   5. The student will volunteer to tidy up the storage room.

_____   6. After listening to several recordings, the student will identify their respective composers.

_____   7. The student will translate a favorite Cambodian poem into English.

_____   8. The student will calculate the length of the hypotenuse.

_____   9. The student will indicate an interest in the subject by voluntarily reading additional library books about earthquakes.

_____   10. The student will successfully stack five blocks.

Answer Key for Exercise 5.11: 2, 3, 6, 7, 8=C, 1, 10=P, 4, 5, 9=A

EXERCISE 5.12: PREPARING MY OWN INSTRUCTIONAL OBJECTIVES

INSTRUCTIONS: The purpose of this exercise is to begin the construction of objectives for your own teaching. For a subject content and grade level of your choice (perhaps from your content outline, Exercise 5.6), prepare 10 specific objectives. (Audience, conditions, and performance level are not necessary unless requested by your course instructor.) Exchange completed exercises with your classmates; then discuss and make changes where necessary.

Subject Field: _____   Grade Level (5–8):_____

1. Cognitive knowledge:

   _____

   _____

   _____

   _____

   _____

2. Cognitive comprehension:

   _____

   _____

   _____

   _____

   _____

3. Cognitive application:

   _____

   _____

   _____

   _____

   _____

4. Cognitive analysis:

   _____

   _____

   _____

   _____

   _____

5. Cognitive synthesis:

   _____

   _____

   _____

   _____

   _____

EXERCISE 5.12 *(continued)*

6. Cognitive evaluation:

_____

_____

_____

_____

_____

7. Affective (low level):

_____

_____

_____

_____

_____

8. Affective (highest level):

_____

_____

_____

_____

_____

9. Psychomotor (low level):

_____

_____

_____

_____

_____

10. Psychomotor (highest level):

_____

_____

_____

_____

_____

USING THE TAXONOMIES

Theoretically, the taxonomies are constructed so that students achieve each lower level before being ready to move to the higher levels. However, because categories and behaviors overlap, as they should, this theory does not always hold in practice. Furthermore, as explained by others (Caine & Caine, 1997), feelings and thoughts are inextricably interconnected; they cannot be neatly separated as might be applied by the taxonomies.

The taxonomies are important in that they emphasize the various levels to which instruction and learning must aspire. For learning to be worthwhile, you must formulate and teach to objectives from the higher levels of the taxonomies as well as from the lower ones. Student thinking and behaving must be moved from the lowest to the highest levels of thinking and behavior. When all is said and done, it is, perhaps, the highest level of the psychomotor domain (creating) to which we aspire.

In using the taxonomies, remember that the point is to formulate the best objectives for the job to be done. In today's schools, using results-driven education models (see page 197 for synonyms), those models describe levels of mastery standards (*rubrics*) for each outcome. The taxonomies provide the mechanism for assuring that you do not spend a disproportionate amount of time on facts and other low-level learning, and can be of tremendous help where teachers are expected to correlate learning activities to one of the school or district's target outcome standards (see Figure 5.7).

Preparing objectives is essential to the preparation of good items for the assessment of student learning. Clearly communicating your performance expectations to students and then specifically assessing student learning against those expectations makes the teaching most efficient and effective, and it makes the assessment of the learning closer to being authentic. This does not mean to imply that you will write performance objectives for everything taught, nor will you always be able to accurately measure what students have learned. As said earlier, learning that is meaningful to students is not as easily compartmentalized as the taxonomies of educational objectives would seem to imply.

Observing for Connected (Meaningful) Learning: Logs, Portfolios, and Journals

In learning that is most important and that has the most meaning to students, the domains are inextricably interconnected. Consequently, when assessing for student learning, both during instruction (formative assessment) and at the conclusion of the instruction (summative assessment), you must look for those connections.

Figure 5.7 Sample school district-expected learning outcomes standards.

Results-driven education helps produce people who are life-long learners, who are effective communicators, who have high self-esteem, and who are:

Problem Solvers

- Are able to solve problems in their academic and personal lives
- Demonstrate higher-level analytical thinking skills when they evaluate or make decisions
- Are able to set personal and career goals
- Can use knowledge, not just display it
- Are innovative thinkers

Self-Directed Learners

- Are independent workers
- Can read, comprehend, and interact with text
- Have self-respect, with an accurate view of themselves and their abilities

Quality Producers

- Can communicate effectively in a variety of situations (oral, aesthetic/artistic, nonverbal)
- Are able to use their knowledge to create intelligent, artistic products that reflect originality
- Have high standards

Collaborative Workers

- Are able to work interdependently
- Show respect for others and their points of view
- Have their own values and moral conduct
- Have an appreciation of cultural diversity

Community Contributors

- Have an awareness of civic, individual, national, and international responsibilities
- Have an understanding of basic health issues
- Have an appreciation of diversity

Ways of looking for connected learning include:

- maintain a teacher's (or team's) log with daily or nearly daily entries about the progress of each student
- students maintain personal learning journals in which they reflect on and respond to their learning
- students assemble personal learning portfolios that document students' thinking, work, and learning experiences.

Dated and chronologically organized items that students place in their portfolios can include notes and communications; awards; brainstorming records; photos of bulletin board contributions and of charts; posters, displays, and models made by the student; records of peer coaching; visual maps; learning contract; record of debate contributions and demonstrations or presentations; mnemonics created by the student; peer evaluations; reading record; other contributions made to the class or to the team; record of service work; and test and grade records.

The use of portfolios and student journals is discussed further in Chapters 7 and 8 respectively.

Character Education and the Domains of Learning

Related especially to the affective domain, although not exclusive of the cognitive and psychomotor domains, is an interest in the development of young adolescents' values, especially those of honesty, kindness, respect, and responsibility, an interest in what is sometimes called *character education* (see discussion and listing of resources that follows). For example, Wynne and Ryan (1997, p. 1) state that "transmitting character, academics, and discipline—essentially, 'traditional' moral values—to pupils is a vital educational responsibility." Thus, if one agrees with that interpretation, then the teaching of moral values is the transmission of character, academics, and discipline and clearly implies learning that transcends the three domains of learning presented in this chapter. Stimulated by a perceived need to reduce student antisocial behaviors (such as drug abuse and violence) and to produce more respectful and responsible citizens, with a primary focus on the affective domain, many middle level schools are developing curricula in character education and instruction in conflict resolution. The ultimate goal of those efforts is to develop students' values that lead to responsible citizenship and moral action.

Teaching Toward Positive Character Development. In what seems a cycle, arising in the 1930s, again in the late 1960s, and in the 1990s and continuing today, interest is high in the development of students' values, especially those of honesty, kindness, respect, and responsibility. Today, this interest is frequently referred to as *character education*. Whether defined as ethics, citizenship, moral values, or personal development, character education has long been a component of public education in this country (Otten, 2000). Stimulated by a perceived need to act to reduce students' antisocial behaviors and produce more respectful and responsible citizens, many schools and districts recently have or are developing curricula in character education with the ultimate goal of "developing mature adults capable of responsible citizenship and moral action" (Burrett & Rusnak, 1993, p. 15).

As a teacher, you can teach toward positive character development in two general ways, by

- providing a conducive classroom atmosphere where students actively and positively share in the decision making
- serving as a model students can proudly emulate.

Acquiring knowledge and developing understanding can enhance the learning of attitudes.

Nevertheless, changing an attitude is often a long and tedious process, requiring the commitment of the teacher and the school, assistance from the community, and the provision of numerous experiences that will guide students to new convictions. Here are some specific practices, most of which are discussed in various places in this resource guide:

- Build a sense of community in the school and in the classroom, with shared goals, optimism, cooperative efforts, and clearly identified and practiced procedures for reaching those goals.
- Collaboratively plan with students action- and community-oriented projects that relate to curriculum themes; solicit student family and community members to assist in projects.
- Make student service projects visible in the school and community.
- Promote higher-order thinking about value issues through the development of students' skills in questioning.
- Sensitize students to issues and teach skills of conflict resolution through debate, role-play, simulations, and creative drama.
- Share and highlight examples of class and individual cooperation in serving the classroom, school, and community.
- Teach students to negotiate; practice and develop skills in conflict resolution, skills such as empathy, problem solving, impulse control, and anger management.

See web listings at the end of this chapter for resources on character education.

LEARNING THAT IS NOT IMMEDIATELY OBSERVABLE

Unlike behaviorists, constructivists do not limit the definition of learning to that which is observable behavior; nor should you. Bits and pieces of new information are stored in short-term memory, where the new information is "rehearsed" until ready to be stored in long-term memory. If the information is not rehearsed, it eventually fades from short-term memory. If it is rehearsed and made meaningful through connections with other stored knowledge, then this new knowledge is transferred to and stored in long-term memory, either by building existing schemata or by forming new schemata. As a teacher, your responsibility is to provide learning experiences that will result in the creation of new schemata as well as the modification of existing schemata.

To be a teacher of young adolescent learners, the challenge is to use performance-based criteria, but simultaneously with a teaching style that encourages the development of intrinsic sources of student motivation, and that allows, provides, and encourages coincidental learning—learning that goes beyond what might be considered predictable, immediately measurable, and representative of minimal expectations.

It has become increasingly clear to many teachers that to be most effective in helping young adolescents to develop meaningful understandings, much of the learning in each discipline can be made more effective and longer lasting when that learning is integrated with the whole curriculum and made meaningful to the lives of the students, rather than when simply taught as an unrelated and separate discipline at the same time each day.

As noted at the start of this chapter, if learning is defined only as the accumulation of bits and pieces of information, then we already know how that is learned and how to teach it. However, the accumulation of pieces of information is at the lowest end of a spectrum of types of learning. For higher levels of thinking and for learning that is most meaningful and longest lasting, the results of research support using: (a) a curriculum where disciplines are integrated and (b) instructional techniques that involve the learners in social, interactive learning, such as project-centered learning, cooperative learning, peer tutoring, and cross-age teaching. When compared with traditional instruction, one characteristic of exemplary middle level instruction today is the teacher's encouragement of dialogue among students in the classroom, to debate, discuss, and explore their own ideas.

INTEGRATED CURRICULUM

People talk about how difficult it is to implement an integrated curriculum, which is taking the standard subject areas and combining them. That is ridiculous. The world is integrated! What is difficult is what schools do every day: unravel the world and all its vast knowledge and put it into boxes called subjects and separate things that are not separate in the real world.

Dennis Littky (2004, p. 29)

When learning about *integrated curriculum* (IC), it is easy to be confused by the plethora of terms that are used, such as *integrated studies, thematic instruction, multidisciplinary teaching, integrated curriculum, interdisciplinary curriculum,* and *interdisciplinary thematic instruction.* In essence, regardless of which of these terms is being used, the reference is to the same thing.

Because the demarcation between the term *curriculum* and the term *instruction* is not always clear, let's assume for the sake of better understanding the meaning of *integrated curriculum,* there is no difference between the two terms, that is, for this discussion,

integrated curriculum and *integrated instruction* will refer to the same thing.

The term **integrated curriculum** (or any of its synonyms mentioned previously) refers to both a way of teaching and a way of planning and organizing the instructional program so the discrete disciplines of subject matter are related to one another in a design that: (a) matches the developmental needs of the learners and (b) helps to connect their learning in ways that are meaningful to their current and past experiences. In that respect, integrated curriculum is the antithesis of traditional, disparate, subject matter-oriented teaching and curriculum designations.

The reason for the various terminology is, in part, because the concept of an integrated curriculum is not new. In fact, it has had a roller-coaster ride throughout the history of education in this country. Over time those efforts to integrate student learning have had varying labels.

Today's interest in curriculum integration has arisen from several inextricably connected sources, especially the four that follow:

a. the success at curriculum integration enjoyed by middle schools since the 1960s

b. the literature-based, whole-language movement in reading and language arts that began in the 1980s [*Note:* Various movements and approaches have been used over the years to try to find the most successful approach to teaching English and the language arts—movements with names such as *whole language, integrated language arts, communication arts and skills, literature-based* and so forth. Whatever the label given, certain common elements and goals prevail: student choice in materials to be read, student reading and writing across the curriculum, time for independent and sustained silent reading in the classroom, use of integrated language arts skills across the curriculum, and use of nonprint materials]

c. the diversity of learners in the regular classroom coupled with growing acceptance of the philosophy that a certain percentage of school dropouts is not a viable assumption

d. recent research in cognitive science and neuroscience demonstrating the necessity of helping students establish bridges between school and life, knowing and doing, content and context, with a parallel rekindled interest in constructivism as opposed to a strictly behaviorist philosophical approach to teaching and learning.

An integrated curriculum approach may not necessarily be the best approach for every school, nor the best for all learning for every student, nor is it necessarily the manner by which every teacher should or must always plan and teach. As evidenced by practice,

Because there are various interpretations to curriculum integration each teacher must make his or her own decisions about its use.

the truth of this statement becomes obvious. And, as you should be well aware of now, it is our belief that a teacher's best choice as an approach to instruction—and to classroom management—is one that is eclectic.

In attempts to connect students' learning with their experiences, efforts fall at various places on a spectrum or continuum, from the least integrated instruction (level 1) to the most integrated (level 5), as illustrated in Figure 5.8. It is not our intent that this illustration be interpreted as going from "worst-case scenario" (far left) to "best-case scenario" (far right), although some people may interpret it in exactly that way. Figure 5.8 is meant solely to show how efforts to integrate fall on a continuum of sophistication and complexity. The following is a description of each level of the continuum.

Level 1 Curriculum Integration

Level 1 curriculum integration is the traditional organization of curriculum and classroom instruction, where teachers plan and arrange the subject-specific scope and sequence in the format of topic outlines, much as you did for Exercise 5.6. If there is an attempt to help students connect their experiences and their learning, then it is up to individual classroom teachers to do it. A student in a school and classroom that has subject-specific instruction at varying times of the day (e.g., language arts at 8:00, mathematics at 9:00, social studies at 10:30, and so on) from one or more teachers is likely learning at a Level 1 instructional environment, especially when what is being learned in one subject has little or no connection with content being learned in

another. The same applies for a student, as found in many junior high schools, who moves during the school day from classroom to classroom, teacher to teacher, subject to subject, from one topic to another. A topic in science, for example, might be "earthquakes." A related topic in social studies might be "the social consequences of natural disasters." These two topics may or may not be studied by a student at the same time.

Level 2 Curriculum Integration

If the same students are learning English/language arts, social studies/history, mathematics, or science using a thematic approach rather than a topic outline, then they are learning at Level 2. At this level, themes for one discipline are not necessarily planned and coordinated to correspond or integrate with themes of another or to be taught simultaneously. At Level 2, the students may have some input into the decision making involved in planning themes and content from various disciplines. Before going further in this presentation of the levels of curriculum integration, let's stop and consider what is a topic and what is a theme.

Integrated Thematic Unit: Topic Versus Theme.   The difference between what is a topic and what is a theme is not always clear. For example, whereas "earthquakes" and "social consequences of natural disasters" are topics, "a survival guide to local natural disasters" could be the theme or umbrella under which these two topics could fall. In addition, themes are likely to be problem-based statements or questions; they often result in a product and are longer in duration than are topics. A theme is the point, the message, or the idea that underlies a study. When compared to a topic, a theme is more dynamic; the theme explains the significance of the study. It communicates to the student what the

Figure 5.8   Levels of curriculum integration.

Least Integrated Level 1	Level 2	Level 3	Level 4	Most Integrated Level 5
Subject-specific topic outline	Subject-specific	Multidisciplinary	Interdisciplinary thematic	Integrated thematic
No student collaboration in planning	Minimal student input	Some student input	Considerable student input in selecting themes and in planning	Maximum student and teacher collaboration
Teacher solo	Solo or teams	Solo or teams	Solo or teams	Solo or teams
Student input into decision making is low.		Student input into decision making is high.		Student input into decision making is very high.

experience means. Although organized around one theme, many topics make up an ITU. Often the theme of a study becomes more clear to students when an overall guiding question is presented and discussed, such as "What could we do to improve our living environment?" or "What happens in our community after natural disasters?"

Some educators predict the integrated curriculum of the future will be based on broad, unchanging, and unifying concepts (i.e., on conceptual themes). If so, it would be the recycling of an approach of the 1960s, as supported by the writings of Jerome Bruner (1960) and implemented in some of the National Science Foundation-sponsored curriculum projects of that era. In fact, there is already action in that direction. For example, forming the basis for the national curriculum standards (discussed earlier in this chapter) for social studies are 10 "thematic strands," including "people, places, and environments," and "power, authority, and governance." The national standards for science education are centered on unifying conceptual schemes, such as "systems, order, and organization" and "form and function." Many of the state curriculum documents are now centered on major concepts and central themes rather than on isolated facts.

Level 3 Curriculum Integration

When the same students are learning two or more of their core subjects around a common theme, such as the theme "natural disasters," from one or more teachers, they are then learning at Level 3 integration. At this level, teachers agree on a common theme, then they separately deal with that theme in their individual subject areas, usually at the same time during the school year. So what the student is learning from a teacher in one class is related to and coordinated with what the student is concurrently learning in another or several others. At Level 3, students may have some input into the decision making involved in selecting and planning themes and content. Some authors may refer to levels 2 or 3 as *coordinated* or *parallel curriculum*.

Level 4 Curriculum Integration

When teachers and students collaborate on a common theme and its content, and when discipline boundaries begin to disappear as teachers teach about this common theme, either solo or as an interdisciplinary teaching team, Level 4 integration is achieved.

Level 5 Curriculum Integration

When teachers and their students have collaborated on a common theme and its content, discipline boundaries are truly blurred during instruction, and teachers of several grade levels and of various subjects teach toward student understanding of aspects of the common theme, then this is Level 5, an *integrated thematic approach*. [*Note:* For detailed accounts of teaching at this level of integration, see Stevenson and Carr (1993).]

Guidelines for integrating topics and for planning and developing an interdisciplinary thematic unit are presented in the next chapter.

Integrated Curriculum in a Standards-Based Environment

Although it is still too early to obtain reliable data on how students in integrated curriculum programs fare on mandatory, state-wide standardized proficiency tests, it should be reassuring to today's classroom teacher to know that students in any type of interdisciplinary or integrative curriculum do as well as, or often times even better than, students in a conventional departmentalized program. Furthermore, this seems to hold true whether the program is taught by one teacher in a self-contained or block-time class or by an interdisciplinary teaching team (Vars & Beane, 2000).

PLANNING FOR INSTRUCTION: A THREE-LEVEL AND SEVEN-STEP PROCESS

Earlier in the chapter it was noted that complete planning for instruction occurs at three levels: the year, the units, and the lessons. There are seven steps in the process. They are as follows:

1. *Course, grade level, and school goals.* Consider and understand your curriculum goals and their relationship to the mission and goals of the school. Your course is not isolated on the planet Jupiter but is an integral component of the total school curriculum.
2. *Expectations.* Consider topics, knowledge, and skills that you are expected to teach, such as those found in the district-wide standards and the course of study.
3. *Academic year, semester, trimester, or quarter plan.* Think about the goals you want the students to reach months from now. Working from your tentative content outline, and with the school calendar in hand, you begin by deciding the amount of time (e.g., the number of days) to be devoted to each topic (or unit), penciling those times into the outline. (Unless you are doing your planning at a computer, you may wish to use a pencil because the times are likely to be modified frequently.)

> You may need to work around mandatory, standardized achievement testing dates in such a way that the testing does not interrupt the flow of student learning.

4. *Course schedule.* This schedule becomes an element in the course syllabus that is presented to parents and students at the beginning (discussed in the next section of this chapter) of the term. However, the schedule must remain flexible to allow for the unexpected, such as the cancellation or interruption of a class meeting, a serendipitous discovery and inquiry by the students, or an extended study of a particular topic.

5. *Plans for each class meeting.* Working from the calendar plan or the course schedule, you are ready to prepare plans for each class meeting, keeping in mind the abilities and interests of your students while making decisions about appropriate strategies and learning experiences. The preparation of daily plans takes considerable time and continues throughout the year as you arrange and prepare instructional notes, demonstrations, discussion topics and questions, classroom exercises, learning centers, guest speakers, materials and equipment, field trips, and tools for the assessment of student learning. Because the content of each class meeting is often determined by the accomplishments of and your reflections upon the preceding one, lessons are never "set in concrete" but need your continual revisiting, reflection, adjustments, and assessment.

6. *Instructional objectives.* Once you have the finalized schedule, and as you prepare the daily plans, you will complete your preparation of the instructional objectives. Those objectives are critical for proper development of the next and final step.

7. *Assessment.* The final step is that of deciding how to assess for student achievement. Included in this component are your decisions about how you will accomplish diagnostic or preassessment (i.e., the assessment of what students know or think they know at the start of a new unit or a new topic), formative assessment (the ongoing assessment on what the students are learning that takes place almost daily during a unit of study), and summative assessment (the assessment of students' learning at the conclusion of a unit of study). Also included in the assessment component are your decisions about assignments (discussed in Chapter 8 and the grading procedures discussed in Chapter 7).

In Chapter 6, you proceed through these steps as you develop your first instructional plan. However, before starting that, let's consider one more topic relevant to the overall planning of the course—the syllabus. There is often confusion about what is and what is not a syllabus.

THE SYLLABUS

A **syllabus** is a written statement of information about the workings of a particular class or course. (See sample

in Figure 5.9.) As a student in postsecondary education, you have seen a variety of syllabi written by professors, each with their individual ideas and personal touches about what general and specific logistic information is most important for students to know about a course. Some instructors, however, err in thinking that a course outline constitutes a course syllabus; a course outline is only one component of a syllabus.

Not all middle level teachers use a course syllabus, at least as is described here, but for reasons that are explored in this discussion, we believe they should. Related to that belief are several questions that are answered next: "Why should teachers use a syllabus?" "What value is it?" "What use can be made of it?" "What purpose does it fulfill?" "How do I develop one?" "Can students have input into its content and participate in its development?" "Where do I start?" "What information should be included?" "When should it be distributed?" "To whom should it be distributed?" and "How rigidly should it be followed?"

Use and Development of a Syllabus

The syllabus is printed information about the class or the course that is usually presented to the parents/guardians and to the students at the start of school or at the start of a course. The syllabus may be developed completely by you or in collaboration with members of your teaching team. As you shall learn, it also can be developed collaboratively with students. As always, the final decision about its development is yours to make. However it is developed, the syllabus should be designed so that it helps establish a rapport among students, parents or guardians, and the teacher; helps students feel more at ease by providing an understanding of what is expected of them; and helps them to organize, conceptualize, and synthesize their learning experiences.

The syllabus should provide a reference, helping eliminate misunderstandings and misconceptions about the nature of the class—its rules, expectations, procedures, requirements, and other policies. It should provide students with a sense of connectedness (often by allowing students to work collaboratively in groups and actually participate in fashioning their own course syllabus).

The syllabus should also serve as a plan to be followed by the teacher and the students, and it should serve as a resource for substitute teachers and (when relevant) members of a teaching team. Each team member should have a copy of every other member's syllabus. In essence, the syllabus stands as documentation for what is taking place in the classroom for those outside the classroom (i.e., parents or guardians, school board members, administrators, other teachers, and students). For access by parents and other interested persons, some teachers include at least portions

Figure 5.9 Sample course syllabus.

English 8　　　　　　　　　　　　　　　　　　　　　　　　　　　*Room 23, Mrs. Biletnikoff*

Course Description

English 8 is a course designed to provide instruction in the areas of reading, analyzing, and writing about literature, while using texts that support the History 8 coursework. Essay writing, especially descriptive writing, is emphasized. In addition to intensive vocabulary study, students will be writing on a daily basis. Also, the students will read 1 million words of outside texts, in addition to their assigned reading. The readings for English 8 are an eclectic mix. The novels that the class will be reading this semester are *April Morning, The Giver,* and *The Diary of Anne Frank.*

Materials Required

Students are required to bring a pen, a pencil, and paper to class each day. Journal binder should be a 2-pocket, 3-prong paper binder. The school provides the vocabulary text and all literary texts.

Goals

- To understand and recognize the various aspects of literature: character, setting, plot, point of view, and theme.
- To increase vocabulary, preparing students for more advanced writing.
- To develop and enhance students' descriptive writing and organizational skills.
- To increase oral and listening skills.

Objectives

- Students will participate in projects, class discussions, journal writing, quizzes, essay writing, and tests that are designed to help them grasp the concepts of plot, setting, character, theme, and other literary devices. Through these activities, students will demonstrate improvement in their writing and oral/listening skills.
- Students will participate in class activities such as sustained silent reading (SSR), reading aloud, and project development to help in their learning of the material.

Assignments

There are weekly vocabulary quizzes. There is also weekly vocabulary homework. Throughout the course, students will be writing journal entries, quickwrites, and essays. All completed and graded work is returned to the corresponding class file. Students are free to check the file before or after class.

Assessment Criteria

- Students will complete weekly vocabulary quizzes.
- Quizzes are administered when the teacher needs to check the students' progress.
- Test dates will be announced in class and class time is used for test preparation.
- Class participation accounts for 15% of the student's grade, therefore absences and tardiness can negatively affect this assessment component.
- Group work is graded, therefore lack of participation can negatively affect the student's grade.

Method of Evaluation

Evaluation is done through oral and written quizzes and tests. In addition, students are evaluated on class participation, assignments, projects, and class discussions. All grades are based on a point system.

Papers, quizzes, and tests	= 50% of total points
Homework	= 20% of total points
Journals	= 15% of total points
Group work and class participation	= 15% of total points

Grading Scale

90–100% of total points	= A 50–69% = D
80–89%	= B <50% = F
70–79%	= C

Grades are posted (by codes, not names) biweekly.

Figure 5.9 (*continued*)

Classroom Behavior and Consequences for Inappropriate Behavior

Students are expected to be prompt, prepared, polite, productive, and positive (the 5 P's). Students may earn 5 points per day by observing the 5 P's guidelines. Students may forfeit their citizenship points by excessive bathroom requests, tardiness, or leaving class without the teacher's approval.
Consequences for inappropriate behavior:

1st infraction = verbal warning
2nd infraction = 15 minutes at time-out and a phone call to parent or guardian
3rd infraction = referral to administration or a call home
4th infraction = administrative referral and possible suspension
Note: Any step in the above process may be skipped at the teacher's discretion.

Attendance

Regular attendance is crucial for success. It enables the student to understand assignments and to take advantage of the guidance provided by the teacher and others. In addition, the students will receive immediate feedback regarding their progress. If a student needs to leave early or enter late, please make arrangements with the teacher beforehand, if possible.

Tardiness

Students are tardy when they are not in their seats when the tardy bell rings. Any student who elects to leave the classroom for any reason takes a tardy for that period. Tardiness affects citizenship as well as the privilege to participate in extracurricular activities before and after school.

Bathroom Privileges

Students are allowed two bathroom passes per quarter. Each pass is redeemed at the time of use. If the student does not use the two passes for the quarter, the student receives 5 extra points per pass with a total of 10 points possible towards their citizenship grade. If a student chooses to use the bathroom beyond the two-pass limit, then that student forfeits the citizenship points (5) for the day.

Make-up

Students may make up assignments one day after returning from an excused absence. All other work is accepted at the teacher's discretion.

Extra Credit Work

There is no "extra credit" work in this class.

Instructional Schedule for English 8, Fall Semester

    Unit I Introduction to the short story (2 weeks)
    Vocabulary, journal, SSR, and outside readings begin
    Unit II *April Morning* (4–5 weeks)
    Unit III *The Giver* (4–5 weeks)
    Unit IV *The Diary of Anne Frank* (4–5 weeks)

Source: Courtesy of Angela Biletnikoff.

of their course syllabus, such as homework assignment specifications and due dates, with the school's website on the Internet.

Usually, the teacher long before the first class meeting prepares the syllabus, at least portions of it. If you maintain a syllabus template on your computer, then it is a simple task to customize it for each group of students you teach. You may find it is more useful if students participate in the development of the syllabus, thereby having an ownership of it and a commitment to its contents. By having input into the workings of a

course and knowing that their opinions count, students usually will take more interest in what they are doing and learning. Some teachers give students a brief syllabus on the first day (see Figure 5.10) and then, collaboratively with the students and other members of the teaching team, develop a more detailed syllabus during the initial days of the start of school.

Shown in Figure 5.11 are steps you can use as a collaborative learning experience where students spend time during the first (or an early) class meeting brainstorming content of their syllabus.

Figure 5.10 How one teacher welcomes students and their parents or guardians.

To Student and Parent/Guardian

Welcome to Sixth Grade—Carmichael School

Your Homeroom will be: Room 18   Your Homeroom Teacher will be: Mrs. Craine

Welcome back! We are looking forward to a productive year of interesting learning experiences to prepare each student for the transition to middle school. The following information will help students and parents/guardians to understand the classroom policies and procedures.

Materials Needed:

Pens (black or blue ink), a binder, dividers, and pencils. Colored pens or pencils are optional but nice to have. Textbooks need to be covered the night the students receive them.

Homework:

Students will have from one to two hours of homework every night, 15 minutes of which will be quiet reading. Please provide a quiet area and a regular study time for your child to complete daily homework assignments. The homework reminder sheet *must* be signed each night. If homework is not ready the next day (1) the student will receive a slip called "unprepared," (2) an area in the classroom will be provided for the student to complete the unfinished work, and (3) when a student receives five unprepareds, an office referral will be given and a phone call made to the parent/guardian.

Rules:

Listen carefully; follow directions; stay on task; respect others and be kind with your words and actions; and turn in homework and classwork on time and be responsible for it being completed and neatly done.

Consequences for breaking a classroom rule:

1. Student receives verbal warning.
2. Student's name is written on the clipboard.
3. If inappropriate behavior continues, student receives a blue card.
4. If two blue cards are received in one week, student receives an orange card and is referred to the office.
5. If inappropriate behavior continues, student receives a purple card, is referred to the office, and is suspended from school.

Source: Courtesy of Shirley Craine.

Content of a Syllabus

A syllabus should be concise, matter-of-fact, uncomplicated, and brief—perhaps no more than two pages—and, to be thorough and most informative, include the following information:

Descriptive information about the class or course. This includes the teacher's name, the course or class title, class period, days of class meetings, beginning and ending times, and room number.

Importance of the course. This information should describe the course, cite the ways students will profit from it, tell whether the course is a required course and from which program in the curriculum (e.g., a core course, an elective, exploratory, or some other arrangement).

Learning targets. This should include major goals, related curriculum standards, and a few objectives.

Materials required. Explain what materials are needed—such as a textbook, notebook, binder, calculator, supplementary readings, apron, safety goggles—and specify which are supplied by the school, which must be supplied by each student, and what materials must be available each day.

Types of assignments that will be given. These should be clearly explained in as much detail as possible this early in the school term. There should be a statement of your estimate of time required (if any) for homework each night. There should also be a statement about where daily assignments will be posted in the classroom (a regular place each day), the procedures for completing and turning in assignments, and (if relevant) for making corrections to assignments after they've been turned in and returned. Include your policy regarding late work. Also, parents/guardians may need to know your expectations of them regarding helping their child with assignments.

Attendance expectations. Explain how attendance is related to achievement grades and to promotion (if relevant) and the procedure for making up missed work (such as one teacher's procedure shown in Figure 5.12.)

Figure 5.11   Steps for involving students in the development of their course syllabus.

Step 1

Sometime during the first few days of the course, arrange students in heterogeneous groups (mixed abilities) of three or four members to brainstorm the development of their syllabus.

Step 2

Instruct each group to spend five minutes listing everything they can think of that they would like to know about the course. Tell students that a group *recorder* must be chosen to write their list of ideas on paper and then, when directed to do so, to transfer the list to the writing board or to sheets of butcher paper to be hung in the classroom for all to see (or on an overhead transparency—a transparency sheet and pen are made available to each group). Tell them to select a group *spokesperson* who will address the class, explaining the group's list. Each group could also appoint a *materials manager,* whose job it is to see that the group has the necessary materials (e.g., pen, paper, transparency, chalk), and a *task master,* whose job it is to keep the group on task and to report to the teacher when each task is completed.

Step 3

After five minutes, have the recorders prepare their lists. When a transparency or butcher paper is used, the lists can be prepared simultaneously while recorders remain with their groups. If using the writing board, then recorders, one at a time, write their lists on areas of the board that you have designated for each group's list.

Step 4

Have the spokesperson of each group explain the group's list. As this is being done, you should make a master list. If transparencies or butcher paper are being used rather than the writing board, you can ask for either as backup to the master list you have made.

Step 5

After all spokespersons have explained their lists, ask the class collectively for additional input. "Can anyone think of anything else that should be added?"

Step 6

You now take the master list and design a course syllabus, being careful to address each question and to include items of importance that students may have omitted. However, your guidance during the preceding five steps should ensure that all bases have been covered.

Step 7

At the next class meeting, give each student a copy of the final syllabus. Discuss its content. (Make copies to distribute to colleagues, especially those on your teaching team; interested administrators; and parents and guardians at Back-to-School night.)

Typical school policy allows that with an excused absence, missed work can be completed without penalty if done within a reasonable period of time following the student's return to school.

Assessment and marking/grading procedures. Explain the assessment procedures and the procedures for determining grades. Will there be quizzes (announced or not?), tests, homework, projects, and group work? What will be their formats, coverage, and weights in the procedure for determining grades? For group work, how will the contributions and learning of individual students be evaluated?

Other information specific to the class or course. Field trips? Special privileges? Computer work? Parental/guardian expectations? Homework hotline? Classroom procedures and expectations should be included here.

If you are a beginning teacher or are new to the school, to affirm that your policies as indicated in the first draft of your syllabus are not counter to any existing school policies, you probably should share your first draft of the syllabus with members of your team, your mentor, or the department chairperson for their feedback.

SUMMARY

In your comparison and analysis of courses of study and teachers' editions of student textbooks, you probably discovered that many are accompanied by sequentially designed resource units from which the teacher can select and build specific teaching units. A resource unit usually consists of an extensive list of objectives, a large number and variety of activities,

Figure 5.12 Procedure established by one teacher for students returning to class after being absent.

I WAS ABSENT—NOW WHAT DO I DO?

1. Go to the back of the room.
2. Check calendar on wall.
3. Open file folder in agenda file box that labels the day you were absent. In this file you will find the *overhead* agenda used that day with the *list of activities, warm-ups, vocabulary, and homework assigned*—this is **very** important so please *refile* this agenda for other students to use as soon as you are finished.
4. Copy warm-ups and vocabulary.
5. *Take one copy of each ditto*—check to make sure you have claimed all of them.
6. Read the agenda on the overhead.
7. Match goals/homework to dittos—did you get everything you need?
8. Record all due dates on your calendar.
9. Ask questions about work after doing 1–8.
10. *Work should be turned in within two days of absence*—multiple days of absences simply means that you can turn in one day's work every two days. After that, work is considered late unless we have made arrangements—so *talk* to me.

You are the one who is responsible for claiming and making up work when you are absent. The file is for your convenience. Do not claim you missed an assignment because you were absent—it doesn't wash in this class!!!!

Other students may have been absent the same day. If you do not find the overhead agenda in the file, check to see if anyone in the class has the agenda. Also, sometimes the agendas are misfiled—check the day before and day after if you don't see the overhead (this is called critical thinking!).

I wonder where that agenda went?

Courtesy: Patricia A. Nelson.

suggested materials, and extensive bibliographies for teacher and students.

As you may have also found, some courses of study contain actual teaching units that have been prepared by teachers of the school district. Beginning teachers and student teachers often ask, "How closely must I follow the school's curriculum guide or course of study?" In this day of statewide achievement testing, the answer is likely to be "very close," but to obtain an accurate answer, you must talk with teachers and administrators of the school before you begin teaching.

In conclusion, your final decisions about what content to teach are guided in various degrees by: (a) discussions with other teachers; (b) review of state curriculum documents, local courses of study, and articles in professional journals; (c) your personal convictions, knowledge, and skills; and (d) the unique characteristics of your students.

In this chapter you learned of the differences among the terms *aims, goals,* and *objectives.* Regardless of how these terms are defined, the important point is this: *Teachers must be clear about what it is they want their students to learn, about the kind of evidence needed to verify their learning, and to communicate those things to the students so they are clearly understood.*

Many teachers do not bother to write specific objectives for all the learning activities in their teaching plans. However, when teachers do prepare specific objectives (by writing them themselves or by borrowing them from textbooks and other curriculum documents) by teaching toward them and assessing students' progress against them, student learning is enhanced; this is called performance-based teaching and criterion-referenced measurement. It is also known as an aligned curriculum. In schools using results-driven education mastery learning models, those models describe levels of mastery standards or rubrics for each outcome or learning target. The taxonomies are of tremendous help in schools where teachers are expected to correlate learning activities to the school's outcome standards, and for today that includes most, if not all, schools.

As a teacher, you will be expected to: (a) plan your lessons well, (b) convey specific expectations to your students, and (c) assess their learning against that specificity. However, because it tends toward high objectivity, there is the danger that such performance-based teaching could become too objective, which can have negative consequences. If young adolescent students are treated as objects, then the relationship between teacher and student becomes impersonal and counterproductive to real learning. Highly specific and impersonal teaching can be discouraging to serendipity, creativity, and the excitement of discovery, to say nothing of its possibly negative impact on the development of students' self-esteem.

Performance-based instruction works well when teaching toward mastery of basic skills, but the concept of mastery learning is inclined to imply that there is some foreseeable end to learning, an assumption that is obviously erroneous. With performance-based instruction, the source of student motivation tends to be extrinsic. Teacher expectations, marks and grades, society, and peer pressures are examples of extrinsic sources that drive student performance. To be a most effective teacher, your very real challenge today is to use performance-based criteria together with a teaching style that encourages the development of intrinsic sources of student motivation and that allows for, provides for, and encourages coincidental learning—learning that goes beyond what might be considered as predictable, immediately measurable, and representative of minimal expectations. In other words, although you must have clear goals and objectives and a routine that students can rely on from day to day, the most effective teachers consider and build upon the interests, experiences, and spontaneous nature of their students. Good teaching is *not* an inhuman experience.

With a knowledge of the content of the middle level school curriculum and the value of instructional objectives, you are now ready to prepare detailed instructional plans with sequenced lessons, the subject of the next chapter.

QUESTIONS FOR CLASS DISCUSSION

1. If you were asked during a middle school teaching job interview, tell how you would differentiate between the terms *curriculum* and *instruction*.
2. Identify and describe various documents that influence the content of the middle grades or middle school curriculum.
3. More frequently in recent years we hear both beginning and experienced teachers complaining that there isn't enough time to teach all curriculum content they are supposed to teach, with less to no time to teach topics they prefer to teach. We hear that they have less and less freedom to decide what is important for children to learn and do and to create learning activities for that learning. That they are told they must spend more time on direct instruction and less on indirect instruction. That there is not enough time for student-initiated exploratory learning. That they have less time during the school year to teach because of the increased amount of time given to testing. That there is less time for students to reflect on what is being learned. That interdisciplinary thematic instruction takes too much time; time they do not have because they must teach the prescribed curriculum to prepare the students for the state proficiency exams given in the spring. And once the spring testing is done it is nearly impossible

to refocus students on further learning—that once the testing is done, the students act as if the school year is over. Do any of these comments sound familiar to you? If so, what do you believe may be causing these concerns? Is there any danger to the profession if the act of teaching becomes so highly prescriptive? How will you plan to counter your own negative thinking as a teacher?

4. A teacher with three years of experience left teaching at age 25 to devote her time to her family. Now, at the age of 50, with three children grown, the former teacher wants to return to grades 7 or 8 classrooms. If this teacher were teaching in your subject field, what will this person find has changed most and what the least? Why? How will the person's teaching schedule today likely be different from that of 25 years ago?
5. With today's emphasis on curriculum standards and high-stakes proficiency testing, the challenge is to design standards and tests that are not so high that many students cannot reach them nor so low they become meaningless and risk boring quicker-learning children. The reality is, for example, on any middle school campus there are students doing algebra and there are students who cannot do simple multiplication, and they're the same age. The question is this: For your subject field (specify which), is one set of standards sufficient or should there be multiple standards, such as a set of minimal standards and another set that will challenge the most capable students? Share your thoughts about this with your classmates.
6. It is sometimes said that teaching less can be better. Think back to your own middle grades schooling. What do you really remember? Do you remember lectures and drill sheets, or do you remember projects, your presentations, the lengthy research you did and your extra effort for artwork to accompany your presentation? Maybe you remember a compliment by a teacher or a compliment by peers. Most likely you do not recall the massive amount of content that was covered. Write a one-page (no longer than) essay expressing and defending your agreement or disagreement with the original statement of this paragraph. Share your essay with those of your classmates.
7. If you were asked in a hiring interview to describe the concept of *integrated curriculum*, what would be your reply?
8. Some people say that it is easier to write learning objectives after a lesson has been taught. What is the significance, if any, of that notion?
9. Describe characteristics of a classroom that enhance affective learning. Do you believe the enhancement of students' affective learning is an important responsibility to you as a teacher of young adolescents? Explain why or why not.
10. Talk with experienced teachers (middle level) of the subject field(s) of your interest and ask what effect, if any, NCLB legislation has had on their curriculum and instruction.

INTERNET RESOURCES

National Curriculum Standards by Content Area with Professional Organizations

- *American Indian Supplements* **http://www.doi.gov/ bureau-indian-affairs.html**

Arts (visual and performing)

- *AAHPERD* **http://www.aahperd.org**
- *MTNA* **http://www.mtna.org**

English/language arts/reading

- *IRA* **http://www.reading.org/**
- *NCTE* **http://www.ncte.org/**

Foreign languages, ACTFL **http://www.actfl.org**

Geography, NCGE **http://www.ncge.org**

Health, AAHPERD **http://www.aahperd.org**

History/social studies

- *National Center for History in the Schools* **http://www.sscnet.ucla.edu/nchs**
- *NCSS* **http://www.ncss.org/**

Mathematics, NCTM **http://www.nctm.org**

Physical education, AAHPERD **http://www.aahperd.org**

Science, NSTA **http://www.nsta.org**

Technology, ISTE **http://www.iste.org**

Character education

- *Character Counts!* **http://www.charactercounts.org**
- *Character Education Partnership* **http://www.character.org**
- *Giraffe Project* **http://www.giraffe.org**

Miscellaneous

- *About controversy in the context of science teaching* **http://scope.educ.washington.edu/**
- *Connected Mathematics Project* **http://www.math.msu.edu/cmp**
- *Excellence in Curriculum Integration through Teaching Epidemiology* **http://www.cdc.gov/excite**
- *First Amendment Schools* **http://www.firstamendmentschools.org**
- *Freedom Forum* **http://www.freedomforum.org**
- *Smartpaper Networks* **http://www.smartpaper.net**
- *Standards state by state* **http://www.statestandards.com**
- *TouchSmart Publishing* **http://www.touchsmart.net**

FOR FURTHER READING

Brady, M. (2004). Thinking big: A conceptual framework for the study of everything. *Phi Delta Kappan, 86,* 276–281.

Cooper, D. (2003). Integrating math and social studies through word problems. *Middle Ground, 6*(3), 43–45.

DeMitchell, T. A., & Carney, J. J. (2005). Harry Potter and the public school library. *Phi Delta Kappan, 87,* 159–165.

Dombchik, L. (2004). Storm busters: A science and technology integrated unit. *Middle Ground, 7*(3), 35–36.

Kellough, R. D., Cangelosi, J. S., Collette, A. T., Chiappetta, E. L., Souviney, R. J., Trowbridge, L. W., & Bybee, R. W. (1996). *Integrating mathematics and science for intermediate and middle school students.* Englewood Cliffs, NJ: Merrill/Prentice Hall.

Kellough, R. D., Jarolimek, J., Parker, W. C., Martorella, P. H., Tompkins, G. E., & Hoskisson, K. (1996). *Integrating language arts and social studies for intermediate and middle school students.* Englewood Cliffs, NJ: Merrill/Prentice Hall.

Lancaster, E. A., & Rikard, G. L. (2002). Across the curriculum learning through movement. *Middle School Journal, 33*(3), 28–33.

Lowe, P. (2004). A new approach to math in the middle grades *Principal, 84*(2), 34–39.

Misulis, K. E. (2004). Planning made easier: Using a content analysis process. *Middle Ground, 7*(3), 27–28.

Pateman, B. (2004). Healthier students, better learners. *Educational Leadership, 61*(4), 70–73.

Reys, B. J., Reys, R. E., & Chavez, O. (2004). Why mathematics textbooks matter. *Educational Leadership, 61*(5), 61–66.

Roberts, P. L., & Kellough, R. D. (2008). *A guide for developing interdisciplinary thematic units.* 4th ed. Upper Saddle River, NJ: Merrill/Prentice Hall.

Seethaler, S., & Linn, M. (2004). Genetically modified food in perspective: An inquiry-based curriculum to help middle school students make sense of tradeoffs. *International Journal of Science Education, 26,* 1765–1785.

Seif, E. (2004). Social studies revived. *Educational Leadership, 61*(4), 54–59.

Smith, T. L., & Thomas, P. B. (2006). Navigating the road to success with every student. *Middle Matters, 14*(5), 1–3.

Stallworth, J. (2006). The relevance of young adult literature. *Educational Leadership, 63*(7), 59–63.

Victor, E., & Kellough, R. D. (2004). *Science K–8: An integrated approach.* 10th ed. Upper Saddle River, NJ: Prentice Hall.

Whitin, D. J., & Whitin, P. (2004). *New visions for linking literature and mathematics.* Reston, VA: National Council of Teachers of Mathematics and the National Council of Teachers of English.

Winn, I. J. (2004). The high cost of uncritical teaching. *Phi Delta Kappan, 85,* 496–497.

6

Preparing an Instructional Plan

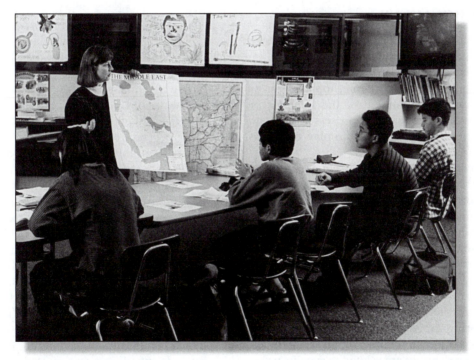

The teacher's edition of the student textbook and other resource materials may expedite your planning but should not substitute for it. You must understand how to create a good instructional plan. In this chapter, you will learn how it is done and will do it.

OBJECTIVES

Specifically, upon completion of this chapter you should be able to:

1. Complete a unit of instruction with sequential lesson plans.

2. Demonstrate understanding of the significance of the planned unit of instruction and the concept of planning curriculum and instruction as an organic process.

3. Differentiate between two types of instructional units—the standard unit and the integrated thematic unit.

4. Demonstrate understanding of the place and role of each of the four decision-making and thought-processing phases in unit planning and implementation.

5. Demonstrate understanding of self-reflection as a common thread important to the reciprocal process of teaching and learning.

6. Demonstrate an understanding of the differences between direct and indirect instruction and the advantages and limitations of each.

7. For a discipline and specific group of young adolescent learners, give examples of learning experiences from each of these categories, and when and why you would use each one: verbal, visual, vicarious, simulated, and direct; and examples of how, why, and when they could be combined.

8. Demonstrate your growing understanding of the meaning of *developmentally appropriate practice.*

9. Demonstrate growing awareness of various styles of teaching and learning and their implications for instructional design.

10. Demonstrate an understanding of the significance of the concepts of learning modalities and learning capacities, and their implications for appropriate educational practice.

THE INSTRUCTIONAL UNIT

The instructional unit is a major subdivision of a course (for one course there are several to many units of instruction) and is comprised of learning activities that are planned around a central theme, topic, issue, or problem. Organizing the content of the semester or year into units makes the teaching process more manageable than when the teacher has no plan or makes only random choices.

The instructional unit is not unlike a chapter in a book, an act or scene in a play, or a phase of work when undertaking a project such as building a house. Breaking down information or actions into component parts and then grouping the related parts makes sense out of learning and doing. The unit brings a sense of cohesiveness and structure to student learning and avoids the piecemeal approach that might otherwise unfold. You can learn to articulate lessons within, between, and among unit plans and focus on important elements while not ignoring tangential information of importance. Students remember "chunks" of information, especially when those chunks are related to specific units.

Although the steps for developing any type of instructional unit are basically the same, units can be organized in a number of ways. For the purposes of this resource guide, let's consider two basic types of units—the standard unit and the integrated thematic unit (ITU)—both of which you are likely to use as a teacher of young adolescents.

A *standard unit* (known also as a *conventional* or *traditional unit*) consists of a series of lessons centered on a topic, theme, major concept, or block of subject matter. Each lesson builds on the previous lesson by contributing additional subject matter, providing further illustrations, and supplying more practice or other added instruction, all of which are aimed at bringing

about mastery of the knowledge and skills on which the unit is centered.

When a standard unit is centered on a central theme, the unit may be referred to as a *thematic unit.* When, by design, the thematic unit integrates disciplines, such as combining the learning of science and mathematics, or combining social studies and English/language arts, or combining any number of disciplines, then it is called an *integrated* (or *interdisciplinary*) *thematic unit* (ITU), or simply, an integrated unit.

Planning and Developing Any Unit of Instruction

Whether for a standard unit or an integrated thematic unit, steps in planning and developing the unit are the same and are described in the following paragraphs.

1. *Select a suitable theme, topic, issue, or problem.* These may be already laid out in your course of study or textbook or already agreed to by members of the teaching team.

2. *Select the goals of the unit and prepare the overview.* The goals are written as an overview or rationale, covering what the unit is about and what the students are to learn. In planning the goals, you should: (a) become as familiar as possible with the topic and materials used; (b) consult curriculum documents, as listed in Chapter 5, for ideas; (c) decide the content and procedures (i.e., what the students should learn about the topic and how); (d) write the rationale or overview, where you summarize what you expect the students will learn about the topic; and (e) be sure your goals are congruent with the goals and standards of the course or grade level program.

3. *Select instructional objectives.* In doing this, you should: (a) include understandings, skills, attitudes, appreciations, and ideals; (b) be specific by avoiding vagueness and generalizations; (c) write the objectives in performance terms; and (d) be as certain as possible that the objectives will contribute to the major learning described in the overview.

4. *Detail the instructional procedures.* These procedures include the subject content and the learning activities, established as a series of lessons. Proceed with the following steps in your initial planning of the instructional procedures.

   a. By referring to curriculum documents, resource units, and colleagues as resources, gather ideas for learning activities that might be suitable for the unit.

   b. Check the learning activities to make sure they will actually contribute to the learning designated in your objectives, discarding ideas that do not.

   c. Make sure the learning activities are feasible. Can you afford the time, effort, or expense? Do you have the necessary materials and equipment? If not, can they be obtained? Are the activities suited to the intellectual and maturity levels of your students?

d. Check resources available to be certain they support the content and learning activities.

e. Decide how to introduce the unit. Provide *introductory activities* to: arouse student interest; inform students of what the unit is about; help you learn about your students—their interests, their abilities, and their experiences and present knowledge of the topic; provide transitions that bridge this topic with that which students have already learned; and involve the students in the planning.

f. Plan *developmental activities* that will sustain student interest, provide for individual student differences, promote the learning as cited in the specific objectives, and promote a project.

g. Plan *culminating activities* that will summarize what has been learned, bring together loose ends, apply what has been learned to new situations, provide students with the opportunity to demonstrate their learning, and provide transfer to the unit that follows.

5. *Plan for preassessment and assessment of student learning.* Preassess what students already know or think they know. Assessment of student progress in achievement of the learning objectives should permeate the entire unit (i.e., as often as possible, assessment should be a daily component of lessons, that is, formative assessment, both formal and informal, is embedded in your teaching. Assessment is the topic of the next chapter.). Plan to gather information in several ways, including informal observations, checklist observations of student performance and their portfolios, and paper-and-pencil tests. Remember, assessment must be congruent with the instructional objectives.

6. *Provide for the materials and tools needed to support the instruction.* The unit cannot function without materials. Therefore, you must plan long before the unit begins for media equipment and materials, references, reading materials, reproduced materials, and community resources. When given ample time to do so, librarians and media center personnel are usually more than willing to assist in finding appropriate materials to support your planned unit of instruction.

Unit Format, Inclusive Elements, and Time Duration

Follow those six steps to develop any type of unit. In addition, two general points should be made. First, although there is no single best format for a teaching unit, there are minimum inclusions. Particular formats may be best for specific disciplines, topics, and types of activities. If you are in student teaching, your program for teacher preparation and/or your cooperating teacher(s) may provide the format you will be expected

to follow. Regardless of the format, in any unit plan the following seven elements should be evident: (1) identification factors, including, for example, grade level, subject, topic, and time duration of the unit; (2) statement of rationale and general goals for the unit; (3) objectives of the unit; (4) materials and resources needed; (5) lesson plans; (6) assessment strategies; and (7) identification of how the unit will attend to student differences, such as variations in students' reading levels, experiential backgrounds, and special needs.

Second, there is no set time duration for a unit plan, although, for specific units, curriculum guides will recommend certain time spans. Units may extend for a minimum of several days or, as in the case of some interdisciplinary thematic units, for several weeks, an entire semester, or even longer. However, be aware that when standard units last more than two or three weeks, they tend to lose the character of clearly identifiable units. Sometimes, in the case of extended duration, units may even overlap. For any unit of instruction, the exact time duration will be dictated by several factors including the topic, problem or theme, the interests and maturity of the students, intensity of the study, and the scope of the learning activities.

THEORETICAL CONSIDERATIONS FOR THE SELECTION OF INSTRUCTIONAL STRATEGIES

As you prepare to detail your instructional plan you will be narrowing in on selecting and planning the instructional activities. In Chapter 2, you learned about specific teacher behaviors that must be in place for students to learn. In the paragraphs that follow, you will learn more, not only about how to implement some of those fundamental behaviors, but also about the large repertoire of other strategies (see Figure 6.1), aids, media, and resources available to you. You will learn about how to select and implement from this repertoire.

Decision Making and Strategy Selection

You must make a myriad of decisions to select and effectively implement a particular teaching strategy. The selection of a strategy depends partially upon your decision whether to deliver information directly (direct, expository, or didactic instruction) or to provide students with access to information (indirect, or facilitative instruction). Direct instruction tends to be teacher-centered, while indirect instruction is more student-centered.

Direct and Indirect Instruction: A Clarification of Terms

By now you are probably well aware that professional education is rampant with its own special jargon, which can be confusing to the neophyte. The use of the term

direct instruction (or its synonym, *direct teaching*), and its antonym, **direct experiences,** are examples of how confusing the jargon can be. The term *direct instruction* (or *direct teaching, expository teaching,* or *teacher-centered instruction*) can also have a variety of definitions, depending on who is doing the defining. For now, you should keep this distinction in mind—do not confuse the term *direct instruction* with the term *direct experience.* The two terms indicate two separate (though not incompatible) instructional modes. The dichotomy of pedagogical opposites shown in Figure 6.2 provides a useful visual distinction of the opposites. While terms in one column are similar, if not synonymous, they are near or exact opposites of those in the other column.

Degrees of Directness

Rather than thinking and behaving in terms of opposites as may be suggested by Figure 6.2, more likely your teaching will be distinguished by "degrees of directness" or "degrees of indirectness." For example, for a unit of instruction, directions for a culminating project may be

given by the teacher in a direct or expository mini-lecture, followed then by a student-designed inquiry that leads to the final project.

Rather than focus your attention on the selection of a particular model of teaching young adolescents, we emphasize the importance of an eclectic model—selecting the best from various models or approaches. As indicated by the example in the preceding paragraph, there will be times when you want to use a direct, teacher-centered approach, perhaps by a mini-lecture or a demonstration. And then there will be many more times when you will want to use an indirect, student-centered, or social-interactive approach, such as the use of cooperative learning and investigative projects. Perhaps there will be even more times when you will be doing both at the same time, such as working with a teacher-centered approach with one small group of students, giving them direct instruction, while another group or several groups of students in areas of the classroom are working on their project studies (a student-centered approach). The information that follows and specific descriptions in Chapters 8–9 will help you make decisions about when each approach is most appropriate and provide guidelines for their use. But first, to assist in your selection of strategies it is important you understand the terms and basic principles of learning summarized as follows.

Figure 6.1   A list of instructional strategies.

Autotutorial	Individualized	Project
Brainstorming	instruction	Questioning
Coaching	Inquiry	Reading
Collaborative	Interactive	partner
learning	media	Review &
Cooperative	Investigation	practice
learning	Journal writing	Role-play
Debate	Laboratory	Self-
Demonstration	investigation	instructional
Diorama	Laser videodisk	module
Discovery	or CD	Script writing
Drama	Learning center	Silent reading
Drill	Lecture	Simulation
Dyad learning	Library/resource	Study guide
Expository	center	Symposium
Field trip	Metacognition	Telecommuni-
Game	Mock-up	cation
Guest	Multimedia	Term paper
presenter	Panel	Textbook
Homework	discussion	Tutorial

Anne Vega/Merrill

Figure 6.2   Pedagogical opposites.

Delivery mode of instruction	versus	Access mode of instruction
Didactic instruction	versus	Facilitative teaching
Direct instruction	versus	Indirect instruction
Direct teaching	versus	Direct experiencing
Expository teaching	versus	Discovery learning
Teacher-centered instruction	versus	Student-centered instruction

Principles of Classroom Instruction and Learning: A Synopsis

A student does not learn to write by learning to recognize grammatical constructions of sentences. Neither does a person learn to play soccer solely by listening to a lecture about soccer. Learning is superficial unless the instructional methods and learning activities are developmentally and intellectually appropriate including: (a) developmentally appropriate for the learners and (b) intellectually appropriate for the understanding, skills, and attitudes desired. Memorizing, for instance, is not the same as understanding. Yet far too often, memorization seems all that is expected of students in many classrooms. The result is low-level learning, a mere verbalism or mouthing of poorly understood words and sentences. The orchestration of short-term memory exercises is not intellectually appropriate, and it is not teaching. A mental model of learning that assumes a brain is capable of doing only one thing at a time is invidiously incorrect (Baker & Martin, 1998; Jensen, 1998).

When selecting the mode of instruction, you should bear in mind basic principles of classroom instruction and learning as shown in Figure 6.3.

TEACHING IN PRACTICE

Students Restless during Direct Instruction

Pat, a social studies teacher, has a class of 28 eighth graders who, during lectures, teacher-led discussions, and recitation lessons, are restless and inattentive, creating for Pat a problem in classroom management. At Pat's invitation, the school psychologist tests the students for learning modality and finds that of the 28 students, 24 are predominately kinesthetic learners.

Questions for class discussion

1. Of what value is this information to Pat?

2. Describe what, if anything, Pat should try as a result of this information.

Conceptual and Procedural Knowledge

Conceptual knowledge (also called *declarative knowledge*) refers to the understanding of relationships and abstractions, whereas *procedural knowledge* entails the recording in memory of the meanings of symbols and rules and procedures needed in order to accomplish tasks. (Motor skills, habits, and perceptual skills are examples of procedural knowledge.) Unless it is connected in meaningful ways for the formation of conceptual knowledge, the accumulation of memorized, procedural knowledge is fragmented, ill fated, and will be maintained in the brain for only a brief time.

To help young adolescents establish conceptual knowledge, the learning for them must be meaningful. To help make learning meaningful for your students, you should use direct and real experiences as often as is practical and possible. Vicarious experiences are sometimes necessary to provide students' with otherwise unattainable knowledge; however, direct experiences that engage all the students' senses and all learning modalities are more powerful. Students learn to write by writing and by receiving coaching and feedback about their progress in writing. They learn to play soccer by playing soccer and by receiving coaching and feedback about their developing skills and knowledge in playing the game. They learn these things best when they are actively (hands-on) and mentally (minds-on) engaged in doing them. This is real learning, learning that is meaningful; it is *authentic learning*. It is the learning that is most developmentally appropriate for young adolescent learners.

Direct versus Indirect Instructional Modes: Strengths and Weaknesses of Each

When selecting an instructional strategy, there are two distinct choices (modes) from which you must make a decision: Should you deliver information to students directly or should you provide students with access to information? (Refer to Figure 6.2.)

Figure 6.3 Basic principles of instruction and learning for teaching young adolescents.

- Although young adolescents differ in their styles of learning and in their learning capacities, each can learn.
- Learning is most meaningful and longest lasting when it is connected to real-life experiences.
- No matter what else you are prepared to teach, you are primarily a teacher of literacy and of thinking, social, and learning skills.
- Physical activity enhances learning. It is advisable that every lesson includes, to some degree, an activity involving the kinesthetic learning modality.
- Students must be actively involved in their own learning and in the assessment of their learning.
- Students need constant, understandable, positive, and reliable feedback about their learning.
- Students should be engaged in both independent study and cooperative learning and give and receive tutorial instruction.
- To a great degree, it is the mode of instruction that determines what is learned and how well it is learned.
- The teacher must hold high expectations for the learning of each student (but not necessarily identical expectations for every student) and not waiver from those expectations.

The *delivery mode* (known also as the *didactic, expository,* or *traditional style*) is to deliver information. Knowledge is passed on from those who know (the teachers, with the aid of textbooks) to those who do not (the students). Within the delivery mode, traditional and time-honored strategies are textbook reading, the lecture (formal teacher talk), questioning, and teacher-centered or teacher-planned discussions.

With the *access mode,* instead of direct delivery of information and direct control over what is learned, you provide students with access to information by working *with* the students. In collaboration with the students, experiences are designed that facilitate the building of their existing schemata and their obtaining new knowledge and skills. Within the access mode, important instructional strategies include cooperative learning, inquiry, and investigative, student-centered project learning, each of which most certainly will use questioning (although the questions more frequently will come from the students than from you or the textbook or some other source extrinsic to the student). Discussions and lectures on particular topics also may be involved. However, when used in the access mode, discussions and lectures occur during or after (rather than precede) direct, hands-on learning by the students. In other words, rather than preceding student inquiry, discussions and lectures *result from* student inquiry, and then may be followed by further student investigation.

You are probably more experienced with the delivery mode. To be most effective as a classroom teacher of young adolescent learners, however, you must become knowledgeable and skillful in using access strategies. You should appropriately select and effectively use strategies from both modes, but with a strong favor toward access strategies. Strategies within the access mode clearly facilitate students' positive learning and acquisition of conceptual knowledge and help build their self-esteem. Thus, from your study of Chapters 8 and 9, you will become knowledgeable about specific techniques so you can make intelligent decisions for choosing the best strategy for particular goals and objectives for your own discipline and the interests, needs, and maturity level of your own unique group of students.

Figures 6.4 and 6.5 provide an overview of the specific strengths and weaknesses of each mode. By comparing those figures you can see that the strengths and weaknesses of one mode are nearly mirror opposites of the other. As noted earlier, although as a teacher you should be skillful in the use of strategies from both modes, for the most developmentally appropriate teaching you should concentrate more on using strategies from the access mode. Strategies within that mode are more student-centered, hands-on, and concrete; students interact with one another and are actually or closer to doing what they are learning to do—that is, the learning is likely more authentic.

Figure 6.4   Delivery mode: Its strengths and weaknesses.

DELIVERY MODE

Strengths
- Much content can be covered within a short span of time, usually by formal teacher talk, which then may be followed by an experiential activity.
- The teacher is in control of what content is covered.
- The teacher is in control of time allotted to specific content coverage.
- Strategies within the delivery mode are consistent with competency-based instruction.
- Student achievement of specific content is predictable and manageable.

Potential Weaknesses
- The sources of student motivation are mostly extrinsic.
- Students have little control over the pacing of their learning.
- Students make few important decisions about their learning.
- There may be little opportunity for divergent or creative thinking.
- Student self-esteem may be inadequately served.

Figure 6.5   Access mode: Its strengths and weaknesses.

ACCESS MODE

Strengths
- Students learn content, and in more depth.
- The sources of student motivation are more likely intrinsic.
- Students make important decisions about their own learning.
- Students have more control over the pacing of their learning.
- Students develop a sense of personal self-worth.

Potential Weaknesses
- Breadth of content coverage may be more limited.
- Strategies are time-consuming.
- The teacher has less control over content and time.
- The specific results of student learning are less predictable.
- The teacher may have less control over class procedures.

Learning that occurs from the use of that mode is longer lasting (fixes into long-term memory). And, as the students interact with one another and with their learning, they develop a sense of "can do," which enhances their self-esteem.

SELECTING LEARNING ACTIVITIES THAT ARE DEVELOPMENTALLY APPROPRIATE FOR YOUNG ADOLESCENT LEARNERS

Returning to our soccer example, can you imagine a soccer coach teaching 9- to 14-year-olds the skills and knowledge needed to play soccer without ever letting them experience playing the game? Can you imagine a science teacher instructing students on how to read a thermometer without ever letting them actually read a real thermometer? Can you imagine a geography teacher teaching students how to read a map without ever letting them put their eyes and hands on a real map? Can you imagine a piano teacher teaching a young adolescent to play piano without ever allowing the child to touch a real keyboard? Unfortunately, still today, too many teachers do almost those exact things—they try to teach students to do something without letting the students practice doing it.

In planning and selecting developmentally appropriate learning activities, an important rule to remember is to select activities that are as close to the real thing as possible. That is **learning through direct experiencing.** When students are involved in direct experiences, they are using more of their sensory input channels, their learning modalities (i.e., auditory, visual, tactile, kinesthetic). And when all the senses are engaged, learning is more integrated and is most effective, meaningful, and longest lasting. This "learning by doing" is *authentic learning*—or, as referred to earlier, *hands-on/minds-on learning*.

STYLES OF LEARNING AND IMPLICATIONS FOR INSTRUCTION

Teachers who are most effective are those who adapt their teaching styles and methods to their students, using approaches that interest the students, that are neither too easy nor too difficult, that match the students' learning styles and learning capacities, and are relevant to the students' lives. This adaptation process is further complicated because each student is different from every other one. All do not have the same interests, abilities, backgrounds, or learning styles and capacities. As a matter of fact, not only do students differ from one another, but also each student's learning style can change to some extent from one day to the next (Harrison, Andrews, & Saklofske, 2003). What appeals to a young adolescent learner today may not have the same appeal tomorrow. Therefore, you need to consider both the nature of young adolescents in general (as reviewed in Chapter 1) and each student in particular. Since you probably have already experienced a recent course in the psychology of learning, what follows is only a brief synopsis of knowledge about learning.

Learning Modalities

Learning modality refers to the *sensory portal* (or input channel) by which a student prefers to receive sensory reception (modality preference), or the actual way a student learns best (modality adeptness). Some young adolescents prefer learning by seeing, a *visual modality*; others prefer learning through instruction from others (through talk), an *auditory modality*; while many others prefer learning by doing and being physically involved, the *kinesthetic modality*, and by touching objects, the *tactile modality*. A student's modality preference is not always that student's modality strength.

While primary modality strength can be determined by observing students, it can also be mixed and can change as the result of experience and intellectual maturity. As one might suspect, modality integration (i.e., engaging more of the sensory input channels, using several modalities at once or staggered) has been found to contribute to better achievement in student learning.

Because many young adolescents neither have a preference or strength for auditory reception, middle level teachers should severely limit their use of the lecture method of instruction, that is, of too much reliance on formal teacher talk. Furthermore, instructions using a singular approach, such as auditory (e.g., talking to the students), cheat students who learn better another way. This difference can affect student achievement. A teacher, for example, who only talks to the students or uses discussions day after day is shortchanging the education of learners who learn better another way, who are, for example, kinesthetic and visual learners.

As a general rule, most young adolescents prefer and learn best by touching objects, by feeling shapes and textures, by interacting with each other, and by moving things around. In contrast, learning by sitting and listening are difficult for many of them.

Some learning style traits significantly discriminate between students who are at risk of not finishing school and students who perform well. Students who are underachieving and at risk need: (a) frequent opportunities for mobility; (b) options and choices; (c) a variety of instructional resources, environments, and sociological groupings, rather than routines and patterns; (d) to learn during late morning, afternoon, or evening hours, rather than in the early morning; (e) informal seating, rather than wooden, steel, or plastic chairs; (f) low illumination, because bright light contributes to hyperactivity; and (g) tactile/visual introductory resources reinforced by kinesthetic (i.e., direct experiencing and whole-body activities)/visual resources, or introductory kinesthetic/visual resources reinforced by tactile/visual resources (Brand, Dunn, & Greb, 2002; Dunn, 1995; Rayneri, Gerber, & Wiley, 2003).

Regardless of the subject(s) you teach, an effective approach is to use strategies that integrate the modalities. When well designed, thematic units and project-based learning incorporate modality integration. In conclusion, then, when teaching any group of young adolescents of mixed learning abilities, modality strengths, language proficiency, and cultural backgrounds, integrating learning modalities is a must for the most successful teaching.

Learning Styles

Related to learning modality is *learning style*, which can be defined as independent forms of knowing and processing information. While some young adolescents may be comfortable with beginning their learning of a new idea in the abstract (e.g., visual or verbal symbolization), most need to begin with the concrete (e.g., learning by actually doing it). Many students prosper while working in groups, while others prefer working alone. Some are quick in their studies, whereas others are slow, methodical, cautious, and meticulous. Some can sustain attention on a single topic for a long time, becoming more absorbed in their study as time passes. Others are slower starters and more casual in their pursuits but are capable of shifting with ease from subject to subject. Some can study in the midst of music, noise, or movement, whereas others need quiet, solitude, and a desk or table. The point is this: People vary in not only their skills and preferences in the way knowledge is received, but also in how they mentally process information once it has been received. This latter is a person's style of learning.

Classifications of Learning Styles. It is important to note learning style is *not* an indicator of intelligence, but rather an indicator of how a person learns. Although there are probably as many types of learning styles as there are individuals, David Kolb (1984) describes two major differences in how people learn: how they perceive situations and how they process information. On the basis of perceiving and processing and earlier work by Carl Jung on psychological types (Jung, 1923), Bernice McCarthy (1997) describes four major learning styles, presented in the following paragraphs.

The *imaginative learner* perceives information concretely and processes it reflectively. Imaginative learners learn well by listening and sharing with others, integrating the ideas of others with their own experiences. Imaginative learners often have difficulty adjusting to traditional teaching, which depends less on classroom interactions and students' sharing and connecting of their prior experiences. In a traditional classroom, the imaginative learner is likely an at-risk student.

The *analytic learner* perceives information abstractly and processes it reflectively. Analytic learners prefer sequential thinking, need details, and value what experts have to offer. Analytic learners do well in traditional classrooms.

The commonsense learner perceives information abstractly and processes it actively. This learner is pragmatic and enjoys hands-on learning. Commonsense learners sometimes find school frustrating unless they can see immediate use for what is being learned. In the traditional classroom, the commonsense learner is likely a learner who is at risk of not completing school, of dropping out.

The *dynamic learner* perceives information concretely and processes it actively. The dynamic learner also prefers hands-on learning and is excited by anything new. Dynamic learners are risk takers and are frustrated by learning if they see it as being tedious and sequential. In a traditional classroom the dynamic learner is likely an at-risk student.

The Three-Phase Learning Cycle

To understand conceptual development and change, researchers in the 1960s developed a Piaget-based theory of learning where students are guided from concrete, hands-on learning experiences to the abstract formulations of concepts and their formal applications. This theory became known as the *three-phase learning cycle* (Karplus, 1974). Long a popular strategy for teaching science, the learning cycle is useful in other disciplines as well, such as art, language arts, mathematics, and social studies (Barojas & Dehesa, 2001; Bevevino, Dengel, & Adams, 1999; Sowell, 1993). The three phases are: (1) the *exploratory hands-on phase*, where students can explore ideas and experience assimilation and disequilibrium that lead to their own questions and tentative answers, (2) the *invention* or *concept development phase*, where, under the guidance of the teacher, students invent concepts and principles that help them answer their questions and reorganize their ideas (i.e., the students revise their thinking to allow the new information to fit), and (3) the *expansion* or *concept application phase*, another hands-on phase in which students try out their new ideas by applying them to situations that are relevant and meaningful to them. [*Note:* The three phases of the learning cycle are comparable to the three levels of thinking (discussed in Chapter 3), described variously by others. For example, in Eisner (1979), the levels are referred to as "descriptive," "interpretive," and "evaluative."] During application of a concept, the learner may discover new information that causes a change in the learner's understanding of the concept being applied. Thus, the process of learning is cyclical.

Variations on the Theme. Recent interpretations or modifications of the three-phase cycle include McCarthy's 4MAT. With the 4MAT system, teachers employ a learning cycle of instructional strategies to try and reach each student's learning style. In the cycle, in the words of McCarthy, learners "sense and feel, they experience, then they watch, they reflect, then they think, they develop theories, then they try out theories, they experiment. Finally, they evaluate and synthesize what they have learned so to apply it to their next similar experience. They get smarter. They apply experience to experiences" (McCarthy, 1990). In this process they are likely using all four learning modalities.

The *constructivist learning theory* suggests learning is a process involving the active engagement of learners who adapt the educative event to fit and expand their individual worldview (as opposed to the behaviorist pedagogical assumption that learning is something done to learners) and accentuate the importance of student self-assessment (DeLay, 1996). In support of that theory, some variations of the learning cycle include a separate phase of assessment. However, because we believe assessment of what students know or think they know should be a continual process, permeating all three phases of the learning cycle, we reject any treatment of assessment as a self-standing phase.

Learning Capacities: The Theory of Multiple Intelligences

In contrast to learning styles, Gardner (1996) introduced what he calls learning capacities exhibited by individuals in differing ways. Originally and sometimes still referred to as multiple intelligences, or ways of knowing, capacities thus far identified are:

- *Bodily/kinesthetic:* ability to use the body skillfully and to handle objects skillfully.
- *Existentialist:* ability to understand and pursue the ultimate philosophical questions, meanings, and mysteries of life.
- *Interpersonal:* ability to understand people and relationships.
- *Intrapersonal:* ability to assess one's emotional life as a means to understand oneself and others.
- *Logical/mathematical:* ability to handle chains of reasoning and recognize patterns and orders.

- *Musical/rhythmic:* sensitivity to pitch, melody, rhythm, and tone.
- *Naturalist:* ability to draw on materials and features of the natural environment to solve problems or fashion products.
- *Verbal/linguistic:* sensitivity to the meaning and order of words.
- *Visual/spatial:* ability to perceive the world accurately and to manipulate the nature of space, such as through architecture, mime, or sculpture.

Many educators believe, and as implied in the presentation of McCarthy's four types of learners, many of the students who are at risk of not completing school are those who may be dominant in a cognitive learning style not in synch with traditional teaching methods. Traditional methods of instruction are largely of McCarthy's analytic style: information is presented in a logical, linear, and sequential fashion. Traditional methods also reflect three of the Gardner types: verbal/linguistic, logical/mathematical, and intrapersonal. Consequently, to better synchronize methods of instruction with learning styles, some teachers and schools (see the Classroom Vignette, "Using the Theory of Learning Capacities") have restructured the curriculum and instruction around Gardner's learning capacities (Bolak, Bialach, & Dunphy, 2005; Campbell & Campbell, 1999), or around Sternberg's Triarchic Theory (English, 1998; Sternberg, 1998). Sternberg identifies seven metaphors for the mind and intelligence (geographic, computational, biological, epistemological, anthropological, sociological, and systems) and proposes a theory of intelligence consisting of three elements: analytical, practical, and creative (Sternberg, 1998; Sternberg, Grigorenko, & Jarvin, 2001).

CLASSROOM VIGNETTE

Using the Theory of Learning Capacities (Multiple Intelligences) and Multilevel Instruction

In one middle school classroom, during one week of a six-week thematic unit on weather, students were concentrating on learning about the water cycle. For this study of the water cycle, with the students' help, the teacher divided the class into several groups of three to five students per group. While working on six projects simultaneously to learn about the water cycle: (1) one group of students designed, conducted, and repeated an experiment to discover the number of drops of water that can be held on one side of a new one-cent coin versus the number that can be held on the side of a worn one-cent coin; (2) working in part with the first group, a second group designed and prepared graphs to illustrate the results of the experiments of the first group; (3) a third group of students created and composed the words and music of a song about the water cycle; (4) a fourth group incorporated their combined interests in mathematics and art to design, collect the necessary materials, and create a colorful and interactive bulletin board about the water cycle; (5) a fifth group read about the water cycle in materials they researched from the Internet and various libraries; and (6) a sixth group created a puppet show about the water cycle. On Friday, after each group had finished, the groups shared their projects with the whole class.

From the preceding information about learning, you must realize at least two important facts:

1. *Intelligence is not a fixed or static reality, but can be learned, taught, and developed.* This concept is important for students to understand, too. When students understand intelligence is incremental, that it is developed through use over time, they tend to be more motivated to work at learning than when they believe intelligence is a fixed entity (Brandt, 2000).
2. *Not all students learn and respond to learning situations in the same way.* A student may learn differently according to the situation or according to the student's ethnicity, cultural background, or socioeconomic status.

A teacher who, for all students, uses only one style of teaching, or who teaches to only one or a few styles of learning day after day, is shortchanging those students who learn better another way.

THE LEARNING EXPERIENCES LADDER

The Learning Experiences Ladder (Figure 6.6) is a visual depiction of a range of kinds of learning experiences from which a teacher may select. Hands-on/minds-on learning is at the bottom of the ladder. At the top are abstract experiences, where the learner is exposed only to symbolization (i.e., letters and numbers) and uses only

Figure 6.6 The Learning Experiences Ladder.

A B S T R A C T

Verbal Experiences

Teacher talk, written words; engaging only one sense; using the most abstract symbolization; students physically inactive. *Examples:* (a) Listening to the teacher talk about tide pools. (b) Listening to a student report about the Grand Canyon. (c) Listening to a guest speaker talk about how the state legislature functions.

Visual Experiences

Still pictures, diagrams, charts; engaging only one sense; typically symbolic; students physically inactive. *Examples:* (a) Viewing slide photographs of tide pools. (b) Viewing drawings and photographs of the Grand Canyon. (c) Listening to a guest speaker talk about the state legislature and show slides of it in action.

Vicarious Experiences

Laser videodisc programs; computer programs; video programs; engaging more than one sense; learner indirectly "doing"; may be some limited physical activity. *Examples:* (a) Interacting with a computer program about wave action and life in tide pools. (b) Viewing and listening to a video program about the Grand Canyon. (c) Taking a field trip to observe the state legislature in action.

Simulated Experiences

Role-playing; experimenting; simulations; mock-up; working models; all or nearly all senses engaged; activity often integrating disciplines; closest to the real thing. *Examples:* (a) Building a classroom working model of a tide pool. (b) Building a classroom working model of the Grand Canyon. (c) Designing a classroom role-play simulation patterned after the operating procedure of the state legislature.

Direct Experiences

Learner actually doing what is being learned; true inquiry; all senses engaged; usually integrates disciplines; the real thing. *Examples:* (a) Visiting and experiencing a tide pool. (b) Visiting and experiencing the Grand Canyon. (c) Designing an elected representative body to oversee the operation of the school-within-the-school program that is patterned after the state legislative assembly.

C O N C R E T E

Note: Earlier versions of this concept were Charles F. Hoban, Sr., et al., *Visualizing the Curriculum* (New York: Dryden, 1937), p. 39; Jerome S. Bruner, *Toward a Theory of Instruction* (Cambridge: Harvard University Press, 1966), p. 49; Edgar Dale, *Audio-visual Methods in Teaching* (New York: Holt, Rinehart & Winston, 1969), p. 108; and Eugene C. Kim and Richard D. Kellough, *A Resource Guide for Secondary School Teaching,* 2nd ed. (Upper Saddle River, NJ: Prentice Hall, 1978), p. 136.

one or two senses (auditory or visual). The teacher lectures while the students sit and watch and hear. Visual and verbal symbolic experiences, although impossible to avoid when teaching, are less effective in assuring that planned and meaningful learning occurs. This is especially so with learners who have special needs, learners with ethnic and cultural differences, and English language learning (ELL) students. Thus, when planning learning experiences and selecting instructional materials, you are advised to select activities that engage the students in the most direct experiences possible and that are developmentally and intellectually appropriate for your specific group of students.

As can be inferred from the Learning Experiences Ladder, when teaching about tide pools (the first example for each step) the most effective mode is to take the students to a tide pool (direct experience), where students can see, hear, touch, smell, and perhaps even taste (if not polluted with toxins) the tide pool. The least effective mode is for the teacher to merely talk about the tide pool (verbal experience, the most abstract and symbolic experience), engaging only one sense—auditory.

Of course, for various reasons—such as time, matters of safety, lack of resources, and/or geographic location of your school—you may not be able to take your students to a tide pool. You cannot always use the most direct experience, so sometimes you must select an experience higher on the ladder. Self-discovery teaching is not always appropriate. Sometimes it is more appropriate to build upon what others have discovered and learned. Although learners do not need to "reinvent the wheel," for young adolescent learners in particular the most effective and longest-lasting learning is that which engages most or all of their senses. On the Learning Experiences Ladder, those are the experiences that fall within the bottom three categories: direct, simulated, and vicarious.

Direct, Simulated, and Vicarious Experiences Help Connect Student Learning

Another value of direct, simulated, and vicarious experiences is they tend to be interdisciplinary; that is, they blur or bridge subject-content boundaries. That makes those experiences especially useful for teachers who want to help students connect the learning of one discipline with that of others and to bridge what is being learned with their own life experiences. Direct, simulated, and vicarious experiences are more like real life. That means the learning resulting from those experiences is authentic.

Now do Exercise 6.1.

FOR YOUR NOTES

EXERCISE 6.1:   CONVERSION OF AN ABSTRACT LEARNING EXPERIENCE TO A DIRECT ONE

INSTRUCTIONS: This exercise is to challenge your creative imagination. Select from your outline done for Exercise 5.6 a topic that is typically taught by the use of symbolization (at or near the top of the Learning Experiences Ladder), then devise a technique by which, with limited resources, that same content would be taught more directly (at or close to the bottom of the ladder). Upon completion of this exercise, share your proposal with your colleagues for their feedback.

1. Grade Level: _____

2. Topic: _____

3. Traditional way of teaching this topic: _____

   _____

   _____

   _____

   _____

   _____

4. Detailed description of how to teach this topic using direct learning experiences: _____

   _____

   _____

   _____

   _____

   _____

   _____

5. Statement about why you believe a direct way of teaching this topic is uncommon: _____

   _____

   _____

   _____

   _____

   _____

6. Ideas resulting from sharing your proposal with others in your class: _____

   _____

   _____

   _____

   _____

   _____

FOR YOUR NOTES

PLANNING AND DEVELOPING AN INTERDISCIPLINARY THEMATIC UNIT

The steps outlined earlier in this chapter are essential for planning any type of teaching unit, including the interdisciplinary thematic unit (ITU), which may consist of smaller subject-specific conventional units developed according to the immediately foregoing guidelines.

The primary responsibility for the development of ITUs can depend on a single teacher or upon the cooperation of several teachers who represent several disciplines. A teaching team may develop from one to several interdisciplinary thematic units a year. Over time, then, a team will have several units that are available for implementation. However, the most effective units are often those that are the most current or the most meaningful to students. This means that ever-changing global, national, and local topics provide a veritable smorgasbord from which to choose, and teaching teams must constantly update old units and develop new and exciting ones.

A caution is to see that one teaching team's unit does not conflict with others at the same or another grade level. If a school has two or more teams at the same grade level that involve the same disciplines, for example, the teams may want to develop units on different themes and share their products. For example, a seventh-grade team must guard against developing a unit quite similar to one that the students had or will have at another grade level. Clear and open communication within, between, and among teams and schools within a school district are critical to the success of interdisciplinary thematic teaching.

Specific Guidelines for Developing an Interdisciplinary Thematic Unit

Specific guidelines to guide you in developing an ITU are presented in the following paragraphs.

Agree on the nature or source of the unit. Team members should view the interdisciplinary approach as a collaborative effort in which all members can participate if appropriate. Write what you want the students to receive from interdisciplinary instruction. Troubleshoot potential stumbling blocks.

Discuss subject-specific standards, goals, and objectives, curriculum guidelines, textbooks and supplemental materials, and units already in place for the school year. Focus on what you are obligated or mandated to teach, and explain the scope and sequence of the teaching so all team members understand the constraints and limitations.

Choose a theme topic and develop a time line. From the information provided by each subject-specialist teacher in the preceding guideline, start listing possible theme topics that can be drawn from within the existing course outlines. Give-and-take is essential here, as some topics will fit certain subjects better than others. The chief goal is to find a topic that can be adapted to each subject without detracting from the educational plan already in place. This may require choosing and merging content from two or more other units previously planned. The theme is then drawn from the topic.

Sometimes themes are selected by the teacher or by a teaching team before meeting the students for the first time. Other times teachers in collaboration with students select them. Even when the theme is preselected,

---

SCHOOL VIGNETTE

A Seventh-Grade ITU at Albert F. Ford Middle School

Seventh-grade students at Ford Middle School (Acushnet, MA) work all year on various projects that constitute a thematic unit about hot air ballooning. The title of the unit is "The Great Balloon Craze." Students read *The Great Balloon Craze,* a nonfiction selection about women who were active in hot air ballooning more than a century ago, and *Airy-Go-Round,* an adventure story of a retired math teacher whose balloon went down and was washed ashore on the island of Krakatoa. Students plot an imaginary journey of their own, create a comic strip, design an imaginary machine, and study and calculate information about three record-breaking balloon voyages. They watch the motive *Around the World in 80 Days* and attend a live theater production of the same title. Students design posters that use persuasive techniques, and that act as ads inviting people in the early 1800s to witness Madame Blanchard's first balloon flight in Paris. A local balloonist gives a live presentation. Students experiment with creating hot air balloon soft sculptures and create watercolors of landscapes and hot air balloons.

Source: Adapted by permission from the Ford Middle School (Acushnet, MA) Web page [Online]. Available at http://www.ultranet.com/~fordms/news.html (March 1, 2001).

with guidance from the teacher, students still should be given major responsibility for deciding the final theme title (name), topics within the theme, and corresponding learning activities. With young adolescents, integrated thematic instruction works best when students have ownership in the study, that is, when they have been empowered with major decision-making responsibility.

The basis for theme selection should satisfy two criteria. The theme should: (a) fit within the expected scope and sequence of mandated content and (b) be of interest to the students. Regarding the first criterion, many teachers have said that when they and their students embarked on an interdisciplinary thematic study they did so without truly knowing where the study would go or what the learning outcomes would be—and they were somewhat frightened by that realization. But when the unit was completed, their students had learned everything (or nearly everything) that the teacher would have expected them to learn were the teacher to use a more traditional approach. And, it was more fun because the students were more intrinsically motivated! See Figure 6.7 for important questions to ask when selecting a theme.

The second criterion is easy to satisfy, as it will most assuredly be when students are truly empowered with decision-making responsibility for what they learn and how they learn it. So, once a general theme is selected (one that satisfies the first criterion), its final title, subtopics, and corresponding procedural activities should be finalized in collaboration with the students.

Establish two time lines. The first is for the team only and is to ensure that each member meets deadlines for specific work required in developing the unit. The second time line is for both students and teachers and shows the intended length of the unit, when it will start, and (if relevant) in which classes it will be taught.

Develop the scope and sequence for content and instruction. To develop the unit, follow the six steps for planning and developing a unit of instruction outlined earlier in this chapter. This should be done by each team member as well as by the group during common planning time so members can coordinate dates and activities in logical sequence and depth. This is an organic process and will generate both ideas and anxiety. Under the guidance of the team leader, members should strive to keep this anxiety at a level conducive to learning, experimenting, and arriving at group consensus.

Share goals and objectives. Each team member should have a copy of the goals and target objectives of every other team member. This helps to refine the unit and lesson plans and to prevent unnecessary overlap and confusion.

Give the unit a name. The unit has been fashioned and is held together by the theme that is chosen. Giving the theme a name and using that name communicates

Figure 6.7 Questions to ask when selecting a theme.

- Is the theme within the realm of understanding and experience of the teachers involved?
- Will the theme interest all members of the teaching team?
- Do we have sufficient materials and resources to supply information we might need?
- Does the theme lend itself to active learning experiences?
- Can this theme lead to a unit that is of the proper duration—not too short and not too long?
- Is the theme helpful, worthwhile, and pertinent to the instructional objectives?
- Will the theme be of interest to students, and will it motivate them to do their best?
- Is the theme one with which teachers are not already so familiar that they cannot share in the excitement of the learning?

to the students that this unit of study is integrated, important, and meaningful to school and to life. Sample names of actual ITUs, their number of lessons, and discipline connections are shown in Figure 6.8.

Share subject-specific units, lesson plans, and printed and nonprinted materials. Exchange the finalized unit to obtain one another's comments and suggestions. Keep a copy of each teacher's unit(s) as a resource, and see if you could present a lesson using it as your basis (some modification may be necessary). Lesson planning is the topic that follows.

Field-test the unit. Beginning at the scheduled time and date, present the lessons. Team members may trade classes from time to time. Team teaching may take place.

Reflect, assess, and perhaps adjust and revise the unit. During planning time, team members should share and discuss their successes and failures and determine what needs to be changed and how and when that should be done to make the unit successful. Adjustments can be made along the way and revisions for future use can be made after completion of the unit.

The preceding are not absolutes and should be viewed only as guidelines. Differing teaching teams and levels of teacher experience and knowledge make the strict adherence to any plan less productive than would be the use of group-generated plans. In practice, the process that works well—one that results in meaningful learning for the students and in their positive feelings about themselves, about learning, and about school—is the appropriate process. For example, some teaching teams use what is sometimes called a *backward design* for their curriculum planning (Wiggins & McTighe, 1998). The procedure is generally as follows: (a) the involved teachers first study the state and district standards; (b) from the standards they select and establish target

Figure 6.8 Sample ITU titles showing their discipline connections and number of lesson plans [These ITUs for use with young adolescents are available in their entirety in Roberts and Kellough listed in the suggested readings at end of this chapter].

Changes: Spring as a Time of Growth, Beauty, and Transformation. Five lessons. Written for primary but adaptable for early middle grades. Art, science, language arts, and mathematics.

Early Civilizations: Dawn of a New Age in Ancient Greece. Eleven lessons. Prepared for grade 6. Literature, geography, mathematics, physical education, science, and social studies.

Migrations: Early Newcomers in North America. Ten lessons. For grades 4 and up. English/language arts, history/social studies, and geography.

---

goals and objectives for their students; (c) they think of projects that will provide opportunities for their students to demonstrate that they have acquired the expected learning; and (d) they finalize their plan with supportive instructional activities.

Developing the Learning Activities: The Heart and Spirit of the ITU

Activities that engage the students in meaningful learning constitute the heart and spirit of the ITU: there are activities that start a unit into motion, that initiate the unit—*initiating activities;* there are the activities that comprise the heart of the unit—*ongoing developmental activities;* and, there are activities that bring the unit to a natural close—*culminating activities.*

The Common Thread

Central to the selection and development of all learning activities for interdisciplinary thematic instruction is a common thread of four tightly interwoven components: (a) the instruction is centered around a big and meaningful idea (theme) rather than on factitious subject areas, (b) the students and the teacher share in the decision making and responsibility for learning, (c) the learning activities are selected so all students are actively engaged in their learning—that is, they are both physically active (hands-on learning) and mentally active (minds-on learning), and (d) there is steady reflection on and frequent sharing of what is being done and what is being learned.

Initiating Activities

An ITU can be initiated by a limitless variety of ways. You must decide which ways are appropriate for your educational goals and objectives, intended time duration, and for your own unique group of students, considering the extent and diversity of their interests, abilities, and skills. You might start with a current event, a community problem, an artifact, a book, a media presentation, or something interesting found on the Internet.

Developmental Activities

Once the ITU has been initiated, students become occupied with a variety of ongoing (developmental) activities. In working with students in selecting and planning the developmental activities, you will want to keep in mind the concept represented by the Learning Experiences Ladder (Figure 6.6) as well as the preselected goals and target objectives.

Culminating Activity

Just as with other types of unit plans, an ITU is brought to close with a culminating activity. Such an activity often includes an exhibition or sharing of the product of the students' study. You could accept the students' suggestions for a culminating activity if it engages them in summarizing what they have learned with others. A culminating activity that brings closure to a unit can give the students an opportunity for synthesis (by assembling, constructing, creating, inventing, producing, or incorporating something) and even an opportunity to present that synthesis to an audience, such as by sharing their product on an existing school website.

With a culminating activity, you can provide the opportunity for students to move from recording information to reporting on their learning. For example, one activity might be for students to take field trips to study something related to the theme, then synthesize their learning after the trip in a way that culminates the study. On field trips, students should be given notepads similar to the ones reporters use and asked to take notes and make sketches of what they learn. They can discuss what questions they have on the ride to the site. They can discuss what they liked and did not like on the ride back to school. After the trip, each student can choose something he or she saw and then build it to scale, so the students can have a scale model of something they saw on the trip that caught their interest. The students could then invite other classes in to examine the scale models and listen to student reports about why an object caught their interest. Students might also present an art show of drawings about the unit's theme, with a narration that informs others about their study. You might also schedule

SCHOOL VIGNETTE

Interdisciplinary Thematic Instruction at West Salem Middle School*

What began as an isolated, single-grade, telecommunications-dependent project for students at West Salem Middle School (Wisconsin) eventually developed into a longer-term cross-grade interdisciplinary program of students and adults working together to design and develop a local nature preserve. Students began their adventure by interacting with explorer Will Steger as he led the International Arctic Project's first training expedition. Electronic online messages, via the Internet, allowed students to receive and send messages to Will and his team in real time. Students delved into the Arctic world, researching the physical environment and the intriguing wildlife, reading native stories and novels about survival, keeping their own imaginary expedition journals, learning about the impact of industrialized society on the Arctic, and conversing with students from around the world. But something very important was missing—a connection between the students' immediate environment and the faraway Arctic.

West Salem Middle School's focus became the local 700-acre lake Neshonoc, an impoundment of the LaCrosse River, a tributary of the Mississippi. Although many students had enjoyed its recreational opportunities, they had never formally studied the lake. The Neshonoc Partners, a committee of parents, community leaders, teachers, students, and environmentalists, was established to assist in setting goals, brainstorming ideas, and developing the program for a year's study of the lake. Right from the start, students showed keen interest in active involvement in the project. A second committee, involving parents, students, and the classroom teacher, met during lunch time on a weekly basis to allow for more intensive discussions about the lake and the overall project.

The team of teachers brainstormed ideas to further develop an interdisciplinary approach to the study of Lake Neshonoc. Special activities, including an all-day "winter survival" adventure, gave students a sense of what real explorers experience. Students learned about hypothermia, winter trekking by cross-country skiing, and building their own snow caves.

For several weeks, students learned about the ecosystem of Lake Neshonoc through field experiences led by local environmentalists and community leaders. Guest speakers told their stories about life on the lake and their observations about the lake's health. Student sketchbooks provided a place to document personal observations about the shoreline, water testing, animal and plant life, and the value of the lake. From these sketchbooks, the best students creations were compiled in books to share electronically with students with similar interests in schools from Russia, Canada, Missouri, South Carolina, Nevada, Wisconsin, and Washington, DC. The opportunity to share findings about their local watershed sparked discussions about how students can make a difference in their own community. Comparative studies gave students a chance to consider how humans and nature impact other watersheds.

West Salem students worked with the local County Parks and Recreation Department to assist in developing a sign marking the new County Park where the nature sanctuary will reside. Students brainstormed design ideas and then constructed a beautiful redwood sign with the help of a local technical educational teacher. Today the sign is a symbol of the partnership that has been established between the students and the community. It is a concrete reminder that together we can work for the common good of the community and the environment. Students celebrated the study of the lake with a closure. Will Steger, along with community leaders, parents, school board members, and staff, commended the students for what is sure to be the start of a long and enduring relationship—a partnership created out of common respect and appreciation for the value of our ecosystem.

*Source: J Wee, "The Neshonoc Project: Profiles in Partnership," *World School for Adventure Learning Bulletin* (Fall 1993): 2–3. Adapted by permission.

a culminating activity that asks students to report on individual projects—the aspect each student formerly reserved for individual study.

Culminating activities serve two purposes. They are opportunities for students to proudly demonstrate and share their learning and creativity in different and individual ways. And, it is from the culminating activity that you, the teacher, can do the summative assessment to determine how well target objectives were met. Examples of actual culminating activities and products of an ITU are endless. For example, the culmination from the study by the students of West Salem Middle School (see the school vignette: "Interdisciplinary Thematic Instruction at West Salem Middle School") was the design and development of a community nature preserve.

Students at King Middle School (Portland, ME) studied the shore life of Maine's Casco Bay for a year. The culminating activity of their study was the writing and publishing of a book that includes their original illustrations and scientific descriptions of the flora and fauna found along the seashore. The book is now in the city's libraries where it can be borrowed for use by anyone taking a walk along the seashore.

For additional ideas for culminating projects, see, "A Collection of More Than 125 Annotated Motivational Teaching Strategies with Ideas for Lessons, Interdisciplinary Teaching, Transcultural Studies, and Student Projects" in Chapter 8.

PREPARING THE LESSON PLAN

As described earlier, one of the steps of instructional planning is the preparation for class meetings. The process of designing a lesson is important in learning to provide the most efficient use of valuable and limited instructional time and the most effective learning for the students that meets the unit goals.

Notice the title of this section does not refer to the "*daily* lesson plan," but rather, "*the* lesson plan." The focus is on how to prepare a lesson plan, one that may, in fact, be a daily plan, or it may not. In some instances, a lesson plan may extend for more than one class period, perhaps two or three days (e.g., the lesson plan shown later in Figure 6.3). In other instances, the lesson plan is in fact a daily plan and may run for an entire class period. In block scheduling, one lesson plan may run for part of, or for an entire 2-hour block of time. See "The Problem of Time" later in this section.

Effective teachers are always planning for their classes. For the long range, they plan the scope and sequence and develop content. Within this long-range planning, they develop units, and within units, they design the activities to be used and the assessments of learning to be done. They familiarize themselves with books, materials, media, and innovations in their fields of interest. Yet, despite all this planning activity, the lesson plan remains pivotal to the planning process.

Consider now the rationale, description, and guidelines for writing detailed lesson plans.

Rationale for Preparing Written Plans

First, *carefully prepared and written lesson plans show everyone—first and foremost your students, then your mentor, colleagues, your administrator, and, if you are a student teacher or teaching intern, your supervisor—that you are a committed professional.* Sometimes, beginning teachers are concerned with being seen by their students using a written plan in class, thinking it may suggest that the teacher has not mastered the material. On the contrary, a lesson plan is tangible evidence that you are working at your job and demonstrates respect for the students, yourself, and for the profession. A written lesson plan shows that preactive thinking and planning have taken place. There is absolutely no excuse for appearing before a class without evidence of being prepared.

Written and detailed lesson plans provide an important sense of security, which is especially useful to a beginning teacher. Like a rudder on a ship, it helps keep you on course. Without it, you are likely to drift aimlessly. Sometimes a disturbance in the classroom can distract from the lesson, causing the teacher to get "off track" or forget an important element of the lesson. A written and detailed lesson plan provides a road map to guide you and help keep you on track.

Written lesson plans help you to be or become a reflective decision maker. Without a written plan, it is difficult or impossible to analyze how something might have been planned or implemented differently after the lesson has been taught. Written lesson plans serve as resources for the next time you teach the same or a similar lesson and are useful for teacher self-evaluation and for the evaluation of student learning and of the curriculum.

Written lesson plans help you organize material and search for "loopholes," "loose ends," or incomplete content. Careful and thorough planning during the preactive phase of instruction includes anticipation of how the lesson activities will develop as the lesson is being taught. During this anticipation you will actually visualize yourself in the classroom teaching your students. Use that visualization to anticipate possible problems.

Written plans help other members of the teaching team understand what you are doing and how you are doing it. This is especially important when implementing an interdisciplinary thematic unit.

Those reasons clearly express the need to write detailed lesson plans. The list is not exhaustive, however, and you may discover additional reasons why written lesson plans are crucial to your teaching. In summary, two points must be made:

- lesson planning is an important and ongoing process
- teachers must take time to plan, reflect, write, test, evaluate, and rewrite their plans to reach optimal performance.

In short, preparing written lesson plans is important work.

Assumptions about Lesson Planning

Not all teachers need elaborate written plans for every lesson. Sometimes effective and experienced teachers need only a sketchy outline. Sometimes they may not need written plans at all. Veteran teachers who have taught the topic many times in the past may need only the presence of a class of students to stimulate a pattern of presentation that has often been successful (though frequent use of old patterns may lead one into the rut of unimaginative and uninspiring teaching and most certainly does not take into full consideration the unique characteristics of the students in the present).

Considering the diversity among middle level teachers, their instructional styles, their young adolescent students, and what research has shown, certain assumptions can be made about lesson planning, as shown in Figure 6.9.

Well-written lesson plans provide many advantages, summarized in Figure 6.10. Naturally, this will require a great deal of work for at least the first year or two, but the reward of knowing that you have prepared and presented effective lessons will compensate for that effort. You can most assuredly expect a very busy first year of teaching.

A Continual Process

Lesson planning is a continual process even for experienced teachers, for there is always a need to keep materials and plans current and relevant. Because no two classes of students are ever identical, today's lesson plan will need to be tailored to the particular needs of each classroom of students. Moreover, because the content of instruction and learning will change as each distinct group of students and their needs and interests give input, and as new thematic units are developed, new developments occur, or new theories are introduced, your objectives and the objectives of the students, school, and teaching faculty will change.

For these reasons, lesson plans should be in a constant state of revision—never "set in concrete." Once the basic framework is developed, however, the task of updating and modifying becomes minimal. If your

Figure 6.9   Important assumptions about lesson planning.

- A plan is more likely to be carefully and thoughtfully plotted during the preactive phase of instruction when the plan is written out.
- Although not all teachers need elaborate written plans for all lessons, all effective teachers do have clearly defined goals and objectives in mind and a planned pattern of instruction for every lesson, whether that plan is written out or not.
- Beginning teachers need to prepare detailed, written lesson plans.
- The depth of knowledge a teacher has about a subject or topic influences the amount of planning necessary for the lessons.
- The diversity of students within today's classroom necessitates careful and thoughtful consideration about individualizing the instruction—these considerations are best implemented when they have been thoughtfully written into lesson plans.
- The skill a teacher has in remaining calm and in following a trend of thought in the presence of distraction will influence the amount of detail necessary when planning activities and writing the lesson plan.
- There is no particular pattern or format that all teachers need to follow when writing out plans—some teacher preparation programs have agreed on certain lesson plan formats for their teacher candidates; you need to know if this is the case for your program.

Figure 6.10   Summary of the advantages of well-written lesson plans.

- Written lesson plans give a teacher an agenda or outline to follow in teaching a lesson
- Written lesson plans give a substitute teacher a basis for presenting appropriate lessons to a class, thereby retaining lesson continuity in the regular teacher's absence
- Written lesson plans are very useful when a teacher is planning to use the same lesson again in the future
- Written lesson plans provide the teacher with something to fall back on in case of a memory lapse, an interruption, or some distraction such as a call from the office or a fire drill
- Using a written plan demonstrates to students that you care and are working for them
- And, perhaps most important, written lesson plans provide beginners security because, with a carefully prepared plan, a beginning teacher can walk into a classroom with confidence and professional pride gained from having developed a sensible framework for that day's instruction.

plans are maintained on a computer, making changes from time to time is even easier.

Well Planned but Open to Last-Minute Change

The lesson plan should provide a tentative outline of the time period given for the lesson but should always remain flexible. A carefully worked plan may have to be set aside because of the unpredictable, serendipitous effect of a "teachable moment" (see the accompanying vignette) or because of unforeseen circumstances, such as a delayed school bus, an impromptu school assembly program, an emergency drill, or the cancellation of school due to inclement weather conditions. Student teachers often are appalled at the frequency of interruptions during a school day and of disruptions to their lesson planning that occur. A daily lesson planned to cover six aspects of a given topic may end with only three of the points having been considered. Although far more frequent than necessary in too many schools (recall Exercise 4.1), these occurrences are natural in a school setting and the teacher and the plans must be flexible enough to accommodate this reality.

TEACHING IN PRACTICE
A Teachable Moment

Casey was teaching an eighth-grade humanities block, a two-hour block course that integrates student learning in social studies, reading, and language arts. On this particular day while Casey and her students were discussing the topic of Manifest Destiny, one of the students raised his hand and, when acknowledged by Casey, asked the question, "Why aren't we [referring to the United States] still adding states? [that is, adding territory to the United States]." Casey immediately replied with "There aren't any more states to add." By responding too quickly, Casey missed one of those "teachable moments," moments when the teacher has the students right where she wants them, that is, where the students are the ones who are thinking and asking questions. What could Casey have done? When was Hawaii added as a state? Why hasn't Puerto Rico become a state? Guam? etc. Aren't those possibilities? Why aren't more states or territories being added? What are the political and social ramifications today and how do they differ from those of the 1800s?

Implementation of Today's Lesson May Necessitate Changes in Tomorrow's Plan. Although you may have your lesson plans completed for several consecutive lessons, as can be inferred by the vignette involving Casey and her students, what actually transpires during the implementation of today's lesson may necessitate last-minute adjustments to the lesson you had planned for tomorrow. More than just occasionally, teachers have discontinued the rest of the week's planned lessons because the feedback received on Tuesday indicated that students didn't comprehend Monday's lesson well enough to move on to the next planned lesson.

Consequently, during student teaching in particular, it is neither uncommon nor unwanted to have last-minute changes penciled in your lesson plan. If, however, penciled-in modifications are substantial and might be confusing to you during implementation of the lesson, then it's better to rewrite the lesson plan.

The greatest pedagogical error of our time is a simplistic insistence on clarity. To spell out every act of education for students so that they are never forced to look deep into themselves and come face to face with the primal "Huh?" is to deny them access to one of the most important parts of their humanity: the right to shape their own destiny.
Andrew K. Davis (2001, p. 789)

The Problem of Time

A lesson plan should provide enough materials and activities to consume the entire class period or time allotted. As mentioned earlier, you must understand that in your planning for teaching you need to plan for every minute of every class period. The lesson plan, then, is more than a plan for a lesson to be taught; it is a plan that accounts for the entire class period or time that you and your students are together in the classroom. Since planning is a skill that takes years of experience to master, especially when teaching a block of time that may extend for 90 or more minutes and that involves more than one discipline and perhaps more than one teacher, as a beginning teacher, rather than run the risk of having too few activities to occupy the time the students are in your classroom you should overplan. One way of assuring that you overplan is to include "if time remains" activities in your lesson plan.

When a lesson plan does not provide sufficient activity to occupy the entire class period or time that the students are available for the lesson, that is when behavior problems mount. Thus, it is best to prepare more than you likely can accomplish in a given period of time. This is not to imply that you should involve the students in meaningless busywork. Young adolescents can be very perceptive when it comes to a teacher who has finished the plan and is attempting to bluff through the minutes that remain before dismissal. And, they are not usually favorably responsive to meaningless busywork.

If you ever do get caught short—as most teachers do at one time or another—one way to avoid embarrassment is to have students work on what we described in Chapter 4 as an *anchor activity* (or *transitional activity*). This is an ongoing assignment, and students understand that whenever they have spare time in class they should be working on it. One decision a teacher must make is whether or not students are going to be mobile during anchor activity work. Another is whether students work alone or can work in small groups. Those are decisions that each teacher must make depending on the circumstances for that teacher.

Anchor activities can include any number of activities, including but not limited to

- journal writing
- lab work, alone or in pairs
- long-term project work, alone or in small groups
- portfolio organization
- review material that has been covered that day or in recent days, alone or in pairs
- work at a learning center
- work on homework for this or another class

Regardless of how you handle time remaining, it works best when you plan for it and write that aspect into your lesson plan. Make sure students understand the purpose and procedures for these anchor assignments.

The Pressure of Standards-Based and High-Stakes Testing and the Felt Need to "Cover" the Prescribed Curriculum

As we prepare this edition of this resource guide we continue with our concern that because of today's heavy pressure on teachers to "teach to the standards," to "cover the curriculum," so that their students do well on the mandated proficiency tests and because for any given grade level or subject there is more content expected to be taught than there is time to teach it, fewer and fewer teachers will even recognize, let alone grasp and run with the already too-few precious teachable moments that occur for every teacher. Your challenge, of course, is to find your way of doing both—that is, to help students accomplish the required learning while not stifling the most meaningful and longest-lasting learning that often is

entirely unpredictable. As we have said before, because it tends toward high objectivity, there is the possibility that such prescriptive teaching could become so objective, that it produces negative consequences. The danger is when the relationship between teacher and student becomes so impersonal. Highly specific and impersonal teaching can be discouraging to serendipity, creativity, and the excitement of discovery, to say nothing of its possible negative impact on the development of young adolescents' self-esteem. Indeed, today's emphasis on standardized testing coupled with the fact that access mode strategies tend to consume more instructional time than do standard expository strategies, access strategies may indeed be too infrequently used in today's classroom (Jorgenson & Vanosdall, 2002).

Caution about "The Weekly Planning Book"

A distinction needs to be made between actual lesson plans and the book for planning that some schools require teachers to maintain and even submit to their supervisors a week in advance (see Figure 6.11). Items that a teacher writes into the boxes in a weekly planning book most assuredly are *not* lesson plans; rather, the pages are a layout by which the teacher writes into the boxes to show what lessons will be taught during the day, week, month, or term. Usually the book provides only a small lined box for time periods for each day of the week. These books are useful for outlining the topics, activities, and assignments projected for the week or term, and supervisors sometimes use them to check the adequacy of teachers' course plans, but they are not lesson plans. Teachers and their supervisors who believe that the notations in the weekly planning book are actual lesson plans are fooling themselves. Student teachers and teaching interns should not use these in lieu of authentic lesson plans.

Figure 6.11 Weekly planning book.

WEEKLY PLANNING BOOK

Teacher _____   Lesson or unit _____

Date	Content	Materials	Procedure	Assessment
Mon				
Tue				
Wed				
Thur				
Fri				

CONSTRUCTING A LESSON PLAN: FORMAT, ELEMENTS, AND SAMPLES

Although it is true that each teacher develops a personal system of lesson planning—the system that works best for that teacher in each unique situation—a beginning teacher needs a more substantial framework from which to work. For that, this section provides a "preferred" lesson plan format (see Figure 6.12). Nothing is hallowed about this format, however. Review the preferred format and samples, and unless your program of teacher preparation insists otherwise, use it with your own modifications until you find or develop a better model. All else being equal, you are encouraged, however, to begin your teaching following as closely as possible this "preferred" format.

FOR YOUR NOTES

Figure 6.12   Preferred lesson plan format with seven components.

---

1. **Descriptive Data**

   Teacher _____ Class _____ Date _____ Grade level _____

   Room number _____ Period _____ Unit _____

   Lesson Number _____ Topic _____

   Anticipated noise level (high, moderate, low)

2. **Goals and Objectives**

   Instructional Goals:

   Specific Objectives:

      Cognitive:

      Affective:

      Psychomotor:

3. **Rationale**

4. **Procedure** (Procedure with modeling examples, transitions, coached practice, etc.)

   Content:

   _____ minutes. Activity 1: Set (introduction)

   _____ minutes. Activity 2:

(continued)

This blank lesson plan format is placed alone so that if you choose, you may remove it from the book and make copies for use in your teaching.

Figure 6.12 (*continued*)

_____ minutes. Activity 3: (the exact number of activities in the procedures will vary)

_____ minutes. Final Activity: (lesson conclusion or closure)

If time remains:

5. **Assignments and Reminders of Assignments**

Special considerations, notes, and reminders to myself:

6. **Materials and Equipment Needed**

Audiovisual:

Other:

7. **Assessment, Reflection, and Revision**

Assessment of student learning:

Reflective thoughts about lesson:

Suggestions for revision:

For Guidance, Reflection, and Reference

While student teaching and during your first few years as an employed teacher, your lesson plans should be printed from a computer, or, if that isn't possible, then written out in an intelligible style. Until you have considerable experience, you need to prepare and maintain detailed lesson plans for guidance, reflection, and reference. There is valid reason to suspect the effectiveness of teachers who say they have no need for a written plan because they have their lessons "in their heads." The hours and periods in a school day range from several to many, as do the number of students in each class. When multiplied by the number of school days in a week, a semester, or a school year, the task of keeping so many things in one's head becomes mind-boggling. Few persons could effectively do that. The guidelines in this book are written for those teachers who want to be effective and exemplary, not mediocre to ineffective.

Basic Elements in a Lesson Plan

The preferred lesson plan format of this resource guide contains the following seven basic elements: (1) descriptive course data, (2) goals and objectives, (3) rationale, (4) procedure, (5) assignments and assignment reminders, (6) materials and equipment, and (7) a section for assessment of student learning, reflection on the lesson, and ideas for lesson revision. Compare those seven elements with those of whatever plan your program of teacher preparation expects you to use. These seven elements need not be present in every written lesson plan, nor must they be presented in any particular order. Nor are they inclusive or exclusive. You might choose to include additional components or subsections. Figure 6.13 displays a completed multiple-day lesson that includes the seven elements and also incorporates many of the developmentally appropriate learning activities discussed in this resource guide.

Following next are descriptions of the seven major elements of the preferred format, with examples and explanations of why each is important.

Descriptive Data

A lesson plan's descriptive data is demographic and logistical information that identifies details about the class. Anyone reading this information should be able to identify when and where the class meets, who is teaching it, and what is being taught. Although as the teacher you know this information, someone else may not. Members of the teaching team, administrators, and substitute teachers (and, if you are the student teacher, your university supervisor and cooperating teacher) appreciate this information, especially when asked to fill in for you, even if only for a few minutes during a class session. Most teachers find out which items of descriptive data are most beneficial in their situation and then develop their own identifiers.

> The mark of a well-prepared, clearly written lesson plan is the ease with which someone else (such as another member of your teaching team or a substitute teacher) could implement it.

As shown in the sample plans of Figures 6.13 (language arts/science/social studies) and 6.14 (physical science), the descriptive data include:

1. *Name of course or class.* These serve as headings for the plan, and facilitate orderly filing of plans.

Language Arts/Science/Social Studies (integrated block class)

Physical Science

2. *Name of the unit.* Inclusion of this facilitates the orderly control of the hundreds of lesson plans a teacher constructs. For example:

Language Arts/Science/ Social Studies	*Unit: Investigative Research and Generative Writing*
Physical Science	*Unit: What's the Matter*

3. *Topic to be considered within the unit.* This is also useful for control and identification. For example:

Language Arts/ Science/Social Studies	Unit: Investigative Research and Generative Writing	*Topic: Writing Response and Peer Assessment via the Internet*
Physical Science	Unit: What's the Matter?	*Topic: Density of Solids*

Anticipated Noise Level. Although not included in the sample lesson plans in this resource guide, the teacher might include in the descriptive data the category of "anticipated classroom noise level," such as "high," "moderate," and "low." Its inclusion, or at least considering the idea, is useful during the planning phase of instruction insofar as thinking about how active and noisy the students might become during the lesson, how you might prepare for that, and whether you should warn an administrator and teachers of neighboring classrooms.

Goals and Objectives

The instructional goals are general statements of intended accomplishments from that lesson. They usually are related to state- and/or district-mandated curriculum standards. This is where that information can be identified and shown.

Teachers and students need to know what the lesson is designed to accomplish. In clear, understandable language, the general goal statement provides that information. From the sample of Figure 6.13, the goals are:

- To collaborate and prepare response papers to peers from around the world who have shared the results of their own experimental research findings and research papers about ozone concentrations in the atmosphere.
- For students worldwide to prepare and publish for worldwide dissemination a final paper about worldwide ozone levels in the atmosphere.

And, from the sample unit of Figure 6.14, goals are:

- Understand that all matter is made of atoms.
- Develop a positive attitude about physical science.

Because the goals are also included in the unit plan, sometimes a teacher may include only the objectives in the daily lesson plan and not the goals. As a beginning teacher, it usually is a good idea to include both.

SETTING THE LEARNING OBJECTIVES

A crucial step in the development of any lesson plan is that of setting the objectives. It is at this point that many lessons go wrong, and where many beginning teachers have problems.

A Common Error and How to Avoid It

Teachers sometimes confuse "learning activity" (*how* the students will learn it) with the "learning objective" (*what* the student will learn as a result of the learning activity). For example, teachers sometimes mistakenly list what *they* intend to do—such as "lecture on photosynthesis" or "lead a discussion on the causes of the Civil War." They fail to focus on just what the learning objectives in these activities truly are—that is, what the students will be able to do (performance) as a result of the instructional activity. Or, rather than specifying what the student will be able to do as a result of the learning activities, the teacher mistakenly writes what the students will do in class (the learning activity)—such as, "in pairs the students will do the 10 problems on page 72"—as if that were the learning objective. While solving the problems correctly may well be the objective, "doing the 10 problems" is not. At the risk of sounding trite or belaboring the point, we emphasize the importance of the teacher being an accurate communicator. If the teacher's stated expectations are fuzzy, then the students may never get it.

When you approach this step in your lesson planning, to avoid error, ask yourself, "What should students be able to do as a result of the activities of this lesson?" Your answer to that question is your objective! Objectives of the lesson are included then as specific statements of performance expectations, detailing precisely what students will be able to do as a result of the instructional activities.

No Need to Include All Domains and Hierarchies in Every Lesson

We have known teachers to worry needlessly over trying to include objectives from all three domains (cognitive, affective, and psychomotor) in every lesson they write. Please understand that not all three domains are necessarily represented in every lesson plan. As a matter of fact, any given lesson plan may be directed to only one or two, or a few, specific objectives. Over the course of a unit of instruction, however, all domains, and most if not all levels within each, should be addressed.

From the lesson shown in Figure 6.13, sample objectives and the domain and level (in parentheses) within that domain are:

- Through cooperative group action, students will conduct experimental research to collect data about the ozone level of air in their environment. (cognitive, application)
- Through the Internet, students will write and share response papers to their peers from other locations in the world. (cognitive, evaluation)
- Students will form judgments about local, regional, and world ozone levels. (affective, organizing)
- Students will create a proposal for worldwide dissemination. (psychomotor, creating)

And, from the lesson illustrated in Figure 6.14, sample objectives are:

- Determine the density of a solid cube. (cognitive, application)
- Communicate the results of their experiments to others in the class. (psychomotor, communicating)

Rationale

The rationale is an explanation of why the lesson is important and why the instructional methods chosen will achieve the objectives. Parents, students, teachers, administrators, and others have the right to know why specific content is being taught and why the methods employed are being used. Prepare yourself well by setting a goal for yourself of always being prepared with intelligent answers to those two questions. This is a proper place to connect the lesson with the mandated benchmark standards.

Teachers become reflective decision makers when they challenge themselves to think about *what* (the content) students are learning, *how* (the learning activities) they are learning it, and *why* (the rationale) it must be learned. As illustrated in the sample unit of Figure 6.14, sometimes the rationale is included within the unit introduction and goals, but not in every lesson plan of the unit. Some lessons are carryovers or continuations of a lesson; we see no reason to repeat the rationale for a continuing lesson.

Figure 6.13 Lesson plan sample: Multiple-day, project-centered, interdisciplinary, and transcultural lesson using worldwide communication via the Internet.

---

1. Descriptive Data

Teacher _____ Class *Language Arts/Science/Social Studies* Date _____ Grade level *5–8*

Unit: *Investigative Research and Generative Writing*

Lesson Topic: *Writing Response and Peer Assessment via Internet*

Time duration: *several days*

2. Goals and Objectives of Unit

Instructional Goals:

2.1. One goal of this lesson is for students to collaborate and prepare response papers for peers around the world who have shared the results of their own experimental research findings and research papers about ozone concentrations in the atmosphere.

2.2. The ultimate goal of this unit is for students around the world to prepare and publish, for worldwide dissemination, a final paper about global ozone levels in the atmosphere.

Objectives:

Cognitive:

a. Through cooperative group action, students will conduct experimental research to collect data about the ozone level of air in their environment. (application)

b. In cooperative groups, students will analyze the results of their experiments. (analysis)

c. Students will compile data and infer from their experimental data. (synthesis and evaluation)

d. Through collaborative writing groups, the students will prepare a final paper that summarizes their research study of local atmospheric ozone levels. (evaluation)

e. Through sharing via the Internet, students will write response papers to their peers at other locations in the world. (evaluation)

f. From their own collaborative research and worldwide communications with their peers, the students will draw conclusions about global atmospheric ozone levels. (evaluation)

Affective:

a. Students will respond attentively to the response papers of their peers. (attending)

b. Students will willingly cooperate with others during the group activities. (responding)

c. Students will offer opinions about the atmospheric level of ozone. (valuing)

d. Students will form judgments about local, regional, and worldwide ozone levels. (organizing)

e. Students will communicate accurately their findings and attend diligently to the work of their worldwide peers. (internalizing)

Psychomotor:

a. Students will manipulate the computer so that their e-mail communications are transmitted accurately. (manipulating)

b. In a summary to the study, students will describe their feelings about atmospheric ozone concentrations. (communicating)

c. The students will ultimately create a proposal for worldwide dissemination. (creating)

3. Rationale

3.1. Important to improvement in one's writing and communication skills are the processes of selecting a topic, decision making, arranging, drafting, proofing, peer review, commenting, revising, editing, rewriting, and publishing the results—processes that are focused on in the writing aspect of this unit.

3.2. Student writers need many readers to respond to their work. Through worldwide communication with peers and dissemination of their final product, this need can be satisfied.

3.3. Students learn best when they are actively pursuing a topic of interest and meaning to them. Resulting from brainstorming potential problems and arriving at their own topic, this unit provides such a topic.

3.4. Real-world problems are interdisciplinary and transcultural; involving writing (English), science, mathematics (data collecting, graphing, etc.), and intercultural communication, this unit is an interdisciplinary transcultural unit.

(continued)

Figure 6.13   *(continued)*

4. Procedure

Content:

At the start of this unit, collaborative groups were established via Intercultural E-mail Classroom Connections (IECC)—(http://www.stolaf.edu/network/iecc)—with other classes from schools around the world. These groups of students conducted several scientific research experiments on the ozone levels of their local atmospheric air. To obtain relative measurements of ozone concentrations in the air, students set up experiments that involved stretching rubber bands on a board, then observing the number of days until the bands broke. Students maintained daily journal logs of the temperature, barometric pressure, wind speed/direction, and the number of days it took for bands to break. After compiling their data and preparing single-page summaries of their results, via the Internet, students exchanged data with other groups. From data collected worldwide, students wrote a one-page summary of what conditions may account for the difference in levels of ozone. Following the exchange of students' written responses and their subsequent revisions based on feedback from the worldwide peers, students are now preparing a final summary report about the world's atmospheric ozone level. The intention is to disseminate worldwide (to newspapers and via the Internet) this final report.

Activity 1: Introduction (__10__ minutes)

Today, in think-share-pairs, you will prepare initial responses to the e-mail responses we have received from other groups around the world. (Teacher shares the list of places from which e-mail has been received.) Any questions before we get started?

As we discussed earlier, here are the instructions: in your think-share-pairs (each pair is given one response received via e-mail), prepare written responses according to the following outline: (a) note points or information you would like to incorporate in the final paper to be forwarded via Internet; (b) comment on one aspect of the written response you like best; (c) provide questions to the sender to seek clarification or elaboration. I think you should be able to finish this in about 30 minutes, so let's try for that.

Activity 2: (__30__ minutes, if needed)

Preparation of dyad responses

Activity 3: (open)

Let's now hear from each response pair.

Dyad responses are shared with whole class for discussion of inclusion in response paper to be sent via Internet.

Activity 4: (open)

Discussion, conclusion, and preparation of final drafts to be sent to each e-mail corresponder to be done by cooperative groups (the number of groups is decided by the number of e-mail corresponders at this time).

Activity 5: (open)

Later, as students receive e-mail responses from other groups, the responses will be printed and reviewed. The class then responds to each, using the same criteria as before, and returns this response to the e-mail sender.

Closure:

The process continues until all groups (from around the world) have agreed upon and prepared the final report for dissemination.

5. Assignments and Reminders

Remind students of important dates and decisions to be made.

6. Materials and Equipment Needed

School computers with Internet access, printers, copies of e-mail responses.

7. Assessment, Reflection, and Revision

Assessment of student learning for this lesson is formative: journals, daily checklist of student participation in groups, writing drafts.

Reflective thoughts about lesson and suggestions for revision:

_____

_____

_____

Figure 6.14   Sample integrated unit plan with one daily lesson for lab science.

UNIT PLAN SAMPLE WITH A DAILY LESSON

Course *Science*

Teacher _____   **Duration of Unit** __*10 days*__

Unit Title __*What's the Matter?*__   **Grade Level** __*Grades 5–8*__

Purpose of the Unit

This unit is designed to develop students' understanding of the concept of matter. At the completion of the unit, students should have a clearer understanding of matter and its properties, of the basic units of matter, and of the source of matter.

Rationale of the Unit

This unit topic is important for building a foundation of knowledge for subsequent courses in science. This can increase students' chances of success in those courses, and thereby improve their self-confidence and self-esteem. A basic understanding of matter and its properties is important because of daily decisions that affect the manipulation of matter. The hands-on laboratory activities in this unit will help students develop their understanding. It is more likely that students will make correct and safe decisions when they understand what matter is, how it changes form, and how its properties determine its use.

Goals of the Unit

The goals of this unit are for students to
1. Understand that all matter is made of atoms.
2. Understand that matter stays constant and that it is neither created nor destroyed.
3. Develop certain basic physical science laboratory skills.
4. Develop a positive attitude about physical science.
5. Look forward to taking other science courses.
6. Understand how science is relevant to their daily lives.

Instructional Objectives of the Unit

Upon completion of this unit of study, students should be able to
1. List at least 10 examples of matter.
2. List the four states of matter, with one example of each.
3. Calculate the density of an object when given its mass and volume.
4. Describe the properties of solids, liquids, and gases.
5. Demonstrate an understanding that matter is made of elements and that elements are made of atoms.
6. Identify and explain one way that knowledge of matter is important to their daily lives.
7. Demonstrate increased self-confidence in pursuing laboratory investigations in physical science.
8. Demonstrate skill in communicating within the cooperative learning group.
9. Demonstrate skill in working with the triple-beam balance.

Unit Overview

Throughout this unit, students will be developing a concept map of matter. Information for the map will be derived from laboratory work, class discussions, lectures, student readings, and research. The overall instructional model is that of concept attainment. Important to this is an assessment of students' concepts about matter at the beginning of the unit. The preassessment and the continuing assessment of their concepts will center on the following:
1. What is matter and what are its properties? Students will develop the concept of matter by discovering the properties that all matter contains (that is, it has mass and takes up space).
2. Students will continue to build on their understanding of the concept of matter by organizing matter into its four major states (that is, solid, liquid, gas, plasma). The concept development will be used to define the attributes of each state of matter, and students will gather information by participating in laboratory activities and class discussions.
3. What are some of the physical properties of matter that make certain kinds of matter unique? Students will experiment with properties of matter such as elasticity, brittleness, and density. Laboratory activities will allow students to contribute their observations and information to the further development of their concept of matter. Density activities enable students to practice their lab and math skills.

(*Source:* Courtesy of Will Hightower.)

(*continued*)

Figure 6.14   (*continued*)

4. What are the basic units of matter, and where did matter come from? Students will continue to develop their concept of matter by working on this understanding of mixtures, compounds, elements, and atoms.

Assessment of Student Achievement

For this unit, assessment of student achievement will be both formative and summative. Formative evaluation will be done daily by checklists of student behavior, knowledge, and skills. Summative evaluation will be based on the following criteria:

1. Student participation as evidenced by completion of daily homework, class work, laboratory activities, and class discussions, and by the information on the student behavior checklists.
2. Weekly quizzes on content.
3. Unit test.

Lesson Number _____   **Duration of Lesson** *1–2 hours*

Unit Title   *What's the Matter?*   **Teacher** _____

Lesson Title   *Mission Impossible*   **Lesson Topic** *Density of Solids*

Objectives of the Lesson

Upon completion of this lesson, students should be able to

1. Determine the density of a solid cube.
2. Based on data gathered in class, develop their own definition of density.
3. Prepare and interpret graphs of data.
4. Communicate the results of their experiments to others in the class.

Materials Needed

1. Two large boxes of cereal and two snack-size boxes of the same cereal
2. Four brownies (two whole and two cut in halves)
3. Four sandboxes (two large plastic boxes and two small boxes, each filled with sand)
4. Two triple-beam balances
5. Several rulers
6. Six handheld calculators
7. Eighteen colored pencils (six sets with three different colors per set)
8. Copies of lab instructions (one copy for each student)

Instructional Procedure with Approximate Time Line

SET (10–15 MINUTES)

Begin class by brainstorming to find what students already know about density. Place the word on the board or overhead, and ask students if they have heard of it. Write down their definitions and examples. Hold up a large box of cereal in one hand and the snack-size box in the other. Ask students which is more dense. Allow them time to explain their responses. Then tell them that by the end of this lesson they will know the answer to the question and that they will develop their own definition of density.

LABORATORY INVESTIGATION (30–60 MINUTES)

Students are divided into teams of four students of mixed abilities. Each member has a role:

1. *Measure master:* In charge of the group's ruler and ruler measurements
2. *Mass master:* In charge of the group's weighings
3. *Engineer:* In charge of the group's calculator and calculations
4. *Graph master:* In charge of plotting the group's data on the graph paper

Each team has eight minutes before switching stations. Each team completes three stations and then meets to make its graphs and to discuss results.

***Station 1:* Cereal Box Density.** Students calculate the density of a large and a small box of cereal to determine whether a larger and heavier object is more dense. The masses versus the volumes of the two boxes are plotted on graph paper using one of the pencil colors.

Figure 6.14 (*continued*)

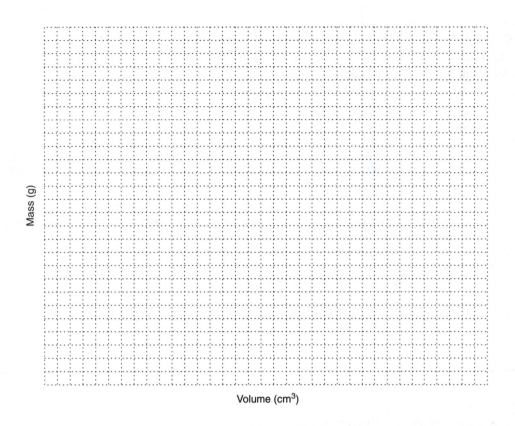

Mass (g)

Volume (cm³)

Instructions

1. The density of any object is determined by dividing its mass by its volume. Density in grams is divided by volume in cubic centimeters. Example: 20 g/10 cm³ ÷ 2 g/cm³.
2. Measure the volume of the small cereal box (length × width × height), and use the balance to determine its mass in grams. The engineer can do the calculations on the calculator. The graph master should graph the results of each trial and connect two points with a straight line.
3. Repeat the procedure using the large box of cereal.
4. The engineer computes the density of both cereal boxes with the calculator and records the results on the proper blank below the graph.

   a. Density of large box of cereal _____

   b. Density of small box of cereal _____

   c. Density of large brownie _____

   d. Density of small brownie _____

   e. Density of large sandbox _____

   f. Density of small sandbox _____

Station 2: Brownie Density. Students calculate the density of a full-size brownie and a half-size brownie. Results are plotted on the same graph as in Station 1, but with the second color.

Instructions

1. The density of any object is determined by dividing its mass by its volume. Density in grams is divided by volume in cubic centimeters. Example: 20 g/10 cm³ ÷ 2 g/cm³.
2. Measure the volume of a small brownie (length × width × height), and use the balance to determine its mass in grams. The engineer can do the calculations on the calculator. The graph master should graph the results of each trial and connect two points with a straight line.

(*continued*)

Figure 6.14   *(continued)*

3. Repeat the procedure using the large brownie.
4. The engineer computes the density of both brownies and records the result on the proper blank.

Station 3: **Sandbox Density.** Students calculate the density of a large and a small box filled with sand. Results are plotted on the graph, but with the third color.

Instructions

1. The density of any object is determined by dividing its mass by its volume. Density in grams is divided by volume in cubic centimeters. Example: 20 g/10 cm^3 ÷ 2 g/cm^3.
2. Measure the volume of the small sandbox (length × width × height) and use the balance to determine its mass in grams. The engineer can do the calculations on the calculator. The graph master should graph the results of each trial and connect two points with a straight line.
3. Repeat the procedure using the large sandbox.
4. The engineer computes the density of both boxes and records the results on the proper blank.

Lab Worksheet. Teams return to their seats to do the graphing, analyze the results, and answer the following questions from their lab sheets:

1. Is a larger, heavier object more dense than its smaller counterpart? Explain your evidence.
2. What is your definition of density?
3. Which is more dense, a pound of feathers or a pound of gold? Explain your answer.

LESSON CLOSURE (10 MINUTES OR MORE)
When all teams are finished, teams should display their graphs, and share and discuss the results.

Concepts

1. Density is one of the properties of matter.
2. Mass and volume are related.
3. Density is determined by dividing mass by volume.

Extension Activities

1. Use a density graph to calculate the mass and volume of a smaller brownie.
2. Explore the story of Archimedes and the king's crown.

Evaluation, Reflection, and Revision of Lesson

Upon completion of this lesson and of the unit, revision in this lesson may be made on the basis of teacher observations and student achievement.

Procedure

The procedure consists of the instructional activities for a scheduled period of time. The substance of the lesson—the information to be presented, obtained, and learned—is the content. Appropriate information is selected to meet the learning objectives, the level of competence of the students, and the grade level or course requirements. To be sure your lesson actually covers what it should, you should write down exactly what minimum content you intend to cover. This material may be placed in a separate section or combined with the procedure section. The important thing is to be sure that your information is written so you can refer to it quickly and easily when you need to.

If, for instance, you intend to conduct the lesson using discussion, you should write the key discussion questions. Or, if you are going to introduce new material using a 10-minute lecture, then you need to outline the content of that lecture. The word *outline* is not used casually—you need not have pages of notes to sift through; nor should you ever read lengthy declarative statements to your students. You should be familiar enough with the content so that an outline (in as much detail as you believe necessary) will be sufficient to carry on the lesson, as in the following example of a content outline

Causes of Civil War
  A. Primary causes
      1. Economics
      2. Abolitionist pressure
      3. Slavery
      4. etc.

B. Secondary causes
1. North-South friction
2. Southern economic dependence
3. etc.

The procedure or procedures to be used, sometimes referred to as the *instructional components*, comprise the *procedure* element of the lesson plan. It is the section that outlines what you and your students will do during the lesson. Appropriate instructional activities are chosen to meet the objectives, to match the students' learning styles and special needs, and to assure that all students have an equal opportunity to learn. Ordinarily, you should plan this section of your lesson as an organized entity having a beginning (an introduction or *set*), a middle, and an end (called the *closure*) to be completed during the lesson. This structure is not always needed, because some lessons are simply parts of units or long-term plans and merely carry on activities spelled out in those long-term plans. Still, most lessons need to include in the procedure the following elements.

a. *introduction*, the process used to prepare the students mentally for the lesson, sometimes referred to as the set (establishes a mind-set), or initiating activity (initiates the lesson)
b. *lesson development*, the detailing of activities that occur between the beginning and the end of the lesson, including the transitions that connect activities
c. plans for *practice*, sometimes referred to as the follow-up—that is, ways that you intend to have students interacting in the classroom (such as individual practice, in dyads, or small groups)—receiving guidance or coaching from each other and from you
d. *lesson conclusion* (or closure), the planned process of bringing the lesson to an end, thereby providing students with a sense of completeness and, with effective teaching, accomplishment and comprehension by helping students to synthesize the information learned from the lesson
e. *timetable* that serves simply as a planning and implementation guide
f. *contingency plan* for what to do if you finish the lesson and time remains
g. *assignments*, that is, what students are instructed to do as follow-up to the lesson, either as homework or as in-class work, providing students an opportunity to practice and enhance what is being learned

Let's now consider some of those elements in detail.

Introduction to the Lesson. Like any good performance, a lesson needs an effective beginning. In many respects, the introduction sets the tone for the rest of the lesson by alerting the students that the business of learning is to begin. The introduction should be an attention-getter. If it is exciting, interesting, or innovative, it can create a favorable mood for the lesson. In any case, a thoughtful introduction serves as a solid indicator that you are well prepared. Although it is difficult to develop an exciting introduction to every lesson taught each day, every day of the school week, there are always a variety of options available by which to spice up the launching of a lesson. You might, for instance, begin the lesson by briefly reviewing the previous lesson, thereby helping students connect the learning. Another possibility is to review vocabulary words from previous lessons and to introduce new ones. Still another possibility is to use the key point of the day's lesson as an introduction and then again as the conclusion. Sometimes teachers begin a lesson by demonstrating a discrepant event (i.e., an event that is contrary to what one might expect), sometimes referred to as a "hook." Yet another possibility is to begin the lesson with a writing activity on some controversial aspect of the ensuing lesson. Sample introductions are:

For U.S. history, study of westward expansion:

- The teacher asks "Who has lived somewhere other than (name of your state)?" After students show hands and answer, the teacher asks individuals why they moved to (name of your state). The teacher then asks students to recall why the first European settlers came to the United States and then moves into the next activity.

For science, study of the science process skill of predicting:

- The teacher takes a glass filled to the brim with colored water (colored so it is more visible) and asks students to discuss and predict (in dyads) how many pennies can be added to the glass before any water spills over the rim of the glass.

In short, you can use the introduction of the lesson to review past learning, tie the new lesson to the previous lesson, introduce new material, point out the objectives of the new lesson, help students connect their learning with other disciplines or with real life, or, by showing what will be learned and why the learning is important, inducing in students motivation and a mind-set favorable to the new lesson.

Lesson Development. The developmental activities that comprise the bulk of the plan are the specifics by which you intend to achieve the lesson objectives. They include activities that present information, demonstrate skills, provide reinforcement of previously learned material, and provide other opportunities to develop understanding and skill. Furthermore, by actions and words, during lesson development you should model the behaviors expected of the students. Students need such modeling. By effective modeling, you can exemplify the anticipated learning outcomes. Activities of this section of the lesson plan should be described in some detail so you will know exactly what it is you plan to do and during the intensity of the class meeting, you do not forget important details and content. It is for this reason you should consider, for example, noting answers (if known) to questions you intend to ask and solutions (if known) to problems you intend to have students solve.

Lesson Conclusion. Having a concise closure to the lesson is as important as having a strong introduction. The concluding activity should summarize and bind together what has ensued in the developmental stage and should reinforce the principal points of the lesson. One way to accomplish these ends is to restate the key points of the lesson. Another is to briefly outline the major points. Still another is to review the major concept. Sometimes the closure is not only a review of what was learned but also the summarizing of a question left unanswered that signals a change in your plan of activities for the next day. In other words, it becomes a *transitional closure*.

Timetable. To estimate the time factors in any lesson can be very difficult, especially for the inexperienced teacher. A useful procedure is to gauge the amount of time needed for each learning activity and make a note of that alongside the activity and strategy in your plan, as shown in the preferred sample lesson plan format. Placing too much faith in your time estimate may be foolish—an estimate is more for your guidance during the preactive phase of instruction than for anything else. To avoid being embarrassed from running out of material, try to make sure you have planned enough meaningful work to consume the entire class period. If nothing else, this may include an anchor activity. Another important reason for including a time plan in your lesson is to give information to students about how much time they have for a particular activity, such as a group activity.

Assignments

When an assignment is to be given, it should be noted in your lesson plan. When to present an assignment to the students is optional, but it should never be yelled as an afterthought as the students are exiting the classroom at the end of the class period. Whether they are to be begun and completed during class time or done outside of class, assignments should be written on the writing board, in a special place on the bulletin board, on the school's website, in each student's assignment log maintained in a binder, and/or on a handout. Take extra care to be sure that assignment specifications are clear to the students. Many teachers give assignments to their students on a weekly or other periodic basis. When given on a periodic basis, rather than daily, assignments

should still show in your daily lesson plans so as to remind yourself to remind students of them.

Once assignment specifications and due dates are given, it is a good idea *not* to make major modifications to them, and it is especially important not to change assignment specifications several days after an assignment has been given. Last-minute changes in assignment specifications can be very frustrating to students who have already begun or completed the assignment; it shows little respect to those students.

Understand the difference between assignments and procedures. An assignment tells students what is to be done, while procedures explain how to do it. Although an assignment may include procedures, spelling out procedures alone is not the same thing as giving an academic assignment. When students are given an assignment, they need to understand the reasons for doing it as well as have some notion of ways the assignment might be done.

Allowing time in class for students to begin work on homework assignments and long-term projects is highly recommended; it provides an opportunity for the teacher to provide individual attention to students. Being able to coach students is the reason for in-class time to begin assignments. The benefits of *coached practice* include being able to: (a) monitor student work so a student doesn't go too far in a wrong direction, (b) help students to reflect on their thinking, (c) assess the progress of individual students, (d) provide for peer tutoring, and (e) discover or create a "teachable moment." For the latter, for example, while observing and monitoring student practice the teacher might discover a commonly shared student misconception. The teacher then stops and discusses that and attempts to clarify the misconception or, collaboratively with students, plans a subsequent lesson centered on focusing on the common misconception.

Special Considerations, Notes, and Reminders

We recommend that in your lesson plan format you have a regular place for special notes and reminders, perhaps in the same location as assignments as illustrated in the preferred format. In that special section that can be referred to quickly, you can place reminders concerning such things as announcements to be made, school programs, assignment due dates, and makeup work or special tasks for certain students. For example, for every student in your class who has an Individualized Education Plan (IEP) you need to specifically describe what you plan to do to ensure the student's success. By consulting the guidelines provided in Chapter 8, you can describe what you will do to accommodate that student.

Materials and Equipment to Be Used

Materials of instruction include books, media, handouts, and other supplies necessary to accomplish the lesson's learning objectives. You must be *certain* that the proper and necessary materials and equipment are available for the lesson; to be certain requires planning. Teachers who, for one reason or another, have to busy themselves during class time looking for materials or equipment that should have been readied before class began are likely to experience classroom control problems. Plus, if it happens very often it demonstrates incompetency and the teacher loses credibility with the students. Teachers want students to be prepared; students expect competent teachers to be prepared.

Assessment, Reflection, and Revision

Details of how you will assess how well students *are learning* (called *formative assessment*) and how well they *have learned* (called *summative assessment*) should be included in your lesson plan. This does not mean to imply that both types of assessment will be in every daily plan. Comprehension checks for formative assessment can be in the form of questions you ask and that the students ask during the lesson (in the procedural section), as well as various kinds of checklists.

For summative assessment, teachers typically use review questions at the end of a lesson (as a closure) or the beginning of the next lesson (as a review or transfer introduction), independent practice or summary activities at the completion of a lesson, and tests.

In most lesson plan formats, for the reflective phase of instruction there is a section reserved for the teacher to make notes or reflective comments about the lesson. Many student teachers seem to prefer to write their reflections at the end or on the reverse page of their lesson plans. As well as useful to yourself, reflections about the lesson are useful for those who are supervising you if you are a student teacher or a teacher being mentored or considered for tenure. Sample reflective questions you might ask yourself are shown in Figure 2.1 (Chapter 2).

Writing and later reading your reflections can provide not only ideas that may be useful if you plan to use the lesson again at some later date, but offer catharsis, easing the tension caused from teaching. To continue working effectively at a challenging task (i.e., to prevent intellectual downshifting, or reverting to earlier learned, lower cognitive level behaviors) requires significant amounts of reflection.

If you have reviewed the sample lesson plan formats, proceed now to Exercise 6.2, where you will analyze a lesson that failed; then, as instructed by your course instructor, do Exercises 6.3 and 6.4.

FOR YOUR NOTES

EXERCISE 6.2: ANALYSIS OF A LESSON THAT FAILED

INSTRUCTIONS: The planning and structure of a lesson are often predictors of the success of its implementation. The purpose of this exercise is to read the following synopsis of the implementation of a lesson, answer the discussion questions individually, and use your responses as a basis for class discussion in small groups about the lesson.

The Setting: Seventh-grade life science class; 1:12–2:07 P.M., spring semester

Synopsis of Events

1:12	Bell rings.
1:12–1:21	Teacher directs students to read from their texts, while he takes attendance.
1:21–1:31	Teacher distributes a photocopy to each student; students are now to label the parts of a flower shown on the handout.
1:31–1:37	Silent reading and labeling of photocopy.
1:37–1:39	Teacher verbally gives instructions for working on a real flower (e.g., by comparing it with the drawing on the handout). Students may use the microscopes if they want.
1:39–1:45	Teacher walks around room, giving each student a real flower.
1:45–2:07	Chaos erupts. There is much confusion, with students wandering around, throwing flower parts at each other. Teacher begins writing referrals, and sends two students to the office for their misbehavior. Teacher is flustered, directs students to spend remainder of period quietly reading from their texts. Two more referrals are written.
2:05–2:07	A few students begin meandering toward the exit.
2:07	End of period (much to the delight of the teacher).

QUESTIONS FOR CLASS DISCUSSION

1. Do you think the teacher had a lesson plan? If so, what (if any) were its good points? Its problems? _____

_____

_____

_____

2. If you believed that the teacher had a lesson plan, do you believe that it was written and detailed? Explain your response. What is your evidence? _____

_____

_____

_____

3. How might the lesson have been prepared and implemented to avoid the chaos? _____

_____

_____

_____

_____

EXERCISE 6.2 *(continued)*

4. Was the format of the lesson traditional? Explain. _____

_____

_____

_____

5. Have you experienced a class such as this? Explain. _____

_____

_____

_____

6. Which teacher behaviors were probable causes of much of the chaos? (Hint: See Chapter 2.) _____

_____

_____

_____

7. What teacher behaviors could have prevented the chaos and made the lesson more effective? _____

_____

_____

_____

8. Within the 55-minute class period, students were expected to operate rather high on the Learning Experiences Ladder (see Figure 6.6). Consider this analysis: 9 minutes of silent reading; 10 minutes of listening; 6 minutes of silent reading and labeling; 2 minutes of listening; 6 minutes of action (the only direct experience); and an additional 22 minutes of silent reading. In all, there were approximately 49 minutes (89 percent of the class time) of abstract verbal and visual symbolization. Is this a problem? _____

_____

_____

_____

_____

9. What have you learned from this exercise? _____

_____

_____

_____

_____

_____

🅟🅟 EXERCISE 6.3A: PREPARING A LESSON PLAN

INSTRUCTIONS: Use the model lesson format or an alternative format that is approved by your instructor to prepare a _____-minute lesson plan (length to be decided in your class) for a grade and course of your choice. After completing your lesson plan, evaluate it yourself, modify it, and then have your modified version evaluated by two or more peers, using Exercise 6.3B for the evaluation, before turning it in for your instructor's evaluation. This exercise may be connected with Exercise 6.4.

EXERCISE 6.3B: SELF- AND PEER ASSESSMENT OF MY LESSON PLAN

INSTRUCTIONS: You may duplicate blank copies of this form for evaluation of the lesson you developed for Exercise 6.3A. Have your lesson plan evaluated by two or more of your peers and yourself. For each of the items below, evaluators should check either "yes" or "no," and write instructive comments. Compare the results of your self-evaluation with the other evaluations.

	No	*Yes*	*Comments*
1. Are descriptive data adequately provided?	_____	_____	_____
2. Are the goals clearly stated?	_____	_____	_____
3. Are the objectives specific and measurable?	_____	_____	_____
4. Are objectives correctly classified?	_____	_____	_____
5. Are objectives only low-order or is higher-order thinking expected?	_____	_____	_____
6. Is the rationale clear and justifiable?	_____	_____	_____
7. Is the plan's content appropriate?	_____	_____	_____
8. Is the content likely to contribute to achievement of the objectives?	_____	_____	_____
9. Given the time frame and other logistical considerations, is the plan workable?	_____	_____	_____
10. Will the opening (set) likely engage the students?	_____	_____	_____
11. Is there a preassessment strategy?	_____	_____	_____
12. Is there a proper mix of learning activities for the time frame of the lesson?	_____	_____	_____
13. Are the activities developmentally appropriate for the intended students?	_____	_____	_____
14. Are transitions planned?	_____	_____	_____
15. If relevant, are key questions written out and key ideas noted in the plan?	_____	_____	_____
16. Does the plan indicate how coached practice will be provided for each student?	_____	_____	_____
17. Is adequate closure provided in the plan?	_____	_____	_____
18. Are needed materials and equipment identified and are they appropriate?	_____	_____	_____

☞

EXERCISE 6.3B *(continued)*

19. Is there a planned formative assessment, formal
    or informal?   _____ _____ _____

20. Is there a planned summative assessment?   _____ _____ _____

21. Is the lesson coordinated in any way with other
    aspects of the curriculum?   _____ _____ _____

22. Is the lesson likely to provide a sense of meaning
    for the students by helping bridge their learning?   _____ _____ _____

23. Is an adequate amount of time allotted to address
    the information presented?   _____ _____ _____

24. Is a thoughtfully prepared and relevant student
    assignment planned?   _____ _____ _____

25. Could a substitute who is knowledgeable follow
    the plan?   _____ _____ _____

Additional comments: _____

_____

_____

_____

_____

_____

_____

_____

_____

_____

_____

_____

_____

_____

_____

_____

_____

_____

PP EXERCISE 6.4: PREPARING AN INSTRUCTIONAL UNIT: BRINGING IT ALL TOGETHER

INSTRUCTIONS: The purpose of this exercise is threefold: (1) to give you experience in preparing an instructional unit, (2) to assist you in preparing an instructional unit that you can use in your teaching, and (3) to start your collection of instructional units that you may be able to use later in your teaching. This assignment will take several hours to complete, and you will need to read ahead in this resource guide. Our advice, therefore, is to start the assignment early, with a due date much later in the course. Your course instructor may have specific guidelines for your completion of this exercise; what follows is the essence of what you are to do.

First, with help from your instructor divide your class into three teams, each with a different assignment pertaining to this exercise. The units completed by these teams are to be shared with all members of the class, for feedback and possible use later.

TEAM 1

Members of this team, individually or in dyads, will develop standard teaching units, perhaps with different grade levels, grades 5–8, in mind. (You will need to review the content of Chapters 7–9.) Using a format that is practical, *each member or pair of this team* will develop a minimum two-week (10-day) unit for a particular grade level, subject, and topic. Regardless of the format chosen, each unit plan should include the following elements:

1. Identification of (a) grade level, (b) subject, (c) topic, and (d) time duration.
2. Statement of rationale and general goals.
3. Separate listing of instructional objectives for each daily lesson. Wherever possible, the unit should include objectives from all three domains—cognitive, affective, and psychomotor.
4. List of materials and resources needed and where they can be obtained (if you have that information). These should also be listed for each daily lesson.
5. Ten consecutive daily lesson plans (see Exercise 6.3A).
6. List of all items that will be used to assess student learning *during* and at *completion* of the unit of study.
7. Statement of how the unit will attend to the diversity of students one is likely to find, such as pertaining to students' reading levels, socioethnic backgrounds, and special needs.

TEAM 2

Following the steps in Exercise 8.1 (Chapter 8), *each member* of this team will develop a self-instructional module.

TEAM 3

In collaboration, members of this team will develop interdisciplinary thematic units. Depending upon the number of students in your class, Team 3 may actually comprise several teams, with each team developing an ITU. Each team should be comprised of no less than two members (e.g., a math specialist and a science specialist) and no more than four (e.g., history/social studies, English/language arts/reading, mathematics, and science).

SUMMARY

You have learned of the importance of learning modalities and instructional modes. You have learned about the importance of providing an accepting and supportive learning environment, as well as about teacher behaviors that are necessary to facilitate student learning beyond that of procedural knowledge.

With this chapter in particular, you continued building your knowledge base about why planning is important and how units with lessons are useful pedagogical tools. Developing units of instruction that integrate student learning and provide a sense of meaning for the students requires coordination throughout the curriculum. Hence, for students, learning is a process of discovering how information, knowledge, and ideas are interrelated so they can make sense out of self, school, and life. Preparing chunks of information into units and units into lessons helps students to process and understand knowledge. You have developed your first unit of instruction and are well on your way to becoming a competent planner of instruction.

In these first six chapters of this resource guide, you have been guided through the preinstructional processes necessary to prepare yourself to teach in a classroom. Later, after you have studied Chapters 7–9 on assessment practices and specific instructional strategies, you may choose to revisit this chapter and to make revisions to your completed unit and lessons. Remember this always: Teaching plans, quite similar to this resource guide, should never be set in concrete, but subject to constant evaluation and revision.

QUESTIONS FOR CLASS DISCUSSION

1. In subject-field discussion groups, list and describe specific considerations you should give to student safety (a topic that this resource guide cannot adequately otherwise address) when preparing instructional plans. Share your lists with other groups. (In doing this you may wish to review Figure 2.3 of Chapter 2.)
2. Explain the importance of the notion that all teachers of young adolescents are teachers of literacy and of thinking, social, and learning skills. Explain why you agree or disagree with that notion. Indicate for your own subject field one way specifically you would address each in your teaching.
3. Give several reasons why both a student teacher and a first-year teacher need to prepare detailed lesson plans. Describe when, if ever, the teacher can or should divert from the written lesson plan.
4. Divide your class into subject-area interest groups. Have each group devise two separate lesson plans to teach the same topic to the same group of students (identified), but one plan uses direct instruction while the other uses indirect. Have groups share the experiences and outcomes of this activity with one another.
5. Explain why, when taught by access strategies, young adolescents learn less content but learn it more effectively. For a teacher using access strategies extensively, could this cause a problem? Explain.
6. Recall one vivid learning experience from your own middle level schooling and reflect on that experience with respect to its position on the Learning Experiences Ladder. In small groups, share your reflection with members of your class. After sharing, discuss what, if anything, can be concluded.
7. From the content outline that you prepared in Chapter 5, select a topic that is typically taught by the use of symbolization (at or near the top of the Learning Experiences Ladder); then devise a technique by which, with limited resources, that same content could be taught more directly (at or close to the bottom of the ladder). Share your proposal with your classmates for their feedback.
8. Explain the importance of organizing instruction into units. Is there ever a time when you might not do so? Share your response with your classmates for their critiques and thoughts.
9. You may want to brainstorm answers to this question in class in small groups involving classmates from various subject-field majors. Identify a lesson typically taught to young adolescents, perhaps a lesson you recently have observed taught. Taking the essence of that lesson, identify nine activities you would include in that lesson, one for each of the nine learning capacities (multiple intelligences) identified earlier in this chapter.
10. Explain why you agree or disagree with the notion that knowing your students well is critical to competent planning for instruction. If you agree with the notion, explain in detail three things you can do in your planning for the first week or two of school to get to better know your students.

INTERNET RESOURCES

Africa Access
   http://www.mcps.k12.md.us/specialprojects/africa_access

Classroom Connect http://www.classroomconnect.com

Copyright free images source http://pics.tech4learning.com

Council of the Great City Schools http://www.cgcs.org

Education World http://www.education-world.com

Eisenhower National Clearinghouse for Mathematics and Science
   http://www.enc.org

FedWorld http://www.fedworld.gov

*GLOBE (Global Learning and Observations to Benefit the
   Environment) Program* http://www.globe.gov

Intercultural E-mail Classroom Connections (IECC)
   http://www.stolaf.edu/network/iecc

Lesson plans for all subjects at http://artsedge.kennedy-
   center.org *and* http://www.pbs.org/teachersource

Lesson plans for mathematics at http://coolmath.com *and at*
   http://mathworld.wolfram.com

Library of Congress http://lcweb.loc.gov/homepage/lchp.html

Opening activity http://www.dailybite.com

The Global Schoolhouse http://www.gsn.org

FOR FURTHER READING

Adams, J., & Bushman, J. H. (2006). Thematic solutions using young adult literature to increase reading comprehension. *Middle School Journal, 37*(4), 25–29

Bintz, W. P., & Moore, S. D. (2003). Using literature to teach factorials. *Mathematics Teaching in the Middle School, 8,* 461–465.

Dombchik, L. (2004). Storm busters: A science and technology integrated unit. *Middle Ground, 7*(3), 35–37.

Eisner, E. (2004). Multiple intelligences: Its tensions and possibilities. *Teachers College Record, 106*(1), 31–39.

Hibbing, A. N., & Rankin-Rickson, J. L. (2003). A picture is worth a thousand words: Using visual images to improve comprehension for middle school struggling readers. *The Reading Teacher, 56,* 758–770.

Kellough, R. D., Cangelosi, J. S., Collette, A. T., Chiappetta, E. L., Souviney, R. J., Trowbridge, L. W., & Bybee, R. W. (1996). *Integrating mathematics and science for intermediate and middle school students.* Englewood Cliffs, NJ: Merrill/Prentice Hall.

Kellough, R. D., Jarolimek, J., Parker, W. C., Martorella, P. H., Tompkins, G. E., & Hoskisson, K. (1996). *Integrating language arts and social studies for intermediate and middle school students.* Englewood Cliffs, NJ: Merrill/Prentice Hall.

McCarthy, B., & McCarthy, D. (2006). *Teaching around the 4MAT cycle.* Thousand Oaks, CA: Corwin Press.

McTighe, J., & O'Connor, K. (2005). Seven strategies for effective learning. *Educational Leadership, 63*(3), 10–17.

Mehigan, K. R. (2005). The strategy toolbox: A ladder to strategic teaching. *The Reading Teacher, 58,* 552–566.

Roberts, P. L., & Kellough, R. D. (2008). *A guide for developing an interdisciplinary thematic unit* (4th ed.). Upper Saddle River, NJ: Prentice Hall.

Whitin, D. J., & Whitin, P. (2004). *New visions for linking literature and mathematics.* Reston, VA: National Council of Teachers of Mathematics and the National Council of Teachers of English.

Wormeli, R. (2006). Differentiating for tweens. *Educational Leadership, 63*(7), 14–19.

7

Assessing and Reporting Student Achievement

Anthony Magnacca/Merrill

Preceding chapters of this resource guide have focused your attention on steps necessary in planning for actual classroom interaction, that is, the planning or preactive phase of instruction. One additional consideration while planning for instruction is that of planning the assessment strategies, and that is the focus of this chapter. That, then is followed by Chapters 8 and 9 that deal specifically with specific interactive or teaching strategies.

The phases of instruction—preactive, interactive, and assessment, each of which involves the teacher's constant reflection—are inextricably intertwined, with each affected by and dependent upon the others. Indeed, teaching and learning are reciprocal processes that depend on and affect one another. Thus, the assessment component of instruction deals with both how well the students are learning and how well the teacher is teaching. One cannot be separated from the other.

Rather than a separate phase, assessment is really an integral and ongoing process in the total educational arena. Curricula, buildings, materials, specific courses, teachers, supervisors, administrators, equipment, and yes, even school board members and politicians at all levels of government—all must be periodically assessed in relation to student learning, the purpose of the school. When gaps between anticipated results and student achievement exist, efforts are made to eliminate those factors that seem to be limiting the educational output or to improve the situation in some other way. Thus, educational progress occurs.

Much concern today is expressed over the use of what is often referred to as **high-stakes assessments**. An assessment is called *high stakes* when use of the assessment's results carry serious consequences, such as a student's grade promotion or graduation from high school rests on the student's performance on a single test. We agree with the many educators who argue that important decisions that affect a student's educational career should not rest on a single test score alone but on multiple sources of data that accumulate over a period of time. We share in the concern that placing high reliance on a single source of data would likely result in an increase, rather than an improvement, in the school dropout rate (Amrein & Berliner, 2003). In a joint announcement, Executive Directors of the National Association of Elementary School Principals (NAESP) and of the National Association of Secondary School Principals (NASSP), stated "Test results should not be used to reward or punish a school, a system, or a state, but instead should be used as diagnostic tools to improve teaching and learning. Tests should not be used for high-stakes purposes or as exit exams" (Ferrandino & Tirozzi, 2001).

However, it is true that to learn effectively, students need to know how they are doing and how they can improve. Similarly, to be an effective teacher, you must be informed about what the student knows, feels, and can do so that you can help the student build on her or his skills, knowledge, and attitudes. Therefore, you and your students need continuous feedback on their progress and problems in order to plan appropriate learning activities and to make adjustments to those already planned. If this feedback says that progress is slow, you can provide alternative activities; if it indicates that some or all of the students have already mastered the desired learning, you can eliminate unnecessary activities and practice for some or all of the students. In short, assessment provides a key for competent teaching, individualized instruction, and effective learning.

The importance of continuous assessment mandates that you are knowledgeable about various principles and techniques of assessment. This chapter explains some of those and shows you how to construct and use assessment instruments. It clarifies terms related to assessment, suggests procedures to use in the construction of assessment items, and identifies the advantages and disadvantages of a variety of types of assessment items and procedures.

It is neither our purpose nor does space in this resource guide allow a consideration of standardized achievement testing. Rather, the focus is on nonstandardized, criterion-referenced tests, tests that you design (or collaboratively design) for your own unique group of students for determination of their level of learning on particular instructional objectives. In no way do we intend to devalue the concern that you as a classroom teacher will have for high-stakes, standardized, norm-referenced, achievement testing. It simply means that our purpose and space in this resource guide do not allow for in-depth attention to that particular topic (for more information about standardized testing, see the recommended readings at the end of this chapter). If relevant to you and your teaching, your school and district will provide special instructions for preparing students and for administering the mandated standardized achievement tests, and analyzing results. For example, with respect to mandated statewide tests, many schools and districts now employ what is referred to as *value-added assessment,* a technique that has teachers and administrators evaluating not only the achievement of individual students but how much "value" teachers add to student learning, taking into account how far behind or how far ahead students are academically upon entering a particular classroom, that is, how much academic growth over time is made by individual children. However, the true worth of value-added assessment and similar techniques is still in question (Vaishnav, 2005).

In addition, this chapter discusses grading and to a limited extent, the reporting of student achievement, two responsibilities that can consume much of a teacher's time. Grading can be both time-consuming and frustrating for teachers. What should be graded? Should grades (or marks) represent student growth, level of achievement in a group, effort, attitude, general behavior, or a combination of these? What should determine grades— homework, tests, projects, class participation and group work, or some combination of these? And, what should be their relative weights? These are just a few of the questions that have plagued teachers, parents/guardians, and the profession for a century or more of education in this nation.

Still today, in too many schools, the grade progress report and final report card are about the only communication between the school and the student's home. Unless the teacher and the school have clearly determined what grades or marks represent, and unless such an understanding is periodically reviewed with each set of new parents or guardians, these reports may create confusion, unrest, and dissatisfaction on the parts of parents/guardians and students and prove to be alienating devices. The grading system and reporting scheme, then, instead of informing parents/guardians may separate even further the home and the school, which do have a common concern—the cognitive, physical, social, and emotional development of the young adolescent.

The development of the student encompasses growth in the cognitive, affective, and psychomotor domains. Traditional, objective paper-and-pencil tests provide only a portion of the data needed to indicate student progress in those domains. Many experts today, as indeed they have in the past, question traditional sources of data and encourage the search for, development of, and use of alternative means to assess more authentically the students' development of thinking and higher-level learning. Although many things are not yet clear, one thing that is clear is that various techniques of assessment with the resultant multiple kinds of data must be used to determine how the student works, what the student is learning, and what the student can produce as a result of that learning. As a teacher, you must develop a repertoire of means of assessing learner behavior and academic progress. Be patient and kind to yourself, for, to become truly skilled in the practices of assessment will take time, practice, and continuous reflection.

Although marks and grades have been a part of school for more than a century, and although it is clear to many experts that the conventional report card with marks or grades falls short of being a developmentally appropriate procedure for reporting the academic performance or progress of young adolescent learners, and although some schools are experimenting with other ways of reporting student achievement in learning, letter grades, especially for middle grades and up, still seem firmly entrenched. However, a variety of systems of assessment and reporting have evolved, are still evolving, and will likely continue to evolve throughout your professional career.

Continuous, authentic, and appropriate assessment and evaluation measures provide evidence about every student's learning progress. Grades alone are inadequate expressions for assessing the many goals of middle level education.

National Middle School Association (2003, p. 27)

OBJECTIVES

Specifically, upon completion of this chapter you should be able to:

1. Demonstrate an understanding of the importance of the assessment component of teaching and learning.
2. Demonstrate an understanding of the concept of authentic assessment.
3. Explain the value of and give an example of a performance assessment that could be used in teaching your subject.
4. Explain why criterion-referenced grading is preferred over norm-referenced grading.
5. Explain how rubrics, checklists, portfolios, and journals are used in the assessment of student learning.
6. Describe the importance of self-assessment and reflection in teaching and learning.
7. Describe means a teacher can use to help students to reduce and manage their text anxiety.
8. Recall guidelines for meeting with parents and guardians.
9. Describe the meaning and importance of the concept of assessment as being *embedded* in daily instruction.

PURPOSES AND PRINCIPLES OF ASSESSMENT

Assessment of achievement in student learning is designed to serve several purposes. These are:

To assist in student learning. This is the purpose usually first thought of when speaking of assessment, and it is the principal topic of this chapter. For the classroom teacher it is (or should be) the most important purpose.

To identify students' strengths and weaknesses. Identification and assessment of students' strengths and weaknesses are necessary for two reasons: to structure and restructure the learning activities and to restructure the curriculum. Concerning the first, for example, data on student strengths and weaknesses in content and process skills are important in planning activities appropriate for both skill development and intellectual development. This is *diagnostic assessment* (known also as *preassessment*). For the second, data on student strengths and weaknesses in content and skills are useful for making appropriate modifications to the curriculum.

To assess the effectiveness of a particular instructional strategy. It is important you understand how well a particular strategy helped accomplish a particular goal or objective. Exemplary teachers continually reflect on and evaluate their strategy choices, using a number of sources—student achievement as measured by assessment instruments, their own intuition, informal feedback given by the students, and, sometimes, informal feedback given by colleagues.

To assess and improve the effectiveness of curriculum programs. Committees composed of teachers and administrators and sometimes parents/guardians, students, and other members of the school and community continually assess components of the curriculum. The assessment is done while students are learning (i.e., formative assessment) and afterward (summative assessment).

To assess and improve teaching effectiveness. To improve student learning, teachers are periodically evaluated on the basis of: (a) their commitment to working with students; (b) their ability to cope with students at a particular age, developmental, or grade level; (c) the achievement of subject-matter knowledge by the students they teach, particularly as related to the mandated state standards; and (d) their ability to show mastery of instructional techniques articulated throughout this resource guide, specifically to those proven developmentally appropriate for teaching young adolescents.

To provide data that assist in decision making about a student's future. Assessment of student achievement is important in guiding decision making about course and program placement, promotion, school transfer, class standing, eligibility for honors and scholarships, and career planning. In many school districts, because of the *No Child Left Behind Act of 2001* this purpose in recent years has assumed increasing prominence.

To provide data in order to communicate with and involve parents/guardians in their children's learning. Parents/guardians, communities, and school boards all share in an accountability for the effectiveness of the learning of the children. Today's schools are reaching out more than ever before and engaging parents/guardians and the community in their children's education. All teachers play an important role in the process of communicating with, reaching out to, and involving parents/guardians and the community.

Because the welfare and, indeed, the future of so many people depend on the outcomes of assessment, it is impossible to overemphasize its importance. For a learning endeavor to be successful, the learner must have answers to basic questions: Where am I going? Where am I now? How do I get where I am going? How will I know when I get there? Am I on the right track for getting there? These questions are integral to a good program of assessment. Of course, in the process of teaching and learning, the answers may be ever-changing, and the teacher and students continue to assess and adjust plans as appropriate and necessary. As you are reminded many times in this resource guide, the exemplary school is in a mode of continuous change and progress.

Based on the questions in the preceding paragraph are the following principles that guide the assessment program and that are reflected in the discussions in this chapter.

- A teacher's responsibility is to facilitate student learning and to assess student progress in that learning, and for that, the teacher is, or should be, held accountable.
- Assessment is a continuous process, imbedded in the teacher's daily instruction. The selection and implementation of plans and activities require continuous monitoring and assessment to check on progress and to change or adopt strategies to promote desired behavior.
- Assessment is a reciprocal process that includes assessment of teacher performance as well as for student achievement.
- Evidence and input data for knowing how well the teacher and students are doing should come from a variety of sources and types of data-collecting devices.
- Reflection and self-assessment are important components of any successful assessment program. Reflection and self-assessment are important if students are to develop the skills necessary for them to assume increasingly greater ownership of their own learning. Reflection and self-assessment are important for the continued and increasing effectiveness of a teacher.
- Students need to know how well they are doing.
- Teachers need to know how well they are doing.
- Parents/guardians need to know how well their children and schools are doing.
- The program of assessment should aid teaching effectiveness and contribute to the intellectual, social, and psychological growth of the children.

THE LANGUAGE OF ASSESSMENT

When discussing the assessment component of teaching and learning it is easy to be confused by the terminology used. The following clarification of terms is offered to aid your reading and comprehension.

Assessment and Evaluation

Assessment is the relative neutral process of finding out what students are learning. **Evaluation** is the more subjective process of making sense of what was found out. For the purposes of this resource guide, we consider the difference between the two terms too slight to really matter.

Measurement and Assessment

Measurement refers to quantifiable data about specific behaviors. Tests and the statistical procedures used to analyze the results are examples. Measurement is a descriptive and objective process; that is, it is relatively free from human value judgments.

Assessment includes objective data from measurement but also other types of information, some of which are more subjective, such as information from anecdotal records and teacher observations and ratings of student performance. In addition to the use of objective data (data from measurement), assessment also includes arriving at value judgments made on the basis of subjective information.

An example of the use of these terms is as follows. A teacher may share the information that Penny Brown received a score in the 90th percentile on the eighth-grade statewide achievement test in reading (a statement of measurement), but may add that "according to my assessment of her work in my language arts class, she has not been an outstanding student" (a statement of assessment).

Validity and Reliability

The degree to which a measuring instrument actually measures that which it is intended to measure is the instrument's **validity**. For example, when we ask if an instrument (such as a performance assessment instrument) has validity, key questions concerning that instrument are:

- Does the instrument adequately sample the intended content?
- Does it measure the cognitive, affective, and psychomotor knowledge and skills that are important to the unit of content being tested?
- Does it sample all the instructional objectives of that unit?

The accuracy with which a technique consistently measures that which it is meant to gauge is its **reliability**. If, for example, you know that you weigh 125 pounds, and a scale consistently records 125 pounds when you stand on it, then that scale has reliability. However, if the same scale consistently records 117 pounds when you stand on it, we can still say the scale has reliability. By this example, then, it should be clear to you that an instrument could be reliable (it produces similar results when used again and again) although not necessarily valid. In this second instance, the scale is not measuring what it is supposed to measure, so although it is reliable, it is not valid. Although a technique might be reliable but not valid, a technique must have reliability before it can have validity. The greater the number of test items or situations on a particular content objective, the higher the reliability. The higher the reliability, the more consistency there will be in students' scores measuring their understanding of that particular objective.

Authentic Assessment: Advantages and Disadvantages

When assessing for student achievement, it is important that you use procedures that are compatible with the instructional objectives that in turn coincide or align with the curriculum standards. This is referred to as **authentic assessment**. Other terms used for authentic assessment are *accurate, active, aligned, alternative,* and *direct*. Although **performance assessment** is sometimes used, performance assessment refers to the type of student response being assessed, whereas authentic assessment refers to the assessment situation. Although not all performance assessments are authentic, assessments that are authentic are most assuredly performance assessments (Oosterhof, 2001).

In English/language arts, for example, although it may seem fairly easy to develop a criterion-referenced test, administer it, and grade it, tests often measure language *skills* rather than language *use*. It is extremely difficult to measure students' communicative competence with a test. Tests do not measure listening and talking very well, and a test on punctuation marks, for example, does not indicate students' ability to use punctuation marks correctly in their own writing.

Instead, tests typically evaluate students' ability to add punctuation marks to a set of sentences created by someone else or to proofread and spot punctuation errors in someone else's writing. An alternative and far better approach is to examine how students use punctuation marks in their own writing (Tompkins & Hoskisson, 1991). An authentic assessment of punctuation, then, would be an assessment of a performance item that involves students in writing and punctuating their own writing. For the authentic assessment of the student's understanding of that which the student has been learning, you would use a performance-based assessment procedure.

Consider another example: "If students have been actively involved in classifying objects using multiple characteristics, it sends them a confusing message if they are then required to take a paper-and-pencil test that asks them to 'define classification' or recite a memorized list of characteristics of good classifications schemes" (Rakow, 1992, p. 3). An authentic assessment technique would be a performance item that actually involves the students in classifying objects. In other words, to obtain an accurate assessment of a student's learning, the teacher uses a performance-based assessment procedure, that is, a procedure that requires students to produce rather than to select a response.

Advantages claimed for the use of authentic assessment include: (a) the direct (also known as performance-based, criterion-referenced, outcome-based, or standards-based) measurement of what students should know and can do and (b) an emphasis on higher-order thinking. On the other hand, disadvantages of authentic assessment include a higher cost, difficulty in making results consistent and usable, and problems with validity, reliability, and comparability.

Unfortunately, a teacher may never see a particular student again after conclusion of a given school semester or academic year, and the effects that teacher had on a student's values and attitudes may never be observed by that teacher at all. In schools where groups or teams of teachers remain with the same cohort of students—as in the increasing popular small learning community concept and looping programs (discussed in Chapter 1)—those teachers often do have an opportunity to observe the positive changes in their students' values and attitudes.

Diagnostic, Formative, and Summative Assessment

Assessing a student's achievement is a three-stage process, involving (as described in the preceding chapter):

Diagnostic assessment (also called preassessment)—the assessment of the student's knowledge and skills *before* the new instruction

Formative assessment—the assessment of learning *during* the instruction

Summative assessment—the assessment of learning *after* the instruction, ultimately represented by the student's final term, semester, or year's achievement grade.

Grades (or marks) shown on unit tests, progress reports, and interim reports are examples of formative evaluation reports. However, an end-of-chapter test or a unit test is summative when the test represents the absolute end of the student's learning of material for that instructional unit.

ASSESSING STUDENT LEARNING: THREE AVENUES

Three general avenues are available for assessing a student's achievement in learning. These include: (1) assess what the student *says*—for example, the quantity and quality of a student's contributions to class discussions; (2) assess what the student *does*—for example, a student's performance (e.g., the amount and quality of a student's participation in the learning activities); and (3) assess what the student *writes*—for example, items in the student's portfolio (homework assignments, checklists, project work, and written tests).

Although your own situation and personal philosophy will influence the levels of importance and weight you give to each avenue of assessment, you should have a strong rationale if you value and weigh the three avenues for assessment differently than one-third each.

Assessing What a Student Says and Does

When evaluating what a student says, you should listen to the student's oral reports, questions, responses, and interactions with others, and observe the student's attentiveness, involvement in class activities, creativeness, and responses to challenges. Notice that we say you should listen and observe. While listening to what the student is saying, you should also be observing the student's nonverbal behaviors. For this you can use narrative observation forms (see Figure 7.1), and you can use observations with checklists and scoring rubrics (see sample checklists in Figures 7.2, 7.4, and 7.5, and sample scoring rubrics in 7.2, 7.3, 7.10, and 7.11) and periodic conferences with the student.

With each technique used, you must proceed from your awareness of anticipated learning outcomes (the instructional objectives), and you must assess a student's progress toward meeting those objectives. That is a **criterion-referenced** assessment.

Observation Form. Figure 7.1 illustrates a sample generic form for recording and evaluating teacher observations of a student's verbal and nonverbal behaviors. With modern technology, such as afforded, for example, by the software program *Learner Profile*™, a teacher can record observations electronically anywhere at any time.

Checklist versus Scoring Rubric. As you can see from Figure 7.2, there is little difference between what is a

Figure 7.1 Form for evaluating and recording student verbal and nonverbal behaviors.

| Student _____ | Course _____ | School _____ |
| Observer _____ | Date _____ | Period _____ |

Objective	Desired Behavior	What Student Did, Said, or Wrote

Teacher's (Observer's) comments:

checklist and what is a rubric: The difference is that rubrics show the degrees for the desired characteristics while checklists usually show only the desired characteristics. The checklist could easily be made into a scoring rubric and the rubric could easily be made into a checklist.

Guidelines for Assessing What a Student Says and Does. When assessing a student's verbal and nonverbal behaviors in the classroom you should:

- Maintain an anecdotal record (teacher's log) book or folder with a separate section in it for your records of each student.
- For a specific activity, list the desirable behaviors.
- Check the list against the specific instructional objectives.
- Record your observations as quickly as possible following your observation. Audio or video recordings,

and, of course, computer software programs can help you maintain records and check the accuracy of your memory, but if this is inconvenient, you should spend time during school, immediately after school, or later that evening recording your observations while they are still fresh in your memory.

- Record your professional judgment about the student's progress toward the desired behavior, but think it through before transferring it to a permanent record.
- Write comments that are reminders to yourself, such as, "Discuss observation with the student," "Check validity of observation by further testing," "Discuss observations with student's mentor" (e.g., an adult representative from the community), and "Discuss observations with other teachers on the teaching team."

Figure 7.2 Checklist and rubric compared.

Sample rubric for assessing a student's skill in listening.

Score Point 3—Strong listener:

   Responds immediately to oral directions

   Focuses on speaker

   Maintains appropriate attention span

   Listens to what others are saying

   Is interactive

Score Point 2—Capable listener:

   Follows oral directions

   Usually attentive to speaker and to discussions

   Listens to others without interrupting

Score Point 1—Developing listener:

   Has difficulty following directions

   Relies on repetition

   Often inattentive

   Has short attention span

   Often interrupts the speaker

Sample checklist for assessing a student's skill in map work:

Check each item if the map comes up to standard in this particular category.

   _____ 1. Accuracy

   _____ 2. Neatness

   _____ 3. Attention to details

Assessing What a Student Writes

When assessing what a student writes, you can use worksheets, written homework and papers, student journal writing, student writing projects, student portfolios, and tests (all discussed later in this chapter). Portfolios, worksheets, and homework assignments are the tools usually used for the formative evaluation of each student's achievement. Tests, too, should be a part of this assessment, but tests are also used for summative assessment at the end of a unit, and also for diagnostic purposes.

Your summative assessment of a student's achievement and any other final judgment made by you about a student can have an impact upon the psychological and intellectual development of that student. Special attention is given to this later in the section titled "Recording Teacher Observations and Judgments."

Guidelines for Assessing Student Writing. Use the following guidelines when assessing what a student writes.

Student writing assignments, test items, and scoring rubrics (see Figure 7.3) *should be criterion-referenced,* that is, they should correlate with and be compatible with specific instructional objectives. Regardless of the avenue chosen, and their relative weights given by you, you must evaluate against the instructional objectives. Any given objective may be checked by using more than one method and by using more than one instrument. Subjectivity, inherent in the assessment process, may be reduced as you check for validity, comparing results of one measuring strategy against those of another.

Read nearly everything a student writes. [*Note:* We are not referring here to student diaries and private journals which are just that—private—and which, in our opinion, should be left at home, not brought to school.] Regarding schoolwork, if it is important for the student to do the work, then it is equally important that you give your professional attention to the product of the

Figure 7.3   Scoring rubric for assessing student writing.

Score Point 4—correct purpose, mode, audience; effective elaboration; consistent organization; clear sense of order and completeness; fluent

Score Point 3—correct purpose, mode, audience; moderately well elaborated; organized but possible brief digressions; clear, effective language

Score Point 2—correct purpose, mode, audience; some elaboration; some specific details; gaps in organization; limited language control

Score Point 1—attempts to address audience; brief, vague, unelaborated; wanders off topic; lack of language control; little or no organization; wrong purpose and mode

Source: Texas Education Agency, *Writing Inservice Guide for English Language Arts and TAAS* (Austin, TX: Author, 1993.)

student's efforts. Of course, in deference to the teacher's productive and efficient use of valuable time, student papers can be read with varying degrees of intensity and scrutiny depending on the purpose of the assignment.

Provide written or verbal comments about the student's work, and be positive in those comments. Rather than just writing "good" on a student's paper, briefly state what it was about it that in your opinion made it good. (Refer to earlier discussion, Chapter 2, about the use of the lone word *good.*) Rather than saying or pointing out that the student didn't do it right, tell or show the student what is acceptable and how to achieve it. For reinforcement, use positive comments and encouragement as frequently as possible.

Think before writing a comment on a student's paper, asking yourself how you think the student (or a parent or guardian) will interpret and react to the comment and if that is a correct interpretation or reaction to your intended meaning.

Avoid writing evaluative comments or grades in student journals (Chandler, 1997). Student journals are for encouraging students to write, to think about their thinking, and to record their creative thoughts. In journal writing, students should be encouraged to write about their experiences in school and out of school and especially about their experiences related to what is being learned. They should be encouraged to write their feelings about what is being learned and about how they are learning it. Writing in journals gives them practice in expressing themselves in written form and in connecting their learning and should provide nonthreatening freedom to do it. Comments and evaluations from teachers might discourage creative and spontaneous expression. You can write simple, empathic comments such as "Thank you for sharing your thoughts," or "I think I understand what makes you feel that way."

When reading student-learning journals, talk individually with students to seek clarification about their expressions. Student learning journals are useful to the teacher (of any subject) in understanding the student's thought processes and writing skills (diagnostic assessment), and should *not* be graded. For grading purposes, teachers may simply record whether the student is maintaining a journal and, perhaps, an assessment regarding the quantity of writing in it, but no judgment should be made about the quality.

When reviewing student portfolios, discuss with students individually the progress in their learning as shown by the materials in their portfolios. As with student learning journals, the portfolio should *not* be graded or compared in any way with those of other students. Its purpose is for student self-assessment and to show progress in learning. For this to happen, students should keep in their portfolios all or major samples of papers related to the course.

Assessment for Affective and Psychomotor Domain Learning

While assessment of cognitive domain learning lends itself to traditional written tests of achievement, the assessment of learning within the affective and psychomotor domains is best suited by the use of performance checklists where student behaviors can be observed in action. However, many educators today are encouraging the use of alternative assessment procedures (i.e., alternatives to traditional paper-and-pencil written testing). After all, in learning that is most important and that has the most meaning to students, the domains are inextricably interconnected. As we emphasized in Chapter 5, learning that is meaningful to students is not as easily compartmentalized as the taxonomies of educational objectives would imply. Alternative assessment strategies include the use of projects, portfolios, skits, papers, oral presentations, and performance tests.

STUDENT INVOLVEMENT IN ASSESSMENT

Students' continuous self-assessment should be planned as an important component of the assessment program. If your students are to progress in their understanding of their own thinking (*metacognition*) and in their intellectual development, then they must receive instruction and guidance in how to become more responsible for their own learning. During that empowerment process, they learn to think well of themselves and of their individual capabilities. To achieve this self-understanding and positive self-esteem requires the experiences afforded by successes, along with guidance in self-understanding and self-assessment.

To meet these goals, teachers provide opportunities for students to think about what they are learning, about how they are learning it, and about how far they have progressed. Specifically, to engage students in the assessment process you can provide opportunities for the students to

- identify learning targets that are especially valued by the students
- help in the planning and design of assessment devices for the units of study
- evaluate the tests (if any) that are furnished by the textbook publisher in terms of how well they match learning targets identified by you and your students, and the benchmark standards provided by your school district
- help interpret assessment results.

To aid in the interpretation of results, students can maintain portfolios of their work, using rating scales or checklists periodically to self-assess their progress, and discuss their self-assessments with their parents/guardians and teacher.

Using Student Portfolios

Portfolios are used by teachers as a means of instruction and by teachers and students as one means of assessing student learning. Although there is scant research evidence to support or refute the claim, educators believe that the instructional value comes from the process of the student's assembling and maintaining a personal portfolio. During that creative process the student is expected to self-reflect, to think critically about what has and is being learned, and is assuming some responsibility for his or her own learning.

Student portfolios fall into three general categories, and the purpose in a given situation may transcend some combination of all three. The categories are:

- *selected works portfolio*, in which students maintain samples of their work as prompted by the teacher
- *longitudinal or growth portfolio*, which is oriented toward outcome-driven goals and includes samples of student work from the beginning and the end of the school term (or thematic unit of study) to exemplify achievement toward the goals
- *passport portfolio*, which contains samples of student work that will enable the student to transition, such as from one grade level to the next or from say middle school to high school.

Student portfolios should be well organized and, depending on the purpose (or category), should contain assignment sheets, class worksheets, the results of homework, project binders, forms for student self-assessment and reflection on their work, and other class materials thought of as important by the students and teacher. Software packages such as *Grady Profile*™ are available for the development of student electronic portfolios.

Portfolio Assessment: Knowing and Dealing with Its Limitations. Although portfolio assessment as an alternative to traditional methods of evaluating student progress has evidenced some popularity in recent years, establishing standards has been difficult. Research on the use of portfolios for assessment indicates that validity and reliability of teacher evaluation are often quite low. In addition, portfolio assessment is not always practical for use by every teacher. For example, if you are the sole art teacher for a middle school and are responsible for teaching art to every one of its 400 students you are unlikely to have the time or storage capacity for 400 portfolios. For your assessment of student learning, the use of checklists, rubrics, and student self-assessment may be more practical.

Before using portfolios as an alternative to traditional testing, you are advised to carefully consider and clearly understand the reasons for doing it and its practicality in your situation. Then choose carefully portfolio content, establish rubrics or expectation standards, anticipate grading problems, and consider and prepare for reactions from parents and guardians.

While emphasizing the criteria for assessment, rating scales and checklists provide students with a means of expressing their feelings and give the teacher still another source of input data useful in assessment. To provide students with reinforcement and guidance to improve their learning and development, teachers can meet with individual students to discuss their self-assessments. Such conferences should provide students with understandable and achievable short-term goals as well as help them develop and maintain adequate self-esteem.

Although almost any instrument used for assessing student work can be used for student self-assessment, in some cases it might be better to construct specific instruments with the student's understanding of the instrument in mind. Student self-assessment and self-reflection should be done on a regular and continuing basis so the student can make comparisons periodically. You will need to help students learn how to analyze these comparisons. Comparisons should provide a student with information previously not recognized about the student's progress and growth.

Using Checklists

One of the items that can be maintained by students in their portfolios is a series of checklists. Checklist items can be used easily by a student to compare with previous self-assessments. Items on the checklist will vary depending on your purpose and subject. (See sample forms, Figures 7.4 and 7.5.) Open-ended questions allow the student to provide additional information as well as to do some expressive writing. After a student has

Figure 7.4 Checklist: Oral report assessment.

Oral Report Assessment Checklist

Did the student	Yes	No	Comments
1. Speak so that everyone could hear?	_____	_____	_____
2. Finish sentences?	_____	_____	_____
3. Seem comfortable in front of the group?	_____	_____	_____
4. Give a good introduction?	_____	_____	_____
5. Seem well informed about the topic?	_____	_____	_____
6. Explain ideas clearly?	_____	_____	_____
7. Stay on the topic?	_____	_____	_____
8. Give a good conclusion?	_____	_____	_____
9. Use effective visuals to make the presentation interesting?	_____	_____	_____
10. Give good answers to questions from the audience?	_____	_____	_____

---

demonstrated each of the skills satisfactorily, a check is made next to the student's name, either by the teacher alone or in conference with the student.

Guidelines for Using Portfolios for Assessment. Following are general guidelines for using student portfolios in the assessment of learning.

- Contents of the portfolio should reflect course goals, learning standards, and target objectives.
- Determine what materials should be kept in the portfolio and announce clearly when (post schedule in room), how, and by what criteria portfolios (post listing of required contents) will be reviewed.
- Portfolio maintenance should be the students' responsibility.
- Portfolios should remain in the classroom.
- Students should be encouraged to personalize their portfolios (e.g., with brightly decorated and tasteful exteriors with the student's photo).
- Students should date all items in their portfolios.
- The portfolio should not be graded or compared in any way with those of other students. Its purpose is for student self-assessment and for showing progress in learning. For this to happen, students should keep in their portfolio all papers, or major sample papers, related to the course. For grading purposes, you can simply record whether or not the portfolio was maintained and, by checklist, whether all items required are in the portfolio.

MAINTAINING RECORDS OF STUDENT ACHIEVEMENT

You must maintain well-organized and complete records of student achievement. You may do this in a

written record book or on an electronic record book. At the very least, the record book should include attendance records and all records of scores on tests, homework, projects, and other assignments.

Daily interactions and events occur in the classroom that may provide informative data about a student's intellectual, emotional, social, and physical development. Maintaining a dated log of your observations of these interactions and events can provide important information that might otherwise be forgotten. At the end of a unit and again at the conclusion of a grading term, you will want to review your records. During the course of the school year, your anecdotal records (and those of other members of your teaching team) will provide important information about the development of each student and ideas for attention to be given to individual students.

Recording Teacher Observations and Judgments

You must think carefully about any written comments that you intend to make about a student. Young adolescents can be quite sensitive to what others say about them, and most particularly to comments about them made by a teacher.

Additionally, we have seen anecdotal comments in students' permanent records that said more about their teachers who made the comments than about the recipient students. Comments that have been carelessly, hurriedly, and thoughtlessly made can be detrimental to a student's welfare and progress in school. Teacher comments must be professional—that is, they must be diagnostically useful to the continued intellectual and psychological development of the student. This is true for any comment you make or write, whether on a student's paper, on the student's permanent school record, or on a message sent to the student's home.

Figure 7.5 Checklist: Student learning assessment for use with interdisciplinary thematic instruction.

Checklist: Interdisciplinary Thematic Unit Learning

Student _____ Date _____

Teacher _____ Time _____

The student	Yes	No	Comments/Evidence
1. Can identify theme, topic, main idea of the unit	_____	_____	_____
2. Can identify contributions of others to the theme	_____	_____	_____
3. Can identify problems related to the unit study	_____	_____	_____
4. Has developed skills in:	_____	_____	_____
Applying knowledge	_____	_____	_____
Assuming responsibility	_____	_____	_____
Categorizing	_____	_____	_____
Classifying	_____	_____	_____
Decision making	_____	_____	_____
Discussing	_____	_____	_____
Gathering resources	_____	_____	_____
Impulse control	_____	_____	_____
Inquiry	_____	_____	_____
Justifying choices	_____	_____	_____
Listening to others	_____	_____	_____
Locating information	_____	_____	_____
Metacognition	_____	_____	_____
Ordering	_____	_____	_____
Organizing information	_____	_____	_____
Problem recognition/identification	_____	_____	_____
Problem solving	_____	_____	_____
Reading maps and globes	_____	_____	_____
Reading text	_____	_____	_____
Reasoning	_____	_____	_____
Reflecting	_____	_____	_____
Reporting to others	_____	_____	_____
Self-assessing	_____	_____	_____
Sharing	_____	_____	_____
Studying	_____	_____	_____
Summarizing	_____	_____	_____
Thinking	_____	_____	_____
Using resources	_____	_____	_____
Working with others	_____	_____	_____
Working independently	_____	_____	_____
(Others unique to the unit)			

Additional teacher and student comments:

As an example, consider the following unprofessional comment observed in one student's permanent record. A teacher wrote, "John is lazy." Describing John as "lazy" could be done by anyone; it is nonproductive, and it is certainly not a professional diagnosis. How many times do you suppose John needs to receive such negative descriptions of his behavior before he begins to believe that he is lazy and as a result acts that way even more often? Written comments like that can also be damaging because they may be read by the teacher who next has John in class and lead that teacher to perpetuate the same expectation of John. To say that John is lazy merely describes behavior as judged by the teacher who wrote the comment. More important, and more professional, would be for the teacher to try to analyze why John is behaving that way, then to prescribe activities that are likely to motivate John to assume more constructive charge of his own learning behavior.

For students' continued intellectual and emotional development, your comments should be useful, productive, analytical, diagnostic, criterion-referenced, and prescriptive. The professional teacher makes diagnoses and prepares prescriptions; a professional teacher does not label students as "lazy," "vulgar," "slow," "stupid," "difficult," or "dumb." The professional teacher sees the behavior of a student as being goal-directed. Perhaps "lazy" John found that particular behavioral pattern won him attention. John's goal, then, was attention (don't we all need attention?), and John assumed negative, perhaps even self-destructive, behavioral patterns to reach that goal. The professional task of any teacher is to facilitate the learner's understanding (perception) of an achievable goal and help the student identify acceptable behaviors positively designed to reach that goal.

That which separates the professional teacher from anyone off the street is the teacher's ability to go beyond mere description of behavior. Keep that in mind when you write comments that will be read by students, by their parents or guardians, and by other teachers.

GRADING AND MARKING STUDENT ACHIEVEMENT

If conditions were ideal (which they are not), and if teachers did their job perfectly (which many of us do not), then all students would receive top marks (the ultimate in mastery or quality learning), and there would be less of a need to talk about grading and marking. Mastery learning implies that some end point of learning is attainable, but there probably isn't an end point. In any case, because conditions for teaching are never ideal and we teachers are mere

> A teacher's concern should not be with deciding which students are better than others but in helping each succeed.

humans, let us continue with this topic of grading that is undoubtedly of special interest to you, to your students, to their parents or guardians, and to school counselors, administrators and school boards, potential employers, providers of scholarships, and college admissions officers.

The term *achievement* is used frequently throughout this resource guide. What is the meaning of the term? Achievement means accomplishment, but is it accomplishment of the instructional objectives against preset standards, or is it simply accomplishment? Most teachers probably choose the former, where the teacher subjectively establishes a standard that must be met in order for a student to receive a certain grade for an assignment, project, test, quarter, semester, or course. Achievement, then, is decided by degrees of accomplishment.

Preset standards are usually expressed in percentages (degrees of accomplishment) needed for marks or ABC grades. If no student achieves the standard required for an *A* grade, for example, then no student receives an *A*. On the other hand, if all students meet the preset standard for the *A* grade, then all receive *A*s. Determining student grades on the basis of preset standards is referred to as *criterion-referenced grading*.

Criterion-Referenced versus Norm-Referenced Grading

While criterion-referenced (or competency-based) grading is based on preset standards, norm-referenced grading measures the relative accomplishment of individuals in the group (e.g., one classroom of seventh-grade language arts students) or in a larger group (e.g., all students enrolled in seventh-grade language arts) by comparing and ranking students, and is commonly known as "grading on a [normal] curve." Because it encourages competition and discourages cooperative learning, for the determination of student grades *norm-referenced grading is not recommended*. Norm-referenced grading is educationally dysfunctional. For your personal interest, after several years of teaching, you can produce frequency-distribution studies of grades you have given over a period of time, but *do not* give students grades that are based on a curve. Grades for student achievement should be tied to performance levels and determined on the basis of each student's achievement toward preset standards. As stated elsewhere, "Teachers who develop success-oriented partnerships with students have no use for grading on a curve. They know they are not the best teacher they can be until every student attains an *A*—demonstrating the highest possible achievement on rigorous high-quality assessments" (Stiggins, 2001, p. 444).

In criterion-referenced grading, the aim is to communicate information about an individual student's progress in knowledge and work skills in comparison to that student's previous attainment or in the pursuit of an absolute, such as content mastery. Criterion-referenced grading is featured in continuous-progress curricula, competency-based curricula, and other programs that focus on quality learning and individualized education.

Criterion-referenced grading is based on the level at which each student meets the specified objectives (standards) for the course or grade level. The objectives must be clearly stated to represent important student learning outcomes. This approach implies that effective teaching and learning result in high grades (*A*s) or marks for most students. In fact, when a mastery concept is used, the student must accomplish the objectives before being allowed to proceed to the next learning task. The philosophy of teachers who favor criterion-referenced procedures recognizes individual potential. Such teachers accept the challenge of finding teaching strategies to help students progress from where they are to the next designated level. Instead of wondering how Sally compares with Juanita, the comparison is between what Sally could do yesterday and what she can do today and how well these performances compare to the preset standard. Such is the purpose of effort today in so-called *value-added assessment,* discussed at the start of this chapter.

Most school systems use some sort of combination of both norm-referenced and criterion-referenced data usage. Sometimes both kinds of information are useful. For example, a report card for a student in the eighth grade might indicate how that student is meeting certain criteria, such as an *A* grade for addition of fractions. Another entry might show that this mastery is expected, however, in the sixth grade. Both criterion- and norm-referenced data may be communicated to the parents or guardians and the student. Appropriate procedures should be used: A criterion-referenced approach to show whether or not the student can accomplish the task, and if so, to what degree, and a norm-referenced approach to show how well that student performs compared to the larger group to which the student belongs. The latter is important data for achievement testing on state standardized testing, some of which is related to NCLB legislation, for college admissions officers, and for committees that appropriate academic scholarships.

Determining Grades

Once entered onto school transcripts, grades have significant impact upon the futures of students. When determining achievement grades for student performance, you must make several important and professional decisions. Although in a few schools, and for certain classes or assignments, only marks such as *E, S,* and *I* or "pass/no pass," are used; percentages of accomplishment and letter grades are used for most middle level schools. For

determining student grades, consider the guidelines presented in the following paragraphs.

At the start of the school term, explain your marking and grading policies first to yourself, then to your students and to their parents or guardians at "back-to-school night," or by a written explanation that is sent home, put on your website, or all three. Share with students and parents/guardians sample scoring and grading rubrics. In addition, include your grading policy in the syllabus.

When converting your interpretation of a student's accomplishments to a letter grade, be as objective as possible. For the selection of criteria for *ABC* grades, select a percentage standard, such as 92 percent for an *A,* 85 percent for a *B,* 75 percent for a *C,* and 65 percent for a *D.* The cutoff percentages used are your decision, although the district, school, program area, team, or department may have established guidelines that you are expected to follow.

For the determination of students' final grades, many teachers use a point system, in which things that students write, say, and do are given points (but not for journals or portfolios, except, perhaps, for whether the student does one or not); then the possible point total is the factor for grade determination. For example, if 92 percent is the cutoff for an *A* and 500 points are possible, then any student with 460 points or more ($500 \times .92$) has achieved an *A.* Likewise, for a test or any other assignment, if the value is 100 points, the cutoff for an *A* is 92 ($100 \times .92$). With a point system and preset standards, the teacher and students, at any time during the grading period, always know the current points possible and can easily calculate a student's current grade standing. Then, as far as a current grade is concerned, students always know where they stand in the course.

Build your grading policy around degrees of accomplishment rather than failure, and where students proceed from one accomplishment to the next. This is *continuous promotion,* not necessarily the promotion of the student from one grade level to the next, but within the classroom. (However, rather than grade-level designations some schools use the concept of continuous promotion from the time of student entry into the school through the student's graduation or exit from it.)

Remember that *assessment* and *grading* are not synonymous. As discussed at the start of this chapter, assessment implies the collection of information from a variety of sources, including measurement techniques and subjective observations. These data, then, become the basis for arriving at a final grade, which in effect is a final value judgment. Grades are one aspect of evaluation and are intended to communicate educational progress to students and to their parents or guardians. To be valid as an indicator of that progress, you *must* use a variety of sources of data for determination of a student's final grade.

About Makeup Work.   Decide beforehand your policy about makeup work, ensuring it is consistent with any school-wide policy standards on the issue that might exist. Students will be absent and will miss assignments and tests, so it is best that your policies about late assignments and missed tests be clearly communicated to students and to their parents or guardians. For makeup work, please consider the following.

Homework Assignments.   We recommend that after due dates have been negotiated or set for assignments no credit or reduced credit be given for work that is turned in late. Sometimes, however, a student has legitimate reasons for not being able to complete the assignment by the due date, and the teacher must exercise a professional judgment in each instance. Although it is important that teachers have rules and procedures—and that they consistently apply those—the teacher is a professional who must consider all aspects of a student's situation and, after doing so, show compassion, caring, and regard for the human situation.

Tests.   If students are absent when tests are given, you have several options. Some teachers allow students to miss or discount one test per grading period. Another technique is to allow each student to substitute a written homework assignment or project for one missed test. Still another option is to give the absent student the choice of either taking a makeup test or having the next test count double. When makeup tests are given, the makeup test should be taken within a week of the regular test unless there is a compelling reason (e.g., medical or family problem) why this cannot happen. Once more than a week has passed, then we recommend an automatic option of one of the choices other than the makeup test. Whatever your policy, be sure it is well stated and understood by students.

Sometimes students miss a testing period, not because of being absent from school but because of involvement in other school activities. In those instances, the student may come in on a makeup day (see section that follows), or may be able to arrange to come in and take the test during another of your class periods, or your prep period, on that day or the next. If a student is absent during performance testing, the logistics and possible diminished reliability of having to readminister the test for one student may necessitate giving the student an alternate paper-and-pencil test or some other option.

Makeup day.   Some middle school teachers set aside an afternoon each week after school, or perhaps during "freeze time" (see Chapter 1), at which time students can come to the classroom and make up quizzes, tests, or other in-class assignments. Sometimes these arrangements are by teaching team or department with teachers taking turns sharing the after-school supervision. Students are responsible for checking with their teacher about what they must make up and for arranging their schedules so that they can remain after school on makeup day to complete their assignments.

Quizzes.   Many teachers give frequent and brief quizzes, as often as every day. As opposed to tests (see next section), quizzes are usually brief (perhaps taking only five minutes of class time) and intended to reinforce the importance of frequent study and review. Sometimes a quiz might be simply for review and not counted toward grades. (However, quizzes should be prepared using the same care and precision as presented in the guidelines that follow in the sections for testing and preparation of assessment items.) When quizzes are given at frequent intervals, no single quiz should count very much toward the student's final grade; therefore, you will probably want to avoid having to schedule and give makeup quizzes for students who were absent when a quiz was given. The following are reasonable options to administering makeup quizzes, and are presented here in order of our preference, with the first being our preferred choice.

- Give a certain number of quizzes during a grading period, say 10, but allow a student to discount a few quiz scores, say 2 of the 10, thereby allowing the student to discount a low score or a missed quiz due to absence, or both.
- Count the next quiz double for a student who missed one due to absence. About the only problem with this option is when a student misses several quizzes. If a student misses several quizzes, then for that student count the unit test a certain and relative percentage greater.

By the way, we see absolutely no positive educational value in using "pop" or unannounced quizzes for use in determining student grades.

Caution about Assigning Zero Credit.   Be cautious before ever assigning a score of zero to a student for a missed or incomplete assignment, test, quiz, or for cheating, especially when using a point system for grading. Depending on the weight of the assignment in relation to the total points possible for the grading period, the assigning of a zero grade can have an extreme negative effect on the student's total grade, thus becoming an act of punishment by the teacher rather than a fair representation of the grade earned (or, in this instance, not earned) by the student. [*Note:* See for example the persuasive argument for using a 4-point rather than 100-point grading system as put forward by Douglas Reeves in the article listed in the suggested readings at the end of this chapter.] This is another example where you, the teacher, must exercise professional judgment. In addition to those mentioned, alternatives to using a zero grade include ignoring the missing grade and calculating the student's final (quarter or semester) percentage grade using, for that student, a lesser total points possible, or, if not counter to school policy, assigning a grade of "incomplete" that gives the student some additional time to complete the work.

TESTING FOR ACHIEVEMENT

One source of information used for determining grades is data obtained from testing for student achievement. There are two kinds of tests, those that are standardized and those that are not.

Standardized (Formal) versus Nonstandardized (Informal) Tests

Whereas *informal tests* are constructed by classroom teachers, *standardized (formal) tests* are those that have been designed by specialists, usually by specialists within commercial testing bureaus, and that are then administered, scored, and interpreted under standard conditions (Linn & Gronlund, 2000). Standardized tests are used by states and districts to determine and compare student achievement, principally in the subjects of reading and mathematics. On usually a state or national level, norms for particular age groups of children are established from its administration to large groups of children. Standardized tests are also used in college entrance requirements. Standardized, norm-referenced tests are best for diagnostic purposes and should not be used for determining student grades.

As said in Chapter 1, the administration of standardized achievement tests and the use of their results are major concerns to classroom teachers and school administrators in particular. In some locales, for example, their salaries and indeed their jobs are contingent on the results of student scores on standardized achievement tests. As we said at the outset of this chapter, it is neither our purpose nor does space in this book allow a consideration of standardized achievement testing. Rather, the focus is on nonstandardized, criterion-referenced tests, ones that you design (or collaboratively design) for your own unique group of students for determination of their level of learning on particular instructional objectives.

Competent planning, preparing, administering, and scoring of tests is an important professional skill. You may want to refer to the guidelines that follow while you are student teaching, then again during your initial years as an employed teacher.

Purposes for Informal Testing

Informal tests can be designed for several purposes, and a variety of kinds of tests and alternate test items will keep your testing program interesting, useful, and reliable. As a college student, you are probably most experienced with testing for measuring for achievement, but as a classroom teacher of young adolescent learners you will use tests for other reasons as well. Additional purposes for testing are:

- to assess and aid in curriculum development
- determiners of teaching effectiveness
- to help students develop positive attitudes, appreciations, and values
- to help students increase their understanding and retention of facts, principles, skills, and concepts
- to motivate students
- to provide diagnostic information for planning for individualization of the instruction
- to provide review and drill to enhance teaching and learning
- sources of informational data for students and their parents/guardians.

Frequency for Informal Testing

First of all, assessment for student learning should be continual; that is, it should be going on every minute of every class day. For grading or marking purposes, it is difficult to generalize about how often to formally test for student achievement, but we believe that testing should be cumulative and frequent. By "cumulative," we mean that each assessment should assess for the student's understanding of previously learned material as well as for the current unit of study; that is, *it should assess for connected learning*. By "frequent," for classes that meet daily we mean as often as once a week. Advantages of assessment that is cumulative include the review, reinforcement, and articulation of old material with the most recent. Advantages of frequent and imbedded assessment include a reduction in student anxiety over tests and an increase in the validity of the summative assessment.

Helping Students Deal with Test Anxiety

Test taking is becoming an increasingly complex and important facet in the educational lives of young people, and begins at an ever-increasing younger age. For example, as early as grade 3 children in many states must pass tests in reading and mathematics to be promoted to the next grade level. Children who are still preteens are now taking the Scholastic Aptitude Test (SAT), an entrance examination requirement for many colleges and universities and usually taken in the junior year of high school. Some young adolescent children take the SAT for the practice while others take it to qualify for talent search programs such as the California State University at Sacramento Talent Search Program or the Johns Hopkins University Center for Talented Youth. Because of increased pressures on young people you may have children in your classroom who knowingly or unknowingly experience and indicate symptoms of text anxiety, symptoms such as sleeplessness, nausea, and headaches. As can be expected from the increased amount of standardized testing nationwide, overall test anxiety in young people of all age groups is reported to be on the increase (Casbarro, 2004; McDonald, 2001). Test anxiety today is a major factor contributing to a variety of negative outcomes (Harris & Coy, 2003). You can help alleviate students' test-related stress by learning and teaching both test-taking strategies and techniques that your students can use to manage their anxiety.

Potential causes of test anxiety in young adolescents include: (a) expectations of the adults in their lives, and the child's fear of not meeting those expectations, (b) peer pressures, and the (c) feeling of lack of control and/or the inability to change one's current life situation.

When working with an anxious student you can help by (a) establishing a rapport with the student whereby the student has confidence in your suggestions and (b) giving specific suggestions to the student such as being positive about the outcomes, use test time efficiently and wisely, be prepared, read directions carefully, making an outline before answering a performance or essay-type question, and to use practice testing.

Finally, to further assist in the learner's control of his/her anxiety help the child learn relaxation techniques, such as deep breathing while counting to 10, stretching out and then contracting body muscles and then relaxing, and thinking of a happy memory. School counselors may know of intervention services for referral of the most serious cases of test anxiety.

If, as a teacher, you believe you too may be experiencing a degree of anxiety, not from having to take tests but from pressure of having to administer state-mandated tests, then you may profit from practicing techniques for stress management, such as those shown in Figure 7.6.

Figure 7.6   Techniques for easing stress.

1. Breathing exercise: Inhale and hold breath while counting to 10, then exhale slowly. Repeat 10 times.
2. Change your environment for a few minutes, either by taking a walk or by closing your eyes and imagining yourself in a wonderful and relaxing place.
3. Stretching exercises: For 5–10 minutes stretch legs, arms, back, shoulders, and neck.

Test Construction

After determining the reasons for which you are designing and administering a test, you need to identify the specific instructional objectives the test is being designed to measure. As you learned in Chapter 5, your written instructional objectives are specific so that you can write assessment items designed to measure against those objectives, and that is referred to as *criterion-referenced assessment.* When the objectives are aligned with specific curriculum standards, as they usually are or should be, then it can also be referred to as *standards-based assessment.*

Thus, the first step in test construction is identification of the purpose(s) for the test. The second step is to identify the objectives to be measured, and the third step is to prepare the test items, assuring you have a balance of question types and not solely low-order recall questions. The best time to prepare draft items is after you have prepared your instructional objectives—while the objectives are fresh in your mind, which means before the lessons are taught. After a lesson is taught you will want to rework your first draft of the test items related to that lesson to make any modifications to the draft items as a result of the instruction that occurred.

Administering Tests

For many young adolescent students, test taking can be a time of high anxiety. They demonstrate test anxiety in various ways. Just before and during testing some are quiet and thoughtful, while others are noisy and disruptive. To more accurately measure student achievement you will want to take steps to reduce their anxiety. To control or reduce student anxieties, consider the following discussion as guidelines for administering tests.

Since many people respond best to familiar routine, plan your assessment program so tests are given at regular intervals and administered at the same time and in the same way. In some schools, days of the week are assigned to departments for administering major tests.

Avoid tests that are too long and that will take too much time. Sometimes beginning teachers have unreasonable expectations of children about their attention spans during testing. Frequent testing with frequent sampling of student knowledge is preferred over infrequent and long tests that attempt to cover everything.

Attend to creature comforts. Try to arrange the classroom so it is well ventilated, the temperature is comfortable, and, when giving paper-and-pencil tests individually, the seats are well spaced. If spacing is a problem, then consider using individual privacy protectors (discussed in Chapter 4), group testing, or using alternate forms of the test, where students seated adjacent to one another have different forms of the same test (e.g., multiple-choice answer alternatives are arranged in different order).

Before distributing the test, explain to students what they are to do when finished, such as quietly begin an anchor activity, because not all of the students will finish at the same time. For many young adolescents it is unreasonable to expect them to just sit quietly after finishing a test; they need something to do. However, as former teachers we, the authors of this book, had no problem with our young adolescent students who, upon finishing a test, wished simply to put their heads down on their desks and rest.

When ready to test, don't drag it out. Distribute tests quickly and efficiently. Once testing has begun, avoid interrupting the students. (It is amazing to us how often teachers interrupt students once the students are at a task, while those same teachers resent being interrupted themselves.) Items or announcements of important information can be written on the board or, if unrelated to the test, held until all are finished with the test. Stay in the room and visually monitor the students. If the test is not going to take an entire class period (and most shouldn't), and it's a major test, then administer it at the start of the class period, if possible, unless you are planning a test review just prior to it (although that seems rather late to conduct a meaningful review; a review just prior to giving the test is likely to upset those who discover they don't know the material like they thought they did). It's improbable that any teacher can effectively teach a lesson with a reasonable degree of student interest in it just prior to or immediately following a major test.

Controlling Cheating

Whatever the causes, some students will try to cheat on tests. There are steps you can take to discourage cheating or to reduce the opportunity and pressure that cause students to cheat. Consider the following.

Preventing Cheating. Space students or, as mentioned earlier, use alternate forms of the test or use privacy protectors. Frequent testing and not allowing a single test to count too much toward a term grade reduce test anxiety and the pressure that can cause cheating. Prepare test questions that are clear and unambiguous, thereby reducing student frustration caused by a question or instructions that students do not understand. As said before, avoid tests that are too long and that will take too much time. During long tests, some students become discouraged and restless, and that is a time when classroom management problems can occur.

By their sheer nature, performance tests can cause even greater pressure on students and can also provide greater opportunity for cheating. When administering performance tests to an entire class it is best to have several monitors, such as members of your teaching team. If that isn't possible, consider testing groups of students rather than individuals. Evaluation of test performance, then, would be based on group rather than individual achievement. However, we tend to agree with those who argue against the use of any kind of assessment of an individual that is based to any degree on group process and functioning. It is very difficult, if not impossible, to rationalize giving an individual student a grade based on a group task.

Consider using open-text and open-notebook tests or allowing each student to prepare a page of notes to use during the test. When students can use their books and notes, it not only reduces anxiety but it helps with their organization of information and the retention of what has been learned. The use of open notes and open-book testing are useful adaptations that are appreciated by many students (Eilertsen & Valdermo, 2000; Nelson, Jaymanthi, Epstein, & Bursuck, 2000).

Stopping Cheating. The preceding paragraphs provide hints to prevent students from cheating. If you suspect cheating is occurring, move and stand in the area of the suspected student. Usually that will stop it.

Dealing with Cheating. When you suspect cheating has occurred, you are faced with a dilemma. Unless your suspicion is backed by solid proof you are advised to ignore it, but keep a close watch on the student the next time to prevent cheating from happening. Think not of your job as *catching* students being dishonest but that of *discouraging* dishonesty. If you have absolute proof that a student has cheated, then you are obligated to proceed with school policy on student cheating, and that may call for a session with the counselor or the student and the student's parent or guardian and perhaps an automatic *F* grade on the test.

Determining the Time Needed to Take a Test

Again, avoid giving tests that are too long and that will take too much time. As a general rule (and we are speaking of teacher-made tests, not about standardized achievement tests or other tests given to students that are out of the teacher's control), testing duration should be limited to 30–40 minutes maximum for children in grades 5 through 8. Preparing and administering effective tests is a skill that you will develop over time. In the meantime, it is best to test frequently and to use tests that sample student achievement rather than try for a comprehensive measure of that achievement.

Some students take more time on the same test than do others. You want to avoid giving too much time, or classroom management problems will result. On the other hand, you don't want to cut short the time needed by students who can do well but need more time to think and to write. As a very general guide, use the table of time needed for different types of test items (Table 7.1). This is only a guide for determining the approximate

Table 7.1 Approximate Time to Allow for Testing as Determined by the Types of Items*

Type of Test Item	Time Needed per Item
Matching	30 seconds per matching item
Completion	30 seconds per item
Multiple-choice	1 minute per item
Completion drawing	2–3 minutes
Arrangement	2–3 minutes
Identification	2–3 minutes
Short explanation	2–3 minutes
Essay and performance	10 or more minutes

(*Students with disabilities and ELL students, of course, may need more time per item, or you may need to administer the test in briefer sessions or provide some other accommodation, depending on the individual's special needs situation.)

amount of time to allow students to complete a test. For example, for a test made up of 10 multiple-choice items, five arrangement items, and two short-explanation items, you would want to plan for about 30 minutes for students to complete the test.

PREPARING ASSESSMENT ITEMS

Preparing and writing the best assessment items is yet another professional skill, and to become proficient at it takes study, time, practice, feedback, and reflection. Because of the importance of an assessment program, you will want to assume this professional charge seriously and responsibly. Although poorly prepared items take no time at all to construct, they will cause you more trouble than you can ever imagine. As a professional, you should take time to study different types of assessment items that can be used and how best to write them, and then practice writing them. Remember, when preparing assessment items, ensure that they match and sufficiently cover the target objectives. In addition, you should prepare each item carefully enough to be reasonably confident that each item will be understood by the student in the manner that you anticipate its being understood. With the diversity of students in today's public school classroom, especially with respect to their proficiency in oral and written English language and the inclusion of students with exceptionalities, this is an especially important point. For your most important tests, such as unit tests and semester exams, ask a trusted colleague or friend to read your test for clarity and errors and to check the test's key for accuracy, something that you and your team members probably should want to do on a regular basis. Finally, after administering a test, you must take time to analyze the results and reflect on the value of each item before ever using that item again.

Classification of Assessment Items

Assessment items can be classified as verbal (oral or written words), visual (pictures and diagrams), and manipulative or performance (handling of materials and equipment; performing). Written verbal items have traditionally been the items most frequently used in testing. However, visual items and visual tests are useful, for example, when working with students who lack fluency with the written word or when testing ELL students.

Performance items and tests are useful when measuring for psychomotor skill development. Common examples are performance testing of a student's ability to carry a microscope or hold a jumping rope in place (gross motor skill) or to focus a microscope or to jump rope (fine motor skill). Performance testing also can and should be part of a wider testing program that includes testing for higher-level thinking skills and knowledge, as, for example, when a student or small group of students are given the problem of creating from discarded materials a habitat for an imaginary animal and then display, write about, and orally present their product to the rest of the class.

As we have previously noted, educators have an interest in this last described form of performance testing as a means of assessing learning that is closer to measuring for the real thing—that is, authentic. In a program for teacher preparation, micro peer teaching and student teaching are examples of performance assessment; that is, assessment practices used to assess the teacher candidate's ability to teach (to perform). It seems axiomatic that assessment of student teaching is a more authentic assessment of a candidate's ability to teach than would be a written (paper-and-pencil test) or verbal (oral test) form of assessment. Although less direct and perhaps less reliable than a checklist observation and analysis of a student teacher actually teaching, an observation of a student teacher's analysis of a video-recorded episode of another teacher's performance would be another way of more authentically assessing a teacher's ability to teach than would be a simple paper-and-pencil test without the visuals provided by the video recording.

Performance Testing

Performance testing is usually more expensive and time-consuming than is verbal testing, which in turn is more time demanding and expensive than is written testing. However, a good program of assessment will use alternate forms of assessment and not rely solely on one form (such as written) and one type of written item (such as multiple choice).

The type of test and items that you use depend upon your purpose and objectives. Carefully consider the alternatives within that framework. To provide validity checks and to account for the individual differences of students, an assessment program should include items from all three types. That is what writers of articles in professional journals are referring to when they talk about *alternative assessment*. They are encouraging the use of multiple assessment items, as opposed to the traditional heavy reliance on objective items, such as multiple-choice questions.

General Guidelines for Preparing for Informal Assessment of Student Learning

Every test that you create and administer to your students should represent your best professional effort. It should be clean and sans spelling and grammar errors. A quickly and poorly prepared test can cause you more grief than you can imagine. One that is obviously hurriedly prepared and wrought with spelling and grammar errors will quickly be frowned upon by discerning parents or guardians. If you are a student teacher, such sloppiness and unprofessional output will certainly bring about an admonishment from your university supervisor and, if it continues, your speedy release from the teacher preparation program. Consider the following general guidelines when preparing to assess for student learning.

- Assure that all objectives or relevant standards are being measured.
- Assure that each item is clear and unambiguous to all students.
- Assure that each item is reliable; that it measures the intended objective. It's usually a good idea to have more than one item measuring for the same objective.
- Because it is time-consuming to write the most effective assessment items, you are advised to maintain a bank of items, with each item coded according to its matching instructional objective and according to its domain of learning (cognitive, affective, or psychomotor), and perhaps according to its level within the hierarchy of a particular domain. Another code could indicate whether the item requires thinking that is recall, processing, or application. Computer software programs are available for this. Ready-made test item banks are available and accompany many programs or textbooks. If you use them, be certain that the items match your course objectives and that they are well written. It doesn't follow that because they were published they are well written nor match what students were

supposed to have learned. When preparing items for your test bank, use your creative thinking and best writing skills. Prepare items that match your objectives, put them aside, think about them, and then work them over again.

- Include several kinds of items and assessment instruments (see 12 types that follow).
- Plan each item to be difficult enough for the poorly prepared student but easy enough for the student who is well prepared.

Attaining Content Validity

To ensure that your test measures what is supposed to be measured, you can construct a table of specifications. A two-way grid indicates behavior in one dimension and content in the other (see Figures 7.7 and 7.8).

In this grid, behavior relates to the three domains: cognitive, affective, and psychomotor. In Figure 7.7, the cognitive domain is divided, according to Bloom's taxonomy, into six categories: knowledge or simple recall, comprehension, application, analysis, synthesis (often involving an original product in oral or written form), and evaluation. The specifications table in Figure 7.7 does not specify levels within the affective and psychomotor domains.

To use a table of specifications, the teacher examining objectives for the unit decides what emphasis should be given to the behavior and to the content. For example, if vocabulary development is a concern for this sixth-grade study of matter and energy, then probably 20 percent of the test on vocabulary would be appropriate, but 50 percent would be unsuitable. This planning enables the teacher to design a test that fits the situation rather than a haphazard test that does not correspond to the objectives either in content or behavior emphasis. Since this is to be an objective test and it is so difficult to write objective items to test affective and psychomotor behaviors, this table of specifications calls for no test items in these areas. If these areas are included in the unit objectives, some other assessment devices must be used to test learning in these domains. The teacher could also show the objectives tested, as indicated within parentheses in Figure 7.7. Then, a check later on inclusion of all objectives is easy.

Preferred by some teachers is the alternative table shown in Figure 7.8. Rather than differentiating among all six of Bloom's cognitive levels, this table separates cognitive objectives into just three levels: those that require simple low-level recall of knowledge, those that require information processing, and those that require application of new knowledge. In addition, the affective and psychomotor domains each are divided into low- and high-level behaviors. A third alternative, not illustrated here, is a table of specifications that shows all levels of each of the three domains.

Figure 7.7 Table of specifications I.

CONTENT	BEHAVIORS								TOTAL
SOCIAL STUDIES GRADE 8	COGNITIVE						AFFEC-TIVE	PSYCHO-MOTOR	
Ancient Greece	*Knowledge*	*Compre-hension*	*Appli-cation*	*Analysis*	*Synthesis*	*Evaluation*			
I. Vocabulary development		2 (1,2)	1 (2)						3
II. Concepts		2 (3,4)	2 (4)						4
III. Applications	1 (5)	1 (5)	1 (5)	1 (5)	1 (5)	1 (5)			6
IV. Problem solving		1 (6)		1 (6)					2
TOTAL	1	6	4	2	1	1			15

Figure 7.8 Table of specifications II.

CONTENT	BEHAVIORS							TOTAL
	COGNITIVE			AFFECTIVE		PSYCHOMOTOR		
	Input	*Processing*	*Application*	*Low*	*High*	*Low*	*High*	
I.								
II.								
III.								
IV.								
TOTAL								

ASSESSMENT ITEMS: DESCRIPTIONS, EXAMPLES, AND GUIDELINES FOR PREPARING AND USING 12 TYPES

This section presents descriptions, advantages and disadvantages, and guidelines for preparing and using 12 types of assessment items. When reading about the advantages and disadvantages of each, you will notice that some types are appropriate for use in direct or performance assessment, while others are not.

Arrangement

Description: Terms or real objects (realia) are to be arranged in a specified order.

Example 1: Arrange the following list of events on a time line in order of their occurrence: Maximilian I elected King of Germany; Maximilian I becomes Holy Roman Emperor; Diet of Augsburg establishes Council of Regency, divides Germany into six regions; Charles I of Spain becomes Holy Roman Emperor; Ferdinand I assumes the title of Holy Roman Emperor.

Example 2: The assortment of balls on the table represents the planets in our solar system. [*Note:* The balls are of various sizes, such as marbles, golf balls, tennis balls, basketballs, and so on, each labeled with a planetary name. A large beach ball is labeled *Sun.*] Arrange the balls in their proper order around the sun.

Advantages: This type of item tests for knowledge of sequence and order, and is good for review, for starting discussions, and for performance assessment. Example 2 is also an example of a performance test item.

Disadvantages: Scoring could be difficult, so be cautious, meticulous, and open to lateral thinking (see Chapter 3) when using this type for grading purposes. For instance, in Example 2, the student could rightfully place either Neptune or Pluto as the outermost planet in the solar system (because of the extreme oval shape of their orbits, Pluto and Neptune alternate in their relative positions from the Sun), or even omit Pluto (most scientists today believe that Pluto is actually the largest or nearest member of a group of icy asteroids found in the outer solar system).

Guideline for use: To enhance reliability, you may need to have students include the rationale for their arrangement on an answer sheet, making it a combined arrangement and short-explanation type of assessment. This is useful for small, heterogeneous group assessment to allow students to share and learn from their collaborative thinking and reasoning.

Completion Drawing

Description: An incomplete drawing is presented and the student is to complete it.

Example 1: Connect the following items with arrow lines to show the stages from introduction of a new bill until it becomes law (items not included here).

Example 2: In the following food web (not included here), draw arrow lines indicating which organisms are consumers and which are producers.

Advantages: This requires less time than would a complete drawing that might be required in an essay item. Scoring is relatively easy although you should be alert and allow for lateral thinking.

Disadvantages: Care needs to be exercised in the instructions so students do not misinterpret the expectation.

Guidelines for use: Use occasionally for diversion, but take care in preparing. This type of assessment can be instructive when assessing for student thinking and reasoning as it can measure conceptual knowledge. Consider making the item a combined completion-drawing, short-explanation type by having students include their rationales for the thinking behind their drawing completion. Be sure to allow space for their explanations. This is useful for small, heterogeneous group assessment to allow students to share and learn from their collaborative thinking and reasoning.

Completion Statement

Description: Sometimes called a "fill-in" item, an incomplete sentence is presented and the student is to complete it by filling in the blank space(s).

Example 1: A group of words that have a special meaning, such as "a skeleton in the closet," is called a(n) _____.

Example 2: To test their hypotheses, scientists and social scientists conduct _____.

Advantages: This type is easy to devise, take, and score.

Disadvantages: When using this type, there is a tendency to emphasize rote memory and to measure procedural knowledge only. Providing a word bank of possible answers is sometimes useful, especially with mainstreamed students, to reduce dependency on rote memory. It is difficult to write this type of item to measure for conceptual knowledge and higher levels of cognition. You must be alert for a correct response that is different from the expected. For instance, in Example 2, although the teacher's key has *experiments* as the correct answer, a student might answer the question with *research, investigations,* or *tests* or some other response that is equally valid.

Guideline for use: Use occasionally for review or for preassessment of student knowledge. Avoid using this for grading unless you can write quality items that extend student thinking beyond mere recall. In all instances, avoid copying items verbatim from the student book. As with all types, be sure to provide adequate space for students' answers, and large spaces for students with motor control difficulties. Try to use only one blank per item and to write so the blank is at the end of the sentence (the reason it is called *completion*) rather than at the front or in the middle. Try also to keep the blanks equal in length. This is useful for small, heterogeneous group assessment to allow students to share and learn from their collaborative thinking and reasoning. Rewriting the item as a statement makes the item a short-answer type, which students might prefer over the completion statement type. Rewritten as short-answer questions, the two examples above would appear as (a) What do we call a group of words that have a special meaning, such as "a skeleton in the closet"? (b) What is it that scientists and social scientists conduct to test their hypotheses?

Correction

Description: This is similar to the completion type, except that sentences or paragraphs are complete but with italicized or underlined words that can be changed to make the sentences correct.

Example 1: <u>There</u> over <u>their</u> with <u>they're</u> friends.

Example 2: 1, 1, 2, 3, 5, 8, *12*, 21, 34, *87*, 89.

Advantages: Use of this type can be enjoyable for teachers and students especially when used for the purposes of preassessment of student knowledge and for review.

Disadvantages: As with completion, correction tends to measure for low-level recall and rote memory (although this is not necessarily the case in Example 2; if a student is unfamiliar with the Fibonacci number series in mathematics, it would be a relatively high-level question). The underlined incorrect items could be so whimsical that they might cause more classroom disturbance than you want.

Guidelines for use: Use occasionally for diversion and discussion. Try to write items that measure for higher-level cognition. Consider making it a combined correction, short-explanation type. Be sure to allow space for student explanations.

Essay

Description: A question or problem is presented, and the student is to compose a response in the form of sustained prose, using his or her own words, phrases, and ideas, within the limits of the question or problem.

Example 1: In the story just read does the author elaborate the setting in great detail or barely sketch it? Explain your response.

Example 2: A healthy green coleus plant sitting in front of you has been planted in fertile soil and sealed in a glass jar. If we place the jar on the window sill, where it will receive strong sunlight, and if we maintain a temperature inside the jar of 60 to 80 degrees Fahrenheit, how long do you predict the plant will live? Justify your prediction.

Advantages: This type of question measures conceptual knowledge and higher mental processes, such as the ability to synthesize material and express ideas in clear and precise written language. It is especially useful in integrated thematic teaching. It provides practice in written expression and can be used in performance assessment, as in the case of Example 2.

Disadvantages: Essay items require a good deal of time to read and score. They tend to provide an unreliable sampling of achievement and are vulnerable to teacher subjectivity and unreliable scoring. Furthermore, they tend to punish the student who writes slowly and laboriously, or who has limited proficiency in the written language but may have achieved as well as a student who writes faster or is more proficient in the language. Essay items tend to favor students who have fluency with words but whose achievement may not necessarily be better. In addition, unless the students have been given instruction in the meaning of key directive verbs and how to respond to them, the teacher should not assume that all students understand such verbs (such as *explain* in the first example and *justify* in the second).

GUIDELINES FOR USING AN ESSAY ITEM

1. When preparing an essay-only test, many questions, each requiring a relatively short prose response (see the short-explanation type), are preferable to a smaller number of questions requiring long prose responses. Briefer answers tend to be more precise, and using many items provides a more reliable sampling of student achievement. When preparing a short prose response essay question, avoid using words verbatim from the student textbook.

2. Allow students adequate test time for a full response.

3. Different qualities of achievement are more likely to be comparable when all students must answer the same questions, as opposed to selecting which they answer from a list of essay items.

4. After preparing essay items, make a tentative scoring key. Decide what key ideas you expect students to identify and how many points you will allot to each.

5. Students should be informed about the relative test value for each item. Point values, if different for each item, can be listed in the margin of the test next to each item.

6. Inform students of the role of spelling, grammar, and sentence structure in your scoring of their essay items.

7. When reading student essay responses, read all student papers for one item at a time in one sitting, and, while doing that, make notes to yourself; then repeat and while reading that item again, score each student's paper for that item. Repeat the process for the next item but modify the order of the pile of papers so you are not reading them in the same order by student. While scoring essay responses, keep in mind the nature of the objective being measured, which may or may not include the qualities of handwriting, grammar, spelling, punctuation, and neatness.

8. To nullify the "halo effect" that can occur when you know whose paper you are reading, have students put their name on the back of the paper or use a number code rather than names on essay papers, so while reading the papers, you are unaware of whose paper is being read.

9. While having some understanding of a concept, many young adolescents are not yet facile with written expression, so you must remember to be patient, tolerant, positive, and prescriptive. Mark papers with positive and constructive comments, showing students how they could have explained or responded better.

10. Prior to using this type of test item, give instruction and practice to students in responding to key directive verbs that will be used (see Figure 7.9).

Grouping

Description: Several items are presented, and the student is to select and group those that are in some way related.

Example 1: Separate the following words into two groups (words are not included here); those that are homonyms, place in group A and those that are not homonyms, place in group B.

Example 2: Circle the figure that is least like the others (showing a wrench, screwdriver, saw, and swing).

Advantages: This type of item tests knowledge of grouping and can be used to measure conceptual knowledge, for higher levels of cognition, and to stimulate discussion. As Example 2 shows, it can be similar to a multiple-choice type item.

Disadvantage: Remain alert for the student who has an alternative but valid rationale for her or his grouping.

Figure 7.9   Meaning of key directive verbs for essay item responses.

Compare asks for an analysis of similarity and difference, but with a greater emphasis on similarities or likenesses.

Contrast asks more for differences than for similarities.

Criticize asks for the good and bad of an idea or situation.

Define means to express clearly and concisely the meaning of a term, as from a dictionary or in the student's own words.

Diagram means to put quantities or numerical values into the form of a chart, graph, or drawing.

Discuss means to explain or argue, presenting various sides of events, ideas, or situations.

Enumerate means to name or list one after another, which is different from "explain briefly" or "tell in a few words."

Evaluate means to express worth, value, and judgment.

Explain means to describe, with emphasis on cause and effect.

Generalize means to arrive at a valid generalization from specific information provided.

Identify means to state recognizable or identifiable characteristics.

Illustrate means to describe by means of examples, figures, pictures, or diagrams.

Infer means to forecast what is likely to happen as a result of information provided.

Interpret means to describe or explain a given fact, theory, principle, or doctrine within a specific context.

Justify means to show reasons, with an emphasis on correct, positive, and advantageous.

List means just that, to simply name items in a category or to include them in a list, without much description.

Outline means to give a short summary with headings and subheadings.

Prove means to present materials as witnesses, proof, and evidence.

Relate means to tell how specified things are connected or brought into some kind of relationship.

Summarize means to recapitulate the main points without examples or illustrations.

Trace means to follow a history or series of events, step by step, by going backward over the evidence.

Guideline for use: To allow for an alternative correct response, consider making the item a combination grouping and short-explanation type, being certain to allow adequate space to encourage student explanations.

Identification

Description: Unknown "specimens" are to be identified by name or some other criterion.

Example 1: Identify each of the trees on our school campus (the trees have been numbered) as to whether it is evergreen or deciduous.

Example 2: Identify by style each of the three poems shown on the screen.

Advantages: Verbalization (i.e., the use of abstract symbolization) is less significant, as the student is working with real materials; it should measure for higher-level learning than simple recall. The item can also be written to measure for procedural understanding, such as for identification of steps in booting up a computer program. This is another useful type for authentic and performance assessments.

Disadvantages: Because of a special familiarity with the material, some students may have an advantage over others; to be fair, "specimens" used should be equally familiar or unfamiliar to all students. This type takes more time than many of the other item types, both for the teacher to prepare and for students to do.

Guidelines for use: Whatever "specimens" are used, they must be familiar to all or to none of the students,

and they must be clear, not confusing. For example, fuzzy photographs or unclear photocopies, dried and incomplete biological specimens, and garbled music recordings can be confusing and frustrating to try to discern. Consider using dyad or team rather than individual testing.

Matching

Description: Students are to match related items from a list of numbered items to a list of lettered choices or in some way to connect the items that are the same or related.

Example 1: In the blank space next to each description in Column A (stem or premises column) put the letter of the correct answer from Column B (answer or response column).

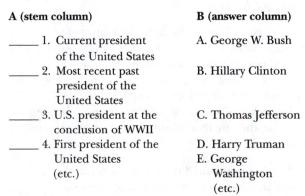

A (stem column)	B (answer column)
_____ 1. Current president of the United States	A. George W. Bush
_____ 2. Most recent past president of the United States	B. Hillary Clinton
_____ 3. U.S. president at the conclusion of WWII	C. Thomas Jefferson
_____ 4. First president of the United States (etc.)	D. Harry Truman
	E. George Washington (etc.)

Example 2: Match items in Column A (stem column) to those in Column B (answer column) by drawing lines connecting the matched pairs.

Column A	Column B
ann/enn	conquer
auto	large
min	self
vic/vinc	small
(etc.)	year
	(etc.)

Advantages: Matching items can measure for ability to judge relationships and to differentiate between similar facts, ideas, definitions, and concepts. They are easy to score and can test a broad range of content. They reduce guessing, especially if one group (e.g., answer column) contains more items than the other; are interesting to students; and are adaptable for performance assessment.

Disadvantages: Although the matching item is adaptable for performance assessment, items are not easily adapted to measuring for higher cognition. Because all parts must be homogeneous, it is possible that clues will be given, thus reducing item validity.

Guidelines for use: The number of items in the response or answer column should exceed the number in the stem or premises column. The number of items in the stem column to be matched should not exceed 10. Fewer is better. Matching sets should have high homogeneity (i.e., items in both columns or groups should be of the same general category; avoid, for example, mixing dates, events, and names). Answers in the response column should be kept short, to one or two words each and should be ordered logically, such as alphabetically. If answers from the response column can be used more than once, which is advised to avoid guessing by elimination, the directions should so state. Be prepared for the student who can legitimately defend an "incorrect" response. To eliminate the paper-and-pencil aspect and make the item more direct, use an item such as "of the materials on the table, pair up those that are most alike."

Multiple Choice

Description: This is similar to the completion item in that statements are presented (the stem)—sometimes in incomplete form—but with several options or alternatives, requiring recognition or even higher cognitive processes rather than mere recall.

Example 1: Of four cylinders with the following dimensions, the one that would cause the highest-pitched sound would be

(a) 4 inches long and 3 inches in diameter
(b) 8 inches long and 3 inches in diameter
(c) 4 inches long and 1 inch in diameter
(d) 8 inches long and 1 inch in diameter

Example 2: Which one of the following is a pair of antonyms?

(a) loud—soft
(b) halt—finish
(c) absolve—vindicate
(d) procure—purchase

Advantages: Items can be answered and scored quickly. A wide range of content and higher levels of cognition can be tested in a relatively short time. This type is excellent for all testing purposes—motivation, review, and assessment of learning.

Disadvantages: Unfortunately, because multiple-choice items are relatively easy to write, there is a tendency to write items measuring only for low levels of cognition. Multiple-choice items are excellent for major testing, but it takes care and time to write quality questions that measure higher levels of thinking and learning.

GUIDELINES FOR USING MULTIPLE-CHOICE ITEMS

1. If the item is in the form of an incomplete statement, it should be meaningful in itself and imply a direct question rather than merely lead into a collection of unrelated true and false statements.

2. Use a level of language that is easy enough for even the poorest readers and those with limited proficiency in English to understand; avoid unnecessary wordiness.

3. If there is much variation in the length of alternatives, arrange the alternatives in order from shortest to longest. For single-word alternatives, consistent use of arrangement of alternatives is recommended, such as by length of answer or alphabetically.

4. Arrangement of alternatives should be uniform throughout the test and listed in vertical (column) form rather than horizontal (paragraph) form.

5. If there is more than one correct response, students should be instructed to identify all responses they believe are correct. Questions that have more than a single correct response should each be worth more than one point, such as a point for each correct response.

6. Incorrect responses (distracters) should be plausible and related to the same concept as the correct alternative. Although an occasional humorous distracter may help relieve text anxiety, along with absurd distracters they should generally be avoided. They offer no measuring value and increase the likelihood of the student guessing the correct response.

7. It is not necessary to maintain a fixed number of alternatives for every item, but the use of less than three

is not recommended. Although it is not always possible to come up with four or five plausible responses, using four or five reduces chance responses and guessing, thereby increasing reliability for the item. If you cannot think of enough plausible distracters, include the item on a test the first time as a completion item. As students respond, wrong answers will provide you with a number of plausible distracters that you can use the next time to make the item a multiple-choice type item.

8. Some mainstreamed students may work better when allowed to circle their selected response rather than writing its letter or number in a blank space.

9. Responses such as "all of these" or "none of these" should be used only when they will contribute more than another plausible distracter. Care must be taken that such responses answer or complete the item. "All of the above" is a poorer alternative than "none of the above" because it needs to have four or five correct answers; also, if it is the right answer, knowledge of any two of the distracters will cue it.

10. Every item should be grammatically consistent. For example, if the stem is in the form of an incomplete sentence, it should be possible to complete the sentence by attaching any of the alternatives to it.

11. The stem should state a single and specific point.

12. The stem must mean the same thing to every student.

13. The item should be expressed in positive form. A negative form can present a psychological disadvantage to students. Negative items are those that ask what is *not* characteristic of something, or what is the *least* useful. Discard the item if you cannot express it in positive terminology.

14. The stem must not include clues that would clue the correct alternative. For example, A four-sided figure whose opposite sides are parallel is called _____.

   (a) a triangle
   (b) an octagon
   (c) a trapezoid
   (d) a parallelogram

Use of the word "parallel" clues the answer.

15. There must be only one correct or best response. However, this is easier said than done (refer to guideline 20).

16. Measuring for understanding of definitions is better tested by furnishing the name or word and requiring a choice among alternative definitions than by presenting the definition and requiring a choice among alternative words.

17. Avoid using alternatives that include absolute terms such as *never* and *always*.

18. Multiple-choice items need not be entirely verbal. Consider the use of realia, charts, diagrams, videos, and other visuals. They will make the test more interesting, especially to students with low verbal abilities or limited proficiency in English. Consequently, they will make the assessment more direct.

19. Once you have composed a series of multiple-choice items or a test comprised completely of this item type, tally the position of answers to be sure they are evenly distributed. This avoids the common psychological habit (when there are four alternatives) of having the correct alternative in the third position. In other words, when alternative choices are A, B, C, and D, or 1, 2, 3, and 4, unless the test designer is aware and avoids it, more correct answers will be in the "C" or "3" position than in any other.

20. Consider providing space between test items for students to include their rationales for their response selections, thus making the test a combination of multiple-choice and short-explanation items. This measures higher levels of cognition and encourages writing. It also provides for the student who can rationalize an alternative that you had not considered plausible, especially possible today with the diversity of cultural experiences represented by students. For example, we recall the story of a math question on a test that asked if a farmer saw eight crows sitting on a fence and shot three of them, how many would be left. Of course, the "correct" response on the answer key was "5." However, one critical thinking student chose "none" as his response, an answer that was marked wrong by the teacher. However, the student was thinking that those crows that were not shot would be frightened and would all fly away, thus he selected "none" as his answer.

21. While scoring, on a blank copy of the test, tally the incorrect responses for each item. Analyze incorrect responses for each item to discover potential errors in your scoring key. If, for example, many students select B for an item for which your key says the correct answer is A, you may have made a mistake on your scoring key or in teaching the lesson.

22. Sometimes teachers attempt to discourage cheating by preparing several versions of the multiple-choice exam with the questions in different order. This could give one group of students an unfair advantage if the order of their questions was in the same sequence that the information was originally presented and learned, and in random order for another group of students. To avoid this, questions should be in random order on every version of the exam.

Performance

Description: Provided with certain conditions or materials, the student solves a problem or accomplishes some other action.

Example 1: Write a retelling of your favorite fable and create a diorama to go along with it.

Example 2: As a culminating project in physical science for a unit on sound, groups of students were challenged to design and make their own musical instruments. The performance assessment included the following:

1. Play your instrument for the class.
2. Show us the part of the instrument that makes the sound.
3. Describe the function of other parts of your instrument.
4. Demonstrate how you change the pitch of the sound.
5. Share with us how you made your instrument.

Example 3: (see Example 2 in "Essay," earlier in this section).

Example 4: Measure and calculate to the nearest centimeter the within-bounds square footage of our basketball court.

Advantages: Performance test item types come closer to direct measurement (authentic assessment) of certain expected outcomes than do most other types. As has been indicated, other types of questions can actually be prepared as performance-type items, that is, where the student actually does what he or she is being tested for.

Disadvantages: This type of test can be difficult and time-consuming to administer to a group of students. Adequate supply of materials could be a problem, scoring may tend to be subjective, and it could be difficult to give makeup tests to students who were absent.

Guidelines for use:

Use your creativity to design and use performance tests, as they tend to measure well the important objectives. To reduce subjectivity in scoring, set up a performance assessment situation as shown in Figure 7.10 and prepare distinct scoring guidelines (rubrics) as discussed in scoring essay-type items and as shown in Figures 7.11 and 7.12.

Figure 7.10 Procedure for setting up a performance assessment situation.

1. Specify the performance objective.
2. Specify the test conditions.
3. Establish the standards or criteria (scoring rubric) for judging the quality of the process and/or product.
4. Prepare directions in writing, outlining the situation, with instructions that the students are to follow.
5. Share the procedure with a colleague for feedback before using it with students.

Short Explanation

Description: The short explanation question is like the essay-type question but requires a shorter answer.

Example 1: Briefly explain in a paragraph why the patriot/colonists were rebelling against England.

Example 2: Briefly explain why organ pipes are made to vary in length.

Advantages: As with the essay type, student understanding is assessed, but this type takes less time for the teacher to read and to score. By using several questions of this type, a greater amount of content can be covered than with a lesser number of essay questions. This type of question is good practice for students to learn to express themselves succinctly in writing.

Disadvantages: Some students will have difficulty expressing themselves in a limited fashion or in writing. They need practice, coaching, and time.

Guidelines for use: This type is useful for occasional reviews and quizzes and as an alternative to other types of questions. For scoring, establish a scoring rubric and follow the same guidelines as for the essay-type item.

True-False

Description: A statement is presented that students are to judge as being accurate or not.

Example 1: A suffix is any bound morpheme added to the end of a root word. T or F?

Example 2: Christopher Columbus discovered America in 1492. T or F?

Advantages: Many items can be answered in a relatively short time, making broad content coverage possible. Scoring is quick and simple. True-false items are good as discussion starters, for review, and for diagnostic evaluation (preassessment) of what students already know or think they know.

Disadvantages: It is sometimes difficult to write true-false items that are purely true or false or to write them without qualifying them in such a way that clues the answer. In the second sample question, for example, the student may question whether Columbus really did discover America or he or she might misunderstand the meaning of "discovering America." Weren't there people already there when he landed? Where, in fact, did he land? What is meant by "America"? Example 2 is poor also because it tests for more than one idea—Columbus, America, and 1492.

Much of the content that most easily lends itself to the true-false type of test item is trivial. Students have a 50 percent chance of guessing the correct answer, thus giving this item type both *poor validity* and *poor reliability*. Scoring and grading give no clue about why the student missed an item. Consequently, the disadvantages of true-false items far outweigh the advantages; *pure true-false items should not be used for arriving at grades.*

Figure 7.11 Sample of a scoring rubric for student project presentation. Possible score = 100. Scorer marks a relevant square in each of the six categories (the horizontal rows), and the student's score for that category is the number within that square.

	14–15	12–13	11	1–10
Professional Presentation	Well organized; smooth transitions between sections; all enthusiastically participate and share responsibility.	Well organized with transitions; students confer/present ideas; group shows ability to interact; attentive discussion of research.	Shows basic organization; lacks transitions; some interaction; discussion focuses mostly on research.	Unorganized, lacks planning; no transitions; reliance on one spokesperson; little interaction; disinterest; too brief.
	14–15	**12–13**	**11**	**1–10**
Engagement of Audience	Successfully and actively engages audience in more than one pertinent activity; maintains interest throughout.	Engages audience in at least one related activity; maintains attention through most of presentation.	Attempts to engage audience in at least one activity; no attempt to involve *entire* audience. May not relate in significant way.	Fails to involve audience; does not maintain audience's attention; no connection with audience. No relationship between activity and topic.
	18–20	**16–17**	**14–15**	**1–13**
Use of Literature	Strong connection between literature and topic; significant, perceptive explanation of literature; pertinent to topic. At least two pieces used.	Clear connection between literature and topic; clear explanation; appropriate to topic. Two pieces used.	Weak connection to topic; unclear explanation; one genre; one piece used.	No connection to topic; no explanation; inappropriate literature; no literature.
	18–20	**16–17**	**14–15**	**1–13**
Knowledge of Subject	Strong understanding of topic; knowledge factually relevant, accurate, and consistent; solution shows analysis of evidence.	Good understanding of topic; uses main points of information researched; builds solution on examination of major evidence.	Shows general understanding; focuses on one aspect, discusses at least one other idea; uses research, attempts to add to it; solution refers to evidence.	Little understanding or comprehension of topic; uses little basic information researched; forms minimal solution; relies solely on own opinions without support.
	18–20	**16–17**	**14–15**	**1–13**
Use of Media	Effectively combines and integrates three distinct forms with one original piece; enhances understanding; offers insight into topic.	Combines two forms with one original piece; relates to topic; connection between media and topic is explained.	Includes two or three forms but no original piece; media relates to topic. Explanation may be vague or missing.	One form; no original piece; connection between media and topic is unclear.
	9–10	**8**	**7**	**1–6**
Speaking Skills	Clear enunciation; strong projection; vocal variety; eye contact with entire audience; presentation posture; solid focus with no interruptions.	Good enunciation; adequate projection; partial audience eye contact; appropriate posture.	Inconsistent enunciation; low projection with little vocal variety; inconsistent posture.	Difficult to understand; inaudible; monotonous; no eye contact; inappropriate posture; interruptions and distractions.

(*Source:* Elk Grove School District, Elk Grove, California.)

Figure 7.12 Sample of a scoring rubric for student research paper. Possible score = 100. Scorer marks a relevant square in each of the six categories (the horizontal rows), and the student's score for that category is the number within that square.

Parenthetical References	**14–15** All documented correctly. Paper's references document a wide variety of sources cited—at least five from bibliography.	**12–13** Most documented correctly. Few minor errors. At least three sources from bibliography are cited.	**11** Some documented correctly. Some show no documentation at all. May not correlate to the bibliography.	**1–10** Few to none are documented. Does not correlate to the bibliography. May be totally absent.
Bibliography and Sources	**14–15** Strong use of library research. Exceeds minimum of five sources. Bibliography is correctly formatted.	**12–13** Good use of library research. Exceeds minimum of five sources. Bibliography has few or no errors in format.	**11** Some use of library research. Meets minimum of five sources. Bibliography is present but may be problematic.	**1–10** Fails to meet minimum standards for library research. Bibliography has major flaws or may be missing.
Mechanics/Format	**14–15** Correct format and pagination. Neat title page, near-perfect spelling, punctuation, and grammar.	**12–13** Mostly correct format and pagination. Neat. Few errors in title page, spelling, punctuation, and grammar.	**11** Errors in format and pagination. Flawed title page. Distracting errors in spelling, punctuation, and grammar.	**1–10** Incorrect format. Title page is flawed or missing. Many errors in spelling, punctuation, and grammar. Lack of planning is obvious. Paper is difficult to read.
Thesis	**9–10** An original and comprehensive thesis that is clear and well thought out. All sections work to support it.	**8** Comprehensive and well-focused thesis, which is clearly stated. All sections work to support it.	**7** Adequate thesis that is understandable but may be neither clear nor focused. It covers the majority of the issues found in the sections.	**1–6** Inadequate thesis that is disconnected from the research or may be too broad to support. May be convoluted, confusing, or absent.
Completeness/ Coherence	**18–20** Paper reads as a unified whole. There is no repetition of information. All sections are in place, and transitions between them are clearly developed.	**16–17** Paper reads as a unified whole with no repetition. All sections are in place, but transitions between them are not as smooth.	**14–15** Paper has required sections. Repetitions may be evident. The paper does not present a unified whole. Transitions are missing or inadequate.	**1–13** Paper lacks one or more sections and makes no attempt to connect sections as a whole unit. Sections may be grossly repetitive or contradictory.
Thinking/Analyzing	**23–25** Strong understanding of the topic. Knowledge is factually relevant, accurate, and consistent. Solutions show analysis of research discussed in paper.	**20–22** Good understanding of the topic. Uses main points of information researched. Solutions build on examination of research discussed in paper.	**17–19** General understanding of topic. Uses research and attempts to add to it; solutions refer to some of the research discussed.	**1–16** Little understanding of topic. Uses little basic information researched. Minimal examination of the topic. Solutions may be based solely on own opinions, without support.

(*Source:* Elk Grove School District, Elk Grove, California.)

For grading purposes, you may use modified true-false items (see guideline 11 following), where space is provided between items for students to write in their explanations, thus making the item a combined true-false, short-explanation type.

GUIDELINES FOR USING TRUE-FALSE ITEMS

1. For preparing a false statement, first write the statement as a true statement, then make it false by changing a word or phrase.
2. Try to avoid using negative statements since they tend to confuse students.
3. A true-false statement should include only one idea.
4. Use close to an equal number of true and false items.
5. Try to avoid using specific determiners (e.g., "always," "all," or "none"), because they usually clue that the statement is false. Also avoid words that may clue that the statement is true (e.g., "often," "probably," and "sometimes").
6. Avoid words that may have different meanings for different students.
7. Avoid using verbatim language from the student textbook.
8. Avoid trick items, such as a slight reversal of numbers in a date.
9. Do not use symbols for the words *true* and *false* (such as + and −) that might be confusing, or have

students write the letters *T* and *F* (sometimes a student does not write the letters clearly enough for the teacher to be able to distinguish which it is). Instead, have students either write out the words *true* and *false* or, better yet, have them simply circle *T* and *F* as indicated by the two previous examples.

10. Proofread your items (or have a friend do it) to be sure that the sentences are well constructed and free from typographical errors.

11. To avoid "wrong" answers caused by variations in thinking, and to make the item more valid and reliable, students should be encouraged to write in their rationale for selecting true or false, making the item a *modified true-false* item. For example,

When a farmer saw eight crows sitting on the fence surrounding his corn field, he shot three of them. Five were left on the fence. T or F? _____

Explanation: _____

In addition to the combined true-false, short-explanation question, modified true-false "sometimes-always-never" items may be used for grading. Here, a third alternative, "sometimes," is introduced to reduce the chance for guessing.

Now do Exercise 7.1 to start developing your skill in writing assessment items. As you work on Exercise 7.1 you may want to correlate it with your previous work on Exercises 5.12, 6.3, and 6.4.

FOR YOUR NOTES

EXERCISE 7.1: PREPARING MY ASSESSMENT ITEMS

INSTRUCTIONS: The purpose of this exercise is to practice your skill in preparing the different types of assessment items discussed in this section. For use in your own teaching, select one specific instructional objective and write assessment items for it. When completed, share this exercise with your colleagues for their feedback. (See Exercises 5.12, 6.3, and 6.4.)

Objective: _____

Grade and subject: _____

1. Arrangement item: _____

_____

_____

_____

_____

2. Completion-drawing item: _____

_____

_____

_____

_____

3. Completion-statement item: _____

_____

_____

_____

_____

4. Correction item: _____

_____

_____

_____

_____

5. Essay item: _____

_____

_____

_____

_____

6. Grouping item: _____

_____

_____

_____

_____

EXERCISE 7.1 *(continued)*

7. Identification item: _____

_____

_____

_____

_____

8. Matching item: _____

_____

_____

_____

_____

9. Multiple-choice item: _____

_____

_____

_____

_____

10. Performance item: _____

_____

_____

_____

_____

11. Short-explanation item: _____

_____

_____

_____

_____

12. Modified true-false item: _____

_____

_____

_____

_____

REPORTING STUDENT ACHIEVEMENT

One of your responsibilities as a classroom teacher is to report student progress in achievement to parents or guardians as well as to the school administration. In some schools the reporting is of student progress and effort as well as of achievement. As described in the discussions that follow, reporting is done in at least two, and sometimes more, ways.

The Grade Report

Periodically a grade report (report card) is issued (generally from four to six times a year, depending upon the school and its type of scheduling). Grade reports may be distributed during an advisory period or they may be mailed to the student's home, or in some instances given only to parents or guardians who must come to the school to get the report card. This grade report represents an achievement grade (formative evaluation). The final report of the semester is also the semester grade, and for courses that are only one semester long it is the final grade (summative evaluation). In essence, the first and sometimes second reports are progress notices; the semester grade is the one that is transferred to the student's transcript of records.

In addition to the student's academic achievement, you must report the student's social behaviors (classroom conduct) while in your classroom. Whichever reporting form is used, you must separate your assessments of a student's social behaviors from the student's academic achievement. Academic achievement (or accomplishment) is represented by a letter (sometimes a number) grade (*A* through *E* or *F*, or *E*, *S*, and *U*, or 1 to 5, and sometimes with minuses and pluses), and the social behavior by a "satisfactory" or an "unsatisfactory" (or by more specific items), or supplemented by teacher-written or computer-generated comments. There may also be a place on the reporting form for teachers to check whether basic grade level standards have been met, especially in reading and mathematics. [*Note:* In some states, California for example, reporting to parents/guardians of a child's standardized achievement testing results is done by a centralized reporting agency, and is outside the individual teacher's or school's responsibility.]

TEACHER PARENTAL/GUARDIAN CONNECTIONS

Study after study shows that when parents or guardians are involved in their child's school and school work, students learn better and earn better grades, and teachers experience more positive feelings about teaching. As a result, schools constantly are searching for improved ways to communicate with and to involve parents/guardians.

Contacting Parents/Guardians

Whenever preparing to establish contact with parents and guardians, try to discover before the contact is made any pertinent information you might need about the home situation, such as, for example, whether there are language barriers or cultural differences you should be aware of, something you can learn about from the very first assignment you give students.

Although it is not always obligatory, some teachers purposefully contact parents or guardians by telephone or by e-mail, especially when a student has shown a sudden turn for either the worse or the better in academic achievement or in classroom behavior. That initiative and contact by the teacher are usually welcomed by parents/guardians and can lead to productive conferences with the teacher. An electronic conference (telephone or e-mail) can save valuable time for both the teacher and the parent/guardian.

Another way of contacting parents/guardians is by letter. Contacting a child's parent/guardian by letter gives time to think and to make clear your thoughts and concerns to that parent/guardian and to invite them to respond at their convenience by letter, by phone, or by arranging to have a conference with you.

In absence of a computer-link assignment/progress report hotline, or in addition to it, most schools have a progress report form that, upon request by a parent/guardian, can be sent home as often as agreed upon by the teacher and the parent/guardian. For example, parents/guardians of children at Kernersville Middle School (Winston-Salem, NC) receive weekly academic updates (L'Esperance & Gabbard, 2001).

Meeting Parents/Guardians

You will meet some of the parents/guardians early in the school year during "back-to-school" night (or "meet the teacher" or "curriculum" night as it is variously called) and throughout the year in individual conferences and later in the year during spring open house. For the beginning teacher, these meetings with parents/guardians can be anxious times. The following paragraphs provide guidelines to help you with those experiences.

Back-to-school (or whatever its cognomen) night is the evening early in the school year when parents and guardians come to the school and meet their children's teachers. The parents and guardians arrive either at the student's homebase or in the auditorium for a greeting and a few words from various school officials and then proceed through a simulation of their child's school day; as a group, they meet each class and each teacher for a few minutes. Later, in the spring, many schools host an "open house" where parents and guardians may have more time to talk individually with teachers, although the major purpose of the open house is for the school and teachers to celebrate and display the work and progress of the students.

At back-to-school night, parents/guardians are eager to learn as much as they can about their children's teachers. You will meet each group of parents/guardians for a brief time, usually about 10 minutes. During that meeting you will provide them with a copy of the course syllabus, make some straightforward remarks about yourself, and talk about the course and its requirements, your expectations of the students, and how they, the parents and guardians, might help.

Although there will be precious little time for questions from the parents/guardians, during your introduction the adults will be delighted to learn that you have your program well planned, are a "task master," appreciate their interest, and welcome their participation. They will be happy to hear your willingness to communicate with them. Parents/guardians will be pleased to know that you are "from the school of the three Fs"—that is, that you are firm, friendly, and fair. For any parent/guardian who indicates an urgent need to talk with you as soon as possible, try to schedule a mutually convenient private conference time in person or via telephone for perhaps later that evening or during the next few days.

Specifically, parents/guardians will expect to learn about your curriculum—goals and objectives, any long-term projects, class size, schedules for tests including any state-required standardized tests, and grading procedures. They will want to know what you expect of them: Will there be homework, and if so, to what extent, if any, should they help their child with it? [*Note:* The answer to the preceding question is in the nature of the help given; parents and other family members should encourage and help facilitate their children doing homework, but they should be careful, however, not to actually do the homework for their child (Marzano, Pickering, & Pollock, 2001).] How can parents/guardians contact you? Try to anticipate other questions. Your principal and colleagues can be of aid in helping you anticipate and prepare for these questions. Of course, you can never prepare for the question or comment that comes from left field. Just remain calm and avoid being flustered (or at least appear so). Ten minutes will pass quickly, and parents and guardians will be reassured to learn you have things under control.

Parent/Guardian Conference

When meeting parents or guardians for conferences, you should be as specific as possible when explaining to a parent/guardian the progress of that person's child in your class. And, again, express your appreciation for their interest. Be helpful to the adult's understanding, and don't saturate the parent/guardian with more information than he or she needs. Resist any tendency to talk too much. Allow time for the parent or guardian to ask questions. Keep your answers succinct. Never compare one student with another or with the rest of the class. If the parent/guardian asks a question for which you do not have an answer, tell the person you will try to find an answer and will contact him or her as quickly as possible, and do it. Have the student's portfolio and other work with you during the parent/guardian conference so you can show the parent/guardian examples of what is being discussed. Also, have your gradebook on hand, or a computer printout of it, but be prepared to protect from the person the names and records of other students.

Sometimes it is helpful to have a three-way conference, a conference with the parent or guardian, the student, and you, or a conference with the parent/guardian, the principal or counselor, and several or all of the student's teachers. If, especially as a beginning teacher, you would like the presence of an administrator or school counselor at a parent/guardian–teacher conference as backup, don't be hesitant to arrange that.

Some middle level educators prefer a *student-led conference*, arguing the advantages resulting from increased student involvement, student goal-setting, student reflection, and student responsibility (Conderman, Ikan, & Hatcher, 2000). Another school reports that when students were put in charge of the conferences parent/guardian attendance at conferences more than doubled (Farber, 1999). Typically, with student-led conferences, students also prepare and share their individual portfolios (Roberts, 2000).

When a parent/guardian asks how she or he may help in the student's learning, the paragraphs that follow offer suggestions for your consideration. Many schools have made special and successful efforts to link home and school. At some schools, through homework hotlines, parents/guardians have phone access to their children's assignment specifications and to their progress in their schoolwork, and parents and guardians with a personal computer and a modem have access to tutorial services to assist students with assignments.

Helping students become critical thinkers, one of the aims of education, is one that parents and guardians can help with by reinforcing the strategies being used in the classroom. Ways to do this are to ask "what if" questions; think aloud as a model for the student's thinking development; encourage the student's own metacognition by asking questions such as, "How did you arrive at that conclusion?" or "How do you feel about your conclusion now?" and asking these questions about the student's everyday social interactions, topics that are important to the student; ask the student to elaborate on his or her ideas; accepting the fact that the student may make mistakes, but encourage the student to learn from them.

Many resources are available for parents/guardians to use at home. The United States government, for example, has a variety of free or low-cost booklets available. For information, contact the Federal Citizen Information Center at the website listed at the end of this chapter.

Dealing with an Angry Parent or Guardian

If a parent or guardian is angry or hostile toward you and the school, the paragraphs that follow offer guidelines for dealing with that hostility.

Remain calm and positive in your discussion with the adult, allowing the person to talk out his or her hostility while you say very little; usually, the less you say the better. What you do say must be objective and to the point of the student's work in your classroom. The parent/guardian may just need to vent frustrations that might have very little to do with you, the school, or even the student.

Do *not* allow yourself to be intimidated, put on the defensive, or backed into a verbal corner. If the parent/guardian tries to do so by attacking you personally, do not press your defense at this point. Perhaps the parent/guardian has made a point that you should take time to consider, and now is a good time to arrange for another conference with the parent/guardian for about a week later. In a follow-up conference, if the parent/guardian agrees, you may want to consider bringing in a mediator, such as another member of your teaching team, an administrator, or a school counselor.

Just as with your students, put up with no foul language from the adult, letting the parent/guardian know that if it continues the conversation is over. Always know where the nearest adult is, so if help is needed you know how to quickly get it. If you at all feel physically threatened, cut the conversation off, reminding the person that it is a felony misdemeanor to cause a disruption at school and that if the feeling of being threatened continues you will call security.

You must *not* talk about other students; keep the conversation focused on the progress of this parent or guardian's child. The adult is not your rival, or should not be. You both share a concern for the academic and emotional well-being of the child. Use your best skills in critical thinking and problem solving, trying to focus the discussion by identifying the problem, defining it, and then arriving at some decision about how mutually to go about solving it. To this end you may need to ask for help from a third party, such as the student's school counselor. If agreed to by the parent, please take that step.

Parents and guardians do *not* need to hear about how busy you are, about your personal problems, or about how many other students you are dealing with on a daily basis, unless, of course, he or she asks. Parents/guardians expect you to be the capable professional who knows what to do and is doing it.

SUMMARY

Assessment is an integral and ongoing factor in the teaching-learning process; consequently, this chapter has emphasized the importance of your including the following in your teaching performance:

- A variety of instruments to collect a body of evidence to most reliably assess the learning of students that focus on their individual development.
- Basing assessment on the target objectives and material that is being or that has been taught.
- Considering your assessment and grading procedures carefully, planning them, and explaining your policies to the students and, when relevant, to parents/guardians.
- Involving students in the assessment process; keeping students informed of their progress.
- Maintaining accurate and clear records of assessment results so that you will have ample data on which to base your judgmental decisions about achievement.
- Returning tests and other papers promptly, reviewing answers to all questions, and responding to inquiries about marks given.
- Striving for objective and impartial assessment.
- Trying to minimize confusion about grades, cheating, and teacher subjectivity by involving students in the planning, reinforcing individual student development, and providing an accepting and stimulating learning environment.

Now, in the two remaining chapters we guide you through the process of choosing and implementing specific strategies for instruction.

QUESTIONS FOR CLASS DISCUSSION

1. Identify a problem in grading that, as a student, you personally experienced in school. What was your perceived cause of the problem? How might it have been avoided? What was the resolution, and how was that resolution arrived at? Was the resolution satisfactory to all concerned? Why or why not?
2. Other than a paper-and-pencil test, identify alternative techniques for assessing student learning during or at completion of an instructional unit.
3. Investigate various ways that middle level schools in your geographic area are experimenting with assessing and reporting student achievement. In what ways, if any, have those assessing and reporting methods changed as a result of mandated standardized achievement testing? Share what you find with your classmates. With your classmates, discuss the pros and cons of various systems of assessing and reporting.
4. When using a point system for determining student grades, is it educationally defensible to give a student a higher grade than that student's points call for? A lower grade? Give your rationale for your answers.

5. Describe any student learning activities or situations that you believe should not be graded but should or could be used for assessment of student learning.

6. List five things you would like to hear from your own child's teachers at back-to-school night. Share and compare your list with those of your classmates. What were the commonalities? How are differences explained?

7. Do you believe that student scores on state-mandated achievement tests adequately portray the success or failure of a particular school? Of a particular teacher? Explain why or why not.

8. Some experts say that rather than teaching to the test, the teacher should test what is taught. Do you see any meaning to that thought? Describe the significance as you see it.

9. When reporting a student's academic achievement, to what extent, if any, do you believe the following should enter into the determination of the student's grades or marks? Effort, behavior, cooperation, and attendance. Defend your position with those of your classmates.

10. What can you learn about the use of "value-added assessment" in middle level schools in your geographic area?

INTERNET RESOURCES

Academy for Educational Development **http://www.aed.org**

Alliance for Parental Involvement in Education
    http://www.croton.com/allpie

ASPIRA Parents for Educational Excellence
    http://www.aspira.org/Apex.html

Family Support America **http://www.familysupportamerica.org**

Federal Citizen Information Center **http://www.pueblo.gsa.gov**

Grady Profile **http://www.aurbach.com**

Institute for Educational Leadership **http://www.iel.org**

Mexican American Legal Defense and Educational Fund
    http://www.maldef.org

National Coalition of Parental Involvement in Education
    http://ncpie.org

Parent Institute, The **http://www.parent-institute.com**

Reading Is Fundamental, Inc. **http://www.rif.org**

Writing assessment scoring rubric
    http://www.state.tn.us/education/tswritingb.htm

Writing assessment Toolkit98
    http://www.nwrel.org/assessment/ToolKit98.asp

FOR FURTHER READING

Benson, B. P., & Barnett, S. P. (2005). *Student-led conferencing using showcase portfolios.* Thousand Oaks, CA: Corwin Press.

Elmore, R. F. (2004). Performance vs. attainment. *Harvard Education Letter, 20*(5), 7–8.

Elston, E. (2004). Beyond report cards: Assessing students on what matters. *Middle Ground, 7*(3), 16–21.

Guskey, T. R. (2005). Mapping the road to proficiency: A table of specifications provides a travel guide to help teachers move students toward mastery of standards. *Educational Leadership, 63*(3), 32–38.

Howe, F., & Simmons, B. J. (2005). *Nurturing the parent-teacher alliance.* Fastback 533. Bloomington, IN: Phi Delta Kappa Educational Foundation.

Jaksec, III, C. M. (2005). *The difficult parent.* Thousand Oaks, CA: Corwin Press.

Kaftan, J. M., Buck, G. A., & Haack, A. (2006). Using formative assessments to individualize instruction and promote learning. *Middle School Journal, 37*(4), 44–49.

McEwan, E. K. (2005). *How to deal with parents who are angry, troubled, afraid, or just plain crazy.* Thousand Oaks, CA: Corwin Press.

Reeves, D. B. (2004). The case against the zero. *Phi Delta Kappan, 84,* 324–325.

Smith, D. B. (2005). Accountability for academics and social responsibility through service learning. *Middle School Journal, 36*(4), 20–25.

Wormeli, R. (2004). Differentiated grading. *Middle Ground, 8*(1), 23–25.

8

Organizing and Guiding Student Learning
Alone and in Groups

Tom Watson/Merrill

Rather than diluting standards and expectations, believing in the learning potential of every student, exemplary schools and teachers are those who are able to effectively modify the key variables of time, methodology, and grouping to help each individual student achieve mastery of the curriculum. These variables can be attuned or modified to better accommodate each learner's needs. Ways in which time is modified were discussed in Chapter 1. Ways of varying the methodology are addressed throughout the book. In this chapter the focus is on ways of grouping young adolescent learners to enhance positive interaction and quality learning for each child.

In the most effective instructional environments, during any given week or even day of school, a student might experience a succession of group settings. Ways of grouping students for quality instruction is the general topic of this chapter, from personalized and individualized instruction to working with dyads, small groups, and large groups. You also will learn how to ensure equality in the classroom, how to use assignments and homework, and how to coordinate various forms of independent and small-group, project-based study. The chapter ends with the presentation of a collection of more than 125 motivational teaching strategies with ideas for lessons, interdisciplinary teaching, transcultural studies, and student projects, what many users of this resource guide have reported as itself well worth the price of the book.

> *Since young adolescents learn best through engagement and interaction, learning strategies involve students in dialogue with teachers and with one another. Teaching approaches should enhance and accommodate the diverse skills, abilities, and prior knowledge of young adolescents, and draw upon students' individual learning styles.*
> National Middle School Association (2003, p. 25)

OBJECTIVES

Specifically, upon completion of this chapter you should be able to:

1. Describe the meaning of *mastery (quality) learning* and its implications for teaching young adolescents.
2. Explain the advantages and disadvantages of various ways of grouping students for quality learning.
3. Explain how the teacher can personalize the instruction to ensure success for each student.
4. Demonstrate an understanding of the meaning and importance of equity in the classroom and how it can be achieved and maintained.
5. Demonstrate an awareness of appropriate curriculum options and instructional practices for specific groups of young adolescent learners.
6. Demonstrate a theoretical and practical understanding of how to effectively use each of these instructional strategies: assignments, homework, written and oral reports, cooperative learning, learning centers, problem-based learning, and projects.
7. Demonstrate your developing understanding of the meaning of *developmentally appropriate practice.*
8. Demonstrate developing skills in recognizing, celebrating, and building upon student diversity.

MASTERY LEARNING AND PERSONALIZED INSTRUCTION

Learning is an individual or personal experience. Yet as a classroom teacher you will be expected to work effectively with students on other than an individual basis—perhaps 25 or more at a time. Much has been written on the importance of *differentiating the instruction*—of individualizing or personalizing the instruction for learners. Virtually all the research concerning effective instructional practice emphasizes greater individualization of instruction (Carroll, 1994). We know of the individuality of the learning experience, and we know that while some young adolescent students are primarily verbal learners, many more are primarily visual, tactile, or kinesthetic learners. As the classroom teacher, though, you find

yourself in the difficult position of simultaneously ministering to many separate and individual learners with individual learning capacities, styles, and preferences.

To individualize the instruction, exemplary middle level schools and teachers use a variety of strategies—small learning communities, advisories, exploratory programs, cooperative learning groups, project-based learning, personalized learning plans, and independent study—to respond to individual student competencies, interests, needs, and abilities. They also use nonconventional scheduling so that teaching teams can vary the length of time in periods and also vary the size of instructional groups and the learning strategies within a given time period.

Common sense tells us that student achievement in learning is related to both the quality of attention and the length of time given to learning tasks. Building upon a model developed earlier by John Carroll (1963), Benjamin Bloom (1987) developed the concept of individualized instruction called **mastery learning,** saying that students need sufficient time on task (i.e., engaged time) to master content before moving on to new content.

Today's Emphasis: Quality Learning for Every Student

Emphasis today is on mastery of content, or quality learning, for every student. By mastery of content, we mean that the student demonstrates his or her use of what has been learned. Because of that emphasis and research that indicates that quality learning programs positively affect achievement, the importance of the concept of mastery learning has resurfaced and is becoming firmly entrenched. For example, the nationwide approach of standards-based instruction relies on a goal-driven curriculum model with instruction that focuses on the construction of individual knowledge through mastery and assessment of student learning against the anticipated outcomes. In some instances, unfortunately, attention may be on the mastery of only minimum competencies; thus, in those instances students may not always be encouraged to work and learn to the maximum of their talents and abilities.

Assumptions about Mastery, or Quality, Learning

Today's concept of mastery, or quality, learning is based on certain assumptions (Battistini, 1995; Horton, 1981):

1. Mastery learning can ensure that students experience success at each level of the instructional process—experiencing success at each level provides incentive and motivation for further learning.
2. Mastery of content, or quality learning, is possible for each learner.

3. Most learning is sequential and logical.

4. Most desired learning outcomes can be specified in terms of observable and measurable performance.

5. Although all students can achieve mastery, to master a particular content some students may require more time than others—the teacher and the school must provide for this difference in time need to complete a task successfully.

6. For quality learning to occur, it is the instruction that must be modified and adapted, not the students—traditional tracking or ability grouping do not fit.

Elements of Any Mastery Learning Model: The Cycle of Teaching

The essence of mastery (quality) learning is the *cycle of teaching,* and contains the following elements:

1. clearly defined target learning objectives with pre-set mastery performance expectations

2. preassessment of the learner's present knowledge

3. instructional component, with a rich variety of choices and options for students

4. frequent practice, reinforcement, and comprehension checks (a form of *formative assessment*), with corrective instruction at each step of the way to keep the learner on track

5. postassessment (*summative assessment*) to determine the extent of student mastery of the learning objectives.

Strategies for Personalizing the Instruction Now!

You can immediately provide personalized instruction by:

* starting the study of a topic from where the students are in terms of what they know (or think they know) and what they want to know about the topic (see "think-pair-share" discussed in Chapter 2; see also KWL and similar strategies in Figure 5.1 of Chapter 5)
* providing students with choices from a rich variety of learning pathways, resources, and hands-on experiences to learn more about the topic
* providing multiple instructional approaches (i.e., using multilevel instruction in a variety of settings, from learning alone to whole-class instruction)
* empowering students with responsibility for decision making, reflection, and self-assessment.

WORKING WITH AND INDIVIDUALIZING THE LEARNING EXPERIENCES FOR SPECIFIC LEARNERS

For working with specific learners, consider the guidelines that follow and refer back to these guidelines often during your preactive (planning) phase of instruction during the first few years of your teaching.

Recognizing and Working with Students with Special Needs

Students with special needs (referred to also as students with exceptionalities) include those with disabling conditions or impairments in any one or more of the following categories: mental, hearing, speech or language, visual, emotional, orthopedic, autism, traumatic brain injury, other health impairment, or specific learning disabilities. To receive special education services, a child must have a disability in one or more of the categories, and by reason thereof, the child needs special education and related services. In other words, not all children who have a disability need services available via special education. For example, a child with a hearing impairment would be entitled to special services when the impairment is so severe that the child cannot understand what is being said even when the child is equipped with a hearing aid.

To the extent possible, students with special needs must be educated with their peers in the regular classroom. Public Law 94-142, the *Education for All Handicapped Children Act (EAHCA) of 1975* (now known as the *Individuals with Disabilities Education Act, IDEA*), and all its amendments that followed including its 2004 revision and reauthorization, mandates all children have the right to a free and appropriate education, as well as to nondiscriminatory assessment. Emphasizing normalizing the educational environment for students with disabilities, legislation requires provision of the least-restrictive environment (LRE) for these students. An LRE is an environment that is as normal as possible.

A Continuum of Differences. It is important to understand that students with disabilities fall along a continuum of learner differences rather than as a separate category of student (Meyer & Rose, 2000). Because of their wide differences, students identified as having special needs may be placed in the regular classroom for the entire school day, called *full inclusion.* Those students may also be in a regular classroom the greater portion of the school day, called *partial inclusion,* or only for designated periods. Although there is no single, universally accepted definition of the term, *inclusion* is the concept that students with disabilities should be included in general education classrooms regardless of whether they can meet grade level academic standards. (The term *inclusion* has largely replaced use of an earlier and similar term, *mainstreaming.*) As a classroom teacher, you will need information and skills specific to teaching learners with special needs who are included in your classes.

Generally speaking, teaching students who have special needs requires more care, better diagnosis, greater skill, more attention to individual needs, and an even greater understanding of the students. The challenges of teaching students with special needs in the regular classroom are great enough that to do it well, you will need

Todd Yarrington/Merrill

specialized training beyond the general guidelines presented here. At some point in your teacher preparation you may be required to take one or more courses in working with special needs learners in the regular classroom.

When a student with special needs is placed in your classroom, your task is to deal directly with the differences between this student and other students in your classroom. To do this, you need an understanding of the general characteristics of different types of special needs learners, to identify the student's unique needs relative to your classroom, and to design lessons that teach to different needs at the same time, called multilevel teaching, a strategy that has been discussed throughout this resource guide.

Just because a student has been identified as having one or more special needs does not preclude that person from being gifted or talented. Gifted students with disabling conditions remain a major group of poorly recognized and underattended-to youth, perhaps because focus on accommodations for their disabilities precludes adequate recognition and development of their gifts and talents (Willard-Holt, 1999).

Congress stipulated in P.L. 94–142 that an Individualized Education Program (IEP) be devised annually for each special needs child. According to that law, an IEP is developed for each student each year by a team that includes special education teachers, the child's parents or guardians, and the classroom teachers. The IEP contains a statement of the student's present educational levels, the educational goals and measurable objectives or benchmarks for the year, specifications for the services to be provided and the extent to which the student should be expected to participate in the regular education program, and the evaluative criteria for the services to be provided. Consultation by special and skilled support personnel is essential in all IEP models. A consultant works directly with teachers or with students and parents/guardians. As a classroom teacher, you may play an active role in preparing the specifications

for the special needs students assigned to your classroom, and assume a major responsibility for implementing the program.

Guidelines for Working with Special Needs Students in the Inclusive Classroom.   Although the guidelines represented by the paragraphs that follow are important for teaching all students, they are especially important for working with special needs students.

- Familiarize yourself with exactly what the special needs of each learner are. Privately ask the special needs student whether there is anything he or she would like for you to know and that you specifically can do to facilitate his or her learning.

- Adapt and modify materials and procedures to the special needs of each student. For example, a student who has extreme difficulty sitting still for more than a few minutes will need planned changes in learning activities. When establishing student seating arrangements in the classroom, give preference to students according to their special needs. Try to incorporate into lessons activities that engage all learning modalities—visual, auditory, tactile, and kinesthetic. Be flexible in your classroom procedures. For example, allow the use of audiorecorders for note taking and test taking when students have trouble with the written language.

- Provide high structure and clear expectations by defining the learning objectives in behavioral terms. Teach students the correct procedures for everything. Break complex learning into simpler components, moving from the most concrete to the abstract, rather than the other way around. Check frequently for student understanding of instructions and procedures, and for comprehension of content. Use computers and other self-correcting materials for drill and practice and for provision of immediate, constructive, and private feedback to the student.

- Exercise your withitness, monitoring students for signs of restlessness, frustration, anxiety, and off-task behaviors. Be ready to reassign individual learners to different activities as the situation warrants. Established classroom learning centers (discussed later in this chapter) can be a big help.

- Have all students maintain assignments for the week or some other period of time in an assignment book or in a folder kept in their notebooks. Post assignments in a special place in the classroom (and perhaps on the school's website) and frequently remind students of assignments and deadlines.

- Maintain consistency in your expectations and in your responses. Special needs learners, particularly, can become frustrated when they do not understand a teacher's expectations and when they cannot depend on a teacher's reactions.

- Plan interesting activities to bridge learning, activities that help students connect what is being learned with their real world. Making that connection helps motivate students and keep them on task.

- Plan questions and questioning sequences, and write them into your lesson plans. Plan questions you ask special needs learners so they are apt to answer them with confidence. Use signals to let students know you are likely to call on them in class (e.g., prolonged eye contact or mentioning your intention to the student before class begins). After asking a question, give the student adequate time to think and respond. Then, after the student responds, build upon the student's response to indicate the student's contribution was accepted as being important.

- Provide for and teach toward student success. Offer students activities and experiences that ensure each student's success and mastery at some level. Use of student portfolios can give evidence of progress and help in building student confidence and self-esteem.

- Provide scaffolded instruction, that is, give each student as much guided or coached practice as time allows. Provide time in class for students to work on assignments and projects. During this time, you can monitor the work of each student while looking for misconceptions, thus ensuring students get started on the right track.

- Provide help in the organization of students' learning. For example, give instruction in the organization of notes and notebooks. Have a three-hole punch available in the classroom so students can place their papers into their notebooks immediately, thus avoiding disorganization and the loss of papers. During class presentations, use an overhead projector with transparencies; students who need more time can then copy material from the transparencies. Ask students to read their notes aloud to each other in small groups, thereby aiding their recall and understanding, and encouraging them to take notes for meaning rather than for rote learning. Encourage and provide for peer support, peer tutoring or coaching, and cross-age teaching (discussed later in this chapter). Ensure the special needs learner is included in all class activities to the fullest extent possible.

TEACHING IN PRACTICE

Help! No Aide Today

Of the 25 children in Hannah's fifth-grade class, one, Aliya, is a special needs child with multiple disabilities including Down's syndrome and severe hearing loss. On this day, Aliya's aide failed to come to school. The aide also failed to notify the school that she would be absent. Hannah is the only adult in class today. Aliya needs to go to the bathroom now. What would you do were you Hannah?

Recognizing and Working with Students of Diversity and Differences

You must quickly determine the language and ethnic groups represented by the students in your classroom. A major problem for recent newcomers, as well as some ethnic groups, is learning a second (or third or fourth) language. While in many schools it is not uncommon for more than half the students to come from homes where the spoken language is not English, standard English is a necessity in most communities of this country if a person is to become vocationally successful and enjoy a full life. Learning to communicate reasonably well in English can take an immigrant child at least a year and probably longer, and from three to seven years to catch up academically in English. By default, then, an increasing percentage of public school teachers in the United States are teachers of English language learning (ELL). Helpful to the success of teaching students who are ELLs are the demonstration of respect for students' cultural backgrounds, long-term teacher-student cohorts (such as, in looping), and the use of active and cooperative learning.

There are numerous programs specially designed for English-language learners. Most use the acronym LEP (limited English proficiency) with five number levels, from LEP 1 that designates non-English-speaking, although the student may understand single sentences and speak simple words or phrases in English, to LEP 5, sometimes designated FEP (fluent English proficiency), for the student who is fully fluent in English, although the student's overall academic achievement may still be less than desired because of language or cultural differences.

Some schools use a "pullout" approach, where a portion of the student's school time is spent in special bilingual classes and the rest of the time the student is placed in regular classrooms. In some schools, LEP students are placed in academic classrooms that use a simplified or "sheltered" English approach. For schools that participate in NCLB legislation (they accept federal funding), ELLs as a subgroup must meet Adequate Yearly Progress (AYP) targets for reading and mathematics proficiency and they must meet Annual Measurable Achievement Objectives (AMAOs) for English-language proficiency.

Regardless of the program and its source of funding, specific techniques recommended for teaching ELL students include:

- Allowing more time for learning activities than one normally would.
- Allowing time for translation by a classroom aide or by a classmate and allowing time for dialogue to clarify meaning, encouraging the students to transfer into English what they already know in their native language.
- Avoiding jargon or idioms that might be misunderstood.
- Dividing complex or extended language discourse into smaller, more manageable units.

- Giving directions in a variety of ways.
- Giving special attention to key words that convey meaning and writing them on the board.
- Maintaining high expectations of each learner.
- Reading written directions aloud, and then writing the directions on the board.
- Speaking clearly and naturally but at a slower-than-normal pace.
- Using a variety of examples and observable models.
- Using simplified vocabulary without talking down to students (Walling, 1993, p. 26).

Language-Minority Students

While they are becoming more competent in English-language usage, LEP students can learn the same curriculum in the various disciplines as native English-speaking students. Although the guidelines presented in the following paragraphs are important for teaching all students, they are especially important when working with language-minority students.

Present instruction that is concrete, and that includes the most direct learning experiences possible. Use the most concrete (least abstract) forms of instruction.

Build upon (or connect with) what the students already have experienced and know. Building upon what students already know, or think they know, helps them connect their knowledge and construct their understandings.

Encourage student writing. One way is by using student journals (discussed later in this chapter). Also help students learn the vocabulary. Assist the ELL students in learning two vocabulary sets: the regular English vocabulary needed for learning and the new vocabulary introduced by the subject content. For example, while learning science a student is dealing with both the regular English-language vocabulary and the special vocabulary of science.

To the extent possible, involve parents or guardians or siblings. Students whose primary language is not English may have other differences about which you will also need to become knowledgeable. These differences are related to culture, customs, family life, and expectations. To be most successful in working with language-minority students, you should learn as much as possible about each student. Parents (or guardians) of new immigrant children are usually truly concerned about the education of their children and may be very interested in cooperating with you in any way possible. In a study of schools recognized for their exemplary practices with language-minority students, the schools were recognized for their friendliness to parents, that is, for welcoming parents in a variety of innovative ways (Minicucci, 1995).

Plan for and use all learning modalities. As with teaching young adolescents in general, in working with language-minority students you need to use multisensory approaches—learning activities that involve students in auditory, visual, tactile, and kinesthetic learning activities.

Provide scaffolded reading experiences, that is a framework of activities for use in prereading (such as preteaching vocabulary and predicting outcomes), during-reading (such as guided reading and silent reading activities), and postreading (such as playacting and writing), of any genre of text (Fitzgerald & Graves, 2005).

Use small group cooperative learning. Cooperative learning strategies are particularly effective with language-minority students because they provide opportunities for students to produce language in a setting less threatening than is speaking before the entire class.

Use the benefits afforded by modern technology. For example, computer networking allows students to write and communicate with peers from around the world as well as participate in "publishing" their classroom work. (See relevant website at the end of this chapter.)

Additional Guidelines for Working with Students of Diverse Backgrounds.   To be compatible with, and be able to teach, students who come from backgrounds different from yours, you need to believe that, given adequate support, all students *can* learn—regardless of gender, social class, physical characteristics, language, religion, and ethnic or cultural backgrounds. You also need to develop special skills that include those in the following guidelines, each of which has been discussed in detail in other chapters. To work successfully and most effectively with students of diverse backgrounds, you should:

- Build the learning around students' individual learning styles. To the extent possible, personalize learning for each student, much like what is done by using the IEP with special needs learners.
- Communicate positively with every student and with the student's parents or guardians, learning as much as you can about the student and the student's culture, and encouraging family members to participate in the student's learning. Involve parents, guardians, and other members of the community in the educational program so all have a sense of ownership and responsibility and feel positive about the school program.
- Establish and maintain high expectations, although not necessarily the same expectations, for each student. Both you and your students must understand intelligence is not a fixed entity, but a set of characteristics that—through a feeling of "I can" and with proper coaching—can be developed.
- Teach individuals by using a variety of strategies to achieve an objective or by using a number of different objectives at the same time (multilevel teaching).
- Use techniques that emphasize collaborative and cooperative learning—that de-emphasize competitive learning.

Recognizing and Working with Students Who Are Gifted

Historically, educators have used the term *gifted* when referring to a person with identified exceptional ability in one or more academic subjects, and *talented* when referring to a person with exceptional ability in one or more of the visual or performing arts (Clark & Zimmerman, 1998). Today, however, the terms more often are used interchangeably, which is how they are used for this resource guide, that is, as if they are synonymous (Callahan, 2001).

Sometimes, unfortunately, in the regular classroom gifted students are neglected (Feldhusen, 1998; Gross, 2000). At least some of the time, it is probably because there is no singularly accepted method for identification of these students. In other words, students who are gifted in some way or another may go unidentified as such. For placement in special classes or programs for the gifted, school districts traditionally have used grade point averages and standard intelligence quotient (IQ) scores. On the other hand, because IQ testing measures linguistic and logical/mathematical aspects of giftedness, it does not account for others and thus gifted students sometimes are unrecognized. They also are sometimes among the students most at risk of dropping out of school (Saunders, 2003).

To work most effectively with gifted learners, their talents first must be identified. This can be done not only by using tests, rating scales, and auditions but also by observations in the classroom, out of the classroom, and from knowledge about the student's life away from school. With those information sources in mind, indicators of superior intelligence are (Schwartz, 1997):

- a strong sense of self, pride, and worth
- ability to assume adult roles and responsibilities at home or at work
- ability to cope with school while living in poverty
- ability to cope with school while living with dysfunctional families
- ability to extrapolate knowledge to different circumstances
- ability to lead others
- ability to manipulate a symbol system
- ability to reason by analogy
- ability to retrieve and use stored knowledge to solve problems
- ability to think and act independently
- ability to think logically
- an understanding of one's cultural heritage
- creativity and artistic ability.

Curriculum Tracking

Every student, not only those identified as being gifted, needs a challenging academic environment. Although grouping and tracking students into classes based on interest and demonstrated ability is still practiced (such as reading groups, grade level retention, accelerated groups, and special education placement), an overwhelming abundance of sources in the literature adamantly opposes the homogeneous grouping of students according to ability, or *curriculum tracking*, as it has long been known. Grouping and tracking do not seem to increase overall achievement of learning, but they do promote inequity (Schwartz, 2000). Tracking is acceptable when it is based upon grouping students according to their interests or vocational aspirations, but tracking students on the basis of race, intelligence, or social class is *not* acceptable and should not be practiced.

Meaningful Curriculum Options: Multiple Pathways to Success

Because of what is now known about learning and intelligence, the trend today is to assume that every student, to some degree and in some area of learning and doing, has the potential for giftedness, and to provide sufficient curriculum options, or multiple pathways, so each student can reach those potentials. That is the reason why, for example, in schools' mission statements (see Chapter 1) today there is usually reference to the school's belief that *all* students can succeed. Clearly, achievement in school increases, students learn more, enjoy learning and remember more of what they have learned when the instruction is developmentally appropriate for the needs of the particular students, and when individual learning capacities, styles, and modalities are identified and accommodated.

To provide relevant curriculum options, a trend in exemplary schools is to eliminate from the school curriculum what have traditionally been the lower and general curriculum tracks and instead provide curriculum options to try and assure a positive environment with success for each student. While attempting to diminish the discriminatory and damaging effects on students believed caused by tracking and homogeneous ability grouping, educators have devised and are refining numerous other seemingly more productive ways of attending to student differences, of providing a more challenging but supportive learning environment, and of stimulating the talents and motivation of each and every student. Because the advantage gained from utilizing a combination of responsive practices concurrently is generally greater than is the gain from using any singular practice by itself, in many instances in a given school the practices overlap and are used simultaneously. These practices are shown in Figure 8.1.

Additional Guidelines for Working with Students with Special Gifts and Talents. When working in the

Figure 8.1   Multiple pathways to success: Productive ways of attending to student differences, of providing a positive and challenging learning environment, and of stimulating the talents, interests, and motivation of each and every student.

- Adult advocacy relationships for each student.
- Assuring bilingual programs are intellectually stimulating and designed for integration with mainstream education.
- Collaborative and cooperative learning opportunities in the classroom.
- Community service learning that is connected in some way to the academic program.
- Curriculum compacting (an enriched or an accelerated study of the curriculum).
- Flexible block scheduling.
- High expectation for each student.
- Integration of appropriate technology into the curriculum.
- Interdisciplinary learning and teaming.
- Looping.
- Mastery learning with instructional scaffolding.
- Opportunity and encouragement for accelerated college entrance.
- Opportunity for academic help for every student.
- Opportunity to attend a high school class while still in the middle grades.
- Opportunity to skip a traditional grade level.
- Peer and cross-age instruction.
- Personal problems assistance.
- Personalized education planning and instruction.
- Recovery opportunities.
- Smaller learning communities.
- Thematic instruction.
- Theme schools.
- Ungraded or multiage grouping.
- Within-class and across-discipline student-centered projects.

regular classroom with a student who has special gifts and talents, you are advised to:

- Collaborate with students in some planning of their personal objectives and activities for learning.
- Emphasize skills in critical thinking, problem solving, and inquiry.
- Identify and showcase the student's special gift or talent.
- Involve the student in selecting and planning activities, encouraging the development of the student's leadership skills.
- Plan assignments and activities that challenge the students to the fullest of their abilities. This does not mean overloading them with homework or giving identical assignments to all students (see discussion of tiered assignments on page 344). Rather, carefully plan so students' time spent on assignments and activities is quality time on meaningful learning.
- Provide in-class seminars for students to discuss topics and problems they are pursuing individually or as members of a learning team.
- Provide independent and self-paced learning, and dyad learning opportunities. Gifted and talented students often prefer working alone or with another gifted student.
- Use curriculum compacting, a process that allows a student who already knows the material to pursue enriched or accelerated study (Willard-Holt, 2003). Plan and provide optional and voluntary enrichment

activities. Learning centers, special projects, learning contracts, and computer and multimedia activities are excellent tools for provision of enriched learning activities.

- Use diagnostic assessments for reading level and subject-content achievement so you are better able to prescribe objectives and activities for each student.

Recognizing and Working with Students Who Take More Time but Are Willing to Try

Students who are slower to learn typically fall into one of two categories: (1) those who try to learn but simply need more time to do it and (2) those who do not try, referred to variously as underachievers, recalcitrant, or reluctant learners. Practices that work well with students of one category are often not those that work well with those of the second—making life difficult for a teacher of 28 students, half who try and half who don't (Kellough, 1970). It is worse still for a teacher of a group of 25 or so students, some who try but need time, one or two who are academically talented, 2 or 3 who have special needs but not the same special needs, a few LEP students, and several who not only seem unwilling to try but who are also disruptive in the classroom. And, by the way, this last example is probably closer to reality for the vast majority of teachers of today's public schools.

Remember this well: just because a student is slow to learn doesn't mean the student is less intelligent;

some students just plain take longer, for any number of reasons. The following guidelines may be helpful when working with a student who is slow, but willing to try:

- Adjust the instruction to the student's preferred learning style, which may be different from yours and from other students in the group.
- Be less concerned with the amount of content coverage than with the student's successful understanding of content that is covered. Teach toward mastery (although this may be antagonistic to modern emphasis on improved student scores on high-stakes assessment tests).
- Discover something the student does exceptionally well, or a special interest, and try and connect the student's learning with that.
- Emphasize basic communication skills, such as speaking, listening, reading, and writing, to ensure the student's skills in these areas are sufficient for learning the intended content.
- Get to know each student, at least well enough that you have empathy for where the person is coming from. For example, as many as half of adolescents from high-poverty inner-city neighborhoods feel hopeless that they will be able to improve their lives (Bolland, 2003). Commit yourself to helping them understand the power of education in finding their way out of such feelings of hopelessness.
- Help the student learn content in small sequential steps with frequent checks for comprehension. Use instructional scaffolding.
- If necessary, help the student to improve his or her reading skills, such as pronunciation and word meanings.
- If using a single textbook, be certain the reading level is adequate for the student; if it is not, then for that student use other, more appropriate, reading materials. Many exemplary middle level teachers maintain a variety of optional texts in their classroom just for this purpose.
- Maximize the use of in-class, on-task work and cooperative learning, with close monitoring of the student's progress. Avoid relying much on successful completion of traditional out-of-class assignments unless you can supply coaching to the student in the classroom.
- Vary the instructional strategies, using a variety of activities to engage the visual, verbal, tactile, and kinesthetic modalities.
- When appropriate, use frequent positive reinforcement, with the intention of building the student's confidence and self-esteem.

Recognizing and Working with Recalcitrant Learners

For working with recalcitrant learners you can use many of the same guidelines from the preceding list, except you should understand that the reasons for these students' behaviors may be quite different from those for the other category of slow learners. Slower-learning students who are willing to try may be slow because of their learning style, because of genetic factors, or a combination of those and any number of other reasons. They are simply slower at learning. But they can and will learn. Recalcitrant learners, on the other hand, may be generally quick and bright thinkers but reluctant even to try because of a history of failure, a history of boredom with school, low confidence level for academic work, a poor self-concept, severe personal problems that distract from school, or any variety and combination of reasons, many of which are emotional/psychological in nature.

Whatever the case, a student identified as being a slow or recalcitrant learner might, in fact, be quite gifted or talented in some way, but because of personal problems, have a history of increasingly poor school attendance, poor attention to schoolwork, poor self-confidence, and an attitude problem. With those factors in mind, consider the following guidelines when working with recalcitrant learners:

- As the school year begins, learn as much about each student as you can. Be cautious in how you do it, though, because many of these students will be suspicious of any interest you show in them. Be businesslike, trusting, genuinely interested, and patient. A second caution: although you learn as much as possible about each student, what has happened in the past is history. Use the information not as ammunition, something to be held against the student, but as insight to help you work more productively with the student.
- Avoid lecturing to these students; it won't work, at least not for awhile.
- Early in the school term, preferably with the help of adult volunteers (e.g., using professional community members as mentors has worked well at helping change the student's attitude from rebellion to one of hope, challenge, and success), work out a personalized education program with each student.
- Engage the students in learning by using interactive media, such as the Internet.
- Engage the students in active learning with real-world problem solving and perhaps community service projects (see the many examples later in this chapter in the list of more than 125 motivational strategies).
- Forget about trying to "cover the subject matter," concentrate instead on student learning of some things well. Practice mastery (although this may go against the grain of modern emphasis on improved student scores on high-stakes achievement tests). A good procedure is to use thematic teaching and divide the theme into short segments. Because school attendance for these students is sometimes sporadic, try personalizing their assignments so they can pick up where they left off and move through the course in an

orderly fashion even when they have been absent excessively. Try assuring some degree of success for each student.

- Help students develop their studying and learning skills, such as concentrating, remembering, and comprehension. Mnemonics, for example, is a device these students respond to positively, and are often quick and creative in inventing their own.
- If using a single textbook, see if the reading level is appropriate; if it is not, then for that student discard the book and select other, more appropriate, reading materials.
- Make sure your classroom procedures and rules are understood at the beginning of the school term and be consistent about following them.
- Maximize the use of in-class, on-task work and cooperative learning, with close monitoring of the student's progress. Do not rely on successful completion of traditional out-of-class assignments unless the student receives coached guidance from you before leaving your classroom.
- Use simple language in the classroom. Be concerned less about the words the students use and the way they use them and more about the ideas they are expressing. Let the students use their own idioms without carping too much on grammar and syntax. Always take care, though, to model proper and professional English yourself.
- When appropriate, use frequent positive reinforcement, with the intention of increasing the student's sense of personal worth. When using praise for reinforcement, however, try to direct your praise to the deed rather than the student.

Recognizing and Working with Abused Children

Child abuse is a grave matter of pressing national concern. Teachers in all states are now legally mandated to report any suspicion of child abuse. It is a serious moral issue not to report such suspicion, and lawsuits for negligence have been brought against educators for not doing so. To report suspicion of child abuse, follow your school's written policy. If there is none, you can telephone 1-800-4-A-CHILD or use the hotline for your state. Proof of abuse is not necessary.

Although physical abuse and certain kinds of neglect, such as improper clothing and inadequate dental care, may be the easiest to spot, other types of abuse such as incest, emotional, and malnutrition can be just as serious. Characteristics of children who are abused or neglected are shown in Figure 8.2. An abused or neglected child in your classroom needs to feel welcome and secure while in the classroom. For additional guidance in working with such a student, contact experts from your local school district (e.g., the school psychologist), and obtain guidelines from your state department of education or from the local Children's Protective Services (CPS) agency.

Figure 8.2 Characteristics of children who may be abused or neglected.

- Abrasions at corner of mouth.
- Below normal in height and/or weight.
- Bruised or swollen lip.
- Difficulty walking or sitting.
- Exhibit self-destructive behavior.
- Exhibit hyperactive or aggressive behavior.
- Exhibit short attention spans and lack of interest in school.
- Exhibit sudden and dramatic changes in behavior.
- Expression of little to no emotion when hurt.
- Falling asleep in class.
- Fear of everyone and everything.
- Fear of going home after school.
- Fear of parent/guardian and other adults.
- Frequently sick and absent from school.
- Frequently tired and often falls asleep in class.
- Indiscriminate craving for attention or affection.
- Odor of alcohol.
- Scars from previous injuries or multiple injuries in various stages of healing.
- Tongue and lip lacerations.
- Unclean, smelling of body wastes.
- Unexpected crying.
- Unexplained burns in various stages of healing.
- Unexplained fractures, lacerations, and bruises.
- Welts, human bite marks, bald spots.
- Withdrawn from adult contact.
- Withdrawn from peer interaction.

LEARNING ALONE

While some students learn well in pairs (dyads), and others learn well with their peers in groups—collaboratively, cooperatively, or competitively—or collaboratively with adults, and others learn well in combinations of these patterns, researchers tell us that more than 10 percent of students learn best alone (Dunn, 1995). Learning-alone students often are gifted, nonconforming, able to work at their own pace successfully, comfortable using media, or seemingly underachieving but potentially able students for whom unconventional instructional strategies, such as *contract learning packages*—that is, agreements between the teacher and individual students to proceed with tasks appropriate to their readiness, interests, or learning profiles in a sequence and at a pace each student selects. For a learning-alone student, instructional packages utilizing a multisensory approach are most apt to encourage and ensure academic success.

The Self-Instructional Module

One technique that can be used to ensure mastery of learning is the self-instructional module (SIM), which is a learning package (written, on audio- or video recording, or on computer) specifically designed with an individual student in mind. It uses small sequential steps, with frequent practice and immediate learning feedback to the student. It is designed to teach a relatively small amount of material, at the mastery level, requiring a brief amount of learning time (about 30 minutes for middle grades students). The SIM can be designed to teach any topic, at any grade level, in any subject, for any domain or combination of domains of learning. Exercise 8.1 is a self-instructional module designed to guide you through the completion of your first SIM.

As instructed by your course instructor, do Exercise 8.1.

FOR YOUR NOTES

PP EXERCISE 8.1: PREPARING A SELF-INSTRUCTIONAL MODULE*

INSTRUCTIONS: The purpose of this exercise is to guide you through the process of preparing a self-instructional module for use in your own teaching. The exercise continues for several pages; it is important that you follow it step by step, beginning with the following boxed-in "cover page."

Self-Instructional Module Number: 1

Instructor's Name: Professor Richard D. Kellough
School: California State University, Sacramento
Course: Methods of Teaching Young Adolescents
Intended Students: Students in Teacher Preparation
Topic: How to Write a Self-Instructional Module
Estimated Working Time: 10 hours

For the challenge of today's classroom . . .

THE SELF-INSTRUCTIONAL MODULE

You are about to embark upon creating and writing a perfect lesson plan. The result of your hard work will be an instructional module in which you will take a lot of pride. More important, you will have learned a technique of teaching that ensures learning takes place. For what more could you ask?

Let us get to the essence of what this self-instructional module (SIM) is: This SIM is about how to write a SIM. The general objective is to guide you gently through the process of preparing and writing your first SIM. Let's begin the experience with background about the history of the SIM.

A History

Research evidence indicates that student achievement in learning is related to time and to the *quality of attention* being given to the learning task. You knew that already! In 1968, Benjamin Bloom developed a concept of individualized instruction called mastery learning, based on the idea that students need sufficient time on task to master

---

☞

EXERCISE 8.1   *(continued)*

content before moving on to new content. Did you know that? _____. (Please read along with a pencil, and fill in the blanks as you go.)

Although Bloom is usually given credit for the concept of mastery learning, the idea did not originate with him. He reinforced and made popular a model developed earlier by John Carroll. In 1968, Fred Keller developed a similar model called the Keller Plan, or the Personalized System of Instruction (PSI). The PSI quickly became a popular teaching technique in the community and four-year colleges. In about 1972, enter Johnson and Johnson (not of the Band-Aid™ family, but Rita and Stuart Johnson), who developed their model of mastery learning and called it the Self-Instructional Package (SIP). Since 1972, I (Richard D. Kellough) have been developing my version, the Self-Instructional Module, which you are now experiencing. As you will learn, *frequent comprehension checks and corrective instructions* are important to the effectiveness of the SIM.

One other thing. There are several devices available to individualize instruction, but the SIM has the flexibility to be adaptable for use at all grade levels, from kindergarten through college. I believe the following to be the reasons for the popularity of this strategy:

- The SIM allows the teacher to *create an experience that ensures learning.* Creating makes you feel good; when your students learn, you feel good—two reasons for the SIM's popularity.
- The SIM is truly *individualized,* because it is a module written for an individual student, with that student in mind as it is being written.
- Although it takes time to prepare, the SIM *requires little financial expenditure,* a fact important to today's teacher.
- Once you have prepared your first SIM, you might see that you have begun a series. Subsequent modules are easier to do, and you may see the value in having a series available.
- With today's emphasis on the *basics,* the SIM is particularly helpful for use in remediation.
- When you finish your SIM, you will have collected the content that could be used for a computer program.
- With today's *large and mixed-ability classes,* teachers need help! Here is time and cost-effective help!
- With emphasis today on competency-based instruction, the SIM makes sense.

How are we doing so far? _____ Are your interests and curiosity aroused? _____ _____ Do you have questions? _____ If so, write them down, then continue.

Questions: _____

_____

_____

_____

What Is the Self-Instructional Module and Why Use It?

The SIM is a learning module designed for an individual student; it is self-instructional (i.e., if you, the teacher, drop dead—heaven forbid—the student can continue to learn), and *it requires about 30 minutes of learning time.* The final module can be recorded on tape, video, or computer disc; it can be written in booklet form; or it can exist in any combination of these.

Here are ways that teachers have found the SIM to be useful:

- As an *enrichment* activity for an accelerated student.
- As a strategy for makeup for a student who has been absent.
- As a strategy for a student in need of *remediation.*
- As a strategy for introducing basic information to an entire class, freeing the teacher to work with individual students, making the act of teaching more *time-efficient,* a particularly significant value of the SIM.
- As a learning experience especially coordinated with manipulatives, perhaps in connection with a science experiment, library work, a computer, a tape recording, a videotape, a DVD, hands-on materials for an activity, or any combination of these.

One other point before we stop and check your comprehension: *The single most important characteristic of the SIM is that it uses small sequential steps followed by immediate and corrective feedback to the learner.* In that respect, the SIM resembles programmed instruction.

EXERCISE 8.1 *(continued)*

  Stop the action!

Let's check your learning with the review questions and instructions that follow.

Comprehension Check 1

Answer the following three questions, then check your responses by reviewing Feedback Check 1. If you answer all three questions correctly, continue the package; otherwise, back up and review.

---

1. How would you define a SIM? _____

_____

_____

2. What is the single most important characteristic of the SIM? _____

_____

3. What is one way that the SIM could be used in your own teaching, a way that currently stands out in your thinking?

_____

_____

Feedback Check 1

1. Although we will continue development of the definition, at this point it should resemble this: The SIM is an individual-ization of learning—teaching strategy that teaches toward mastery learning of one relatively small bit of content by building upon small, sequential steps and providing corrective feedback throughout.
2. Referring to the small, sequential steps, followed by immediate and corrective feedback.
3. Your answer is probably related to one of those listed earlier but it could differ.

How Does the SIM Differ from Other Kinds of Learning Packages?

Another characteristic of the SIM is the *amount of learning contained in one module.* Each SIM is designed to teach a relatively small amount of material, but to do it well. *This is a major difference in the SIM from other types of learning activity packages.*

And, in case you have been wondering about what the SIM can be designed to teach, I want to emphasize that it *can be designed*

- For any topic,
  - At any grade level,
    - In any discipline,
      - For cognitive understanding,
        - For psychomotor development, and
          - For affective learning.

That probably brings to your mind all sorts of thoughts and questions. Hold them for a moment, and let's do another comprehension check.

☞

EXERCISE 8.1   *(continued)*

 Stop the action and check your learning.

Comprehension Check 2

Answer the following two questions, then check your responses in the feedback box that follows.

---

1. How does the SIM differ from other self-contained learning packages?

    _____

    _____

    _____

2. Although teachers frequently emphasize learning that falls within the cognitive domain, is it possible for the SIM to be written to include learning in the psychomotor and affective domains? Yes or no? _____

Feedback Check 2

1. Length of learning time is shorter for the SIM, and it is written with an individual student in mind. It is written to teach one thing well, to one student.
2. The SIM *can* be written for any domain, although evaluation is trickier for the affective and for the highest-level psychomotor.

Perhaps we should now say a word about what we mean when we use the expression *teach one thing well*—that is, to explain what is meant by mastery learning. Theoretically, if the package is being used by an individual student, performance level expectation is 100 percent. In reality, performance level will most likely be between 85 and 95 percent, particularly if you are using the SIM for a group of students rather than an individual. That 5–15 percent difference allows for human errors that can occur in writing and in reading.

Now that you have learned what the SIM is—and how this learning strategy differs from other learning activity packages—it is time to concentrate on developing your SIM. Please continue.

SIM DEVELOPMENT

How Do I Develop a SIM?

As with any good lesson plan, it takes time to develop an effective SIM. Indeed, preparation of your first SIM will test your imagination and writing skills! Nevertheless, it will be time well spent; you will be proud of your product. *It is important that you continue following this module, step by step; do not skip parts, or I will assume no responsibility for your final product! Understand?* _____ Development of your SIM emphasizes the importance of

- Writing the learning objectives clearly, precisely, and in behavioral terms.
- Planning the learning activities in small, sequential steps.
- Providing frequent practice and learning comprehension checks.
- Providing immediate feedback, corrective instruction, and assurance to the learner.
- Preparing evaluative questions that measure against the learning objectives.

As you embark on preparing what may be the perfect lesson plan, keep in mind the following two points:

1. Prepare your first SIM so it will take no more than

---

30 minutes for young adolescents

EXERCISE 8.1 *(continued)*

2. Use a *conversational tone* in your writing. Write in the first person, as though you are talking directly to the student for whom it is intended. For example, when speaking of the learning objectives, use *You will be able to* rather than *The student will be able to*. Keep in mind that you are communicating with one person rather than with an entire class (even though you may be preparing your package for entire class use). It helps to pretend that you are in a one-on-one situation tutoring the student at the writing board.

Stop the action, and again check your learning.

Comprehension Check 3

Answer the following two questions; then check your responses in Feedback Check 3.

---

1. What maximum learning-time duration is recommended? _____

2. What major item of importance has been recommended for you to keep in mind as you write your SIM?

_____

_____

Feedback Check 3

1. Approximately 30 minutes.
2. Write in the first person, as if you are speaking directly to the student.

Now that I have emphasized the *length of learning time* and *the personalization of your writing*, here are other important reminders.

1. Make your SIM attractive and stimulating. Consider using cartoons, puns, graphics, scratch-and-sniff stickers, and interesting manipulatives. Use your creative imagination! Use both cerebral hemispheres!

Add sketches, diagrams, modules, pictures, magazine clippings, humor, and a conversational tone, as students appreciate a departure from the usual textbooks and worksheets.

2. Use colleagues as resource persons, brainstorming ideas as you proceed through each step of module production.

During production, use your best cooperative learning skills.

☞

EXERCISE 8.1   *(continued)*

3. The module should not be read (or heard) like a lecture. It *must* involve small sequential steps with frequent practice and corrective feedback instruction (as modeled in this module).

"*. . . and with the course material broken down into small, self-instructional units, students can move through at individual rates.*"

4. The module should contain a variety of activities, preferably involving all four learning modalities—*visual, auditory, tactile,* and *kinesthetic.*

5. Vary margins, indentations, and fonts so the final module does not have the usual textbook or worksheet appearance with which students are so familiar. Build into your module the "Hawthorne Effect."

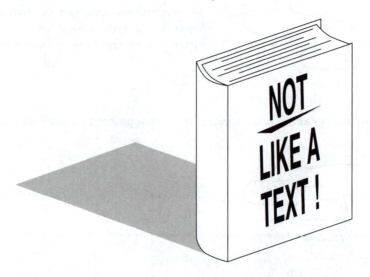

EXERCISE 8.1 *(continued)*

Note about the cosmetics of your SIM: My own prejudice about the SIM is that it should be spread out more than the usual textbook page or worksheet. Use double-spaced lines, varied margins, and so on. Make cosmetic improvements after finishing your final draft. Write, review, sleep on it, write more, revise, add that final touch. This modular packet that you are using has been "toned down" and modified for practical inclusion in this textbook.

---

6. Your SIM does not have to fit the common 8 1/2″ × 11″ size. You are encouraged to be creative in the design of your SIM's shape, size, and format.
7. Like all lesson plans, the SIM is subject to revision and improvement after use. Use your best creative writing skills. *Write, review, sleep on it, Write more, revise, test, revise. . . .*

Perhaps before proceeding, it would be useful to review the preceding points. Remember, too, the well-written module *will ensure learning.* Your first SIM will take several hours to produce, but it will be worth it!

Proceed with the steps that follow.

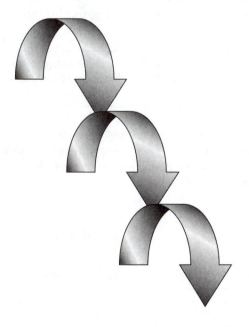

EXERCISE 8.1 *(continued)*

Steps For Developing Your SIM

Instructions: It is important that you proceed through the following module development step by step.

One thing you will notice is that immediately after writing your learning objectives, you will prepare the evaluative test items; both steps precede the preparation of the learning activities. That is not the usual order followed by a teacher when preparing lessons, but it does help to ensure that test items match objectives. Now, here we go! *Step by step,* please.

Note: From here on, write on separate paper for draft planning.

Step 1. Prepare the cover page. It should include the following items:

- Instructor's name (that is you)
  - School (yours)
    - Class or intended students (whom it's for)
      - Topic (specific but not wordy)
        - Estimated working time

For a sample, refer to the beginning of this module. You can vary the design of the cover page according to your needs.

Step 2. Prepare the instructional objectives. For now, these should be written in specific behavioral terms. Later, when writing these into your module introduction, you can phrase them in more general terms.

Recommended is the inclusion of at least one attitudinal (affective) objective, such as "Upon completion of this module, you will tell me your feelings about this kind of learning."

Step 3. **Comprehension Check 4**

Share with your colleagues what you have accomplished (with steps 1 and 2) to solicit their valuable feedback and input.

Step 4. Depending on feedback (from step 3), *modify items 1 and 2,* if necessary. For example, after listing the learning instructions, you may find that you really have more than one module in preparation, and within the list of objectives you may find a natural cut-off between modules 1 and 2. You may discover that you have a *series* of modules begun.

Step 5. Prepare the pretest. If the learner does well on the pretest, there may be no need for the student to continue the module. Some modules (like this one) may not include a pretest, though most will. And if this is your first SIM writing experience, I think you *should* include a pretest.

Suggestion: The pretest need not be as long as the posttest but should include a limited sample of questions to determine whether the student already knows the material and need not continue with the module. A pretest also serves to set the student mentally for the SIM.

Step 6. Prepare the posttest. The pretest and posttest could be identical, but usually the pretest is shorter. It is important that both pretest and posttest items actually test against the objectives (of step 2). Try to keep the items objective (e.g., multiple-choice type), avoiding as much as possible the use of subjective test items (e.g., essay type), but do include at least one item measuring an affective objective (see boxed item in step 2).

Important reminder: If your module is well written, the student should achieve 85–100 percent on the posttest.

Step 7. **Comprehension Check 5**

Share with colleagues your pretest and posttest items (providing a copy of your objectives) for suggested improvement changes before continuing to the next step.

EXERCISE 8.1 *(continued)*

Use the following space to write notes to yourself about ideas you are having and regarding any materials you may need to complete your module.

Dear Self—

Good work so far! Before continuing, take a break.

It is time to stop working for a while . . .   . . . and go play!

Step 8. Okay, enough play; it is time to prepare the text of your SIM. This is the "meat" of your module—what goes between the pretest and the posttest. It is the INSTRUCTION. *Reminder:* For the SIM to be self-instructional, the learner should be able to work through the module with little or no help from you.

An important ingredient in your module is the *directions.* The module should be self-directed and self-paced. Therefore, each step of the module should be clear to the learner, making you, the instructor, literally unnecessary. *Everything needed by the learner to complete the module should be provided with the module.*

☞

EXERCISE 8.1   *(continued)*

Use small, sequential steps with frequent practice cycles, followed by comprehension checks and corrective feedback. Make it fun and interesting with a variety of activities for the student, activities that provide for learning in several ways, from writing to reading, from viewing a video tape to drawing, from listening to a tape recording to doing a hands-on activity. And be certain the activities correlate with the learning objectives. The learning cycles should lead to satisfaction of the stated objectives, and the posttest items *must* measure against those objectives.

Step 9. **Comprehension Check 6**

Test your package. Try it out on your colleagues as they look for content errors, spelling and grammar errors, and clarity, as well as offer suggestions for improvement. Duplicate and use the SIM Assessment Form provided at the end of this exercise.

Stop the Action! Congratulations on the development of your first SIM! However, two additional steps need your consideration.

Step 10. Revise, if necessary. Make appropriate changes to your SIM as a result of the feedback from your colleagues. Then you are ready to give your SIM its first real test—try it out on the student for whom it is intended.

Step 11. Further revisions. This comes later, after you have used it with the student for whom it was originally intended. Like any other well-prepared lesson or unit plan, it should always be subject to revision and to improvement, never "set in concrete."

SIM ASSESSMENT FORM

1. Module identification
   Author: _____

   _____

   _____

   Title of SIM: _____

   _____

   _____

2. Module Objectives: Do they tell the student

   a. What the student will be able to do? _____

   _____

   _____

   _____

   _____

   b. How the student will demonstrate this new knowledge or skill? _____

   _____

   _____

   _____

   _____

   Is there a clear statement (overview or introduction) of the importance, telling the learner what will be learned by completing the module?

   _____

   _____

   _____

   _____

3. Pretest

   _____

   _____

   _____

   _____

   _____

   _____

4. Activities (practice cycles)

Are small sequential steps used? _____

_____

_____

_____

Are there frequent practice cycles, with comprehension checks and corrective feedback to the learner?

_____

_____

_____

_____

5. Posttest: Does it test against the objectives? _____

_____

_____

_____

_____

6. Clarity and continuity of expression: _____

_____

_____

_____

_____

7. Is the module informative, attractive, and enjoyable? _____

_____

_____

_____

_____

8. Additional comments useful to the author of this module: _____

_____

_____

_____

_____

LEARNING IN PAIRS

It is sometimes advantageous to pair students (dyads) for learning. Four types of dyads are described as follows.

Peer tutoring, mentoring, and cross-age coaching. Peer mentoring, tutoring, or peer-assisted learning (PAL) is a strategy whereby one student tutors another. It is useful, for example, when one student helps another who has limited proficiency in English or when a student skilled in math helps another whom is less skilled. It has been demonstrated repeatedly that peer tutoring is a significant strategy for promoting active learning (Bacon, 2005; Thrope & Wood, 2000). Cross-age coaching is a strategy whereby one student coaches another from a different, and sometimes lower, grade level (Jacobson et al., 2001; Potenza, 2003). This is similar to peer tutoring, except that the coach is from a different age/grade level than the student being coached.

Paired team learning. Paired team learning is a strategy whereby students study and learn in teams of two. Students identified as gifted work and learn especially well when paired. Specific uses for paired team learning include drill partners, science buddies, reading buddies, book report pairs, summary pairs, homework partners, project assignment pairs, and elaborating and relating pairs.

Think-pair-share (see Chapter 2).

The Learning Center

Another significantly beneficial way of pairing students for instruction (as well as of individualizing the instruction and learning alone and integrating the learning) is by using the learning center (LC) or learning station. [*Note:* Whereas each learning center is distinct and unrelated to others, learning stations are sequenced or in some way linked to one another, as discussed in the TEAMS approach that follows.] The LC is a special area located in the classroom where one student (or two, if student interaction is necessary or preferred at the center; or as many as four or five students in the case of learning stations) can quietly work and learn at the student's own pace more about a special topic or to improve specific skills. All materials needed are provided at that center, including clear instructions for operation of the center.

Whereas the LC used to be thought of as belonging to the domain of elementary school teachers with self-contained classrooms, now, with block scheduling and longer class periods in many middle schools and high schools, the LC has special relevance and usefulness for all teachers, regardless of grade level. In the words of a teacher of French and Spanish at Bailey Middle School (Austin, TX),

As other teachers in our district have begun to use center techniques, I hear comments such as, "The students are so excited," and "There was none of the chaos I was afraid of." In using centers as a teaching tool, I have found that students are eager to participate in all class work and excited about speaking a new language both inside and outside the classroom. (Voelzel, 2000)

The value of learning centers as instructional devices undoubtedly lies in the following facts. LCs can provide instructional diversity. While working at a center, the student is giving time and quality attention to the learning task (learning toward mastery) and is likely to be engaging his or her most effective learning modality, or integrating several modalities or all of them.

Learning centers are of three types. In the *direct-learning center*, performance expectations for cognitive learning are quite specific and the focus is on mastery of content. In the *open-learning center*, the goal is to provide opportunity for exploration, enrichment, motivation, and creative discovery. In the *skill center*, as in a direct-learning center, performance expectations are quite specific, but the focus is on the development of a particular skill or process.

In all instances, the primary reason for using a learning center is to individualize—that is, to provide collections of materials and activities adjusted to the various readiness levels, interests, and learning profiles of students. Other reasons to use an LC are to provide: 1) a mechanism for learning that crosses discipline boundaries; 2) a special place for a student with exceptional needs; 3) opportunities for creative work, enrichment experiences, and multisensory experiences; and 4) the opportunity to learn from learning packages that utilize special equipment or media of which only one or a limited supply may be available for use in the classroom (e.g., science materials, a microscope, a computer, a DVD player, or some combination of these).

To adapt instruction to the curriculum and to students' individual needs and preferences, it is possible to design a learning environment that includes several learning stations, each of which uses a different medium and modality or focuses on a special aspect of the curriculum. Students then rotate through the various stations according to their needs and preferences (Reiser & Butzin, 2000).

> Learning centers should always be used for educational purposes, *never* for punishment.

To construct an LC you can be as elaborate and as creative as your time, imagination, and resources allow. Students can even help you plan and set up learning centers, which will relieve some of the burden from your busy schedule. The following paragraphs present guidelines for setting up and using this valuable instructional tool.

The center should be designed with a theme in mind, preferably one that integrates the students' learning by providing activities that cross discipline boundaries. Decide the purpose of the center and give the center a name, such as "the center for the study of wetlands," "walking tour of Jerusalem," "patterns in nature," "the United Nations," "sound editing," "our state capitol," "the center for worldwide communication," or "history of the overseas highway," and so on. The purpose of the center should be clearly understood by the students.

The center should be designed so as to be attractive, purposeful, and uncluttered and should be identified with an attractive sign. Learning centers should be activity-oriented (i.e., dependent on the student's manipulation of materials, not just paper-and-pencil tasks).

Topics for the center should be related to the instructional program—for review and reinforcement, remediation, or enrichment. The center should be self-directing (i.e., specific instructional objectives and procedures for using the center should be clearly posted and understandable to the student user). An audio- or videocassette or a computer program is sometimes used for this purpose. The center should also be self-correcting (i.e., student users should be able to tell by the way they have completed the task whether or not they have done it correctly and have learned).

The center should contain a variety of activities geared to the varying abilities and interest levels of the students. A choice of two or more activities at a center is one way to provide for this.

Materials to be used at the center should be maintained at the center, with descriptions for use provided to the students. Using SIMs (Exercise 8.1) with LCs works well. Materials should be safe for student use, and you or another adult should easily supervise the center. Some centers may become more or less permanent centers, that is, remain for the school term or longer, whereas others may change according to what is being studied at the time.

LEARNING IN SMALL GROUPS

Small groups are those involving three to five students, in either a teacher- or a student-directed setting. Using small groups for instruction, including the cooperative learning group (CLG), enhances the opportunities for students to assume greater control over their own learning, sometimes referred to as *empowerment.*

Purposes for Using Small Groups

Small groups can be formed to serve a number of purposes. They might be useful for a specific learning activity (e.g., *literature circles*, where students who have read the same self-selected story or novel discuss their reading (Scott, 1994), or *reciprocal reading groups*, where students take turns asking questions, summarizing, making predictions about, and clarifying a story (Slater & Horstman, 2002). Or they might be formed to complete an activity that requires materials that are of short supply, to

Scott Cunningham/Merrill

complete a science experiment or a project, only lasting as long as the project does. Teachers have various rationales for assigning students to groups. Groups can be formed by grouping students according to: (a) personality type (e.g., sometimes a teacher may want to team less-assertive students together in order to give them the opportunity for greater management of their own learning), (b) social pattern (e.g., sometimes it may be necessary to break up a group of rowdy friends, or it may be desirable to broaden the association among students), (c) common interest, (d) learning styles (e.g., forming groups of either mixed styles or of styles in common), or (e) according to their abilities in a particular skill or their knowledge in a particular area. One specific type of small-group instruction is the cooperative learning group.

COOPERATIVE LEARNING

More than a century ago, Lev Vygotsky studied the importance of a learner's social interactions in learning situations, concluding that learning is most effective when learners cooperate with one another in a supportive learning environment under the careful guidance of a teacher. Cooperative learning, group problem solving, problem-based learning, and cross-age tutoring are instructional strategies used by teachers that have grown in popularity as a result of research evolving from the work of Vygotsky (1962, 1978).

The Cooperative Learning Group (CLG)

The *cooperative learning group* is a heterogeneous group (i.e., mixed according to one or more criteria, such as ability or skill level, ethnicity, learning style, learning capacity, gender, and language proficiency) of three to five students who work together in a teacher- or student-directed setting, emphasizing support for one another. Oftentimes, a CLG consists of four students of mixed ability, learning styles, gender, and ethnicity, with each member of the group assuming a particular role. Teachers usually change the membership of each group several to many times during the year.

The Theory and Use of Cooperative Learning

The theory of cooperative learning is that when small groups of students of mixed backgrounds and capabilities work together toward a common goal, members of the group increase their friendship and respect for one another. As a consequence, each individual's self-esteem is enhanced, students are more motivated to participate in higher-order thinking, and academic achievement is accomplished. In short, the effective use of heterogeneous cooperative learning helps students grow academically, socially, and emotionally (Schniedewind & Davidson, 2000; Slavin, 1996).

There are several techniques for using cooperative learning (see, for example, Coelho, 1994; Johnson, Johnson, & Holubec, 1998; Sharan & Sharan, 1992). Yet the primary purpose of each is for the groups to learn—which means, of course, that individuals within a group must learn. Group achievement in learning, then, is dependent upon the learning of individuals within the group. Rather than competing for rewards for achievement, members of the group cooperate with one another by helping one another learn so that the group reward will be a good one. Normally, the group is rewarded on the basis of group achievement, though individual members within the group can later be rewarded for individual contributions. Because of peer pressure, when using CLGs you must be cautious about using group grading. For grading purposes, bonus points can be given to all members of a group; individuals can add to their own scores when everyone in the group has reached preset standards. The preset standards must be appropriate for all members of a group. Lower standards or improvement criteria could be set for students with lower ability so everyone feels rewarded and successful. To determine each student's term grades, individual student achievement is measured later through individual students' results on tests and other criteria, as well as through each student's performance in the group work.

Roles within the Cooperative Learning Group

It is advisable to assign roles (specific functions) to each member of the CLG. (The lesson plan shown in the unit plan of Figure 6.16, Chapter 6, shows the use of a CLG activity using assigned roles for a lesson in science.) These roles should be rotated, either during the activity or from one time to the next. Although titles may vary, five typical roles are:

- Group facilitator—role is to keep the group on task.
- Materials manager—role is to obtain, maintain, and return materials needed for the group to function.

- Recorder—role is to record all group activities and processes, and perhaps to periodically assess how the group is doing.
- Reporter—role is to report group processes and accomplishments to the teacher and/or to the entire class. When using groups of four members, the roles of recorder and reporter can easily be combined.
- Thinking monitor—role is to identify and record the sequence and processes of the group's thinking. This role encourages metacognition and the development of thinking skills.

It is important that students understand and perform their individual roles, and that each member of the CLG performs her or his tasks as expected. No student should be allowed to ride on the coattails of the group. To give significance to and to reinforce the importance of each role, and to be able to readily recognize the role any student is playing during CLG activity, one teacher made a trip to an office supplier and had permanent badges made for the various CLG roles. During CLGs, then, each student attaches the appropriate badge to her or his clothing.

What Students and the Teacher Do When Using Cooperative Learning Groups

Actually, for learning by CLGs to work, each member of the CLG must understand and assume two roles or responsibilities—the role he or she is assigned as a member of the group, and that of making sure all others in the group are performing their roles. Sometimes this requires interpersonal skills that young adolescents have yet to learn or to learn well. This is where the teacher must assume some responsibility, too. Simply placing students into CLGs and expecting each member and each group to function and to learn the expected outcomes may not work. In other words, skills of cooperation must be taught, and if all your students have not yet learned the skills of cooperation, then you will have to teach them. This doesn't mean that if a group is not functioning you immediately break up the group and reassign members to new groups. Important to group learning is learning the process of how to work out conflict. For a group to work out a conflict may require your assistance. With your guidance the group should be able to discover the problem that is causing the conflict, then identify some options and mediate at least a temporary solution. If a particular skill is needed, then, with your guidance, students identify and learn that skill.

When to Use Cooperative Learning Groups

CLGs can be used for problem solving, investigations, opinion surveys, experiments, review, project work, test making, or almost any other instructional purpose. Just as you would for small-group work in general, you can use CLGs for most any purpose at any time.

Cooperative Group Learning, Assessment, and Grading

Normally, the CLG is rewarded on the basis of group achievement, though individual members within the group can later be rewarded for individual contributions (see Figure 8.3). Because of peer pressure, when using CLGs, you must be cautious about using group grading (Guskey, 1996; Kagan, 1995). Some teachers give bonus points to all members of a group to add to their individual scores when everyone in the group has reached preset criteria. In establishing preset standards, the standards can be different for individuals within a group, depending on each member's ability and past performance. It is important that each member of a group feel rewarded and successful. For determination of students' report card grades, individual student achievement is measured later through individual results on tests and other sources of data.

Why Some Teachers Experience Difficulty Using CLGs

Sometimes, when they think they are using CLGs, teachers have difficulty and either give up trying to use the strategy or simply tell students to divide into groups for an activity and call it cooperative learning. As emphasized earlier, for the strategy to work, each student must be given training in and have acquired basic skills in interaction and group processing and must realize that individual achievement rests with that of their group. And, as true for any other strategy, the use of CLGs must not be overused—teachers must vary their strategies.

For the use of CLGs to work well, advanced planning and effective management are a must. Each student must be assigned a responsible role within the group and be held accountable for fulfilling that responsibility. And, when a CLG activity is in process, groups must be continually monitored by the teacher for possible breakdown of this process within a group. In other words, while students are working in groups the teacher must exercise skills of withitness. When a potential breakdown is noticed, the teacher quickly intervenes to help the group get back on track.

LEARNING IN LARGE GROUPS

As defined for purposes of this resource guide, large groups are those that involve more than five students, usually the entire class. Most often, they are teacher-directed. Student presentations and whole-class discussions are two techniques that involve the use of large groups.

Student Presentations

Students should be encouraged to be presenters for discussion of the ideas, opinions, and knowledge obtained from their own independent and small-group study. Several techniques encourage the development of certain skills and intelligent behaviors, such as the skills of studying and organizing material, discovery, discussion, rebuttal, listening, analysis, suspending judgment, and critical thinking. Possible forms of discussions involving student presentations are described as follows:

- *Debate.* The debate is an arrangement in which oral presentations are made by members of two opposing teams on topics preassigned and researched. The speeches are followed by rebuttals from each team (Koenig, 2001).
- *Jury Trial.* The jury trial is a discussion approach in which the class simulates a courtroom, with class members playing the various roles of judge, attorneys, jury members, bailiff, and court recorder.
- *Panel.* The panel is a setting in which four to six students, with one designated as the chairperson or moderator, discuss a topic about which they have studied, followed by a question-and-answer period involving the entire class. The panel usually begins with each panel member giving a brief opening statement.
- *Research Report.* One or two students or a small group of students gives a report on a topic that they investigated, followed by questions and discussion by the entire class.
- *Roundtable.* The roundtable is a small group of three to five students who sit around a table and discuss among themselves (perhaps with the rest of the class listening and later asking questions) a problem or issue that they have studied. One member of the panel may serve as moderator.
- *Symposium.* Similar to a roundtable discussion but more formal, the symposium is an arrangement in which each student participant presents an explanation of his or her position on a preassigned topic researched by the student. Again, one student should serve as moderator. After the presentations, questions are accepted from the rest of the class.

To use these techniques effectively, students may need to be coached by you—individually, in small groups, or in whole-class sessions—on how and where to gather information; how to listen, take notes (Marzano, Pickering, & Pollock, 2001), select major points, organize material, and present a position succinctly and convincingly (see Figure 8.4); how to play roles; and how to engage in dialogue and debate with one another.

Whole-Class Discussion

Direct, whole-class discussion is a teaching technique used frequently by most or all teachers. On this topic,

Figure 8.3 Sample scoring rubric for assessing individual students in a cooperative learning group project. Explanation for use: Possible score = 50. Scorer marks a relevant square in each of the five categories (horizontal rows), and student's score for that category is the small number in the top right corner within that square.

	9–10	8	7	1–6
Goals	Consistently and actively helps identify group goals; works effectively to meet goals.	Consistently communicates commitment to group goals; carries out assigned roles.	Sporadically communicates commitment to group goals; carries out assigned role.	Rarely, if ever, works toward group goals or may work against them.
Interpersonal Skills	Cooperates with group members by encouraging, compromising, and/or taking a leadership role without dominating; shows sensitivity to feelings and knowledge of others.	Cooperates with group members by encouraging, compromising, and/or taking a leadership role.	Participates with group but has own agenda; may not be willing to compromise or to make significant contributions.	May discourage others, harass group members, or encourage off-task behavior. Makes significant changes to others' work without their knowledge or permission.
Quality Producer	Contributes significant information, ideas, time, and/or talent to produce a quality product.	Contributes information, ideas, time, and/or talent to produce a quality product.	Contributes some ideas, though not significant; may be more supportive than contributive; shows willingness to complete assignment but has no desire to go beyond average expectations.	Does little or no work toward the completion of group product; shows little or no interest in contributing to the task; produces work that fails to meet minimum standards for quality.
Participation	Attends daily; consistently and actively utilizes class time by working on the task.	Attends consistently; sends in work to group if absent; utilizes class time by working on the task.	Attends sporadically; absences or tardies may hinder group involvement; may send in work when absent; utilizes some time; may be off task by talking to others, interrupting other groups, or watching others do the majority of the work.	Frequent absences or tardies hinder group involvement; fails to send in work when absent; wastes class time by talking, doing other work, or avoiding tasks; group has asked that member be reproved by teacher or removed from the group.
Commitment	Consistently contributes time out of class to produce a quality product; attends all group meetings as evidenced by the group meeting log.	Contributes time out of class to produce a quality product; attends a majority of group meetings as evidenced by the group meeting log.	Willing to work toward completion of task during class time; attends some of the group meetings; may arrive late or leave early; may keep inconsistent meeting log.	Rarely, if ever, attends group meetings outside of class or may attend and hinder progress of the group; fails to keep meeting log.

Source: Courtesy of Susan Abbott, Pam Benedetti, and Carleen Smith, Elk Grove School District, Elk Grove, California.

Figure 8.4 Sample scoring rubric for small-group or individual presentation.

PRESENTATION SCORING RUBRIC

5. Presentation was excellent. Project clearly understood and delivery organized.
   - Made eye contact throughout presentation.
   - Spoke loud enough for all to hear.
   - Spoke clearly.
   - Spoke for time allotted.
   - Stood straight and confidently.
   - Covered at least five pieces of important information.
   - Introduced project.
   - All members spoke.

4. Presentation was well thought out and planned.
   - Made eye contact throughout most of presentation.
   - Spoke loud enough and clearly most of the time.
   - Spoke nearly for time allotted.
   - Covered at least four pieces of important information.
   - Introduced project.
   - All members spoke.

3. Adequate presentation. Mostly organized.
   - Made eye contact at times.
   - Some of audience could hear the presentation.
   - Audience could understand most of what was said.
   - Spoke for about half of time allotted.
   - At least half of team spoke.
   - Covered at least three pieces of important information.
   - Project was vaguely introduced.

2–1. Underprepared presentation. Disorganized and incomplete information.
   - No eye contact during presentation.
   - Most of audience were unable to hear presentation.
   - Information presented was unclear.
   - Spoke for only brief time.
   - Covered less than three pieces of information.
   - Project was not introduced or only vaguely introduced.

---

you should consider yourself an expert. Having been a student in formal learning for at least 15 years, you are undoubtedly knowledgeable about the advantages and disadvantages of whole-class discussions, at least from your personal vantage point. So, explore your knowledge and share your experiences by responding to Exercise 8.2A. Then do Exercise 8.2B, where guidelines for using whole-class discussion will be generated.

EXERCISE 8.2A: WHOLE-CLASS DISCUSSION AS A TEACHING STRATEGY: WHAT DO I ALREADY KNOW?

INSTRUCTIONS: It is the purpose of this exercise to build your knowledge about using whole-class discussions by sharing experiences and knowledge with your classmates. Answer the following questions, and then share your responses with classmates, perhaps first in small discussion groups and then in the large group.

1. Your subject field: _____

2. For what reasons would you hold a whole-class discussion? _____

   _____

   _____

   _____

   _____

3. Assuming that your classroom has movable seats, how would you arrange them? _____

   _____

   _____

   _____

4. What would you do if the seats were not movable? _____

   _____

   _____

   _____

5. What rules would you establish before starting the discussion? _____

   _____

   _____

   _____

6. Should student participation be forced? Why or why not? If so, how? _____

   _____

   _____

   _____

7. How would you discourage a few students from dominating the discussion? _____

   _____

   _____

   _____

   _____

EXERCISE 8.2A (continued)

8. What preparation should the students and the teacher be expected to make before beginning the discussion?

_____

_____

_____

9. How would you handle digression from the topic? _____

_____

_____

_____

10. Should students be discussion leaders? Why or why not? If so, what training, if any, should they receive, and how?

_____

_____

_____

_____

_____

11. What teacher roles are options during a class discussion? _____

_____

_____

_____

_____

12. When is each of these roles most appropriate? _____

_____

_____

_____

13. When, if ever, is it appropriate to hold a class meeting for discussing class procedures, not subject matter?

_____

_____

_____

14. Can brainstorming be a form of whole-class discussion? Why or why not? _____

_____

_____

_____

_____

_____

EXERCISE 8.2A *(continued)*

15. What follow-up activities would be appropriate after a whole-class discussion? On what basis would you decide to use each? _____

_____

_____

_____

16. What sorts of activities should precede a class discussion? _____

_____

_____

_____

17. Should a discussion be given a set length? Why or why not? If so, how long? How is the length to be decided?

_____

_____

_____

_____

18. Should students be graded for their participation in class discussion? Why or why not? If so, how? On what basis? By whom? _____

_____

_____

_____

19. For effective discussions, 10 to 12 feet is the maximum recommended distance between participants. During a teacher-led discussion, what can a teacher do to keep within this limit? _____

_____

_____

_____

20. Are there any pitfalls or other points of importance that a teacher should be aware of when planning and implementing a whole-class discussion? If so, explain them and how to guard against them. _____

_____

_____

_____

EXERCISE 8.2B: WHOLE-CLASS DISCUSSION AS A TEACHING STRATEGY: BUILDING ON WHAT I ALREADY KNOW

INSTRUCTIONS: Having shared your responses to Exercise 8.2A with your classmates, now individually answer the first two questions below. Then, as a group, use all three questions to help you generate a list of five general guidelines for the use of whole-class discussion as a strategy for teaching young adolescent students in the classroom. Share your group's guidelines with the whole class. Then, finally, as a class, derive a final list of general guidelines.

1. How effective was your small-group discussion in sharing Exercise 8.2A? _____

_____

_____

_____

_____

_____

_____

_____

2. What allowed for or inhibited the effectiveness of that small-group discussion? _____

_____

_____

_____

_____

_____

_____

_____

3. How effective is this small-group discussion? Why? _____

_____

_____

_____

_____

_____

_____

_____

EXERCISE 8.2B *(continued)*

GENERAL GUIDELINES GENERATED FROM SMALL-GROUP DISCUSSION

1. _____
   _____

2. _____
   _____

3. _____
   _____

4. _____
   _____

5. _____
   _____

GENERAL GUIDELINES: FINAL LIST DERIVED FROM WHOLE CLASS

_____

_____

_____

_____

_____

_____

_____

_____

_____

_____

_____

_____

_____

_____

_____

_____

_____

_____

FOR YOUR NOTES

EQUALITY IN THE CLASSROOM

Especially when conducting direct, whole-group discussions, it is easy for a teacher to fall into the trap of interacting with only "the stars," or only those in the front of the room or on one side, or only the most vocal and assertive. You must exercise caution and avoid falling into that trap. To ensure a psychologically safe and effective environment for learning for every person in your classroom, you must attend to all students and try to involve all students equally in all class activities. You must avoid any biased expectations about certain students, and you must avoid discriminating against students according to their gender or some other personal characteristic.

To guarantee equity in interaction with students, many teachers have found it helpful to ask someone (perhaps a member of your teaching team) secretly to tally classroom interactions between the teacher and students during a class discussion. After an analysis of the results, the teacher arrives at decisions about his or her own attending and facilitating behaviors. Such an analysis is the purpose of Exercise 8.3. You are welcome to make blank copies and share them with your teaching colleagues.

In addition to the variables mentioned at the beginning of Exercise 8.3, the exercise can be modified to include responses and their frequencies according to other teacher–student interactions, such as your calling on all students equally for responses to your questions or to assist you with classroom helping jobs, or your chastising students for their inappropriate behavior.

Ensuring Equity

In addition to the advice given in Chapter 3 about using questioning, there are many other ways of assuring that students are treated fairly in the classroom, including the following:

- During whole-class instruction, insist that students raise their hands and be called on by you before they speak.
- Have and maintain high expectations, although not necessarily identical expectations, for all students.
- Insist on politeness in the classroom. For example, a student can be shown appreciation—such as with a sincere "thank you" or "I appreciate your contribution," with whole-class applause, or with a handshake or a genuine smile—for her or his contribution to the learning process.
- Insist students are allowed to finish what they are saying without being interrupted by others. Be certain that you model this behavior yourself.
- Keep a stopwatch handy to unobtrusively control the wait time given for each student. Although at first this idea may sound impractical, it works.
- Use a seating chart attached to a clipboard, and next to each student's name, make a tally for each interaction you have with a student. This also is a useful way to maintain records of students' contributions to class discussion. The seating chart can be laminated so it can be used day after day simply by erasing the marks of the previous day.

Now, do Exercise 8.3, through which you will examine a teacher's behavior with students according to gender or some other personal characteristic.

FOR YOUR NOTES

EXERCISE 8.3: TEACHER INTERACTION WITH STUDENTS ACCORDING TO STUDENT GENDER

INSTRUCTIONS: The purpose of this exercise is to provide a tool for the analysis of your town interactions with students according to gender. To become accustomed to the exercise, you should do a trial run in one of your university classes, then use it during your student teaching, and again during your first years of teaching. The exercise can be modified to include: (1) the amount of time given for each interaction, (2) the response time given by the teacher according to student gender, and (3) other student characteristics, such as ethnicity.

This activity can be used to check for teacher interaction with many kinds of student differences. For example, you can use the activity to check teacher interaction between students of different language or cultural backgrounds, students from different economic backgrounds, and students with different academic ability levels.

Prior to class, select a student (this will be you during the trial run recommended above) or an outside observer, such as a colleague, to do the tallying and calculations as follows. Ask the person to tally secretly the interactions between you and the students by placing a mark after the name of each student (or on the student's position on a seating chart) with whom you have verbal interaction. If a student does the tallying, that person should not be counted in any one of the calculations.

Exact time at start: _____

Exact time at end: _____

Total time in minutes: _____

Total in class today = _____   Girls = _____   Boys = _____

                                                    % Girls = _____   % Boys = _____

Tally of Interactions

With girls	With boys

Total Interactions = _____

% with girls = _____   % with boys = _____

Teacher Reflections and Conclusions: _____

_____

_____

_____

_____

LEARNING FROM ASSIGNMENTS AND HOMEWORK

An *assignment* is a statement of what the student is to accomplish and is tied to a specific instructional objective. Assignments, whether completed at home or at school, can ease student learning in many ways, but when poorly planned they can discourage the student and upset an entire family. *Homework* can be defined as any out-of-class task that a student is assigned as an extension of classroom learning. Like all else that you do as a teacher, it is your professional responsibility to think about and plan carefully any and all homework assignments you give to students.

Before giving students any assignment, consider how you would feel were you given the assignment, how you would feel were your own child given the assignment, about how much out-of-class time you expect the assignment to take, and to what extent, if any, parents and guardians and other family members should or could be involved in assisting the student with the assignment.

The time a student needs to complete assignments beyond school time will vary depending upon many variables; the very general rule of thumb has been to expect a child to spend 5 nights a week doing about 10 minutes of homework per grade level, which means a fifth grader would spend about 50 minutes doing homework, a sixth grader 60 minutes, a seventh grader 70 minutes, and so on.

Purposes for Assignments

Purposes for giving homework assignments can be any of the following: to constructively extend the time that students are engaged in learning, to help students to develop personal learning, to help students develop their research skills, to help students develop their study skills, to help students organize their learning, to individualize the learning, to involve parents and guardians in their children's learning, to provide a mechanism by which students receive constructive feedback, to provide students with the opportunity to review and practice what has been learned, to reinforce classroom experiences, and to teach new content.

Guidelines for Using Assignments

To use assignments, consider the guidelines in the following paragraphs. While an assignment is a statement of what the student is to accomplish, procedures are statements of how to do something. Although students may need some procedural guidelines, especially with respect to your expectations on an assignment, generally, you will want to avoid supplying too much detail on how to accomplish an assignment.

Plan early and thoughtfully the types of assignments you will give (e.g., daily and long-range; minor and major; in class, at home, or both; individual,

paired, or group), and prepare assignment specifications. Assignments must correlate with specific instructional objectives and should never be given as busywork or as punishment. For each assignment, let students know what the purposes are; for example, whether the assignment is to prepare the student for what is to come in class, to practice what has been learned in class, or to extend the learning of class activities.

Use caution in giving assignments that could be controversial or could pose a hazard to the safety of students. In such cases (especially if you are new to the community), before giving the assignment it is probably a good idea to talk it over with members of your teaching team, the departmental chair, or an administrator. Also, for a particular assignment, you may need to have parental or guardian permission and/or support for students to do it, or be prepared to give an alternate assignment for some students.

Provide differentiated, tiered, or optional assignments—assignment variations given to students or selected by them on the basis of their interests and learning capacities (Willard-Holt, 2003). Students can select or be assigned different activities to accomplish the same objective, such as read and discuss, or they can participate with others in a more direct learning experience. After their study, as a portion of the assignment, students share what they have learned. This is another example of using multilevel teaching.

Teachers have found it beneficial to prepare personalized study guides with questions to be answered and activities to be completed by the student while reading textbook chapters as homework. One advantage of a study guide is that it can make the reading more than a visual experience. A study guide can help to organize student learning by accenting instructional objectives, emphasizing important points to be learned, providing a guide for studying for tests, and encouraging the student to read the homework assignment.

Teachers need to understand that not only can homework help students learn factual information, develop study skills, and involve parents or guardians as facilitators in their child's education, but it can also overwhelm students and cause them to dislike learning, encourage them to take shortcuts, such as copying others' work, and prevent them from participating in extracurricular activities. Teachers sometimes underestimate just how long it will take a student to complete a homework assignment or how a particular assignment can disrupt the relationships in the child's home. With these considerations in mind, think carefully about all homework assignments before making them.

Some students find homework and assignments very difficult, especially those students who have limited English proficiency, special needs, and those who have little to no support from home. As an aid to these students in particular and to any student in general, many teachers use student volunteers to serve as *homework helpers* to assist other students both during class and after school, perhaps by exchanging telephone numbers or e-mail addresses. In some schools, teachers also use older students and even paid college students and adults as mentors.

As a general rule, homework assignments should stimulate thinking by arousing a student's curiosity, raising questions for further study, and encouraging and supporting the self-discipline required for independent study.

Determine the resources that students will need to complete assignments, and check the availability of these resources. This is important; students can't be expected to use that which is unavailable to them. Many will not use that which is not readily available.

Avoid yelling out assignments as students are leaving your classroom. When giving assignments in class, you should write them on a special place on the writing board, give a copy to each student, require that each student write the assignment into his or her assignment folder (an expectation in many schools), or include them in the course syllabus, taking extra care to be sure that assignment specifications are clear to students and to allow time for students to ask questions about an assignment. It's important that your procedure for giving and collecting assignments be consistent throughout the school year.

Students should be given sufficient time to complete their assignments. In other words, avoid announcing a new assignment that is due the very next day. As a general rule, assignments should be given much earlier than the day before they are due.

Although not always possible, try to avoid changing assignment specifications after they are given. Especially avoid changing them at the last minute, such as changing an assignment that is due tomorrow but was made weeks ago. Changing specifications at the last minute can be very frustrating to students who have already completed the assignment, and it shows little respect for those students.

We believe that time in class should be provided for students to begin work on homework assignments, so the teacher can give them individual attention (called *guided* or *coached practice*). Your ability to coach students is the reason for in-class time to begin work on assignments. The benefits of this coached practice include being able to monitor student work so that a student does not go too far in a wrong direction; help students reflect on their thinking; assess the progress of individual students; and discover or create a "teachable moment." For example, while monitoring students doing their work, you might discover a commonly shared student misconception. Then, taking advantage of this teachable moment, you stop and talk about that and attempt to clarify the misconception.

If the assignment is important for students to do, then you must give your full and immediate attention to the product of their efforts. Read almost everything that students write. Students are much more willing to do homework when they believe it is useful, when it is treated as an integral component of instruction, when it is read and evaluated by the teacher, and when it counts in the grading (see "How to Avoid . . ." that follows).

Provide feedback about each student's work, and be positive and constructive in your comments. Always think about the written comments that you make to be relatively certain they will convey your intended message to the student. When writing comments on student papers, consider using a color other than red, such as green or blue. Although to you this may sound trite, to many people red brings with it a host of negative connotations (e.g., blood, hurt, danger, stop), and children often perceive it as punitive.

Most routine homework assignments should not be graded for accuracy, only for completion. Rather than giving a percentage or numerical grade, with its negative connotations, teachers often prefer to mark assignment papers with constructive and reinforcing comments and symbols they have created for this purpose.

Regardless of subject taught, you must give attention to the development of students' reading, listening, speaking, and writing skills. Attention to these skills must also be obvious in your assignment specifications and your assignment grading policy. Reading is crucial to the development of a person's ability to write. For example, to foster higher-order thinking, students in any subject can and should be encouraged to write (in their journals, as discussed later in this chapter), or draw representations of, their thoughts and feelings about the material they have read.

Opportunities for Recovery

Using the concept of mastery (quality) learning would seem to us to dictate the need for a policy whereby students are able to revise and resubmit assignments for reassessment and grading. Although it is important to encourage positive initial efforts by students, sometimes, for a multitude of reasons, a student's first effort is inadequate or is lacking entirely. Perhaps the student is absent from school without legitimate excuse, or the student does poorly on an assignment or fails to turn in an assignment on time, or at all. Although accepting late work from students is extra work for the teacher, and although allowing the resubmission of a marked or tentative-graded paper increases the amount of paperwork, many teachers report that it is worthwhile to give students the opportunity for recovery and a day or so to make corrections and resubmit an assignment for an improved score. However, out of regard for students who do well from the start and to encourage a best first

---

CLASSROOM VIGNETTE

Late Homework Paper from an At-Risk Student

A student turned in a class assignment several days late, and the paper was accepted by the teacher without penalty, although the teacher's policy was that late papers would be severely penalized. During the week that the assignment was due, the student had suffered a miscarriage. In this instance, her teacher accepted the paper late sans penalty because the student carried a great deal of psychological baggage and the teacher felt that turning in the paper at all was a positive act. If the paper had not been accepted, or had been accepted only with severe penalty to her grade, then, in the teacher's opinion, the student would have simply quit trying and probably dropped out of school altogether.

---

effort, it is probably unwise to allow a resubmitted paper to receive an *A* grade (unless, of course, it was an *A* paper initially).

Students sometimes have legitimate reasons for not completing an assignment by the due date. (Consider the classroom vignette "Late Homework Paper from an At-Risk Student.") It is our opinion that the teacher should listen and exercise professional judgment in each instance. As someone once said, there is nothing democratic about treating unequals as equals. The provision of recovery options seems a sensible and scholastic tactic.

How to Avoid Having So Many Papers to Grade That Time for Effective Planning Is Restricted

A waterloo for some beginning teachers is that of being buried beneath mounds of homework to be read and marked, leaving less and less time for effective planning. To keep this from happening to you, consider the following suggestions. Although, in our opinion, the teacher should read almost everything that students write, papers can be read with varying degrees of intensity and scrutiny, depending on the purpose of the assignment. For assignments that are designed for learning, understanding, and practice, you can allow students to check them themselves using either self-checking or peer checking. During the self- or peer checking, you can walk around the room, monitor the activity, and record whether a student did the assignment or not, or, after the checking, you can collect the papers and do your recording. Besides reducing the amount of paperwork for you, student self- or peer checking provides other advantages: it allows students to see and understand their errors; it encourages productive peer dialogue; and it helps them develop self-assessment techniques and standards. If the purpose of the assignment is to assess mastery competence, then the papers should be read, marked, and graded only by you or by you and members of your teaching team.

Caution About Using Peer Checking. Peer checking can, however, be a problem. Sometimes during peer checking of student work, students may spend more time watching the person checking their paper than they do accurately checking the one given to them. And use of peer checking does not necessarily allow a student to see or understand his or her mistakes.

Of even greater concern is the matter of privacy. Even though the U.S. Supreme Court (on February 19, 2002) ruled unanimously that students may grade each other's work in class without violating federal privacy law, when Student A becomes knowledgeable of the academic success or failure of Student B, Student A, the "checker," could cause emotional or social embarrassment to Student B. It is our opinion that peer checking of papers should be done only for the editing of classmates' drafts of stories or research projects, making suggestions about content and grammar, but not assigning a grade or marking answers right or wrong.

PROJECT-CENTERED LEARNING: GUIDING LEARNING FROM INDEPENDENT AND GROUP INVESTIGATIONS, PAPERS, AND ORAL REPORTS

For the most meaningful student learning to occur, independent study, individual writing, student-centered projects, and oral reports should be major features of your instruction. There will be times when the students are interested in an in-depth inquiry of a topic and will want to pursue a particular topic for study. This undertaking of a learning project can be flexible—an individual student, a team of two, a small group, or the entire class can do the investigation. The *project* is a relatively long-term investigative study from which students produce something called the culminating presentation. It is a way for students to apply what they are learning. The *culminating presentation* is a final presentation that usually includes an oral and written presentation accompanied by a hands-on item of some kind (e.g., a display,

Figure 8.5 Sample choices for culminating presentation.

After reading *(name of novel),* students make a culminating presentation that is focused on representing various themes and events as depicted in the novel. Students may choose from the following:

1. Story in a shoebox — A representation of major events in the novel through the presentation of various symbolic objects.
2. Poster board presentation — A poster board designed with at least five different events depicted and titled appropriately. May use miniature drawings or graphics.
3. Sketching/drawing — A collection of detailed drawings depicting at least five major events in the novel.
4. Model — A model depicting the geography that serves as the setting of the novel.
5. Play or skit — A 5 to 8 minute play or skit performed by the student(s) in class with a script for the teacher to follow. Must involve at least one major event from the novel.

play or skit, book, song or poem, multimedia presentation, diorama, poster, maps, charts, and so on). See culminating presentations in Figure 8.5.

Values and Purposes of Project-Centered Learning

The values and purposes of encouraging project-centered learning are to: develop individual skills in cooperation and social-interaction; develop student skills in writing, communication, and in higher-level thinking and doing; foster student engagement, independent learning and thinking skills; optimize personal meaning of the learning to each student by considering, valuing, and accommodating individual interests, learning styles, learning capacities, and life experiences; provide an opportunity for each student to become especially knowledgeable and experienced in one area of subject content or in one process skill, thus adding to the student's knowledge and experience base and sense of importance and self-worth; provide an opportunity for students to become intrinsically motivated to learn because they are working on topics of personal meaning, with outcomes and time lines that are relatively open-ended; provide an opportunity for students to make decisions about their own learning and to develop their skills in managing time and materials; and provide an opportunity for students to make an important contribution. As has been demonstrated time and again, when students choose their own projects, integrating knowledge as the need arises, motivation and learning follow naturally (McCullen, 2000; Tassinari, 1996).

Guidelines for Guiding Students in Project-Centered Learning

In collaboration with the teacher, students select a topic for the project. Some experts suggest planning projects backward, that is by first identifying the desired results (the objectives), then determining acceptable evidence, followed lastly by planning the learning experience

(Fagan & Sherman, 2002). Regardless, what you can do is to stimulate ideas and provide anchor studies (also called model or benchmark examples). You can stimulate ideas by providing lists of things students might do, by mentioning each time an idea comes up in class that this would be a good idea for an independent, small-group, or class project, by having former students tell about their projects, by showing the results of other students' projects, by suggesting Internet resources and readings that are likely to give students ideas, and by using class discussions to brainstorm ideas.

Sometimes a teacher will write the general problem or topic in the center of a graphic web and ask the students to brainstorm some questions. The questions will lead to ways for students to investigate, draw sketches, construct models, record findings, predict items, compare and contrast, and discuss understandings. In essence, this kind of brainstorming is the technique often used by teachers in collaboration with students for the selection of an interdisciplinary thematic unit of study.

Allow students to individually choose whether they will work alone, in pairs, or in small groups. If they choose to work in groups, then help them delineate job descriptions for each member of the group. For project work, groups of four or less students usually work better than groups of more than four. Even if the project is one the whole class is pursuing, the project should be broken down into parts with individuals or small groups of students undertaking independent study of these parts.

You can keep track of the students' progress by reviewing weekly updates of their work. Set deadlines with the groups and meet with groups daily to discuss any questions or problems they have. Based on their investigations, the students will prepare and present their findings in culminating presentations.

Provide coaching and guidance. Work with each student or student team in topic selection, as well as in the processes of written and oral reporting. Allow students to develop their own procedures, but guide their preparation of work outlines and preliminary drafts, giving them constructive feedback and encouragement along the way. Aid students in their identification of potential resources and in the techniques of research. Assist the students, for example, in their understanding of the concepts of accuracy and reliability.

Your coordination with the library and other resource centers is central to the success of project-centered teaching. Frequent drafts and progress reports from the students are a must. With each of these stages, provide students with constructive feedback and encouragement. Provide written guidelines and negotiate time lines for the outlines, drafts, and the completed project.

Promote sharing by insisting that students share both the progress and the results of their study with the rest of the class. The amount of time allowed for this sharing will, of course, depend upon many variables. The value of this type of instructional strategy comes not only from individual contributions but also from the learning that results from the experience and the communication of that experience with others. For project work and student sharing of the outcomes of their study, some teachers have their students use the KWHLS strategy (see Chapter 5), where the student identifies what he/she already *K*nows about the topic of study, *W*hat he/she wants to learn, *H*ow the student plans to learn it, then what he/she *L*earned, and how the student will *S*hare with others what was learned from the study.

Without careful planning, and unless students are given steady guidance, project-based teaching can be a frustrating experience for both the teacher and the students, and especially for a beginning teacher who is inexperienced in such an undertaking. Students should do projects because they want to and because the project seems meaningful. Therefore, students with guidance from you should decide what project to do and how to do it. Your role is to advise and guide students so they experience success. If the teacher or teaching team lays out a project in too much detail, that then is a procedure rather than a student-centered project. There must be a balance between structure and opportunities for student choices and decision making. Without frequent progress reporting by the student and guidance and reinforcement from the teacher, a student can become frustrated and quickly lose interest in the project. What do we mean when we say "frequent"? In our opinion, as a general rule, progress reports from students should be weekly.

Writing as a Required Component of Project-Centered Learning

Provide options but insist that writing be a component of each student's work. Research examining the links among writing, thinking, and learning has helped emphasize the importance of writing. Writing is a complex intellectual behavior and process that helps the learner create and record his or her understanding—that is, to construct meaning.

When teachers use project-centered teaching, a paper and an oral presentation are usually automatically required of all students. It is recommended that you use the *I-Search paper* instead of the traditional research paper. Under your careful guidance, the student: (a) lists things that she would like to know, and from the list selects one, which becomes the research topic; (b) conducts the study while maintaining a log of activities and findings, which becomes a process journal; (c) prepares a booklet that presents the student's findings, and that consists of paragraphs and visual representations; (d) prepares a summary of the findings, including the significance of the study and the student's personal feelings; and (e) shares the project as a final oral report with the teacher and classmates.

Assessing the Final Product

The final product of the project, including papers, oral reports, and presentations should be graded. The method of determining the grade should be clear to students from the beginning, as well as the weight of the project grade toward each student's term grade. Provide students with clear descriptions (rubrics) of how evaluation and grading will be done. Evaluation should include meeting deadlines for drafts and progress reports. The final grade for the study should be based on four criteria: (a) how well it was organized, including meeting draft deadlines; (b) the quality and quantity of both content and procedural knowledge gained from the experience; (c) the quality of the student's sharing of that learning experience with the rest of the class; and (d) the quality of the student's final written or oral report. For oral presentations, a sample scoring rubric and a checklist are shown in Figures 7.3 and 7.4, respectively, and for scoring rubrics for other aspects of project study see Figures 7.11 and 7.12 in Chapter 7.

WRITING ACROSS THE CURRICULUM

Because writing is a discrete representation of thinking, every teacher should consider himself or herself to be a teacher of writing. In exemplary schools, by using multiple technologies to teach writing—paper and pencil, e-mail, listservers, and software packages (Yancey, 2004)—student writing is encouraged in all subjects, at all grade levels, across the curriculum. For example, Burns (2004) suggests that a teacher of mathematics give writing assignments that fall into these four categories: maintaining journals or logs, solving problems, explaining mathematical ideas, and writing about learning processes. Oftentimes, and especially with the current prominence of standardized writing assessments, all teachers of a particular school, and even district, are expected to assess students' papers using the same scoring rubric (Baldwin, 2004).

Kinds of Writing

A student should experience a variety of kinds of writing rather than the same form, class after class, year after year. Perhaps most important is that writing should be emphasized as a process that illustrates one's thinking, rather than solely as a product completed as an assignment.

Writing and thinking develop best when a student experiences, during any school day, various forms of writing to express their ideas, such as the following:

Autobiographical incident. The writer narrates a specific event in his or her life and states or implies the significance of the event.

TEACHING IN PRACTICE

Students Who Supposedly Can't Write, Try—and They Can! Mr. Mayo Uses Blogs to Encourage Student Writing*

Last year, I set up blogs for eight students in a remediation class I teach. The students in this class had failed one or more parts of the fifth-grade Standards of Learning state test here in Virginia. They lose an elective in sixth grade and have to take this remediation class to work on their reading and writing skills. These are the students who supposedly can't write. Well, they can, and they did. They wrote a lot once they had their own blogs.

Each student assumed a nickname for an online blog identity. My first assignment: Write about your favorite hobby. It ended up being the most productive writing day of the entire semester.

Here's Shiloh, a.k.a. Kangaroo, on her favorite hobby, canoeing:

> "Whin I cone whith my dad in his cone he sters and I have to whouch for rocks. He gets rilly mad if we hit one. You may not think it is easy to brake a cone, but this one man hit a rock on one of the tuffest rivers and the cone got raped aroun a ruck. It was cool looking. My dad jumd on it and poped the dint rit out."

Here's another sample from Cody, a.k.a. Fox. He's writing about his favorite hobby, BMX biking:

> "My favorite thing to do is bikeing. I like to bike that I have a biking club. My biking clubs name is The Ghost Rider Kings. We are very good. We can do some good tricks. We can do indos, ghost riders, skids, Biddle caps, snakes. I can do the Biddle cap very good."

When asked to write about something they love to do, the students wrote enthusiastically. The writing was fun and purposeful. Blogs make student writing more accessible. With blogs, students know that what they write is going to be immediately published. They take their writing more seriously.

Here's a quote from, Todd, a.k.a. Giraffe, about writing on his blog:

> "I used to hate writing but now I like it the day I came I was angry that I was in remediation and knew it would be boring but I was wrong and waited until we actually started the class. Now I know that if I am here for the rest of the year I will just learn more and more."

My remediation students were amazed at the amount of writing they did on their blogs. They regularly scrolled up and down the screen reading and marveling at everything they had written. They talked to each other about what they had written, and compared entries.

As students begin to accumulate a large amount of writing, they begin to feel more confident. They also begin to see themselves as writers. Not only were they interested in their own blogs, they became curious about what others were up to. The clean and accessible format of the writing naturally builds curiosity. Students talk spontaneously to each other about their writing and their ideas. They actually start to point out sentence-level errors to each other as they discuss their writing.

Student blogs help create a sense of community by making student writing accessible to anyone who has Internet access. With blogs, a student's peers, relatives, teachers, and administrators are invited to watch a student's growth. The more people who read a student's work, the more likely they are to talk to that student about their writing. This helps create a sense of community that is otherwise hard to imagine. Parents can check in whenever they feel like it to see what their kids are doing in school and interested parties get a candid sense of student writing in their true voices. This helps establish a dialogue between parent and child and draws parents into the classroom in a new way. With blogs, students are more likely to care about what they write because they have a built-in audience.

This experience has convinced me that blogs can be a powerful motivator to get students to write, and to take their writing more seriously. For the next school year, I am setting up blogs for all 120 of my students, and will ask my students to write on their blogs as much as possible. The only restriction that might exist would be caused by the limited availability of laptop computer carts.

---

*Courtesy of George Mayo.

Evaluation. The writer presents a judgment on the worth of an item—book, movie, artwork, consumer product—and supports this with reasons and evidence.

Eyewitness account. The writer tells about a person, group, or event that was objectively observed from the outside.

Firsthand biographical sketch. Through incident and description, the writer characterizes a person he or she knows well.

Interpretation. The writer conjectures about the causes and effects of a specific event.

Problem solving. The writer describes and analyzes a specific problem and then proposes and argues for a solution.

Report of information. The writer collects data from observation and research and chooses material that best represents a phenomenon or concept.

Story. Using dialogue and description, the writer shows conflict between characters or between a character and the environment.

Student Journals

Many teachers across the curriculum have their students maintain journals in which the students keep a log of their activities, findings, and thoughts (i.e., *process journal*), and write their thoughts about what it is they are studying (*response journal*). Actually, commonly used are two types of response journals: dialogue journals and reading-response journals. *Dialogue journals* are used for students to write anything that is on their minds, perhaps on a website (see sample entries of sixth graders in the box on page 349), or in a written binder on the right side page, while peers, teachers, and parents or guardians respond on the left side page, thereby "talking with" the journal writer (Werderich, 2002). *Response journals* are used for students to write (and perhaps draw—a "visual learning log") their reactions to whatever is being studied.

Purpose and Assessment of Student Journal Writing.

Normally, academic journals are *not* the personal diaries of the writer's recollection of daily events and the writer's thoughts about the events. Rather, the purpose of journal writing is to encourage students to write, to think about their writing, to record their creative thoughts about *what they are learning*, and to share their written thoughts with an audience—all of which help in the development of their thinking skills, in their learning, and in their development as writers. Students are encouraged to write about experiences, both in school and out, that are related to the topics being studied. They should be encouraged to record their feelings about what and how they are learning.

Journal writing provides practice in expression and should *not* be graded by the teacher. Negative comments and evaluations from the teacher will discourage creative and spontaneous expression by students. Teachers should read the journal writing and then offer constructive and positive feedback, but teachers should avoid negative comments or grading the journals. For grading purposes, most teachers simply record whether or not a student does, in fact, maintain the required journal. The National Council of Teachers of English (NCTE) has developed guidelines for journal writing.

A COLLECTION OF MORE THAN 125 ANNOTATED MOTIVATIONAL TEACHING STRATEGIES WITH IDEAS FOR LESSONS, INTERDISCIPLINARY TEACHING, TRANSCULTURAL STUDIES, AND STUDENT PROJECTS

Today's young adolescents are used to multimillion-dollar productions on television, stage, CDs and DVDs, arcade games, and the movie screen. When they come to school, into your classroom, and are subjected each day to something short of a high-budget production, it is little wonder that they sometimes react in a less than highly motivated fashion. No doubt, today's youth are growing up in a highly stimulating instant-action society, a society that has learned to expect instant electronic communication, instant information retrieval, instant headache relief, instant meals, instant gratification, instant replays, and perhaps, in the minds of many youth, instant high-paying employment with signing bonuses for jobs that entail more fun than hard work. In light of this cultural phenomenon, we are on your side: The classroom teacher is on the firing line each day and is expected to perform—perhaps instantly and entertainingly, but most certainly in a highly competent and professional manner—in situations that are far from ideal. In any case, you must gain your students' attention before you can teach them.

In this, the final section of this chapter, you will find the presentation of an annotated list of ideas, many of which have been offered over recent years by classroom teachers. (See also website listings at the conclusion of this chapter.) Although the ideas are organized according to discipline, and some may be more appropriate for one group of students or grade level than another, you may profit from reading all entries for each field. Although a particular entry might be identified as specific to one discipline, it might also be useful in others (many of them can be used in interdisciplinary teaching—for example, number one can clearly be combined with mathematics and science, as well as art), or it might stimulate a creative thought for your own stock of motivational techniques, such as an idea for a way to utilize the theory of multiple learning capacities, to incorporate technology, or to emphasize the multicultural aspect of a lesson in math, social studies, or whatever the central discipline or theme of a lesson or unit of instruction.

The Visual and Performing Arts

1. As part of a unit combining design or creativity with science, have students design, construct, and decorate their own kites. Designate a launch date and time.

2. Use lyrics from popular music to influence student work in class, such as putting the lyrics into pictures.

3. Utilize the outdoors or another environment, such as a shopping mall, for a free drawing experience.

4. Invite a local artist who has created a community mural to speak to the class about the mural. Plan and create a class mural, perhaps on a large sheet of plywood or some other location approved by the school administration. For example, at Chartiers Valley Intermediate School (Pittsburgh, PA), for more than a decade, as a culminating project in the school's visual arts program, each fifth-grade class has contributed its own section to a growing mural in the school cafeteria.

5. Create a mandala to demonstrate the importance of individual experience, as in interpreting paintings and interpreting poetry.

6. Study masks. Collect books, magazines, posters, films, videos, computer software programs, and other sources that show different kinds of masks people around the world wear. Ask students to identify the similarities and differences in the masks. Have them research the meanings that mask characters have in various cultures. Have students design and create their own masks to illustrate their own personalities, cultures, and other characteristics.

7. As a portion of a unit on the creative process, have each student draw or sketch on a piece of paper, then pass it on to the next person, and that person will make additions to the drawing. Instructions could include "improve the drawing," "make the drawing ugly," "make the drawing 17th century," and "add what you think would be necessary to complete the composition."

8. Instructions for students: Imagine that you're a bird flying over the largest city you have visited. Draw a "sensory" map of what you see, hear, smell, feel, and taste.

9. Assign each student a different color. Have the students arrange themselves into warm and cool colors and explain their decisions (why blue is cool, etc.). Discuss people's emotional responses to each of the colors.

10. Watch video of dances from various countries and cultures. Invite students to identify similarities and differences. Ask them to research the meanings and occasions of particular dances.

11. Challenge students to discover ways that music, art, and dance are used in their community.

12. Find a popular song liked by the students. Transpose the melody into unfamiliar keys for each instrument. This makes the student want to learn the song, but in the process the student will have to become more familiar with his or her instrument.

13. Set aside one weekend morning a month and hold small, informal recitals (workshops) allowing students to participate/observe the performance situation(s) among their peers and themselves. Students might be told previously about these "special days" and encouraged to prepare a selection of their own choosing.

14. Play a group-activity rhythm game, one such as the "Dutch Shoe Game," to get students to cooperate, work together, and enjoy themselves using rhythm. Participants sit in a circle, and as the song is sung, each person passes one of his or her shoes to the person on the right in rhythm to the music. Shoes continue to be passed as long as verses are sung.

15. Choose a rhythmical, humorous poem or verse to conduct as if it were a musical work. The students read the poem in chorus while you stand before them and conduct. Students must be sensitive to the intonation, speed, inflection, mood, and dynamics that you expect them to convey in their reading.

16. Organize a Retired Senior Citizens Volunteer Program (RSCVP) with senior citizens presenting folk art workshops with students, and where the students and seniors work together to create artwork for the school and community.

17. Students from Elkhorn Area Middle School (Elkhorn, WI) organized an Improv Troupe, which creates and performs unscripted, improvisational skits about social issues relevant to today's youth (Reedy, 2001).

Family and Consumer Economics, Foods, and Textiles

18. Often the foods we like originated from another area of our country or another place in the world. Have the students identify such foods and from where they came—foods such as spaghetti, enchiladas, fajitas, wontons, tacos, quiches, croissants, teriyaki, fried rice, pizza, hot dogs, hamburgers, noodles, tomatoes, chocolate, potatoes, hoagies, chop suey, ice cream cones, submarines, and poor boys. Have them list the names and origins, and place pictures of the food in place on a large world map.

19. Take photos of class members at special events such as dinners, fashion shows, field trips, and projects. Build a scrapbook or bulletin board with these and display on campus or on the school website and at the spring open house or in a display case at school or in a shopping mall store window.

20. Plan thematic units on cultural foods, using the traditions, costumes, and music of a particular culture. Have the students decorate the room. Invite guests

such as the principal, school board president, and city mayor for a visit and perhaps tasting treat.

21. Have a committee of students plan and create a school display of pictures of 100-calorie portions of basic nutritional foods and popular fad foods that contain only empty calories. Do the same with pictures of foods and their specific carbohydrate contents.

22. Pin the names of different garments on the backs of students. Students are then to sort themselves into different wash loads.

23. For a clothing unit, hold a "new look day." Ask each student to bring in an idea of something that can be done to give clothes a new look, a fun touch, or an extended wearing life. Ideas may include appliqués, embroidery, tie-dye, batik, colorful patches, and restyling old clothes into current or creative fashions.

24. Have the students research, create, write, practice, and present skits on topics such as consumer fraud and identity theft.

25. Periodically have students plan a menu, prepare the food, and serve it to invited senior citizens from the community.

26. Organize a program with senior citizens and students working together on a community garden.

27. Plan a program at a senior citizens' center whereby students and seniors work together on planning and decorating the center for special occasions and holidays.

28. With your students, plan a community service program. For example, at Discovery Middle School (Vancouver, WA), students provide childcare, cross-age tutoring, and companionship to preschool, elementary school, and elderly clients at off-campus locations.

29. Have students work on a project about culture and how culture affects our lives, such as the way we dress, eat, worship, celebrate, and communicate.

30. Challenge students to plan ways to educate the school and surrounding community about topics such as general nutrition, the new food pyramid, and exercise.

31. Learn about and plan with your students an "edible schoolyard" (see website at the end of this chapter) such as that tended by the more than 900 students of Martin Luther King, Jr. Middle School (Berkeley, CA).

English, Languages, and the Language Arts

32. Organize a paper or electronic letter writing activity between senior citizens and your students.

33. For a unit on the Renaissance, have students create a wall-to-wall mural depicting a village of the times. Teams of students can research customs, costumes, and architecture. Others may paint or draw.

34. On a U.S. road map, have students find the names of places that sound "foreign" and categorize the names according to nationality or culture. Students could research when and how places got their names.

35. Set up this problem to enhance understanding of parts of speech. Provide several boxes (shoeboxes work fine) containing different parts of speech. Each student is to form one sentence from the fragments chosen from each box, being allowed to discard only at a penalty. The students then nonverbally make trades with other students to make coherent and perhaps meaningfully amusing sentences. A student may trade a noun for a verb but will have to keep in mind what parts of speech are essential for a sentence. Results may be read aloud as a culmination to this activity.

36. Students can match American English and British English words (or any other combination of languages), such as cookies and biscuits, hood and bonnet, canned meat and tinned meat, elevator and lift, flashlight and torch, subway and tube, garbage collector and dustman, undershirt and vest, sweater and jumper, and gasoline and petrol. Have students compare pronunciations and spellings.

37. English words derive from many other languages. Have students research and list some, such as ketchup (Malay), alcohol (Arabic), kindergarten (German), menu (French), shampoo (Hindi), bonanza (Spanish), piano (Italian), kosher (Yiddish), and smorgasbord (Swedish).

38. For an exercise in objective versus subjective writing, after a lesson on descriptive writing, bring to class a nondescript object, such as a potato, and place it before the class. Ask them to write a paragraph either describing the potato in detail, that is, its color, size, markings, and other characteristics, or describing how the potato feels about them.

39. Read a story to the class but without ending. Then ask the students (as individuals or in think-write-share-pairs) to invent and write their own endings or conclusions.

40. Challenge students to create an advertisement (decide for radio, TV, Internet, or print medium) using a propaganda device of their choice.

41. Invite students (individually or in pairs) to create and design an invention and then to write a "patent description" for their invention.

42. Using think-write-share-pair, invite students to write a physical description of some well-known public figure, such as a movie star, politician, athlete, or musician. Other class members may enjoy trying to identify the "mystery" personality from the written description.

43. A bulletin board may be designated for current events and news in the world of writers. New books and recordings as well as reviews may be included. News of poets and authors (student authors and poets, too) may also be displayed.

44. Everyone has heard of or experienced stereotyping. Ask students to list stereotypes they have heard and examples they find in media. Have students discuss these questions: Have you ever felt stereotyped? How do you suppose stereotypes come to be? Does stereotyping have any useful value? Can it be harmful?

45. Remove the text from a newspaper comic strip and have the students work in pairs to create the story line, or, give each pair a picture from a magazine and have the pair create a story about the picture.

46. Use newspaper and Internet want ads to locate jobs as a base for completing job application forms and creating letters of inquiry.

47. To develop language and listening skills use video recording equipment to record student-written employer-employee role-play situations, interview for jobs, or child-parent situations.

48. Invite students to choose a short story from a text and write it into a play and perform the play for their family members.

49. To begin a poetry unit, ask students to bring in the lyrics to their favorite songs. Show how these fit into the genre of poetry.

50. Invite students to analyze commercial advertisements that might be classed as "ecopornographic," that is, ads for the product that is potentially damaging to our environment.

51. Have students analyze commercial advertisements for the emotions to which they appeal, for the techniques used, and for their integrity. Try the same thing with radio, youth magazines, theater advertisements, websites, and other media.

52. Change the learning environment by moving to an outdoor location, and ask students to write poetry to see if the change in surroundings stimulates or discourages their creativeness. Discuss the results. For example, take your class to a large supermarket, a mall, a lake, a forest, or an athletic stadium to write.

53. Use your state's seal to initiate the study of the concept of interpretations. Have students analyze the seal for its history and the meaning of its various symbols. Do the same with a dollar bill.

54. Provide puppets in native costume for students to use in practicing dialogue when learning a language or in developing language skills.

55. Have students use the Internet to establish communication with students from another place in the world.

56. As a class or small-group project, design a page on your school website.

57. Use drama to build language arts and thinking skills. Have students write dialogue, set scenes, and communicate emotions through expressive language and mime.

58. Establish a community-service learning literacy project. For example, students from your school could serve as mentors to local elementary school children to help the children develop their reading and comprehension skills.

59. A teacher uses a digital camera to take pictures of her students acting out scenes from a book being read in class. She prints the photos and asks the students to describe their actions in words. From this activity the students then create their own books.

60. Invite your students to create and write a movie script by viewing any 5- to 10-minute scene taken from a film and then writing a script for that scene.

61. Students from a school in Arizona became pen pals with inner-city students from Toledo, OH. Not only did the experience prove beneficial for their lessons in language arts but also promoted their knowledge about their city and state, resulting in cross-curricular learning (Lemkuhl, 2002).

62. Challenge your students to look for, create, and collect *palindromes*, a series of words or sentences, or numbers, that read the same backward or forward. Examples are the names *Ava* and *Otto*, the words *racecar* and *solos*, the date *4.04.04*, and the year *2002*.

Mathematics

63. Collaboratively plan with students a role-play unit where members role-play the solar system. Students calculate their weights, set up a proportion system, find a large field, and as a culmination to the project actually simulate the solar system, using their own bodies to represent the sun, planets, and moons. Notify local media of the culminating event.

64. Encourage students to look for evidence of the (Leonardo Pisano) Fibonacci number series (i.e., 1, 1, 2, 3, 5, 8, 13, 21, etc., where each number is gotten by adding the two previous numbers), both within and outside of mathematics, such as in nature and in manufactured objects. Here are examples of where evidence may be found: piano keyboard, petals of flowers, spermatogenesis and oogenesis. Perhaps your students might like to organize a Fibonacci Club and through the Internet establish communication with similar clubs around the world.

65. After students research the history of the cost of a first-class, U.S. postage stamp, ask them to devise ways of predicting its cost by the year they graduate from high school, the year they become grandparents, or some other target year.

66. Provide students a list of the frequencies of each of the 88 keys and strings on a piano (a local music store can provide the information). Challenge students to derive an equation to express the relation between key position and frequency. After they have done this, research and tell them about the Bösendorfer piano (Germany) with its nine extra keys at the lower end of the keyboard. See if students can predict the frequencies of those extra keys.

67. Using a light sensor to measure the intensity of a light source from various distances, have students graph the data points and then, with their scientific calculators, find the relevant equation.

68. Students at George Washington Middle School (Alexandria, VA) participate in a parachute creation contest. Using plastic from trash bags, string, and a bobby pin as the skydiver, the challenge is to design a parachute with the least surface area and longest hang time (Mann, 2000).

69. Establish a service-learning project, mentoring children of lower grades.

70. Teach your students how to play chess. Invite the students to plan chess moves for homework, using combination theory and probability. In collaboration with an art or shop teacher, some students may wish to extend the study by creating their own chessboards and pieces.

71. Invite your students to survey and map the school grounds.

72. Invite your students to research, design, build, and decorate their own canoes, such as done by students at Floyd Dryden Middle School (Juneau, AK).

Physical Education

73. Ask your students to choose, individually (or in dyads), a famous athlete they most (or least) admire. A short report will be written about the athlete. The student will then discuss the attributes and/or characteristics that they admire (or dislike) in the athlete, and how they feel they can emulate (or avoid) those qualities. After all pairs of students have made their presentations, as a class devise two lists, one of common attributes admired, the other of qualities to avoid.

74. Challenge students, in small learning groups, to create an exercise routine to their favorite music recording and share it with the class. Then, have them discuss how they arrived at decisions along the way.

75. Divide your class into groups. Given the basic non-locomotor skills, have each group come up with a "people machine." Each student within the group is hooked up to another demonstrating a nonlocomotor skill and adding some sort of noise to it. Have a contest for the most creative people machine.

76. Give students a chance to design a balance-beam routine that has two passes on the beam and that must include: front support mount, forward roll, leap, low or high turn, visit, chassé, and cross-support dismount. These routines will be posted to show the variety of ways the different maneuvers can be put together.

77. Divide the class into groups. Challenge each group to create a new game or activity for the class, using only the equipment they are given. Let the class play their newly created games.

Science

78. Challenge students to create and test their own science tools and materials, such as microscopes using stems of bamboo with a drop of water in each end or litmus indicators using the petals of flowers.

79. Record sounds of the environment. Compare and write about day versus night sounds, fall versus spring sounds, foggy day versus sunny day sounds, busy mall versus residential backyard sounds, single residential dwelling versus multiple residential dwelling sounds.

80. With appropriate permissions and adult supervision, plan an overnight campout in which students must "live off the land" with only sleeping bags, clothing, and other essentials (water), and no electronics. (Take a cell phone for emergency purposes.)

81. Plan a yearlong project where each student, or small group of students, must develop knowledge and understanding of some specific piece of technology. Each project culmination presentation must have five components: visual, oral, written, artistic, and creative.

82. Invite students to identify and use a social relationship, such as landlord-tenant relationships, to create a role-play simulation of predator-prey relationships.

83. For a life science class, on the first day of class give each student one live guppy in a test tube and one live cactus plant in a three-inch pot. Tell the students that the minimum they each need to pass the course is to bring their pet plant and fish back to you during the final week of school, alive.

84. If you are a life science teacher, make sure your classroom looks like a place for studying life rather than a place of death, that is displays live plants and animals, rather than only preserved ones.

85. With each student playing the role of a cell part, have students set up and perform a role-play simulating parts of cells.

86. Divide your class into groups, and ask each group to create an environment for an imaginary organism using discarded items from the environment. By asking questions, each group will try and learn about the other groups' "mystery" organism.

87. Have each student, or student pair, "adopt" a chemical element. The student then researches that element and becomes the class expert whenever that particular substance comes up in discussion. There could be a special bulletin board for putting up questions on interesting or little-known facts about the elements.

88. Milk can be precipitated, separated, and the solid product dried to form a very hard substance that was, in the days before plastic, used to make buttons. Challenge your students to make their own buttons from milk.

89. As a class or interdisciplinary team project, obtain permission and "adopt" a wetland area or some other environmental project that is located near the school.

90. Invite students to research the composition and development of familiar objects. For example, the ordinary pencil is made of cedar wood from the forests of the Pacific Northwest. The graphite is often from Montana or Mexico and is reinforced with clays from Georgia and Kentucky. The eraser is made from soybean oil, latex from trees in South America, reinforced with pumice from California or New Mexico, and sulfur, calcium, and barium. The metal band is aluminum or brass, made from copper and zinc, and mined in several states of the United States and in several provinces of Canada. The paint to color the wood and the lacquer to make it shine are made from a variety of different minerals and metals, as is the glue that holds the wood together.

91. Invite students to locate and design large posters to hang on the classroom walls that show the meaning of words used in science that are not typical of their meaning in everyday language usage—the words *theory* and *Spanish moss* are examples.

92. To bridge cultural differences, allow students to design large posters to hang on the classroom walls showing potential differences in perceptions or views according to ethnoscience and formal science.

93. With your students, plan a community-service project. For example, students of the Powder River County School District (Broadus, MT) adopted community flower gardens and conduct an annual food drive for the needy. At Great Falls Middle School (Montague, MA), students research and produce television documentaries on subjects related to energy. The documentaries are broadcast on the local cable channel to promote energy literacy in the school and community. Students at Baldwyn Middle School (Baldwyn, MS) plan and care for the landscaping of the local battlefield/museum.

94. Sometimes projects become ongoing, permanent endeavors with many spin-off projects of shorter duration. For example, what began as a science classroom project at W. H. English Middle School (Scottsburg, IN) has become what is perhaps the largest animal refuge shelter in the Midwest.

95. Invite students to research and produce TV documentaries on subjects related to energy, or on a health-related topic. To promote energy or health-related literacy in the school and surrounding community, a local TV channel might be willing to broadcast the documentaries.

96. During their study of atomic theory, have students read and discuss J. R. Hersey's *Hiroshima* (Random House, 1989).

97. Ask students to inquire as to whether a nearby zoo or botanical garden or commercial nursery, has an animal or plant loan program.

98. Have a group of students research from the Internet and library the literature and report on the plant *Morinda citrifolia*. Have them share their findings with the rest of the class.

99. Have students use bobblehead toys to explore force and motion (Foster, 2003).

Social Studies/History

100. Invite the students to organize an improvisation troupe to create and perform skits about social issues relevant to today's youth. Perform the skits at school events, parent-teacher organization meetings, and for community groups.

101. In collaboration with your students, develop a yearlong three-phase project. During the first phase, students individually research the question, "Who Am I?"; during the second phase, "Who Are They?"; and during the third phase, "Who Are We?" Multimedia presentations should be included in the students' culminating presentation.

102. Organize an Intergenerational Advocacy program, in which students and senior citizens work together to make a better society for both groups (MacBain, 1996). For example, at Burns Middle School (Owensboro, KY), students work in collaboration with a retired senior volunteer program to develop their understanding of personal and social responsibilities.

103. Initiate a service-learning project where, for an extended period of time, students work directly with community organizations and agencies. For example, at John Ford Middle School (St. Matthews, SC), students incorporate the Constitutional Rights Foundation "City Youth" program into the curriculum, helping to make decisions about areas of the community that need improvement.

104. During their study of Ancient Egypt, invite students to create and build their own model pyramids; in science, students could study simple machines that will help in their pyramid building.

105. Invite students to plan how they would improve their living environment, beginning with the classroom, moving out to the school, home, community, state, nation, and finally the global.

106. Start a pictorial essay on the development and/or changes of a given area in your community, such as a major corner or block adjacent to the school. This is a study project that could continue for years and that has many social, political, and economic implications.

107. Invite your students in small groups or as a class project to build a model that represents their community.

108. Start a folk hero study. Each year ask, "What prominent human being who has lived during (a particular period of time) do you most (and/or least) admire?" Collect individual responses to the question, tally results, and discuss. After you have done this for several years, you may wish to share with your class for comparison and discussion purposes the results of your surveys of previous years.

109. Start a sister class program. Establish a class relationship with another similar class from another school around the country or the world, perhaps by using the Internet.

110. During their study of westward expansion, challenge students to organize a role-play of a simulated family movement to the West in the 1800s. What items would they take? What would they toss out of the wagon to lighten the load? Where would they stop and settle? Or would they stop, turn around, and return to their point of origin? What issues would enter into their decision making?

111. Invite students to collect music, art, or athletic records from a particular period of history. Have them compare their collections with the music, art, or recordings of today and predict the music, art, or recordings of the future.

112. Using play money, establish a capitalistic economic system within your classroom. Salaries may be paid for attendance and bonus income for work well done, taxes may be collected for poor work, and a welfare section established somewhere in the room.

113. Divide your class into small groups, and ask that each group make predictions as to what world governments, world geography, world social issues, world health, world energy, or some other related topic will be like some time in the future. Let each group give its report, followed by debate and discussion. With guidance from the school administration, plant the predictions in some secret location on the school grounds for a future discovery.

114. As an opener to a unit on the U.S. Constitution, have students design their own classroom (or school) "Bill of Rights."

115. On one day, behave toward your students in class as if your class were a socialist society; the next day as if they were a fascist society; and on another day as a communist society, etc. At the end of the simulation, have students discuss and compare their feelings and thoughts about each day's experience.

116. Using Legos™ or sugar cubes as construction blocks, and with assigned roles, challenge students to simulate the building of the Great Wall of China.

117. At Indian Trail Junior High School (Addison, IL) all eighth graders and teachers from not only social studies but various other content areas, including English, mathematics, physical education, and science, work together on a "real world,"

problem-based project titled the Inspector Red Ribbon Unit. The unit focuses on a social problem that has truly occurred too many times—the prom night automobile accident.

118. Establish a caring and antiviolence program. For example, students in Lynn Haven, Florida, work as tutors/mentors with elementary school children to help boost confidence and self-esteem among both groups of students.

119. During an interdisciplinary thematic unit of study (the history and literature of the medieval period of Europe), have students study and build model castles.

120. With guidance from three teachers using a common philosophical approach based on Glasser's Choice Theory, Reality Therapy, and ideas from his book *The Quality School*, students of eighth-grade history at Longfellow Middle School (La Crosse, WI) designed and built their own middle school nation (Frost, Olson, & Valiquette, 2000).

121. During a study of U.S. history students are given this assignment for an activity titled "Creating a Candidate." The assignment is done in student dyads. "Research electronic and print media about the progressive movement in early state history. Determine relevant issues a candidate for governor of the state in 1910 would need to address. Create a fictitious candidate. Your exhibition must include: (a) an election poster, (b) a slogan, (c) a theme song that you must sing, and (d) a five-minute platform speech addressing the issues, your proposed solutions, and the position of your opponents."

122. During their study of the U.S. Constitution, invite students to organize debates on current issues, such as gun control and civil rights.

123. In collaboration with other classes, invite your students to design and implement a school-wide conflict resolution program.

124. Plan time each week for students to comment on the week's classroom activities, or to compliment a peer.

125. Organize a study to determine how well students who have arrived in the United States from other countries are integrated into your community and school's culture.

126. Invite students to research, identify, and discuss current plagiarism and copyright issues.

SUMMARY

This chapter has continued the development of your repertoire of teaching strategies. As you know, young adolescents can be quite peer-conscious, can have relatively short attention spans for experiences in which they are uninterested, and prefer experiences that are multisensory and require activity. Most are intensely curious about things of interest to them. Cooperative learning, student-centered projects, and teaching strategies that emphasize shared discovery and inquiry (discussed in the next and final chapter) within a psychologically safe environment encourage the most positive aspects of thinking and learning. Central to your strategy selection should be those strategies that encourage students to become independent thinkers and skilled learners who can participate in the planning, structuring, regulating, and assessing of their own learning and learning activities.

QUESTIONS FOR CLASS DISCUSSION

1. Using modern software to enhance their project presentations, students are learning to put their presentations on computerized visual shows that they fill with colorful animation, bold topic headings and neat rows of points they wish to make, each introduced with a highlight mark. Some educators are concerned that too often young people become fixated on fonts and formats and other aspects of the technology without actually giving much deep thought to the content of their presentations. Share your experiences and opinions about this.

2. Do you have concerns about using project-based teaching and not being able to cover all the content you believe should be covered? Think back to your own schooling. What do you really remember? Most likely you remember projects, yours and other students' presentations, the lengthy research you did, and your extra effort for the artwork to accompany your presentation. Maybe you remember a compliment by a teacher or a pat on the back by peers. Most likely you do not remember the massive amount of content that was covered. Discuss your feelings about this with your classmates. Share experiences and concerns.

3. It is an aphorism that to learn something well students need time to practice it. There is a difference, however, between solitary practice and coached practice. Describe the difference and conditions where in your teaching you would use each.

4. Divide into teams of four, and have each team develop one learning center for a specified use in a particular subject and group of young adolescents. Set up and share the LCs in your college classroom.

5. Explain how a teacher can tell when he or she is truly using cooperative learning groups for instruction as opposed to traditional, small-group learning.

6. When a student is said to be on task, does that necessarily imply that the student is mentally engaged? Is it possible for a student to be mentally engaged although not on task? Explain your answers.

7. What concerns you most about teaching the diversity of students you are likely to have in a classroom? Share those concerns with others in your class. Categorize your group's concerns. By accessing an Internet teacher bulletin board see what kinds of problems middle level classroom teachers are currently concerned about. Are assessment practices, curriculum expectations, scheduling, grading, group learning, and classroom management high in frequency of concern? Are the concerns of teachers as expressed on the Internet similar to yours? As a class, devise a plan and time line for attempting to ameliorate your concerns.

8. For a specific grade level (identify it, 5–8) and subject (identify), what classroom activities would be particularly well suited to a whole-class configuration? Which ones are best suited for small groups? For each, explain why.

9. Describe three things you will do to help students develop their writing skills.

10. Of the more than 125 motivational ideas listed in this chapter, name 5 that you would most like to try in your teaching. Share your list with others in your class, discussing what most interests you about each of your selections.

INTERNET RESOURCES

Miscellaneous

Digital cameras
http://members.ozemail.com.au/~cumulus/digcam.htm

Gender bias http://www.american.edu/sadker

Global Schoolhouse http://www.gsh.org

globalEDGE™ http://globaledge.msu.edu

Intercultural E-Mail Classroom Connections
http://www.iecc.org/

Learning theories http://tip.psychology.org/theories.html

PBS Teacher Source http://www.pbs.org/teachersource

Teachers Net Lesson Bank http://teachers.net/lessons

The Library in the Sky http://www.nwrel.org/sky

Weblogging service http://www.typepad.com

Webpage creation www.marshall-es.marshall.k12.tn.us/jobe/webpage.html

What Kids Can Do http://wkcd.org

Arts

American Alliance for Theatre & Education
http://www.aate.com

The Funkamentals http://www.funkamentals.org

The Hip-Hop Circuit: Teachers http://www.hiphopcircuit.com

Hip-Hop in the Classroom http://www.domingoyu.com/

Music Education Resource Links
http://www.isd77.k12.mn.us/resources/staffpages/shirk/k12.music.html

TheatreLink http://www.theatrelink.org

World Wide Arts Resources http://wwar.com/

Environmental Issues

World Bank http://www.worldbank.org/depweb

History/Social Studies

American Women's History
http://frank.mtsu.edu/~kmiddlet/history/women.html

Best of History Websites http://www.besthistorysites.net

Choices Program http://www.choices.edu/index.cfm

Civics Online http://civics-online.org

Facing History and Ourselves http://facinghistory.org

FedWorld **http://www.fedworld.gov**

Historical Text Archive **http://historicaltextarchive.com**

History Net **http://www.thehistorynet.com**

Houghton-Mifflin Social Studies Center
    http://www.eduplace.com/ss/

Links to lesson plans, unit plans, thematic units, and resources
    http://www.csun.edu/~hcedu013/index.html

Mexico Online **http://www.mexonline.com**

National Council for the Social Studies
    http://www.socialstudies.org

U.S. History, From Revolution to Reconstruction
    http://grid.let.rug.nl/~welling/usa/usa.html

Language and Literacy

Language links
    http://polyglot.lss.wisc.edu/lss/lang/langlink.html

*National Clearinghouse for English Language Acquisition &
    Language Instruction Education Programs*
    http://www.ncela.gwu.edu

Second language learning **http://www.sdkrashen.com**

Mathematics

Math Activities **http://www.k111.k12.il.us/king/math.htm**

Math Archives **http://archives.math.utk.edu**

Math Forum **http://www.mathforum.org**

Mega Mathematics **http://www.c3.lanl.gov/mega-math**

PlaneMath **http://www.planemath.com**

Show-Me Project **http://www.showmecenter.missouri.edu**

Science, Food, and Health

*Centers for Disease Control and Prevention; National Center on
    Birth Defects and Developmental Disabilities*
    http://www.cdc.gov/ncbddd

Columbia Education Center lesson plan collection
    http://www.col-ed.org/cur/science.html#sci1

Dive and Discover **http://www.divediscover.whoi.edu**

The Edible Schoolyard **http://www.edibleschoolyard.org**

Electric Universe **http://ameren.electricuniverse.com**

Electronic Zoo **http://netvet.wustl.edu/e-zoo.htm**

*EXCITE (Excellence in Curriculum Integration through
    Teaching Epidemiology* **http://www.cdc.gov/excite**

LifeQuest Expedition **http://www.thequestnetwork.com**

National Institutes of Health http://science.education.nih.gov

National Institute on Alcohol Abuse and Alcoholism
    http://www.niaaa.nih.gov

Stanford Solar Center **http://solar-center.stanford.edu**

Windows to the Universe **http://www.windows.umich.edu**

Publishers of Student Writing

New Moon (for girls ages 8–14) **http://www.newmoon.org**

Potato Hill Poetry **http://www.potatohill.com**

Stone Soup **http://www.stonesoup.com/index.html**

What If (for Canadians) **http://www.whatifmagazine.com**

Service Learning

Learning In Deed **http://www.learningindeed.org**

National Service-Learning Clearinghouse
    http://www.servicelearning.org

National Service-Learning Exchange
    http://www.nslexchange.org

FOR FURTHER READING

Bailey, L. (2005). Understanding Chris to teach him more effectively. *Middle School Journal, 37*(2), 37–46.

Bernt, P. W., Turner, S. V., & Bernt, J. P. (2005). Middle school students are co-researchers of their media environment: An integrated project. *Middle School Journal, 37*(1), 38–44.

Carrier, K. A. (2005). Key issues for teaching English language learners in academic classrooms. *Middle School Journal, 37*(2), 4–9.

Curtin, E. M. (2006). Lessons on effective teaching from middle school ESL students. *Middle School Journal, 37*(3), 38–45.

Cuthbert, A., & Slotta, J. (2004). Designing a web-based design curriculum for middle school science: The WISE "Houses in the Desert" Project. *International Journal of Science Education, 26* (7), 821–844.

Daniel, V. A. H., Stuhr, P. L., & Ballengee-Morris, C. (2006). Suggestions for integrating the arts into the curriculum. *Art Education, 59*(1), 6–11.

Garbe, G., & Guy, D. (2006). No homework left behind. *Educational Leadership, 63,* 1–6. *Helping All Students Succeed,* ASCD online journal at www.ascd.org:80/portal/site/ascd.

Halderson, J. (2006). Podcasting: Connecting with a new generation. *Middle Ground, 10*(1), 18–21.

Hill, J. D., & Flynn, K. M. (2006). *Classroom instruction that works with English language learners.* Alexandria, VA: Association for Supervision and Curriculum Development.

Johnson, C. (2005). Making instruction relevant to language minority students at the middle level. *Middle School Journal, 37*(2), 10–14.

Kasten, W. C., & Wilfong, L. G. (2005). Encouraging independent reading with ambience: The book bistro in middle and secondary school classes. *Journal of Adolescent and Adult Literacy, 48,* 656–664.

Kenkel, S., Hoelscher, S., & West, T. (2006). Leading adolescents to mastery. *Educational Leadership, 63*(7), 33–7.

Miller, P. C., & Endo, H. (2004). Understanding and meeting the needs of ESL students. *Phil Delta Kappan, 85,* 786–791.

Morgan, B., & Odam, D. (2006). Stories from tween classrooms. *Educational Leadership, 63*(7), 38–41.

Ohl, T., & Cates, W. (2006). The nature of groups: Implications for learning design. *Journal of Interactive Learning Research, 17,* 71–89.

Peterson, S., & Belizaire, M. (2006). Another look at roles in literature circles. *Middle School Journal, 37*(4), 37–43.

Smith, T. W., & Lambie, G. W. (2005). Teachers' responsibilities when adolescent abuse and neglect are suspected. *Middle School Journal, 36*(3), 33–39.

Wormeli, R. (2006). Differentiating for tweens. *Educational Leadership, 63*(7), 14–19.

CHAPTER 9

Additional Strategies and Strategy Integration

Anthony Magnacca/Merrill

Perhaps no other strategy is used more by teachers than is teacher talk, so we begin this final chapter of the resource guide with a presentation of guidelines for using that vital and significant instructional strategy.

A strategy related to teacher talk is the demonstration, which is addressed later in the chapter, followed by guidelines for other important strategies, namely, inquiry and discovery, and games. Finally, in keeping with the developmentally important practice of integrating the learning for young adolescents, we cap the book with a discussion of ways of doing that.

Whether you are a beginning or experienced teacher, one way to collect data and improve your effectiveness is through periodic assessment of your teaching performance. This can be done either by an evaluation of your teaching in the real classroom or, as you have learned, if in a teacher education program, by a technique called micro peer teaching. The latter is the final exercise of this chapter, indeed of this resource guide, a type of final performance assessment for your study of this resource guide, especially of the final two chapters.

OBJECTIVES

Specifically, upon your completion of this chapter you should be able to:

1. Make an effective demonstration performed either by yourself, by some students, or collaboratively between you and students.
2. Demonstrate an understanding of the relationship among problem solving, discovery, and inquiry.
3. Explain ways of integrating strategies for integrated learning.
4. Demonstrate when and how to use inquiry for student learning.
5. Describe when and how to use teacher talk for instruction.
6. Demonstrate your knowledge of advantages and disadvantages of each of seven categories of games for learning.

TEACHER TALK: FORMAL AND INFORMAL

Teacher talk encompasses both lecturing *to* students and talking *with* students. A lecture is considered formal teacher talk, whereas a discussion with students is considered informal teacher talk.

Cautions in Using Teacher Talk

Whether your talk is formal or informal, there are certain cautions that you need to be mindful of. Perhaps the most important is that of *talking too much*. If a teacher talks too much, the significance of the teacher's words may be lost because some students will tune the teacher out.

Another caution is to avoid *talking too fast*. Young adolescents can hear faster than they can process into comprehension what they hear. It is a good idea to remind yourself to talk at a reasonable pace and to check frequently for student comprehension of what you are talking about. And, when working with ELL students, you will want to talk even more slowly and do more frequent checks for comprehension. It is also important to remember that your one brain is communicating with many student brains, each of which responds to sensory input (auditory in this instance) at varying rates. Because of this, you will need to pause to let words sink in and you will need to pause during transitions from one point or activity to the next.

A third caution is to be sure you are being *heard and understood*. Sometimes teachers talk in too low a pitch or use words that are not understood by many of the students, or both. You should vary the pitch of your voice, and you should stop and help students with their understanding of vocabulary that may be new to them.

A fourth caution is to remember that *just because students have heard something before does not necessarily mean that they understand it or learned it*. From the earlier discussions of learning experiences (such as "The Learning Experiences Ladder" in Chapter 6), remember that although verbal communication is an important form of communication, because of its reliance on the use of abstract symbolization, it is not a very reliable form of communication. Teacher talk relies on words and on skill in listening, a skill that is not mastered by many young adolescents (or many adults for that matter). For that and other reasons, to ensure student understanding, it is good to reinforce your teacher talk with either direct or simulated learning experiences.

A related caution is to *resist believing that students have attained a skill or have learned something that was taught previously by you or by another teacher*. During any discussion (formal or informal), rather than assuming that your students know something, you should ensure they know it. For example, if the discussion and student activity involve a particular math skill or thinking skill, then you will want to make sure that students understand how to use that skill.

Still another problem is *talking in a humdrum monotone*. Students need teachers whose voices exude enthusiasm and excitement (although not to be overdone) about the subject and about teaching and learning. Such enthusiasm and excitement for learning are contagious. A voice that demonstrates genuine enthusiasm for teaching and learning is more likely to motivate students to learn.

A final caution is *just because your speaking (auditory output) channel is engaged doesn't mean that you should disengage your sensory input channels*. This is another time when the competent teachers' skills of withitness and overlapping are apparent. While a competent teacher is talking, that teacher is still seeing and listening and capable of changing her or his physical location in the classroom.

Keep those cautions in mind as you study the general principles and specific guidelines for the productive and effective use of teacher talk.

Teacher Talk: General Guidelines

Certain general guidelines should be followed whether your talk is formal or informal. First, *begin the talk with an advance organizer*. *Advance organizers* are introductions that mentally prepare students for a study by helping them make connections with material already learned or experienced—a *comparative organizer*—or by providing students with a conceptual arrangement of what is to be learned—an *expository organizer* (Ausubel, 1963). The value of using advance organizers is well documented by research (see, for example, Good & Brophy, 2003). An advance organizer can be a brief introduction or statement about the main idea you intend to convey and how it is related to other aspects of the students' learning (an expository organizer), or it can be a presentation of a discrepancy to arouse curiosity (a comparative organizer, in this instance causing students to compare what they have observed with what they already knew or thought they knew). Preparing an organizer helps you plan and organize the sequence of ideas, and its presentation helps students organize their own learning and become motivated about it. An advance organizer can also make their learning meaningful by providing important connections between what they already know and what is being learned.

Second, *your talk should be planned so that it has a beginning and an end, with a logical order between.* During your talk, you should reinforce your words with visuals (discussed in the specific guidelines that follow). These visuals may include writing unfamiliar terms on the board (helping students learn new vocabulary); visual organizers; and prepared graphs, charts, photographs, and various audiovisuals.

Third, *pacing is important.* Your talk must move briskly, although not too fast. For many beginning teachers, the ability to pace the instruction is a difficult skill (the tendency among many beginning teachers is to talk too fast and too much), but one that improves with experience. Until you have developed your skill in pacing lessons, you may need to remind yourself during lessons to slow down and provide silent pauses (allowing for think-time) and frequent checks for student comprehension. Specifically, your talk should:

- Be brisk, though not too fast, but with occasional slowdowns to change the pace and to check for student comprehension. Allow students time to think, to ask questions, and to make notes (Marzano, Pickering, & Pollock, 2001).
- Have a time plan. A talk planned for, say, 10 minutes, if interesting to students, will probably take longer. If not interesting to them, it will probably take less time.
- Always be planned with careful consideration given for the characteristics of the students. For example, if you have a fairly high percentage of ELL students or of students with exceptionalities, then your teacher talk may be less brisk, sprinkled with even more visuals, repeated statements and simpler word use, and frequent checks for student comprehension.

Fourth, *encourage student participation.* Their active participation enhances their learning. This encouragement can be planned as questions that you ask or as time allowed for students to comment and ask questions or as some sort of a visual and conceptual outline that students complete during the talk.

Fifth, *plan a clear ending (closure).* Be sure your talk has a clear ending, followed by another activity (during the same or next class period) that will help secure the learning. As for all lessons, you want to strive for planning a clear and mesmerizing beginning, an involving lesson body, and a firm and meaningful closure.

Teacher Talk: Specific Guidelines

> *The most successful learning strategies are ones that involve each student personally. When students routinely assume the role of teacher, and teachers demonstrate that they are still learners, a genuine learning community is present.*
>
> National Middle School Association (2003, p. 16)

Specific guidelines for using teacher talk are presented in the following paragraphs.

Understand the various reasons for using teacher talk. Teacher talk, formal or informal, can be useful to discuss the progress of a unit of study, explain an inquiry, introduce a unit of study, present a problem, promote student inquiry or critical thinking, provide a transition from one unit of study to the next, provide information otherwise unobtainable to students, share the teacher's experiences, share the teacher's thinking, summarize a problem, summarize a unit of study, and teach a thinking skill by modeling that skill.

Clarify the objectives of the talk. Your talk should center around one idea. The learning objectives, which should not be too numerous for one talk, should be clearly understood by the students.

Choose between informal and formal talk. Although an occasional formal cutting-edge lecture may be appropriate for some groups of young adolescents, spontaneous, interactive informal talks of 5 to 12 minutes are preferred. You should *never* give long lectures with no teacher-student interaction. A formal period-long noninteractive lecture, common in some college teaching, is developmentally inappropriate when teaching young adolescents. On the other hand, to arouse student interest and to provide new information in relatively small and intellectually digestible chunks, a lecture of 5–12 minutes duration may be appropriate. If, during your student teaching, you have doubts or questions about your selection and use of a particular instructional strategy, discuss it with your cooperating teacher or your university supervisor, or both. When you have doubts about the appropriateness of a particular strategy, trust your intuition—without some modification, the strategy probably is inappropriate.

Vary strategies and activities frequently. Perhaps most useful as a strategy for recapturing student attention is to change to an entirely different strategy or learning modality. For example, from teacher talk (a teacher-centered strategy) you would change to a student activity (a student-centered strategy). Notice that changing from a lecture (mostly teacher talk) to a teacher-led discussion (mostly more teacher talk) would not be changing to an entirely different modality. Figure 9.1 provides a comparison of different changes.

TEACHING IN PRACTICE
When Student Attention Begins to Drift

Today's young adolescents are used to electronic interactions as well as "commercial breaks," and the capacity to "surf channels" to find something of personal interest—for many lessons, especially those that are teacher-centered, after about eight minutes student attention is quite likely to begin to waft, to begin to "channel surf." For that eventuality, you need lesson elements planned to recapture student attention. These planned elements can include:

* analogies to help connect the topic to students' experiences
* humor
* pauses for emphasis and to allow information to register
* sensory cues, such as eye contact and proximity (as in your moving around the room)
* verbal cues, such as voice inflections and name dropping
* visual cues, such as the use of overhead displays, charts, board drawings, excerpts from CDs, realia, and body gestures.

Question for Class Discussion

1. Can you think of other elements or techniques that could be used to recapture waning student attention, perhaps specific to your subject field? Share and discuss your ideas with your classmates.

As a generalization, when using teacher-centered direct instruction, with most groups of young adolescents you will want to change the learning activities about every 8 to 15 minutes. (That is one reason that in the preferred lesson plan format we offer in Chapter 6, you find space for at least four activities, including the introduction and closure.) This means that in a 50- or 60-minute time block, for example, you should probably plan three or four *sequenced* learning activities, with some that are teacher-centered and many others that are more student-centered. In a 90-minute block, plan five or six learning activities.

In exemplary middle level classrooms, rather than using teacher-centered direct instruction, teachers often have several activities *concurrently* being performed by individuals, dyads, and small groups of students (i.e., the teachers use multitasking or multilevel instruction). Multilevel instruction is particularly important for use during long block periods, called *macroperiods*, typically a couple hours in length.

Prepare and use notes as a guide to yourself for your talk. Planning your talk and preparing notes to be used during formal and informal teacher talk is important—just as important as is implementing the talk with visuals. There is absolutely nothing wrong with using notes during your teaching. You can carry them on a clipboard, perhaps a neon-colored one that gives students a visual

focus as you move around the room. Your notes for a formal talk can first be prepared in narrative form; for class use, though they should be reduced to an outline form. *Talks to students should always be from an outline, never read from prose.* The only time that a teacher's reading from prose aloud to students is appropriate is when reading a brief, published article (such as in science or social studies) or portions of a story or a poem (such as in reading/English/language arts).

In your outline, use color-coding with abbreviated visual cues to yourself. You will eventually develop your own coding system, though keep whatever coding system you use simple lest you forget what the codes are for. Consider these examples of coding:

* Where media will be used, mark *M*, or *V* for *visual*, or *PP* for *PowerPoint*™
* Where transition of ideas occur and you want to allow silent moments for ideas to sink in, mark *P* for *pause*, *T* for a *transition*, and *S* for moments of *silence*
* Where you intend to stop and ask a question, mark *TQ* for *teacher question*, or *TQ(student name)* when you intend to ask the question of a particular student
* Where you plan *reviews* and *comprehension checks*, mark *R* and *CS*
* Where you plan *small-group work*, mark *SG*, or for *cooperative learning group work*, mark *CLG*
* Where you plan to have a *discussion*, mark *D*
* Where you plan to switch to an *investigatory* activity, mark *I*
* Where you want to stop and allow time for *student questions*, mark *SQ* or *?*

Share your note organization with your students. Sharing with them how you organize for your work is important modeling for them for their organization of their own learning and doing. Teach the students how to take notes and what kinds of things they should write down, including how to summarize. Teaching students note taking and summarizing skills is to help them with what researchers refer to as "two of the most useful academic skills students can have" (Marzano, Pickering, & Pollock, 2001, p. 29). Use colored chalk or markers to outline and highlight your talk; encourage your students to use colored pencils for note taking, so their notes can be color-coded to match your writing board notes. This serves not only to enhance their learning but keeps them productively and kinesthetically occupied during the instruction.

Rehearse your talk. Using your lesson plan as your guide, rehearse your talk using a video recorder, or rehearse it while talking into a mirror or to a roommate. You may want to include a time plan for each subtopic to allow you to gauge your timing during implementation of the talk.

Avoid racing through the talk solely to complete it by a certain time. It is more important that students understand

Figure 9.1   Recapturing student attention by changing the instructional strategy.

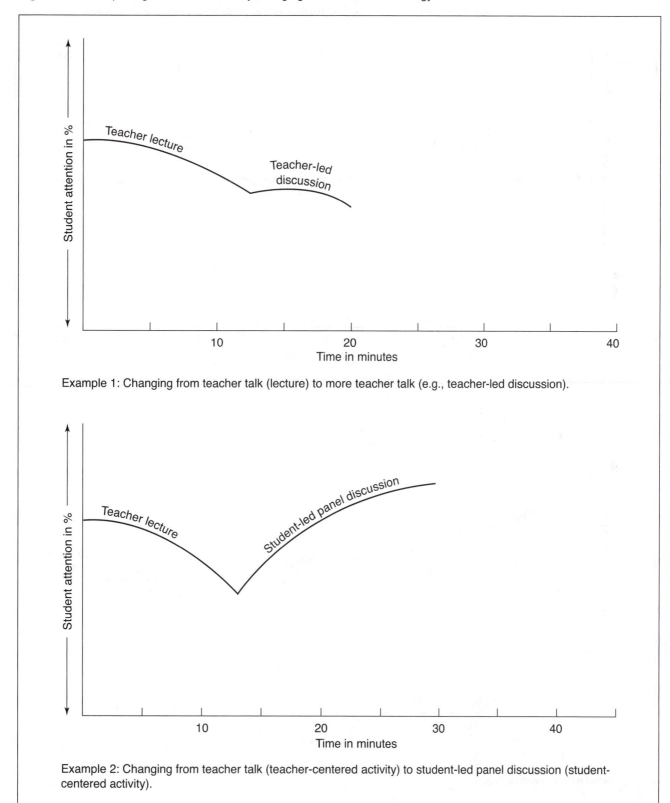

Example 1: Changing from teacher talk (lecture) to more teacher talk (e.g., teacher-led discussion).

Example 2: Changing from teacher talk (teacher-centered activity) to student-led panel discussion (student-centered activity).

(continued)

Figure 9.1   (*continued*)

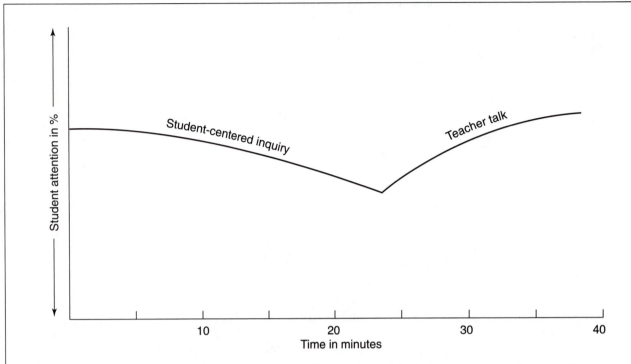

Example 3: Changing from inquiry (student-centered) to teacher-talk fueled by student questions from inquiry.

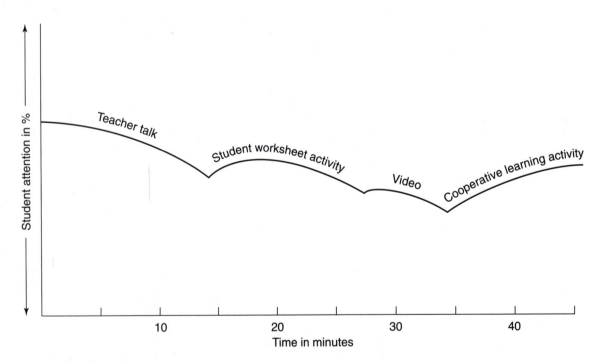

Example 4: Changing from teacher talk (teacher-centered activity) to cooperative learning activity (student-centered activity).

some of what you say than that you cover it all and they understand little or none of it. If you do not finish, continue it later.

Augment your talk with multisensory stimulation and allow for think-time. Your presentation should not rely too much on verbal communication. When using visuals, do not think that you must be constantly talking; after clearly explaining the reason for using a particular visual, give students sufficient time to look at it, think about it, and ask questions about it. The visual is new to the students, so give them time to take it in.

Carefully plan the content of your talk. The content of your talk should supplement and enhance that found in the student textbook rather than simply rehash content from the textbook. Students may never read their book if you tell them in an interesting and condensed fashion everything that they need to know from it.

Monitor your delivery. Your voice should be pleasant and interesting to listen to rather than a steady, boring monotone or a constantly shrieking, irritating, high pitch. On the other hand, it is good to show enthusiasm for what you are talking about, for teaching and learning. Occasionally use dramatic voice inflections to emphasize important points and meaningful body language to give students a visual focus. So as not to appear phony, practice these skills so they become second nature.

When teaching a large group of students (by "large group," we mean more than eight students), *avoid standing in the same spot for long periods of time.* (When teaching young adolescents, we consider 10 minutes in the same spot to be a long time.) Be mobile! Even during direct instruction, you need to monitor student behavior and to engage occasional signal interference (as discussed in Chapter 4). As a matter of fact, when teaching young adolescents it is especially during extended periods of direct instruction that a beginning teacher's skills in withitness and overlapping behaviors are likely to be most put to the test.

View the vocabulary of the talk as an opportunity to help students with their word morphology. Words you use should be easily understood by the students, though you should still model professionalism and help students develop their vocabulary—both the vocabulary of your special discipline and the more general vocabulary of the English language. During your lesson planning, predict when you are likely to use a word that is new to most students, and plan to stop to ask a student to explain its meaning and perhaps demonstrate its derivation. Help students with word meaning. This assists students with their remembering. Remember, regardless of subject or grade level, *every teacher is a teacher of language arts.* Knowledge of word morphology is an important component of skilled reading and includes the ability to generate new words from prefixes, roots, and suffixes. For some students, nearly every subject in the curriculum is basically a foreign language. That is cer-

tainly true for some English-language learners, for whom teacher talk, especially formal teacher talk, should be used sparingly, if at all. As we have repeated often throughout this resource guide, every teacher of young adolescents has the responsibility of helping students learn how to learn, and that includes helping students develop their word comprehension skills, reading skills, thinking and memory skills, and their motivation for learning.

Give thoughtful and intelligent consideration to student diversity. While preparing your talk (during the preactive phase of your instruction), consider students in your classroom who are culturally and linguistically different and those who have special needs. Personalize the talk for them by choosing your vocabulary carefully and appropriately, speaking slowly and methodically, repeating often, and by planning meaningful analogies and examples and relevant audio and visual displays.

Use familiar examples and analogies to help students make relevant connections (bridges). Although this sometimes takes a great deal of creative thinking as well as action during the planning phase of instruction, it is important that you do your best to connect the talk with ideas and events with which the students are already familiar. The most effective talk is one that makes frequent and meaningful connections between what students already know and what they are learning, which bridges what they are learning with what they have experienced in their lives. Of course, to do this well means you need to "know" your students (see "Get to Know Your Students as People" in Chapter 4).

Establish eye contact frequently. Your primary eye contact should be with your students—always! That important point cannot be overemphasized. Only momentarily should you look at your notes, your visuals, the projection screen, media equipment, the writing board, and other adults or objects in the classroom. Although you may raise your eyebrows in doubt when you read this, it is true and it is important that with practice you can learn to scan a classroom of 25 students, establishing eye contact with each student about once every 60 seconds. To "establish" eye contact means that the student is aware that you are looking at him or her. Frequent eye contact can have two major benefits. First, as you "read" a student's body posture and facial expressions, you obtain clues about that student's attentiveness and comprehension. Second, eye contact helps to establish rapport between you and a student. A look with a smile or a wink from the teacher to a student can say so much! Be alert, though, for students who are from cultures where eye contact is infrequent or unwanted and could have negative consequences. In other words, don't push it!

Frequent eye contact is easier when using a screen display (such as with the overhead projector or a

PowerPoint™ presentation) than when using the writing board. When using a writing board, you have to turn at least partially away from your audience; you may also have to pace back and forth from the board to the students in order to retain that important proximity to them.

As said at the start of the discussion of teacher talk, while lecturing on a topic, you must remain aware and attentive to everything that is happening in the classroom (i.e., to student behavior as well as to the content of your lecture). No one truly knowledgeable about it ever said that good teaching is easy. But don't dismay; with the knowledge of the preceding guidelines and with practice, experience, and intelligent reflection, you will in time develop the skills.

DEMONSTRATION

Most young adolescents like demonstrations because the person doing the demonstration is actively physically engaged in a learning activity rather than merely verbalizing about it. Demonstrations can be used to teach any subject and for a variety of reasons. The teacher demonstrates role-playing in preparation for a social studies simulation. Select students demonstrate how they solved a problem. A language arts/English teacher demonstrates clustering to students ready for a creative writing assignment. A life science teacher demonstrates the coarse and fine focus adjustments when using a microscope. The physical education teacher or student volunteer demonstrates the proper way to serve in volleyball.

Reasons for Using Demonstrations

A demonstration can be designed to serve any of the following functions, and the reason(s) for using a particular demonstration should be communicated to the students.

- assist in recognizing a solution to an existing problem; to bring an unusual closure to a lesson or unit of study
- conservation of time and resources (as opposed to the entire class doing that which is being demonstrated)
- establish discrepancy recognition
- establish problem recognition
- give students an opportunity for vicarious participation in active learning
- illustrate a particular point of content
- introduce a lesson or unit of study in a way that grabs the students' attention
- model or demonstrate a skill, such as a skill in sports, inquiry, thinking, note taking, summarizing, social behavior, library use, or a skill useful in conflict resolution

- model or demonstrate proper use of equipment, such as a microscope or a trampoline
- reduce potential safety hazards (where the teacher demonstrates with materials that are too dangerous for students to handle)
- review or summarize a topic or unit of study
- test a hypothesis

Guidelines for Using Demonstrations

When planning a demonstration, consider the following guidelines.

Decide the most effective way to conduct the demonstration. It might be a verbal or a silent demonstration by a student or the teacher, by the teacher with a student helper, by a student with the teacher as helper, to the entire class or to small groups, or by some combination of these, such as first by the teacher followed by a repeat of the demonstration by a student or succession of students.

Be sure that the demonstration is visible to all students. To accomplish this, some classrooms use overhead mirrors or video cameras connected to large-screen television monitors. Otherwise, a raised demonstration table will probably suffice. This reminds us of the middle school teacher we have long known who had built in the middle of his classroom a raised platform or stage, about 10 feet square. We have always been impressed with the positive usefulness that a permanent classroom stage seemed to provide, mostly as a center of visual focus for the students.

Practice with the materials and procedure before demonstrating to the students. During your practice, try to prepare for anything that could go wrong during the real demonstration; if you don't, as Murphy's Law states, if anything can go wrong, it probably will. Then, if something does go wrong during the live demonstration, use that as an opportunity for a teachable moment; engage the students in working with you to try to figure out what went wrong, or if that isn't feasible, then go to Plan B (an *emergency alternate plan* that you made during lesson planning—always a good idea when planning a demonstration or the use of media).

Consider your pacing of the demonstration, allowing for enough student wait-see-and-think time. At the start of the demonstration, explain the learning objectives. Remember this familiar adage: Tell them what you are going to do, show them, and then help them understand what they saw. As with any lesson, plan your closure and allow time for questions and discussion. During the demonstration, as in other types of teacher talk, use frequent stops to check for student understanding.

Consider using special lighting to highlight the demonstration. (One teacher uses a "recycled" slide projector as a spotlight.) And finally, be sure the demonstration table and area are free of unnecessary objects that could distract, be in the way, or pose a safety hazard.

With potentially hazardous demonstrations, such as might occur in physical education or science classes, you must *model* proper safety precautions.

INQUIRY TEACHING AND DISCOVERY LEARNING

Intrinsic to the effectiveness of both inquiry and discovery is the assumption that students would rather actively seek knowledge than receive it through traditional direct instruction (i.e., information delivery) methods such as lectures, demonstrations, worksheets, and textbook reading. Although inquiry and discovery are important teaching tools, there is sometimes confusion about exactly what inquiry teaching is and how it differs from discovery learning. The distinction should become clear as you study the following section discussing these two important tools for teaching and learning.

> Experiences afforded by inquiry help students understand the importance of suspending judgment and also the tentativeness of answers and solutions to problems. With those intelligent understandings, students eventually are better able to deal with life's ambiguities.

Although inquiry and discovery are well recognized as valuable teaching tools, they do tend to consume more instructional time than do traditional methods of information delivery (direct instruction). Coupled with that and the current emphasis on standardized testing, classroom use of inquiry and discovery methods may be in jeopardy (Jorgenson & Vanosdall, 2002).

Problem Solving

Perhaps a major reason why inquiry and discovery are sometimes confused is that, in both, students are actively engaged in problem solving. **Problem solving** can be thought of as the ability to recognize, identify, define, or describe a problem, determine the preferred resolution, identify potential solutions, select strategies, test solutions, evaluate outcomes, and revise any of these steps as necessary (Costa, 1985).

Inquiry versus Discovery

Problem solving is *not* a teaching strategy but a high-order intellectual behavior that facilitates learning. What a teacher can and should do is provide opportunities for students to identify and tentatively solve problems. Experiences in inquiry and discovery can provide those opportunities. With the processes involved in inquiry and discovery, teachers can help young adolescents develop the skills necessary for effective problem solving. Two major differences between discovery and inquiry are (a) who identifies the problem and (b) the percentage of decisions that are made by the students. Table 9.1 shows three levels of inquiry, each level defined according to what the student does and decides.

It should be evident from Table 9.1 that what is called *Level I inquiry* is actually traditional, didactic, workbook and "cookbook" teaching, where both the problem and the process for resolving it are identified and defined *for* the student. The student then works through the process to its inevitable resolution. If the process is well designed, the result is inevitable, because the student "discovers" what was intended by the writers of the program. This level is also called *guided inquiry* or *discovery*, because the students are carefully guided through the investigation to (the predictable) "discovery."

Level I is, in reality, a strategy within the delivery mode, the advantages of which were described in Chapter 6. Because Level I inquiry is highly manageable and the learning outcome is predictable, it is probably best for teaching basic concepts and principles. Students who never experience learning beyond Level I are missing an opportunity to engage their highest mental operations, and they seldom (or never) get to experience more motivating, real-life problem solving. Furthermore, those students may come away with the false notion that problem solving is a linear process, which it is not. As illustrated in Figure 9.2, true inquiry is cyclical rather than linear. For that reason, Level I is not true inquiry because it is a linear process. Real-world problem solving is a cyclical rather than linear process. One enters the cycle whenever a discrepancy or problem is observed and recognized, and that can occur at any point in the cycle.

True Inquiry

By the time students are in their young adolescent years, they should be provided school experiences for true inquiry, which begins with *Level II inquiry*, where students actually decide and design processes for their inquiry. In true inquiry, there is emphasis on the tentative nature of conclusions, which makes the activity more like real-life problem solving, where decisions are always subject to revision if and when new data so prescribe.

Table 9.1 Levels of Inquiry Adapted from Schwab, 1962, p. 55

	Level I	Level II	Level III
Problem Identification	By teacher or textbook	By teacher or textbook	By student
Process of Solving the Problem	Decided by teacher or text	Decided by student	Decided by student
Identification of Tentative Solution	Resolved by student	Resolved by student	Resolved by student

Figure 9.2   The inquiry cycle.

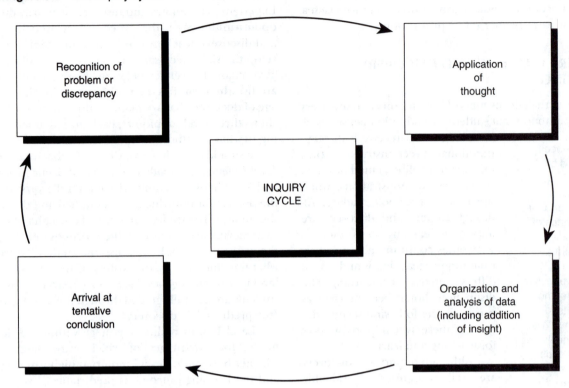

REAL-LIFE SCENARIO

Problem Solving and Decision Making in the Real World Is an Integrated and Interdisciplinary Inquiry Activity

During any given day or specified time period, teacher and students can look at a problem or subject of study from the point of view of many separate disciplines. Such an interdisciplinary approach has been adopted not only by educators but by other professionals as well. It is the mode of meaningful learning and real-life problem solving.

For example, consider the fact-finding and decision-making approach of public officials in Colorado when confronted with making decisions about projects proposed for watersheds in their state. While gathering information, the officials brought in Dave Rosgen, a state hydrologist. Rosgen led the officials into the field to demonstrate specific ways by which he helped control erosion and rehabilitate damaged streams. He took the officials to Wolf Creek, where they donned high waders. Rosgen led the group down the creek to examine various features of that complex natural stream. He pointed out evidence of the creek's past meanders—patterns that he had incorporated into his rehabilitation projects. In addition to listening to this scientist's point of view, the public officials listened to other experts to consider related economic and political issues; for example, before making final decisions about projects that had been proposed for watersheds in that state.

During interdisciplinary thematic units, students study a topic and its underlying ideas as well as related knowledge from various disciplines on an ongoing basis. The teacher, sometimes with the help of students and other teachers and adults, introduces experiences designed according to ideas and skills from various disciplines—just as Rosgen introduced information from hydrology—to develop literacy skills through the unit. For instance, the teacher might stimulate communication skills through creative writing and other projects. Throughout the unit, the students are guided in exploring ideas related to different disciplines, to integrate their knowledge.

At *Level III inquiry,* students recognize and identify the problem as well as decide the processes and reach a conclusion. In project-centered teaching, students are usually engaged at this level of inquiry. By the time students are in middle grades, Level III inquiry should be a major strategy for instruction, which is often the case in schools that use cross-age teaching and interdisciplinary thematic instruction. But, it is not easy; like most good teaching practices it is a lot of work. But also like good teaching, the intrinsic rewards concomitant with the fact that students achieve meaningful learning, make the effort worthwhile. As exclaimed by one teacher using interdisciplinary thematic instruction with student-centered inquiry, "I've never worked harder in my life, but I've never had this much fun, either."

The Critical Thinking Skills of Discovery and Inquiry

In true inquiry, students generate ideas and then design ways to test those ideas. The various processes used represent the many critical thinking skills. Some of those skills are concerned with generating and organizing data; others are concerned with building and using ideas. Figure 9.3 provides four main categories of these thinking processes and illustrates the place of each within the inquiry cycle.

Some processes in the cycle are discovery processes, and others are inquiry processes. Inquiry processes include the more complex mental operations (including all of those in the idea-using category). Project-centered teaching provides an avenue for doing that, as does problem-centered teaching.

Inquiry learning is a higher-level mental operation that introduces the concept of the discrepant event, something that establishes *cognitive disequilibrium* (using the element of surprise to challenge students' prior notions, sometimes called *naïve theories*) to help students develop skills in observing and being alert for discrepancies (Echevarria, 2003). Such a strategy provides opportunities for students to investigate their own ideas about explanations. Inquiry, like discovery, depends upon skill in problem solving; the difference between the two is in the amount of decision-making responsibility given to students. Experiences afforded by inquiry help students understand the importance of suspending judgment and also the tentativeness of answers and solutions. With those intelligent understandings, students eventually are better able to deal with life's ambiguities. When students are not provided these important educational experiences their education is incomplete.

One of the most effective ways of stimulating inquiry is to use materials that provoke students' interest.

Figure 9.3 Inquiry cycle processes.

Cindy Charles/Photo Edit Inc.

These materials should be presented in a nonthreatening, noncompetitive context, so students think and hypothesize freely. The teacher's role is to encourage students to form as many hypotheses as possible and then support their hypotheses with reasons. After the students suggest several ideas, the teacher should begin to move on to higher-order, more abstract questions that involve the development of generalizations and evaluations. True inquiry problems have a special advantage in that they can be used with almost any group of students. Members of a group approach the problem as an adventure in thinking and apply it to whatever background they can muster. Background experience may enrich a student's approach to the problem, but is not crucial to the use or understanding of the evidence presented to that student. Locating a Colony, Figure 9.4, is a Level II inquiry. As a class, do the inquiry now.

INTEGRATING STRATEGIES FOR INTEGRATED LEARNING

In today's exemplary classrooms for young adolescents, instructional strategies are combined to establish the most effective teaching-learning experience. For example, in an integrated language arts program, teachers are interested in their students' speaking, reading, listening, thinking, study, and writing skills. These skills (and not textbooks) form a holistic process that is the primary aspect of integrated language arts.

In the area of speaking skills, oral discourse (discussion) in the classroom has a growing research base that promotes methods of teaching and learning through oral language. These methods include cooperative learning, instructional scaffolding, and inquiry teaching.

In cooperative learning groups, students discuss and use language for learning that benefits both their content learning and skills in social interaction. Working in heterogeneous groups, students participate in their own learning and can extend their knowledge base and cultural awareness with students of different backgrounds. When students share information and ideas, they are completing difficult learning tasks, using divergent thinking and decision making, and developing their understanding of concepts. As issues are presented and responses are challenged, student thinking is clarified. Students assume the responsibility for planning within the group and for carrying out their assignments. When needed, the teacher models an activity with one group in front of the class, and when integrated with student questions, the modeling can become inquiry teaching. Activities can include any from a variety of heuristics (a *heuristic* is a tool used in solving a problem or understanding an idea), such as the following:

Brainstorming. Members generate ideas related to a keyword and record them. Clustering or chunking, mapping, and the Venn diagram (all discussed in the following paragraphs) are variations of brainstorming.

Chunking or clustering. Groups of students apply mental organizers by clustering information into chunks for easier manipulation and remembering.

Comparing and contrasting. Similarities and differences between items are found and recorded.

Inferring. For instance, students assume the roles of different people (real or fictional) and infer their motives, personalities, and thoughts.

Memory strategies. The teacher and students model the use of acronyms, mnemonics, rhymes, or clustering of information into categories to promote learning. Sometimes, such as in memorizing the Social Security number, one must learn by rote information that is not connected to any prior knowledge. To do that, it is helpful to break the information to be learned into smaller chunks, such as dividing the eight-digit Social Security number into smaller chunks of information (with, in this instance, each chunk separated by a hyphen). Learning by rote is also easier if one can connect that which is to be memorized to some prior knowledge. Strategies such as these are used to bridge the gap between rote learning and meaningful learning and are known as *mnemonics* (Mastropieri & Scruggs, 1998; Raschke, Alper, & Eggers, 1999; van Hell & Mahn, 1997). Sample mnemonics are:

- The notes on a treble staff are *FACE* for the space notes and *Empty Garbage Before Dad Flips* (*EGBDF*) for the line notes. The notes on the bass staff are *All Cows Eat Granola Bars* for space notes and *Grizzly Bears Don't Fly Airplanes* (*GBDFA*) for line notes.
- The names of the Great Lakes are *HOMES* for *H*uron, *O*ntario, *M*ichigan, *E*rie, and *S*uperior.
- To remember when to use "affect" versus "effect," remember *RAVEN* for *R*emember *a*ffect (is a) *v*erb, *e*ffect (is a) *n*oun.

Figure 9.4 Locating a colony: A Level II inquiry.

Presentation of the Problem. In groups of three or four, students receive the following information.

Background. You (your group is considered as one person) are one of 120 passengers on the ship, the *Prince Charles.* You left England 12 weeks ago. You have experienced many hardships, including a stormy passage, limited rations, sickness, cold and damp weather, and hot, foul air below deck. Ten of your fellow immigrants to the New World, including three children, have died and been buried at sea. You are now anchored at an uncertain place, off the coast of the New World, which your captain believes to be somewhere north of the Virginia Grants. Seas are so rough and food so scarce that you and your fellow passengers have decided to settle here. A landing party has returned with a map they made of the area. You, as one of the elders, must decide at once where the settlement is to be located. The tradesmen want to settle along the river, which is deep, even though this seems to be the season of low water levels. Within 10 months they expect deep-water ships from England with more colonists and merchants. Those within your group who are farmers say they must have fertile, workable land. The officer in charge of the landing party reported seeing a group of armed natives who fled when approached. He feels the settlement must be located so that it can be defended from the natives and from the sea.

Directions, step one: You (your group) are to select a site on the attached map that you feel is best suited for a colony. Your site must satisfy the different factions aboard the ship. A number of possible sites are already marked on the map (letters *A–G*). You may select one of these locations or use them as reference points to show the location of your colony. When your group has selected its site, list and explain the reasons for your choice. When each group has arrived at its tentative decision, these will be shared with the whole class.

Directions, step two: After each group has made its presentation and argument, a class debate is held about where the colony should be located.

Notes to teacher: For the debate, have a large map drawn on the writing board or on an overhead transparency, where each group's mark can be made for all to see and discuss. After each group has presented its argument for its location and against the others, we suggest that you then mark on the large map the two,

three, or more hypothetical locations (assuming that, as a class, there is no single favorite location yet). Then take a straw vote of the students, allowing each to vote on her or his own independently, rather than as members of groups. At this time you can terminate the activity by saying that if the majority of students favor one location, then that, in fact, is the solution to the problem—that is, the colony is located wherever the majority of class members believe it should be. No sooner will that statement be made by you than someone will ask, "Are we correct?" or "What is the right answer?" They will ask such questions because, as students in school, they are used to solving problems that have right answers (Level I inquiry teaching). In real-world problems, however, there are no "right" answers, though some answers may seem better than others. It is the process of problem solving that is important. You want your students to develop confidence in their ability to solve problems and understand the tentativeness of "answers" to real-life problems.

Source: Adapted by permission from unpublished material provided by Jennifer Devine and Dennis Devine.

- To remember when a vowel is not pronounced, use "When vowels go walking, the first one does the talking."
- To remember when to use "principle" versus "principal," remember "The principal is your pal."
- Visual mnemonics are useful too, such as remembering that Italy is shaped in the form of a boot.

Outlining. Each group completes an outline that contains some of the main ideas but with subtopics omitted.

Paraphrasing. In a brief summary, each student restates a short selection of what was read or heard.

Reciprocal teaching. In classroom dialogue, students take turns at summarizing, questioning, clarifying, and predicting (Carter, 1997; Marzano, Pickering, & Pollock, 2001; Palincsar & Brown, 1984).

Review. While frequent review of material being learned is essential, it is most effective when the students are actively involved in planning and implementing the review as opposed to their being passive respondents to a review conducted by the teacher (Wolfe, 2001).

Study strategies. Important strategies that should be taught explicitly include vocabulary expansion, reading and interpreting graphic information, locating resources, using advance organizers, adjusting one's reading rate, and skimming, scanning, and study reading (Choate & Rakes, 1998).

Visual tools. A variety of terms for visual tools useful for learning have been invented (some of which are synonymous), such as brainstorming web, cluster, cognitive map, conflict map, graphic organizer, mind mapping web, semantic map, spider map, thinking process map, Venn diagram, and visual scaffold. Visual tools are separated into three categories according to purpose: (a) *brainstorming tools* (such as mind mapping, webbing, and clustering) for the purpose of developing one's knowledge and creativity; (b) *task-specific organizers* (such as life cycle diagrams used in life science, decision trees used in mathematics, and text structures in reading); and (c) *thinking process maps* for encouraging cognitive development across disciplines (Hyerle, 1996). It is the latter about which we are interested here.

Based on Ausubel's (1963) theory of meaningful learning, thinking process mapping has been found useful in helping students change prior notions (i.e., their misconceptions or naïve views). It can help students in their ability to organize and to represent their thoughts, as well as to help them connect new knowledge to their past experiences and precepts (Novak, 1990; Novak, 1998; Plotnick, 1997; van Boxtel, van der Linden, Roelofs, & Erkens, 2002). Simply put, concepts can be understood as classifications that attempt to organize the world of objects and events into a smaller number of categories. In everyday usage, the term *concept* means idea, as when someone says, "My concept of love is not the same as yours." Concepts embody a meaning that develops in complexity with experience and learning over time. For example, the concept of love that is held by a second grader is unlikely to be as complex as that held by an eleventh grader. Thinking process mapping is a graphical way of demonstrating the relationship between and among concepts.

Typically, a thinking process map refers to a visual or graphic representation of concepts with bridges (connections) that show relationships. Figure 9.5 shows a partially complete thinking process map done by an integrated science and social studies class, where students have made connections of concept relationships related to fruit farming and marketing. The general procedure for thinking process mapping is to have the students: (1) identify important concepts in materials being studied, often by circling those concepts; (2) rank the concepts from the most general to the most specific; and (3) arrange the concepts on a sheet of paper, connect related ideas with lines, and define the connections between the related ideas.

One specific type of thinking process map is the *vee map.* This is a V-shaped road map completed by students, as they learn, showing the route they follow from prior knowledge to new and future knowledge.

Prognostication about what may
    be known in the future   →

Listing of what is known today   →

What we knew when we began
    our quest   →

Venn diagramming is a thinking process mapping tool for comparing concepts or, for example, two stories, to show similarities and differences. Using stories as an example, a student is asked to draw two circles that intersect and to mark the circles one and two and the area where they intersect three. In circle one, the student lists characteristics of one story, and in circle two she or he lists the characteristics of the second story. In the area of the intersection, marked three, the student lists characteristics common to both stories.

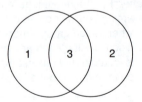

Venn diagrams can be useful for assessing for higher-order thinking. For example, the sample assessment item in Figure 9.6 assesses for the student's understanding of the concepts of the universe, planets, and the Earth's moon. For scoring or marking the

Figure 9.5 Partially completed thinking process map.

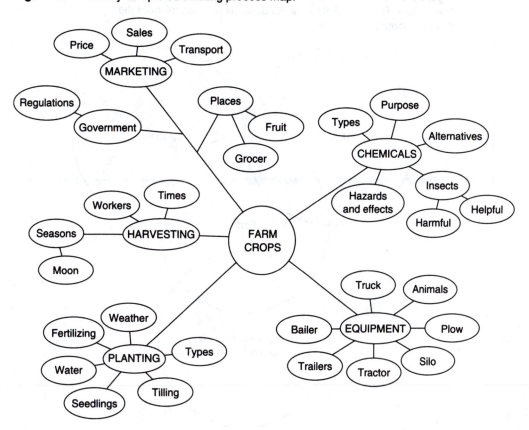

student's response, each possible response has a maximum score of 3, one point for three distinct responses that are obvious elements of the item.

The *visual learning log* (VLL) is another kind of road map completed by students showing the route they follow from prior knowledge to new and future knowledge, except that the VLL consists of pictograms (free-form drawings) that each student makes and that are maintained in a journal.

The value of the above discussed representations is believed to be because they engage what psychologists refer to as the "dual-coding" theory of information storage (Pavio, 1971, 1990), that knowledge is stored in the brain in two forms, a linguistic form and a nonlinguistic form, the latter of which is stored as mental pictures and as sensory sensations (Marzano, Pickering, & Pollock, 2001). Again, the oft-repeated message and central theme of this resource guide is that when teaching young adolescents the most effective and longest-lasting learning is not that of verbiage alone but that which engages most or all of their senses.

To further explore inquiry teaching and integrated learning, complete Exercise 9.1.

Figure 9.6 Sample assessment item using Venn diagramming.
Instructions: From the diagram write down all you can tell from the
diagram about planet Earth.

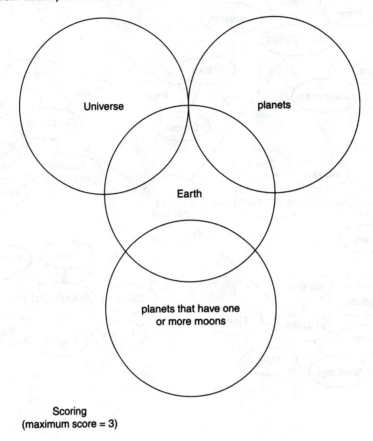

Scoring
(maximum score = 3)

Response	Score
Earth is in the Universe	1
Earth is a planet	1
Earth has at least one moon	1

EXERCISE 9.1: A STUDY OF INQUIRY AND STRATEGY INTEGRATION

INSTRUCTIONS: The purpose of this exercise is to analyze the Locating a Colony inquiry (the Level II inquiry of Figure 9.4 that you did with your classmates) and the discussion in the text about integrating strategies and then to synthesize that information for use in your own teaching. We suggest that you first answer the questions of this exercise and then share your answers with others in your discipline (in groups of about four). Finally, share your group's collective responses with the entire class.

1. My subject field and middle level grade interest:

2a. How I could use the Locating a Colony inquiry (for what purpose, goals, or objectives)?

2b. Content in my class that students might be expected to learn from doing the Locating a Colony inquiry:

3. In what way could I involve my students in reciprocal teaching while doing the Locating a Colony inquiry?

4. How brainstorming could be used while doing the Locating a Colony inquiry:

5. How clustering could be used while doing the Locating a Colony inquiry:

6. How thinking process mapping could be used while doing the Locating a Colony inquiry:

☞

EXERCISE 9.1   *(continued)*

7. How outlining could be used while doing the Locating a Colony inquiry:

8. How comparing and contrasting could be used while doing the Locating a Colony inquiry:

9. How paraphrasing could be used while doing the Locating a Colony inquiry:

10. How reviewing and summarizing could be used while doing the Locating a Colony inquiry:

11. How memory strategies could be used while doing the Locating a Colony inquiry:

12. How inferring could be used while doing the Locating a Colony inquiry:

13. What other skills could be taught while doing the Locating a Colony inquiry? For each, describe how.

EDUCATIONAL GAMES

Devices classified as educational games include a wide variety of learning activities, such as simulations, role-play and sociodrama activities, mind games, board games, computer games, and sporting games—see section that follows—all of which provide valuable learning experiences for participants. That is, they are experiences that tend to involve several senses and involve several learning modalities, tend to engage higher-order thinking skills, and tend to be quite effective as learning tools.

Of all the arts, drama involves the learner-participant most fully—intellectually, emotionally, physically, verbally, and socially. Interactive drama, which is role-playing, a simplified form of drama, is a method by which students can become involved with literature.

CLASSROOM VIGNETTE

Science Students Write and Stage a One-Act Play

Early in the year, in preparation for a unit on the study of oxygen and other gases, Robert told the 28 students in his seventh-grade physical science class that, if they were interested, he would like for them to plan, write, and stage a one-act play about the life of Joseph Priestley, the theologian and scientist who in 1774 discovered what he called "dephlogisticated air," later named *oxygen* by Lavoisier. Furthermore, the students would be given one week to plan. The play would be presented and video recorded in class. The students accepted Robert's idea with enthusiasm and immediately went about the task of organizing and putting their ideas into motion. They took on the challenging task with such vigor and seriousness that they asked Robert for an additional three days to prepare. Sean, a bright student who was really more interested in theatre than science, was selected by the students to play the role of Priestley and to be the director. Other students played lesser roles. Students with special interest in writing wrote the play. Those with interest in art and stagecraft assumed the task of designing and preparing the set, while another assumed the role of sound stage manager. The resulting 60-minute presentation was more successful than Robert, and perhaps the students, could ever have anticipated. By request of the school principal, the students put on the play two more times, once for the entire student body, and a second time for the school's parent-teacher-student organization. Both performances resulted in standing ovations. During the performance before the PTO, the student production was simultaneously recorded by the local cable television network and later played several times over the community cable channel. Robert later said that during this experience the students learned far more content than they ever would have via his traditional approach to the topic. In addition, these students were highly motivated in learning science for the entire rest of the year. Several years later, Sean graduated with honors from the University of California with a degree major in theatre and a minor in chemistry.

Simulations, a more complex form of drama, serve many of the developmental needs of young adolescents. They provide for interaction with peers and allow students of differences to work together on a common project. They engage students in physical activity and provide them the opportunity to try out different roles, which help them better understand themselves. Role-play simulations can provide concrete experiences that help students to understand complex concepts and issues, and they provide opportunities for exploring values and develop skill in decision making. Indeed, in the not so distant future because it involves a learning that is powerfully effective, that young people are familiar with, and that is based on the best of what we know about how children learn, we are likely to see greater use of technology-based simulation games in teaching (Foreman, 2004).

Educational games can play an integral role in interdisciplinary teaching and, as indicated in the scenario that follows, serve as valuable resources for enriching the effectiveness of students' learning. As with any other instructional strategy, the use of games should follow a clear educational purpose, have a careful plan, and be congruent with the instructional objectives.

Classification of Educational Games

What are educational games? Seven types of games fall under the general heading of "educational games."

TEACHING IN PRACTICE

Games in the Classroom and the Underperforming Student*

High-stakes state assessments have recently spotlighted the underperforming student. Faced with the probability of barring a large number of students from graduation, one teacher found a unique way to get students excited about studying the language arts and math skills required for the state tests.

The teacher was assigned to teach a special class for those students who were likely to fail the state test. The students, including a good number of special needs students and students still learning English, were generally apathetic toward trying again to learn what they had failed to learn in math and English class.

They were apathetic, that is, until their teacher told them, "Put away your pencils and notebooks. Today we're going to play a video game!" After a demonstration by the teacher of how the game worked, the students, every one of them, were concentrating hard on achieving the best score in the class . . . on a video game. In a few minutes, Jacinto, one of the more competitive students, exclaimed, "I beat the game!" The teacher recorded Jacinto's score and encouraged Jacinto to try to beat the game in fewer than 100 seconds. Jacinto accepted the challenge.

Did the students know that they were learning math? Certainly. The goal of the game was to state the range and domain (e.g., $22 < y < 97$ and $65 < x < 144$) of 10 randomly displayed functions. Once a student earned an *A* for "beating the game," they were encouraged to earn another *A* by turning in a time of under 100 seconds. Toward the end of the period, Jacinto and four other students were vying for the lowest time. When the dismissal bell rang, Ana had beaten Jacinto by one second, but the real reward was when they were asked to express the range and domain of a function on the state math assessment test.

*Source: The teacher Mark Greenberg, is now an English teacher at North High School (Phoenix, AZ). By permission.

Table 9.2 shows the seven types, with characteristics and examples of each.

Functions of Educational Games

Games can be powerful tools for teaching and learning. A game can serve several of the following functions, and the function(s) of a particular game being used should be communicated to the students.

- add variety and change of pace, providing a break from the usual rigors of learning
- assess student learning
- encourage lateral thinking
- encourage learning through peer interaction
- enhance student self-esteem
- enhance student social relationships
- motivate students
- offers learning about real-life issues through simulation and role-playing
- provide learning through tactile and kinesthetic modalities, as well as through linguistics
- provide problem-solving situations and experiences
- provide skill development and motivation through computer usage
- provide skill development in inductive thinking
- provide skill development in verbal communication and debate
- reinforce convergent thinking
- review and reinforce subject-matter learning
- stimulate critical thinking
- stimulate deductive thinking
- teach both content and process.

Sources for useful educational games include professional journals (see Figure 9.7) and the Internet. Web sources of commercially available educational games for use in teaching are shown at the end of the chapter. Now, according to instructions by your course instructor, do Exercise 9.2.

Table 9.2   Classification of Educational Games

Type	Characteristics	Examples
1. Pure game*	Fun	*Ungame, New Games*
2. Pure contest	Stimulates competition; built-in inefficiency[†]	Political contests, (e.g., U.S. presidential race)
3. Pure simulation*	Models reality	Toddler play; Think-time and the art of questioning (Exercise 3.2 of this resource guide.)
4. Contest/game	Stimulates competition; fun; built-in inefficiency	Golf; bowling; *Trivial Pursuit*
5. Simulation/game*	Models reality; fun	*SIMCITY; Our Town's Planning Commission Meeting*[§]
6. Contest/simulation	Stimulates competition; models reality; built-in inefficiency	Boxcar Derby of Akron, OH
7. Simulation/game/contest	Models reality; fun; stimulates competition; built-in inefficiency	*Careers, Life, Monopoly*

[*]These game types do not emphasize competition and, therefore, are particularly recommended for use in the classroom as learning tools.

[†]This means that rules for accomplishing the game objective make accomplishment of that objective less than efficient. For example, in golf the objective is to get the ball into the hole with the least amount of effort; but to do that, one has to take a peculiarly shaped stick (the club) and hit the ball, find it, and hit it again, continuing that sequence until the ball is in the hole. Yet, common sense tells us that the best way to get the ball into the hole with the least amount of effort would be to simply pick up the ball and place it by hand into the hole.

[§]See J. V. Vort, "Our Town's Planning Commission Meeting," *Journal of Geography 96*(4):183–190 (July–August 1997).

Figure 9.7   Sample professional journals with educational games.

Barlow, A. T. (February 2002). Reviewing made fun! *Mathematics Teacher, 95*(2), 98.

Bassett, J. (Winter 1997). The Pullman Strike of 1894. *OAH Magazine of History, 11*(2), 34–41. Role-play simulation.

Faden, M. & Christopher, A. (June–July 2005). Go eat. *Edutopia, 1*(5), 32. A meal-planning card game.

Howle, M. J. (March 1997). Play-party games in the modern classroom. *Music Educators Journal, 83*(5), 24–28. Introduces games popular on the 19th-century American frontier.

LeNoir, D. W. (May 2003). "There's nothing to eat!" A half-dozen ways to find writing ideas. *English Journal, 92*(5), 25–29.

Levy, T. (September 1995). The Amistad incident: A classroom reenactment. *Social Education, 59*(5), 202–208.

Luque-Ekrich, M. (March 2003). Idea: The rapid memory game: Por and para. *Hispania, 86*(1), 133–137.

May, K. (September 2002). Science signature game. *Science Scope, 26*(1), 42–43.

Moyer, P. S., & Bolyard, J. J. (February 2003). Classify and capture: Using Venn diagrams and tangrams to develop abilities in mathematical reasoning and proof. *Mathematical Teaching in the Middle School, 8*(6), 325–330. Game of classifying objects.

Rotter, K. (January/February 2004). Modifying "Jeopardy!" games to benefit all students." *Teaching Exceptional Children, 36*(3), 58–62.

Van Dresar, V. J. (May 2002). Opening Young Minds to Closure Properties. *Mathematics Teacher, 95*(5), 326–328.

FOR YOUR NOTES

PP EXERCISE 9.2: DEVELOPING A LESSON USING INQUIRY LEVEL II, THINKING SKILL DEVELOPMENT, A DEMONSTRATION, OR AN INTERACTIVE LECTURE—MICRO PEER TEACHING II

INSTRUCTIONS: The purpose of this exercise is to provide an opportunity for you to create a brief lesson (about 20 minutes of instructional time, but to be specified by your instructor) designed for a specific grade level and subject and to try it out on your peers for their feedback in an informal (i.e., nongraded) micro peer teaching demonstration.

Divide your class into four groups. The task of the members of each group is to prepare lessons (individually) that fall into one of the four categories: Level II inquiry, thinking level, demonstration, and interactive lecture. Schedule class presentations so that each class member has an opportunity to present his or her lesson and to obtain feedback from class members about it. For feedback, class members who are the "teacher's" audience can complete the assessment rubric shown on page 382 (by circling one of the three choices for each of the 10 categories) and give their completed forms to the teacher for use in analysis and self-assessment. Before your class starts this exercise, you may want to review the scoring rubric and make modifications to it that the class agrees on.

To structure your lesson plan, use one of the sample lesson plan formats presented in Chapter 6; however, each lesson should be centered on one major theme or concept and should be planned for about 20 minutes of instructional time.

Group 1: Develop a Level II inquiry lesson.
Group 2: Develop a lesson designed to raise the level of student thinking.
Group 3: Develop a lesson that involves a demonstration.
Group 4: Develop a lesson that is an interactive lecture.

EXERCISE 9.2   *(continued)*

PEER AND SELF-ASSESSMENT RUBRIC FOR USE WITH EXERCISE 9.2

For: _____   Group: _____

	1	0.5	0
1. Lesson beginning	effective	less effective	not effective
Comment:			
2. Sequencing	effective	less effective	rambling
Comment:			
3. Pacing of lesson	effective	less effective	too slow or too fast
Comment:			
4. Audience involvement	effective	less effective	none
Comment:			
5. Motivators (e.g., analogies, verbal cues, humor, visual cues, sensory cues)	effective	less effective	not apparent
Comment:			
6. Content of lesson	well chosen	interesting	boring or inappropriate
Comment:			
7. Voice of teacher	stimulating	minor problem	major problems
Comment:			
8. Vocabulary used	well chosen	appropriate	inappropriate
Comment:			
9. Eye contact	excellent	average	problems
Comment:			
10. Closure	effective	less effective	unclear/none
Comment:			

Other Comments:

SUMMARY

Central to your selection of instructional strategies for teaching young adolescents should be those that encourage students to become independent thinkers and skilled learners who can help in the planning, structuring, regulating, and assessing of their own learning and learning activities. This final chapter has presented guidelines for some of the most frequently used and useful ways of helping young adolescents become independent thinkers and skilled learners.

This final chapter of this resource guide ushers in an important transition in your professional career, a career that as emphasized in the introduction of the final MPT exercise is really only beginning. Throughout your teaching career, you will continue improving your knowledge and skills in all aspects of teaching and learning.

We wish you the very best in what is to be the first chapter in your new career. Be the very best teacher that you can be. The nation, indeed the world, and its young adolescents need you.

—Richard Kellough
—Noreen Kellough

QUESTIONS FOR CLASS DISCUSSION

1. Many cognitive researchers agree that students should spend more time actively using knowledge to solve problems and less time reading introductory material and listening to teachers. Describe the meaning of this statement and how you now feel about it with respect to your decision to become a teacher of young adolescents. Do you expect to act on their suggestion? Explain why not, or how you will do it.

2. Explain the meaning of *integrating strategies for integrated learning*.

3. Are there any cautions that, as a teacher, you need to be aware of when using games for teaching? If there are, describe them.

4. Explain some specific ways you can help students develop their skills in thinking and learning. Explain how you will determine that students have raised their skill level in thinking and learning.

5. From chapter 3, select one of the characteristics of intelligent behavior and (for a grade level of your choice and time limit as decided by your class) write a lesson plan for helping students develop that behavior. Share or teach your lesson to others in your class for their analysis and suggestions.

6. Test scores typically do not measure skills and intelligent behaviors such as critical thinking, persistence, cooperation, ingenuity, patience, creativity, originality, and flexibility in thinking. How should students who demonstrate achievement in intelligent behaviors be recognized?

7. Return to your response to question number 3 at the end of Chapter 2. Modify it if necessary. Share your modifications with those of your classmates.

8. Recent years have seen a tremendous growth in gaming, and for many young adolescents, technology-centered games are a component of their everyday lives. Explain the impact of games, if any, in your own life. Considering these facts, what do you predict for the near future in public school teaching for the use of video, computer or on-line games for teaching?

9. Think back about your own schooling. What is one demonstration that you observed that stands out as being most impressive to you, in either a negative or a positive way? Identify one or two characteristics of that demonstration that made it so. Share your conclusion with your classmates. From your sharing, what conclusions can be made about using demonstrations for teaching and learning.

10. Can you recall from your own schooling any participation in educational games that made a positive impact on your learning? If so, identify which of the seven types of games it was and one or two characteristics that made the effect positive. Share your conclusion with your classmates.

INTERNET RESOURCES

Ampersand Press **http://www.ampersandpress.com/**

Aristoplay **http://www.aristoplay.com/**

Creative Teaching Associates **http://www.mastercta.com/**

Dawn publications **http://www.dawnpub.com/**

Harcourt Brace School Publishers
   http://www.harcourtbrace.com/

Latz Chance Games **http://www.latzchancegames.com/**

Novostars Designs **http://www.novostar.com/**

Prufrock Press **http://www.prufrock.com**

The Sims **http://www.maxis.com**

Summit Learning **http://www.summitlearning.com/pg1.htm**

Teacher-Created Materials
   **http://myconsumerguide.com/teacher_created_
   materials.htm**

Visual learning mapping software **http://www.ihmc.us** *and*
   http://www.inspiration.com

FOR FURTHER READING

Albright, L. K., & Arail, M. (2005). Tapping the potential of teacher read-alouds in middle schools. *Journal of Adolescent and Adult Literacy, 48,* 582–591.

Beamon, G. W. (2002). Guiding the inquiry of young adolescents. *Middle School Journal, 33*(3), 19–27.

Cole, S. (2002). Take a risk with earth science inquiry. *Science Scope, 25*(4), 48–51.

Dass, P. M., Kilby, D., & Chappell, A. (2005). Scientific inquiry and real-life applications bring middle school students up to standards. *Middle School Journal, 36*(5), 20–29.

Eagleton, M., Guinee, K., & Langlais, K. (2003). Teaching Internet literacy strategies: The hero inquiry project. *Voices from the Middle, 10*(3), 28–35.

Galus, P. (2003). Playing games. *Science Scope, 26*(7), 33–34.

Howes, E. V., Hamilton, G. W., & Zaskoda, D. (2003). Linking science and literature through technology: Thinking about interdisciplinary inquiry in middle school. *Journal of Adolescent & Adult Literacy, 46,* 494–504.

Moore, S. D., & Blintz, W. P. (2002). From Galileo to Snowflake Bentley: Using literature to teaching inquiry in middle school science. *Science Scope, 26*(1), 10–14.

Moyer, P. S., & Bolyard, J. J. (2003). Classify and capture: Using Venn diagrams and tangrams to develop abilities in mathematical reasoning and proof. *Mathematics Teaching in the Middle School, 8,* 325–330.

Olson, J. C. (2003). Interdisciplinary projects enhance teaching and learning. *Mathematics Teaching in the Middle School, 8,* 260–266.

Pogrow, S. (2004). Supermath: An alternative approach to improving math performance in grades 4 through 9. *Phi Delta Kappan, 86,* 297–303.

Shaffer, D. W., Squire, K. R., Halverson, R., & Gee, J. P. (2005). Video games and the future of learning. *Phi Delta Kappan, 87,* 104–111.

Shreve, J. (2005). *Let the games begin. Video games, once confiscated in class, are now a key teaching tool. If they're done right.* San Rafael, CA: George Lucas Educational Foundation.

Van Eck, R. (2006). The effect of contextual pedagogical advisement and competition on middle-school students' attitude toward mathematics and mathematics instruction using a computer-based simulation game. *Journal of Computers in Mathematics and Science Teching, 25,* 165–195.

White, S. H., O'Brien, J. E., Smith, A., Mortensen, D., & Hileman, K. (2006). A history lab environment in the classroom brings the standards to life. *Middle School Journal, 37*(4), 4–10.

Wilhelm, J. D. (2006). The age for drama. *Educational Leadership, 63*(7), 74–77.

References

Albert, L. (1989, rev. 1996). *A teacher's guide to cooperative discipline: How to manage your classroom and promote self-esteem.* Circle Pines, MN: American Guidance Service.

Allen, R. (2003). An early taste of college: Accelerated learning with support motivates urban students. *Education Update, 45,* 1, 3, & 8.

Amrein, A. L., & Berliner, D. C. (2003). The testing divide: New research on the intended and unintended impact of high-stakes testing. *Peer Review, 5*(2), 21–32.

Armstrong, T. (1998). *Awakening genius in the classroom.* Alexandria, VA: Association for Supervision and Curriculum Development.

Arth, A., et al. (2004). Present imperfect. *Principal Leadership, 4.* Retrieved July 10, 2004, from http://www.principals. org/publications/pl/pl_present_imperfect_0404.cfm.

Ashton, P., & Webb, R. (1986). *Making a difference: Teacher's sense of efficacy and student achievement.* New York: Longman.

Astington, J. W. (1998). Theory of mind goes to school. *Educational Leadership, 56*(3), 46–48.

Ausubel, D. P. (1963). *The psychology of meaningful learning.* New York: Grune & Stratton.

Bacon, S. (2005). Reading coaches: Adapting an intervention model for upper elementary and middle school readers. *Journal of Adolescent & Adult Literacy, 48,* 416–427.

Baker, J. C., & Martin, F. G. (1998). *A neural network guide to teaching,* Fastback 431. Bloomington, IN: Phi Delta Kappa Educational Foundation.

Baldwin, D. (2004). A guide to standardized writing assessment. *Educational Leadership, 62*(2), 72–75.

Banks, J. A. (1999). Multicultural and citizenship education in the new century. *School Administrator, 56,* 8–10. Retrieved March 19, 2004, from http://www.aasa.org/SA/may9901/htm.

Barojas, J., & Dehesa, N. (2001). Mathematics for social scientists: Learning cycles and teaching strategies. *Industry & Higher Education, 15,* 269–277.

Barron, J. B., & Sternberg, R. J. (Eds.). (1987). *Teaching thinking skills: Theory and practice.* New York: W. H. Freeman.

Battistini, J. (1995). *From theory to practice: Classroom application of outcome-based education.* Bloomington, IN: ERIC Clearinghouse on Reading, English, and Communication.

Bevevino, M. M., Dengel, J., & Adams, K. (1999). Constructivist theory in the classroom: Internalizing concepts through inquiry learning. *Clearing House, 72,* 275–278.

Black, S. (1998). Learning on the block. *American School Board Journal, 185*(1), 32–34.

Black, S. (2004). All together now. *American School Board Journal, 191*(3), 40–42.

Bloom, B. S. (Ed.). (1984). *Taxonomy of educational objectives, book 1, cognitive domain.* White Plains, NY: Longman.

Bloom, B. S. (1987). *Human characteristics and school learning.* New York: McGraw-Hill.

Bobek, B. L. (2002). Teacher resiliency: A key to career longevity. *Clearing House, 75,* 202–205.

Bolak, K., Bialach, D., & Dunphy, M. (2005). Standards-based, thematic units integrate the arts and energize students and teachers. *Middle School Journal, 36*(5), 9–19.

Bolland, J. M. (2003). Hopelessness and risk behaviour among adolescents living in high-poverty inner-city neighbourhoods. *Journal of Adolescence, 26,* 145–158.

Bracey, G. W. (2003). April foolishness: The 20th anniversary of a Nation at Risk. *Phi Delta Kappan, 84*(8), 616–621.

Brand, S., Dunn, R., & Greb, F. (2002). Learning styles of students with attention deficit hyperactivity disorder: Who are they and how can we teach them? *Clearing House, 75,* 268–273.

Brandt, R. (2000). On teaching brains to think: A conversation with Robert Sylwester. *Educational Leadership, 57*(7), 72–75.

Brogan, B. R., & Brogan, W. A. (1995). The Socratic questioner: Teaching and learning in the dialogical classroom. *Educational Forum, 59,* 288–296.

Brooks, J. G., & Brooks, M. G. (1993). *In search of understanding: The case for constructivist classrooms.* Alexandria, VA: Association for Supervision and Curriculum Development.

Brown, J. L., & Moffett, C. A. (1999). *The hero's journey.* Alexandria, VA: Association for Supervision and Curriculum Development.

Bruner, J. S. (1960). *Process of education.* Cambridge, MA: Harvard University Press.

Burns, M. (2004). Writing in math. *Educational Leadership, 62*(3), 30–33.

Burrett, K., & Rusnak, T. (1993). *Integrated character education.* Fastback 351. Bloomington, IN: Phi Delta Kappa Educational Foundation.

Caine, R. N. (2000). Building the bridge from research to classroom. *Educational Leadership, 58*(3), 59–61.

Caine, R. N., & Caine, G. (1997). *Education on the edge of possibility.* Alexandria, VA: Association for Supervision and Curriculum Development.

California Middle Grade Task Force. (1987). *Caught in the middle: Educational reform for young adolescents in California public schools.* Sacramento, CA: California State Department of Education.

Callahan, C. M. (2001). Beyond the gifted stereotype. *Educational Leadership, 59*(3), 42–46.

Campbell, L., & Campbell, B. (1999). *Multiple intelligences and student achievement: Success stories from six schools.* Alexandria, VA: Association for Supervision and Curriculum Development.

Canter, L., & Canter, M. (1992). *Assertive discipline: Positive behavior management for today's schools.* Santa Monica, CA: Lee Canter & Associates.

Carroll, J. (1963). A model of school learning. *Teachers College Record, 64,* 723–733.

Carroll, J. M. (1994). The Copernican plan evaluated. *Phi Delta Kappan, 76*(2), 105–113.

Carter, C. J. (1997). Why reciprocal teaching? *Educational Leadership, 54*(6), 64–68.

Casbarro, J. (2004). Reducing anxiety in the era of high-stakes testing. *Principal, 83*(5), 36–38.

Center for Education Policy. (August, 2004). *State high school exit exams: A maturing reform.* Washington, DC: Author.

Chandler, A. (1997). Is this for a grade? A personal look at journals. *English Journal, 86*(1), 45–49.

Choate, J. S., & Rakes, T. A. (1998). *Inclusive instruction for struggling readers.* Fastback 434. Bloomington, IN: Phi Delta Kappa Educational Foundation.

Ciardiello, A. V. (2000). Student questioning and multidimensional literacy in the 21st century. *Educational Forum, 64,* 215–222.

Clark, G., & Zimmerman, E. (1998). Nurturing the arts in programs for gifted and talented students. *Phi Delta Kappan, 79,* 747–751.

Coelho, E. (1994). *Learning together in the multicultural classroom.* Portsmouth, NH: Heinemann.

Combs, A. W. (Ed.). (1962) *Perceiving, behaving, becoming: A new focus for education.* 1962 Yearbook. Arlington, VA: Association for Supervision and Curriculum Development.

Conderman, G., Ikan, P. A., & Hatcher, R. E. (2000). Student-led conferences in inclusive settings. *Intervention in School and Clinic, 36*(1), 22–26.

Costa, A. L. (1991). *The school as a home for the mind.* Palatine, IL: Skylight Publishing.

Costa, A. L. (Ed.). (1985). *Developing minds: A resource book for teaching thinking.* Alexandria, VA: Association for Supervision and Curriculum Development.

Costa, A. L., & Kallick, B. (2000). *Discovering and exploring habits of mind, book 1 of habits of mind: A developmental series.* Alexandria, VA: Association for Supervision and Curriculum Development.

Danforth, E. L. (2003). Mixed signals. *American School Board Journal, 190*(7), 30–32.

Daniels, E. (2005). On the minds of middle schoolers. *Educational Leadership, 62*(7), 53–54.

Danielson, C., & McGreal, T. I. (2000). *Teacher evaluation to enhance professional practice.* Alexandria, VA: Association for Supervision and Curriculum Development, and Princeton, NJ: Educational Testing Service.

Davis, A. K. (2001). The politics of barking and the state of our schools. *Phi Delta Kappan, 82,* 786–789.

De Bono, E. (1970). *Lateral thinking: Creativity step by step.* New York: Harper & Row.

DeLay, R. (1996). Forming knowledge: Constructivist learning and experiential education. *Journal of Experiential Education, 19*(2), 76–81.

Dewey, J. (1902). *The child and the curriculum.* Chicago: The University of Chicago Press.

Dewey, J. (1910). *How we think.* Boston, MA: Heath.

Dreikurs, R., & Cassel, P. (1972). *Discipline without tears.* New York: Hawthorne Books.

Dreikurs, R., Grunwald, B. B., & Pepper, F. C. (1982). *Maintaining sanity in the classroom: Classroom management techniques* (2nd ed.). New York: Harper & Row.

Dryfoos, J. (2002). Full service schools: Creating new institutions. *Phi Delta Kappan, 83,* 393–399.

Dunn, R. (1995). *Strategies for educating diverse learners.* Fastback 384. Bloomington, IN: Phi Delta Kappa Educational Foundation.

Echevarria, M. (2003). Anomalies as a catalyst for middle school students' knowledge construction and scientific reasoning during science inquiry. *Journal of Educational Psychology, 95,* 357–374.

Educational Leadership. (1999). The constructivist classroom, the entire November theme issue. *Educational Leadership, 57.*

Edwards, C. H. (1997). *Classroom discipline and management* (2nd ed.). Upper Saddle River, NJ: Prentice Hall.

Eilertsen, T. V., & Valdermo, O. (2000). Open-book assessment: A contribution to improved learning? *Studies in Educational Evaluation, 26*(2), 91–103.

Eisner, E. W. (1979). *The educational imagination.* New York: Macmillan.

Eisner, E. W. (2002). The kind of schools we need. *Phi Delta Kappan, 84,* 579.

Elder, L., & Paul, R. (1998). The role of Socratic questioning in thinking, teaching, and learning. *Clearing House, 71,* 297–301.

Elias, M. J. (2001). Easing transitions with social-emotional learning. *Principal Leadership, 1,* 1–4. Retrieved April 1, 2001, from http://www.nassp.org/news/pl_soc_emo_lrng_301.htm.

Englert, C. S., & Mariage, T. V. (1991). Making students partners in the comprehension process: Organizing the reading "POSSE." *Learning Disability Quarterly, 14*(1), 123–138.

English, L. (1998). Uncovering students' analytic, practical, and creative intelligences: One school's application of Sternberg's triarchic theory. *School Administrator, 55*(1), 28–29.

Fagan, H., & Sherman, L. (2002). Starting at the end: Alaska project-based learning expert Helena Fagan insists that good projects are designed "backward"—that is, what do we want kids to know when they're done? *Northwest Education, 7*(3), 30–35.

Farber, P. (1999). Speak up: Student-led conference is a real conversation piece. *Middle Ground, 2*(4), 21–24.

Feldhusen, J. F. (1998). Programs for the gifted few or talent development for the many? *Phi Delta Kappan, 79*, 735–738.

Ferrandino, V. L., & Tirozzi, G. N. (May 23, 2001). Test driven or data driven. NAESP *Principal Online.* Retrieved August 10, 2004, from http://www.naesp.org.

Findley, N. (2002). In their own ways. *Educational Leadership, 60*(1), 60–63.

Fiscus, L. (2005). Student voice in school leadership. *Middle Ground, 8*(3), 22–24.

Fitzgerald, J., & Graves, M. F. (2005). Reading supports for all. *Educational Leadership, 62*(4), 68–71.

Foreman, J. (2004). Game-based learning: How to delight and instruct in the 21st century. *Educause Review, 39*(5), 50–66.

Foster, A. S. (2003). Let the dogs out: Using bobble head toys to explore force and motion. *Science Scope, 26*(7), 16–19.

Frahm, R. A. (October 7, 2004). School officials, in survey, fault education law. *Hartford Courant.* Retrieved October 12, 2004, from www.courant.com.

Franklin, J. (2002). Taking up the challenge: Safeguarding the shelves of school libraries. *Curriculum Update, 44*(8), 1, 3 & 8.

Freiberg, H. J. (Ed.). (1997). *Beyond behaviorism: Changing the classroom management paradigm.* Boston: Allyn & Bacon.

Freiberg, H. J. (Ed.). (1999). *Perceiving behaving becoming: Lessons learned.* Alexandria, VA: Association for Supervision and Curriculum Development.

Freidenberg, E. Z. (1963). *The vanishing adolescent.* New York: Dell.

Frost, R., Olson, E., & Valiquette, L. (2000). The wolf pack: Power shared and power earned—building a middle school nation. *Middle School Journal, 31*(5), 30–36.

Gabriel, A. E. (1999). Brain-based learning: The scent of the trail. *Clearing House, 72*, 288–290.

Gagné, R. M., Briggs, L. J., & Wager, W. W. (1994). *Principles of instructional design* (4th ed.). New York: Holt, Rinehart & Winston.

Gardner, H. (1996). Multiple intelligences: Myths and messages. *International Schools Journal, 15*(2), 8–22.

Gathercoal, F. (1997). *Judicious discipline* (4th ed.). San Francisco, CA: Caddo Gap Press.

Geelan, D. R. (1997). Epistemological anarchy and the many forms of constructivism. *Science and Education, 6*(1–2), 15–28.

George, P. (2005). The big picture: Year-round schooling. *Middle Ground, 8*(4), 19.

Ginott, H. G. (1971). *Teacher and child.* New York: Macmillan.

Glasser, W. (1965). *Reality therapy: A new approach to psychiatry.* New York: Harper & Row.

Glasser, W. (1969). *Schools without failure.* New York: Harper & Row.

Glasser, W. (1986). *Control theory in the classroom.* New York: Harper & Row.

Glasser, W. (1990). *The quality school: Managing students without coercion.* New York: Harper & Row.

Glasser, W. (1993). *The quality school teacher.* New York: HarperPerennial.

Glasser, W. (1997). A new look at school failure and school success. *Phi Delta Kappan, 78*, 597–602.

Goleman, D., Boyatzis, R., & McKee, A. (2002). *Primal leadership: Realizing the power of emotional intelligence.* Boston: Harvard Business School Press.

Good, T. L., & Brophy, J. E. (2003). *Looking in classrooms* (9th ed.). New York: Allyn & Bacon.

Goos, M., & Galbraith, P. (1996). Do it this way! Metacognitive strategies in collaborative mathematics problem solving. *Educational Studies in Mathematics, 30*, 229–260.

Gordon, D. T. (2002). Curriculum access in the digital age. *Harvard Education Letter, 18*(1), 1–5.

Gordon, T. (1989). *Discipline that works: Promoting self-discipline in the classroom.* New York: Penguin.

Gross, M. U. M. (2000). Exceptionally and profoundly gifted students: An underserved population. *Understanding Our Gifted, 12*(2), 3–9.

Guskey, T. R. (Ed.). (1996). *Communicating student learning.* Alexandria, VA: Association for Supervision and Curriculum Development.

Harrington-Lueker, D. (1997). Emotional intelligence. *High Strides, 9*(4), 1, 4–5.

Harris, H. L., & Coy, D. R. (2003). *Helping students cope with text anxiety.* ED479355. Greensboro, NC: ERIC Clearinghouse on Counseling and Student Services.

Harrison, G., Andrews, J., & Saklofske, D. (2003). Current perspectives on cognitive and learning styles. *Education Canada, 43*(2), 44–47.

Harrow, A. J. (1977). *Taxonomy of the psychomotor domain.* New York: Longman.

Haynes, C. C., Chaltain, S., Ferguson, Jr., J. E., Hudson, Jr., D. L., & Thomas, O. (2003). *The First Amendment in schools.* Alexandria, VA: Association for Supervision and Curriculum Development and Nashville, TN: First Amendment Center.

Helfand, D., & Rubin, J. (online Nov. 8, 2004). Few parents move their children out of failing schools. *Los Angeles Times.* Retrieved November 8, 2004, from www.latimes.com.

Heller, D. A. (2004). *Teachers wanted: Attracting and retaining good teachers.* Alexandria, VA: Association for Supervision and Curriculum Development.

Henry J. Kaiser Family Foundation. (September 2004). Children, the digital divide, and federal policy. *Issue Brief.*

Herman, B. E. (2004). *The revival of K–8 schools.* Fastback 519. Bloomington, IN: Phi Delta Kappa Educational Foundation.

Hoffman, D., & Levak, B. A. (2003). Personalizing schools. *Educational Leadership, 61*(1), 30–34.

Hopping, L. (2000). Multi-age teaming: A real-life approach to the middle school. *Phi Delta Kappan, 82*, 270–272 & 292.

Horton, L. (1981). *Mastery learning.* Fastback 154. Bloomington, IN: Phi Delta Kappa Educational Foundation.

Hough, D. L. (1989). *Middle level education in California: A survey of programs and organizations.* Riverside, CA: University of California, Educational Research Cooperative.

Hyerle, D. (1996). *Visual tools for constructing knowledge.* Alexandria, VA: Association for Supervision and Curriculum Development.

Hyman, L. A., & D'Allessandro, J. (April 11, 1984). Oversimplifying the discipline problem. *Education Week, 3*(29), 24.

Jackson, A. W., & Davis, G. A. (2000). *Turning points 2000: Educating adolescents in the 21st century.* New York: Teachers College Press.

Jacobson, J., Thrope, L., Fisher, D., Lapp, D., Frey, N., & Flood, J. (2001). Cross-age tutoring: A literacy improvement approach for struggling adolescent readers. *Journal of Adolescent & Adult Literacy, 44,* 528–536.

Jensen, E. (1998). *Teaching with the brain in mind.* Alexandria, VA: Association for Supervision and Curriculum Development.

Johnson, D. W., Johnson, R., & Holubec, E. (1998). *Cooperation in the classroom* (3rd ed.). Edina, MN: Interaction Book Co.

Joiner, L. L. (2003). Where did we come from? *American School Board Journal, 190*(4), 30–34.

Jones, F. (1987). *Positive classroom discipline.* New York: McGraw-Hill.

Jorgenson, O., & Vanosdall, R. (2002). The death of science? What we risk in our rush toward standardized testing and the three R's. *Phi Delta Kappan, 83,* 601–605.

Jung, C. G. (1923). *Psychological types.* New York: Harcourt Brace.

Kagan, S. (1995). Group grades miss the mark. *Educational Leadership, 52*(8), 68–71.

Kalina, B. (2004). The benefits of block scheduling. *Middle Matters, 12*(2), 6.

Karplus, R. (1974). *Science curriculum improvement study,* teacher's handbook. Berkeley: University of California.

Kellough, R. D. (1970). The humanistic approach: An experiment in the teaching of biology to slow learners in high school—an experiment in classroom experimentation. *Science Education, 54,* 253–262.

Kellough, R. D. (1994). *A resource guide for teaching: K–12.* New York: Macmillan.

Kellough, R. D., & Kellough, N. G. (1999). *Middle school teaching: A guide to methods and resources.* (3rd ed.). Upper Saddle River, NJ: Merrill/Prentice Hall.

Kellough, R. D., & Roberts, P. L. (1994). *A resource guide for elementary school teaching: planning for competence* (3rd ed.). New York: Macmillan.

Kelly, E. B. (1994). *Memory enhancement for educators.* Fastback 365. Bloomington, IN: Phi Delta Kappa Educational Foundation.

Kim, E. C., & Kellough, R. D. (1983). *A resource guide for secondary school teaching* (3rd ed.). New York: Macmillan.

Kim, E. C., & Kellough, R. D. (1991). *A resource guide for secondary school teaching* (5th ed.). New York: Macmillan.

Koenig, M. (2001). Debating real-world issues. *Science Scope, 24*(5), 19–23.

Kohlberg, I. (1981). *The meaning and measurement of moral development.* Worcester, MA: Clark University Press.

Kohn, A. (1993). *Punished by rewards.* New York: Houghton Mifflin.

Kolb, D. A. (1984). *Experiential learning: Experience as a source of learning and development.* Upper Saddle River, NJ: Prentice Hall.

Kounin, J. (1970). *Discipline and group management in classrooms.* New York: Holt, Rinehart and Winston.

Krathwohl, D. R., Bloom, B. S., & Masia, B. B. (1964). *Taxonomy of educational goals, handbook 2, affective domain.* New York: David McKay.

Lemkuhl, M. (2002). Pen-pal letters: The cross-curricular experience. *Reading Teacher, 55,* 720–722.

L'Esperance, M. E., & Gabbard, D. (2001). Empowering *all* parents. *Middle Ground, 56*(1), 83–85.

Linn, R. L., & Gronlund, N. E. (2000). *Measurement and assessment in teaching* (8th ed.). Columbus, OH: Merrill/Prentice Hall.

Littky, D. (2004). *The big picture.* Alexandria, VA: Association for Supervision and Curriculum Development.

Long, D., Drake, K., & Halychyn, D. (2004). Go on a science quest. *Science & Children, 42*(2), 40–45.

Luttrell, W., & Ward, J. (2004). The "n-word" and the racial dynamics of teaching. *Harvard Education Letter, 20*(5), 4–6.

MacBain, D. E. (1996). *Intergenerational education programs.* Fastback 402. Bloomington, IN: Phi Delta Kappa Educational Foundation.

Mann, L. (2000). Recalculating middle school math. *Education Update, 42*(1), 2–3, 8.

Manning, M. L., & Bucher, K. T. (2001). Revisiting Ginott's congruent communication after thirty years. *Clearing House, 74*(4), 15–18.

Marzano, R. J. (1992). *A different kind of classroom: Teaching with dimensions of learning.* Alexandria, VA: Association for Supervision and Curriculum Development.

Marzano, R. J., & Marzano, J. S. (2003). The key to classroom management. *Educational Leadership, 61*(1), 6–13.

Marzano, R. J., Pickering, D. J., & Pollock, J. E. (2001). *Classroom instruction that works: Research-based strategies for increasing student achievement.* Alexandria, VA: Association for Supervision and Curriculum Development.

Mastropieri, M. A., & Scruggs, T. E. (1998). Constructing more meaningful relationships in the classroom: Mnemonic research into practice. *Learning Disabilities Research & Practice, 13*(1), 138–145.

McCarthy, B. (1990). Using the 4MAT system to bring learning styles to schools. *Educational Leadership, 48*(2), 33.

McCarthy, B. (1997). A tale of four learners: 4MAT's learning styles. *Educational Leadership, 54*(6), 47–51.

McCarty, P., Ostrem, J., & Young, P. (2004). Saving teachers' voices. *Principal, 82*(2), 56–57.

McCullen, C. (2000). In project-based learning, technology adds a new twist to an old idea. *Middle Ground, 3*(5), 7–9.

McDonald, S. (2001). The prevalence and effects of test anxiety in school children. *Educational Psychology: An International Journal of Experimental Educational Psychology, 21*(1), 89–101.

McEwan, B., & Gathercoal, P. (2000). Creating peaceful classrooms: Judicious discipline and class meetings. *Phi Delta Kappan, 81,* 450–454.

McEwin, C. K., Jenkins, D., & Dickinson, T. S. (1996). *America's middle schools: A 25 year perspective.* Columbus, OH: National Middle School Association.

McIntosh, M. E., & Draper, R. J. (1996). Using the question-answer relationship strategy to improve students' reading of mathematics texts. *Clearing House, 69*(3), 154–162.

Meier, D. (2005). The student-teacher relationship: Our most important "data" source. *Harvard Education Letter, 21*(3), 7–8.

Mesmer, H. A. E., & Hutchins, E. J. (2002). Using QARs with charts and graphs. *Reading Teacher, 56*(1), 21–27.

Meyer, A., & Rose, D. H. (2000). Universal design for individual differences. *Educational Leadership, 58*(3), 39–43.

Minicucci, C., et al. (1995). School reform and student diversity. *Phi Delta Kappan, 77,* 77–80.

Murdock, T. B., & Miller, G. (2003). Teachers as sources of middle school students' motivational identity: Variable-centered and person-centered analytic approaches. *Elementary School Journal, 103,* 383–399.

National Middle School Association. (1995). *This we believe: Developmentally responsive middle level schools.* Columbus, OH: Author.

National Middle School Association. (2003). *This we believe: Successful schools for young adolescents.* Columbus, OH: Author.

National Middle School Association. (2004). *National Middle School Association performance-based standards for initial middle level teacher preparation.* Columbus, OH: Author.

Nelsen, J. (1987). *Positive discipline* (2nd ed.). New York: Ballantine Books.

Nelsen, J., Lott, L., & Glenn, H. S. (1993). *Positive discipline in the classroom: How to effectively use class meetings and other positive discipline strategies.* Rocklin, CA: Prima Publishing.

Nelson, J. S., Jaymanthi, M., Epstein, M. H., & Bursuck, W. D. (2000). Student preferences for adaptations in classroom testing. *Remedial and Special Education, 21*(1), 41–52.

Newton, B. (1978). Theoretical basis for higher cognitive questioning—an avenue to critical thinking. *Education, 98*(3), 286–290.

Novak, J. D. (1998). *Learning, creating, and using knowledge: Concept maps as facilitative tools in schools and corporations.* Mahwah, NJ: Lawrence Erlbaum.

Novak, J. D. (1990). Concept maps and vee diagrams: Two metacognitive tools to facilitate meaningful learning. *Instructional Science, 19*(1), 29–52.

Ogle, D. M. (1986). K-W-L: A teaching model that develops active reading of expository text. *Reading Teacher, 39*(6), 564–570.

Oosterhof, A. (2001). *Classroom applications of educational measurement* (3rd ed.). Upper Saddle River, NJ: Merrill/Prentice Hall.

Otten, E. H. (2000). *Character education.* ED444932. Bloomington, IN: ERIC Clearinghouse for Social Studies/Social Science Education.

Palincsar, A. S., & Brown, A. L. (1984). Reciprocal teaching of comprehension—fostering and comprehension-monitoring activities. *Cognition and Instruction, 1,* 117–175.

Paulson, A. (2004). An education rebellion stirring. *The Christian Science Monitor.* Retrieved February 12, 2004, from http://www.csmonitor.com/2004/0211/p01s02-ussc.html.

Pavio, A. (1971). *Imagery and verbal processing.* New York: Holt, Rinehart & Winston.

Pavio, A. (1990). *Mental representations: A dual coding approach.* New York: Oxford University Press.

Perlstein, L. (2004). What you should know about middle schoolers. *Principal, 83*(5), 60–61.

Phillips, C. (2000). A sense of wonder: Young philosophers in San Francisco ponder age-old questions. *Teaching Tolerance, 17,* 36–39.

Piaget, J. (1970). *Science of education and the psychology of the child.* New York: Orion.

Piaget, J. (1972). *The psychology of intelligence.* Totowa, NJ: Littlefield Adams.

Piaget, J. (1977). *The development of thought: Elaboration of cognitive structures.* New York: Viking.

Plotnick, E. (1997). *Concept mapping: A graphical system for understanding the relationship between concepts.* ED407938. Syracuse, NY: ERIC Clearinghouse on Information and Technology.

Potenza, S. A. (2003). Science buddies. *Science and Children, 40*(4), 40–43.

Queen, J. A., Blackwelder, B. B., & Mallen, L. P. (1997). *Responsible classroom management for teachers and students.* Upper Saddle River, NJ: Merrill/Prentice Hall.

Rakow, S. J. (1992). Assessment: A driving force. *Science Scope, 15*(6), 3.

Raschke, D., Alper, S., & Eggers, E. (1999). Recalling alphabet letter names: A mnemonic system to facilitate learning. *Preventing School Failure, 43*(2), 80–83.

Rayneri, L. J., Gerber, B. L., & Wiley, L. P. (2003). Gifted achievers and gifted underachievers: The impact of learning style preference in the classroom. *Journal of Secondary Gifted Education, 14*(4), 197–204.

Redfield, D., & Rousseau, E. (1981). A meta-analysis of experimental research on teacher questioning behavior. *Review of Educational Research, 51*(2), 237–245.

Reedy, P. A. (2001). Improv and the middle school. *Principal, 80*(4), 52.

Reents, J. N. (2002). Isolating 9th graders. *School Administrator, 59*(3), 14–19.

Reiser, R. A., & Butzin, S. M. (2000). Using teaming, active learning, and technology to improve instruction. *Middle School Journal, 32*(2), 21–29.

Robb, L. (2002). Multiple texts: Multiple opportunities for teaching and learning. *Voices from the Middle, 9*(4), 28–32.

Roberts, K. (2000). Conferencing with confidence: Suggestions for using portfolios in student-led conferences. *Ohio Reading Teacher, 34*(2), 34–39.

Robinson, F. P. (1961). *Effective study.* (Rev. ed.). New York: Harper & Brothers.

Rowe, M. B. (1974). Wait time and reward as instructional variables, their influence on language, logic and fate control: Part I. Wait time. *Journal of Research in Science Teaching, 11*(2), 81–94.

Saunders, C. L. (2003). Case study: A gifted child at risk. *Journal of Secondary Gifted Education, 14*(2), 100–106.

Schank, R. C. (2000). A vision of education for the 21st century. *T.H.E. Journal, 27*(6), 43–45.

Schneider, E. (2000). Shifting into high gear. *Educational Leadership, 58*(1), 57–60.

Schniedewind, N., & Davidson, E. (2000). Differentiating cooperative learning. *Educational Leadership, 58*(1), 24–27.

Schon, D. A. (1983). *The reflective practitioner: How professionals think in action.* New York: Basic Books.

Schumaker, J. B., Denton, P. H., & Deshler, D. D. (1984). *The paraphrasing strategy.* Lawrence, KS: Edge Enterprises.

Schwab, J. J. (1962). *The teaching of science as enquiry.* Cambridge, MA: Harvard University Press.

Schwartz, S. (1997). *Strategies for identifying the talents of diverse students.* ED410323. New York: ERIC Clearinghouse on Urban Education.

Schwartz, W. (1999). *Preventing violence by elementary school children.* ERIC/CUE Digest Number 149. New York: ERIC Clearinghouse on Urban Education.

Schwartz, W. (Ed.). (2000). *New trends in language education for hispanic students.* ED442913. New York: ERIC Clearinghouse on Urban Education.

Scott, J. E. (1994). Literature circles in the middle school classroom: Developing reading, responding, and responsibility. *Middle School Journal, 26*(2), 37–41.

Sharan, Y., & Sharan, S. (1992). *Cooperative learning through group investigation.* New York: Teachers College Press.

Shortt, T. L., & Thayer, Y. V. (1998). Block scheduling can enhance school climate. *Educational Leadership, 56*(4), 76–81.

Simpson, E. J. (1972). *The classification of educational objectives in the psychomotor domain. The psychomotor domain: Volume 3.* Washington, DC: Gryphon House.

Skinner, B. F. (1968). *The technology of teaching.* New York: Appleton-Century-Crofts.

Skinner, B. F. (1971). *Beyond freedom and dignity.* New York: Knopf.

Slater, W. H., & Horstman, F. R. (2002). Teaching reading and writing to struggling middle school and high school students: The case for reciprocal teaching. *Preventing School Failure, 46*(4), 163–166.

Slavin, R. E. (1996). Cooperative learning in middle and secondary schools. *Clearing House, 69,* 200–204.

Smerdon, B. A., Burkam, D. T., & Lee, V. E. (1999). Access to constructivist and didactic teaching: Who gets it? Where is it practiced? *Teachers College Record, 101*(1), 5–34.

Sosniak, L. (2001). The 9% challenge: Education in school and society. *Teachers College Record.* Retrieved May 7, 2001, from http://www.tcrecord.org.

Sowell, J. E. (1993). Approach to art history in the classroom. *Art Education, 46*(2), 19–24.

Sternberg, R. J. (1998). Teaching and assessing for successful intelligence. *School Administrator, 55*(1), 30–31.

Sternberg, R. J., Grigorenko, E. L., & Jarvin, L. (2001). Improving reading instruction: The triarchic model. *Educational Leadership, 58*(6), 48–51.

Stevenson, C., & Carr, J. F. (Eds.). (1993). *Integrated studies in the middle grades.* New York: Teachers College Press.

Stiggins, R. J. (2001). *Student-involved classroom assessment* (3rd ed.). Upper Saddle River, NJ: Prentice Hall.

Stright, S. D., & Supplee, L. H. (2002). Children's self-regulatory behaviors during teacher-directed, seat-work, and small-group instructional contexts. *Journal of Educational Research, 95*(4), 235–244.

Sullivan, P. (1998). The PTA's national standards. *Educational Leadership, 55*(8), 43–44.

Sunderman, G. L., & Kim, J. (2004). Inspiring vision, disappointing results: Four studies on implementing the No Child Left Behind Act. *The Civil Rights Project of Harvard University.* Retrieved February 6, 2004, from http://www.civilrightsproject.harvard.edu.

Tassinari, M. (1996). Hands-on projects take students beyond the book. *Social Studies Review, 34*(3), 16–20.

Terry, M. (2004). One nation, under the designer. *Phi Delta Kappan, 86*(4), 265–270.

Thames, D. G., & York, K. C. (2003). Disciplinary border crossing: Adopting a broader, richer view of literacy. *The Reading Teacher, 56,* 602–609.

Thrope, L., & Wood, K. (2000). Cross-age tutoring for young adolescents. *Clearing House, 73,* 239–242.

Tobin, K. G. (1984). The effect of extended wait time on discourse characteristics and achievement in middle school grades. *Journal of Research in Science Teaching, 21,* 779–791.

Tompkins, G. E., & Hoskisson, K. (1991). *Language arts: Content and teaching strategies.* Upper Saddle River, NJ: Prentice Hall.

United States Department of Education. (1997). *Tried and true: Tested ideas for teaching and learning from the regional educational laboratories.* Washington, DC: Office of Educational Research and Improvement.

Vaishnav, A. (2005). Adding value to student assessment. *Harvard Education Letter, 21*(5), 1–3.

van Boxtel, C., van der Linden, J., Roelofs, E., & Erkens, G. (2002). Collaborative concept mapping: Provoking and supporting meaningful discourse. *Theory into Practice, 41*(1), 40–46.

van Hell, J. G., & Mahn, A. C. (1997). Keyword mnemonics versus rote rehearsal: Learning concrete and abstract foreign words by experienced and inexperienced learners. *Language Learning, 47,* 507–546.

Vars, G. F., & Beane, J. A. (2000). *Integrative curriculum in a standards-based world.* ED441618. Champaign, IL: ERIC Clearinghouse on Elementary and Early Childhood Education.

Vavilis, B., & Vavilis, S. L. (2004). Why are we learning this? What is this stuff good for, anyway? *Phi Delta Kappan, 84,* 282–287.

Villa, R. A., & Thousands, J. S. (Eds.). (1995). *Creating an inclusive school.* Alexandria, VA: Association for Supervision and Curriculum Development.

Voelzel, L. (2000). Making foreign language instruction the center of attention. *Middle Ground, 4*(2), 44–46.

Vygotsky, L. (1962). *Thought and language.* Cambridge, MA: MIT Press.

Vygotsky, L. (1978). *Mind in society: The development of higher psychological processes.* (Edited by M. Cole, V. John-Steiner, S. Scribner, & E. Souberman). Cambridge: Harvard University Press.

Walker, M. L. (1995). Help for the "fourth-grade slump"—SRQ2R plus instruction in text structure or main idea. *Reading Horizons, 36*(1), 38–58.

Walling, D. R. (1993). *English as a second language: 25 questions and answers.* Fastback 347. Bloomington, IN: Phi Delta Kappa Educational Foundation.

Want, M. C., Haertel, G. D., & Walberg, H. J. (1993). What helps students learn? *Educational Leadership, 51*(4), 74–79.

Wassermann, S. (1999). Shazam! You're a teacher. *Phi Delta Kappan, 80,* 464, 466–468.

Weasmer, J., & Woods, A. M. (2000). Shifting classroom ownership to students. *Middle School Journal, 32*(2), 15–20.

Weertz, M. (2002). The benefits of theme schools. *Educational Leadership, 59,* 68–71.

Werderich, D. E. (2002). Individualized responses: Using journal letters as a vehicle for differentiated reading instruction. *Journal of Adolescent & Adult Literacy, 4*(8), 5, 746–754.

Wiggins, G., & McTighe, J. (1998). *Understanding by design.* Alexandria, VA: Association for Supervision and Curriculum Development.

Wiles, J., & Bondi, J. (2001). *The New American Middle School* (3rd ed.). Upper Saddle River, NJ: Merrill/Prentice Hall.

Willard-Holt, C. (1999). *Dual exceptionalities.* EDE574. Reston, VA: ERIC Clearinghouse on Disabilities and Gifted Education.

Willard-Holt, C. (2003). Raising expectations for the gifted. *Educational Leadership, 61*(2), 72–75.

Wolfe, P. (2001). *Brain matters.* Alexandria, VA: Association for Supervision and Curriculum Development.

Wynne, E. A., & Ryan, K. (1997). *Reclaiming our schools: Teaching character, academics, and discipline* (2nd ed.). Upper Saddle River, NJ: Prentice Hall.

Yancey, K. B. (2004). Using multiple technologies to teach writing. *Educational Leadership, 62*(2), 38–40.

Glossary

ability grouping The assignment of students to separate classrooms or to separate activities within a classroom according to their perceived academic abilities. *Homogeneous grouping* is the grouping of students of similar abilities; *heterogeneous grouping* is the grouping of students of mixed abilities.

accountability Reference to the concept that an individual is responsible for his or her behaviors and should be able to demonstrate publicly the worth of the activities carried out.

adolescence The period of life from the onset of puberty to maturity, terminating legally at the age of majority, generally the ages of 12 to 20, although young or early adolescence may start as soon as age 9.

advance organizer Preinstructional cues that encourage a mental set; used to enhance retention of content to be studied.

advisor-advisee Common to many middle schools, the (sometimes referred to as *homebase* or *advisory*) program that provides each student with opportunity to interact with peers about school and personal concerns and to develop a meaningful relationship with at least one adult.

affective domain The area of learning related to interests, attitudes, feelings, values, and personal adjustment.

alternative assessment Assessment of learning in ways different from traditional paper-and-pencil objective testing, such as a portfolio, project, or self-assessment. See *authentic assessment.*

American Federation of Teachers (AFT) A national professional organization of teachers founded in 1916, currently affiliated with the American Federation of Labor and Congress of Industrial Organizations (AFL-CIO). Recently merged in at least two states with the NEA.

anticipatory set See *advance organizer.*

articulation Term used when referring to the connectedness of the various components of the formal curriculum— *vertical articulation* refers to the connectedness of the K–12 curriculum, and *horizontal articulation* refers to the connectedness across a grade level.

assessment The relatively neutral process of finding out what students are or have learned as a result of instruction.

at risk General term given to a student who shows a high potential for not completing school.

authentic assessment The use of assessment procedures (usually portfolios and projects) that are compatible with the instructional objectives. Also referred to as *accurate, active, aligned, alternative, direct,* and *performance assessment.*

behavioral objective A statement of expectation describing what the learner should be able to do upon completion of the instruction.

behaviorism A theory that equates learning with changes in observable behavior.

block scheduling The school programming procedure that provides large blocks of time (e.g., two hours) in which individual teachers or teacher teams can organize and arrange groupings of students for varied periods of time, thereby more effectively individualizing the instruction for students with various needs and abilities.

brainstorming   An instructional strategy used to create a flow of new ideas, during which judgments of the ideas of others are forbidden.

CD-ROM (compact disc-read only memory)   Digitally encoded information (up to 650 MB of data that can include animation, audio, graphics, text, and video) permanently recorded on a compact (4.72 inch 12 cm in diameter) disc.

character education   Focuses on the development of the values of honesty, kindness, respect, and responsibility.

classroom control   The process of influencing student behavior in the classroom.

classroom management   The teacher's system of establishing a climate for learning, including techniques for preventing and handling student misbehavior.

closure   The means by which a teacher brings the lesson to an end.

coaching   See *mentoring*.

cognition   The process of thinking.

cognitive disequilibrium   The mental state of not yet having made sense out of a perplexing (discrepant) situation.

cognitive domain   The area of learning related to intellectual skills, such as retention and assimilation of knowledge.

cognitive psychology   A branch of psychology devoted to the study of how individuals acquire, process, and use information.

cognitivism   A theory that holds that learning entails the construction or reshaping of mental schemata and that mental processes mediate learning. Also known as *constructivism*.

common planning time   A regularly scheduled time during the school day when teachers who teach the same students meet for joint planning, parent conferences, materials preparation, and student evaluation.

comprehension   A level of cognition that refers to the skill of understanding.

computer-assisted instruction (CAI)   Instruction received by a student when interacting with lessons programmed into a computer system. Known also as computer-assisted learning (CAL).

computer literacy   The ability at some level on a continuum to understand and use computers.

computer-managed instruction (CMI)   The use of a computer system to manage information about learner performance and learning-resources options in order to prescribe and control individual lessons.

constructivism   See *cognitivism*.

continuous progress   An instructional procedure that allows students to progress at their own pace through a sequenced curriculum.

convergent thinking   Thinking that is directed to a preset conclusion.

cooperative learning   A genre of instructional strategies that use small groups of students working together and helping each other on learning tasks, stressing support for one another rather than competition.

core curriculum   Subject or discipline components of the curriculum considered as being absolutely necessary. Traditionally these are English/language arts, mathematics, science, and social science. However, the *No Child Left Behind Legislation of 2001* includes these as the core subjects: English, reading or language arts, mathematics, science, foreign language, civics and government, economics, arts, history, and geography.

covert behavior   A learner behavior that is not outwardly observable.

criterion   A standard by which behavioral performance is judged.

criterion-referenced assessment   Assessment in which standards are established and behaviors are judged against the present guideline, rather than against the behaviors of others.

critical thinking   The ability to recognize and identify problems, to propose and to test solutions, and to arrive at tentative conclusions based on the data collected.

curriculum   Originally derived from a Latin term referring to a racecourse for the chariots, the term still has no widely accepted definition. As used in this text, curriculum is that which is planned and encouraged for teaching and learning. This includes both school and nonschool environments, overt (formal) and hidden (informal) curriculums, and broad as well as narrow notions of content—its development, acquisition, and consequences.

curriculum standards   Statements of the essential knowledge, skills, and attitudes to be learned.

deductive learning   Learning that proceeds from the general to the specific. See also *expository learning*.

detracking   An effort to minimize or eliminate separate classes or programs for students who are of differing abilities.

developmental characteristics   A set of common intellectual, psychological, physical, and social characteristics that, when considered as a whole, indicate an individual's development relative to others during a particular age span.

developmental needs A set of needs unique and appropriate to the developmental characteristics of a particular age span.

diagnostic assessment See *preassessment*.

didactic teaching See *direct instruction*.

differentiated instruction Varying the methods and content of instruction according to individual student differences and needs.

direct experience Learning by doing (applying) that which is being learned.

direct instruction Teacher-centered expository instruction, such as lecturing or a teacher-guided group discussion.

direct intervention Teacher use of verbal reminders or verbal commands to redirect student behavior, as opposed to nonverbal gestures or cues.

direct teaching See *direct instruction*.

discipline The process of controlling student behavior in the classroom. The term has been largely replaced by the terms *classroom control* or *classroom management*. It is also used in reference to the subject taught (e.g., language arts, science, mathematics, and so forth).

discovery learning Learning that proceeds from identification of a problem, through the development of hypotheses, the testing of the hypotheses, and the arrival at a conclusion. See also *critical thinking*.

divergent thinking Thinking that expands beyond original thought.

downshifting Reverting to earlier learned, lower-cognitive-level behaviors.

DVD (digital versatile disc) Like a CD-ROM but with a much greater storage capacity.

early adolescence The developmental stage of young people as they approach and begin to experience puberty. This stage usually occurs between 10 and 14 years of age and deals with the successful attainment of the appropriate developmental characteristics for this age span.

eclectic Utilizing the best from a variety of sources.

effective school A school where students master basic skills, seek academic excellence in all subjects, demonstrate achievement, and display good behavior and attendance. Known also as an *exemplary school*.

elective High-interest or special needs courses that are based on student selection from various options.

elementary school Any school that has been planned and organized especially for children of some combination of grades kindergarten through 6. There are many variations; for example, a school might house preschool children through grades 7 or 8 and still be called an elementary school.

empathy The ability to understand the feelings of another person.

equality Considered to be same in status or competency level.

equity Fairness and justice, that is, impartiality.

evaluation Like assessment, but includes making sense out of the assessment results, usually based on criteria or a rubric. Evaluation is more subjective than is assessment.

exceptional child A child who deviates from the average in any of the following ways: mental characteristics, sensory ability, neuromotor or physical characteristics, social behavior, communication ability, or multiple handicaps. Also known as a special needs child and special education student.

exemplary school See *effective school*.

exploratory course A course designed to help students explore curriculum experiences based on their felt needs, interests, and abilities.

expository learning The traditional classroom instructional approach that proceeds as follows: presentation of information to the learners, reference to particular examples, and application of the information to the learner's experiences.

extended-year school Schools that have extended the school-year calendar from the traditional 180 days to a longer period, such as 200 days.

extrinsic motivators Motivation of learning by rewards outside of the learner, such as parent and teacher expectations, gifts, certificates, stamps, and grades.

facilitating behavior Teacher behavior that makes it possible for students to learn.

facilitative teaching See *indirect instruction*.

family See *school-within-a-school*.

feedback Information sent from the receiver to the originator that provides disclosure about the reception of the intended message.

flexible scheduling Organization of classes and activities in a way that allows for variation from day to day, as opposed to the traditional, fixed schedule that does not vary from day to day.

formative evaluation Evaluation of learning in progress.

goal, course A broad, generalized statement about the expected outcomes of a course.

goal, educational A desired instructional outcome that is broad in scope.

goal, student A statement about what the student hopes to accomplish.

goal, teacher A statement about what the teacher hopes to accomplish.

hands-on learning Learning by actively doing.

Hawthorne effect Says that trying something new will show positive effects at first simply because of the interest demonstrated when something new is tried. Name derived from first notice of the effect in 1962 at the Hawthorne plant of Western Electric in Cicero, Illinois.

heterogeneous grouping A grouping pattern that does not separate students into groups based on their intelligence, learning achievement, or physical characteristics.

high school A school that houses students in any combination of grades 9–12.

high-stakes assessment An assessment is called high stakes if use of the assessment's results carry serious consequences, such as a student's grade promotion rests on the student's performance on one test, or the student's graduation from high school rests on the student's performance on a single test.

holistic learning Learning that incorporates emotions with thinking.

homogeneous grouping A grouping pattern that separates students into groups based on common characteristics, such as intelligence, achievement, or physical characteristics.

house See *school-within-a-school*.

inclusion The commitment to the education of each special needs learner, to the maximum extent appropriate, in the school and classroom the student would otherwise attend.

independent study An instructional strategy that allows a student to select a topic, set the goals, and work alone to attain them.

indirect instruction Student-centered teaching using discovery and inquiry as learning strategies.

individualized instruction The self-paced process whereby individual students assume responsibility for learning through study, practice, feedback, and reinforcement with appropriately designed instructional modules.

inductive learning Learning that proceeds from specifics to the general. See also *discovery learning*.

inquiry learning Like discovery learning, except the learner designs the processes to be used in resolving the problem.

inservice teacher Term used when referring to credentialed and employed teachers.

instruction Planned arrangement of experiences to help a learner develop understanding and to achieve a desirable change in behavior.

instructional module Any freestanding instructional unit that includes these components: rationale, objectives, pretest, learning activities, comprehension checks with instructive feedback, and posttest.

integrated (interdisciplinary) curriculum Curriculum organization that combines subject matter traditionally taught independently.

interdisciplinary instruction Instruction that combines subject-matter disciplines traditionally taught independently.

interdisciplinary team An organizational pattern of two or more teachers representing different subject areas. The team shares the same students, schedule, areas of the school, and the opportunity for teaching more than one subject.

interdisciplinary thematic unit (ITU) A thematic unit that crosses boundaries of two or more disciplines.

intermediate grades Term sometimes used to refer to grades 4 through 6. An intermediate school, for example, is an elementary school that houses children of grades 4 through 6.

internalization The extent to which an attitude or value becomes a part of the learner. That is, without having to think about it, the learner's behavior reflects the attitude or value.

interscholastic sports Athletic competition between teams from two or more schools.

intervention A teacher's interruption to redirect a student's behavior, either by direct intervention (e.g., by a verbal command) or by indirect intervention (e.g., by eye contact or physical proximity).

intramural program Organized activity program that features events between individuals or teams from within the school.

intrinsic motivation Motivation of learning through the student's internal sense of accomplishment.

intuition Knowing without conscious reasoning.

junior high school A school that houses grades 7–9 or 7–8 and that has a schedule and curriculum that resemble those of the senior high school (grades 9–12 or 10–12) more than they do those of the elementary school.

lead teacher The member of a teaching team who is designated to facilitate the work and planning of that team.

leadership team A group of teachers and administrators, and sometimes students, designated by the principal or elected by the faculty (and student body) to assist in the leadership of the school.

learning The development of understandings and the change in behavior resulting from experiences. For different interpretations of learning, see *behaviorism* and *cognitivism.*

learning center (LC) An instructional strategy that utilizes activities and materials located at a special place in the classroom and is designed to allow a student to work independently at his or her own pace to learn one area of content. See also *learning station.*

learning modality The way a person receives information. Four modalities are recognized: visual, auditory, tactile (touch), and kinesthetic (movement).

learning resource center The central location in the school where instructional materials and media are stored, organized, and accessed by students and staff.

learning station (LS) Like a learning center, except that where each learning center is distinct and unrelated to others, learning stations are sequenced or in some way linked to one another.

learning style The way a person learns best in a given situation.

literacy The ability to read, write, speak, listen, and think critically.

looping An arrangement in which the cohort of students and teachers remain together as a group for several or for all the years a child is at a particular school. Also referred to as multiyear grouping, multiyear instruction, multiyear placement, and teacher-student progression.

magnet school A school that specializes in a particular academic area, such as science, mathematics, technology, the arts, or international relations. Also referred to as a *theme school.*

mainstreaming Placing an exceptional child in regular education classrooms for all (inclusion) or part (partial inclusion) of the school day.

mandala A diagram, usually circular, with spiritual and ritual significance.

mastery learning The concept that a student should master the content of one lesson before moving on to the content of the next.

measurement The process of collecting and interpreting data.

mentoring One-on-one coaching, tutoring, or guidance to facilitate learning.

metacognition Planning, monitoring, and evaluating one's own thinking. Known also as *reflective abstraction.*

micro peer teaching (MPT) Teaching a limited objective for a brief period to a small group of peers for the purpose of evaluation and improvement of particular teaching skills.

middle grades Grades 5 through 8.

middle level education Any school unit between elementary and high school.

middle school A school that has been planned and organized especially for students of ages 10 to 14, and that generally includes grades 5 through 8, although many varied patterns exist. For example, a school might include only grades 7 and 8 and still be called a middle school.

minds-on learning Learning in which the learner is intellectually active, thinking about what is being learned.

misconception Faulty understanding of a major idea or concept. Also known as a naïve theory and conceptual misunderstanding.

modeling The teacher's direct and indirect demonstration, by actions and by words, of the behaviors expected of students.

multicultural education A deliberate attempt to help students understand facts, generalizations, attitudes, and behaviors derived from their own ethnic roots as well as others. In this process, students unlearn racism and biases and recognize the interdependent fabric of society, giving due acknowledgment for contributions made by its members.

multilevel instruction See *multitasking.*

multilevel teaching See *multitasking.*

multimedia The combined use of sound, video, and graphics for instruction.

multiple intelligences A theory of several different intelligences, as opposed to just one general intelligence; intelligences that have been described are verbal/linguistic, musical, logical/mathematical, naturalist, visual/spatial, bodily/kinesthetic, interpersonal, and intrapersonal.

multipurpose board A writing board with a smooth plastic surface used with special marking pens rather than chalk. Sometimes called a visual aid panel, the board may have a steel backing and then can be used as a magnetic board as well as a screen for projecting visuals.

multitasking The simultaneous use of several levels of teaching and learning in the same classroom, with students working on different objectives or different tasks leading to the same objective. Also called *multilevel teaching.*

naïve theory See *misconception.*

National Education Association (NEA) The nation's oldest professional organization of teachers, founded in 1857 as the National Teachers Association and changed in 1879 to its present name. Recently merged in at least two states (Montana and Minnesota) with the AFT.

norm-referenced Individual performance is judged relative to overall performance of the group (e.g., grading on a curve), as opposed to being criterion-referenced.

orientation set See *advance organizer.*

overlapping A teacher behavior where the teacher is able to attend to more than one matter at once.

overt behavior A behavior that is outwardly observable.

peer tutoring An instructional strategy that places students in a tutorial role in which one student helps another learn.

performance assessment See *authentic assessment.*

performance-based instruction Instruction designed around the instruction and assessment of student achievement against specified and predetermined objectives.

performance objective See *behavioral objective.*

portfolio assessment An alternative approach to evaluation that assembles representative samples of a student's work over time as a basis for assessment.

positive reinforcer A means of encouraging desired student behaviors by rewarding those behaviors when they occur.

preassessment Diagnostic assessment of what students know or think they know prior to the instruction.

preservice Term used when referring to teachers in training, as opposed to inservice teachers, teachers who are employed.

probationary teacher An untenured teacher. After a designated number of years in the same district, usually three, upon rehire the probationary teacher receives a tenure contract.

procedure A statement telling the student how to accomplish a task.

psychomotor domain The domain of learning that involves locomotor behaviors.

realia Real objects used as visual props during instruction, such as political campaign buttons, plants, memorabilia, art, balls, and so forth.

reciprocal teaching A form of collaborative teaching where the teacher and the students share the teaching responsibility and all are involved in asking questions, clarifying, predicting, and summarizing.

reflection The conscious process of mentally replaying experiences.

reflective abstraction See *metacognition.*

reliability In measurement, the consistency with which an item or instrument is measured over time.

rubric An outline of the criteria used to assess a student's work.

rules In classroom management, rules are the standards of expectation for classroom behavior.

schema (plural: schemata) A mental construct by which the learner organizes his or her perceptions of situations and knowledge.

school-within-a-school Sometimes referred to as a *house, cluster, village, pod,* or *family,* it is a teaching arrangement where one team of teachers is assigned to work with the same group of about 125 students for a common block of time, for the entire school day, or, in some instances, for all the years those students are at that school.

secondary school Traditionally, any school housing students for any combination of grades 7 through 12.

self-contained classroom Commonly used in the primary grades, it is a grouping pattern where one teacher teaches all or most subjects to one group of children.

self-instructional module (SIM) An completely self-contained instructional package that has been designed for an individual student to master a specific and relatively brief quantity of content on his or her own and at the student's own pace.

self-paced learning See *individualized learning.*

senior high school Usually a high school that houses only students in grades 9 to 12 or 10 to 12.

sequencing Arranging ideas in logical order.

simulation An abstraction or simplification of a real-life situation.

special needs student See *exceptional child.*

standards See *curriculum standards.*

student teaching A field experience component of teacher preparation, traditionally the culminating experience, where the teacher candidate practices teaching children while under the supervision of a credentialed teacher and a university supervisor.

summative assessment Assessment of learning after instruction is completed.

teacher leader See *lead teacher.*

teaching See *instruction.*

teaching style The way teachers teach; their distinctive mannerisms complemented by their choices of teaching behaviors and strategies.

teaching team A team of two or more teachers who work together to provide instruction to the same group of students, either alternating the instruction or team teaching simultaneously.

team teaching Two or more teachers working together to provide instruction to a group of students.

tenured teacher After serving a designated number of years in the same school district (usually three) as a probationary teacher, upon rehire the teacher receives a tenure contract, which means that the teacher is automatically rehired each year thereafter unless the contract is revoked by either the district or the teacher and for specific and legal reasons.

terminal behavior   That which has been learned as a direct result of instruction.

thematic unit   A unit of instruction built on a central theme or concept.

theme school   See *magnet school.*

think-time   See *wait time.*

tracking   The practice of the voluntary or involuntary placement of students in different programs or courses according to their ability and prior academic performance. See also *ability grouping.*

traditional teaching   Teacher-centered direct instruction, typically using lectures, discussions, textbooks, and worksheets.

transescence   A no-longer-popular term referring to the stage of human development, usually thought of as ages 10 to 14. It is the middle school years, which begins before the onset of puberty and extends through the early stages of adolescence. Students in this stage of development have been referred to variously as the *transescent, preadolescent, preteen, in-betweenager,* and *tweenager.*

transition   In a lesson, the planned procedures that move student thinking from one idea to the next or that move their actions from one activity to the next. With reference to schooling, transitions are the times when a student moves from one level of school to the next.

untracking   See *detracking.*

validity   In measurement, the degree to which an item or instrument measures that which it is intended to measure.

village   See *school-within-a-school.*

wait time   In the use of questioning, the period of silence between the time a question is asked and the inquirer (teacher) does something, such as repeats the question, rephrases the question, calls on a particular student, answers the question him- or herself, or asks another question. Also referred to as *think-time.*

whole-language learning   A point of view with a focus on seeking or creating meaning that encourages language production, risk taking, independence in producing language, and the use of a wide variety of print materials in authentic reading and writing situations.

withitness   The teacher's timely ability to intervene and redirect a student's inappropriate behavior.

year-round school   A school that operates as is tradition, which is with 180 school days, but the days are spread over 12 months rather than the usual 10. Most common is the nine-weeks on, three-weeks off format.

young adolescent   The 10- to 14-year-old experiencing the developmental stage of early adolescence.

Index

NMSA Standards	INTASC Principles

Chapter 1

1. Middle level teacher candidates understand the major concepts, principles, theories, and research related to young adolescent development, and they provide opportunities that support student development and learning.
2. Middle level teacher candidates understand the major concepts, principles, theories, and research underlying the philosophical foundations of developmentally responsive middle level programs and schools, and they work successfully within these organizational components.
6. Middle level teacher candidates understand the major concepts, principles, theories, and research related to working collaboratively with family and community members, and they use that knowledge to maximize the learning of all young adolescents.

2. The teacher understands how children learn and develop, and can provide learning opportunities that support their intellectual, social, and personal development.
10. The teacher fosters relationships with school colleagues, parents, and agencies in the larger community to support students' learning and well-being.

Chapter 2

1. Middle level teacher candidates understand the major concepts, principles theories, and research related to young adolescent development, and they provide opportunities that support student development and learning.
2. Middle level teacher candidates understand the major concepts, principles, theories, and research underlying the philosophical foundations of developmentally responsive middle level programs and schools, and they work successfully within these organizational components.
5. Middle level teacher candidates understand and use the major concepts, principles, theories, and research related to effective instruction and assessment, and they employ a variety of strategies for a developmentally appropriate climate to meet the varying abilities and learning styles of all young adolescents.
6. Middle level teacher candidates understand the major concepts, principles, theories, and research related to working collaboratively with family and community members, and they use that knowledge to maximize the learning of all young adolescents.
7. Middle level teacher candidates understand the complexity of teaching young adolescents, and they engage in practices and behaviors that develop their competence as professionals.

6. The teacher uses knowledge of effective verbal, nonverbal, and media communication techniques to foster active inquiry, collaboration, and supportive interaction in the classroom.
9. The teacher is a reflective practitioner who continually evaluates the effects of his/her choices and actions on others (students, parents, and other professionals in the learning community) and who actively seeks out opportunities to grow professionally.
10. The teacher fosters relationships with school colleagues, parents, and agencies in the larger community to support students' learning and well-being.

Chapter 3

4. Middle level teacher candidates understand and use the central concepts, tools of inquiry, standards, and structures of content in their chosen fields, and they create meaningful learning experiences that develop all young adolescents' competence in subject matter and skills.
5. Middle level teacher candidates understand and use the major concepts, principles, theories, and research related to effective instruction and assessment, and they employ a variety of strategies for a developmentally appropriate climate to meet the varying abilities and learning styles of all young adolescents.

1. The teacher understands the central concepts, tools of inquiry, and structures of the discipline(s) he or she teaches and can create learning experiences that make these aspects of subject matter meaningful to students.
4. The teacher understands and uses a variety of instructional strategies to encourage students' development of critical thinking, problem solving, and performance skills.

Chapter 4

1. Middle level teacher candidates understand the major concepts, principles theories, and research related to young adolescent development, and they provide opportunities that support student development and learning.
5. Middle level teacher candidates understand and use the major concepts, principles, theories, and research related to effective instruction and assessment, and they employ a variety of strategies for a developmentally appropriate climate to meet the varying abilities and learning styles of all young adolescents.
7. Middle level teacher candidates understand the complexity of teaching young adolescents, and they engage in practices and behaviors that develop their competence as professionals.

5. The teacher uses an understanding of individual and group motivation and behavior to create a learning environment that encourages positive social interaction, active engagement in learning, and self-motivation.

Chapter 5

2. Middle level teacher candidates understand the major concepts, principles, theories, and research underlying the philosophical foundations of developmentally responsive middle level programs and schools, and they work successfully within these organizational components.

7. The teacher plans instruction based upon knowledge of subject matter, students, community, and curriculum goals.
10. The teacher fosters relationships with colleagues, parents, and agencies in the community to support students' learning and well-being.